Apalachee

D1300457

Ripley P. Bullen Monographs in Anthropology and History
Number 7
The Florida State Museum

Apalachee

The Land between the Rivers

John H. Hann

University Presses of Florida
University of Florida Press / Florida State Museum
Gainesville

The author thanks the following publishers for permission to use material:

The Academy of American Franciscan History for Mark F. Boyd, "Documents: Further Consideration of the Apalachee Missions," *The Americas* 9 (April 1953): 459–479.
The Carnegie Institution of Washington for the map in figure 2.2 from Verne Chatelain, *The Defenses of Spanish Florida, 1565 to 1763* (1941).
The South Carolina Department of Archives and History for Alexander S. Salley, ed., *Journal of the Commons House of Assembly of South Carolina, Nov. 20, 1706–Feb. 8, 1706/7* (1939) and Salley, ed., *Records in the British Public Records Office Relating to South Carolina*, vol. 5 (1947).
The University of Texas Press for Garcilaso de la Vega, *The Florida of the Inca,* translated and edited by John Grier Varner and Jeannette Johnson Varner (1951).

Library of Congress Cataloging-in-Publication Data

Hann, John H.
  Apalachee: the land between the rivers.

  (Ripley P. Bullen monographs in anthropology and
history; no. 7)
  Bibliography: p.
  Includes index.
  1. Apalachee Indians.   2. Indians of North America—
Florida—History.   3. Florida—History—1565–1763.
I. Title. II. Series.
E99.A62H36   1987   975.9′00497   87–2163
ISBN 0–8130–0854–9 (alk. paper)

UNIVERSITY PRESSES OF FLORIDA is the central agency for scholarly publishing of the State of Florida's university system, producing books selected for publication by the faculty editorial committees of Florida's nine public universities: Florida A&M University (Tallahassee), Florida Atlantic University (Boca Raton), Florida International University (Miami), Florida State University (Tallahassee), University of Central Florida (Orlando), University of Florida (Gainesville), University of North Florida (Jacksonville), University of South Florida (Tampa), University of West Florida (Pensacola).
  Orders for books published by all member presses should be addressed to University Presses of Florida, 15 NW 15th Street, Gainesville, FL 32603.

Contents

Figures

Tables

Foreword

NEARLY forty years have passed since the pioneering excavations of John Griffin at the site of the seventeenth-century Spanish mission of San Luis, reported along with Hale Smith's excavations at the Ayubale mission site in Jefferson County and Mark Boyd's translation of contemporary Spanish documents. Their book, *Here They Once Stood*, published by the University of Florida Press in 1951, laid out a solid foundation for subsequent archaeological and historical study of Florida's mission period and contributed significantly to the development of what has now come to be known as historical archaeology. In their preface, Boyd, Smith and Griffin expressed the hope "that similar studies will be conducted, to the end that the documentary sources may be enriched by the data recovered by excavation and the archaeological objects may be enlivened by the insight provided by contemporary documents."

In 1983, when the site of San Luis came into public ownership, the Florida Department of State was charged with the responsibility of researching, interpreting and managing the 50-acre property for the public benefit. We were presented with the unique opportunity to develop a long-term program of archaeological and historical research that would not only improve our understanding of Florida's early Spanish history, but also present the story of the Apalachee missions to the public through exhibits, educational programs, and publications. San Luis Archaeological and Historical Site has now been open to the public for more than three years, and thousands of visitors have toured the grounds, viewed the excavations in progress, and, we hope, left with a better understanding of Florida's Indian and Spanish history. Much work remains to be done before San Luis achieves its full potential as a center for Spanish Colonial research and interpretation, but John Hann's book represents a milestone in the long-term effort to understand and present to the public a full account of seventeenth-century life in the Apalachee province and follows directly out of the task defined so long ago by Boyd, Smith, and Griffin.

Apalachee: Land Between the Rivers grew out of an initial review of readily available documents and translations about the site of San Luis that was intended simply to guide the archaeologists in their general understanding of the site and the interpretation of the preliminary archaeological excavations. In the middle 1970s, John Hann had translated excerpts of documents related to the Apalachee missions to supplement the results of earlier archaeological work at a number of mission sites conducted by B. Calvin Jones and L. Ross Morrell. As the potential of the documents became more apparent, the scope of the project increased, and John Hann took on the task of organizing his results into a book-length manuscript. The importance of the completed study was recognized by Jerald Milanich, Bullen Series editor, in 1985, and the manuscript was accepted for publication soon thereafter. The Bureau of Archaeological Research is pleased to join the Florida State Museum in making this book available to the public.

Apalachee presents the fullest account available of any indigenous Florida Indian tribe and illustrates how profoundly Spanish and Indian cultures in Florida were interrelated in the seventeenth century. Although the documentary record is rich, the book provides an account of the famed Apalachee Indians that depicts a way of life much different from their aboriginal way of life before Spanish contact. It is clear from this study that the Apalachee Indians, the Franciscan missionaries and the Spanish soldiers comprised a complicated triangle, each side possessing its own cultural system of goals and desires. As we approach the quincentennial celebration of the first European contact with the Native American people of the New World, much attention will be focused on Florida's early history. We may now recognize from Hann's work the rich and complex nature of at least one aspect of this history and perhaps appreciate more fully the life of the Spaniard and the Indian in early Florida.

James J. Miller
Florida Division of Historical Resources,
Bureau of Archaeological Research

Preface

AMONG Florida's historic sites from the First Spanish Period, San Luis de Talimali probably ranks as the most important after St. Augustine. It was the site of one of the largest of the mission centers, home to a Spanish garrison and the governor's deputy for the area, location of an impressive fortification, jumping-off point for Spanish contact with the natives to the west and north-west of Apalachee, and abode for a small number of Spanish ranchers. From at least the middle of the seventeenth century until the destruction of the missions in 1704, the province of Apalachee headed by San Luis contained the majority of Florida's missionized Indians. Population figures from 1675 indicate that Apalachee by then held more than three-fourths of Florida's mission population.

The 50-acre property on which was located much of the core area of San Luis has been purchased for the people of the State of Florida under the Conservation and Recreation Lands Trust Fund program. Management of the property and responsibility for its preliminary development as a historic and archaeological site have been entrusted to the secretary of state through the Division of Historical Resources under the terms of a lease from the trustees of the Internal Improvement Trust Fund. The site, opened to the public in March 1985, is to be explored systematically under the guidance of Gary Shapiro, director of archaeology, and under the supervision of Jim Miller, chief of the Bureau of Archaeological Research.

This work had its genesis in the immediate need for a compilation of current knowledge about the Apalachee Indians, the activity that took place in Apalachee during the historic period, and the fate of the province's people after the destruction of the missions in 1704. Based on historical sources and on published archaeological research on Apalachee sites, this study is designed to serve as a guide for the archaeologists exploring the site of the fort, mission, and village of San Luis, for the personnel charged with interpreting the site for the general public, and for scholars and the general public who would like to learn more about the aboriginal and the European inhabitants of this area of northwest Florida during the historic period.

In the use of this work it should be kept in mind that the principal corpus of research on which it is based was tailored to meet somewhat narrow specifications, namely, primary sources providing information on site location and appearance and data of ethnographic interest. Although available published documents and secondary sources have substantially lessened the handicap, this study is only a first step toward what the subject deserves and needs. It is offered in the spirit of the remark attributed by Henry Dobyns to Sherburne F. Cook that "One either uses such data as may be available and learns something, however inadequate, or abjures such data and learns nothing."

Further research is needed in the various collections of Spanish documents held by the P. K. Yonge Library of Florida History of the University of Florida, in the transcriptions made by John Tate Lanning held by the Library of the University of Missouri at St. Louis, and in the holdings of the archives of Cuba and Mexico. Ultimately there is need for a search in the Archive of the Indies and in the other repositories of documents from the First Spanish Period for additional material on the Apalachee region and for specific documents mentioned in, but not found in, existing microfilm and photostat collections held in the United States.

Current investigation at the San Luis site offers a unique opportunity to explore the native dwellings and the council house of an Apalachee mission site under circumstances that could be particularly rewarding. Neither the dwellings nor the council house of a principal mission village has been explored. The San Luis site is particularly interesting because of indications that it became the location of the native village associated with the Spanish garrison and the mission of San Luis about 1656, a generation after the establishment of the first mission in the region. If indications prove true, and if it was not the site of an existing village, it will provide an unparalleled opportunity to search for changes in village layout, building style, and technique introduced under Spanish influence. There will be opportunities for comparisons with the results of explorations at one of the Patale sites, results that are being prepared for publication by the Bureau of Archaeological Research. An even greater potential for comparisons may arise from the ongoing exploration of two Patale sites under the direction of Rochelle Marrinan of the Department of Anthropology of Florida State University. Because one of the Patale sites appears to have been abandoned relatively early in the mission period, the portrait of native life that its exploration reveals could serve as a foil against which to assess the magnitude of the Spanish-influenced changes at San Luis after 1656. These projects, in conjunction with other work under the direction of the Bureau of Archaeological Research and Florida State University's Department of Anthropology, promise a new age of discovery for the Apalachee region, based on the foundation established over the past two decades by the work of state archaeologists L. Ross Morrell and B. Calvin Jones.

On the problem of how to spell the native component of the village names and other Indian terms, I have adopted my version of what seemed to be commonly used spellings in the documents consulted. My standard spellings of such native words are included in the glossary and appendixes. This standard will be adhered to in the body of the text. But in reproducing the various mission lists, I have spelled the village names as they appear on my 1976 transcriptions of the lists. Variant names given to the mission villages and some of the variant spellings of the native components of those village names are noted in appendix 3. For the spelling of Spanish names, where diversity also occurs, I have adopted a standard version, choosing the variant that most closely approximates modern usage unless that variant was rarely used by the person concerned or by his contemporaries.

The initial research for this study was performed at the P. K. Yonge Library of Florida History in 1976, when I prepared a series of translations and synopses of documents dealing with Apalachee for Florida's Division of Archives, History and Records Management. I gratefully acknowledge the unstinting assistance that I received from the P. K. Yonge Library's director, Elizabeth Alexander, from her staff, and, during a two-week visit in 1985, from Bruce S. Chappell, archivist. Except for that visit, my recent research has been confined to the holdings of the Florida State Library and the Florida State University Library, supplemented by what is available at the former through interlibrary loan. I am grateful for the assistance of the staffs of both libraries. I wish to express my gratitude as well to the director of the Manuscript Division of the Library of Congress, the South Carolina Division of Archives and History, and the Public Records Office, whom I contacted by mail in an unsuccessful effort to get closer to the original copies of Colonel James Moore's two letters describing his destruction of most of the Apalachee missions. I am most grateful for the encouragement and support I have received from Randall Kelley and Ross Morrell, director and assistant director, respectively, of the Division of Archives, History and Records Management during the time this book was written; Jim Miller, chief of the Bureau of Archaeological Research; Louis Tesar, who painstakingly read the initial draft of this study; Charles Poe, who has prepared the illustrations; and Calvin Jones, Gary Shapiro, and many other colleagues in the Bureau of Archaeological Research and in the Museum of Florida History, who have made their expertise available.

Introduction

AMONG Florida's inland areas, the Tallahassee hills region is one of the few that has attracted Indians since their first appearance in Florida. From early times this land between the Rivers Ochlockonee and Aucilla served as the eastern anchor of what archaeologists designate as the Northwest culture area, comprising all the lands from Mobile Bay east through Apalachee Bay to the Aucilla River and inland to the vicinity of the Alabama and Georgia borders. As Florida's natives developed more advanced cultures and more complex societies, the region around Tallahassee remained one of the areas of most intense activity. That process culminated when the region became the locale for one and possibly two major Mississippian ceremonial centers. After the decline and abandonment of those centers, this land between the rivers continued to hold a large population even though most of the rest of the Northwest culture area was depopulated as the prehistoric period was coming to an end (Milanich and Fairbanks 1980).

As the historic period began, the Apalachee controlled that area of favored land. They were described thus in a recent general survey of Florida archaeology: "Historically the most important group in the Northwest region was the powerful Apalachee, settled on the red clay hills near where Tallahassee now stands. The fertile clay and loam soils of the hills supported the heaviest, most concentrated population in the state" (Milanich and Fairbanks 1980:24).

The first Spaniards to explore Florida extensively were drawn to the same region. Pánfilo de Narváez journeyed north to the province from Tampa Bay in 1528. Hernando de Soto wintered there from October 1539 until early March 1540. In the second quarter of the seventeenth century, the region became the center of intense mission activity by Spanish Franciscan friars. From the mid-seventeenth century, Apalachee was clearly the most important of the Florida

1

mission provinces, and, within Apalachee, San Luis was the most important of the missions.

For half a century the mission village of San Luis de Talimali headed that province of 14 or 15 missions and over 40 settlements. It occupied one of the commanding hills in the Tallahassee area, two miles west of the present state capital complex. From the appointment of the first deputy-governor for Apalachee in the 1640s, the site apparently was the residence of that officer and from the mid-1650s housed the small garrison as well. The principal chief of what was then known as San Luis de Inhayca established his village there in 1656 in order to be near the Spaniards. From that time the site contained a church for the natives, a convent for the friars, a cemetery, an Indian village of unknown size, a principal council house, and a ball court. Soon thereafter it acquired a blockhouse described as "a fortified country house" that served as the deputy governor's residence. In the 1670s, and perhaps earlier, a number of Spaniards who were not soldiers settled there to establish ranches or to trade in the products of the province. Its elaborate fort was built only during the last decade of the mission's existence in response to the growing threat from the English in South Carolina and from the neighboring non-Christian Indians who had come under the Carolinians' influence.

In 1675 the mission of San Luis held 1,400 natives out of the province's total of over 8,000, making it the largest mission center in the province. But this population was spread over its satellite villages as well as the principal village of San Luis de Talimali.

As Spain's westernmost outpost in Florida until almost the end of the seventeenth century, San Luis and the province it headed were the stepping-off point for numerous exploratory or commercial or military expeditions into the region west and northwest of Apalachee.

When the Europeans arrived, the Apalachee lived in somewhat permanent villages, relying heavily on agriculture for their subsistence. Controlling the territory between the Aucilla and lands some distance beyond the Ochlockonee River, they were a distinct group, politically and culturally, recognized as such both by themselves and by other Indian groups far to the south.

As a result of the fierce and determined hostility the Apalachee manifested toward the first Spanish intrusions into their territory in the second quarter of the sixteenth century, the Spaniards made no additional attempts to contact them until early in the next century. By that time the Apalachee's self-sufficiency had abated enough to permit some among them to request the presence of Franciscan friars in some of their villages. Although friars began visiting the easternmost villages in Apalachee in 1608, the authorities did not launch a formal effort to evangelize the province and to bring it into the Spanish ecumene effectively until 1633, when they dispatched two friars to begin such an effort. Five years later the first soldiers made a temporary appearance. During the early 1640s, the Spanish effort expanded significantly, occasioning a revolt in 1647 in which the insurgents torched seven of the eight mission complexes in existence and killed three friars and the governor's deputy and his family. A loyal Christian element enabled the Spaniards to regain control soon thereafter, and during the following quarter century the Apalachee appear to have been thoroughly Christianized. A number of non-Apalachee groups entered the province during that period, most of whom also formed mission villages there.

As in other frontier areas of the Spanish Empire, the mission was the Crown's principal agency for winning the allegiance and obedience of the natives. In the years following the discovery of the New World, the popes gave the Spanish and Portuguese monarchs control over the church there in all matters except doctrine and internal discipline; in exchange, the Crown pledged to promote and support the evangelization of the natives. The Crown controlled the flow of missionaries, paid their passage to Florida, furnished them a stipend as if they were soldiers, and bore some of the cost of equipping the mission churches. Despite the church's transformation into an agency of the Crown under this regime, relations between the friars and the Crown's political authorities were frequently stormy. This was particularly true in Apalachee, where the presence of the soldiers and the locus of control and disciplining of the natives became seriously contended issues.

After the virtual completion of the conversion of Apalachee by the early 1670s, the friars and the political authorities began to look west and northwest to the natives beyond Apalachee's borders; but the arrival of the first English settlers at Charleston during the same period thwarted these efforts at expansion. Ignoring the century-long presence of the Spaniards at St. Augustine and the string of missions along the Georgia coast, the British monarch, in a charter granted to the proprietors of the Carolina colony, set the new colony's southern limit below St. Augustine to encompass almost all of the Florida natives and missions then under Spanish control.

This charter set the stage for a quarter century of conflict that was to culminate in the destruction of all the missions beyond St. Augustine. Averse to submitting to the disciplined life of the missions and to the surrender of much of their native culture that this entailed, and attracted by the prospect of English trade, most of the Creek tribes to the north and northwest of Apalachee threw off their allegiance to the Spanish monarch by preemptorily ousting the friars who appeared and welcoming the English traders. The Florida governors' efforts to counter these moves with threats and force led to open hostilities and the migration of many of the Creek to sites closer to the English settlements where they might strengthen their ties with the English and be less subject to Spanish pressures. The appearance of the French on the lower Mississippi late in the century and their founding of Mobile at the start of the new century made the Carolinians even more determined to eliminate the Spanish presence in Florida before the two Latin rivals could join forces to block the English drive toward the Mississippi and the Gulf of Mexico.

The outbreak of the War of the Spanish Succession provided the excuse for an overt move against St. Augustine and the missions. By mid-1704 most of St. Augustine, except for the fort, and all but two or three of Apalachee's missions had been destroyed. Many of the missions' inhabitants had been killed, enslaved, or forced to migrate, and many at San Luis's garrison had been killed or captured. Under the threat of additional attacks by a superior enemy, the remaining soldiers and most of the remaining natives abandoned the province.

After a brief review of what is known about prehistoric Apalachee, I will explore the encounter between the Apalachee and the first European intruders, the establishment and growth of the missions among the Apalachee, the culture and customs of the historic Apalachee, their political structure at the village level, their language, the mission economy, population trends, interaction and acculturation of Indian and Spaniard, the demoralization of the natives that paved the way for the destruction of the missions, and the dispersion and extinction of the Apalachee as a distinct people.

Chapter 1

The Famed Land of Apalachee

> The Province of Apalache, which had great fame
> wheresoever we went.—Hernández de Biedma 1904(2):5

BIEDMA'S description of Apalachee aptly reflects the experience of the first Spaniards to explore inland in Florida in 1528 under Narváez and in 1539 under de Soto. When Narváez found Indians with articles of gold at the head of Tampa Bay, he inquired of them where the gold had come from. They indicated by signs a province called Apalachen, far from there, giving the Spaniards to understand that it was very rich (Núñez Cabeza de Vaca 1966:24). Eleven years later Hernando de Soto was lured northward by the same tale.

This fabled land of Apalachee stretched less than 40 miles from east to west and no more than that from north to south (figs. 1.1, 1.2). It comprised the land from the west bank of the Aucilla River to a little west of the Ochlockonee and from the Gulf coast to the vicinity of the Georgia border or a little further. Despite their confinement to this circumscribed portion of North Florida, the Apalachee's name became attached to the most important geographical feature of the eastern United States, the Appalachian Mountains. The mountains were identified by that name at least as early as the 1560s by René Laudonnière. William P. Cumming noted that "During the last quarter of the sixteenth century this name became the most popular designation for the southeastern area; it continued to be used by continental geographers until well into the eighteenth century, when it appears as a kind of generic term for the Indian country back of the foreign settlements" (1958:10).

The people of Apalachee whom Narváez and de Soto met were renowned for their valor and ferocity as well as for their prosperity. As de Soto's men moved northward, the natives close to that region warned the Spaniards that

5

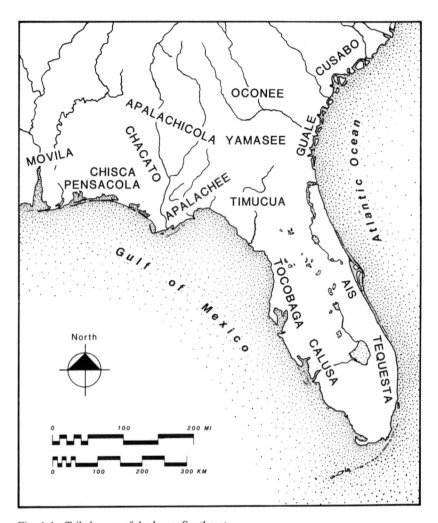

Fig. 1.1. Tribal areas of the lower Southeast.

the Apalachee "would shoot them with arrows, quarter, burn, and destroy them" (Vega 1951:175). The predictions proved accurate. The de Soto chroniclers commented repeatedly on the persistence and ferocity of the Apalachee attacks throughout the months they wintered in that land (Fernández de Oviedo y Valdéz 1904:89; Vega 1951:254–259). On leaving the Apalachee's territory, so vivid was these Spaniards' remembrance of that unrelenting ferocity that, when they reached neighboring Altapaha, Garcilaso recorded that de Soto "resolved to be the first to examine this new land because he wished to ascertain if its inhabitants were as cruel and warlike as those of Apalache" (Vega 1951:267). Another Spaniard, who began a long captivity among Florida's Indians only a few years after de Soto's expedition, saw a different side to the Apalachee character. He paid them even greater tribute in a remarkably prophetic prediction about their mission potential: "They are archers; but by sending them cloth by an experienced and capable linguist their friendship may be easily won. They are the best Indians in Florida; superior to those of Tocobaga, Carlos, Ais, Tegesta and the other countries I have spoken of" (d'Escalante Fontaneda 1976:38).

The people who were the recipients of these tributes were descendants of the Fort Walton peoples of the region and possessed a culture similar to that identified with the Mississippian ceremonial centers. The Apalachee territory possessed at least two multimound centers, one near Lake Jackson and the other near Lake Miccosukee. Like the better-known Moundville and Etowah complexes, these centers are believed to have been abandoned a short time before the Europeans arrived. However, only the Lake Jackson mounds have been investigated enough to permit any dating. The Lake Miccosukee mounds possibly could date to the Woodland period. The persistence of the fame of the Apalachee when Narváez and de Soto landed in south Florida may have been the result in part of the afterglow from a more glorious time when the authorities at one or the other of these centers held sway over a larger territory than that controlled by the historic Apalachee (B. Calvin Jones, personal communication, April 19, 1984; Payne 1981:29–31). With this perspective the "gold" was probably ornaments of hammered copper, which were found as grave goods at Lake Jackson.

Some interpret the lack of specific mention of mounds in association with the Apalachee villages visited by Narváez and de Soto as confirmation not only that the centers had been abandoned but also that the villages had been moved farther south in the Tallahassee hills, where most of the missions appear to have been located. Those who take that position point out that the chroniclers did record the existence of such features elsewhere (Tesar 1980:174, 181). Others interpret Garcilaso's mention of mounds at Osachile as an indication that they were to be found everywhere in Florida in proximity to the major villages in view of the chronicler's statement that "It is fitting that we describe the location and plan of the town of Osachile with the idea of giving some conception of the site and arrangement of the rest of the towns of this great kingdom called Florida . . . as they differ little or nothing from each other" (Vega 1951:170).

Just prior to and during the early historic era, the Apalachee had some ceramic influences from late Lamar peoples from central Georgia with whom

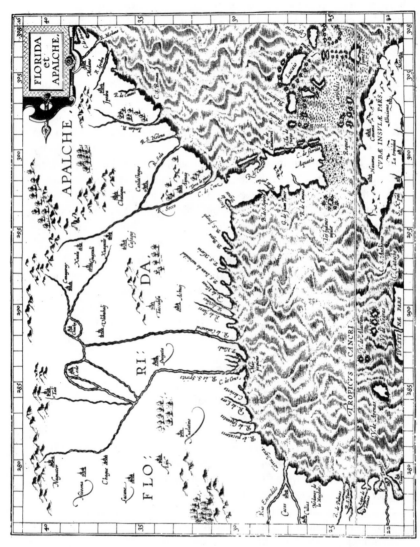

Fig. 1.2. The Wytfliet map of Florida and Apalache, 1597. From a copy in the Florida State University Library.

they had probably merged (Milanich and Fairbanks 1980:193–199; Tesar 1980:169–171). John Scarry, characterizing this transition as the Velda phase, suggests that the changes in the ceramic assemblage may indicate social and political turmoil and a shift in external alliances. Such upheaval forced an abandonment of the mound centers and of the use of exotic sumptuary goods such as the celts and copper plates found in Mound 3 of the Lake Jackson site. Despite this turmoil, however, this Apalachee chiefdom encountered by the first Europeans remained a prestigious complex chiefdom under the new ruling faction (Scarry 1986). Like many others among the tribes of the Southeast, the Apalachee spoke a Muskogean language. Most scholars believe it to be a dialect of the Hitchiti spoken by a number of the tribes living immediately to the north of the Apalachee territory in historic times (Milanich and Fairbanks 1980:228).

The reports of the de Soto expedition in particular provided the earliest details of the Mississippian maize-growing culture that characterized Apalachee and the Southeast in general at that time. Those reports are especially important in that they portray the culture before it had been affected substantially by the European intrusion, except possibly for European- and African-introduced diseases. With the exception of d'Escalante Fontaneda's memoir, the records have so far revealed no other contact between Europeans and the Apalachee until early in the seventeenth century. It is possible that survivors from shipwrecks made their way to Apalachee, as Fontaneda claimed to have done. Archaeologists report Spanish artifacts in some late Fort Walton sites in Apalachee. These, of course, could have been obtained by trade with the natives of South Florida, where shipwrecks commonly occurred, or could have come from the Narváez or de Soto expeditions (Milanich and Fairbanks 1980:227).

The shortage of personnel and the remoteness of Apalachee were doubtless partly responsible for this long hiatus in the Spaniards' contact with the Apalachee. An even more important reason was the markedly hostile reception of both the Narváez and the de Soto expeditions. All of the accounts of these two expeditions highlight the hostility of the Apalachee. Garcilaso's pithy tribute sums up the Spaniards' reluctantly admiring recollection of this people: "By these incidents, one may perceive the savagery and at the same time the audacity of the Indians of that province, for certainly their actions proved that they knew to dare and not to fear" (Vega 1951:250).

As the seventeenth century began, for reasons not known, many native groups in the Florida and Georgia hinterland began to express interest in giving obedience to Spain's monarch and in being Christianized (López 1602; Pareja 1602). In November 1607 two friars reported that "even villages in Apalachee are now requesting ministers" (Pareja and Peñaranda 1607). Perhaps some of the natives were impressed by the tenacity with which the friars continued their work after the massacre of five of their number in the Guale rebellion of 1597, or perhaps they admired the stoic calmness with which the murdered friars met their fate. For others, the interest reflected renewed political strife between contending elite factions (Scarry 1986). For some, perhaps, it was fear that the military odds were about to turn against them as they saw perennial enemies acknowledging Spanish sovereignty.

The fearful natives had no cause for alarm. Spanish policy discouraged anything more than token arming of the natives. Crown directives forbade offensive alliances even with Christian natives and severely restricted even defensive involvement in native wars. The governor reported in 1608 that he had sent forces to Potano to assist the Christian natives there, because a large number of pagan Indians were advancing to make war on them; the Crown was moved to issue this cautious instruction: "Tell him how it has been ordered that, if a battle breaks out, the people whom he has sent are to position themselves in such a way that under no circumstances will it be necessary for them to wage an offensive war, and, that they are to do only what is necessary to support and defend the natives who are vassals of His Majesty." The instructions counseled moderation, prudence, and reflection in such actions and closed with the reminder that the king wished to spread the gospel "without recourse to arms and soldiers and only by means of the ministers and preachers of the gospel, who, when they wish to undertake these conversions are to go alone without an escort of soldiers" (Ibarra 1608).

The redoubtable Fray Martín Prieto led the first renewal of contact with the Apalachee in 1608. Only one year after his arrival in Florida in 1605, he and a companion had set out to begin the evangelization of the Potano. His companion was cowed by the hostility and threats of the natives, and Fray Prieto mercifully sent him back to St. Augustine a few weeks after their arrival. For the next five or six months Fray Prieto labored alone, making daily visits to three of the four villages in the district to teach the catechism. He endured jostling, jeers, and taunts from the majority of the natives for some time before the number who came to learn began to grow. By 1607 he had baptized over half the people in those three villages, and another friar was engaged in the conversion of the fourth. Buoyed by that success, Fray Prieto began making frequent visits to the neighboring Timucua province of Utina. As the friars began an intensive effort in 1608 to Christianize all of western Timucua, he saw that region's long-standing war with Great Apalachee, as he described it, as an obstacle to the progress of their work. Despite some initial opposition to the project from the head chief of the Utina, he resolved to try to end the war.

Fray Prieto dispatched two Apalachee prisoners held by the Timucua at

Cotocochuni to Apalachee ahead of him to inform its people that he was coming on a mission of peace. He followed them to Ivitachuco, the easternmost Apalachee village, accompanied by the head chief of Utina, the chiefs of the Timucua villages in the vicinity of Apalachee, and 150 warriors from Potano and Utina. He found the entire population of the province led by some seventy chiefs assembled there to greet him and estimated the crowd at over 36,000.[1] The peace mission received a friendly reception. Ivitachuco's seventy-year-old chief, opening the conclave, spoke at great length in favor of peace. Fray Prieto then presided over a meeting of the chiefs of the two peoples, all of whom agreed on peace. As the most important of the Apalachee chiefs and as host, the Ivitachucan leader addressed the assembly anew, expressing his joy that peace had been established. After they had feasted, the assembled Apalachee chieftains appointed the *cacique* of the village of Inihayca to visit the governor at St. Augustine (Oré 1936:114–117). An account of these events written by the governor in 1609 indicates that the chief of Inihayca was the brother of the chief of Ivitachuco.

Although Fray Prieto reported that half or more of Apalachee's numerous population desired to become Christian, no permanent Spanish presence in the province was established for another 25 years. Intermittent contact continued, at least to 1612 and probably thereafter, although on a reduced scale. In that year Fray Lorenzo Martínez, superior of the Florida Franciscans, reported that the friars visiting Apalachee were receiving warm appeals to establish a permanent presence there. When informed that there were no missionaries available to serve them, the Indians insisted that the friars set up a cross before leaving and indicate a site where they might build churches to be ready when the friars should become available (Martínez 1612). That the Ivitachucan mission was dedicated to San Lorenzo might mean that a church was built there at the time and so named as a tribute to the Franciscans' superior who had lobbied the king to support the immediate evangelization of the Apalachee (Martínez 1612). San Francisco de Ocone is another site where a church was likely erected. In 1657 its inhabitants claimed that theirs was the first place in Apalachee where Christianity had been established (Rebolledo 1657a).

Fray Martínez reported that the Franciscans' decision to defer establishment of a permanent mission enterprise among the Apalachee was based not

1. Following the opinion that prevailed among scholars when he wrote—that Florida's native population was never large—Father Maynard Geiger suggested that Fray Prieto may have erred considerably in estimating the number of chiefs and the size of the crowd. If, however, the term was used loosely to include both the chief and his second-in-command, 70 should be a conservative figure. A 1647 document mentions that Apalachee then had over 40 chiefs. The subsequent listing of the mission villages and their satellites verifies the reliability of the latter figure. Modern scholars are disposed to accept such estimates of the population's size.

only on the lack of manpower but also on the distance involved, the consequent problem of supply, the need for soldiers in a fortified post to lend support, and the unruliness of some of the Indians, who did not obey their chiefs well.[2] And the friars hinted that there was opposition to the coming of the priests (Martínez 1612; Pareja, Martínez, et al. 1617).

The governor was more explicit. He noted that in Apalachee the chiefs were not given much respect, and that for this reason the friars had twice been forced to leave (Fernández de Olivera 1612b). Meeting as a body five years after the governor's statement, the religious gave more detail concerning these problems.

> The governor . . . has decided . . . not to send any religious to Apalachee because it is so far away and because it is necessary to locate a settlement or blockhouse with soldiers in that land for support and so that there would be foodstuffs for the religious, especially because it is impossible to carry those provisions overland from . . . St. Augustine or to assist them or to support them with what they need. And for this [reason] the religious, who went to see the land have returned, in addition to the fact that some of the Indians obey their chiefs poorly, and the chiefs would like to gain control of their Indians with the aid and support of Your majesty. (Florida Friars in Chapter 1617)

They went on to note that there were friars working along the frontier with Apalachee who were intent on learning the language of their province. That some of the chiefs were among those most desirous of a permanent Spanish presence in order to bolster their control over their tribesmen was doubtless one of the reasons for the hostility shown to the friars.

Other reasons for that hostility were indicated by Fray Luis Gerónimo de Oré when he stressed the need for soldiers: "In Apalachee the priests . . . are not able to have peace with the Indians, for there is much for which they should be taken to task; for instance the extirpation of their immoral practices which are of the worst kind" (Oré 1936:118). Efforts to prohibit polygamy and casual sexual unions were a major source of friction between the friars and the natives. The Guale rebellion 20 years earlier had been sparked by a friar's attempt to deprive the heir to a major chieftainship of his rights of succession because he would not abandon his polygamous habits after becoming a Christian. In his statement, the governor also cited the lack of guarantees that the friars would be protected from hostile caciques and Indians, noting

2. Lack of manpower does not seem to have been a valid reason, inasmuch as over 20 new friars had arrived just a few weeks before.

also the ample opportunity for conversions closer to St. Augustine. This was probably a reference to the missionization of the Utina, Potano, and Fresh Water Timucua, which was well under way at the time (Fernández de Olivera 1612b; Milanich and Proctor 1978:71–77).

It is not clear whether all the talk of the need for soldiers to accompany the friars represented a change in royal policy or whether it was simply another illustration of the colonial officials' policy of "*obedezco pero no cumplo.*" [3] In any event the two friars who began the permanent effort to Christianize Apalachee in 1633 went without an armed escort (Rebolledo 1657a:109).

Presumably these transitory contacts continued until the launching of that effort on October 16, 1633. That Pedro Muñoz and Francisco Martínez, the two friars entrusted with that mission, were described by Governor Luis Horruytiner as knowing the language like natives indicates that they had some experience there. Such contact is also reflected in Bushnell's observation that, since 1625, Timucua Alta (Utina and Ustaqua) and Apalachee had served as primary sources of maize for St. Augustine. Governor Horruytiner's remarks, as well as those of his immediate successors, suggest that the prospect that the Apalachee would solve St. Augustine's chronic food and labor shortages was an important consideration in his launching of the permanent mission effort (Bushnell 1978b:4; Horruytiner 1633; Menéndez Marquez and Horruytiner 1647; Vega Castro y Pardo 1639a). Fray Muñoz appears to have been an excellent choice for the mission. Presumably he was young, as he had arrived in Florida only in 1626. During the 1657 visitation, when the governor encouraged criticism of the friars that would undermine their effort to thwart his policy of expanding the Spanish military presence in Apalachee, Fray Muñoz was one of the two friars singled out for praise by the natives. The chief of Ivitachuco spoke of him as having catechized them with great love. Such was the esteem in which he was held there that one of the village's leaders adopted the name Pedro Muñoz as his own (Rebolledo 1657a:100–101).

Nothing is known of the circumstances that surrounded the arrival of these two friars. Indeed, with the exception of the years 1655–1657, the first 40 years of the Apalachee mission period are largely a great void. Available documents do not even indicate which of the native villages were the first to receive the friars' attention. It is likely that a village such as Inihayca, whose chief went to St. Augustine in 1608 to pledge the province's loyalty to Spain's monarch, would be among the first to be missionized. This may be reflected in the choice of San Luis as the Christian name of the village in tribute to Luis

---

3. *Obedezco pero no cumplo* means "I obey but do not enforce." Recourse was had regularly to this principle to ignore royal orders on the grounds that the king would reverse an unwise decision once he became aware of its harmful consequences.

Horruytiner, the governor who launched the mission effort in Apalachee. Ivitachuco, because of its geographic position, its political importance, and its role in the events of 1608, seems another likely site for one of the first missions. That the chief of Ivitachuco in 1657 was the only Apalachee then given the title of "don" and that Ivitachuco possessed two of the four literate Apalachee among the ruling class (Rebolledo 1657a:100) might also be interpreted as indications of its primacy and early missionization.[4]

The only mission whose foundation date has been determined is San Cosme and San Damián de Cupaica. In 1639 Cupaica's chief (described as the lord of over 200 vassals), accompanied by two Indian leaders, journeyed to St. Augustine to be baptized, with the governor as his godfather. The chief, christened Baltasar, was then given a friar. It is not clear whether he was an additional friar or a reassignment of one of the two already in the province, whose number had not been augmented as late as 1639 (Vega Castro y Pardo 1639a). This mission appears to have been given the incumbent governor's name, Damián. If that were the case, it could be an additional indicator that San Luis was an early foundation, possibly named for Luis Horruytiner, who governed from 1633 to 1638.

The first report on the progress of the conversions was made in 1635. Out of a reputed population of 34,000 the report claimed 5,000 baptisms, a total that seems rather inflated (Friar 1635). In 1639 the governor reported over 1,000 baptisms, remarking that conversions were increasing there more rapidly than elsewhere (Vega Castro y Pardo 1639a).

The first soldiers followed the friars to Apalachee about 1638, in the governorship of Damián de Vega Castro. The chiefs' remarks during the 1657 visitation indicate that soldiers had been present for many years, although not continuously. They apparently remained in or near Apalachee for most of the time until 1651, when the interim governor, Pedro Benedit Horruytiner, withdrew them at the insistence of the friars, who claimed that the soldiers were a hindrance to the progress of their work. When the Apalachee revolted in 1647, the soldiers appear to have been stationed at Governor Ruíz de Salazar's wheat farm between Ivitachuco and Asile. It is not clear whether the soldiers had any common domicile in these early days. They spent part of their time visiting some, but not all, of the villages in the province. On those occasions they were lodged and fed in the village's principal council house as any other guest would have been (Rebolledo 1657a:passim, 1657b:40–42; San Antonio et al. 1657a:107–109).

---

4. The other two literate Apalachee were San Luis's militia captain and the royal interpreter Diego Salvador, whose village of origin is not indicated. The clear, firm signatures of the two Ivitachucans, reflecting confidence and long practice, contrast sharply with the nervous scrawl of the captain from San Luis.

It is possible that trouble among the natives brought about the dispatch of the first soldiers in 1638. Barcia noted for that year that "The Indians of Apalachee warred on the Spaniards, and the governor of Florida opposed them with few men. . . . But despite the small number of men the governor was able to secure from the fort, he humbled the Indians' pride, forcing them to withdraw to their provinces, where he continued to pursue them to good effect" (González de Barcia Carballido y Zúñiga 1951:218). Most authorities have assumed that Barcia was talking about the 1647 revolt and assigned it to the wrong year, as he does not mention that revolt. This is probably the case as there is no reference to a revolt in 1638 in the extant primary sources. But the conjunction of the Barcia reference and the sending of the first soldiers raises the possibility that there was some minor disturbance during that year that provided the pretext for the dispatch of the first soldiers.

The deputy governorship for Apalachee was created in the mid-1640s. In May 1643, shortly after being nominated, Governor Salazar Vallecilla asked for the authority to appoint a lieutenant-governor. The first one was appointed after he arrived in Florida in April 1645. This man, Claudio Luis de Florencia, reached Apalachee in time to perish, along with his wife and children, in the 1647 uprising (Benavides 1722; Royal Officials 1647a; Ruíz de Salazar y Vallecilla 1643, 1645).

One of the problems flowing from the establishment of the Apalachee missions and the placement of soldiers there was that supplies for both groups and gifts for the Indians had to be sent via a long overland route. These gifts played a role in converting the natives and securing their loyalty to Spain. Even greater problems arose from the transport of Apalachee's surplus produce to St. Augustine and Havana and from the opening of trade with other tribes to the west and northwest of Apalachee. As early as 1637 Governor Horruytiner commented that the mission effort could not survive or progress unless a suitable port was found on the Apalachee coast. He reported that he had been sending pilots overland to Apalachee to take soundings, using locally obtained canoes to search for a feasible landing spot for oceangoing vessels (Horruytiner 1637). Two years later, on April 8, 1639, Horruytiner's successor, Governor Castro y Pardo, dispatched a frigate that made the first run from St. Augustine to the Apalachee coast in fewer than 13 days, opening the prospect that St. Augustine's chronic shortage of foodstuffs could be relieved by easy access to Apalachee's abundance (Vega Castro y Pardo 1643).

The establishing of a port in Apalachee proved to be a mixed blessing for St. Augustine. Ships began sailing directly between Havana and the Apalachee coast. In 1643 the governor complained that such ships, coming ostensibly to bring supplies to the missionaries, were taking on cargoes of Apalachee's produce without paying taxes on it (Vega Castro y Pardo 1643). More to the point, the friars had become competitors with the governor and his soldiers, who served as his factors, in this trade with the Apalachee and with neighboring tribes to the west and north. This commercial competition was one of the important elements that generated the bitter feelings between the clergy and the soldiers and that reached a climax in the mid-1650s under Governor Rebolledo (Rebolledo 1657a:passim).

As part of his plan for the development of Apalachee, Governor Castro y Pardo opened contacts with the province's neighboring tribes in an effort to bring peace to the region and thereby expand the possibilities for trade. In 1639 he ended a war between the Apalachee and the neighboring Chacato, Apalachicola, and Amacano,[5] commenting that this achievement was particularly extraordinary because the Chacato had never before been at peace with anybody. He strove less successfully to curb incursions by Indians called Ysisca or Chisca,[6] whom he portrayed as being especially warlike and nomadic, wandering freely through the entire area then comprising Spanish Florida. At that time a group of them reportedly journeyed 200 leagues to St. Augustine to render obedience to the Spanish monarch (Vega Castro y Pardo 1643). Several years later members of this tribe helped spark a revolt against the Spaniards in Apalachee. Governor Castro y Pardo's successor continued the policy of reaching out to bring the neighboring tribes into obedience to the Spanish authorities, going in person into the province of Apalachicola (Leturiondo 1672; Ruíz de Salazar y Vallecilla 1657).

Sometime in the first half of the 1640s the mission effort among the Apalachee expanded dramatically. In mid-1643 the governor reported optimistically that conversions there were increasing greatly (Vega Castro y Pardo 1643). Before 1647 the number of friars had risen to eight, and eight of the village chieftains out of a total of more than 40 had become Christians, allowing the establishment of *doctrinas* in their villages (Royal Officials 1647a). Although there is no direct evidence to that effect, probably most, if not all, of the chiefs mentioned as converts were principal chiefs. All the doctrinas visited by the governor in 1657 were in principal villages.

Early in 1647 a serious uprising halted this progress and briefly eliminated the Spanish presence. Three of the friars perished along with the governor's lieutenant and the lieutenant's family. The rebels torched seven churches and convents along with the mission crosses. The revolt began on February 19 in the new frontier mission of San Antonio de Bacuqua. Those who perished apparently had assembled there to celebrate the feast day of the mission's pa-

---

5. The Amacano had expressed interest in being Christianized when the friars arrived in 1633.
6. He described the Chisca as not having any known settlements and as living in the wilderness. A generation later one large band of them shared a large palisaded settlement in West Florida with some Chacato and Pansacola.

tron saint. Five friars were able to escape because of assistance from some of the Christian natives. Some of the sources said that the soldiers had escaped because they were out in their wheat plantings. They escaped probably because those plantings were located on Governor Salazar's wheat farm, which lay on the eastern border of Apalachee rather than in Apalachee proper on land belonging to the chief of Asile (Benavides 1722; Royal Officials 1647a, 1647b; Ruíz de Salazar y Vallecilla 1657).[7]

The available records do not indicate where the Spaniards who survived the revolt fled while the rebels were in control of the province. It is likely that they retreated well into Timucua territory. On learning of this debacle, the authorities at St. Augustine hastily dispatched a force of 31 soldiers, who recruited 500 warriors in Timucua as allies. Before this force reached Apalachee a much larger rebel force engaged them in a struggle that lasted from eight o'clock in the morning until five o'clock in the afternoon.[8] The Spaniards claimed to have put the rebels to flight finally but said that, having exhausted their shot, they made no attempt to pursue them. They left a considerable quantity of lead on the battlefield, having fired 2,700 balls from their 30 muskets in the course of the day. In fact, the Spaniards, leaving the insurgents in control of the province, returned to St. Augustine believing that additional forces would have to be recruited in Cuba. They speculated that a number of expeditions might be necessary to bring the region back under control and that a permanent garrison of 30 to 40 soldiers might be needed to maintain calm once it had been restored.

At the time of the uprising, Francisco Menéndez Marquez, one of the royal officials who had been governing Florida in lieu of the suspended Governor Ruíz de Salazar, was in Guale to deal with the unrest that disturbed that province also. On his return, while plans were being formulated to raise a larger force to retake Apalachee, Menéndez Marquez hastened to western Timucua with a few troops. He hoped to see what could be done, in conjunction with the loyal Christians there, to contain any additional rebel forays into that province. On arriving at the frontier, he learned that the rebels had been struck with fear from their losses in the recent encounter and had been disheartened by the rapidity of the Spanish response. The rebels had not anticipated such a rapid response, inasmuch as the Spaniards' Timucua allies were then occupied with the planting of their crops. The non-Christianized Apalachee and their Chisca allies had hoped for sufficient time to consolidate

7. It was apparently less than a league from the Apalachee border. But as some of the royal officials at this time considered Asile to be part of Apalachee, the farm is spoken of in some documents as being in Apalachee.
8. The rebel force was described variously as more than 8,000 and as "a multitude." The 8,000 figure is, no doubt, an exaggeration.

their support among the Christian Apalachee and to form alliances with other non-Christian provinces to resist the reassertion of Spanish control. Emboldened by this intelligence and desiring to thwart the rebels' strategy, Menéndez Marquez secretly crossed into Apalachee, with 21 soldiers and 60 Timucuan warriors whom he felt could be spared from the spring planting. Within a month, supported by the loyal Christians in Apalachee, he persuaded the rebels, both Christians and non-Christians, to surrender and to hand over the leaders of the revolt for trial. Twelve of them, who were considered most guilty, were executed in Apalachee, and 26 others were sentenced to some years of forced labor in the royal works. The rest received a general pardon granted in exchange for the province's obliging itself (in the words of the Spanish officials)

to send the Indians that were indicated to them for the *repartimiento*[9] for the royal works and tasks connected with St. Augustine's fort, to which they had been unwilling to subject themselves prior to this, for which they were greatly needed, because most of those from the other Christian provinces had died off, leaving these poor soldiers now unable to sustain their families, because they had no one to make some plantings of corn. (Menéndez Marquez 1648; Menéndez Marquez and Horruytiner 1647; Royal Officials 1647a, 1647b; Ruíz de Salazar y Vallecilla 1647)

In reporting this denouement, the Spanish officials commented that the collapse of the uprising had stimulated a rekindling of Christian fervor among the faithful and had moved many of the non-Christians to seek baptism, noting that now they were raising crosses everywhere with the same joy and enthusiasm with which they had burned them shortly before. By February 1648 the seven burned churches had been rebuilt. The authorities lamented the lack of clerical manpower to translate this fervor into conversions, noting that only two friars could be sent to replace the three who had been killed and the five others who had died there since their arrival (Menéndez Marquez 1648; Menéndez Marquez and Horruytiner 1647).

The sudden expansion of the missions and the fears that it aroused among the unconverted and recently converted, along with the increasing labor demands flowing from the growth of the Spanish presence and the economic activity it generated, created a climate favorable to the outbreak of revolt. The instigation for the uprising came from the non-Christian Apalachee and from

9. A system of forced paid labor for a specified time, developed to extract labor deemed necessary for the common good from natives culturally unaccustomed to providing it voluntarily or consistently.

Chisca in the area. The latter used threats of death to press the Christians into joining them. The available documents do not reveal what success they had among the Christians, but the Spaniards were fearful that their efforts might meet success, alluding to the fact that many were new converts and as fickle in nature as some of the earlier converts from that province. Some probably had accepted the new faith without a full understanding of the change in the old customs and life-style that their decision entailed. Once they had made such a commitment, many of the friars were not at all hesitant about insisting that it was irrevocable—even to the point of chasing down apostates who fled to the woods or to neighboring tribes in order to maintain their old ways. One governor, who was particularly interested in winning over the Chisca to a Spanish allegiance, saw that their nomadism and warlike ways would make them ideal bounty hunters for bringing back fugitive Christian natives (Moreno Ponce de León 1648a, 1648b; Royal Officials 1647a; Vega Castro y Pardo 1639b).

In their postmortems, the Spaniards attributed the uprising to a variety of causes. Friars pointed to the fears aroused by the beginning of Spanish settlement and farming activity and to the increasing labor demands it entailed. Officials and soldiers leveled the same charges at the friars and spoke also of some of the friars' abusive treatment of the Indians, especially of the Indian leaders. They indicted the friars as well for their outlawing of many of the natives' traditions such as their ball game, dances, and recourse to the shaman. The declining number of gifts distributed by the Spanish authorities had added to the dissatisfaction. The importation of supplies for the expanding missions and for the soldiers, the growing volume of trade goods, and the shipping out of the region's produce all led to the increased use of the Indians for the unpopular work of cargo bearing. Governor Ruíz de Salazar's wheat, corn, and cattle operation was indicated as a major source of the natives' grievances. The steady decline of the population of the older mission areas of Timucua and Guale brought mounting pressure for Apalachee participation in the repartimiento labor system (Moreno Ponce de León 1648a, 1648b; Pérez 1646; Royal Officials 1647a, 1647b; Ruíz de Salazar y Vallecilla 1645, 1657; Vega Castro y Pardo 1643).

The diverse reports to the king on the principal causes of the natives' unrest set off a debate that raged for more than a decade and manifested a steadily widening division of opinion among the Spaniards in Florida. It is epitomized in a remark of one of the soldiers in Apalachee in 1657: "The damned priests [are so opposed] to what the Spaniards, or to put it better [to what] your excellency does and proposes" (Rebolledo 1657a:116). Some of the friars stressed the greed of the governors and the presence of the soldiers, alleging that they were merely factors for the governors for the assembling of stores of corn, beans, and skins for shipment to St. Augustine and a burden on and bad example to the natives. The friars accused most of the governors, from Castro y Pardo on, of this abuse, singling out Salazar y Vallecilla as the worst offender. His large corn- and wheat-growing farm received particularly sharp criticism from the friars, who eventually secured its dismantlement by an elected acting governor. The friars accused Governor Vallecilla of using unnecessary official trips as a cover for forcing the natives to carry supplies to his ranch on the pretext that the work requested was for the service of the king. Although the governor had brought in a few slaves from Cuba for this enterprise, the transport of its supplies and produce as well as the work on the ranch itself required Indian labor also. The friars charged these governors with bringing the natives to St. Augustine loaded down as though they were horses or mules. On one such expedition under Vallecilla's successor, they alleged that, of the 200 who set out from Apalachee, no more than ten returned to their homes, the others having died of hunger and exposure either in St. Augustine or on the trail (Bushnell 1981:81–82; Gómez de Engraba 1657a:127–128, 1657b:128–129; Matter 1972:254–257; Moral et al. 1657; Moreno Ponce de León 1648a; Royal Cedula 1651). In the wake of a 1656 rebellion in Timucua, some friars lodged similar charges against the incumbent governor, Diego de Rebolledo (Matter 1972:185–186; Rebolledo 1657a:107–124).

The governors, and Rebolledo particularly, responded in kind, accusing the friars of many of the same charges by eliciting complaints against the friars from the native leaders. Governor Rebolledo's visitation record is a litany of such charges. Although that record leaves the impression that the Apalachee received some coaching from the governor, it also makes it evident (if it is reliable) that some of the friars were at times equally consumed with greed at the expense of the Indians and equally unconcerned with their health and welfare, dispatching the natives on trading expeditions into nonmissionized territory under onerous circumstances, insisting that the natives trade only with them and not with the soldiers, and forbidding the natives to trade directly with the merchants on the ships from Havana. When the ships arrived, friars allegedly attempted to buy up all the trade goods they brought and then sell them to the Indians at twice the price the Indians would have paid at dockside. Then, to make matters worse, those friars required the Indians to transport to the coast without pay the foodstuffs and skins they accumulated in this commerce; the lay traders on the ships were accustomed to compensate them for their labor in moving those goods to the coast (Matter 1972:257–258; Prado 1654; Rebolledo 1657a:passim).

Not unexpectedly, these conflicting charges left the authorities in Spain nonplussed about who was truly at fault and what remedies should be adopted. In 1648 the Crown approved the dispatch of 200 horses from Cuba which, a friar reported, the island's inhabitants had offered to donate to relieve Florida's natives of the increasingly onerous cargo bearing (Moreno Ponce de León 1648b; Royal Cedula 1648). But there is no evidence that these horses reached Florida. To resolve the continuing disputes and confusion, the Crown instructed a treasury official at St. Augustine, José de Prado, to investigate the trouble secretly, without advising the governor of his commission. Prado attributed the revolt principally to the Indians' resentment of the abusive use of them as cargo bearers. Among the Timucua (and probably among the neighboring Apalachee as well), cargo bearing was regarded as particularly odious and was relegated to the women, the young, and, above all, to so-called hermaphrodites. The last group was particularly despised and was given various unpleasant tasks. It was probably the association of cargo bearing with this last group, as well as the hardships involved, that made that labor so resented by the proud native who considered himself a warrior and a man. Prado suggested bringing in 50 mules as a long-term remedy. For the short term, after observing that some continued cargo bearing was essential to supply St. Augustine and its soldiers with food and to bring supplies to the friars, he suggested an immediate prohibition on using the Indians to carry trade goods. He rejected the friars' allegations against Governor Vallecilla's grain and cattle operations. But he agreed that the other charges made by the friars were well founded, particularly the complaints that sometimes in cold weather the natives died on the trail from the exertions to which they were subjected. He noted that only rarely were they paid for their work, and then it was with something of little value such as a knife.

Despite the Crown's order of secrecy, Prado gave the governor an opportunity to defend his conduct. He asked Rebolledo for his comments concerning these grievances voiced by the natives and by the friars in their behalf. Prado enclosed the governor's reply in his report to the king. In that reply, the governor, while professing a concern for the Indians' welfare, maintained that the customary use of Indian labor was a practical necessity in order to maintain the colony. Although it is not clear if Prado showed his report to the governor, Rebolledo's conduct during the 1657 visitation indicates that, by that time at least, he was aware of its tenor. The Apalachee leaders' unanimity, under Rebolledo's apparent guidance, in portraying the soldiers as no less than angels and in asserting that they never imposed on the Indians in any fashion seems to be a directed response to Prado's charge that when the governors sent out soldiers, the Indians were required to sustain them and to work for them without pay. The complaints against the friars' trading activities seem to be similarly inspired. The friars charged that the governor invented the complaints against them to deflect attention from his own misdeeds and to make the friars seem responsible for the revolt in Timucua. So striking is the contrast between the saintly conduct attributed to the soldiers and the disreputable conduct ascribed to some of the friars that the reader is left with the feeling that the soldiers should have been wearing the friars' robes and that many of the friars were fitter candidates for the barracks or even for prison than for the religious life (Prado 1654; Rebolledo 1657a:passim; San Antonio et al. 1657b). That Rebolledo was capable of falsifying such evidence is suggested strongly by the Council of the Indies' appraisal of the complaints against the governor by soldiers as well as by friars (Council of the Indies 1657a, 1657b:130–135).

Most of the traditional secondary sources speak of a second uprising in Apalachee in 1656 or 1657, in conjunction with the revolt that broke out in Timucua in 1656. That the Timucuan revolt did not spread to Apalachee is clear from primary sources. In September 1657 six friars reported that Timucua launched its revolt expecting that Apalachee would join in and that Apalachee had indeed been on the verge of revolt itself. That it did not join they attributed to God in "inspiring one of the most important of the chiefs of that province not to go along with the decision of the rest, who had already resolved [on revolt], and to seek to calm them" (San Antonio et al. 1657b). Soldiers commissioned by Governor Rebolledo to investigate rumors of impending trouble (and also probably to look for fugitive Yustaga) reported unequivocally that all the rumors of imminent revolt in Apalachee were inventions of the priests, for the purpose of thwarting the governor's plans to enlarge the military force there and to build a fort. One soldier remarked that "this is the sum total of the uprising in Apalache, because I do not find any other"; another, in playing down the threat of revolt, attributed the rumors to "Timucuan gossips who have assumed that they [the Apalachee] are ready to revolt because they asked them to" (Rebolledo 1657a:118). And the governor himself, writing in 1657 about his having 26 of the leading Apalachee as his houseguests, stated clearly that their loyalty was the principal reason that Apalachee did not participate in the recent revolt in Timucua (Rebolledo 1657a:112). The absence of revolt in Apalachee at this time was reflected equally clearly in a 1664 note to the king in which some friars protested the continued presence of the soldiers, whose main function, they maintained, was to conduct trading expeditions to the non-Christians. The burdens this activity placed on the Indian, they complained, was the main reason for the recent uprising in Timucua and for moving Apalachee to the edge of revolt at that time (Franciscan Friars 1664). The threat of revolt in the province seemed to have been real, or at least was so perceived by some of the friars. During this crisis, six friars hastily departed for Havana on a ship that was lost at sea (Rebolledo 1657a:112).

During this decade of conflict, Florida's natives were traumatized as well by a series of epidemics that killed uncounted thousands between 1649 and

1659. Up until 1657, Apalachee was not as severely affected as were Guale and Timucua (Moreno Ponce de León 1651; Rebolledo 1655, 1657a:111; Ruíz de Salazar y Vallecilla 1650). Late in 1659 the incoming governor reported that a recent epidemic of measles had killed 10,000 Indians. If that figure is accurate, many of the victims must have been Apalachee. In 1657 Governor Rebolledo had remarked that the epidemics prior to that year left few people in either Guale or Timucua (Aranguíz y Cotes 1659; Rebolledo 1657a:111).

Governor Rebolledo himself was one of the casualties of the decade of conflict. The Council of the Indies was gravely alarmed by the 1656 revolt and by the demographic disasters that preceded and followed it. Moved by the criticisms leveled at the governor by the friars and by others, the council, in June 1657, took the unusual step of recommending the immediate removal and imprisonment of Governor Rebolledo, blaming him for having created a situation that seemed to threaten the total loss of the Florida missions (Council of the Indies 1657a). The council reiterated its recommendation a few weeks later, despite a plea by Rebolledo's agent in Spain that the Crown suspend its decision. In the name of justice and equity the agent insisted that Rebolledo have an opportunity to defend himself and that his accusers first be required to furnish proof of their allegations (Council of the Indies 1657c:135–138). The deposed governor had no opportunity to vindicate himself, dying shortly after he had been imprisoned.

Although this period was not the "Golden Age" that it has been called (Gannon 1983:49; Spellman 1965), as the 1650s drew to a close a period of accommodation appears to have begun that was to last for a quarter of a century or so.[10] The encounter phase between Spaniard and Apalachee had ended. The mission system and the Spanish military presence in Apalachee appeared to be solidly rooted and acquiesced to by most of the natives despite the loss in 1657 of so many friars versed in their language. A decade later a Spaniard boasted that the area west of St. Augustine through the province of Apalachee had been Christianized thoroughly. The authorities began to push the "rim of Christendom" westward and northwestward to embrace the Chacato and the Apalachicola, who, as early as Governor Ruíz de Salazar's visit to their territory in the mid-1640s, reputedly had expressed an interest in being catechized (Leturiondo 1672; Ruíz de Salazar y Vallecilla 1657). A routine had been established that persisted until it was disturbed and then destroyed by the Carolinians and by the native neighbors of the Apalachee who entered the English orbit.

10. The period 1660–1675 is one of those for which the least amount of documentation of events occurring in the missions is available.

Chapter 2

Villages and Missions of Apalachee and Apalachicola

> Thenceforward the country was well inhabited, producing
> much corn, the way leading by many habitations like
> villages.—Elvas 1904:47

> In addition to the principal town, there were many more
> scattered throughout the vicinity at a half-league, one, one
> and a half, two and at times three leagues apart. Some
> comprised fifty or sixty dwellings and others a hundred
> more or less, not to mention another great number which
> were sprinkled about and not arranged as a town.—Vega
> 1951:184

ALTHOUGH de Soto and his men spent five months wintering in Apalachee,
the chroniclers of that sojourn provided little information about the settlement
pattern there that is more specific than what is contained in epigraph to this
chapter. Unlike references to the other areas in which they tarried or even to
many through which they passed rapidly, few of the Apalachee villages are
described in any detail, and only four or five are mentioned by name: Ivitachuco, the province's eastern portal; an intermediary village or villages referred to by the names Uzela and Calahuchi; a western village identified variously as Anhayca Apalache, Iniahico, and Iviahica; and a settlement named
Ochete, six leagues from Anhayca on the way to the coast.[1] Ivitachuco and
Anhayca became mission centers a century later, but Ochete, Uzela, and Cal-

1. This distance is taken from the Fidalgo de Elvas's original Portuguese edition of 1557 rather
   than from the English translation by Buckingham Smith, which gives the distance as 8 leagues.
   The Fidalgo edition placed Anhayca 10 leagues from the coast.

24

ahuchi were never mentioned by those names during the mission era. One of the chroniclers described Anhayca as the seat of the lord of all that country (Elvas 1904:46–47; Fernández de Oviedo y Valdéz 1904:78–79; Hernández de Biedma 1904:6–7; Vega 1951:175–184). Both the archaeological evidence and later historical documents confirm the image of a territory heavily sprinkled with sizable villages, hamlets, and individual farmsteads.

De Soto reached Ivitachuco only a few hours after crossing the Aucilla River (Fernández de Oviedo y Valdéz 1904:79). It appears to have been a settlement of some importance even then as it is one of two settlements named by the four de Soto chroniclers whose work has survived. Garcilaso described it as a village of 200 large, strong houses, noting that it contained many small ones as well, which lay about the center like suburbs. He described Anhayca as having 250 large houses. In describing the settlement pattern, the chroniclers agree in general that it consisted of rather small villages dispersed over the countryside with some located close to one another, as satellites to a main village. They also agree on seeing individual isolated homesteads scattered among the planted fields, which are portrayed as extensive (Elvas 1904:47; Vega 1951:138, 184). Villages do not appear to have been fortified with palisades. Neither the Narváez nor the de Soto account mentions palisades in Apalachee, and de Soto found it necessary to add some sort of fortification to the village he chose for his winter quarters (Vega 1951:193–194).

The same general pattern seems to have persisted until a century later, in the early years of the mission era, and to have remained substantially intact until the destruction of the Apalachee settlements in 1704 (Rebolledo 1657a:passim; Solana 1687a:17–39; Solana 1702). The houses are pictured as made of thatch of grass or palm leaves. The de Soto chroniclers noted that the Apalachee structures were more like those in east and south Florida than those belonging to their Hitchiti and Muskogee relatives to the north. They observed an abrupt change in the style of the habitations beginning with the first village de Soto encountered after heading north from Apalachee (Elvas 1904:53; Hernández de Biedma 1904:9–10).

Although general agreement marks the early descriptions of Apalachee, some striking divergences emerge as well. Cabeza de Vaca's Apalachee differs notably from that presented by de Soto's chroniclers. Garcilaso's Anhayca Apalachee was a settlement of 250 large, good houses, surrounded by many smaller villages scattered about the countryside at varying distances. The satellite villages ranged in size from 50 to 60 up to approximately 100 dwellings (Vega 1951:184).

The Fidalgo's narrative paints a similar image of a main town surrounded by satellite villages, remarking that "the Campmaster, whose duty it is to divide and lodge all the men, quartered them about the town at a distance of half a league to a league apart." The image of a relatively compact main town is suggested by the Fidalgo's comment that "on Saturday, November 29, in a high wind an Indian passed through the sentries . . . and set fire to the town, two portions of which were instantly consumed" (Elvas 1904:47). Cabeza de Vaca's settlement of Apalachen, supposedly the largest in Apalachee, is a hamlet of 40 "small and low houses reared in sheltered places out of fear of the great storms that continuously occur in the country"; its buildings were made of straw and surrounded by "dense timber, tall trees, and numerous water pools where there were so many fallen trees and of such size as to greatly obstruct and impede circulation" (Núñez Cabeza de Vaca 1964:25–26). In Cabeza de Vaca's Apalachee, ponds and lakes appear to have been everywhere. There were ponds near the village of Apalachen where they stayed, and there was another village on the other side of one of those ponds. The Indians used those bodies of water to attack and retreat, and Narváez's men were unable to cope with those tactics. Cabeza de Vaca considered the country to be inhabited thinly (1964:25–29).

It is possible that Cabeza de Vaca's appreciation for the land was distorted by the enfeebling illness that afflicted the Spaniards and by their failure to find the gold that they had been led to expect. Although it was midsummer when they were in Apalachee, he inexplicably described the land as very cold (Núñez Cabeza de Vaca 1964:27). The de Soto accounts made no mention of ponds or lakes in the area as a whole or in the various villages, and they made no comment on fallen timber or difficulties in moving about. Those accounts describe the land as populous. Garcilaso was struck by the differences between the accounts. He suggested that the Narváez expedition may never have penetrated far from the seacoast but had remained in the rough and swampy lowlands where the woods were dense and passage was difficult, conditions even de Soto's men commented on when they went in search of the coast from Apalachee (Vega 1951:185–186).[2]

The site of the Anhayca Apalachee, where de Soto wintered, has not yet been identified, but almost all researchers agree that it is located in the Leon County area (Tesar 1980(1):338). Louis Tesar, author of a 1980 study of this problem, concluded that it is somewhere in the vicinity of Tallahassee, ruling out the San Luis de Talimali mission site as well as the Lake Jackson site favored by earlier authorities (Tesar 1980(1):301). In interpreting the chronicler's estimates of the distances they had traveled, Tesar relied exclusively on the 2.63-mile legal league. If he had employed the common league of 3.45

2. Garcilaso, of course, was not an eyewitness to the events and places that he was describing, but he interviewed a participant extensively and had access to the manuscripts prepared by two additional eyewitnesses, Juan Coles and Alonso de Carmona.

miles, used at times in the sixteenth century, he would have put this site farther west than he thought possible when he excluded the San Luis and the
Lake Jackson areas as possibilities.

One of the names applied to de Soto's winter quarters, and possibly both
names, survived into the early mission period. The name Anhayca Apalache,
applied by the Fidalgo to the region's head village, reappears in the account of
Fray Prieto's peacemaking foray into Apalachee territory in 1608, which was
described in chapter 1. On that occasion the chiefs assembled at Ivitachuco
delegated the chief of Inihayca to go to St. Augustine to give allegiance to the
Spanish authorities. Friar Maynard Geiger, who translated this account of the
event, commented that Inihayca probably was the Anhayca Apalache mentioned by the Fidalgo (Oré 1936:115–117). The name reappeared almost a
half century later in the account of Governor Rebolledo's 1657 visitation of
the province. That account lists the mission villages by their native names for
the first time. San Luis was then called San Luis Xinayca, a rendering almost
identical with the Inihayca of 1608, and on a second occasion in the same
document it was called San Luis Nixaxipa (Rebolledo 1657a).[3] Just as the de
Soto chroniclers' Anhayca was probably a garbled version of Inhayca, their
Iniahico or Iviahica could also be representations of Nijajipa, as apprehended
by European ears new to the speech of Florida's natives. The later name of
San Luis de Talimali appears in the records only in 1675.

Prior to the start of the mission period, there is no other significant mention of Apalachee or its people. The only statements are some passing and
questionable references to Apalachee's limits, the number of settlements it
contained, and its population. In 1601 the governor spoke of Apalachee's borders extending to the vicinity of Panuco in Mexico. In 1608 a friar described
the province as having 107 towns. A 1617 estimate placed the population at
about 30,000 (Gerónimo 1617; López 1602; Méndez de Canço 1601b; Peñaranda 1608). As noted earlier, there is a pronounced lack of identification of
individual Apalachee villages both for the period of informal contacts between 1608 and 1633 and for the first 22 years after the commencement of the
formal mission effort in 1633. The records reveal the establishment of the San
Damián de Cupaica mission in 1639 after the baptism of that village's chief in
St. Augustine. That the Bacuqua mission was founded before 1647 is known
from its having been the site where the Apalachee uprising began on February
19 of that year. Seven other missions, unnamed, existed at this time. All but
one were put to the torch during the rebellion.

The mission of Ivitachuco is mentioned in a 1651 deed drawn up there

---

3. In seventeenth-century Spanish, the letter *x* could represent either a *j* or an *r*. Inasmuch as the
   Muskogean languages did not have an *r*, the names most likely are Jinayca and Nijajipa.

giving Governor Ruíz de Salazar's son title to the lands on which the governor had founded his wheat and cattle ranch. The chief's literacy indicates that the mission had been in existence for some time. The governor's hacienda was described as bordering "on the new place of Bittachuco," which suggests that the village had been moved recently (Benavides 1722; Ruíz de Salazar y Vallecilla 1657; Vega Castro y Pardo 1639b). It is to be presumed that the eight missions that existed when the revolt began at Bacuqua included all but two of the nine missions named on the first formal listing of the Apalachee missions in 1655. Two of those eight missions of 1647 were Cupaica and Bacuqua. San Luis, Ivitachuco, and Ocone probably constituted another three of these early missions, and Patale seems to be a likely candidate. Recent archaeological exploration of one of the two known Patale sites indicates that it belongs to the early mission period and that it was abandoned by about mid-seventeenth century. Presently there is no basis for conjecture on which two of the remaining four known to have been founded by 1655 (Aspalaga, Ayubale, Ocuia, and Tomole) were already established in 1647.

In the absence of any evidence that the Florida inland missions followed the reduction approach common in other mission regions at this time, it has usually been assumed that the friars erected their churches and convents in the preexisting principal villages. (*Reducción* involved the concentration of native populations at sites usually chosen by the priests to facilitate conversion and acculturation. The priests provided the means of subsistence initially to attract the natives.) For Apalachee in particular, the size of the principal villages, the sedentary nature of the people, the compactness of the territory, and the density of its population all militated against the adoption of a reduction approach. Later, after the missions had been established, some Apalachee mission villages moved. San Antonio de Bacuqua moved in 1657, avowedly because of the exhaustion of the soil and of easily available firewood at the existing site (Rebolledo 1657a:90–91). More is known about the reasons for the moving about of Timucua's people. Timucua's experience suggests that most of Apalachee's other site changes probably were dictated by secular rather than religious authorities or by the natives' own economic interests.

The earliest list, composed after the beginning of the mission effort in Apalachee, is a relatively complete catalog of the Apalachee missions and their distances from St. Augustine (table 2.1). The 1657 list (table 2.2) reveals that Bacuqua was the only such site omitted from the earlier list. Bacuqua may have been omitted because it had neither a church nor a friar (when the governor visited the village in 1657, its chief noted that the village had neither). Alternatively Bacuqua may have been left off the 1655 list merely because it was not meant to be a complete enumeration of the missions that had been

Table 2.1. The mission list of 1655

Village	Distance from St. Augustine (leagues)
San Miguel de Asile (Timucua)	75
San Lorenzo de Apalache [Ivitachuco]	75
San Francisco de Apalache [Oconi]	77
La Concepción de Apalache [Ayubale]	77
San Josef de Apalache [Ocuia]	84
San Juan de Apalache [Aspalaga]	86
San Pedro y San Pablo de Apalache [Patale]	87
San Cosme y San Damián [Cupaica]	90
Coaba in the Apalache chain of mountains	150
San Luis de Apalache	88
San Martín de Apalache [Tomole]	87

SOURCE: Diez de la Calle 1659.
NOTE: There are some differences among the versions of this document in the Lowery Collection, the Buckingham Smith Collection, and M. Serrano y Sanz's *Documentos historicos*. In the Lowery version, San Lorenzo is said to have a population of 2500. The mission at Coaba does not appear on Lowery's and Smith's lists. Both Lowery and Serrano y Sanz give Patale as San Pedro y San Pablo de Kpal.

Table 2.2. The mission list of 1657

Principal village	Satellites
San Damián de Cupaica	Nicapana, San Cosme, San Pedro, Faltassa, San Lucas
Santa María de Bacucua	Guaca
San Pedro de Patali	Ajamano,[a] Talpahique
San Juan de Aspalaga	Pansacola, Sabe, Nipe (or Jipe or Sipe)
San Luis de Xinayca or Nixaxipa	Abaslaco, San Francisco
San Martín de Thomole	Ciban, San Diego, Samoche
San Joseph de Ocuya	Sabacola, Ajapaxca, Chali
San Francisco de Ocone	San Miguel
Santa María de Ayubale	Cutachuba
San Lorenço de Ybitachuco	San Juan, San Pablo, San Nicolas, Ajapasca

SOURCE: Rebolledo 1657a: passim.
a. Possibly Ayamano.

founded up to that time. At least two Timucua missions founded before 1655 were not mentioned and possibly more (Hann 1986; Rebolledo 1657a:90–91).

The missions' distances from St. Augustine are probably only rough estimates rather than accurate measurements. It is somewhat puzzling that Asile, supposedly located east of the Aucilla River,[4] is given the same distance from St. Augustine as Ivitachuco, situated west of the river. From later lists, the two villages are known to have been two leagues or 5.2 miles apart.

Table 2.1 is the only mission list whose origin or raison d'être is unknown. It appears in a rare work published in 1659 by a cleric known to have served in Guatemala, not in Florida. The village list of 1657 stems from Governor Rebolledo's visitation of the province during January and February of that year. It is the most complete of the lists in that it mentions not only the ten principal villages that were mission sites at that time but also at least 25 of their satellite villages, indicating the head village within whose jurisdiction they fell. Christian and native names are given for the ten principal villages. Sixteen of the satellite villages are identified by native name alone, the other nine only by saints' names. Altogether, the list identifies 35 of the more than 40 settlements said to be in the province a decade earlier. In subsequent documents one additional principal village and possibly four other satellite villages are mentioned, for a total of 40 (Florencia 1695; Leturiondo 1678; Paiva 1676).

Such a large number of villages in Apalachee's compact territory suggests a continuation of the settlement pattern depicted by the de Soto chronicles more than a hundred years earlier, that is, main villages surrounded by satellite villages. Despite the depletion of the population by epidemics, this pattern seems to have persisted to the end of the century, in contrast to most of Timucua where the number of villages shrank steadily.

As noted, the native portion of the name of the head village, San Luis de Jinayca, is almost identical to that of de Soto's time, Anhayca. Despite the similarity in names, the Jinayca of 1657 probably did not occupy the same site as did de Soto's Anhayca. Correspondence appended to the 1657 visitation record reveals that the chief of San Luis had moved his village the previous year (Rebolledo 1657a:116–117). Nonetheless there is an intriguing possibility that the Spaniards chose the San Luis site as their headquarters because it had such a historic association. It seems probable that for their own security the Spaniards would have chosen a location in the general vicinity of the principal chief's earlier village.

The 1657 documents make no specific mention of San Luis as the head village, although there are intimations that its chief played a leadership role. This role might be inferred, first of all, from the Spanish decision to locate the

4. Calvin Jones has identified a mission site west of the Aucilla River as an Asile site.

garrison and the blockhouse there. Several letters by Spanish soldiers in Apalachee indicate that the San Luis chief was in some way a leader of the province. At the same time, other passages indicate that decisions were reached in a collegial fashion by a vote of all the chiefs. One of the soldiers' letters reveals that other Apalachee chieftains were jealous of the chief of San Luis because of his relationship with the Spaniards. Moreover, his leadership of the Apalachee opposition to involvement in the recent revolt in Timucua caused ill feelings toward him among the Yustaga and among the Apalachee who sympathized with their plight (Rebolledo 1657a:115–119). Although there is no concrete evidence pointing in that direction, Governor Ruíz de Salazar's choice of the lands between Asile and Ivitachuco as the location for his hacienda and, particularly, his stationing of the soldiers on the ranch might be interpreted as an indication that he had intended to make the Ivitachuco region the site of Spanish headquarters for the province. The 1647 killing of the lieutenant and his family may have cast a cloud over western Apalachee.

The 1657 record also provides the Christian names of a number of the leading Indians of each village. It names the chief of the principal village, if he was present, and the chiefs of the satellite villages. For several of the villages the name of the *inija,* or second in command, was also noted, and occasionally the names of additional leading men were catalogued. The governor visited only the principal village of each jurisdiction, requiring the chiefs and other leading men of the satellite villages to appear before him in the principal lodge of their head village. Governor Rebolledo seems to have invited only the leaders to his assemblies (Rebolledo 1657a:passim), in contrast to the 1694 visitation in which all or most of the population seems to have participated.

This 1657 visitation record also contains a number of anomalies. Rebolledo concluded his visitation of Apalachee at Asile, recording it as under the jurisdiction of Apalachee, although elsewhere Asile has been clearly identified as a Timucua village. Bacuqua was identified as Santa María de Bacuqua, but on all subsequent lists the name appeared as San Antonio de Bacuqua. The name change may have accompanied the village's move to a new site. During the visitation the settlement's leaders received permission to move the village to another site one-half league away.

San Luis was referred to by two distinct native names, Jinayca and Nijajipa. When Rebolledo arrived at Aspalaga, the leaders were away for the *Junumelas.*[5] Rebolledo left word that Aspalaga's leaders should appear at San Luis on January 22, 1657, the day set for the visitation there. At that session, the village was first referred to as San Luis de Jinayca. When the Aspalagans assembled there, the name was rendered as San Luis de Nijajipa. In 1657 only

5. Probably the *Hurimelas,* or fire-hunt, described by Bishop Calderón.

two satellites were mentioned for San Luis, Abaslaco and San Francisco. A generation later San Luis was said to have three satellites, San Francisco, San Bernardo, and San Agustín. In the 1680s it was spoken of as having four villages under its jurisdiction.

Because the 1657 list represents an itinerary recording the visitation day at each mission, some inferences about village location can be drawn from it. The governor began the visitation at Cupaica (presented in 1655 as the farthest from St. Augustine) and proceeded to Bacuqua, Patale, Aspalaga, San Luis, and Tomole, in that order, before going to the more easterly villages. There the order of visitation was Ocuia, Oconi, Ayubale, and Ivitachuco. The governor visited Tomole on January 23. Almost two weeks passed before he resumed the visitation at Ocuia on February 5. Common sense suggests that the governor chose this itinerary because the first six villages were relatively close together in the western part of the province, and in going from Cupaica to Bacuqua to Patale and to Aspalaga he did not pass over any other villages. On several later itineraries, the visitation of Aspalaga was associated with the easterly group and sandwiched between Ocuia and Oconi. This change suggests that Aspalaga had been moved eastward before the appearance of the next mission list a generation later.

For the period 1657–1672 there is almost no documentation for the progress of the Apalachee missions. Two remarks during the period suggest that there was a lull in missionary activity for a time and that little progress was made in advancing conversions. Initially this may have been a result of the loss of six friars who drowned when they left Apalachee for Havana during the troubled days of the 1656 uprising in Timucua. A 1672 document states tersely that all the Indians from Apalachee eastward have been Christianized in contrast to the Apalachicola to the west. Although completely non-Christian, they had sworn obedience to the Spanish Crown and traded peacefully with the soldiers from Apalachee who frequented their villages.

By 1672 the number of Apalachee mission villages had grown by one, to 11 containing 8,000 to 9,000 Indians served by 11 friars. The new village was Santa Cruz de Capoli, also known as Santa Cruz de Ychuntafun or Santa Cruz y San Pedro de Alcantara de Ychutafon (Díaz Vara Calderón 1675; Franciscan Commissary General 1673; Leturiondo 1672; Moreno 1673). The 11 villages were all of the strictly Apalachee mission villages.

After completing the missionization of the Apalachee, the friars began to reach out to other groups both within the province of Apalachee and in the territory to its west and northwest, the so-called province of Apalachicola, parts of which at times were referred to as the province of the Chacato. During Governor Ruíz de Salazar's visit to that province in the 1640s, both the Apalachicola and the Chacato reportedly had requested friars. In the early 1660s bands of Chacato again requested baptism (Díaz Vara Calderón 1675:8–9; Hita Salazar 1675b; Ruíz de Salazar y Vallecilla 1657; Valverde and Barreda 1674). It is reported that subsequently a large unidentified band of Indians who lived far to the west (and were probably Creek) also requested that missionaries come to live among them.

At the invitation of the Franciscan provincial, some 3,000 to 4,000 of this unidentified band were said to have come from a distance of 100 leagues to form a chain of nine settlements along the Apalachicola River six leagues from the sea. The villages were described as two leagues apart from each other but with the first and the last separated by a distance of only eight leagues. One of the friars reporting this development commented that the provincial, aware of the lack of friars in Florida, went to Havana to find some. The provincial dispatched Fray Alvaro de Navia and Fray Andrés de Armas to Florida, seemingly to establish a mission among the migrants. However, no further mention is made of villages, people, or missions in this area along the lower Apalachicola, not even in Bishop Calderón's letter, despite the fact that he went out of his way to learn about the tribes to the west and northwest of Apalachee and to list their villages if possible. The only mention of a mission that could conceivably be a fruit of his effort is that of Santa Cruz de Sabacola, which was founded on the Apalachicola River at about that time. However, it was on the upper part of the river, and its inhabitants appear to have come down from a site on the Chattahoochee. The friar refers to the river on which these newcomers settled as "a river which is called 'of Apalachee' which is six leagues distant from the sea toward the west," undoubtedly the Apalachicola or one of its tributaries (Franciscan Commissary General 1673; Moreno 1673). There are some striking parallels between these 1673 references and the data from the Lamhatty account as presented by Swanton (1922:130–31). In a recent survey, Nancy Marie White found no historic period aboriginal sites in the middle and lower valley of that river, noting that "Curiously enough, few historic aboriginal sites have been located from about the midpoint of the valley and downstream. . . . strangest of all there is no evidence for Lower Creek/Seminole occupation" (White 1986:7).

At the same time, mission activity was initiated among several groups of non-Apalachee Indians living within the territory of the Apalachee: the Tama, Yamasee, Capara, Amacano, and Chine. The result was the establishment of a number of new missions in Apalachee and in the territory to the west of it in 1674 and 1675. The documents give no indication of how long these non-Apalachee groups had been living within the province. In 1633 the Amacano were mentioned as having approached the province seeking baptism, but there is no further reference to them until the 1670s. From their own land the Tama had asked for friars as early as 1619 (Díaz Vara Calderón 1675:8–9; Hita

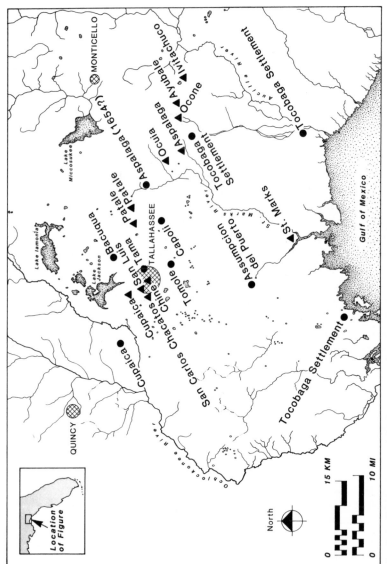

Fig. 2.1. Southern part of Apalachee province showing locations of mission villages (see appendix 8). ▲ = definite identification of mission site. ● = location of site based on documentary sources.

Table 2.3. Fernández de Florencia's mission list of 1675

Mission	Population	Location
San Luis	1400	(1 league from there to)
San Damián de Acpayca	900	(2 leagues to)
San Antonio de Bacuqua	120	(2 leagues to)
San Pedro de Patale	500	(4 leagues to)
San Joseph de Ocuya	900	(1.5 leagues to)
San Juan de Aspalaga	800	(1 league to)
San Francisco de Oconi	200	(0.5+ league to)
Concepción de Ayubale	800	(1.5 leagues to)
San Lorenço de Ybitachuco	1200	(1.5 leagues to Asile)
Candelaria (La Tama and Yamassee)	300	(1.5+ leagues from San Luis and 2 leagues to)
San Martín de Tomole	700	(2+ leagues to)
Santa Cruz de Ytuchafun	60	
Assumption of Our Lady	300	(on the path to the sea from San Luis— for Capara, Amacano, and Chine)
Nativity of Our Lady (?)	40	(2 leagues from San Luis to a river by which one goes to the Province of Apalachicole)
San Nicolas de Tolentino	100 Chacto	(10 leagues from the river and 4 leagues to)
San Carlos	300 Chacto	(both missions are no more and two religious are in these two places)
And on the said River of Sta Cruz another		

Source: Fernández de Florencia 1675a.
Note: Referred to in the text also as the lieutenant's list.

Salazar 1675b; Salinas 1619). It is possible that the Tama and at least some of the Yamasee moved into the province soon after 1662. In that year the governor reported that a group of Chichimeco who said they were from Jacan wreaked havoc on Guale and then passed to the provinces of La Tama and Catufa.

The new missions first appear in two 1675 lists. One, prepared by Apalachee's lieutenant, Juan Fernández de Florencia, was forwarded to Spain by Governor Pablo de Hita Salazar (table 2.3). The other was the product of the episcopal visitation made by Gabriel Díaz Vara Calderón (table 2.4).

Tables 2.3 and 2.4 represent the development of the western Florida missions at their height, and being from the same year they invite comparison. A quick glance at the lists reveals discrepancies in the distance between some villages. The bishop, who appears to have been less precise than the lieutenant in giving distances, rounded all his distances to whole numbers. The lieutenant, at times, gave the distance in half leagues or, when the fraction was

Table 2.4. Bishop Calderón's mission list of 1675

Mission	Location
Asyle	(2 leagues to)
San Lorenzo de Hibitachuco	(first village of this province; 1 league to)
La Concepción de Ayubali	(1 league to)
San Francisco de Oconi	(1 league to)
San Juan de Aspalaga	(2 leagues to)
San Joseph de Ocuya	(4 leagues to)
San Pedro de Patali	(2 leagues to)
San Antonio de Bacuqua	(2 leagues to)
San Damián de Cupahica	(also called Escambí; 1 league to)
San Luis de Talimali	(the largest of all; 1 league to)
La Purificación de Tama	(called Yamases; 1 league to)
San Martín de Tomoli	(2 leagues to)
Santa Cruz de Capole	(also called Chuntafu)
Assumpción del Puerto	(4 leagues from Tomoli; inhabited by Chine, Pacara, and Amacano)
Missions in the Province of Apalachicoli[a]	
La Encarnación a la Santa	
Cruz de Sabacola	(12 leagues from the River Agna)
San Nicolás	(a Chacato mission; 9 leagues from Encarnación on the northern frontier; about 30 inhabitants)
San Carlos	(a Chacato mission; 3 leagues from San Nicolás; about 100 inhabitants)

SOURCE: Diaz Vara Calderón 1675:8–9.

a. The bishop placed the boundary between the provinces at the Agna River, which is the Ochlockonee.

small, used the expression 1+ or 2+ leagues. However, not all the differences can be explained in this fashion. Equally obvious are some differences in the names of the missions. The bishop's Purificación de Tama is the same mission as the lieutenant's Candelaria. Assumpción del Puerto (of the Port) and Assumption of Our Lady appear to be the same mission. The two lists also differ in that the lieutenant's list includes Nativity of Our Lady, which does not appear on the bishop's list. A last point on which the two lists differ is the size of the population of the Chacato missions.

The discrepancies concerning Candelaria are the easiest to account for. The bishop claimed to have founded the mission of Purificación de Tama in 1675 on February 2, which is Candlemas Day or the feast of the Presentation of the Christ-child in the Temple. For the mother of Jesus this was the occasion for the Jewish rite of purification, so we have the differing names of Purificación and Candelaria. In the matter of distances the bishop locates Purificación de Tama one league from both San Luis and San Martín, whereas the lieutenant placed Candelaria one-half league from San Luis and two leagues from San Martín. The larger discrepancy of one league between the two lists for Candelaria's distance from San Martín may have occurred because this new mission was composed of two distinct villages, one for the Tama and another for the Yamasee, and because the two authors chose different villages as their points of reference. The difference could also have resulted from the bishop's use of round numbers, as the lieutenant placed Candelaria a little *more* than one-half league from San Luis. Indeed all of the discrepancies involving distances in Apalachee are small enough to be accounted for in this fashion.

In addition to their minor difference in the rendering of the name of Assumption of Our Lady, the bishop and the lieutenant disagreed about the time of its founding. The lieutenant said 1674, the bishop 1675. It is likely that the mission was established by the friars in 1674 but that the church was consecrated by the bishop on January 27, 1675. He would probably have considered the date of consecration as the official date of its founding, embellishing the truth a bit in claiming credit for having established the mission. The two authorities differed as well in their rendering of the name of one of the groups who lived at this mission. The bishop gave their name as Pacara, the lieutenant as Capara. The lieutenant also noted that the mission was composed of three separate villages.

The two authorities differed as well in their description of the Chacato missions. The lieutenant placed San Nicolás ten leagues from the Apalachicola River compared to the bishop's nine leagues. The lieutenant placed San Nicolás and San Carlos four leagues apart, the bishop three. The lieutenant gave the two villages far larger populations than did the bishop. In view of the lieutenant's familiarity with the area, his estimates of the distances were probably more reliable. He was corroborated in 1693 by Governor Torres y Ayala in his account of his overland trek from San Luis to Pensacola Bay. However, the governor's companion, Fray Barreda, who also knew the land well, having founded the mission at San Nicolás, put the distance at eight leagues.

The divergences in population figures are easier to explain. The lieutenant's figures probably represent the villages' populations when the missions were founded in mid-1674, whereas the bishop's figures represent either the number of Christians he confirmed or the resident population at the time of his visit in 1675. Because there was revolt at those missions in the fall of 1674, much of the population had probably left before the bishop arrived. That reality is reflected in the lieutenant's remark that both missions "are no more." The abandonment of these missions by both the friars and the natives was confirmed two years later by the Apalachee's account of their 1677 expedition against a Chisca settlement in western Florida. The expedition passed the site of both villages, reporting that the villages had been abandoned and implying that they had been abandoned for some time. By the time of the expedition the Chacato had established a village within Apalachee. It was probably composed of the Christian remnant from the two missions who feared attack from the Chisca, who had been involved in the trouble at those missions (Barreda 1693:267; Diáz Vara Calderón 1675:8–9; Fernández de Florencia 1675a, 1678; Torres y Ayala 1693a:230–231).

A last point on which the two lists diverge is the fourteenth mission mentioned by the lieutenant. The bishop did not mention the lieutenant's Nativity of Our Lady, and the lieutenant referred only obliquely to the bishop's Santa Cruz de Sabacola. It is probable that Nativity of Our Lady was founded after the bishop's departure; the lieutenant stated that it was founded in 1675. It did not appear on any subsequent list, and its precarious situation at the time of its founding seems to be implied in the lieutenant's remark that it "today has very few people . . . which may be as many as forty persons" (Fernández de Florencia 1675a). There seems to be no ready explanation for the lieutenant's failure to mention the Sabacola mission more clearly. Its founding was contemporaneous with the founding of the Chacato missions. The friar, whose assault by disgruntled natives touched off the Chacato revolt, retreated to the Sabacola mission after surviving being attacked with a hatchet. But it is Sabacola that the lieutenant referred to in his closing line: "And on the said River of Sta. Cruz another [friar]" (Fernández de Florencia 1675a, 1675b).

The two lists from 1675 are among the more informative of the mission lists. The familiar name San Luis de Talimali first appeared on the bishop's list. The bishop spoke of San Luis as the principal village of the province. He described it as the residence of a military officer who lived in a country house defended by pieces of ordnance and a garrison of infantry. The lieutenant gave the population of each mission in round numbers, which presumably represent the population of the principal village and the satellite villages under its jurisdiction. Accordingly, the figure of 1,400 for San Luis does not indicate the size of San Luis alone because those 1,400 people were distributed over at least three satellite villages as well. It is not clear at this time whether it will ever be possible to determine the manner of distribution of that population for any of the Apalachee villages.

Communal structures on Apalachee mission sites have not been excavated sufficiently to discover whether their size might be a guide to the size of the village they served or if there is any correlation between the size of these structures and the documented population of the villages in 1675. Bishop Calderón's description of the principal council house as large enough in most villages to accommodate 2,000 to 3,000 persons suggests a certain uniformity and a size that was more than adequate for the entire population of Apalachee's largest mission jurisdiction in that era. Investigation of the site of the council house at San Luis revealed a huge structure easily capable of containing the adult portion of the population of 1,400 in 1675 as well as a substantial number of guests (Shapiro 1985b; personal communication 1986). Unfortunately there is no similar description of the size of the mission churches that would indicate whether they were designed to shelter the entire population of a particular mission. Bishop Calderón's remark that "They attend mass with regularity at 11 o'clock on the holy days they observe" might be interpreted to suggest that the churches were that large. However, the published results of the archaeological exploration of the Aspalaga site suggest a church that would be small for a mission that had 800 people within its jurisdiction in 1675. Allowing 2.25 square feet per person, one would find it difficult to fit 400 persons (standing) in the portion of the structure that is believed to have been the church proper. On the other hand, the larger churches of the two Patale sites appear to be more than adequate for the 500 persons listed for Patale in 1675 (Díaz Vara Calderón 1675:13–14; B. Calvin Jones, personal communication 1985; Morrell and Jones 1970; Shapiro 1985a).

The distances between villages given on these 1675 lists provide a relatively clear view of the spatial distribution of the principal villages. Although the 1675 image coincides generally with the less precise ones of 1655 and 1657, it differs sharply from the earlier ones in reference to Aspalaga. Whatever Aspalaga's location earlier, both 1675 lists place it in the eastern constellation of villages between Ocuia and Oconi and closer to the more easterly Oconi than to Ocuia. In 1675 a four-league gap separated Ocuia from Patale, its nearest neighbor in the western constellation. On the 1655 list Aspalaga was two leagues farther away from St. Augustine than was Ocuia and nine leagues farther away from St. Augustine than was Oconi. At 86 leagues distance, Aspalaga was only one league closer to St. Augustine in 1655 than was Patale at 87. Governor Rebolledo's passage from Patale to Aspalaga projects the same image. One must conclude that, between 1657 and 1675, Aspalaga was moved eastward by a considerable distance. One might also conclude that Ocuia was moved eastward to some degree. In 1655 Ocuia was seven leagues farther from St. Augustine than was Oconi. By the lieutenant's calculations, in 1675 Oconi and Ocuia were only 2.5 leagues apart.

A comparison of the 1675 lists with the list of 1655 also shows different distances between Cupaica and San Luis. In 1675 the two villages were one league apart. In 1655 Cupaica was two leagues farther from St. Augustine than was San Luis. As Calvin Jones has observed, the 1655 figures are probably rough estimates, so no conclusions can be reached about such relatively minor differences. But inasmuch as it is known that San Luis Jinayca was moved in 1656, the difference might indicate the radius within which the earlier site of San Luis was located. The difference suggests that in 1656 the new San Luis was moved west or west-northwest of the old site.

The lieutenant's list itself presents some problems that require comment. The last part of the name of his fourteenth mission, Nativity of Our Lady, is abbreviated and is not very legible. The first part of the abbreviation clearly is "Nra." for *Nuestra,* followed by what appears to be "ge." Boyd, in transcribing this passage, rendered it as "La Natividad de Nra. Gracia" as though it were written out thus rather than abbreviated. Because "Nativity of Our Grace" does not sound like a plausible name for a mission, I have presumed that what appears to be "ge" is a badly copied "Sra." for "Señora-Lady."

In the same footnote Boyd remarked that the Spanish text here and in the two paragraphs following apparently contained instances of omissions and garbling attributable either to the lieutenant or to some copyist. For example, Boyd assumed that the river mentioned in association with Nativity of Our Lady as being two leagues from San Luis was the Apalachicola, and he objected with reason that this possibility was absurd. He commented that "This leads to the suspicion that the word '*veinte*' was omitted from before '*dos.*' A statement of twenty-two leagues would be reasonable." Boyd seemed to overlook the fact that the Ochlockonee was two leagues distance from San Luis. Though one would not normally say that one went to the province of Apalachicola by way of the Ochlockonee, the Ochlockonee is on the way to that province. In addition, 22 leagues seems to be too great a distance to accommodate the Apalachicola as the river in question. On his 1693 trip to Pensacola Bay, Governor Torres y Ayala described the distance of the trail from the Ochlockonee to the Apalachicola as 12 leagues, as did Bishop Calderón (Boyd 1948:186).

In the same footnote Boyd observed further, concerning the lieutenant's remark about the Chacato missions that "They are no more," that it "does not make sense with its context." In fact, it makes excellent sense; those missions among the Chacato had been abandoned, as has been noted.

In 1675 the province possessed only eight friars to serve the fourteen mission centers within Apalachee. Those friars ministered to a total population of at least 8,220 natives, 640 of whom were non-Apalachee.

Although only a little more than two years had elapsed since the composition of the 1675 lists, only 12 of the 17 missions of 1675 were visited by Domingo de Leturiondo (table 2.5). One nonmission village that was not mentioned in 1675, the Tocobagan settlement at Wacissa, was also visited. Eleven of the 12 missions were the traditional missions inhabited by Apalachee, and Taman Candelaria was the twelfth.

Leturiondo began the visitation by holding a general assembly of the leaders of all the villages at Tomole. The record does not indicate whether he held

Table 2.5. Leturiondo's mission list of 1677

Mission or village	Date visited	Satellites mentioned
Nuestra Señora de la Candelaria de la Tama	Dec. 24, 1677	
San Luis de Talimali		San Francisco, San Bernardo, San Agustín
San Cosme y San Damián de Cupaica	Dec. 29, 1677	Nicupana, Yfalcasar
San Antonio de Bacuqua	Dec. 31, 1677	
San Pedro y San Pablo de Patale	Dec. 31, 1677	
San Joseph de Ocuya	Jan. 2, 1678	
San Juan de Aspalaga	Jan. 3, 1678	
San Francisco de Ocone	Jan. 5, 1678	Culcuti
Santa Cruz de Ychutafun	Jan. 6, 1678	
Nuestra Señora de la Concepción de Ayubale	Jan. 7, 1678	
San Lorenzo de Hivitachuco	Jan. 9, 1678	
Place of the Tocopacas	Jan. 9, 1678	
San Martín de Tomole (General Assembly)	Dec. 22, 1677	Samoche, San Diego

SOURCE: Leturiondo 1678.

a particular visitation at Tomole before proceeding to Candelaria and, in order, the other villages indicated on this list, closing with the visitation of the Tocobagan settlement. The record of the visitation contains more details on that closing session than on most of the others.

Leturiondo described the Tocobaga as living along the channel of the Wacissa River "mixed together with other nations" whom he did not identify. He held a formal visitation in this village even though it was not a mission center. He chided its people for not yet having become Christian, even though they had been living among Christians for many years. The Tocobaga replied that they had not resisted becoming Christians but that no one, lay or clerical, had come to teach them the new faith. As a consequence, they continued, they had only a confused knowledge of the good news it brought. Even so, they pointed out, at least 18 or 20 of their number had become Christians on their deathbeds and had been buried in the church of Ivitachuco.

The motive for Leturiondo's visitation of this nonmission village appears to have been an order he carried from the governor commanding the Tocobaga to close the channel of the Wacissa (and possibly to move from that region), lest they be captured by the English or other pirates and be forced to serve as guides for an attack on the missions by that route.

Leturiondo accepted the Tocobaga's arguments that they were safer living along the Wacissa in one large group than they would be in smaller settlements scattered along the coast. They indicated that they would be in scattered smaller settlements if they were forced to abandon their role as the transporters of the produce from eastern Apalachee and western Yustaga that was sent to St. Augustine by canoe via the Suwannee route. They noted that the main channel was already closed off with trees and that they were able to slip in and out by a concealed side channel. Leturiondo counted 348 men, women, and children who inhabited this Tocobaga village.

Although Leturiondo included this non-Christian village on his itinerary, he failed to visit at least two villages of Christian non-Apalachee that were probably in existence at the time of his visitation of the province. One was the Chine settlement mentioned on the 1675 lists, and the other was a Chacato settlement that had been formed a little to the west of San Luis after 1675. They may have been included in the visitation at San Luis since both were located on lands under the jurisdiction of its chief. Only two months before Leturiondo's arrival, the existence of these settlements was revealed when San Luis drew recruits from them in September 1677 for an expedition against the Chisca. The Apalachicola village of Santa Cruz de Sabacola on the west bank of the Apalachicola River was not mentioned by Leturiondo either, even though it still existed at the time of the attack against the Chisca. In view of these omissions, it is not clear what conclusions can be drawn from Leturiondo's failure to mention either the village of the Assumption of Our Lady or that of the Nativity of Our Lady, both of which appeared on the 1675 lists (Fernández de Florencia 1678; Leturiondo 1678).

Although the reference is enigmatic, the continued presence of Yamasee in the province is implied in the visitation record. In the document appointing Leturiondo as visitor, Governor Hita Salazar included these words: "and he commissioned him that in the place of San Luis of the Province of Apalachee, where there resides and lives some Yamasee chiefs and Indians, that he join them all together and hold a *visita,* just as in the rest of the places." This passage could mean that the Yamasee were living at San Luis or on lands that were within the jurisdiction of San Luis. In 1675 Yamasee were mentioned as being part of the Mission of Candelaria, which may have been established on lands under the jurisdiction of San Luis.

The visitation record reveals the continued existence of the satellite villages attached to each Apalachee mission village. It states that each main village had three or four smaller satellite villages joined to it and, using San Luis as an example, mentions San Francisco, San Bernardo, and San Agustín as its satellites. Cupaica's Nicopana and Faltassa appear again as do Tomole's Samoche and San Diego. The record shows Culcuti as an additional satellite for Aspalaga beyond those mentioned in 1657.

The regulations that Leturiondo promulgated at the end of the visitation restricted the Indians' freedom of movement from village to village. Anyone desiring to move had to obtain permission from the chief of his village and from the lieutenant in Apalachee. Moves to the frontier village of Bacuqua, however, were excepted to some degree on the grounds that it was open to attack and, therefore, in need of people; it had only 120 inhabitants in 1675. Such moves in the past, Leturiondo noted, had been motivated too often by a desire to escape the consequences of some crime or to evade work or other community responsibilities.

Leturiondo selected Tomole as the site for the general assembly of Apalachee's native leaders with which he opened the visitation. In his announcement of the meeting, Leturiondo stated that there the leaders might freely voice any complaints, petitions, or suggestions for the improvement of conditions in the region that they wished. Under his guidance, the assembly's principal business was the reopening of discussion on the measure outlawing the Apalachee's ball game (see chapter 3 and appendix 2). Each of the chiefs spoke on the issue in turn in an order corresponding to the ranking of their villages. The chief of Ivitachuco was the first to speak, but unfortunately the record did not indicate the order in which the other chiefs appeared. The discussion closed with a renewal of the prohibition of the game. Leturiondo also used the occasion to thank those who had taken part in the recent campaign against the Chisca and exhorted them to act with equal valor in such challenges that might arise in the future. He urged the Apalachee to show mercy to any who surrendered and to the women and the children, authorizing that they be held as slaves of their captors. He declared that any who had enslaved rather than killed them were legitimate *norocos,* whose preeminence was to be respected.[6]

The list in table 2.6 is one of the two that have been most widely disseminated. Swanton (1922:110) reproduced it but omitted the term *Señor* that precedes the missions named for male saints. He rendered Aspalaga as Ospalaga but presented Ocuux as Ocuia without comment. Significantly this listing confirms the continued existence of two of the non-Apalachee missions in Apalachee that Leturiondo had failed to mention in 1677, the villages of the Chine and of the Chacato. That the Chine mission was known by the name of San Pedro in 1680 suggests that the Chine had moved from Assumpción del Puerto, which they had shared with the Amacano and the Pacara in 1675. Assumpción, referred to in 1675 as on the road to the sea, is believed to have

---

6. As the syntax of his statement is rather muddy, it is not clear whether this is what he said or whether he was simply declaring that those who participated in the campaign should be considered *norocos* (warriors who had killed three people).

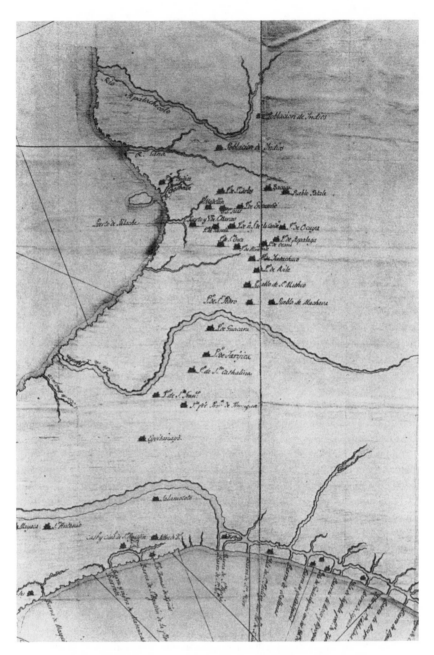

Fig. 2.2. The Alonso Solana map of 1683. Source: Chatelain 1941, map 7.

Table 2.6. Marques Cabrera's mission list of 1680

Señor San Lorenço de Ybithachucu
Nuestra Señora de la Purissima Concepción de Ajubali
Señor San Francisco de Oconi
Señor San Joan [sic] de Aspalaga
Señor San Joseph de Ocuux [sic]
Señores San Pedro y San Pablo de Patali
Señor San Antonio de Bacuqua
Señores San Cosme y San Damián de Yecambí
Señor San Carlos de los Chacatos: a new conversion
Señor San Luis de Talimali
Nuestra Señora de la Candelaria de la Tama: a new conversion
Señor San Pedro de los Chines: a new conversion
Señor San Martín de Tomoli
Santa Cruz y San Pedro de Alcantara de Ychutafun

SOURCE: Marques Cabrera 1680.

been in the vicinity of Wakulla Springs (B. Calvin Jones, personal communication, April 19, 1984). Such a location might well put it in the vicinity of de Soto's Ocute.

In 1677 the Chine settlement was at a place called Chacariz lying within San Luis's jurisdiction (Fernández de Florencia 1678). It is possible that the fear of an English attack expressed by Leturiondo at Wacissa in 1677 had led to the abandonment of Assumption for more secure locations farther inland. In 1680 the Chacato mission probably occupied the site just west of San Luis, where it is shown in the 1683 Solana map (fig. 2.2).

The continued absence of Assumption and of Nativity of Our Lady from this 1680 list suggests that these missions may have ceased to exist at least as early as late 1677. The continued absence of the Sabacola mission will be discussed later.

The Solana map of 1683

The 1683 map is the only graphic portrayal I have seen of Apalachee's settlement pattern that was made while the missions were flourishing.[7] The map (fig. 2.2) has been attributed to an Alonso Solana. That such maps were scarce in Spain is suggested by the Crown's request for this map. The loss of St. Catherines Island and the Florida government's plans for the reoccupation

7. I have seen references to a map of Florida drawn in the late 1660s, and there is mention in one of Bishop Calderón's letters of a map having been drawn during his visit.

and resettlement of the island gave rise to the Crown's request for a map drawn to scale by which to assess the advisability of the Florida governor's suggestion. The evidence for Solana's qualification for the task and for the desire to portray Apalachee accurately is minimal. On forwarding the completed map to the Crown, Governor Marques Cabrera himself vouched for the accuracy of the latitudes and ground distances, remarking that he had been on Florida's Gulf coast and traveled through Apalachee and Timucua. The map's portrayal of the Apalachicola River is somewhat disconcerting, however, with its turn to the west where it should have forked into the Flint and the Chattahoochee, which do not appear on the map. Perhaps the best that can be said for the map is the remark by the person who has researched its genesis: "The map he [the king] asked for was a superbly drawn sketch rather than the accurate scaled map he desired. Yet, despite shortcomings, Solana's map gave quite a fair idea of the extent of the king's dominion overseas. More important, however, it recorded for posterity the knowledge that the men at St. Augustine had of the land under their jurisdiction in 1683" (Arana 1964:258–266).

The map's portrayal of the 11 traditional Apalachee villages and Taman Candelaria conforms to the pattern reflected in the 1675 lists. The Chacato village of San Carlos is placed just to the west of San Luis, where later documentary evidence put it. The map also depicts a number of mystery villages. One was given the name Medellín, which appears in no other source. In view of its location, Medellín could be the Chine mission, which is not mentioned by name in the legend. The three other mystery villages are identified simply as Indian settlements, all west of Apalachee. The one close to the coast in the vicinity of present-day Carabelle, just to the west of a short stream named the Rio Chachave, may have been a Tocobaga village, as early eighteenth-century maps show one in that area. The village north of the Apalachicola River may have been either the Chacato village or the Sabacola village known to have been located in that region at that time.

The next document giving a picture of Apalachee's village pattern is a 1687 register of the Indian carpenters who worked on a ship-building project on the Tacabona River toward the coast. It lists the workers by name, giving their village of origin, the number of days they worked, and the wages they received. Although it obviously was not meant to be a complete listing of the villages, all of the 11 traditional Apalachee missions were represented except Aspalaga. No carpenters were drawn from the non-Apalachee villages. Cupaica was identified by the name Icabí. In an associated document San Luis was mentioned as having four satellite villages at this time (Chuba 1687:31; Matheos 1687a:77; Vi Ventura 1686:67).

The Evanescent Sabacola

One of the mysteries of this period is the fate of what seem to be a number of villages bearing the name Sabacola that appear and then disappear. Bishop Calderón mentioned a non-Christian village on the Apalachicola River that formerly was called Santa Cruz de Sabacola el Menor (the Lesser). The bishop had dedicated the church there on February 28, 1675, at which time the mission's name had been changed to La Encarnación a la Santa Cruz de Sabacola. Residing there by that time, according to the bishop, was another group of Sabacola whom he identified as "the Great Cacique of the province, with his vassals from Sabacola el Grande" (the Greater), whom the bishop had converted. The bishop expected that the new mission would become a large town inasmuch as the Apalachicola villages along the Chattahoochee 30 leagues to the north had expressed an interest in becoming Christian. Among those villages was another Sabacola (Díaz Vara Calderón 1675:9).

This Sabacola mission was located on the upper Apalachicola, just below the confluence of the Flint and the Chattahoochee. Swanton, however, noted that native tradition placed this tribe nearer the Gulf coast at some period in its history, observing that the tradition seems to be supported by the Lamhatty map and by the journal of a Spanish captain who explored the coast from St. Marks to Pensacola in 1693. Lamhatty, Swanton stated, appears to give the name Sabacola to the Choctawhatchee, while the Spanish captain recorded that the eastern mouth of the Apalachicola was called "Sabacola" (Milán Tapia 1693:288). It is not clear what conclusions can be drawn from such nomenclature, as Apalachee itself had a village named Sabacola and another named Pansacola, and the aforementioned Spanish captain gave the name Chicasses to the Choctawhatchee and noted that the Ochlockonee was known as the Claraquachine (Milán Tapia 1693:283, 291). Swanton also identified the 1675–era village of Nativity of Our Lady on the Ochlockonee with the Sawokli, his name for the Sabacola, but he did not give his grounds for that assumption (Swanton 1946:180).

When the expedition against the Chisca stopped at the Sabacola mission in 1677, the settlement was referred to simply as Santa Cruz, the name that the Spaniards sometimes gave to the Apalachicola River. Baltasar, the village chief, identifying himself as a recent but fervent convert, joined the expedition with six of his warriors. Correlation of the trail references given at this time with those furnished by Governor Torres y Ayala in 1693 indicates that the Sabacola mission was located on the west bank of the Apalachicola close to the point where the Apalachicola divides into the Chattahoochee and the Flint (Barreda 1693:266–267; Fernández de Florencia 1678; Torres y Ayala 1693a:230). The mission was not mentioned during Leturiondo's visitation, which occurred only several months after the return of the anti-Chisca expedition.

In 1679 Fray Juan Ocón, who had been pastor of the above-mentioned Sabacola mission in 1675, was sent with two recently arrived friars to establish a mission at the village of Sabacola on the middle Chattahoochee a few leagues below the falls. Three days after their arrival, they were ordered out by the cacique of Caveta, who was the head chief of the Apalachicola. Governor Salazar instructed his lieutenant in Apalachee, Juan Fernández de Florencia, to make no reprisals against the Apalachicola and to continue to treat them as friends (Bolton 1925a:119; Hita Salazar [1679], 1680a; Royal Officials 1680). His successor, however, the more militant and irascible Juan Marques Cabrera, sent two friars accompanied by 11 soldiers back to Sabacola. They were received in a hostile fashion and withdrew after a few months of waiting for the Indians' attitude to change. Governor Cabrera's threats led to a compromise under which the Christianized Sabacola moved downriver from the middle Chattahoochee, where the Apalachicola villages were then clustered, to the confluence of the Flint and Chattahoochee. There they established a mission of Santa Cruz de Sabacola near a recently formed Chacato mission called San Carlos de los Chacatos (Bolton 1925b:46–47; Marques Cabrera 1682). Some, if not all, of the inhabitants of this new village came from the Chacato village near San Luis, which is known to have been abandoned sometime before 1694 (Florencia 1695).

Bolton and Lanning seem to treat the Sabacola mission of the 1680s as an entirely new foundation, making no reference to the evanescent mission of 1674–1677 that was located on or near the same spot. The Solana map of 1683 does not register a Santa Cruz de Sabacola or a Chacato mission at the confluence of the Flint and Chattahoochee, though it shows an Indian settlement there. During these years the upriver village of Sabacola El Grande appears to have been abandoned completely by its inhabitants. Bolton referred to the *chicasa* of Sabacola El Grande in discussing the two forays through the Apalachicola country in 1685 by Antonio Matheos, the governor's lieutenant in Apalachee. In mentioning the village chiefs who accepted Matheos's invitation to parley with him at Caveta and the four recusant chiefs whose villages Matheos burned, Bolton made no mention of Sabacola except to indicate that Matheos had crossed the Chattahoochee at Sabacola on his second expedition (Bolton 1925b:47, 51, 79; Lanning 1935:177–178).

In 1686, Marcos Delgado, leading an expedition westward in search of La Salle's followers, crossed the Apalachicola River near the confluence of the Flint and the Chattahoochee. In his report, he mentioned only the village of Christian Chacato. However, the lieutenant in Apalachee, writing to the governor some weeks later to report on the expedition, stated that he had heard nothing since Delgado left Sabacola and that none of the Sabacola Indians that Delgado had taken with him as porters had yet returned to their village (Boyd 1937:22, 6). Sabacola reappears on a 1689 mission list in hybridized form as San Carlos de Çabacola. As the name San Carlos had earlier been attached to a Chacato mission in the area, the name change of the Sabacola village might indicate that the settlement's 30 families were drawn from both tribes. It should be noted, however, that in the area there was a separate village of 70 families named San Nicolás de los Chacatos (Ebelino de Compostela 1689). In 1690 the village was identified as Savacola Chuba or Big Sabacola, but it was not mentioned on the mission lists of 1694, 1697, or 1698 (Quiroga y Losada 1690b).

When Governor Torres y Ayala passed through this region in 1693, he crossed the Apalachicola at the site of the Chacato village, but neither he nor Friar Barreda made any mention of the Sabacola in their journals (Barreda 1693:266–267; Torres y Ayala 1693a:230). It is not clear that any conclusion can be drawn from this omission, however, as Savacola Chuba was located a little above the confluence of the Flint and the Chattahoochee.

In 1694 the Chacato village on the Apalachicola was attacked by a force of 50 warriors who were Sabacola, Apalachicola, and Tiquepache. The attackers killed five of the Chacato and carried off 42 to sell to the Carolinians as slaves. The survivors took refuge at Escambé, which was apparently still located west of the Ochlockonee. Only Chacato were mentioned as being among the refugees (Florencia 1695; Torres y Ayala 1695). Swanton noted that just over a decade later, the Sabacola themselves were carried off by hostile Indians allied to the English (Swanton 1946:180).

The implications of Diego Peña's remark in 1716 about the linguistic affiliation of the Sabacola are unexplored at present. After noting that Caveta and Casista spoke Muskogee, Peña stated that the rest of the Lower Creek villages spoke the same language, except for Sabacola which had a distinct language and also spoke Apalachee (Boyd 1949:25).

The bishop's tabulation of the mission villages (table 2.7) agrees substantially with the 1680 list and with that projected by the 1683 map. San Carlos de los Chacatos is the only mission in Apalachee that appeared on those two earlier lists and is not found among the bishop's count of the Apalachee missions. The attachment of the name "San Carlos" to the Sabacola village suggests that some of the Chacato from San Carlos in Apalachee may have settled there. Neither San Nicolás nor Sabacola was mentioned on the 1680 list or the 1683 map. The list was composed by the bishop on the basis of information that he had requested from the priests of his diocese so that he might inform the king of the composition of the diocese. To convert the number of families into individuals, the bishop noted that he multiplied the number of families by

Table 2.7. Bishop Compostela's mission list of 1689

Village	Number of families
San Lorenzo de Hivitachuco	200
Concebción de Ayubale	250
San Fran Oconi	80
San Juan de Aspalaga	50
S^n Joseph de Ocuya	200
Sta Cruz de Hichutafun	30
San Martín de Tomoli	130
Nra. Señora de la Tama	80
San Pedro de los Chines	30
San Luis de Talimali	300
S^n Pedro y S Pablo de Patali	120
S Antonio de Bacucua	50
San Damián de Yscambí	400
Total	1920
New province	
San Nicolás de los Chacatos	70
San Carlos de Çabacola	30
Total	100

SOURCE: Ebelino de Compostela 1689.

five. The Chacato probably abandoned the site in Apalachee soon after the drafting of the 1683 map, as documents associated with the Delgado expedition of 1686 show the presence of both the Chacato and the Sabacola along the upper Apalachicola River at that time. A comparison of the population figures supplied by the bishop with those given by the lieutenant in 1675 raises some intriguing questions that will be discussed in the chapter on Apalachee population.

There is no indication of the reason for the concentration of clerical manpower in only five of the fourteen villages known to exist at that time (table 2.8). Although a governor early in the seventeenth century had advocated the concentration of friars in only a few villages, the scant available evidence on clerical assignment indicates that generally one friar was assigned to each mission. In a 1690 document on clerical assignments, it was mentioned specifically that the villages of the Chacato, the Chine, Ocon [*sic*], Capoli, Bacuqua and the Tocobaga settlement at Wacissa did not have a friar. Aspalaga, Tomoli, Ocuia, Cupaica, and Tama were not mentioned at all, although the place identified as "Convent of San Pedro" probably was associated with Cupaica. Cupaica had a satellite village named San Pedro. Its 400 families would seem to have required the stationing of a friar there, particularly as the village seems to have been located west of the Ochlockonee River

Table 2.8. List of villages with attendant priests, 1690

Village	Priests
Convent of San Luis	Antonio de los Ángeles, Pedro Galíndez, and Martín de Alacano
Convent of Ayubale	Pedro Lacaxo Bernal and Diego Gonçález
Convent of San Pedro	León de Lara and Francisco de Nogales
Convent of Patali	Francisco Camacho and Luis de Seçar (Cezar)
Convent of Savacola Chuba	Pedro Hace and Matheo de Argüelles
Convent of Ybitachuco	Francisco de Bargas (Vargas) and Miguel Martorell

at that time so it did not have access to the services of a friar from one of the missions that was staffed.

Two friars, one each from Ivitachuco and San Luis, were mentioned as having recently requested changes of assignment. Fray González had found San Luis unhealthy, and Fray Alacano had been unhappy during his stay at Ivitachuco. The time appears to have been one of low morale among at least some of the friars in Apalachee, and it was a period of sharp dissension between the friars and the governors. The governor was sharply critical of the recent transfer to Rome of a Fray Juan Angel from the Tama mission, alleging that he was one of the few friars skilled in its people's language. Tama's new pastor, the governor complained, soon impelled most of his parishioners to flee to the woods by his brutal use of the whip on errant natives (Luna 1690a, 1690b; Quiroga y Losada 1691a).

The visitation record from which the list in table 2.9 is drawn is perhaps the most useful of the three available for Apalachee. As the product of a visitation, it represents an itinerary like those of 1657 and 1677. The 14 villages mentioned appear to be a complete tally. As noted earlier, the Chacato village on the Apalachicola had been attacked before the visitation, and the survivors were domiciled temporarily at Escambé. The refugees informed the visitor that, after they had made a trip to some unspecified destination, they wished to reoccupy the site on which they had lived some time earlier, which was one-half league from San Luis on land that was within that village's jurisdiction. To that end, the leaders of San Luis prepared a formal agreement making the Chacato a free gift of the use of the land for farming but imposing some obligations and limitations on the hunting of game and gathering of wild fruits and nuts. It is not known whether they reoccupied the site near San Luis. The village of the Chine appears under a new name, San Antonio rather than San Pedro. This change may indicate that since 1689 it had moved to a new site. The visitation record reveals another probable moving of the site of Escambé.

Table 2.9. Florencia's visitation list of 1695

Village or ranch	Description
San Cosme y San Damián de Escambí	Refugee Chacato living there
San Antonio de Bacuqua	
Ranch of Our Lady of the Rosary	Property of Marcos Delgado
San Pedro y San Pablo de Patali	
San Joseph de Ocuia	Fray Manuel de Mendoza its friar; Usunaca Sebastian, chief of Ichasli, living there
Ranch of San Joseph de Upalucha	Property of Joseph Salinas
San Francisco de Oconi	
Hivitachuco	Visitation for Wacissa's Tocobaga held at Ivitachuco
Nuestra Señora de la Concepción de Aiubale	
Santa Cruz de Capoli	Only 20 men, some elderly
San Juan de Azpalaga	
San Martín de Tomoli	House of Pedro Torres was half a league distant from it
Nuestra Señor de la Candelaria	
San Antonio de los Chines	
San Luis de Talimali	Its satellite, Abaslaco, mentioned; refugee Chacato at Escambí arranged to reoccupy the site of their former village half a league from San Luis
Ranch of San Juan de Ochania	Property of Juan Sánchez de la Paz Cuchillada

Source: Florencia 1695.

The journals from Governor Torres y Ayala's overland trek to Pensacola Bay in 1693 indicate that at some time before that date Escambé had moved from its location one league north of San Luis to a site that was three leagues northwest of that provincial headquarters and one league west of the Ochlockonee River. Nothing is known of the circumstances of that move except that it was made after 1686. At the time of the 1686 Delgado expedition, Escambé seems to have been still east of the Ochlockonee. During the 1694–1695 visitation Escambé's chief requested permission to return to the site that Escambé had occupied earlier, presumably the site one league north of San Luis. That it moved to that location is not certain, however, as the visitation record does not provide any information about the location of the former village site. On a

1697 list, Escambé was still situated three leagues from San Luis and two from Bacuqua. That could be interpreted to indicate that Escambé still lay west of the Ochlockonee. It would mean a move by Bacuqua, though, because two leagues was the distance between Escambé and Bacuqua when Escambé was only one league from San Luis. In requesting the permission to move, Escambé's chief complained that the soil at the present site was too sterile to produce enough to feed the village. The visitor assented to the move on the condition that the village leaders gave consent (Barreda 1693:266; Boyd 1937; Florencia 1695; Menéndez Marquez and Florencia 1697; Torres y Ayala 1693a:230; Torres y Ayala and Royal Officials 1697).

A unique feature of the 1694 list is the mention of a number of Spanish ranches. The ranch owners are identified, and the locations of some of the ranches in relation to certain Indian villages are indicated because the Indians had lodged complaints that the stock from those ranches was damaging their crops. The location of the residence of one other Spaniard is indicated.

The chief of Bacuqua complained that herds belonging to three Spanish ranchers, Diego Ximénez, Francisco de Florencia, and Marcos Delgado, grazed close to his village and destroyed its crops. Patale's chief lodged a similar complaint against Delgado's stock. Delgado's ranch of Our Lady of the Rosary appears to have been established by 1677 on the site abandoned by Bacuqua in 1657. In response to the visitor's orders, Delgado moved his ranching operation to a chicasa of Patale that was four leagues from San Luis and about one and one-half leagues from his former ranch site. Ximénez chose as his new ranch site a chicasa of Escambé, located three leagues from San Luis and five leagues from his former ranch. That site points to the trans-Ochlockonee Escambé as the probable location of the new ranch. Francisco de Florencia used his influential family connections to continue grazing his cattle without concern for the natives' crops (Hinachuba and Andrés 1699: 24–26; Ponce de León 1702:27–29; Zúñiga y Zerda 1700a:84, 89, 96).

Like the 1657 visitation record, that of 1694–1695 presents the names of a number of chiefs and leading men of the Apalachee villages. It also preserves the names of twenty-nine ordinary Indians who were living apart from their wives because of their work in areas outside of Apalachee. As might be expected, the easternmost village of Ivitachuco had the greatest number of absent husbands, a total of nine. San Luis seems to have had no married men away from home who were missed by their wives. An unspecified number of single men were also indicated as working outside of the province on a contract basis.

By this time, some of the leading Indians as well as the Spaniards possessed farms and cattle ranches in areas that were at some distance from their own villages. This fact is reflected in the visitor's prohibition of the presence of single women at such places to serve the peons and married women at such places unless they were accompanied by their husbands.

Among the other regulations issued by the visitor, one forbade the Indians from moving from villages on the royal road to villages not on the road, but none of the villages in either category was identified. At this time, Escambé, Bacuqua, and Patale seem to have been on the frontier of the province on the trails used by the neighboring non-Christian natives who came to Apalachee to trade. One of the visitor's regulations ordered those villages not to detain such non-Christian Indians when they arrived but to hurry them on to the lieutenant at San Luis. In a 1702 document, Ocuia was also mentioned as being on the frontier and as being "away from the road" as well. At that time, the lieutenant suggested that Ocuia should be removed to the road to make it more accessible to relief in case of attack (Romo de Urisa 1702). That it was a target for attack in 1703 would seem to confirm its remoteness.

The 1697 list (table 2.10) has some interesting anomalies to plague the archaeologist's attempts to locate and identify village sites. It does not reflect the projected resettlement of the Chacato spoken of during the Florencia visitation. This may mean that they had not yet returned from the planned trip they mentioned in 1695 or it may simply signify that the rebuilt village had no church and that they attended Mass at nearby San Luis or at the place of the Chine, who probably spoke the same language as the Chacato. It is easier to evaluate the anomalies in the 1697 list when it is compared with the lists from 1675, 1677, and 1695 (table 2.11).

The 1677 and the 1695 lists are itineraries. Tomole was the starting point in 1677 because the general assembly was held there to open the visitation. The 1675 list is that of the lieutenant, Fernández de Florencia. Numbers between settlement names represent the distances in leagues between those settlements. In 1695 Florencia held a visitation of the Tocobaga, but he had them travel the one league from Wacissa to Ivitachuco rather than go to their village, as Leturiondo had done in 1678. Assumption, which was the home of the Chine in 1675, was on the path to the sea from San Luis and, according to Bishop Calderón, four leagues from Tomole.

The first and most obvious of the anomalies in the 1697 list (table 2.10)—that giving the distance from San Luis to St. Augustine as 80 leagues—is the easiest to explain. On the 1655 list that distance was given as 88 leagues. In 1697 the distance was not intended as a measure of the exact location of San Luis but as a general statement of the median distance of the province from St. Augustine. On a number of occasions, that figure of 80 leagues was used when the person was speaking of Apalachee in general.

A striking anomaly on the 1697 list is the distance between Bacuqua

Table 2.10. The mission list of 1697

Name of mission	Location	Attendant priest
San Luis	80 leagues from St. Augustine	Fray Joseph de Rueda
Escabí	3 leagues from San Luis	Fray Pedro de Aze
Vacuqua	2 leagues from Escabí	Fray Manuel de Mendoza
Ocuya	9 leagues from Vacuqua	Fray Pedro Galíndez
Oconi	3 leagues from Ocuya	Fray Luis de Vargas
Vitachuco	2 leagues from Oconi	Fray Juan de Villalva
Ayubale	1 league from Vitachuco	Fray Rodrigo de la Barrera
Capoli	3 leagues from Ayubale	No friar
Patale	1.5 leagues from Capoli	No friar
Aspalaga	1.5 leagues from Patale	Fray Joseph Valero
Tomole	1.5 leagues from Aspalaga	Fray Salvador Buerno
La Tama	1.5 leagues from Tomole	Fray Doningos Santos
Place of the Chines	0.5 leagues from Tama	Fray Francisco de León
Asile	2 leagues from Vitachuco	No friar

SOURCE: Torres y Ayala and the Royal Officials Menéndez Marquez and Florencia 1697.

(given in table 2.11 as Vacuqua) and Ocuya, a full nine leagues. Since both 1675 lists show that distance to be only six leagues—two from Bacuqua to Patale and four from Patale to Ocuya—it is obvious that either Bacuqua or Ocuya had moved at some time during the 22-year interval. An arresting feature of this anomaly is that the jump was made directly from Bacuqua to Ocuya while Patale was mentioned in association with Capoli, Aspalaga, and Tomole. On almost every earlier list the order was Cupaica, Bacuqua, Patale, and Ocuya. This change may indicate that Patale had slipped southward or that Bacuqua had been moved so far north that it was no longer practical to proceed from Bacuqua to Ocuia by way of Patale. Such a possibility is strengthened by the 1698 visitation record. The visitor's hasty trek through the province took him from Ocuya to Bacuqua to Cupaica and thence to San Luis, Tomole, Aspalaga, Patali, and Capoli, in that order.

Another anomaly of the 1697 list is the placement of Aspalaga. In 1675 Aspalaga and Patale had been five and one-half leagues apart with Ocuya between them as a buffer. On the 1697 list Aspalaga and Patale are only one and one-half leagues apart. In 1675 and on most other lists Aspalaga was bracketed between Ocuia and Oconi. On the 1695, 1697, and 1698 lists, Ocuia and Oconi follow each other directly, while Aspalaga is sandwiched between Patale and Tomole on the latter two and between Tomole and Capoli on the first.

Table 2.11. Comparison of mission lists of 1695, 1697, 1675, and 1677

1695	1697	1675	1677
			Tomole
			↓
			Tama
			↓
	San Luis	San Luis	San Luis
	↓↑ 3	↓↑ 1	↓
Escambi	Escabi		
↓	↓↑ 2	Acpayca	Cupaica
		↓↑ 2	↓
Bacuqua	Vacuqua	Bacuqua	Bacuqua
↓		↓↑ 2	↓
Patali	↓↑ 9	Patale	Patale
↓		↓↑ 4	↓
Ocuia	Ocuya	Ocuya	Ocuya
↓	↓↑ 3		
Oconi	Oconi		
↓	↓↑ 2		
Hivitachuco	Vitachuco		
↓	↓↑ 1		
Aiubale	Ayubale	↓↑ 1.5	↓
↓	↓↑ 3		
Capoli	Capoli		
	↓↑ 1.5		
↓	Patale		
	↓↑ 1.5		
Azpalaga	Aspalaga	Aspalaga	Aspalaga
↓	↓↑ 1.5	↓↑ 1	↓
Tomoli	Tomole	Oconi	Ocone
	↓↑ 1.5	↓↑ 0.5+	
	La Tama		
↓		Ayubale	↓
		↓↑ 1.5	
		Ybitachuco	
	↓↑ 0.5	Ytuchafun	Ychutafun
		↓↑ 2+	↓
		Tomole	Ayubale
		↓↑ 2	↓
Candelaria		Candelaria	Hivitachuco
↓			↓
Chines	Chines	↓↑ 0.5+	Tocopacas
↓			
San Luis		San Luis	
		↓↑	
		Assumpcion	

NOTE: Numbers between settlement names are distances in leagues. Bishop Calderón's list of 1675 gives a distance of 4 leagues from Tomole to Assumpcion.

This change definitely suggests that Aspalaga had slipped southward. In 1716, however, Diego Peña, who seems to have made a point of mentioning the missions whose ruins he passed, listed only Tomole and La Tama for the three-league stretch between Patale and San Luis. That Aspalaga had been moved at some time is confirmed by a 1704 document telling of the second assault on Apalachee during that year. In describing an encounter with the enemy, the lieutenant mentioned that one of the enemy casualties was a rebel Apalachee whom he identified as Pedro, son of the cacique of Aspalaga the old (Solana 1704a:50–55). And the visitor's sojourn at the ranch of St. Joseph of Upalucha in 1695 between his visits to Ocuia and Oconi suggests that that ranch may have been established on the former site of Aspalaga that lay between those two missions.

An additional possible discrepancy between this 1697 list and those of 1675 involves the distance between Tomole and Capoli. Both 1675 lists gave the distance as two leagues. In 1697 the trek from Capoli to Tomole by way of Patale and Aspalaga covered four and one-half leagues. This route, of course, may not have been the most direct one, but it was the one taken in reverse order by the visitor in 1698.

Although the extrapolation of the distance between Tomole and San Luis from the data of the 1675 and the 1697 lists gives the same result of two and one-half leagues in both instances, this result is possibly at odds with Irving Leonard's rendition of a 1693 statement by Fray Barreda. On coming to the Apalachee coast with Governor Torres y Ayala, the friar gave the following account of their passage to San Luis:

After getting into port, we landed and took lodgings in some wretched huts where we remained until boats were brought from the province to transport us to a village within the same jurisdiction called *Tomoly*. This hamlet, where we spent Corpus Christi day, is about six leagues from Apalachee through beautiful open pine groves. In the afternoon of the holy day of our Lord mentioned, the journey was made to the village of San Luis de Talmaly through a district furrowed with ploughed fields two leagues from Tomoly. (Barreda 1693:265)

The resolution hinges on what the friar meant by Apalachee. Here the term seems to refer to their point of embarkation on the coast, but, usually, the term was used to signify San Luis or the mission area in general.

The last listing of the mission villages before their destruction (table 2.12) originated from an extraordinary visitation of the provinces of Timucua and Apalachee apparently in response to the volume of complaints that the governor was receiving. The governor instructed Captain Juan de Ayala y Escobar

Table 2.12. Ayala's visitation list of 1698

Place	Day in February visited	Chief	Headmen
San Lorenzo de Ibitachuco	12	Field Master Don Patricio Ygnhac Chuba	Niquichasli Antonio and Aque Ju$^{\circ}$
Ayubale	13	Ushina(?) Coaleixo	MiChasle Ebanjelista and Hina Adrian
Oconi	14	Hina Alonso	Osonaca Ju$^{\circ}$ and Hina Alonso
Ocuya	14	Osunaca Lorenzo	Ymixa Mexia and Cui Bernardo
Bacucua	14	Usuñaca(?) Mexía	Hina Felipe
Escabí	15(?)	Hina Bicente	Esfana Labentura and Bis(?) Bautista
San Luis	15	Osunaca Andrés	Michasli Francisco and Mila Ysfani Alonso
Thomoli	16	Osonaca Alonso	Ysfania Alonso and Cui Patriburio
Espalaga [sic]	16	Osonaca Benito	Ysfani Bentura and Bi Ju$^{\circ}$
Patali	16	(no names given)	
Capoli	17	Hina Chuba Adrián	Sabacola Feliziano and Cui Esteban

SOURCE: Ayala y Escobar 1698.
NOTE: Ju$^{\circ}$ probably stands for "Juan."

to gather information secretly from the village headmen and from the Indians in general concerning the propriety of the lieutenant's conduct toward them. The questioning of the leaders of the 11 traditional Apalachee missions elicited no complaints whatsoever against the incumbent, Captain Jacinto Roque Pérez, or against the other Spanish residents of the province. The native leaders, doubtless, were taken aback when they saw whom the governor had dispatched to look into their complaints against a number of members of Apalachee's Spanish community. Inasmuch as some of the worst abusers of the Indians were the numerous Florencias, the family of Lieutenant Roque Pérez's wife, the imperious Juana Caterina de Florencia, and, inasmuch as the *visitador*, Ayala, was himself related to the Florencias by marriage, the reticence of the natives is understandable. They knew that complaints to Ayala would not bring relief and that they might bring retribution from the lieutenant against those who complained.

It is not clear whether Ayala y Escobar's restriction of his visitation to the 11 settlements inhabited by Apalachee is an indication that the Tama and Chine villages' leaders attended the visitation at San Luis without being noted in the rather brief record left by the visitor.

The ineffectuality of Ayala y Escobar's visitation is reflected vividly in an early 1699 letter to the king. In it the chiefs of Ivitachuco and San Luis reported that the natives of San Luis had withdrawn from that village into the woods because their places had been seized for the Spaniards and because they were subjected to continual demands for unpaid labor at the houses of the lieutenant and of other Spanish settlers. That Joachín Florencia saw fit to inspect three of the ranches in 1694–1695 probably indicates that each had a sizable work force. Don Antonio Ponce de León, a friend of the Apalachee Indians and a spokesman for them, also mentioned having seen "in the vicinity of San Luis the houses of the Indians located at a league's distance because their building sites and fields have been taken by the Spanish settlers" (Hinachuba and Andrés 1699).

In their letter to the king the chiefs voiced a number of additional grievances. They complained that, after having been required to build the fort at San Luis with their own tools and without compensation for their labor (even having to supply their own food), they were then compelled to use the remaining timbers to build houses for a brother-in-law of the lieutenant and for other Spanish settlers at San Luis. The chiefs also stated that, at the instigation of the incumbent lieutenant, a former lieutenant there, Captain Juan Fernández de Florencia, had established a ranch of cattle, swine, and horses that was wreaking havoc on the Indians' fields. They added that those fields had also been damaged by the stock of two of Florencia's brothers-in-law who resided with him (Hinachuba 1699; Hinachuba and Andrés 1699). A subsequent letter indicated that the governor's lieutenant had done nothing to remedy the problems highlighted in the 1694–1695 visitation despite the visitor's orders that within a specified period all such ranches would be removed to a minimum distance of three to four leagues from such villages, as the law required (Ponce de León 1702).

The chiefs' letter brought a relatively prompt response from the monarch. He ordered the governor to investigate their allegations and to act decisively to bring an end to such abuses, if they existed, as he presumed they did (Royal Cedula 1700). But nothing effective seems to have been done by the royal authorities in Florida. Early in 1702 Don Antonio Ponce de León found it necessary to write to the king anew, informing him that the destruction of the Indians' crops by the Spanish settlers' cattle continued unabated and that the Indians continued to be impressed to work for the Spaniards without compensation. Ponce de León reported that during the inspection no charges were placed before Ayala y Escobar because he was related by marriage to the abusers of the Indians in Apalachee and that when he left the Indians were greatly discontented. This report refers to a second extraordinary visitation entrusted to Ayala y Escobar in 1701 to investigate the charges made by Apalachee's two principal chiefs in their 1699 letter and by Ivitachuco's chief alone in a subsequent letter. In view of the ties between those settlers and the authorities, Ponce de León suggested that the only effective remedy would be the removal of the Spanish settlers from the province (Ponce de León 1702). St. Augustine's pastor had made the same recommendation about two years earlier in a printed memorial to the king (Leturiondo 1700).

By contrast, action had been taken by this time to move two of the offending Spanish ranches that provoked the complaints of the natives during the 1694–1695 Florencia visitation. Marcos Delgado's ranch, situated between Patale and Bacuqua, had been moved rather promptly to a chicasa of Patale and his herd of swine to a spot five leagues from San Luis. By 1699 the ranch of Diego Jiménez had been relocated five leagues away from its former site to occupy a chicasa of Escambé, which was three leagues from San Luis. Francisco de Florencia, the third rancher against whom the natives of Bacuqua had complained during the visitation, made no move to relocate his ranch, however. He was confident, apparently, that the lieutenant, to whom he was related by marriage, would not enforce the decree against him even though the visitador, Joaquín de Florencia, had made the lieutenant subject to a 50-ducat fine for nonenforcement of these decrees (Florencia 1695; Hinachuba 1699; Ponce de León 1702; Zúñiga y Zerda 1700a:84, 86, 89, 92–93). It is possible that, to avoid compliance with impunity, Francisco de Florencia and the lieutenant availed themselves of the legal pretext that Florencia did not own the land on which he ran his cattle. During the residencia of Governor Torres, that argument—that the records did not show that Florencia possessed such a ranch—was used to justify the governor's not having acted to see that the ranch was relocated (Zúñiga y Zerda 1700a:16).

Between 1701 and 1714, Spain and much of Europe were embroiled in the struggle over the succession to the Spanish throne and for its resources in Europe and throughout the world. The Crown's supervision of developments in the overseas territories was impaired severely, especially in peripheral areas such as Florida. It was a time when the local Spanish authorities were most in need of the loyal support of the natives, especially in areas where the proximity of hostile English settlements and Indians allied with the English presented a serious challenge to the Crown. In Apalachee the natives were grievously alienated and severely demoralized not only by the abuses of the Spanish settlers but also by a string of other developments that had begun in the early 1680s, which shall be examined in chapter 10.

Writing immediately after the destruction of the missions, the Spanish authorities at St. Augustine spoke of there having been 14 villages in Apalachee on the eve of this calamity, but they did not identify them (Council of War 1704). On the basis of the 1695 and 1697 lists, there could be 15 villages to be accounted for, if one counts the Tocobaga settlement and if one presumes that the Chacato refugees at Escambé in 1694 carried out their plans to settle near San Luis after taking their projected trip. No Chacato village is mentioned in the 1697 or 1698 lists, but documents dating from 1699 and 1702 indicate the presence of Chacato in the area in those years (Hinachuba 1699; Zúñiga and Zerda 1700a, 1702). Ocuia may not be included in the 14 because it had been destroyed earlier in 1703. The Spanish authorities may not have counted the Tocobaga settlement in making their calculation because it was not a mission site.

In any event, the authorities interpret the somewhat muddy English and Spanish records on the destruction of the Apalachee missions to indicate that all of the missions except San Luis and Ivitachuco were either occupied or destroyed between 1703 and mid-1704, when the few surviving Spaniards and the Apalachee Indians who remained loyal withdrew from the province, considering their position there untenable. The Spaniards themselves destroyed San Luis and its fort before retreating at the end of July 1704. Ivitachuco had escaped attack by paying a ransom to Colonel James Moore. It is presumed that its inhabitants destroyed it when they joined the other survivors in withdrawing from the province (Boyd 1951:12–18; Bushnell 1979:9–13; Jones 1972).

When the Spaniards and the natives at Ivitachuco and San Luis withdrew from the province, the only natives mentioned as remaining were a few of the former inhabitants of Escambé. They welcomed the third invasion force of 1704, which was already on its way to the province when the Spanish remnant abandoned San Luis. Two days after the Spanish withdrawal, that force arrived, killing or imprisoning those remaining from Escambé (Zúñiga y Zerda 1704d, 1704e:65–68).

Except for the Chacato who migrated to Mobile, little is known of the fate of the non-Apalachee who had been living in the province. The governor identified Tama as one of the missions whose people were carried off by the invaders. Another mission, which he called Ocatoses, suffered the same fate; its identity is not known (Zúñiga y Zerda 1705). As the Chine village was only one-half league from San Luis, its people may have survived and been included among the Chacato who moved westward. The Tocobaga may have survived the initial onslaughts of 1704 because they were non-Christian and were shielded by their proximity to Ivitachuco. If they remained in the area, they probably fell victim during the subsequent years to one or another of the raiding parties that pushed deeper and deeper into central and southern Florida. By 1711, as the insatiable English demand for slaves propelled the invaders to the very tip of the peninsula, even the Keys Indians had learned to fear the name Yamasee (Valdés 1711). When the Spaniards returned to St. Marks in 1718, they found no more than two dozen Tocobaga in the area; these Tocobaga had pledged allegiance to the chief of Caveta in a bid for survival. Fearing that this pledge would not protect them from death or enslavement at the hands of the Cavetans, the Spanish commander dispatched several soldiers to Wacissa via Ayubale to bring the Tocobaga to San Marcos (Primo de Rivera 1718a).

One year after the abandonment of the province, Admiral Landeche, after marching to San Luis from St. Marks, conducted a brief reconnaissance of the part of Apalachee in the vicinity of the former headquarters. He left a rough map showing the locations of St. Marks and the villages of the Chinos [*sic*], Escambé, and Bacuqua in relation to the fort at San Luis. At San Luis he found part of the stockade still standing but no trace of the nearby villages to which he sent infantry details accompanied by persons familiar with the region. They simply accepted on faith, he said, their guide's statement that there had been villages at those sites (Landeche 1705). On its face, the admiral's statement seems to mean that there was absolutely no trace of the former villages, but that does not seem to be the case. Americans who visited San Luis in the 1820s and 1830s claimed to have been able to see some signs of the San Luis settlement even then.

Diego Peña appears to have been the first Spaniard to traverse the province after its destruction. On his 1716 journey to the country of the Apalachicola, he listed a considerable number of former mission sites that he passed or on which he camped for the night. He mentioned in this abbreviated list of the former mission villages the following chicasas (Boyd 1949:15–19):

Ivitachuco and
Ayubale, presented as being one league apart, after which he passed
Capoli on his way to
Patale, where he camped for the night, and on the next day passing
Tomole and
La Tama, while covering the three leagues to
San Luis, where he spent the following night, journeying on the next
   day
to the prairie of Ocalquire (Lake Jackson prairie), which extends for
   more than a league, where they saw over 300 buffalo and a few cows,
   and where they camped for two nights because of the heavy rain before passing on to

Escambé, where they spent the night, it having taken them all day to
   cover the distance of one plus leagues because of the difficulty they
   experienced in crossing the Rio de Lagna (Ochlockonee), but making
   four leagues the next day to camp near a pond, after crossing the Rio
   de Palos (Little River), while following the old road to
Savacola, the chicasa of which was now the place of Chislacasliche,
   which they reached after marching one league to the Flint at its
   juncture with the Apalachicola and crossing the Flint and going on
   about half a league farther.

In telling of his overland trek to St. Marks, José Primo de Rivera mentioned in 1718 only the chicasa of Tomole where he stopped to hunt (Primo de
Rivera 1718a). In discussing a plan for reestablishing an inland Spanish settlement in Apalachee on the site of the former village of Tama, a document included in a 1732 letter to the king by Governor Antonio de Benavides lists 13
of Apalachee's former mission villages and nine of the Timucua villages that
were on the royal road. For Apalachee it noted that (Benavides 1732)

The thirteen places of Apalachee Indians of which the said province was
composed are the following and they are 1, 2, 3, and 4 leagues distant
from one another.

In the duplicate:

	San Luis
	Bagugua
	Patale
Chines	
Chacattos	
	Chatos
	Latama (place chosen for the settlement and store[?])
	Tomole
Ocuia	ô Cuya
Espalaga	Espalaga
Ocone	ô Cone
	Capole
Aiobale	Ayubale
Y Bitta chuco	Bitachuco

The words "In the duplicate" are written in English, presumably by Buckingham Smith while he was making the copy of the document. It is not clear

Table 2.13. Lists and itineraries as indicators of village location and sequence

1655 mission list	leagues from St. Augustine
Azile	75
Ivitachuco	75
Oconi	77
Ayubale	77
Ocuia	84
Aspalaga	86
Patale	87
Tomole	87
San Luis	88
Cupaica	90

1657 itinerary	
January 17	Cupaica
January 19	Bacucua
January 19	Patale
January 20	Aspalaga
January 22	San Luis
January 23	Thomole
February 5	Ocuia
February 6	Oconi
February 6	Ayubale
February 7	Ybitachuco
February 8	Azile

1675 mission list of Calderón	leagues to	
Asyle	2	Hibitachuco
Hibitachuco	1	Ayubali
Ayubali	1	Oconi
Oconi	1	Aspalaga
Aspalaga	2	Ocuya
Ocuya	4	Patale
Patale	2	Bacuqua
Bacuqua	2	Cupahica
Cupahica	1	San Luis
San Luis	1	Tama
Tama	1	Tomoli
Tomoli	2	Capoli
Tomoli	4	Assumpción del Puerto

1675 mission list of Hita Salazar			1677 itinerary		1680 mission list of Marques Cabrera
	leagues to				
San Luis	1	Cupaica	No date	San Luis	Ybithachucu
Cupaica	2	Bacuqua	December 22	Tomole	Ajubali
Bacuqua	2	Patale	December 24	Candelaria	Oconi
Patale	4	Ocuya		San Luis	Aspalaga
Ocuya	1.5	Aspalaga	December 29	Cupaica	Ocuux
Aspalaga	1	Oconi	December 31	Bacuqua	Patali
Oconi	0.5+	Ayubale	December 31	Patale	Bacuqua
Ayubale	1.5	Ivitachuco	January 2	Ocuia	Yecambí
Ivitachuco	1.5	Azile	January 3	Aspalaga	San Carlos de los Chacatos
			January 5	Oconi	San Luis
			January 6	Capole	Tama
San Luis	0.5+	Tama	January 7	Ayubale	Chines
Tama	2	Tomoli	January 9	Ivitachuco	Tomoli
Tomoli	2+	Capoli	January 9	Tocopacas	Ychutafun
San Luis on the		Assumption of			
path to the sea		Our Lady			

(continued on next page)

Table 2.13 (continued)

1689 mission list of Compostela	1693 itinerary			1694 itinerary	
		leagues to			
Hivitachuco	San Marcos		Tomole	November 19	Hivitachuco
Ayubale	Tomole	6	San Luis	November 19	Aiubale
Oconi	San Luis	3	Ilcombe	November 20	Capoli
Aspalaga	Ilcombe	12	NW to Chacatos village	November 20	Aspalaga
Ocuya	Chacatos village	1	Palos or Taluga River	November 20	Tomoli
Hichutafun	Chacatos village	5	Calistobe Spring	November 20	San Luis
Tomoli	Calistobe Spring	5	former site of San Nicolás	November 21	Tama
Tama				November 24	Escabí
Chines				November 26	Bacuqua
San Luis	SOURCE: Leonard 1939.			November 28	Patale
Patali				November 28	Ocuia
Bacucua				December 1	Oconi
Yscambí					
San Nicolas de los Chacatos					
San Carlos de Çabacola					

NOTE: This itinerary is the route taken by the official who preceded Joaquín de Florencia to set the time for the visitation of each village and to make the preliminary announcements.

1694 visitation itinerary of Florencia		1697 mission list			1716 itinerary of Diego Peña
			leagues to		
November 25	Escabí	San Luis	3	Escabí	Ivitachuco
November 27	Bacuqua	Escabí	2	Vacuqua	Ayabale
November 27	Delgado Ranch	Vacuqua	9	Ocuya	Capoli
November 29	Patali	Ocuya	3	Oconi	Patale
November 29	Ocuia	Oconi	2	Vitachuco	Tomole
December 1	Upalucha Ranch	Vitachuco	1	Ayubale	La Tama
December 2	Oconi	Ayubale	3	Capoli	San Luis
December 3	Hivitachuco	Capoli	1.5	Patali	Ocalquire Prairie (Lake Jackson)
December 4	Aiubale	Patali	1.5	Aspalaga	Ochlokonee River
December 5	Capoli	Aspalaga	1.5	Tomole	Escambé
December 6	Aspalaga	Tomole	1.5	La Tama	Across mouth of the Flint River
December 7	Tomole	La Tama	0.5	Chines	Savacola (Chislacaliche's Town) [a]
December 7	Candelaria				
December 7	Chines				
December 9	San Luis				
No date	Ochania Ranch				
December 10	San Luis General Assembly				

a. This settlement was located a little above the confluence of the Flint and the Chattahoochee rivers about a half league from the west bank of the Flint on the former site of the settlement of Christian Sabacolans. Diego Peña mentioned stopping for the night at Patale, San Luis, the Ocalquire Prairie, Escambé, and Savacola (Boyd 1949).

whether the names were duplicated in this fashion in the original. For some reason Cupaica was omitted from the listing.

In a curious document written in 1740, a scribe at St. Augustine described the Apalachee countryside, suggesting the division of Florida into entailed estates to be awarded along with titles of nobility in order to attract European settlers. Departing from Fort St. Marks and heading north toward the lands of Caveta, he wrote that his route took him through sandy and swampy flax fields suitable for cattle to the chicasa of the Chacato, which was six leagues from the fort at St. Marks. From there to San Luis there was a league of clayey farmland dotted with hills. And from San Luis to the River of the Chacato[8] and the mouth of the Flint it was 12 leagues. He then described the land starting from St. Marks and heading toward Ivitachuco along the road to St. Augustine as seven leagues of low and marshy flax lands good for cattle. Then, using Ivitachuco as his point of reference, he remarked that in the vicinity of that settlement there had been other villages—Ayubale, Capoli, Aspalaga, Patale, Bacuqua, Tomole, La Tama, and Santa Cruz—which were spread over eight leagues of very fertile lands, and there were others named Escambé, Ocuia, and Ocone inhabited by Apalachee, and also the Chacato, the Ocatacos (?), and the Tabacos (?) (Castilla 1740).[9]

Summary

Until disaster struck in the form of invasions in 1704, Apalachee's 11 mission centers inhabited by Apalachee and the four mission villages of the Tama, Chine, and Chacato and the Tocobaga settlement had demonstrated remark-

8. This is probably the Chattahoochee, which may have been named for the Chacatos. In one early document it was spelled Chactahoochee. There are other interpretations for the origin of the name, one, that it is from the Creek for "red," which is *chate,* as in *Iste-chate,* "red man" (see Hawkins 1982b:7).

9. The last two names, Ocatacos and Tabacos, are not very legible, so this rendering is open to question. The name Ocatacos is quite close to Ocatoses, one of the five places mentioned by the governor as among those whose inhabitants were carried off by Moore. By a process of elimination it may be adjudged to be a geographical place-name for the village of the Chine, which is the only known village or people not mentioned here by Castilla by its usual name, particularly as he includes Ocatacos among the non-Apalachee. The Tabaco are possibly meant to be the Tocobaga. And it is worthy of note that he specifically mentions Ocone as being a settlement of Apalachee. Because the Chine on several occasions were associated with maritime navigation, and because their village was designated as being on the road to the sea, this name may mean "water" people or some other such association with water. There is a remote possibility that Tabaco may be a corruption of Tavasa. On one occasion late in the mission period some of the Tavasa expressed interest in moving into Apalachee, and the Lamhatty account put some Tavasa near the Lower Apalachicola before 1706 (Swanton 1922:130). In 1707 Indians named Ocatazes allied to the Spaniards lived just outside the fort at Pensacola.

able staying power, contrasting favorably with other mission areas. Most of the other areas were prostrate demographically and losing villages steadily within a half century or less of the onset of their missionization. Only Timucuan Yustaga seems to have paralleled Apalachee in longevity.

Although the overall number of villages in Apalachee remained stable, there is evidence that a number of them relocated. During the mission era, Cupaica, Bacuqua, Patale, Aspalaga, San Luis, and the Chine and the Chacato are known to have moved. There is good evidence that Ocuia moved as well. As shown in table 2.13, until 1689, mission lists followed a pattern in the enumeration of the missions, whether the lists were derived from a known itinerary or not: Cupaica to Bacuqua to Patale to Ocuia to Aspalaga to Oconi to Ayubale to Ivitachuco as the primary route and Cupaica to San Luis to Tama to Tomole to Capoli to Ayubale to Ivitachuco as a secondary route. The beginning of a shift in the pattern is discernible in the 1689 list and is revealed fully in the 1697 list in which Patale and Aspalaga are linked with Capoli and Tomole rather than with Ocuia and Bacuqua. In the later lists, the early secondary route appears to have achieved primacy.

Chapter 3

Apalachee Culture and Customs

THE AVAILABLE documents provide little information about the culture and customs of the Apalachee before the mission era, but we do know that theirs, like most southeastern tribes, was a matrilineal society. Positions of authority, such as the chieftainship and the post of inija or second in command, passed not to the son of the deceased chief but to his nephew, the son of his eldest sister (Leturiondo 1678; Matheos [1687b]). Despite some Spanish criticism of the practice, the custom seems to have survived intact until the destruction of the Apalachee villages in 1704. In contrast to the Timucua and Guale during the mission era, there is no indication that an Apalachee woman ever succeeded to the chieftainship or other leadership posts. The Apalachee were matrilocal as well; husbands seem to have been required to reside in the village of their wives unless the wife consented to a different arrangement (Florencia 1695:63–64).

Under the matrilineal system among the Apalachicola, responsibility for custody, education, and discipline of the children, as well as the provision of clothing for them, rested completely with the mother and her family; the father was not involved. Presumably this was also the case among the Apalachee (Hawkins 1982a:83–84). The survival of this custom was possibly reinforced by the absences of many husbands who had long-term contracts to work outside the province, leaving their wives and children to fend for themselves at home. In 1695 the visitor Florencia forbade married men to accept long-term employment that took them away from their families, broadening article 4 of the constitution of the 1682 diocesan synod, which forbade the employment of married Indians in St. Augustine under such conditions (Leon n.d.). But there is no other evidence that the Spanish authorities sought to impose the Christian ideal of paternal responsibility on the matriarchially oriented Apalachee.

It was common for the Apalachee to scalp their enemies killed in battle, as it was for the southeastern Indians in general. The attempt by some anthropologists to argue that scalping was not indigenous lacks historical foundation. The de Soto chronicles establish clearly that the Apalachee scalped their European victims during their first contact with the intruders. Christianization of the tribe led to some curbing of the practice, but its survival is reflected in its prohibition by the Spanish authorities as late as 1701 (Zúñiga y Zerda 1701). A notable example of its disuse is the 1677 campaign against the Chisca by the warriors of San Luis and Escambé. On that occasion the native leaders resisted pressure from their men to allow scalping of the slain enemy (Fernández de Florencia 1678). One reason for the survival of the practice was the link between the achievement of warrior status, known as *tascaia*, and the killing of an enemy. Exhibition of the slain enemy's scalp was the standard manner of demonstrating one's prowess and right to be admitted to the warrior class. It was the custom to display such scalps in the main council house and to hold a scalp dance to celebrate the warrior's deed. During the dance the warrior wore a crown fashioned out of birds' beaks and the hair of deer and other wild animals. Advancement within the warrior ranks to the status of noroco and *nicoguadca* depended on killing additional enemies, three scalps to attain the former, ten for the latter, three of which had to be taken from a warrior above the entry-level rank. The nicoguadca of the Apalachee may have been the equivalent of the Apalachicola's "Great Warrior." After the ceremony the warriors attached the scalps to their bows or to a staff. This round of killings became self-perpetuating: it was incumbent on the victim's village or clan to avenge his death by slaying someone from the killer's family, village, or clan (García 1695; Junta of War 1705; Leturiondo 1678; Peña 1706; Zuñiga y Zerda 1701). Just before the destruction of the missions, St. Augustine's pastor recorded the survival of these customs:

The Indians of those provinces, and principally the Apalache, have been and are the most valiant of all those lands. . . . They also use some hatchets that they bear attached to the leather belt worn about the waist [*en la petrina*] with which they remove the scalp of those whom they kill and they carry it to the council house on a pine branch as an indication of their victory. There they hang it up and they dance the war dance for many days. They are so bloodthirsty that, if some Indian from their village is killed by one from another, they do not rest until they revenge the killing either on the one who did it or on someone else from his village. In order to give battle they dress themselves elaborately, after their usage, painted all over with red ochre and with their heads full of multicolored feathers. (Leturiondo [1700]:199–200)

The best-known feature of Apalachee culture is sports, particularly one of their ball games. They had at least three different games: the game of chunkey,

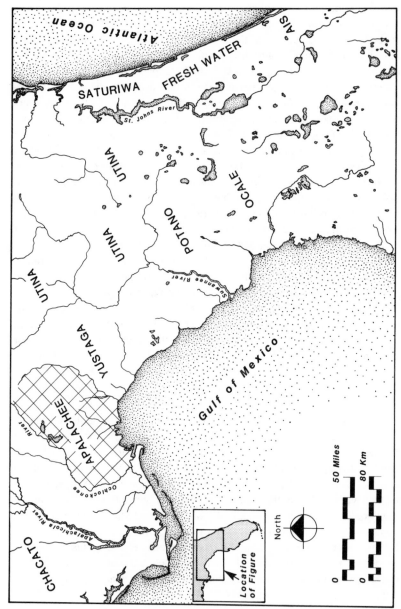

Fig. 3.1. Tribal groups of Timucua.

which they shared with a number of other tribes;[1] a ball game for women played with cane rackets; and the game known best by its Spanish name, *el juego de pelota*, or, simply, the ball game. The title of the ball game manuscript (appendix 2), from which our knowledge of the game derives, proclaims that the Apalachee shared the game with the neighboring Yustaga from time immemorial (fig. 3.1). All the Timucua as far east as Potano seem to have been addicted to the sport (Leturiondo 1678). The coastal Timucua's game pictured by the French was distinct. Boys played a milder intramural version of the Apalachee game.

Considerable information on this game has survived because of the research done by two literate Hispanicized natives, who served as interpreters, and the animosity that San Luis's pastor developed toward the game in the mid-1670s. The marked non-Christian religious overtones of the pregame ceremonies and the game itself and the superstitious practices associated with both, along with the game's brutality, aroused the suspicions and eventually the hostility of many clergy. As early as the 1650s and probably earlier, some friars had forbidden their parishioners to play the game. In response to the natives' complaints, Governor Rebolledo (during his 1657 visitation) explicitly forbade the clerics to ban this native game. In 1675, appalled by the brutality exhibited in the milder juvenile version of the game, which he had witnessed, Bishop Calderón reinvigorated the opposition to the game by issuing a ban on playing it. But Friar Juan de Paiva, then the pastor at San Luis, persuaded him to rescind the ban. Possibly inspired by this incident or by Friar Paiva, the two interpreters then conducted an inquiry into the origins of the game and the ceremonies and customs associated with it. They incorporated their findings in a report, usually referred to as the *cuaderno*, or notebook, that was critical of the game. Perturbed by scruples over the wisdom of his intercession with the bishop, Friar Paiva began to observe the game more critically. Influenced by his observances and above all by the two interpreters' report, Friar Paiva became convinced that the game was evil in itself and in its consequences. Inspired by this change of heart, he wrote a treatise condemning the game. He based the treatise largely on the interpreters' findings but incorporated his own observations as well, and he developed new arguments to win wider support for its prohibition throughout the province. Juan Fernández de Florencia, then the governor's lieutenant in Apalachee, lent his support to the effort to eliminate the game. Nonetheless, elements in both the native and the Spanish communities continued to defend the game and to press for the lifting of the new ban. When Domingo de Leturiondo arrived for his visitation of the province, held in the village of Tomole in late 1677, he

---

1. *Quisio* is the term used for it in the ball game manuscript. It is not clear whether this is the Spanish or the native name for the game.

made the issue of the ball game the principal business of the general assembly of all the leaders of the province. Lending his support to the campaign against the game, he incorporated Friar Paiva's manuscript into the visitation record.[2]

The ball game was a village affair. Its pregame ceremonies and preparations involved the entire community. Of the raising of the ball post and the ceremonies surrounding it, Friar Paiva remarked, "It was their greatest festival." Although referring to the Creek, the following comment aptly captures the spirit and intensity with which the Apalachee approached the game: "Far more than a sport, the intertown ball games called by the Creek 'the younger brother of war' provided ways for young men to gain honors in time of peace" (Green 1979:10). Among the mission-era Apalachee this function probably assumed even more importance as Christianization and the Spanish promotion of peace between them and the neighboring tribes lessened the incidence of warfare for almost half a century. Green suggested as well that the Creek game served to maintain peace and solidarity among the people of a single town (Green 1979:10). It is interesting that those who opposed the banning of the Apalachee game in the mid-1670s advanced a similar argument as a reason to justify the continuation of the games.

The ball game was also an integral part of the aboriginal religious observance. In particular, the ceremonies surrounding the raising of the goalpost had strong religious overtones, moving Friar Paiva to characterize the pole as "this ballpost of the devil." Similarly, the preparations for the game included a number of prescribed rituals suggestive either of religious associations or superstitious beliefs. The practices indicative of the latter were viewed as necessary to guarantee or at least to enhance the chances of victory. Although most of the practices with religious associations had fallen into disuse, they were a major factor in the friars' hostility toward the game.

The ball game also provided an outlet for the natives' penchant for gambling. Wagers made on the outcome of the game ranged up to a family's entire possessions, including even its food supply for the winter. In this aspect and in those which made it a substitute for war, the Apalachee ball game seems to have some possible parallels with the Aztecs' Xochiyaotl or Flowery Wars and with the game played on the well-known Mayan ball court.

The basic components of the game were a tall goalpost (fig. 3.2) surmounted by an eagle's nest containing a stuffed eagle and a few shells; a small hard buckskin ball, slightly larger than a musket ball, filled with dried mud into which human hair was occasionally mixed; and two teams of varying

2. Unless indicated otherwise by a footnote citation, all the information presented here on the ball game was drawn from the writer's transcription of the Stetson photostat of the ball game manuscript contained in the 1677–1678 Leturiondo visitation record. In this chapter, information drawn from that source is not explicitly referenced to that transcription. The entire text of the ball game manuscript appears in appendix 2.

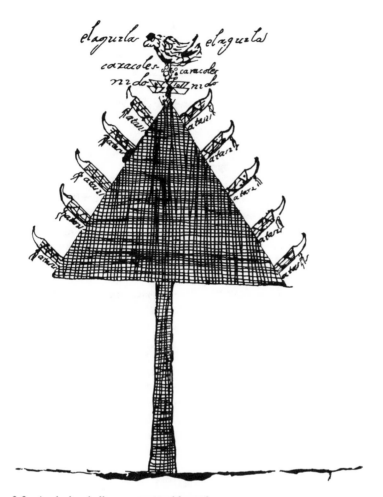

Fig. 3.2. Apalachee ball game post and legends.

size. The number of players varied with the size of the villages playing, but sides of 40 or 50 were typical. In contrast to the parallel games of the Creek and the Timucua, no instruments but the human hand and foot were used to propel the ball. The foot was used exclusively for hurling the ball at the post. The players dressed only in a deerskin loincloth. They painted their bodies in colors associated with the dominant clans of the town, at times using a fetid greasy stew as the vehicle for the body paint, and they braided their hair. Apparently one strike (point) was awarded each time the post was struck with the ball propelled by the foot. If the ball lodged in the eagle's nest, the feat counted for two strikes. Victory went to the first team to achieve eleven strikes.

At the start of the game all the players bunched together on the field, as Friar Paiva put it, "like a clump of pine cones," waiting for a village leader to toss the ball to them. As soon as someone caught the ball, a general melee ensued as the rival hordes of players struggled with one another to possess it. This mob scene was graphically portrayed in the ball game manuscript:

> And they fall upon one another at full tilt. And the last to arrive climb up over their bodies, using them as stairs. And, to enter, others step on their faces, heads, or bellies, as they encounter them taking no notice [of them] and aiming kicks without any concern whether it is to the face or to the body, while in other places still others pull at arms or legs with no concern as to whether they may be dislocated or not, while still others have their mouths filled with dirt. When this pileup begins to become untangled, they are accustomed to find four or five stretched out like tuna; over them are others gasping for breath, because, inasmuch as some are wont to swallow the ball, they are made to vomit it up by squeezing their windpipe or by kicks to the stomach. Over there lie others with an arm or a leg broken. [See appendix 2 for complete translation of this section.]

Some of those described above as being stretched out like tuna apparently were prostrated by the heat. The game was played only during the summer, starting at midday or two in the afternoon, probably because of its association with the placation of the deified forces of nature vital to a good crop. Father Paiva described the players' faces as ruddy, as if they were aflame, and said buckets of water were used to revive them. The friar saw in this action one of the causes of the natives' high mortality, remarking, "What kind of remedy is this, when they have their pores open in this fashion? How can these wretches stay alive thus? Accordingly, they are destroying themselves and this nation is being extinguished. And all this is only a sketch."

Violence often was not confined to the game itself. Paiva reported that of five successive games at San Luis, "not one concluded without becoming a live war," which apparently spread to the spectators. Only the presence of soldiers, he concluded, prevented serious incidents. Among the injuries produced by the brutality of the game, he catalogued broken legs, permanently maimed hands, broken ribs, and the loss of sight in an eye. It was not unknown, he affirmed, for people to be killed in the course of the game, asserting that he was aware of two such deaths in the plaza of San Luis.

Friar Paiva went on to mention that those who defended the game argued that it was good policy for some villages to be in conflict with others and that this was merely healthy competition and not something morbid. Bushnell suggested that this intervillage rivalry had become intense by 1677, especially between San Luis and most of the rest of Apalachee. According to Bushnell, this rivalry was responsible for the cold shoulder shown San Luis's call in 1677 for volunteers for a punitive expedition against the Chisca of western Florida who had been making hostile forays into Apalachee (Bushnell 1978b:9). Only the chief of nearby Cupaica responded, bringing 70 warriors with him. Ayubale, Tomole, and Aspalaga contributed a total of six men, who went without any encouragement from their chiefs. The two non-Apalachee settlements of the Chine and the Chacato, which were located on lands belonging to San Luis, furnished eight and ten men, respectively (Fernández de Florencia 1678). The official report on this expedition gives no explanation for the other villages' disinterest, but Hawkins's remark concerning the decisions for war among the Creek suggests another possible explanation: "It is seldom a town is unanimous, the nation never is; and within the memory of the oldest man among them, it is not recollected that more than one half the nation have been for war at the same time or taken as they express it, the war talk" (Hawkins 1982b:72).

Proceeding in accord with a prescribed ritual, villages formally challenged each other to a ball game. The messenger was to appear in the guise of a raccoon.[3] He wore a raccoon's tail and something like horns on his head. He painted his face red and his body black with superimposed streaks of red, with the result, as Paiva put it, that he appeared to be the devil himself. The messenger carried some noisemakers with him, such as rattles, small bells, or cowbells. If the rival village accepted his challenge, he would return to his village on the run, sounding the rattle and bells with great éclat. If the challenge were declined, he slunk back quietly with his instruments tied to a pole slung over his shoulder. Paiva does not indicate how often these challenges were presented or accepted, except obliquely, remarking that the Spanish authorities had to intervene at times so that the playing of the game did not lead to the neglect of the crops. The friar did not indicate whether the messenger's colors described here were peculiar to San Luis or were used by messengers from all the villages. The colors used by the players themselves differed from village to village and, apparently, were based on the colors of the animals that were totems of the predominant clans in the village (Bushnell 1978b:13).

In preparation for the game, an elaborate series of rituals was observed in order to avoid defeat and to enhance the chances of victory. These rituals constituted a set of rules to be obeyed. The first rule required the players to assemble in the main council house or around the goalpost to maintain a vigil during

---

3. The Spanish word used here, *tejon*, means badger. But, inasmuch as the badger is not known to have been an inhabitant of the region in historic times, raccoon seems to be a more appropriate translation.

the night before the game, talking very quietly and occasionally howling like wolves. Flat, low benches made of hollowed-out logs were placed there so that they might sit facing the village with which they were to play. For the placing of the players' seats during the game itself, recourse was had to the interpretation of the dreams of several elderly men who would be awakened early in the morning to be questioned on the nature of their dreams. A new fire was to be lit and then reserved for the preparation of the ceremonial *onsla,* or gruel, for the *usinulo* ("beloved one") and for lighting his tobacco. Before the game this fire was carried out to the playing field and placed in front of it. Except for a prescribed number of spoonfuls of onsla, the usinulo was to fast on the day before the game and to smoke a special mixture of tobaccos composed of the natives' *acchuma fino* and *atabac.* The chief was to fast on the night before the game, taking only copious amounts of *cacina,* a tealike beverage, and smoking the same mixture as the usinulo. The chief was to advise the players during the night, exhorting them to risk their very lives in the quest for victory. The players, in turn, were to ply the chief steadily with cacina to the point of making him nauseated. The team was to enter the field with a few less than the agreed-upon complement of players. If this move induced their rivals to suggest that they complete the roster by choosing some young men from the bystanders, their chances for winning were improved. The people of the village were also supposed to maintain a vigil known as "sleeping the ball." If any of the villagers felt misgivings about their chances for victory, they could enhance their odds by burying a scalp under the rivals' goalpost. If they threw the scalp into their rivals' fire, that would serve as an even more effective charm. Collectively, this array of charms to influence the game's outcome was known as the *chacalica.*

To nullify these charms, the rival village would adopt countermeasures known as the chacalica chacalica.[4] The most striking of these measures was the preparation of a fetid stew made by cooking a turkey, squirrel, or raccoon for three or four days. This foul, greasy mixture would be blended with the clays the Indians used to paint themselves. The object of this was to upset their rivals and thereby neutralize the rivals' magic as the players began to pass out. A less odiferous countermeasure sometimes resorted to was a potion of finger-length sticks tied in a bundle and cooked in a pot of special cacina. The number of sticks equaled the number of players on the rival team. The cacina for this ceremony was to be made from leaves of trees in the inland forests rather than from the coastal plant that was customarily used. This magic was supposed to make the opposing players weak. While the game was in progress, the pot had to be kept covered or the team would certainly lose the game.

---

4. In the ball game manuscript, this native term is followed by its equivalent in Spanish, the *contra de la contra* or "the against, or counter, of the counter."

For the raising of the ball post, an even more elaborate ritual, pregnant with religious symbolism and magical formulas, was prescribed. The goalpost depicted in the Paiva manuscript is like a flagpole on its lower portion and has the appearance of a flat Christmas tree on the upper portion. The edges of the upper portion are adorned with a series of equidistant sassafras pegs, five to a side. Suspended from the outer edge of each peg is what appears to be a short tassel, and inscribed below each of the ten pegs in a minuscule script is the word *atari*. The other inscriptions on this drawing are in Spanish, so this word is probably Spanish as well. The letter *r* in the word seems to rule out its being an Apalachee name. Although there appears to be no such word in modern Spanish, it may well be an obsolete derivative of the verb *atar,* meaning "to tie," and may indicate that the grapevines used to raise the post were tied to those pegs or that the decorations placed on the post were tied there. The top bears an eagle's nest, a stuffed eagle, and some small spiral shells. Paiva's remark "because a pole like the one you see, this is set up in all the places, with the baubles with which they decorate it and which they hang from it" seems to indicate that additional insignia adorned the post. The prescribed ritual for raising the post had to be observed meticulously in order to avoid bad luck for the villages in the games played under it. Once the post was raised, it was probably left in place until it was brought down by the forces of nature. The posts appear to have been struck by lightning frequently. Paiva reported that during the late 1660s and early 1670s, lightning struck and burned the posts at San Luis, Bacuqua, and Patale. This event is especially fitting as there was an association in the Apalachee pantheon between the game and its goalpost and the gods identified with rain and thunderstorms. One of the myths recorded by Paiva suggests that a purpose of the games was to assure adequate rains for the crops.

The rituals for setting up a goalpost were elaborate. Once the pole's basic frame had been assembled, but before the sassafras pegs were attached, the crown was to be put in place facing the east. The hole for raising the pole had to face west. The eagle atop the pole also had to face the setting sun. Only grapevines were to be used in raising the pole. These were in memory of the vines used by the game's patron, Nicoguadca, to divert the snakes in one of the trials he endured. For some time before the raising of the pole, warriors were to dance around the pole to the sound of a drum, occasionally howling like dogs, at other times barking, and at still others making wolflike noises. In one of the earlier translations of this passage, these warriors were presented as having to dance to the *sun* with a tambourine. However, the Spanish text here is very clearly "Avian de estar las tascaias vailando *al son de* um tamboril al rededor al palo," meaning to the sound of a drum around a pole.

For the actual raising of the post, groups of men and women were to pull on the vines from different sides. The warriors were to continue their dance during the raising of the pole, and they were to be joined by six women and by six additional warriors. During this ceremony no woman was to remain in her house. A young unmarried woman, carrying the lacrosse-like stick used in the women's ball game, was to perform some unspecified ceremony beneath the pole in memory of Nicotaijulo, the mother of Nicoguadca. As the pole was about to be set in place, the usinulo was to pay reverence to the pole in a ceremony known as the *gua*. Placing his hands together as a Christian would to pray, the usinulo uttered the word "gua" three times, then poured a libation of cacina to the pole. He also performed other unspecified rituals at this time. Paiva viewed the rituals performed by the usinulo as an idolatrous worship of the pole and of the gods of lightning and rain with which it and the game were associated. A final rule stipulated that a human skull or scalp be placed at the foot of the post in honor of Ytonanslac, the founder of the game and the patron of the players.

The ritual for the raising of the pole also prescribed that a dance be held on the night before that event. For that evening the usual taboos governing sexual conduct were suspended. Paiva described this feature of the ceremony: "As a guarantee of good luck for the season, any man had carte-blanche to touch, fondle, etc. any of the women who came, whether they were married or single." The headman, he remarked, went about exhorting the women not to defend themselves against these advances lest the village lose all the games it played under that pole and lest their husbands and brothers and leaders thereby lose everything they owned, referring to the natives' custom of making substantial wagers on the outcome of the game.

The musketball-sized missile used in the game was to be made of buckskin from the animal's hooves in order to give the one who caught the ball the speed of the deer. During the mission era, Sunday afternoon was the favorite time for the game. The sources say nothing about the size or preparation of the playing field. The observation that the players often had their mouths filled with dirt as they struggled for possession of the ball indicates that it was cleared of vegetation rather than grassy. There are indications as well that the village's central plaza was the playing field, as it was with the Creek later. Neutral fields were chosen on occasion, possibly to lessen the distance to be traveled by the "visiting" team. The ball game manuscript mentions a game between San Luis and Ivitachuco having been played at Ocuia. The entire population of the village customarily attended the game. Paiva commented in shocked tones about the lack of family supervision and togetherness that characterized these outings.

Once it was announced that there was a ball game, they all foolishly ran to see it. They went whichever way they chose. The husband took off by

one path, the wife by another. And if they had a daughter or sons, each
one chose his own path, except that they all went to see the ball [game].
The husband did nothing to prevent his wife or his children from going
with whomever they pleased and to wherever they pleased. [See appendix 2 for complete translation of this section.]

Such conduct would be incomprehensible to seventeenth-century Spanish society, whose self-respecting members closely circumscribed the movements of
wives and daughters and chaperoned them almost everywhere they went.

The emptying of the villages was also an occasion for thefts from the deserted dwellings. Their open doorways were covered at most by a few branches,
useful only for keeping out animals.

If Friar Paiva is to be believed, not all the prospective players were eager
to participate. They often had to be cajoled into playing by entreaties or by a
gift of something with which to wager. Skilled players were especially pam-
pered. To keep them in the village, they were given a house, their fields were
planted for them, and their misdeeds were winked at by the village authorities.

Paiva's account of the ceremonies associated with the game as well as his
litanies detailing its evils are straightforward and informative. The manuscript
is less satisfactory as a source of information on the symbolism, mythology,
and religious overtones of the ball game and its appurtenances. In particular,
his account of the myths concerning the origins of the game in the tribe's remote past are disjointed and confusing. The following is the basic story line of
that mythic account.

In the days when all the Apalachee were non-Christian, there were two
chiefs who lived in neighboring villages. One bore the name Ochuna Nicoguadca, which signifies the lightning bolt. The other, Ytonanslac, was an
elderly and wise leader. (Paiva indicated that his name also was identified with
one of the native gods.) Ytonanslac had an orphaned granddaughter, Nicotaijulo, whose name signified "woman of the sun." Every day she was sent by
the village leaders to fetch water. In the course of this employment she became pregnant and gave birth to a son and hid him among some bushes, where
the panther, the bear, and the blue jay found him. Having introduced the
mythic protagonists, Father Paiva proceeded with the story.

And they brought him to Itonanslac, his great-grandfather. And they
told him how his granddaughter, Nicotaijulo, had given birth to that
child. He then ordered that they should not say anything to anybody or
reveal that his granddaughter had given birth. He was given the name
Chita. They do not know what it means, nor have I been able to discover
it. He was reared to the age of twelve with this name, and [then] it was

changed, and he was given another, which was Oclafi, Baron of water. This is their way of speaking. He was reared with that name until the twentieth year. And [then], it was taken from him and he was given another, which was eslafiayupi. Neither did they know what this one meant.[5] They say they are ignorant of it. The which young man excelled everyone in courage and in his skill with the bow and arrow and the game of *quicio* [chunkey], which all these nations play, which is [played] with two long poles about three yardsticks in length and a flat and round stone.

Ochuna Nicoguadca harbored suspicions that that young man was the son of Taijulo, because his shamans had told him or prognosticated, as we would say, that the son to which Nico taijulo gave birth was destined to kill him. And in order [to learn] if perchance this was so, he tried to see if he might kill him. And he set the following three traps for him, so that he might perish in one.

Take note that the Ytonanslaq had commanded his great-grandson that, concerning everything that they ordered him to do or that happened, that it was important for him that he should let him know about it before he obeyed it. And, accordingly, [when] he was ordered first, that he should go to a certain place, where there was a large and very deep sinkhole, that he should obtain flints there for arrowheads, and that they should not be from any other place, the young man went at once and told his great-grandfather of what they were ordering him [to do]. And he said to him, son, this spring is very deep. You cannot obtain the flints from it without risking your life. He gave him some beads [made] of shell and told him to give those beads to a little bird that would be there diving and ask for the flints from it. And so he went, gave it the beads, and asked it for them [the flints]. And it gave them [to him], and he brought them to Ochuna Nicoguadca. [See appendix 2 for complete translation of this section.]

Ochuna Nicoguadca then gave his nemesis two more dangerous tasks to perform. The young rival was to bring some bamboo for arrow shafts from a canebrake filled with venomous snakes and some fledgling eagles from a certain treetop nest. When Eslafiayupi, aided by the advice of his great-grandfather, returned unscathed and successful, Ochuna Nicoguadca concluded that he could not kill him in this fashion and then arranged that they

---

5. Evelyn Peterson suggested that Father Paiva's native informants may well have known the meanings of these names but would not tell the uninitiated because they occupied so exalted a niche in the Apalachee's mythology.

should play the ball game. This portion of the myth ends with the comment "This is how it had its beginning and it is in this fashion."

At this point in the manuscript Paiva digressed to explain, at length, how the challenge was presented, how the game was played, and other aspects of the game. On returning to the story line, he recounted that "His players having come together, Ytonanslac gave them the rules so that they would not lose." After listing the first four of those rules, Paiva resumed the story line.

They entered the plaza and, on being asked if their people were assembled and at full strength, those on Ytonanslac's side said "no," that they were short so many people. The rivals told them that they should choose from those young men who were in the vicinity. They called to eslafiayupi, the son of Nicotaijulo, he who killed the eagle and tricked the snakes, etc., and who gave the appearance of being ill, leaning up against a post, wrapped with a cloak of feathers. And upon his entering the game, the battle was begun. And when those of Ytonanslac had reached seven, eslafiayupi let out a thunderous roar and they were all terrified. And eslafiayupi was recognized for Nicoguadca, who is the Lightning-flash, son of Nicotaijulo and of the sun, who is nico. And since then it has remained for an omen that the first who arrived at seven would win because Nicoguadca helped him. And the rivals lose heart at once. And they were accustomed to tell this story every night, sometimes in the council house and sometimes under the ballpost. [See appendix 2 for a complete translation of this section.]

The next paragraph is confusing because Paiva uses pronouns without clearly establishing their antecedents and because the protagonists share the name Nicoguadca. Consequently, the various translators of this manuscript have differed in their renditions of this paragraph. According to my reading of the Spanish text, the story proceeds as follows:

After having lost at the ball [game], Ochuna Nicoguadca challenged Nicoguadca to play at el quisio [chunkey], which is the game, which at the beginning, I said all these nations play, which is with a stone and two poles, for, as I say, he challenged Nicoguadca, and having won from him all that he had, they say that he tried to ensnare him and he pretended to the aforesaid Ochuna Nicoguadca that he was thirsty and wanted to go to drink. And they say nicoguadca hit the ground with the stick's sharp end [and] made water spring forth, and said to him, "Drink." At this point he pretended to need to relieve himself. And Nicoguadca fashioned a little thicket for him and said, "Over here." And

finally he said he was going to light a tobacco and entered into a house
and opened a hole [in the wall] and fled to Apalachocolo. And Nicoguadca then went in search of him with his warriors. And they say that
he formed much fog, cold mists, [and] frost, etc. But despite it all he
vanquished him and killed him and his warriors. And his vassals fashioned the ball pole for him that is shown here on this page. [See appendix 2 for a complete translation of this section.]

Others who have wrestled with this muddy text have presented versions of this
episode that differ from mine to some degree. (The Spanish text of this paragraph appears in appendix 2 for those who wish to translate it for themselves.)

If my rendition of the Spanish text is correct, it indicates that at the end of
the struggle it was the younger Nicoguadca who perished rather than Ochuna
Nicoguadca, whose death at the hands of the younger man had been foretold
by the older man's shaman. Such a resolution of the plot seems contrary to the
logic of a traditional European story line, which would call for victory by the
new Nicoguadca. Influenced perhaps by such a consideration, Bushnell presented a version of this episode in which Ochuna Nicoguadca pretended to be
thirsty (Bushnell 1978b:11). In my transcript of the Spanish text, there is no
question that it was the younger Nicoguadca who pretended to be thirsty. The
phrase "fingio *al* tal Ochuna Nicoguadca que tenia sede" (he pretended to the
said Ochuna Nicoguadca that he was thirsty), assuming it is a faithful rendition of the original text, can only mean that Ochuna Nicoguadca was the indirect object of the verb *fingio,* "he pretended." Concerning the regular use of
the preposition *a* before nouns denoting definite persons, which are used as
direct objects, George E. McSpadden comments in his *Introduction to Spanish Usage*, "Because of the flexibility of Spanish word order, this personal *a*
construction is often the means of distinguishing the object from the subject.
It is therefore most important to be able to recognize and use this construction" (1956:50). The *a* can serve the same function before nouns used as indirect objects. Also in Bushnell's version of the pursuit passage, Ochuna Nicoguadca, rather than the younger Nicoguadca, was caught and killed by his
rival. On this point, Bushnell admits that her interpretation is conjectural because of the unclear pronoun references in the text and, I would add, the fact
that the rivals shared the name Nicoguadca.

I agree with Bushnell that any interpretation of the pursuit passage must
be conjectural. Some of the problems with this text probably result from its
being a myth that was translated into Spanish from Apalachee, in which the
interpreters probably recorded it, by a friar whose polemical work was inspired by a certain amount of passion. Accordingly, it is difficult to determine
definitively which Nicoguadca triumphed. A strict adherence to the rules of

grammar and the maintenance of logical sequence would make the younger Nicoguadca the author of the various strategems for escape and the one who fled and was caught and killed by the elder one, Ochuna Nicoguadca. On the other hand, the logic of the story line would favor victory by the younger one, for the pole was dedicated to Ytonanslac. To effect this, his and the young Nicoguadca's vassals would have to have survived. I lean toward the younger Nicoguadca as the one who triumphed. Whichever Nicoguadca emerged as victor, in the wake of the elimination of one of the Nicoguadcas, the vassals of the victorious Nicoguadca fashioned the goalpost in his honor.[6]

The myth concludes in this fashion. When Nicoguadca wished to die, he called together all his leaders to inform them that he was going to die, telling them that whoever wished to become Nicoguadca and to remain in his place had to kill seven tascaias or warriors and three *hitas tascaias* (a special category of warriors). Having done so, he would be Nicoguadca. At this point Friar Paiva interrupted the narrative with a related anecdote.

> As my children have told me, those from San Luis that not long ago there died an Indian named Talpagana Luis, who had a staff or club the size of a *benoble*, and on the tip of the said pole, some scalps, and some painted. And I asked who [or possibly, what] that was. And they told me that he [or it] was *Itatascaia* and now they have confessed to me that he was Nicoguadca.
>
> While I was priest of this *doctrina*, the year of seventy-one, I left [to become] guardian of the convent of St. Augustine. And during this time, while the Reverend Fray Francisco Maillo was its priest, this Indian died, and they still tell me that he said he would have to come back and burn the ball post. As though by the just judgments of God Our Lord, a lightning bolt fell that year and burned that of San Luis. And another year, another fell and burned that of Bacuqua, it having happened two years before that another had fallen in Patale and burned another pole? [*sic*]. [See appendix 2 for a complete transcription of this section.]

Returning to the story of the Nicoguadca's death, Friar Paiva reported that Nicoguadca instructed his vassals that as soon as he died, they should put his body in some big pots with squash, melons, and watermelons, fill the pots

---

6. Here Bushnell has "erected the palo de pelota," and Peterson has "invented the ball post." If either phrase is taken literally, it would seem to suggest that they played the first game without a goalpost. This in turn raises the question of how they achieved a score. It probably means simply that they dedicated the existing one to the god Nicoguadca and decorated it in some fashion to indicate that.

with water, and boil them well so that he might be converted into steam, in order that, when they had planted their fields, he might remember them and return to give them water. He said, "And accordingly, when you hear it thunder, it is a sign that I am coming." Paiva closed with the remark "And thus, they say, did he go, and that he did it. And up to the present, they, and particularly the old ones, continue to believe that when it thundered Nicoguadca was on his way to give them water."

From this paragraph it is clear why the friars asserted that this ball game had religious overtones and symbolism. It seems to have been associated with the forces of nature, through the sun-god, the rain-god, and the lightning-bolt-god, the most vital powers to an agricultural people. Among the Creek a thunder-god enjoyed a prominent position in the pantheon. The suggestion of his successive incarnations in noted human warriors might imply that Nicoguadca was a messenger of the gods or a lesser god—but was still a very important personage to placate, both to ensure rain and to avoid harmful lightning strikes, definitely a consideration for a hilltop-dwelling people in an area prone to cloud-to-ground lightning. From the viewpoint of European theogony, there is an unusually strong element of human volition in the transmogrification of the ambitious superwarrior into Nicoguadca. When the reigning Nicoguadca was ready to die, he assembled his leaders and told them that whoever *wished* to become Nicoguadca should follow certain steps. Several references to sun and lightning suggest that they associated the lightning bolt or its god with the sun-god and recognized it or him, or both, as a harbinger of rain. The second incarnation of Nicoguadca in the ball game origin myth is the offspring of the sun and the "Woman of the sun,"[7] and the name for the sun, Nico, is part of the name for the lightning bolt, Nicoguadca. That the game was played only during the summer and that it was so identified with the sun-god and rain-god suggest that the playing of the game was not only a form of sport and a means of projecting a village's power and enjoyment of divine favor but also was designed to assure good crops.

Paiva had always had some misgivings about the game, but in view of the royal policy forbidding interference with native customs that were not contrary to Christian law, he had not felt that his qualms were sufficiently grave to warrant prohibition of the game. When Bishop Calderón banned the game in 1675, Paiva had even intervened in support of the game, persuading the bishop to rescind the ban. However, because he had observed the game more

7. Laudonnière noted that the Timucua used the expression "daughters of the sun" but gave no indication that the term had any special religious connotation. Among the Inca, those among the "chosen women" who were consecrated to the service of the sun god became "Virgins of the Sun" or Mamacuna, and their high priestess was considered the wife of the Sun (Mason 1957: 181).

closely and inquired into its origins and the practices associated with it, he began to have second thoughts about his stand before the bishop. He also perceived potentially disastrous political consequences resulting from the intervillage hostility awakened by the game. His concern is evident in his remark that in 1676 "the province was on the point of being lost, all as a result of this game. My conscience began to bother me with the weight of scruples concerning them [his reasons for defending the game] and to make me responsible for everything that could happen." Bushnell attributed Paiva's concern in this matter to the 1675 Chisca-influenced revolt among the newly converted Chacato and to a Chisca raid on Ivitachuco in 1676. The friar had been directly involved in the revolt, having served as a peacemaker to bring it to an end (Bushnell 1978b:8; Hita Salazar 1675a).

The raid on Ivitachuco and other attacks by the Chisca in the vicinity of San Luis had kept the inhabitants of that region in a continual state of alarm during the spring and early summer of 1677. These attacks were the principal motive for the Apalachee's retaliatory expedition against the Chisca after the harvest that year (Fernández de Florencia 1678). Although the authorities used the unrest among the Chacato as an argument for fortifying the port of Apalachee to instill respect among the Apalachicola, the unrest does not seem to have been the threat Paiva believed it to be. If the threat had been that serious, both Ivitachuco's failure to participate in the retaliatory expedition and the lieutenant's lack of involvement in it seem inexplicable, despite any ill feelings toward San Luis because of its performance on the playing field.

Nevertheless these threats influenced Friar Paiva's position on the game's harmlessness, and he began to question various village interpreters about the game. Two of the interpreters in particular, Diego Salvador, the government's interpreter, and Juan Mendoza, parish interpreter and a native leader at San Luis, worked diligently to assemble information on this topic.[8] Salvador, who wrote the report, consulted the chief of Samoche (a satellite village of Tomole) and an inija of Oconi as his major sources. Mendoza turned to his father, who told him the entire story, having witnessed the raising of a post in San Diego (another of Tomole's satellite villages). In light of their having to consult older authorities, rather than relying on their own experience, and because the friars apparently had contact with little beyond the playing of the game itself, we can assume that many of the pregame ceremonies and rituals surrounding the raising of the ball post had fallen into disuse. Diego Salvador had been on the scene in a leadership role since 1656 at least, having served as royal interpreter in the 1657 visitation of Apalachee and Timucua. The In-

8. There is some confusion concerning the position of Mendoza, who is referred to as chief of San Luis by Bushnell. I believe the *holata* in his name was a surname rather than a title of office. His position will be discussed in more detail in chapter 4.

dians who opposed the extinction of the game advanced the argument that the ceremonies recorded by Diego Salvador had once existed but were no longer practiced. Undoubtedly certain vestiges of these ceremonies did survive, particularly some on the night before the game, such as staying awake all night, howling like wolves, and kindling the new fire, all of which Paiva said he or other friars had witnessed. In reference to the "sleeping of the ball" he recorded that, in a certain village to which he had gone one Sunday as a substitute for the absent pastor, he found the Indians in despair over their chances of winning an upcoming game. They attributed their recent losses of two successive games to their having abandoned that pagan practice. They said they were denied the chance to try a Christian substitute because the church was closed to them on Saturday night. Paiva also recorded that he had seen the painting of the body of the runner sent to present the challenge to a game to a rival village. He also noted that upon witnessing the raising of a ball post with grapevines, he offered ropes to the Indians. They declined the offer, saying the grapevines were stronger and used also in memory of the hoops that Eslafia-yupi made to distract the snakes.

Fortified with this research, Paiva began his campaign for the formal abolition of the ball game. At an assembly of the leaders of San Luis and its satellite villages, Diego Salvador read the account of his and Juan Mendoza's findings, and Paiva proposed that they quit the ball game, presenting his own arguments. After a delay they acceded to his request but apparently with some reluctance. Bushnell speculated that Paiva then composed a first draft of the extant ball game manuscript using the notebook of Diego Salvador and Juan Mendoza and his own reminiscences. He did this to win the support of the governor, his agents, and the Franciscan provincial for a ban on the game that would include all of Apalachee and Yustaga (Bushnell 1978b:13–14). In the meantime, his campaign met with some success among other Indian leaders, as a number of caciques pulled down the ball posts in their villages and erected crosses in their place. The governor's deputy for Apalachee, Captain Juan Fernández de Florencia, summoned the native leaders to a meeting and conveyed the governor's appreciation for the steps they had taken. Diego Salvador assured the Indians of the validity of Paiva's charges against the game, and then a number of the sympathetic leaders spoke, affirming their belief in Diego Salvador's assurances. Nonetheless, strong opposition to the proscription of the game continued. The dissidents argued that the game as then played had been stripped of its pagan superstitions and religious connotations. While rejecting that argument out of hand, Paiva, in a moment of candor, admitted that the game was so strongly rooted in the native mores that its complete abolition would require a prolonged effort, one equal to that necessary for the natives to reject seeing the shaman when they were ill. A joint effort over time by the lieutenant and the priest was needed to instill fear in the Indian through the certainty of reproach and punishment in the wake of any transgression.

At this point, Bushnell suggested, Paiva met the strongest resistance to his crusade from Spaniards rather than from Indians. As evidence she cited Paiva's reference to a letter sent to the governor: "They tell me that it is one of the reasons that they wrote to the governor, asking that he not abolish the game. I do not know that it is true. I only know that it was told to me by a trustworthy person." The writers of the letter argued that it was good politics "that some places should be at odds with others" and develop fierce rivalries and suggested that, if the Indians' game was taken from them, they would refuse to work or dig their fields (Bushnell 1978b:14–15). In the ball game manuscript there is no clear antecedent to indicate whether the "they" who wrote the letter were Indians or Spaniards. In her translation of this passage, Peterson identified "they" as Indians. Inasmuch as there is no antecedent referring to Spaniards but only to Indians, the rules of grammar favor Peterson's interpretation. The argument given, however, seems to be one that would more likely be advanced by Spaniards. Furthermore, a statement by Paiva from an earlier paragraph seems to support Bushnell's argument to some degree at least: "And despite all this, [its abolition] has not failed to arouse its controversies. Not on the part of the Indians." It is likely that opposition to the game's abolition was voiced by members of both communities.

Bushnell theorized that the emergence of the Spanish opposition to his campaign provoked Paiva to compose a revised version of the ball game manuscript, emphasizing the social evils resulting from the game rather than its pagan overtones, which he had stressed in the putative earlier version. Using the techniques of biblical Higher Criticism, she based this judgment on internal evidence in the extant ball game manuscript, which she perceived as showing two fairly distinct layers. She remarked that "As completed on 23 September, 1676, the Pelota Manuscript, with its Salvador-Mendoza source, and what might be called its 'Proto' and 'Deutero' elements, is as endlessly fascinating and disputable as an ancient scroll. Certainly, it is a translator's nightmare; full of flashbacks and derailings, copyists' errors, garbled syntax and unanchored pronouns, not to speak of smatterings of Apalache, Timucuan, and Latin" (Bushnell 1978b:14–15). Having worked with that manuscript, I can heartily agree with the latter part of her observation. Interesting as her theory of "Proto" and "Deutero" is, however, I believe that other simpler alternatives can explain adequately the difficulties and peculiarities of the manuscript. Obviously, it was written in haste, combining elements from the interpreters' account and Paiva's reminiscences and current observations, when Paiva's passions on the subject were inflamed. These circumstances would account for many of those problems of garbled syntax and disjunction.

Other syntactical problems might be attributed to the writers' languages. The interpreters' report was probably written in Apalachee, and the extant copy of the ball game manuscript was prepared by a Spaniard fluent in the Apalachee tongue (Captain Juan Fernandez de Florencia, who, perhaps, was thinking in Apalachee in dealing with some of these passages). The one extant example of a translation from Apalachee, the letter to the Spanish monarch written on January 21, 1688, by the chiefs of Apalachee in their native tongue and translated literally by the friar who put it into Spanish, illustrates the problems of syntax that might arise.

Opposition to the abolition of the game appears to have remained strong despite Paiva's energetic campaign, the support it received from the governor, lieutenant, and provincial, and the cooperation of many chiefs, who replaced goalposts with crosses. Paiva's account of the meeting of the chiefs convoked by the lieutenant indicates that it was designed as much to squelch that opposition as to commend the chiefs who had heeded Paiva's admonitions. When Domingo de Leturiondo began his formal visitation of the province in December 1677, abolition of the game was his major topic at the general assembly of all the caciques and leaders in Tomole, where he opened his inspection of the province. After acknowledging their discontent and speaking in favor of the elimination of the game, he invited each of the chiefs to express his feelings freely so that the matter might be resolved definitively. Beginning with the chief of Ivitachuco, who spoke first, they all agreed that there was justification for abolition of the game and suggested that opposition came mainly from the professional players, who made it their principal activity. Buttressed by that support, Leturiondo, acting in the governor's name, again declared the ball game outlawed throughout the province of Apalachee. At San Luis on December 6, Leturiondo requisitioned the copy of the ball game manuscript that had been made by Florencia so that he could include it among the official papers of the visitation in order that future generations would know why the game had been abolished.

It is not clear whether Leturiondo's prohibition of the game was effective or not. Paiva had reported confidently in 1676: "Blessed be God. The game has been abolished with all love and calm. The Indians themselves with loud voices [recognize] how good this is for their souls as well as for their bodies." The fact that just over a year later Leturiondo saw fit to reopen the debate suggests that the game had not disappeared everywhere. There is some evidence that Leturiondo's prohibition was no more successful than Paiva's. The next governor, Juan Marques Cabrera, informed the Crown early in 1681 that, shortly after assuming power, he had accomplished what none of his predecessors had been able to: he got the Indians to give up the playing of the ball game simply by explaining to them its diabolical content. In view of that scant effort, one might legitimately wonder whether he was any more successful. The memory of the game was still sufficiently alive in 1682 to merit a repetition of its condemnation at the synod of the Diocese of Santiago de Cuba (Bushnell 1978b:18; Leon n.d.). In the 1694 visitation of the province, one of the inspector's routine exhortations to the assembled villagers was "Let them declare whether they practice and maintain among themselves any customs and abuses from their past that results in harm to their souls, and whether they keep the orders and prohibitions that have been issued concerning the ball game, and whether they have ordered them kept." In the course of the inspection there was no complaint or record that the ball game was still being played anywhere in the province of Apalachee.

When the visitador Leturiondo carried his campaign against the game into western Timucua, he found the leaders of the provinces of that region far less compliant than their Apalachee neighbors. On arriving at San Miguel de Asile on January 10, 1678, he summoned the chiefs of Yustaga to a general assembly to be held on January 15 at San Pedro de Potohiriba.[9] Early in that meeting Leturiondo suggested that, inasmuch as the ball game had been proscribed in Apalachee, it would be fitting that it should cease in Yustaga as well. He pointed out that, on the supposition that it was the same game, it could be presumed to contain the same evils. The Yustagan leaders promptly informed him that their version of the game was not tainted by the superstitions that surrounded the one played in Apalachee. Leturiondo ignored this reply and appealed to them as people who had long been Christians to set an example, lest their continuing to play should weaken the resolve of the Apalachee and sow discord. The Yustaga held firm, arguing that they had no other games or entertainment to fill the void that would result from the extinction of an institution so deeply rooted in their past. Among them, they insisted, the game was played without contention, violence, or frauds. Bowing to their persistence, Leturiondo agreed to leave the resolution of the matter to the political and ecclesiastical authorities at St. Augustine. The Yustaga pledged to suspend the playing of the game until they heard from those authorities. Bushnell said it is not known what decision those authorities reached, but one would expect them to have supported Leturiondo, if he had pressed the issue. Both Governor Cabrera's letter and the 1682 synodal proscription of the game indicate that the proscription applied to all of Florida. When Leturiondo intro-

9. In her article on the ball game, Bushnell stated that he "summoned the chiefs of Ustaqua and Utina to San Pedro de Potohiribe." In the visitation record I saw no evidence that anyone other than the leaders from Asile, San Matheo, Machaba, and Potohiriba attended that general assembly at Potohiriba. However, they may well have done so, as there was no mention of a general assembly having been held for Utina during the visitation of its individual villages. For the Potano region, by contrast, such a general assembly was held.

duced this issue at another general assembly held at San Francisco de Potano, the leaders gathered there also firmly opposed his prohibition of the ball game. Again both sides agreed to leave the resolution of the question to the authorities at St. Augustine (Bushnell 1978b:16–18; Leturiondo 1678:587–610). This development suggests that all the western Timucua, not merely the Yustaga, shared the game with the Apalachee.

Spanish documents reveal the Apalachee's continued resort to the shamans who served as healers, whom the Spaniards called *curanderos,* but none of the references describe their practices for healing clients. The Spaniards severely punished those who used their services, at times with sentences of forced labor (Paiva 1676). These shamans were among the native dignitaries whose fields were tilled by the community labor pool. In their drive to eradicate the healers' practices and the Indians' continued recourse to them, the Spanish authorities forbade the provision of this financial reward to the shamans (Florencia 1695:51). Despite the Spaniards' antipathy, the shamans seem to have survived until the destruction of the missions in 1704. As late as 1694–1695, Florencia included the following among the regulations he published at the conclusion of his visitation: "15th—that they are not to consent to, tolerate, or conceal curing after the pagan manner; and if any one of the natives practices it, let him be punished at the discretion of the lieutenant; and let the cacique see to this with great vigilance; and they are not to sow or dig the field for such curanderos as is the practice" (Florencia 1695:87).

Dancing played a major role in the social life of the Apalachee, serving ceremonial or ritual functions, as in the ceremonies accompanying the raising of the ball post, as well as providing amusement for the participants. There are no descriptions of their dances, however. The most frequent mention of dancing is in regard to the persistent attempt by friars to prohibit or curtail it severely. The Spanish authorities prohibited some of the dances as lewd and indecent but protected the natives' right to continue others, despite the desire of some of the friars to prohibit all the traditional dances. Only in Lent was all dancing prohibited. Despite the friars' surveillance some of the dances considered lewd even by the Spaniards appear to have survived until the end of the seventeenth century. Bishop Calderón noted that the friars attended such festivities "in order to prevent indecent and lewd conduct." Florencia found it necessary to repeat the prohibition in 1695 and to stipulate that the lieutenant should summon the responsible cacique for punishment "each and every time that they practiced them and consent to them" (Días Vara Calderón 1675:13; Florencia 1695:87).

The ball game manuscript indicates that body painting for ceremonial purposes was practiced by the Apalachee. Its use by warriors going into battle is indicated in this passage: "In order to give battle they [the Apalachee] dress themselves elaborately, after their usage, painted all over with red ochre and with their heads full of multicolored feathers" (Leturiondo 1700). The use of body painting at other times is not mentioned, but it seems likely. It may even have been a general practice, as it appears to have been among the neighboring Timucua. There is no indication that the Apalachee practiced the more permanent tattooing of designs on the body attributed to the Timucua by the French in the 1560s. The degree to which body painting survived the pressures of acculturation is unknown. The remark of the French who observed that the Apalachee exiles at Mobile had little of the savage about them except their language might indicate that body painting had fallen into disuse by the end of the mission era.

The presence of various shell ornaments for arm and leg bands, ear pins, and gorgets at Fort Walton sites in the area indicates that similar items were used by the Apalachee in historic times (Smith 1956:123). The use of beads made out of snail shells is mentioned in passing in the ball game manuscript.

One of the important traditional customs of the Indians of the Southeast, the busk, or green corn, ceremony, inexplicably is not mentioned in the records as a celebration by the Apalachee. Because of the native religious rituals associated with such a ceremony, it would have been viewed with hostility by the friars, and, accordingly, would probably have been prohibited or regulated. One would expect to find complaints by the native leaders about these restrictions at one or another of the visitations, yet none is stated. The exiles at Mobile are said to have held a great celebration accompanied by Catholic religious services, feasting, dancing, and the wearing of masks. The French and the neighboring tribes were invited to this event to commemorate the feast of St. Louis (San Luis), just as it was the Creek custom to invite other towns to the busk ceremony. St. Louis's feast day falling late in August was possibly close enough to the busk season to have absorbed and replaced the native ceremony. And San Luis's position as head town would have facilitated the process (Hudson 1976: 293, 366). There are also indications that the Iberian churches' Fiestas Juaninas were adopted by the Apalachee.[10] These semisecular and semireligious celebrations, occurring in late June, could also have been occasions for the Christianization and absorption of the busk. A major feature of the busk ceremony, the kindling of the new fire, had a strong rival in the Catholic ritual for Holy Saturday, which involves a ceremonial kindling and blessing of the new fire symbolizing Christ's resurrection and the new dispensation associated with it. The existence of this Christian counterpart would

10. The Fiestas Juaninas were a celebration held in honor of four saints, John, Peter, Paul, and
    Anthony, whose feasts fell in the month of June in the church calendar. The feast of St. Peter
    and St. Paul was a holy day of obligation for the Christian natives of Spanish Florida
    (Leon n.d.).

have facilitated abandonment of the native ceremony without any major resistance.

Not much is known about the marriage practices of the Apalachee before the mission era. Presumably they shared the mores of their Apalachicola cousins concerning marriage, divorce, adultery, polygamy, and concubinage. Hawkins observed that among the Apalachicola, when a man desired to marry, he sent a female relative such as his mother or sister to make the proposal to the female relations of the woman whom he had selected. If she and her maternal relatives assented, the prospective bridegroom then displayed his abilities as a provider by assembling a blanket and whatever other articles of clothing he could produce and by assisting his wife in the planting of her crop, by building a house, and by securing some meat through the hunt. He placed all of these in the possession of his future wife or her family. Once the woman's family accepted the proposed match, he could go to her house as soon as he chose, but it appears that before they were considered so fully married that the penalties for adultery could apply, the wife had to accept his offering from the hunt and prepare and serve it to him before witnesses. If his wife consented, a man might take more than one wife. Before marriage a woman was permitted to enter casual unions as she chose. Once a firm marriage alliance was established, there were harsh penalties for adultery if the family or clan of the aggrieved party chose to press the matter (Hawkins 1982b:73–74; Hudson 1976: 198–201). For Apalachee, the evidence is equivocal. In mission times, at least, some Apalachee seem to have had a more relaxed attitude toward this failing. The irascible lieutenant in Apalachee for much of the 1680s, Antonio Matheos, remarked in shocked tones:

> And not holding it as a matter of pride, they do not consider it an outrage that their wives commit adultery. And the most they do in that case is to advise the lieutenant, and, on punishing the delinquents, they return to their houses with their wives and often in the company of the offender, as I have seen and witnessed many times, with such calmness and lack of embarrassment that it is as if such a thing had never occurred. (Matheos 1687b)

The visitors' constant warnings that the native authorities should be vigilant in preventing and punishing concubinage suggests that casual unions among the unmarried were permitted (Florencia 1695:50–52; Rebolledo 1657a:91). On the other hand, friars in Apalachee, arguing against the presence of soldiers, described Apalachee men as "most jealous" about their wives, daughters, and sisters (Moral et al. 1657). Among the Apalachicola, at least until the marriage produced children, divorce was easy to obtain on the request of either partner during the period of the busk each year. A man could not marry anyone within his own clan or in his father's lineage (Hawkins 1982b:73).

Because of the Christian precepts in the matter and their contrast with these native practices, under the closely supervised mission regime profound changes were imposed on the Apalachee's customs. The degree of this control is reflected in a 1695 regulation by the visitor Florencia. He remarked that he had been informed that on the farms and cattle ranches of both the Spaniards and the natives in Apalachee married and single women were present to serve the peons. He noted that this had already been prohibited because of the scandals and offense to God and harm to souls that it occasioned, and he ordered that only married women accompanied by their husbands be permitted to live or work under such circumstances. Husbands, similarly, were prohibited from accepting any long-term employment that separated them from their wives and families, and Spaniards, Negroes, and mulattos were forbidden by the 1682 synod to detain married Indians sent to St. Augustine beyond the time prescribed under the repartimiento (Florencia 1695:87; Leon n.d.).[11]

Abortion appears to have been practiced among some of North Florida's Indians, if not among the Apalachee. During the 1694 visitation, at San Matheo in Timucua, Florencia passed judgment on a married woman living apart from her husband, who had been denounced for having terminated several pregnancies by aborting them with *verudises* that she took for that purpose because of the anxiety that she was experiencing. He imposed no penalty for her past offenses, but he left instructions that she was to be given 50 lashes and to have her hair cropped if she repeated the offense (Florencia 1695: 91–92).

11. The sixth and nineteenth regulations he issued for Timucua provided, respectively: "Let them not consent to married Apalachino Indians being in this province under the penalty of 25 ducats to be paid by the chiefs and the lieutenants who consent to it, but, rather, let them make them return to their villages that they may lead a conjugal life with their wives" and "During Lent, let the lieutenants take care to gather together all the Apalachino Indians in these parts and to send them to their native lands so that they may go to Confession and let it be with one of their companions; and, afterward, if they wish, they may return, provided they are not married."

Chapter 4

Apalachee Political Structure

THE SIXTEENTH-CENTURY accounts of Spanish contacts with the Apalachee reveal little about the political structure of their territory. Two large villages, Ivitachuco and Anhayca Apalache, seem to have anchored either end of their densely settled area. Numerous other villages seem to have been scattered around these eastern and western termini in the form of rough arcs or semicircles reaching toward one another. A relatively unsettled and uncultivated area separated them (Elvas 1904:46–47; Fernández de Oviedo y Valdéz 1904:78–79; Hernández de Biedma 1904:6; Vega 1951:181–184). The clumping of the mounds of the earlier period in two major complexes near Lakes Jackson and Miccosukee also suggests that, if the mounds were contemporaneous, the Apalachee were divided into an eastern and a western component.

The chief of the western terminus, where de Soto wintered, was spoken of as the lord of that country, and Ivitachuco was characterized as being subject to Apalachee. Inasmuch as the Spaniards found Ivitachuco in flames and appear to have had little contact with its people after the initial hostile encounters, there is no evidence to show that its chiefs then occupied the leadership position, in prestige at least, that they enjoyed during mission times. It is interesting to note that the size of the village depicted by Garcilaso, 200 large houses and many small ones (Vega 1951:138), indicates that it was a settlement second only to Anhayca Apalache in size, which Garcilaso described as having 250 houses. The mention of Ivitachuco by all of the chroniclers might indicate that it made a special impression on their minds beyond its being the first Apalachee village they encountered. Garcilaso spent the better part of nine chapters describing events that occurred at Ivitachuco. It is difficult, however, to ascertain what parts of Garcilaso's account represent flights of fancy. His remarks about Ivitachuco and his account of events there must be

96

approached with particular caution because they differ sharply in many details from the accounts presented by other chroniclers. Most disconcerting is his placing Ivitachuco a considerable distance to the east of Apalachee and his description of the time of the burning of the village, which differs from that recorded by the other de Soto chroniclers.

Their narratives tell us nothing about the nature of the overlordship wielded by the chief of Apalachee. There is no indication that he was able to organize the people of the province for a massive effort to drive out the Spaniards. The natives' attacks seem to have been mounted independently by each village unit. There is evidence, however, of a tight cultural unity among the villages, and this probably had some political foundation. None of the Apalachee broke ranks to come to terms with the intruders. The natives of faraway regions of Florida saw them as a homogeneous regional unit and referred to them as Apalachee rather than as Ivitachuca, Anhayca, or Uzela. De Soto's followers were impressed by the natives' pride in being known as Apalachee. This unity was probably a pale reflection of the political situation that prevailed in an earlier time, that of the Fort Walton peoples. Then the Lake Jackson complex was the headquarters or "capital city" of a Mississippian culture whose chief, archaeologists believe, was at the apex of a political structure that was more strongly centralized than it appears to have been in de Soto's time (Milanich and Fairbanks 1980:197).

In a recent paper, John Scarry described that political structure in some detail. The "Lake Jackson phase," he believes, existing "from the twelfth through the fifteenth centuries," was a complex chiefdom for much of its existence and distinguished by "a well-developed settlement hierarchy with four or more classes of settlements" and a clear distinction between the elite and commoners. The grave goods associated with the elite burials from Mound 3, he noted, "included specialized craft items, symbols of office and parts of uniforms. Many were manufactured outside the Lake Jackson chiefdom or consisted of nonlocal materials. They demonstrate that the rulers of the Lake Jackson chiefdom participated in a prestige economy that included the elite of other systems. They were sumptuary goods, intended to identify the chiefs, remind everyone of the presumably divine source of their power, and reinforce the distinctions between the chief and his subjects" (Scarry 1986).

Indications are stronger for a political system unifying the villages when friendly formal contacts between the Spaniards and the Apalachee were initiated at the start of the seventeenth century than those reflected in the de Soto chronicles. When Friar Martín Prieto, accompanied by a number of Timucua chieftains, came to Ivitachuco in 1608 to negotiate a peace between the warring Apalachee and Timucua, allegedly the entire population of the province assembled there to welcome the visitors. Once peace had been agreed upon, the assembled Apalachee chieftains in concert delegated the chief of Inihayca to go to St. Augustine to visit the governor. The Inihayca chief was apparently a brother of the Ivitachuca leader, who spoke for the province at this assembly (Ibarra 1609; Oré 1936:114–117). The rule of these two leading towns by brothers might indicate that their family or clan represented something of a noble line. This view conforms to the pattern Hawkins attributed to the Apalachicola, that the *mico,* "peace leader," and the great warrior, "war leader," were often brothers or brothers-in-law (Hawkins 1982a:15).

Unfortunately, we do not have surnames for many of the chiefs or many indications of blood ties among the chiefly class, particularly for this early period. Most of those that we do have involve the family that was dominant at Ivitachuco. In the Rebolledo visitation the Ivitachucan leader signed his name as Don Luis Ybitachucu. In 1688 one of his successors signed his name as Don Bentura Ybitachuco, *holahta,* while his successor signed his name variously as Don Patricio Hinachuba, Don Patricio Ynhac Chuba, and Nan hula chuba, don Patricio (Ayala y Escobar 1698; Bushnell 1979:17; Chiefs of Apalachee 1688; Hinachuba and Andrés 1699; Rebolledo 1657a:102). These surnames are probably metamorphosed forms of Ybitachuco. In 1677 a Bernardo Hinachuba was the principal cacique of Cupaica, while one of the important leaders at San Luis in the period 1677–1678 was Don Matheo Chuba (Fernández de Florencia 1678; Leturiondo 1678:547; Solana 1687b:28–29). The Rebolledo visitation also indicates that other members of this family held positions of power, namely, Gaspar, the chief of Asile who was an uncle of the chief of Ivitachuco, as were Andrés, the cacique of San Juan (a satellite village of Ivitachuco), and Lourenço Moreno, the captain of Ivitachuco's militia. The same source identifies Don Luis Ybitachuco as "the greatest and most important of all the cacique-nephews of the said Andrés and Lourenco" (Rebolledo 1657a:101–102, 112), implying that there were additional nephews holding chieftainships at that time. In 1694 an Adrián Hinachuba was installed as the principal chief at Santa Cruz de Capoli as successor to another Patricio Hinachuba, who died in 1687 (Florencia 1695:69). The choice of the name Andrés for the man who was chief at San Luis in the 1690s could indicate a connection with the Asile-Ivitachuco line, as might also the fact that in 1657 the chiefs of both San Luis and Ivitachuco bore the name Luis. However, the 1690s Andrés was an Usunaca, not a Hinachuba. Usunaca is the other native surname that appears repeatedly in the second half of the mission period among the chiefs and would-be chiefs.

During the mission period the two chieftainships of San Luis and Ivitachuco or their incumbents, or both, seem to have enjoyed a higher status than those of the remainder of the villages. The chiefs of both were referred to repeatedly as the most important among the chiefs of the province. Leaders such as Matheo Chuba and Juan Mendoza who served at San Luis in leadership roles, without being chief in name, also received designations as the province's most important leaders (Chuba 1687:31; Guerrero 1687:104–105; Luxán 1687:111–113; Roque Pérez 1687:32–33). It is not clear whether it is significant that Ivitachuco's chief is the only one indisputably known to have been a chief, who used the title *holata* rather than the more common Arawakian-derived term *cacique* introduced by the Spaniards. It is worthy of note that in the one text in Apalachee that we have, the term *holahta* is used to designate the king as their "great chief," thus, *Pin holahta chuba pin Rey* (literally, "Our chief great, our King"). Holahta was also applied to the governor in this document. The other village chiefs who were able to sign their names used the term *cacique* to designate their positions (Chiefs of Apalachee 1688).

The origin of the title *holahta* is open to question as this term was used as well by the Timucua. The sixteenth-century Guale, by contrast, as well as the later Muskhogean-speaking Creek, used the term *mico*. The term used most commonly by the Apalachee was the Arawakian term *cacique*.

The relative status of the chiefs of these two most important centers is more difficult to resolve. For the mission period there seems to be little doubt that the chiefs of Ivitachuco enjoyed a higher status than did the chiefs of San Luis. Tesar has suggested that Ivitachuco possibly secured this position for itself as a distributor of Spanish goods to the rest of the province. Although there is no documentary evidence to support this supposition, it could explain Ivitachuco's apparent rise in status over the heir to de Soto's Anhayca. It is noteworthy that as early as 1608, Ivitachuco's chief was referred to as "the greatest of all."

The chief of Ivitachuco is referred to as the most important of all the Apalachee chiefs far more often than is the leader of San Luis. The beginning of a 1699 letter to the king by the chiefs of Ivitachuco and San Luis clearly reveals each chief's status: "Don Patricio Hinachuba, the principal cacique of the Province of Apalachee, and Don Andrés, cacique of San Luis, in the name of all the province, and for themselves" (Hinachuba and Andrés 1699). As a co-signatory, Don Andrés acknowledged the status of principal chief of the province claimed by Don Patricio. Equally compelling is the evidence from the 1677 debate held by the visitor Leturiondo on the abolition of the Apalachee's ball game. The chiefs addressed the assembly in the order of the ranking of their villages. The chief of Ivitachuco was the first to speak (Leturiondo 1678:541–542). In a 1702 letter to the king, Antonio Ponce de León, a Spaniard who served as a spokesman for the Indians, similarly designated Don Patricio as "the greatest of all the caciques of the Province of Apalachee" (Ponce de León 1702). It might be noted as well that in the 1657 visitation, Ivitachuco's chief was the only one ennobled with the Spanish title of *don*. Only in later times were all the chiefs and at least some of the other leaders accorded that status. The components of the names of the town and the family— Ivitachuco and Hinachuba—may also indicate their stature.[1] *Chuba* and *chuco* mean "great" or "powerful." There is some indication that *hina* means "power." If Brian Boniface is correct that the name of the Timucuan town Ivitanayo means "white lake" in Timucuan (Boniface 1971:110), then the name Ivitachuco might mean "Great White" in the sense of principal White, or Peace, Town. This interpretation is tenuous inasmuch as another source has associated the color black with Ivitanayo, illustrating the pitfalls of such efforts. The de Soto chroniclers' assessment of Anhayca's chief as lord of that province may be unreliable as the judgment of newcomers. And if the institution of War and Peace towns prevailed, the war precipitated by de Soto's arrival would make Inhayca's chief lord of the land as the great war leader. That the 1608 peace negotiations took place at Ivitachuco may also have some significance in this respect, though use of that site may have been a function of its proximity to the Timucuan border. There is no indication that the special status of the leaders of these two villages gave them any power over the chiefs of the other major villages, except the influence inherent in being looked to as leaders.

Accordingly, the native political structure at the height of the mission period in the second half of the seventeenth century consisted of 11 largely autonomous major villages that were also mission centers. The ten known to have been in existence in 1657 had one to five satellite villages that were spoken of as being "within their jurisdiction." It is not clear what power, if any, the chief of the major village exercised over the satellite villages within his jurisdiction beyond the leadership of the district's warriors, the apportionment of repartimiento labor quotas, and the direction of activities in which the whole community was involved, such as the "fire hunt," or Junumelas, and labor in the community fields.

The meager evidence that exists suggests that the villages functioned as oligarchical democracies in which all members of the leadership were on something of an equal footing or, at least, no great gap separated the chief from the other more important leaders. It is not clear what influence, if any, the Spanish presence had in strengthening or diminishing the control of the chiefs over their villages. At the time of the friars' first contacts with the Apalachee early in the seventeenth century, the governor spoke of Apalachee as a land where the chiefs were not given very much respect. From 1608 to 1612,

---

1. Ivitachuco is apparently the only Apalachee town that bore the same name as its chief. Elsewhere in Florida, chief and town commonly bore the same name.

friars withdrew twice when the chiefs who had invited them to their villages could not control those who were opposed to their presence. As the chiefs' failure may be attributable to many factors, no conclusions can be drawn about its significance.[2] One can only note that in Spanish eyes the chiefs lacked power and that that description sounds similar to the situation portrayed by Hawkins concerning the Creek at the end of the eighteenth century. It would then seem likely that the Spanish authorities would support the strengthening of the chief's power in order to facilitate their own task, because their control of the ordinary Indian was exercised through the native leadership. This view is reflected in the visitors' admonition to the villagers to obey their chiefs.

On the other hand, the new demands for labor made by the native leadership to satisfy Spanish needs and the occasional humiliation of native leaders by the friars, the lieutenant, or the lieutenant's haughty wife must have placed strains on the chiefs' abilities to maintain the respect and obedience of their tribes. The only clear image we have of the functioning of the decision-making process within the Apalachee's local leadership is reflected in the report on the 1677 Apalachee expedition from San Luis against the Chisca. Both the decision to launch the expedition and the decisions on attack strategy were made collectively by the leaders after they had held a discussion (Fernández de Florencia 1678). In religious matters in mission times, whenever a chief or other leader neglected his religious duties, such as missing Mass for no good reason, the other members of the leadership class functioned as a peer-pressure group to force the errant Christian into line (Fernández de Florencia 1678; Florencia 1695:71–77). The principal chief's position was one of greater dignity as he was always referred to as "the principal cacique of the district." It was he who spoke for the village before the Spanish authorities, and in the chief's absence the spokesman was his second-in-command, the inija, rather than one of the chiefs of the satellite villages.[3] Among the Apalachicola, according to Bartram, "The next man in order of dignity and power is the great war chief; he represents and exercises the dignity of the mico in his absence, in council." Bartram does not appear to have noticed the existence of the henihi. Also, it is not clear that the great war chief he refers to is the chief of the major Red, or War, Town. He goes on to observe, "There are many of these war chiefs in a town or tribe, who are captains or leaders of military

2. Gary Shapiro, for instance, suggested that the ones viewed as chiefs by the Spaniards may only have been the ambitious leaders of satellite villages who saw the invitation to the friars as a means of advancing their own interests and that such a usurpation of authority was the cause of the unruliness.

3. The Spaniards used many variant spellings of this term, including hinija, jinija, enija, and inixa.

parties." He notes that the mico who goes on a military expedition heads the army and serves as war chief (Bartram 1955:390).

For Apalachee there is no explicit mention of a native war chief. On at least one occasion, the natives referred to the lieutenant as their "war chief." It is possible that Juan de Mendoza and Matheo Chuba's anomalous positions at San Luis (they seem to have acted as chief without being chief in name) resulted in part from their being great war chiefs in the sense portrayed by Bartram.

Population figures given for the major villages include the population of all the Apalachee villages within the jurisdiction of that principal village. Functions such as the visitation were held in the principal village's council house, and the district's population assembled there. In contrast, general assemblies of the leaders of all the Apalachee villages were not always held at San Luis. Tomole was the site of the one held during Leturiondo's visitation.

This political structure probably prevailed in substantially the same form in the premission era, inasmuch as it was the Crown's policy not to interfere with native institutions as long as they posed no threat to overall Spanish control or to Christian morals or beliefs. Indeed, the Crown relied on the native political structure on the local level, co-opting it in effect, to maintain its control and to supply Spanish demands for labor, goods, and military support.

The jurisdiction of the major villages had a definite territorial component. It is revealed in the documentary references to groups of non-Apalachee such as the Chine and the Chacato, whose villages are described on two occasions to be within the jurisdiction of San Luis. There seems to be no justification for speaking of them as "invaders," as some authorities do. It is clear that their presence was acquiesced in or welcomed by the Spanish authorities. In the case of the Chacato, a formal contract was elaborated between them and the cacique of San Luis, spelling out the rights and the obligations of the Chacato and granting them permission to settle within the territory belonging to San Luis, on a site some of them had occupied at an earlier period (Fernández de Florencia 1678; Florencia 1695:71–73). This concept of specific village lands appears as well in a complaint by one Apalachee village that the inhabitants of a neighboring village were hunting on their lands (Leturiondo 1678:558).

What is not clear is whether the lands of the various villages were coterminous or whether, in the less densely settled areas, there were unclaimed lands between those belonging to specific villages. The number of non-Apalachee groups that were allowed to settle in the province suggests that the latter was the case.

The political status of these non-Apalachee settlements in relation to the Apalachee among whom they lived is unclear. There are indications that the leaders at San Luis exerted some pressure on the Chacato and the Chine living within their jurisdiction to commit some warriors for the 1677 expedition against the Chisca. The Taman village of Candelaria was about as close to San Luis as the places of the Chine and Chacato, but there is no indication that they were bound to San Luis. The one possible exception occurs in the instructions that Governor Pablo de Hita Salazar gave to Leturiondo for the latter's 1677-1678 visitation of the province. The governor mentioned that there were some Yamasee chiefs and Indians living in the place of San Luis and instructed Leturiondo to assemble them and to hold a visitation among them in the same fashion that he did in the rest of the places. The visitation record contains no other mention of Yamasee. However, Leturiondo's visitation of Taman Candelaria may have included those Yamasee, as that mission was spoken of in 1675 as made up of Tama and Yamasee. If so, the governor may have been speaking loosely in saying that the Yamasee were living in the place of San Luis, indicating only that they were residing on lands that pertained to the jurisdiction of San Luis. Whatever their status in relation to the Apalachee leaders, these settlements were sufficiently autonomous in the eyes of the Spanish authorities to merit being designated as mission centers and to receive separate treatment during the visitation, in contrast to the satellite villages of the Apalachee mission centers.

Each of the Apalachee villages, whether it was the major village at the head of the district or one of the satellite villages, had a chief who was the highest ranking native official. The position of chief was hereditary. Under the prevailing matriarchal system, upon the death of a chief his position passed to the eldest of his nephews by his eldest sister, rather than to his own sons. In contrast to some other areas of Florida, there is no evidence that women ever succeeded to chieftainships or to other positions of authority in Apalachee. There is evidence, however, that this principle of hereditary succession was not an ironclad rule. It could be ignored in the face of the covetousness of an ambitious leader or in the case of the unsuitableness of the hereditary candidate. This is illustrated clearly in a case brought before Leturiondo in 1677 during his visitation of Cupaica.

Nicolás Tafunsaca, inija of Nicupana,[4] claimed the chieftainship of Cupaica's satellite village of Faltassa,[5] alleging that he had been cheated of his birthright about eight years earlier through the manipulations of the incumbent chief, Odunaca Pedro García. Nicolás and an older brother, Feliciano, who had since died, were the nephews of the deceased chief, Tafunsaca

4. Nicupana was another satellite village of Cupaica.
5. In this document the name of the village is rendered as Yfalcasar. Faltassa is the spelling used in the Rebolledo visitation and in a third document subsequent to the Leturiondo visitation record.

Martín, who, on his deathbed, had expressly declared them his heirs and made it known that he wished the chieftainship to pass to them. That he found it necessary to reinforce their claim in this manner might suggest that it was not uncommon for the hereditary principle to be ignored. It also suggests that the chief had a voice in determining whether the hereditary principle should be honored. The Tafunsaca brothers had been away when their uncle died, and one of the four leading men of the village, who had served under Tafunsaca Martín, spread malicious reports to make the brothers appear unqualified for the position. He charged the pair with maliciously using their neighbors' hogs as targets to sharpen their skills at archery, and, thereby, he convinced his colleagues that he was a better choice for the post. They elected him as the new chief and presented his name to the lieutenant for approval, saying that he was the rightful heir. The usurping chief's colleagues were not entirely innocent participants; the only one surviving at the visitation in 1677 was deemed worthy of punishment for his part in the affair.

When Nicolás returned to Faltassa, he found Odunac installed as chief and determined to remain so. In presenting his case, Nicolás Tafunsaca rounded up an impressive array of witnesses to support his claims. These included the principal chief of Cupaica, Bernardo Hinachuba, and the parish interpreter, Tafunsaca Bauptista, who had been present at the bedside of the dying Tafunsaca Martín when he had designated his nephews as his successors. Confronted with this evidence, even the intruder, Odunaca, confessed his usurpation. As a consequence, he was deposed and Nicolás installed in his place (Leturiondo 1678:547–548).

Although the son of an incumbent chief did not enjoy any rights of succession, his position seems to have been one of some prestige, particularly if he were the son of a principal chief. In that case he bore the title of usinulo. Special roles were assigned to him both in the pregame ceremonies for the ball game and in the ceremonies that accompanied the raising of a goalpost. There is a suggestion in the ball game manuscript that in the absence of a son, the post of usinulo might be filled by a daughter of the chief (Paiva 1676).

The prominent role of the chief and the usinulo in the rituals associated with the ball game might indicate that the chief and his family exercised priestly as well as political power in pre-Christian times. This dual role may account for the leaders' support of Paiva's campaign to abolish the game. The greater Hispanization of the leaders would have made them more susceptible to his arguments.

It seems that much of the chief's work was ceremonial or involved his serving as spokesman for his village, but the documentation on this point is minimal. He presided over the ceremonies preceding the ball game and encouraged the players. During the mission era he spoke for the village at the official visitation and was usually the person who gave speeches. When he was able, he led the native troops in forays against enemies and in defense of the home territory, and again he took the lead in exhorting them to fight with valor. Decisions about whether to launch an expedition and which tactics to adopt in the course of the adventure, however, were discussed with other leaders and, apparently, reached by a vote of the majority. The chief was responsible for the disciplining of errant Indians belonging to his village and for selecting the quota of Indian workers for the repartimiento on public projects and private farms. Although he served as commander-in-chief of the native militia from his village, in Spanish times at least he was not necessarily the professional leader of the military forces. More often than not, that post was occupied by a separate individual who held the rank of captain in the Spanish infantry (Fernández de Florencia 1678; Florencia 1695; Leturiondo 1678; Matheos 1687b:50–60; Rebolledo 1657a:93,100; Solana 1687a:17–39).

The chiefs and the other members of the leadership cadre enjoyed certain privileges of office. The chief had the right to the skins of all the bears killed on the lands under the jurisdiction of his village. Gifts distributed by the Crown, such as guns and clothing, were reserved for the leaders, with the chief, naturally, receiving the most coveted of the gifts. Booty captured in forays against other Indians or against English traders also was divided among the leaders. The fields for the support of the chief's household and for the households of other members of the leadership group (including the parish interpreter and even, at times, it seems, some of the more skillful ball players) were worked by the common Indians.

From these or from other sources the members of this leadership group were sometimes able to accumulate considerable quantities of foodstuffs. For Antonio Matheos's second expedition into the Apalachicola country in 1685 in pursuit of the English traders operating there, the native leaders who took part supplied the food for the force of 600 Spaniards and Indians. They did this in the expectation of receiving a share of the booty as compensation.

Chiefs and other leaders were exempt from the labor tribute and from the demeaning forms of punishment such as whipping. A major grievance of the natives that incited the 1656 rebellion in Timucua was that Governor Rebolledo ignored the privileged status of the native leaders. He ordered them to come to St. Augustine to work and to bring three *arrobas* of food on their backs. The chiefs insisted that as long as they had vassals to do such work, it would be demeaning for them to do so. It is not clear whether these social distinctions were as sharp before the mission era or whether they were intensified by the Spanish influence. The de Soto chroniclers portrayed the social status of the chiefs of some of Florida's other groups as one of definite privilege that set them apart from the rest. During the mission era at least, the chiefs claimed the right to alienate village lands that supposedly were not needed by the village. Many of the leadership group were given or assumed the title of "don" which put them into the class of minor nobility (Aranda y Avellaneda 1687:101–113; Florencia 1695; Gomez de Engraba 1657a, 1657b:127–129).

Most of the village's day-to-day administrative duties were handled by the official known as the inija, who was second in rank to the chief.[6] In the absence of the chief, he assumed the functions of the chief, at least in serving as spokesman for the other leaders in dealing with the Spanish authorities. He handled such chores as assignments for sentry duty and patrol work and conducted inspections to see that those duties were fulfilled properly.

As *chacal* he performed such tasks as assigning workers for the community fields and determining the way those fields should be planted, assigning workers for the fields of the padre and the church, and also probably assigning laborers for the repartimiento quota.[7] If they were always coterminous, the duties of the inija as chacal seem to have been similar to those of the *fiscal* in the Spanish cabildo. In documents dealing with Apalachee Province the Spanish authorities seem to have used the terms *fiscal* and *chacal* interchangeably, even referring to the royal fiscals as *chacales reales* (Florencia 1695; Matheos 1687b:50–60; Rebolledo 1657a:96; Solana 1687a:17–39). There are fleeting indications that in mission times the inija may have been the keeper of the town's records and the tribe's traditions. In their inquiry into the origins of the ball game, the two interpreters mentioned the inijas of Oconi and Ivitachuco as two of their principal sources. In a dispute over the chieftainship of Abaslaco, a would-be chief said Matheo Chuba could attest to the legitimacy of his claim. When questioned by the visitor Florencia, Chuba denied knowing any-

6. According to Bushnell the title was applied loosely to chiefs as well. In her article on Patricio Hinachuba, Bushnell mentions that usinulo and inija were among the titles that he used. Of course, it is possible that before becoming chief of Ivitachuco he held the position of inija in some other village as Nicolás Tafunsaca had before his installation as chief of Faltassa. I have seen no evidence of such commingling of titles.

7. It is not clear whether the post of chacal was always held by the inija. These terms do not seem to have been used interchangeably. The documents leave the impression that when an inija is referred to as a *chacal*, the writer is talking about only one aspect of his duties as inija. For example, in a discussion of one of Lieutenant Antonio Matheos's many interferences with the administration of the village of San Luis, he is reported to have temporarily reduced the number of chacals for San Luis's satellite villages from four to two. He was forced to restore the number to four, bowing to the natives' insistence that one was needed for each village. In the case of the two dismissed chacals there is no indication that they are talking about the inija of those satellite villages. There are indications in this document as well that San Luis itself had subordinate chacales in addition to the inija-chacal. The term *chacal* is probably of Mexican origin.

thing about the matter and referred Florencia to the inija Bentura to resolve the dispute (Florencia 1695; Paiva 1676).

Hawkins remarked on the existence among the Apalachicola of an official similar to the inija (whom Corkran calls the henihi), observing that the traders called him the "second man." Hawkins, however, portrays the position as held collectively by a group known as the *Enehau Ulgee* ("people second in command"), who sat in the mico's cabin on the left. They were in charge of the town's public works, such as the public buildings, the construction of houses for new settlers, and the work in the fields. Preparation of the black drink was one of their special duties (Hawkins 1982a:15). For the Apalachee there is no equally clear reference to such a collectivity, but the mention of San Luis's possession of four chacales in addition to its principal inija-chacal suggests a similar institution, as does the four-man council at Faltassa that installed the usurper Odunac Pedro García. While Hawkins speaks of the head of this group as "second in command," Corkran comments that among the Creek the *Tastanage,* or "head warrior," was next to the mico in prestige and influence (Corkran 1967:14). It is possible that in mission times those who held commissions as captains or fieldmasters were the Apalachee equivalent of the Tastanage. As shall be noted shortly, two such individuals at San Luis seem to have enjoyed prestige of that caliber and even to have overshadowed the nominal chief.

Another native official of considerable prestige, at least during the mission era, was the village or parish interpreter, known as the *atequi.* For the friars who did not speak the Indians' language, he served as translator for sermons, confessions, catechetical instructions, and other religious activities. He also served as a language instructor for the neophyte missionary and, at times, even directly handled the teaching of the catechism. The San Luis parish interpreter in the 1670s and 1680s, Juan de Mendoza, appears to have been particularly active in this respect, even serving as acolyte. Indeed, he was so involved with church affairs that, along with Matheo Chuba, he became the butt of Antonio Matheos's gibes about his close clerical ties. The fact that Juan de Mendoza is referred to as one of the province's most important leaders indicates that the position of interpreter also carried some prestige for a leader of his standing to assume the position (Fernández de Florencia 1678; Matheos 1687b:50–60; Paiva 1676; Solana 1687a:17–39). In Cupaica in 1669, the parish interpreter was a member of the Tafunsaca family. Two members of this family were chiefs of Faltassa and one of these was inija of Nicopana before assuming the chieftainship.

The parish interpreter along with the parish fiscal also served as eyes and ears for the priest, seeing to it that the Indians of the parish satisfied their religious obligations and lived in accordance with Christian moral principles. As compensation for the interpreter's work, the ordinary Indians of the parish tilled one or more fields for his support. In one of his many intrusions into the established routine of the villages, Antonio Matheos attempted to deprive Juan de Mendoza of this reward.

On the parish level in some places, the friar had still another lay assistant known as the fiscal. In the one situation where he is mentioned, he had the duty of assigning Indians to run errands for the friar. In this case the errand involved carrying a package to a Timucuan village. The fiscal probably supervised the planting, harvesting, and disbursement of the food supply for the support of the friar and the church. He was probably the Iberian equivalent of the Anglo-Saxon beadle. The post of sacristan was an additional clerical position filled by the natives.

In addition to the parish interpreters, there was a special royal interpreter for handling such government business as visitations and judicial inquiries. During the mid-1670s proscription of the ball game, two interpreters, Diego Salvador, the royal interpreter, and Juan de Mendoza, the San Luis parish interpreter, seemingly on their own initiative, did most of the research that fueled Friar Paiva's campaign for the elimination of the game (Bushnell 1978b:2, 10; Florencia 1695; Leturiondo 1678; Matheos 1687b:50–60; Paiva 1676; Rebolledo 1657a: passim; Solana 1687a:17–39).

There is conflicting evidence about the role of Juan Mendoza at San Luis during the 1670s and the 1680s. Bushnell twice identifies him as chief at San Luis. First, she says, "When cacique Juan Mendoza called for volunteers to help San Luis and its satellite San Damián fight the Chisca," and the second mention is, "Juan Mendoza, holata of San Luis, atequi for the church and captain in the militia" (Bushnell 1978b:9–10). A document appearing on page 583 of the Leturiondo visitation (in association with the ball game manuscript) was signed Diego Salvador and Holata Juan Mendoza. The latter also signed his name in that fashion a dozen years later in the famous 1688 letter written in the Apalachee language. In Buckingham Smith's facsimile of the Apalachee text it appears as "holahta Ju Mendoza." If one interprets this literally to indicate that he ruled as chief at San Luis from 1677 to 1688, some explanations are called for because other documents from this period clearly and positively identify Francisco Luis as the principal chief at San Luis (Chuba 1687:31; Guerrero 1687:104–105).

In the face of that and other problems, a more acceptable conclusion seems to be that the term *Holata* preceding Mendoza's name is a family surname rather than a title of office. In that same 1688 letter, the chief of Ivitachuco also attached the word *holahta* to his name, but he used it as a suffix rather than a prefix, thus, "D^n B^m yBita chuco holahta." In rendering these signatures for the Spanish version of the letter, the priest who translated it from the Apalachee presented them in this fashion: "Don Matheo Chuba=holata=Juan Mendoza=Don Bentuxa Casique de Ybitachua=Don Alonso Pastrana" (Chiefs of Apalachee 1688). That the priest chose to translate one of the holahtas as "cacique," while leaving the other in its native form, suggests that one was a title of office and the other a surname. It is noteworthy that every signer of the 1688 letter except Mendoza was given the title of "don" and that all except Matheo Chuba and Mendoza were given the title of "cacique."

Far more telling in support of the assumption that Mendoza's "holata" did not signify chieftainship is the fact that Mendoza is never explicitly identified by the Spaniards as "chief of San Luis" when others in the same passages are identified as "cacique of Cupayca," or "cacique of Abaslaco," or "principal ynixa of San Luis." In those instances, when Juan Mendoza is spoken of or introduced as a witness, he is identified as "the parish interpreter at San Luis," or "an Indian leader," or "Captain Juan de Mendoza." The highest title given him is "one of the province's most important leaders" (Fernández de Florencia 1678; Guerrero 1687:104–105; Labora 1677:583; Mendoza 1687: 38; Pastrana 1687:34; Don Patricio 1687:38–39). To my knowledge, Mendoza never received the title "don" at a time when it was being handed out rather freely to people such as the chiefs of Capole and Patale, as well as to Matheo Chuba. The possibility remains, of course, that he was chief de facto, if not in name, for much of the period and vain enough to assume the title. His devotion to the friars and to the Spaniards would make him a logical choice on their part. Friar Paiva referred to Mendoza and Diego Salvador as "men who were considered the most worthy of trust there have been."

In the title to the report on the expedition against the Chisca, the leaders are identified as "principal leaders who are Juan Mendoza, Matheo Chuba, Bernardo, the cacique of Cupayca, and Bentura, the Inija of San Luis." Bushnell stated that Mendoza functioned as chief of the expedition. In the body of the report, the lieutenant Florencia records his appointment of the principal officers thus: "Juan Mendoza, captain of this place of San Luis, and Matheo Chuba, fieldmaster, and Don Bernardo, *cacique* and *captain* [italics mine] of the place of San Damián de Cupayca, and Bentura, Ynija of this place." Although Mendoza is mentioned first on both occasions, he is identified only as captain, in contrast to Don Bernardo. During the attack on the Chisca's palisaded village, Matheo Chuba assisted by two unnamed captains led the main body of the Apalachee force under the banner, while Captains Bernardo and Mendoza (mentioned in that order) led the attack on the east and west flanks, respectively (Fernández de Florencia 1678).

Prestigious as the position of parish interpreter might be, it seems a little unusual that a man who was principal chief of the important village of San Luis would stoop, in effect, to occupy it. Again in the 1680s documents associated with the removal of the lieutenant Antonio Matheos, Juan de Mendoza is mentioned repeatedly, but he is never given the title of chief. It is the team of Matheo Chuba and the inija Bentura who seem to be acting then as the leaders at San Luis. While being introduced as a witness in the process against Matheos, Mendoza is identified simply as "Captain Juan de Mendoza, who is of the natives of the said province and one of its most important leaders." Even more indicative of his nonchiefly status at San Luis is a complaint made by Mendoza himself. He claimed that Matheos had deprived him of his salary as parish interpreter and had hindered and prevented "the Indians from planting for him, as they were accustomed to do, the said lieutenant ordering *the leaders* [emphasis added] not to consent to this, and saying that if the said Captain Juan de Mendoza wishes to eat, let him plant" (Chuba 1687:31; Matheos 1687b:52 ff.; Mendoza 1687:38; Roque Pérez 1687:32–33). As chief he already would have had people to plant for him.

While testifying against Antonio Matheos under oath, Matheo Chuba spoke clearly of approaching Matheos in the company of the inija Bentura, the cacique of Abaslaco, and Francisco Luis, whom he identifies as the principal cacique of that place. One of the Spanish soldiers who testified spoke of Matheo Chuba as governor of the said place, but he called Mendoza simply "an Indian leader" and then referred to the "other Francisco, the principal cacique of San Luis" (Chuba 1687:31; Roque Pérez 1687:32–33). In 1695, while Mendoza still held the position of captain at San Luis, Usunaca Andrés is mentioned clearly as its principal chief (Florencia 1695).

This "deposition" of Mendoza from his alleged chieftainship at San Luis does not resolve all the problems concerning its chieftainship during this period. In speaking of the chiefs who went to St. Augustine to complain against the lieutenant, Pedro Luxán, a Spanish soldier who testified against Matheos, characterized Matheo Chuba as "principal cacique of the province" and Bi Bentura, the inija, as "second in rank after the principal cacique." Another Spaniard referred to Matheo Chuba as "a leading Indian and governor of this place." And in telling of Matheos's having put Matheo Chuba and his partner Bentura in irons, the same witness mentioned that the Indians of the village went to consult with the pair as "their heads and governors to ask what they should do." Matheo Chuba himself, on the same occasion that he identified Francisco Luis as principal cacique, styled himself "governor of that place" (Chuba 1687:31; Luxán 1687:111–113; Roque Pérez 1687:32–33).

That title "governor" provides the solution to the problem. Juan de Pueyo's 1695 visitation of Guale portrays the "governor" as the man who governed the village even though he might not be a cacique or mico or at least not the cacique whom one would expect to be in charge. In the Guale village of Santa Clara de Tupique, the official known as the *alaiguita* was governor of the village in 1695, even though another man held the hereditary title of mico of Tupiqui. He had been stripped of the power pertaining to the title because of his incapacity to rule. Antonio, the alaiguita of Tupiqui, was given no title except governor and alaiguita (Pueyo 1695:116–120, 125–128). Matheo Chuba's position at San Luis in the 1680s was similar. It is possible that Mendoza played a similar role in the late 1670s, although there is no equivalent documentation to support that thesis.

Such leaders' rise to power might suggest that clerical support and friendly relations with other sectors of the Spanish community played a part in their eclipsing of the rightful leader during this era. Both Matheo Chuba and Mendoza were taunted by Matheos for their clerical ties. Chuba, in his testimony, recalled that in one of his encounters with the lieutenant, Matheos remarked, "You have been very involved in the convent. It would be best that you become sacristan." Mendoza complained that for two years the lieutenant had constantly made fun of him for his work for the church as catechist, acolyte, and language teacher to the friars (Chuba 1687:31; Mendoza 1687:38). Both held military commissions from the Spanish authorities. Mendoza's role in bringing about the outlawing of the ball game probably would have won him additional favor in both official and clerical circles, as the lieutenant, Juan Fernández de Florencia, supported that move. Matheo Chuba was revealed as enjoying considerable sympathy among the Spaniards in his difficulties with the lieutenant. Their rise to power, however, probably flowed from Chief Francisco Luis's incapacity and the support of other native leaders, as was the case in the alaiguita's accession to power in Tupiqui. If Guale's lieutenant in 1695 is to be believed, the alaiguita was not at all a Hispanophile (Jaen 1695:passim).

If the Francisco Luis who was principal chief in the 1680s was the same Francisco Luis who governed in 1657, age or infirmity could have been a factor responsible for his retiring ways, though in the mid-1680s he was still fit enough to contemplate a trip to St. Augustine. Both the Apalachicola and the Timucua had provisions for a chief to select an assistant when he so desired, whether for reasons of age, infirmity, or any other cause. Hawkins remarks that among the Apalachicola the chief selected the man who appeared best qualified to him and submitted his name to his counselors, who did or did not approve his choice (Florencia 1695:90–93; Hawkins 1982a:69). The Apalachee probably had a similar arrangement.

At San Luis both of the native leaders who overshadowed or replaced the nominal chief in the 1670s and 1680s were leaders in the village's native militia. As seems to have been customary for such leaders, they held captains' commissions in the Spanish infantry. In some villages the chief held that commission. At Ivitachuco in 1657 and in San Luis from the mid-1670s into the 1690s, someone other than the principal chief held that position (Fernández de Florencia 1678; Mendoza 1687:38; Rebolledo 1657a:93, 100). It is not clear whether this phenomenon of chiefs who did not also lead the villages' warriors antedated the mission era. Corkran, citing Bartram, notes that among the Creek, "It sometimes happens that the king (mico) is war-chief and high-priest, and then his power is very formidable and sometimes dangerous to the liberty of citizens." This attempt to avoid abuse of power may have been a reason for separating the function in the larger, more important towns such as San Luis and Ivitachuco.

A number of these militia leaders bore exclusively Spanish names such as Lourenço Martín, Antonio García, Juan de Mendoza, and Alonzo Pastrana, who was a chief as well. These four men were also literate, and their Hispanicization and literacy suggest that they may have been products of St. Augustine's school for interpreters or that some may have been mestizos or that they were natives born and reared in St. Augustine, as was Juan Bernardo Pueyo's Mocama interpreter for the 1695 visitation (Jaen 1695: 169).

These four leaders were often mentioned by name and title during the visitation. A number of other classes of village leaders were noted as being present; they were not identified, just lumped together under the category "other village leaders." They no doubt included some of the prestigious warriors, respected elders, members of the chief's family, and, earlier in the mission period, possibly the medicine maker (Bushnell 1978b:2, 10; Leturiondo 1678; Rebolledo 1657a: passim).

Hawkins and others reveal that among the neighboring Apalachicola, the mico, or chief, and the heniha, or second-in-command, shared decision making with a band of numerous counselors made up of the important warriors, active and retired, the members of the mico's family, the important assistants of the heniha, and other elders of distinction. Among the Apalachee, representatives of these groups undoubtedly were to be found among the anonymous "other leaders." As far as is known, however, there appears to be among the Apalachee no parallel to the elaborate political architecture that characterized the Creek square ground with its four separate cabins: one for the mico and his counselors on the west side with its open front facing east; one for the warriors on the north side; one for the beloved men on the south side; and one for the young people on the east side. In addition, the Creek had another nearby public building known as the rotunda; it served at times as a meeting place for the mico and his counselors and as a ceremonial center for dancing and for certain religious rites. In warm weather the Creek used the square ground and the cabins around it for such activities, but in cold weather they retreated to the rotunda (Fernández de Florencia 1678; Florencia 1695; Hawkins 1982a: 68–72). Among the Apalachee the principal council house appears to have been used for all of these functions year-round. In his description of a typical Florida village, the only major communal structure mentioned by Bishop Calderón was the council house, or great *bujio*. It was round, built of wood, and covered with straw, and it had a very large opening at the top. "Most of them," the bishop commented, "can accommodate from 2,000 to 3,000 persons." He added that they were "furnished all around the interior with niches called *barbacoas*, which serve as beds and as seats for the caciques and chiefs, and as lodgings for soldiers and transients. Dances and festivals are held in them around a great fire in the center" (Diaz Vara Calderón 1675:13). The 1985 and 1986 excavations at San Luis have revealed just such a circular structure 36 meters in diameter. Paralleling the exterior wall below the edges of the niches or barbacoas, the 1985 excavation unearthed 19 cob-filled smudge pits spaced at regular intervals. The expectations that this feature would be found all the way around the interior wall were borne out during the 1986 excavation. The remains of the principal fire indicate that it was placed on the same level as the floor rather than in a fire pit. The fire remains were so shallow that they would have been lost had that portion of the site ever been plowed (Gary Shapiro, personal communications, October 1985, May 1986). This structure is remarkably similar in detail to the one portrayed by Bartram for the Creek, including the large, evenly spaced central support posts and benches around the inside of the exterior wall (Shapiro 1985b:16–18). In the council house it was the prerogative of the chief to sit on the principal barbacoa or bench (Florencia 1695:66–67).

In theory, the native leaders were free to manage their day-to-day affairs without interference from the Spanish authorities, civil or religious. In practice, the governor's lieutenant in Apalachee did intrude at times in the daily affairs of the village, especially in San Luis in such matters as disciplining the Indians and directing labor. The friars, to an even greater degree, seem to have interfered in these matters of Indian administration. The Indian leaders could and often did complain to the lieutenant and to the governor about the friars' intrusions, especially during the governors' visitations. Intrusions and abuses of power by the lieutenant or by the governor himself were more difficult for the Indians to deal with and took longer to remedy. If the governor proved to be unresponsive, they could appeal to the other royal officials in St. Augustine and ultimately to the king, either through the friars and secular clergy or through the royal officials. When the volume of complaints was serious enough, it sometimes brought about the removal of a lieutenant, the deposition of a governor, or, in one case, a harried governor's desertion of his post (Bushnell 1981:135; Solana 1687a:17–39).

As the governor's deputy, the lieutenant was the supreme authority in the province, exercising executive, legislative, judicial, and military power. He was responsible for maintaining the loyalty of the natives, securing good order, defending the province, promoting economic growth, dispatching labor levies to St. Augustine, providing justice, and resolving disputes. To meet the last two responsibilities, he was to make a circuit of the settlements under his jurisdiction every four months. The major guarantee for his proper fulfillment of these duties was the visitation of the province by the governor or by an inspector delegated by the governor. This visit took place once during the governor's term and consisted of an inquiry into the state of affairs in the province that provided an opportunity for the natives to voice any complaints they might have against the lieutenant, the soldiers, the friars, or their own leaders. When the complaints were serious and numerous, the governor might send a special inspector to hold an inquiry without waiting until the regular visitation. But as the lieutenant was appointed by the governor, more often than not such a move was merely a gesture to deter criticism. That the friars could go over the head of the governor and appeal directly to the authorities in Spain was an additional check (Florencia 1695; Leturiondo 1678; Rebolledo 1657a: passim).

Throughout the Habsburg period, churchmen in the New World were able to make their views known to people in Spain who had influence in the decision-making process. For most of the reign of Charles II (1665–1700), that entree to the "corridors of influence, if not of power," as John Lynch expressed it, was even greater (Lynch 1964(2):230). At the death of Philip IV, Charles, the heir to the throne, was a sickly four-year-old child, mentally disturbed and mentally subnormal. Because those conditions lasted for most of his life, even as an adult he never controlled the government in any real sense. Lynch noted that "Government was first controlled by his mother, the queen regent. . . . As she was weak of character and scrupulous of conscience, she inevitably took counsel of her confessor, not only on faith and morals, but also on matters of government" (Lynch 1964(2):237). This confessor became one of the last of a line of seventeenth-century *validos*, or favorites, who functioned as prime ministers. Although he was soon ousted because of his unacceptable origins (he was Austrian by birth and not a member of the aristocracy) and the aristocracy soon moved into the political vacuum created by Charles II's incapacity, the church remained one of the most privileged sectors of society. Its upper ranks were filled largely by members of the aristocracy (Lynch 1964(2): 229–230, 236–237).

The available documentation does not reveal whether the Spanish authorities ever intervened to remove any of the native leaders of Apalachee from their positions. One suspects that some native leaders were involved in the 1647 uprising. If so, it is likely that they were among those executed or sentenced to hard labor. Such circumstances would seem to be the only ones in which the royal officials could safely remove an Indian leader and not leave themselves open to complaints and eventual punishment in the wake of the *residencia* to which all Spanish officials were obliged to submit. Among the powers given to Leturiondo for his 1677–1678 visitation was "the full and ample jurisdiction in his Majesty's name to punish, install in office or remove caciques."

Equally difficult to assess is the impact of the Spanish intrusion on altering the natives' political system or on influencing ascension to the post of cacique in cases where the designated heir lost out to a usurper. At some point in the mission period, if not from its beginning, it appears to have become customary for a village council to secure an approbatory nod from the governor's deputy before a new cacique was installed. What happened if the governor's lieutenant withheld or threatened to withhold that nod of approval? In the case of the disputed chieftainship of Faltassa, the usurper, who held power for eight years before being removed by the visitor Leturiondo, had been installed with the approval of the lieutenant. During the 1694 visitation, Joaquín de Florencia dealt with a complaint from Hinachuba Adrián, the legitimate heir to the head chieftainship of Capoli, that he had not been given possession of that post. The visitation record does not explain why that had happened or how long the delay had been. But on receiving testimony that Adrián's claim was justified, Florencia ordered his installation as chief.

It is difficult to assess the political effect of the conferral of military titles such as captain and field master on selected native leaders. The interpreter Juan Mendoza held the rank of captain. He was referred to by one Spaniard as "one of the most important leaders." Matheo Chuba held the title of field master, as did Luis de Ybitachuco in 1651. Bernardo Hinachuba was both head cacique and captain at Cupaica. Don Andrés, the successor to the lackluster Chief Francisco Luis, was issued the title of "governor" (Florencia 1695; Leturiondo 1678; Rebolledo 1657a:93, 100, 1657b; Solana 1687a:17–39). One wonders if he sought it so that he would not be similarly overshadowed.

Another Spanish-introduced novelty that may have had some political impact was the art of writing. Several of the more influential and active leaders at the cacique and subcacique level were literate. All of the Ivitachucan chiefs whose names we know were literate, as were Juan Mendoza, Diego Salvador, and Matheo Chuba, although judging from his nervous scrawl, the latter was not very adept or practiced at writing.

For whatever reason, the pattern of native leadership seems to have become more complex at San Luis during the 1680s.[8] There were chacals at San

8. Of course, we may simply have more detailed knowledge of the leadership for this period, rather than an indication of change.

Luis distinct from the inija. Bip Bentura was referred to as principal inija and head chacal. The title "principal" seems to imply the existence of another inija. He may have been Matheo Chuba, who, at times, seemed to be doing work normally done by an inija.

Of course, the other inija or inijas may have been those of the satellite villages. One possible reason for the development of a more complex leadership structure may have been the stepped-up military activity from the middle 1670s into the 1690s, especially during the late 1680s. This activity necessitated the prolonged absence of many of the leaders who were responsible for the direction of the day-to-day activities of the village. The natives of San Luis, naturally, were called on to participate in many of these expeditions. Matheo Chuba and Bentura along with Juan de Mendoza and the chief of Cupaica, Bernardo Ynachuba, were the principal organizers and leaders of the 1677 expedition against the Chisca. San Luis's chief is not even mentioned in connection with that enterprise. Chuba and Bentura orchestrated the barrage of complaints against Antonio Matheos that effected his removal as the governor's deputy, and they were among the principal targets of his tyrannical acts (Fernandez de Florencia 1678; Leturiondo 1678; Solana 1687a:17–39).

A significant political consequence of the Spanish intrusion was a more regimented existence for the natives, whether they were leaders or workers. During the latter part of the mission era at least, Indians journeying to St. Augustine were required to carry passports showing that they were authorized to be away from their villages. Similarly, before returning to their villages, upon completing whatever work or business they had been sent to do, they needed a document or signature from the governor. The potential for abusing the system, should a governor want to keep a worker there beyond his time, is obvious. Theoretically at least, Indian leaders needed the permission of that official even when they wished to lodge a complaint against an official such as the lieutenant, Antonio Matheos. One wonders whether the very seeking of that permission was an attempt to intimidate the errant official into mending his ways. The lieutenant's permission was required as well for travel to the villages of non-Christian natives to the west and northwest, but that requirement was probably less of a restraint because the traveler did not have to pass any Spanish control points or worry about meeting Spaniards at his destination, unless the deputy governor happened to have soldiers there on a trading mission (Quiroga y Losada 1691a). This regimentation extended to other aspects of the natives' life once the mission regime had been well established. Permission of the authorities was required to move from village to village and from villages on the royal road to others that were not on that road.

Another annoying facet of this regimentation was the labor repartimiento's requirement that the ordinary Indian be available periodically for compulsory, compensated labor, either for government projects or on the farms of Spanish soldiers. As most of the government building projects and most of the soldiers were at St. Augustine, the laborer selected for this service was required to move temporarily to that center where, in most cases, he would live in some sort of temporary shelter. While performing such mandated labor the native was not able to bargain concerning the compensation he would receive but was paid the relatively low wage set by the authorities. Wages were often devalued further by the employer paying the Indians in goods rather than money—which allowed the employer to inflate the value of the goods or, even worse, pass off goods of little or no utility or of the poorest quality, which no one else wanted. Indians selected for the duty of carrying the bedding and other baggage for soldiers traveling on orders of the governor received no compensation at all unless the soldier voluntarily chose to give the porter something. The restriction on the natives' travel to St. Augustine is doubtless one of the factors that permitted the Spanish settlers to eliminate most of the native competition from the trade in hogs, chickens, butter, and bacon, etc., during the last years of the seventeenth century (Leturiondo [1700]:177–179, 183).

The only effective way the natives could escape this regimentation was to take the drastic step of leaving their homeland to live with some neighboring tribe, a psychologically wrenching experience, as well as a dangerous one. This regimentation and the exploitation associated with it as well as Spain's failure to provide adequately for the defense of the region were all elements contributing to the departure of so many of the Apalachee with Colonel James Moore in the wake of his 1704 attack on the province. For a catalog of native leaders whose names appear in the records and available biographical data, see appendix 11.

Chapter 5

The Apalachee Language

TO DATE, only one text of any length in the Apalachee language has surfaced to serve as an indicator of the linguistic ancestry of its speakers and as a guide to situating Apalachee within the broad family of Muskogean languages. That text is a letter to the Spanish king written by the chiefs of Apalachee in 1688 and was translated at that time into Spanish by Fray Marcelo de San Joseph. The text and the translation were published more than a century ago by Buckingham Smith, who also provided an English translation of the Spanish version of the letter. The Spanish version, fortunately, was a literal translation designed, as Fray Marcelo put it, to present it "just as it is and sounds' (San Joseph 1688). The only other current source of knowledge of the language is a few isolated words, many of them from Friar Paiva's ball game manuscript. Caution must be used in dealing with the Indian words used by the Spaniards in describing things in Apalachee, for some of those words are Arawak or Timucua rather than Apalachee.

The Stetson Collection has photostats of a Spanish copy of the letter, which differs considerably in spelling from the version reproduced by Buckingham Smith. The differences are quite numerous and follow a pattern that seems to rule out the possibility of their being attributed to random errors on the part of the transcriber.

There may be other documents in the Apalachee language buried in Spanish or Cuban archives. In *A Migration Legend of the Creek Indians,* Alfred Gatschet mentions the reputed existence of two such documents in a Cuban archive. Other documents originally written in the Apalachee language are the ball game manuscript, composed in the mid-1670s by two literate Apalachee who served as interpreters (Bushnell 1978b:10), and, almost contemporaneous with it, the 1677 report on the expedition against the Chisca, written by Captain Juan Fernández de Florencia, the governor's deputy in the province.

118

Florencia recorded the native leaders' report to him on their return, taking it down in their language.

Over the years there has been considerable diversity of opinion concerning where Apalachee belongs in relation to the other languages of the Muskogean family. Swanton, comparing the Apalachee and the Apalachicola who lived in the town of Apalachicola, describes the latter as Hitchiti-speaking, the former as speaking a dialect distinct from Hitchiti within the Southern Division of the general Muskogean family (Swanton 1922:11, 130). Milanich and Fairbanks, on the other hand, identified the language as Muskogean, commenting that "most researchers agree that their language was a dialect of Hitchiti, which today is the language of the Seminoles" (Milanich and Fairbanks 1980:228). Kathleen Deagan considered the Apalachee to be affiliated linguistically with the Hitchiti group of Muskogean languages (Deagan 1976). *The Handbook of American Indians* holds the Apalachee to be "linguistically more nearly related to the Choctaw than to the Creek" (Haas 1978:282). Gatschet concluded that "The Hitchiti, Mikasuki and Apalachi languages form a dialectic group distinct from Creek and the western dialects, and the people speaking them must once have had a common origin." He went on to suggest that the province of Apalachee probably once included "the upper part or the whole of the Chatahuchi river basin" (Gatschet 1969:74–76). Crawford observed that "Apalachee was perhaps closer to Alabama and Koasati than to the other Muskogean languages" (Crawford 1975:26). This view seems to be borne out by the statement of one of the Frenchmen who had contact with the Apalachee refugees in Mobile soon after they arrived there; he described their language as a mixture of Alibaman and Spanish (McWilliams 1953:135). Mooney held that Apalachee was closer to Choctaw than it was to Creek, while Toomey, in the same vein, compared a specimen of the Apalachee text with other Muskogean languages and noted that Apalachee has its roots in Choctaw, resembles Hitchiti in its structure, and differs phonetically "from Northern Choctaw very much as does Houma and Alibamu." He concluded that Apalachee became separated from Old Choctaw at least several centuries before the arrival of Columbus (Crawford 1975).

In her article "The Position of Apalachee in the Muskogean Family," Mary Haas presents what seems to be the most reasoned analysis of the relationship of Apalachee to its related languages within the Muskogean family. She divided the extant Muskogean languages into a Western Division, containing only Choctaw and Chickasaw, and an Eastern Division, embracing all the rest. Starting from Proto-Muskogean forms, she illustrated two of the major phonological considerations that are the basis for distinguishing a Western and an Eastern Division within the family of Muskogean languages. Then she showed with several Apalachee words that it follows the pattern of Hitchiti,

Creek, Seminole, and Alabama-Koasati, rather than the pattern of Choctaw. Having established that Apalachee belongs to the Eastern Division, she turned her attention to either finding its closest relatives within that Eastern Division or establishing that it represents a subdivision by itself. In the Eastern Division she noted three subdivisions, Alabama-Koasati, Hitchiti-Mikasuki, and Creek-Seminole. She then showed that Apalachee probably belongs with the first, or Alabama, subdivision, based particularly on the fact that the other two subdivisions always *suffix* personal pronominal elements used in the conjunction of active verbs, while Apalachee, along with Alabama-Koasati and Choctaw, *prefixes* such elements. The subject seems to merit more study; her arguments mention certain anomalies that show other elements linking the subdivision to Choctaw and linking it more closely to the other Eastern Division languages. Overall, however, the evidence seems to place it in the Alabama-Koasati subdivision. In a final elucidation she noted that in this Alabaman subdivision, Apalachee is one of three separate languages, whereas the other two subdivisions contain only slightly variant dialects of one language. She concluded that Apalachee may be closer to Alabama proper than to Koasati but that she did not have sufficient material on Alabama to confirm her suspicions (Haas 1978:282–293).

Mark F. Boyd's articles on the Diego Peña expeditions provide some insights on the relationship between the language of the Apalachee and that of some of the native peoples with whom they had the closest contact. Diego Peña's remarks establish clearly that Apalachee was related closely enough to Hitchiti as to be serviceably understandable to the Hitchiti-speakers among the Apalachicola. On his first expedition in 1716, Diego Peña's Apalachee interpreter, the Spanish ensign Don Diego de Florencia, addressed the Apalachicola for him (Boyd 1949:23–25, 1952:113–114, 117). During his second expedition, however, he employed two interpreters. One, a Spaniard translated his words into Apalachee, and the other, Adrián, the chief of Bacuqua, translated the Apalachee version into Uchisi (Boyd 1952:117). Uchisi is believed to be a Hitchiti tongue.

Considering the length of their contact with the Apalachee, the Spaniards made few comparisons of the Apalachee language with the tongues of the neighboring tribes. In 1673 two friars mentioned the need in St. Augustine for religious personnel who understood the languages of Apalachee, Timucua, and Guale so that the needs of the Indians there might be addressed. They remarked that the three languages were so different that few of the friars understand all of them (Somoza and Madrigal 1673). A letter from the early 1690s implies that Taman was sufficiently distinct from Apalachee to rule out the use of a friar versed in the latter to meet the needs of the Tama at Candelaria. Governor Quiroga complained about the transfer to Rome of Fray

Juan Angel, whom he characterized as skilled in the Tahaman (Taman) language. Because of the lack of priests who knew the tongue, Quiroga remarked that the mission remained without a friar for one and a half years, during which time many of the Tama fled to the woods (Quiroga y Losada 1690b).

There are some fragmentary references to the relationship between Apalachee and Timucuan. The languages were sufficiently distinct to require the first missionaries who contemplated working in Apalachee to learn the Apalachee language (Horruytiner 1633). However, the two languages seem to have shared a few words. In 1695 there was an investigation into the reported disappearance and possible murder of a putative Christian Chacato woman in the Timucua village of San Pedro de Potohiriba. For the questioning of the Yustagan and the Apalachee witnesses, separate interpreters were used for the two tongues (García 1695:172 ff.). On the other hand, during Rebolledo's visitation of 1657 and Leturiondo's inspection of 1677–1678 the same interpreter was used for both Timucua and Apalachee; this use seems to have been made possible by the linguistic skills of the royal interpreter, Diego Salvador, a literate Apalachee Indian.

During Leturiondo's visitation, Salvador served also as the interpreter at Candelaria, then inhabited by Tama and Yamassee. It is not clear whether this occurrence was an indication of his linguistic skill or of the fact that the languages of the Tama and Yamassee were close enough to Apalachee to make a separate interpreter unnecessary. It is possible that the leaders of those tribes had learned sufficient Apalachee to understand Diego Salvador's presentations of the visitor's questions and orders. In the 1694 visitation, another Apalachee interpreter, Hubabat Gaspar, also served in the Taman village. If the Tamans spoke Hitchiti, as Swanton suggested, it might explain the use of the same interpreter. Hubabat served as interpreter in the Chine village as well. Unfortunately, there is no mention of the name of the interpreter for the 1694 visitation of the Tocobaga (Florencia 1695; Leturiondo 1678; Rebolledo 1657a; Swanton 1922:83).

The Chacato language appears to have defied Diego Salvador's skills. During the inquiry into the 1675 Chacato revolt, he was part of a two-man interpreting team; he translated the Spanish official's words into Apalachee so that a Chacato versed in Apalachee, a man named Chacta Alonso, could then translate them into the Chacato tongue (Fernández de Florencia 1675a).[1] Similarly in 1694, for the questioning of the Chacato temporarily domiciled at Escambé, a separate interpreter was employed rather than Hubabat Gaspar (Florencia 1695:56–57). On the other hand, in the course of the 1677 Apala-

---

1. As this inquiry was a judicial process, it is possible that higher levels of communication skills were required by custom or law.

chee expedition against the Chisca, a number of Christian Chacato recruited as guides became discontented over the privations they were forced to endure and began to discuss plans among themselves for deserting the expedition. The Apalachee within earshot were able to understand them (Fernández de Florencia 1678). The Choctaw presumably spoken by the Chacato may have been related closely enough to Apalachee to be grasped by the Apalachee. It is, however, more likely that some of the Apalachee had had enough contact with the Chacato living among them to be conversant with their tongue. The fact that Pansacola was a common Apalachee surname as well as the name of an Apalachee satellite village suggests some affinity between the two people or their language.

The sparse evidence concerning the affiliation of the Chacato is difficult to evaluate. They appear to have been closely associated with the Pansacola, and a brief reference to them by Governor Juan Marques Cábrera seems to imply that they were closely related (Marques Cábrera 1686a). Some authorities identify the Chine as a branch of the Chacato. The Chacato seem to have been closely related politically to the Chisca as well, and, if one accepts the theory that the Chisca and the Yuchi or Uchee are the same people, then they are in close association with the mostly Hitchiti-speaking lower towns among the Apalachicola. Lanning, in particular, made this point, remarking that the Chacato, when first reported by the Spaniards around 1639, were described as living near the middle course of the Chipola River and west of the Apalachicola. He then pointed out that "Their history was tied up, however, with the Georgia tribes" (Lanning 1935:171).

There is, in addition, the evidence from the oft-repeated tale of the Chacato woman in the era of the destruction of the missions.[2] She first brought the news of the genocide planned for the Apalachee by the Apalachicola and their English mentors. About 1701 she had been carried off from Apalachee to the Apalachicola country by a Christian Sabacolan. While living in the village of Achito, she witnessed a meeting of all the leaders of the Apalachicola towns. In this meeting the Apalachicola planned the extermination of the Christian Apalachee in conjunction with the English move in 1702 to eliminate the Spanish presence at St. Augustine (Albuquerque 1703). Her ability to understand a detailed account of their campaign plans suggests that she had a good grasp of the language of the Apalachicola, perhaps because it was similar to her own or perhaps because she had become skilled in Apalachee during her stay among its people. It is possible that her knowledge of Apalachee enabled her to understand the Hitchiti-speaking Apalachicola. Of course, there is yet

2. The woman returned to Apalachee with her story in October 1702, just after the disastrous rout of the Spanish-led 800-man Apalachee force at the Flint River by an English-led Creek force.

another possibility—that her information came via the Sabacolan who had carried her off.

During Leturiondo's visitation of the Tocobaga village of Wacissa, the Tocobaga's language defied Diego Salvador's skills. He was part of the interpreting team on that occasion, but he was also joined by Manuel Ruíz, described as being of the Tocobaga's tongue. Presumably he also knew Timucua or Apalachee. In 1695 there was no mention of an interpreter being used for the Tocobaga.

In his comments on the languages of the various Apalachicola settlements, Diego Peña, after remarking that most of the southernmost towns spoke the same language (Hitchiti), noted that Sabacola had a distinct language. He then added that they also spoke Apalachee (Boyd 1949:25), giving no indication of the reason for their bilingualism. Contemporaneously, Governor Juan de Ayala y Escobar identified Chislacaliche (Cherokeeleechee) as chief of the province of the Uchise (Ayala y Escobar 1717b:36, 53). Swanton identified him as chief of Apalachicola (1922:131– 32; 1946:92).

Inasmuch as many of the Indians of the Southeast, as members of the general Muskogean family, were related linguistically, they shared a number of words whose form had not changed substantially from their Proto-Muskogean roots. The most familiar examples are some of the words for officials such as inija, which was shared by the Apalachee, the Chacato, and the Apalachicola. The word for "favored son of the chief," *usinulo,* was also shared by the same three groups, although, in both cases, with a slight variance in form among the Apalachicola. The word for "interpreter" used by the Spaniards was *ate-qui* for the Apalachee and Chacato, *yatiki* for the Creek, and *athequi* for the Timucua. The word for "principal chief," *holahta,* was shared by the Apalachee and the Timucua. *Chuco,* the Apalachee word for "great" or "principal," appears in a number of slightly variant forms in the languages of the neighboring tribes. *Is-te-puc-cau-chau thlucco,* Hawkins noted, was the Creek term for "Great Leader" and *Tustunnuggee thlucco* their term for "Great Warrior" (Hawkins 1982b:70, 72). It appears again as a variant in Bartram's title of "Mico Chlucco" for the Long Warrior, King of the Seminoles. In the organization of the reprisals against those most responsible for the 1597 revolt in Guale, one of the places in Georgia to which the mico of Asao appealed for aid was Ytochuco. Swanton (1922) identified it as a Gualean town. Although the word for "former village site," *chicasa,* was different than the one used by the Timucua, *ycapacha,* the number of words shared by the Apalachee and the Timucua raises some questions, particularly because most authorities consider the Timucua to be a non-Muskogean people. As soon as he crossed into Apalachee, Peña began to use the word *chicasa* rather than the word *ycapacha,* which he had used for the sites of former Timucua villages.

Ivitachuco is paralleled by Timucua's Ivitanayo. Mutual influences can also be inferred from the title of the ball game manuscript, which said the game was traditional in Apalachee and Yustaga, and in their sharing the custom of building round structures rather than the rectangular structures of most of their neighbors.

In mission times the Spaniards almost invariably spelled the name of the province Apalache. On a number of occasions when the name was being used by native speakers or by Europeans steeped in the Indian tongues, the name is rendered as Abalache. It is spelled in this way by Fontaneda, by the friar who translated the one extant text in Apalachee, and by the Apalachee chieftains who composed that text in their native tongue. In the native script it is written and broken as "Aba lah chi."

Over the years various individuals have advanced interpretations of the meaning of such tribal names as Apalachee, Caddo, and Calusa. Swanton gave the meaning of Apalachee as "people on the other side" (of a river, presumably, he adds), or "allies" (Swanton 1946:216). Bartram stated that the Creek's name for the king of England was Ant-apala-mico-chucco, meaning "the great king over or beyond the great water" (Bartram 1955:388), which seems to support Swanton's suggestion. J. Clarence Simpson, working on the assumption that the words from which Apalachee was formed might have had the same meaning in Apalachee as in Choctaw, advanced two words from the latter as possible keys to the significance of the name. The first is *Apelachi*, "help or helper," which by extension could include "ally." The other is Apelichi, "the place in which to rule, preside, or govern." Simpson considered the last to be the most plausible, based on the Fidalgo de Elvas's assertion that the chief of Anhayca Apalache was lord of all that country (Simpson 1956:24). One scholar has suggested that a slight variation on that meaning could be "people of the center," which is particularly interesting because of its possible association with the earlier Lake Jackson ceremonial center. However, it is perilous to attempt to divine the meaning and significance of native terms from languages that are no longer spoken and for which there are few surviving words. One of the more striking illustrations of the potential pitfalls of such ventures are the two absolutely contradictory suggestions concerning the meaning of the name of the Timucuan settlement of Ivitanayo. Boniface suggested that the name meant "White Lake," and Simpson stated that Gatschet believed Ivitanayo to be a Timucuan name meaning "Black Lake" (Simpson 1956:62).

The letter in Apalachee does not give us any indication as to whether their name for God the Creator paralleled the Apalachicola's "Master of Breath." Although the name of God appears a number of times, the Apalachee writer invariably used the Spanish *Dios* rather than whatever equivalent word they may have had in their own tongue. This usage contrasts with their usage of the word "king," which appears in both the Spanish form *rey* and the native *holahta chuba*. This use of the Spanish word Dios may indicate that they lacked a concept of the divinity close enough to the Judeo-Christian concept to be adequate, or simply that the friars frowned on any association of the Christian concept with the native one.

Chapter 6

The Apalachee Economy

WHEN THE FIRST Europeans arrived, the Apalachee were already a sedentary people, depending primarily on agriculture for their food supply but also relying on fish, game, and wild fruit and nuts to supplement what they grew. In contrast to the Spaniards' reports that the natives of coastal Florida and Georgia led a nomadic existence for several months each winter as they searched the woods for food, there is no mention of such a practice among the Apalachee. Possibly it was this sedentary trait that made Fontaneda see them as excellent mission material.

The Spaniards found Apalachee, in comparison to the surrounding regions, to be rather densely peopled. So great was the region's reputation for productivity among the Indians of peninsular Florida that they reported it to the Spaniards as an incentive for them to move to the north. On reaching Apalachee they found those reports to be true. The chroniclers of the de Soto expedition remarked on the extensive fields of corn, beans, squash, and other vegetables that they encountered along the roadside, and although it was still early in the fall they also found caches of dried venison. Their decision to winter there was based largely on the adequacy of the stored supplies of foodstuffs, which they were able to seize within a relatively short distance of the Apalachee's head village, appropriated for their winter quarters.

The natives' clothing was minimal, a deerskin loincloth for the men and a skirt woven of Spanish moss for the women. For the winter cold they had cloaks or capes of animal skins or furs. They made garments also from fibers extracted from the roots and bark of various trees and from the feathers of birds.

Neither the first explorers nor the Spaniards of the mission era provide much information about the native techniques for producing their abundance of foodstuffs. The best source of information is the observations of Bishop

126

Calderón. He noted that the natives cleared the fields of grass and weeds during January by setting fire to them. The original clearing of trees and underbrush probably was done in a similar fashion, reminiscent of a process used by the American aborigines as far away as southern Brazil. The method, the so-called *coivara*, "swidden" or "slash-and-burn" technique, is still practiced at times by the *caboclos* of Brazil's backlands. It involves cutting most of the larger trees, ringing the remainder, and cutting the underbrush. When the area has dried sufficiently, it is burned to leave the land clear for planting. Bishop Calderón reported that such preparation of the fields was combined with a form of hunting called hurimelas, in which much of the village's population would surround the area to be burned and slay the deer, wild ducks, and rabbits fleeing the fire. Inasmuch as the bishop was talking about the Christianized Indians of Florida, in general, that name may not be the Apalachee name for the practice. There is an apparent reference to this practice during Rebolledo's visitation, when it was called Junumelas; it also took place in January (Díaz Vara Calderón 1675:12–13; Rebolledo 1657a:92). The bishop mentioned that the planting was done in April, observing that the ground was prepared by the men and that the sowing of the seed was done by the women. The Europeans' wheat was planted by the natives in October and harvested in June. He noted that everyone in the community worked to plant the chiefs' fields. Friars in Apalachee described the planting and cultivating as involving a "first, second, and third *caba* (digging)" and the guarding of the fields as an integral part of farm work (Moral et al. 1657). There is no mention of the tools used by the Apalachee to prepare the soil, but they probably used a mattocklike instrument similar to the one the Timucua are described as employing. The Spaniards introduced an iron mattocklike hoe.

The Apalachee cultivated tobacco and gathered the leaves of the yaupon holly growing near the coast for the preparation of cacina, a tea that also had ceremonial uses. They had no alcoholic beverages and even during mission times did not adopt them; the bishop noted that their only drink other than cacina was water, remarking specifically that they did not touch wine or rum (Díaz Vara Calderón 1675:12–13; Laudonnière 1975:15; Paiva 1676:576).

Corn was consumed in a number of ways: as a lye-hominy porridge made with ashes, in little cakes made of cornmeal, in a thin gruel, onsla, or a thick gruel, *atole*, and, on journeys, as toasted or parched corn flour. Like the Apalachicola, the Apalachee probably had several varieties of corn, each used for a different purpose. Adair noted that the Apalachicola had three varieties: first "the smaller sort of Indian corn, which usually ripens in two months," which they planted as soon as the weather permitted; second, one that was "yellow and flinty, which they call hommony-corn"; third, "the largest, of a very white and soft grain termed bread-corn" (Adair 1930:435–437). Whether coincidentally or not, Alonso de Leturiondo noted that for the payment of the tithe in Florida, maize was divided into the three categories of "principal maize, second class [maize], and then that of the puny ears (*de redrojo*)," observing further that "of these three categories, they only pay on the principal." Although the ears of the second category were smaller, this kind of maize ordinarily was produced in far greater quantity than was the principal maize (Leturiondo [1700]:191). Late-eighteenth-century observers of the Apalachicola mention a number of boiled soft breads made by combining the green corn or flour extracted from the corn with chestnuts, beans, or sweet potatoes. Thin cakes mixed with bear oil were baked on thin broad stones or broad flat pieces of pottery made for that purpose. After extracting the oil from hickory nutmeats, the residue, or "milk," was combined with flour to make a nutbread (Adair 1930:437; Díaz Vara Calderón 1675:12; Fernández de Florencia 1678; Garcia 1902:192; Hawkins 1982b:26; Paiva 1676:576). The Apalachee probably had similar foods. The prominence of the *cazuela* bowl among the pottery remains suggests that stews were common in their diet. In the 1650s a wrathful friar from Patale smashed a number of pots of food being prepared for guests who had been invited from San Luis to a repast at Bacuqua before attending a concurrent fiesta at Patale. The bishop seems to suggest that normally only the well-to-do could afford game and fish as part of their diet (Díaz Vara Calderón 1675:12–13; Rebolledo 1657a:90).

Some indication of daily food consumption is given in two references to daily portions that the natives considered to be short rations. Fray Alonso Moral stated that it was the general practice of employers of the Indian workers sent to St. Augustine to give them "very short rations such as . . . only two pounds of corn a day." In 1693 Governor Torres y Ayala mentioned that the Apalachee who accompanied him to Pensacola Bay asked to be allowed to return to their homes soon after they arrived there, expressing dissatisfaction with the rations they received when the food supply began to run low. The governor said the ration was the same as that issued to the Spaniards up to then, "two pounds of ground corn and a pound of meat" (Moral 1676; Torres y Ayala 1693a:238).

Those who have viewed or examined skeletal remains of mission-era Apalachee have remarked on their apparent robustness. One interesting source of such information that is to be published derives from Widmer's study of remains from one of the Patale sites. Preliminary analysis of a limited number of skeletal remains suggests that the population represented in his study was composed of healthy individuals with an adequate diet (Widmer 1985). By contrast, Widmer's preliminary analysis of burial remains from Lake Jackson that belong to the late Fort Walton period indicates that even the high-status individuals among those ancestors of the mission Apalachee were not as well nourished as were ordinary individuals of the mission period (B. Calvin Jones, personal communication, June 1985). Speaking of the mission Indians in general, Bishop Calderón remarked, "They are fleshy and rarely is there a small one" (Díaz Vara Calderón 1675:12).

Similarly, Clark Spencer Larsen's detailed analysis of remains from St. Catherines Island found marked signs of dietary stress for the precontact agricultural period as compared to the pre-agricultural period. But there was pronounced stress as well among the mission-era Guale of the island and "a decline in quality of life and overall well-being," although paradoxically some data suggest that "there may have been a rebound, especially with regard to body-size and bone strength (cross-sectional geometric properties) and demographic parameters" (Larsen 1987:7–9).

In addition to corn, Alonso de Leturiondo mentioned a number of other sources of starch utilized by the natives:

Other types of roots and fruit also grow there, which are called *Ache, Zebaca,* and *Pinoco,* which the Indians use a great deal, even though they have the regular wheat of that land, which is maize; but they are so strong and poisonous that, if they do not process them very well, the people burst open, as two Indians did burst open four years ago because they did not properly prepare the small fruit of the *Pinoco.* But the root of the *Ache,* which is similar to the Yucca, well processed, yields a flour whiter than that from wheat; and, by pounding it in a hand mortar, throwing water on it, the pungency and poison is removed, and it is possible to make everything from the dough that can be made from wheat, without one being able to distinguish them either in the whiteness or in the flavor. And it is a very good bread and much more desirable than that which is made from maize, but if it is not processed well, the dough comes out very black, and, if the pungency is not removed, the mouth is set afire and they are in danger of bursting; and the removal of this root or tuber requires a lot of work because it grows in mudholes (*variales*) full of water, and the entire tuber has so many roots, like a horse's mane or like hair, that in order to pull it out of the ground some very strong levers are needed. . . . Likewise, the Indians make bread from the bitter acorn. (Leturiondo [1700]:201–202)

In 1646 a friar mentioned ache in a similar context, noting that when food was scarce at St. Augustine, the Spaniards braved hordes of mosquitoes to go out to the ponds in search of ache roots (Pérez 1646). Almost a century earlier both Fontaneda and Laudonniére reported a substantial trade in a certain root from which an excellent bread could be made. This root was grown in a fresh-water lake called Sarrope (Larson 1980:199; Lorant 1965:58). The ache may have been the *Uc-lau-wau-he-aha,* or bog potato, of the Creek described by Hawkins as growing in old beaver ponds in thick, boggy places. These appear to have been usually gathered rather than planted.

Despite Leturiondo's detailed description of ache and the processing it required, the plant's identity is difficult to establish. The name *ache* resembles *ă:hî,* the Mikasuki Seminole word for tuber or enlarged root (Sturtevant 1954:437). This suggests zamia, which was used for coontie, but ache's aquatic habitat rules it out. Many of the more obvious edible roots from aquatic habitats known to have been used by the Indians, such as Wapato or Arrowhead (*Sagittaria*), sweet flag (*Acorus calamus*) and groundnut (*Apios*), are ruled out by their lack of one or more of the characteristics Leturiondo attributed to ache such as toxicity, pungency, hairy roots, and difficulties of extraction. Wapato and groundnut were boiled or roasted like a potato rather than converted into flour (Fernald and Kinsey 1958:86–89, 121–122, 252–255; Medsger 1957:169–170, 173–175, 187–188; Widmer, personal communication, March 3, 1986). The more common smilax fail the test because they are inhabitants of dry or sandy soil and produce a red flour rather than a white one, although Hale Smith did produce a white flour from one variety (Fernald and Kinsey 1958:141–142; Medsger 1957:198; Smith 1951d:139). Tuckahoe or green arrow arum and golden club (*Orontium aquaticum*) seem to come the closest to meeting the requirements of aquatic habitat, pungency, processing, hairy roots, and use for flour (Fernald and Kinsey 1958:113–116, 119–121; Medsger 1957:196–197).

Leturiondo also describes the gathering and processing of cacina, remarking that the name of the drink comes from the small tree the leaves of which are used to make it. The leaves were roasted or parched in jars (*hollas*) over a fire. Then, according to Leturiondo, "They break it up and when it is well ground up they pour water on it and they let it boil, and then they filter it and drink it hot" (Leturiondo [1700]:202). Preparching the leaves is further suggested by another incident involving a surly friar. The friar, deciding that there was an undue delay in serving him his draught of cacina in the council house at San Luis, set about with a cudgel to smash both the jars in which it was brewed and the jugs in which the roasted cacina was distributed (Rebolledo 1657a). The Spaniards of Florida became as addicted to this drink as did their counterparts in Paraguay and on the pampas of the Rio de la Plata and of southern Brazil to the similar native tea known as *yerba mate.* For the ceremonial consumption of cacina associated with the ball game, an inland forest variety of the yaupon was used rather than the coastal shrub (Leturiondo [1700]:202; Paiva 1676:570). The popularity of the coastal variety is no doubt reflected in the name Cazina Point given to one of the headlands at the mouth of the St. Marks River (Milan Tapía 1693:283, 304). It is not clear whether the distinction made by the natives corresponds to the modern botanical distinction between *Ilex vomitoria Aiton*, or yaupon, and *Ilex cassine* L.,[1] or dahoon holly (Hu 1979:25–37). Spanish sources use the name cacina rather than the currently popular "Black Drink" employed by the Carolinians.

Another native beverage, used particularly for refreshment and for nourishment on journeys, was made by infusing in water a meal composed of ground nuts, maize, dried persimmons, and blueberries. Said to check both hunger and fatigue (Leturiondo [1700]:202), it is probably the refreshment referred to as *tolocano*.

In his recent work on Native American population, Henry Dobyns pointed to acorns as one of aboriginal Florida's major potential food sources (Dobyns 1983:69–70). Use of acorns by various Florida tribal groups and by the Spaniards themselves in times of need is well documented (García 1902:190–192; Larson 1980:186; Leturiondo [1700]:202; Pérez 1646). Identifying the acorns used specifically as "bitter acorns," Alonso de Leturiondo described the processing of those acorns for making bread. After the husks had been removed the acorns were ground in a hand mill and the resulting meal was buried underground in pits, a practice that removed the bitterness and other harmful elements. The purified meal was then formed into small loaves and placed on "something like wooden spits that were placed over the fire." When cooked, Leturiondo attested, the bread was sweet and delicious (Leturiondo [1700]: 202). Not all Spaniards found acorn bread so palatable. In 1595 a group of starving shipwrecked Spaniards found the Gualean variety so sharp tasting and bitter as to be inedible despite their hunger (García 1902:191–192). Although the Apalachee were renowned as the most intensive cultivators of maize in Florida during the Mississippi period (Larson 1980:214), they relied on acorns as well. In the early 1650s, an Apalachee chieftain objected to Governor Ruíz de Salazar y Vallecilla's cattle operation on the coastal lowlands below Asile and Ivitachuco because it threatened foodstuffs obtained from that area, such as acorns and palm berries (*uva de palms*) (Manuel, Chief of Asile [1654]; Medina 1651). In 1716, Diego Peña observed that the chicasas of the mission villages of Apalachee contained many fruit trees, listing acorns among the products of those orchards along with figs, peaches, pomegranates, quinces, persimmons, and chestnuts (Boyd 1949:18).

The Apalachee probably extracted cooking oil from those acorns. The Apalachicola are known to have used both the acorn and the hickory nut for that purpose, and Hawkins specified that he saw red oak acorns used for oil. After drying the acorns on reed mats and hulling them, they beat the acorns

1. Some authorities deny that there is any botanical distinction (Hudson 1979).

into a fine powder in a mortar and then mixed the powder with water. After letting this mixture stand overnight, they used a feather to skim off the oil that rose to the top. A bushel of acorns yielded about one pint of oil (Hawkins 1982b:31). It may be only coincidence, but the front area of the present San Luis archaeological site, where part of the village was located, had a considerable number of red oaks as well as hickories; most of the red oaks were lost in a hurricane in late 1985.

Oil from hickory nuts was produced similarly except that the nutmeat flour mixed with water was kneaded and the oil was removed as it rose to the top. Hawkins found this oil as pleasant to the palate as olive oil. It was expensive, however, compared to butter (Hawkins 1982:38). Others have mentioned cooking as part of the process for the extraction of the oil.

Lard and butter are the only cooking fats or oils mentioned in the Spanish records for Apalachee. It is likely that after the introduction of hogs and cattle, animal fats largely replaced the expensive labor-intensive oil from nuts, which probably became a luxury item used only on special occasions. Although lard and butter are mentioned among Apalachee's exports, the one reference that we have to the Apalachee's use of these commodities occurs in the financial record of a galley-building project on the Tacabona River. Two of the three foodstuffs purchased for consumption by the natives were lard and beans (Leturiondo [1700]:200; Matheos 1687a:50–60).[2]

Both Adair and Hawkins mentioned the use of bear oil or lard for cooking. Adair added that during its rendering it was mixed with plenty of sassafras and wild cinnamon to keep it sweet from one winter to another (Adair 1930:437, 446). In view of the prevalence of sassafras in the Apalachee's territory, their use of it for the same purpose seems probable.

With the introduction of the hog, acorns assumed greater indirect importance as a food source because they were a major element in the hog's diet. Acorns were also an important food for Apalachee's deer.

The fabled productiveness of the Apalachee region was one of the principal reasons for the launching of Spain's formal effort to Christianize the people in 1633. Apalachee's surplus, it was hoped, would remedy St. Augustine's chronic food shortages, especially on occasions when the supply ships bringing the annual subsidy were lost or delayed. On the Indians' side, the interest in being Christianized also had both a material and a spiritual basis. Before the mission era the Apalachee probably had already acquired a taste for European goods obtained by trade with neighboring Indians who had contact with the Spaniards or with Spanish shipwrecks. From 1608 on, doubt-

---

2. Corn was the third item purchased. *Manteca*, which I translated as lard, could be translated as butter also. There is no mention of meat.

less, some such goods were received as gifts by chiefs and other leaders who visited St. Augustine to pay their respects to the governor and to pledge their allegiance to the king. The Crown allocated a certain sum annually for such gifts to the natives, having learned from its experience with the formidable Chichimec of northern Mexico that winning the natives' submission with gifts was far less costly and more effective than subduing them by force.

It is not known how soon after the arrival of the Spaniards in Apalachee in 1633 the formal introduction of European crops, fruits, stock animals and fowl began. Based on discoveries elsewhere, however, it is probable that some of these introductions antedated the permanent European presence, particularly items such as hogs, chickens, and peaches that found ready acceptance among the natives. Mark Williams's exploration of the Joe Bell site, at the junction of the Apalachee and the Oconee rivers in a relatively remote section of north-central Georgia, revealed peach pits to be the second most common plant food remains from the second quarter of the seventeenth century (Williams 1984:425–427, 434, 456). He has indicated that peaches had spread so rapidly among the natives that when the English arrived at Jamestown in 1607, the Indians of that region had already acquired them via trade routes extending back to Spanish Florida (personal communication). In his treks through the Creek country Hawkins frequently noted the existence of peach trees in settlements.

It is known that the Apalachee's contact with the Spaniards led to a considerable expansion of the variety of fruits and vegetables produced in the region. Before the arrival of the Europeans the natives had gathered grapes, nuts, persimmons, plums, and blackberries, drying some of the last two for winter use. They gathered and toasted the leaves of the yaupon holly for their tea, and they grew tobacco. After contact with the Spaniards, in addition to wheat they grew barley, peas, chickpeas, sugarcane, new strains of tobacco, figs, strawberries, sweet nuts, chestnuts, pomegranates, peaches, persimmons, quinces, cultivated varieties of grapes, and other fruits. There is no mention of whether wine making was attempted in the region or whether citrus fruits were introduced (Boyd 1949:18; Castilla 1740; Leturiondo [1700: 200–201]; Paiva 1676).

A possible indication of the early introduction of items such as hogs and chickens is that, as early as the governorship of Damián de Vega Castro y Pardo (1638–1645), trade between Apalachee and Cuba had grown sufficiently to move the royal officials at St. Augustine to press for the stationing of customs officers at St. Marks. The officers were to collect duties on the goods shipped in and out of that port and to block the introduction of contraband goods. Unfortunately for our knowledge of that trade, those officers did not remain there long. Later the governors' lieutenants in Apalachee were directed to collect duties from the visiting ships, but there is little evidence that those injunctions were carried out (Bushnell 1981: 81–82; Rebolledo 1657a: 89, 120–121).

It is not known whether early trade involved the introduction of anything more than the usual cloth, tools, glass beads, bells, and flour, which were among the principal items that the natives desired and the Spanish authorities were willing to furnish. In 1675 Bishop Calderón mentioned knives, scissors, axes, hoes, hatchets, large bronze rattles, glass beads, cheap blankets, coarse cloth, clothing, and other trifles as the most common articles of trade (Díaz Vara Calderón 1675:13). The earliest mention of the introduction of European crops and animals other than the hogs and horses brought by Narváez and de Soto occurred in connection with Governor Salazar Vallecilla's experimental wheat farm, which flourished from 1645 until 1650. Six square leagues had been allegedly put under cultivation. For this operation the governor had imported two experienced slaves, eight horses and mules, 11 yokes of draft oxen, a millstone, and the necessary plows and harrows. Upon the death of the governor, the operation was purchased for the Crown by his successor, but upon his death shortly thereafter, at the request of the Franciscans, his successor dismantled the operation. The Franciscans blamed the governor's operation and the presence of Spanish soldiers similarly engaged in wheat planting for the uprising in Apalachee in 1647. Although this wheat planting is spoken of at times as having taken place in Apalachee, it occurred on the province's eastern border rather than in Apalachee. However, the planters relied heavily on native labor for their operations, and some of that labor came from Apalachee. Although the black slaves, farm tools, and most of the stock were auctioned off when the ranch was dismantled, it is not clear who obtained control of these items. Wheat produced by the governor was saved for seed, and corn grown on the ranch was consumed by the workers. The seed for starting the plantings was imported from New Spain, but some of the wheat from the last planting was harvested by the friars and the Apalachee chiefs. From that time on, wheat appears to have been grown in Apalachee on a small scale to meet local needs and for occasional export to Havana (Bushnell 1981:82; Rebolledo 1657c, 1657d:230–234, 310–316, 355–360; Royal Officials 1647a).

The Crown approved the importation of 200 horses from Cuba in the late 1640s to relieve the Indians of cargo-bearing, but there is no evidence that these horses reached Florida. At some time before 1657, the friar Miguel Sánchez, who had been stationed at Ocuia, had a horse and some other stock at the mission, the first reference to the presence of European farm animals in Apalachee since de Soto's stay there. Until sometime after the mid-1650s, not many horses or mules had reached Apalachee. Their absence and the consequent abuse of the Indians as cargo bearers were the reasons most often given for the 1647 uprising, and it was a frequent complaint of the natives during Rebolledo's 1657 visitation of the province (Franciscan Friars 1664; Prado 1654; Rebolledo 1657a:97–98). Indeed, horses seem to have been scarce at that time even in the original centers of Spanish settlement.

A horse was worth 100 pesos in Florida in 1651; by 1682 their value had fallen to 25 pesos (Bushnell 1978a:429; Rebolledo 1657d:230–234). Horses for the wheat farm were imported from Cuba, and eight were sold for 100 pesos each when the farm was dismantled. It is not clear how quickly effective steps were taken to meet Florida's need for transport animals, but during the last quarter of the century, horses were sufficiently numerous in Apalachee to have become an article of trade between the Apalachee Indian leaders and the Apalachicola. According to the Spanish authorities, the Apalachicola sought horses primarily for sale to the English traders as packhorses.

A number of the complaints presented to the visitor Florencia in 1694–1695 involved damage to the native villagers' crops from horses and other stock from the ranches of a number of Spanish settlers. Other complaints (involving the selling and trading of horses, making and loaning of pack saddles, and breaking in of horses) reflect the ownership of horses and cattle by either individual Indian leaders or by their villages; the village of Ocuia and an individual Indian from the village of Patale are mentioned as the owners of cattle. This visitation record also mentions Indian chiefs as the owners of cattle ranches (Florencia 1695; Zúñiga 1702). Just after the turn of the century the ownership of horses had become sufficiently widespread among the chiefs to enable the governor to ask the chiefs to furnish 25 horses and be confident that they would be forthcoming (Boyd, Smith, and Griffin 1951:45).

Nevertheless, as late as 1693, the newly arrived governor, Laureano de Torres y Ayala, making preparations at San Luis for his overland expedition to Pensacola Bay, remarked how difficult it was to transport corn and other cargo, which he had brought from Mexico, from the port of St. Marks to San Luis because of the shortage of horses. On that expedition he used 76 horses, most of them collected in Apalachee. In contrast with imported corn, meat for the expedition was purchased in Apalachee: more than two tons of salt beef, three steers for consumption by the infantry on their march from St. Marks to San Luis, and three calves for consumption while the troops were in San Luis. By this time cheese was being manufactured in the area as well, and 22 cheeses were purchased for the trip. The supplier of these victuals was the Spanish rancher Marcos Delgado. In his journal Governor Torres y Ayala mentioned that as soon as the corn was brought up to San Luis "it was sent out to several villages in this locality where milling is done so that it could be ready as soon as possible for the expedition" (Torres y Ayala 1693a:229; Delgado 1693:254). It is not clear whether San Luis lacked the facilities for such milling (other than the Indians' mortar and pestle) or that it could not handle the quantity involved in the short space of time available. At midcentury Governor Ruíz de Salazar had imported millstones from the Canary Islands for his wheat farm. Torres y Ayala's account indicates that the raising of cattle and the use of beef and dairy products was well established in Apalachee by the early 1690s.

The development of the cattle industry and the production of a number of other foodstuffs for sale to St. Augustine and elsewhere seem to have occurred even earlier in Apalachee. So vigorously had the Indians' production of hogs flourished that by 1670 an Apalachee hog could be purchased in St. Augustine for about four pesos, the cost of a poncho or middling woolen blanket. As early as 1651 four pesos a head was paid for the 45 hogs from Governor Ruíz de Salazar's farm. Writing about 1700, Alonso de Leturiondo remarked that in the period before 1670, stimulated by the demand for their produce, the Indians had increased greatly their stock-raising, hunting, and planting and gathering to supply bacon, butter, nuts and other goods for St. Augustine. In the 1670s, however, a number of Spanish families acquired land in Apalachee, encouraged by a governor who reputedly saw it as a way of reducing the number of "useless mouths" in his poverty-stricken city.

Hoping to corner the market on such produce, especially that for hogs, the new settlers began to raise hogs and also to buy them from the Indians. If they could achieve a monopoly, they could raise the price for hogs in St. Augustine. When necessary, they used violence or other pressure to secure their objective, taking advantage of the Indians' natural reticence in dealing with Spaniards and their fear of the consequences if they crossed someone who was well connected. As a result of the settlers' maneuvers, pigs, which sold for four pesos in 1670, rose steadily in price to 10, 16, 20, and even 25 pesos by 1700. Many of the natives were pressured out of hog production and trading; those who persisted began to charge as much as the Spaniards did for hogs shipped to St. Augustine, but those who were forced to sell the hogs in Apalachee at the monopolists' low prices became increasingly disenchanted, forming, Leturiondo noted, "a poor opinion of the Spaniards." The result was a steadily decreasing supply at a continually rising price (Leturiondo [1700]:177–178).

During his visitation in the mid-1690s, Joaquín de Florencia attempted to deal with supply problems by issuing regulations for trade with St. Augustine. First, he stipulated that the lieutenants were not to consent to changes in the prices for the products of the land or for other goods unless the item was one for which such changes were customary. He also stipulated that the chiefs were to be charged with this concern. Second, he ordered that the natives be encouraged to raise every type of stock, large and small, as long as they did not do it in an area where the stock might harm the cornfields. His regulations did not resolve the problems of short supply and high prices. Writing about six years later, Leturiondo suggested that the only remedy would be the removal of all Spaniards from Apalachee, other than the soldiers and the friars, and a prohibition on the soldiers' trading hogs. The raising and selling of hogs would be left to the Indians under a system of controlled prices whereby the price would be returned to and held at the four-peso level (Florencia 1695; Leturiondo [1700:178–179]; Rebolledo 1657d:230). The prohibition of trading by the soldiers was probably well founded. In the inquiry in 1686 into the conduct of the infamous Antonio Matheos, one of the soldiers, Lorenzo Guerrero, testified that he had been sent to the Apalachee villages by Matheos to buy pigs and hens for the lieutenant's table and for making lard, which Matheos sold. It was implied that the governor was involved in these dealings, because he had sent the trade goods used to purchase the pigs and hens (Guerrero 1687:104–105).

While the price of hogs spiraled upward, the price of cattle was falling in Florida. In 1651 the large plow-oxen from Governor Ruíz de Salazar's farm sold for 40 pesos each. In 1693, in Apalachee, Marcos Delgado had received eight pesos each for his three steers and three pesos each for the calves; the hide alone brought four reales, or one-half peso (Delgado 1693:254; Rebolledo 1657d:230). According to Bushnell, by 1702 a Florida steer was worth only two pesos (Bushnell 1978a:429). The reason for the difference in prices is not entirely clear.

Apalachee did not supply beef to St. Augustine. The La Chua ranch in Timucuan territory was the city's main source of meat. Hides and tallow appear to have been the principal export products of Apalachee's cattle industry, and Havana provided the market for them. According to Boniface, the statistics on these exports indicate that at least as early as 1675, before the arrival of the civilian ranchers in Apalachee, there were already sufficient cattle in the province to permit 150 hides and 150 arrobas (3,800 pounds) of tallow to be sent to Havana. Because such hides were used commonly to wrap bundles of tobacco and other commodities in this era, the production was probably considerably larger. Early in 1681 another ship was loaded with 700 hides at St. Marks. In 1685, a ship carried away 100 of Apalachee's chickens, 110 hams, 35 jars of lard, 300 deerskins, 44 bushels of corn, and 60 arrobas of pine tar (Boniface 1971:150, 200–201). There is no indication in the available records that cattle on the hoof were sold to the neighboring Apalachicola, although horses were. In 1698–1699 the nine Spanish cattle ranches in Apalachee paid a tax of 61 calves to the Crown. The Indian cattle owners were exempt from this tax (Boniface 1971:147).

In describing Spanish ranching practices in Florida, Boniface noted that in spring and summer, cattle evidently were pastured on the seasonally flooded grasslands referred to as savannas (Boniface 1971:147). Once the corn had been harvested, the cattle could be turned loose to forage in those fields. In the 1690s the natives of several villages complained that foraging was taking place while the corn was still growing. In the winter it was the custom to allow the cattle to retreat into the woods to forage on the browse and on the weeds and grasses that would escape frosts longer than in the open fields. Ordered to move his cattle, hogs, and horses from the vicinity of Bacuqua and Patale within a three-month grace period, the rancher Marcos Delgado used this practice as an excuse to request that the grace period be extended to six months, affirming that "at the moment [early December] all the cattle are in the woods, incapable of being conveyed to different lands and because only in the spring can this move be made on account of the abundance of pasture." He specified the month of May as the suitable time for this move (Florencia 1695:79). Springtime apparently was the time for rounding up and branding these open-range cattle. The calves were not branded until they were one year old (Boniface 1971:150).

Under the law such ranches had to be at least three leagues distant from any native village. For the new site for his ranch Delgado asked for a grant of 1.5 leagues of land near a region known as Nicasoco or Usobile, where he was already pasturing a herd of wild horses.[3] This site, he affirmed, was more than four leagues distant from all the villages (Florencia 1695:79). Delgado obeyed the order to move his cattle, having asked the governor on December 16, 1695, for lands to which to move his stock-raising operations. During the residencia for Governor Torres y Ayala, a number of witnesses testified that Delgado had indeed moved his ranch. Two witnesses specified that the move had been made to lands belonging to the chicasa of Patale, which was four leagues from San Luis and approximately 1.5 leagues from the site of his former ranch. That it was sufficiently remote from the native villages seems to be indicated by the fact that he is not mentioned in either of Patricio Hinachuba's letters as an owner whose cattle were still wreaking havoc on the villagers' crops (Hinachuba 1699:26–27; Hinachuba and Andrés 1699:24–26; Zúñiga y Zerda 1700a:84, 89, 96).

In the course of the residencia the accountant Juan de Pueyo certified that in 1690 Delgado had supplied 20 young steers valued at 200 pesos for the

3. In the deed for Governor Ruíz de Salazar's wheat farm, some woods bearing the name Nicasoco were mentioned as the farm's northern boundary. If this was the same Nicasoco as the one mentioned by Delgado, his request was denied because the site of his new cattle ranch was only four leagues from San Luis on a former site of Patale.

garrison then stationed at the fort in Apalachicola as payment for the four leagues of land for his first cattle ranch. Presumably, he was granted a similar expanse on his move to the former site of the village of Patale. Pueyo also recorded that Delgado had paid an additional 50 pesos for another league of land in Patale, which was, undoubtedly, the separate ranch five leagues from San Luis to which he moved his herd of swine.

The visitor granted Delgado's request that he be allowed to keep his house where it was at that time, which was listed on the 1693 bill of sale as Bacuqua (Florencia 1695:79; Zúñiga y Zerda 1700a:31–32). The implication of his request is that his house was somewhere on his existing ranch; it was probably outside of the village but within the jurisdiction of Bacuqua. Before learning of the site to which Delgado had moved his ranch, I had speculated that the site of the village of Bacuqua, abandoned by its inhabitants in 1657, probably would have been an attractive one for a ranch headquarters a generation later and that Delgado's first ranch might have been located there. It would have a source of water nearby for both humans and animals. Heavy cutting of firewood in the vicinity of Bacuqua had deforested the immediate area, so the abandoned fields would probably have been slow to return to forest since there were few standing trees nearby to reseed them. Because the site of the first ranch was only one-half league distant from the new one, the first residence could be said, without straining logic, to be at Bacuqua. Both Delgado's ranch and another one recorded as having been relocated at this time were moved to the abandoned sites of former villages.[4] This relocation seems to support my surmise that such locales would be ideal for ranching.

Throughout the greater part of the mission period, the most important economic product and export of the Apalachee region seems to have been the labor exacted of the natives under various pretenses by the friars, the soldiers, the Spanish settlers, and, most important, the Spanish authorities in the name of the crown. During the first 15 years of the mission era, the Apalachee firmly resisted pressure from the authorities to accept the labor repartimiento and thereby assume the obligation to provide laborers for government building projects in St. Augustine and for working the lands of the soldiers there. During these early years both the friars and the governors managed to persuade the native leaders who had become Christians to provide some Indians to serve as cargo bearers. These Indians carried the soldiers' bedding and supplies and brought in the goods needed to sustain the friars and to equip new

4. Diego Ximénez was the other Spanish rancher recorded as having moved his operation in compliance with the visitor's orders. Ximénez chose the chicasa of Escabí that was three leagues from San Luis and five leagues distant from the site of his earlier ranch. Ximénez was recorded as having made his request for the new lands at Escabí only on December 24, 1699, four years after he was ordered to move.

churches and convents. During the first few years, when there were only two friars and five or six soldiers at most, this service probably was not a major imposition. The demand for porters undoubtedly became more onerous as the clerical population expanded in the early 1640s, as Governor Salazar Valle-cilla's expedition into the Apalachicola country established commercial relations between the Spaniards and those tribes, and as his large wheat farm was being established. Under some pretext considerable numbers of Apalachee were induced or forced to work on the establishment of the governor's ambitious enterprise.

This labor certainly was one of the factors responsible for the uprising of 1647. That revolt, in turn, gave the Spanish authorities the opportunity to break the Apalachee's resistance to the labor repartimiento. As punishment for the revolt and the killing of the governor's deputy and family and three of the friars, 12 Indians were executed and others who were deeply involved in the uprising were sentenced to terms at forced labor. As reparation the chiefs agreed to furnish a yearly contingent of paid laborers to assist the Spaniards at St. Augustine under the repartimiento labor system.

The Spaniards viewed ordinary natives as a labor pool for them to exploit in exchange for the protection afforded the natives by Spanish arms and for the alleged benefits of Christianity and European culture. When the Apalachee chieftains agreed to supply the labor forces, they had considered it only a temporary expedient in reparation for the revolt and for the destruction associated with it. But the Spaniards continued these demands yearly, until the destruction of the missions in 1704. As the native populations of Guale and Timucua dwindled, the labor burden was borne to an increasing degree by the Apalachee. Their participation in the labor repartimiento contributed to the decline of Apalachee's population because it exposed the workers to new diseases in St. Augustine at a time when they were weakened by the rigors of carrying heavy cargo on their backs for 200 miles and because they were separated from their wives for prolonged periods of time. In 1676 Fray Alonso Moral, a 33-year veteran of the Florida missions, provided the following graphic portrait of the evils associated with this labor system:

> All the natives of those provinces suffer great servitude, injuries, and vexations from the fact that the governors, lieutenants, and soldiers oblige them to carry loads on their shoulders to the Province of Apalachee and to other areas and also to bring loads from those regions to the fort of St. Augustine. And it usually happens that to enhance their own interests they pretend that this work is in Your Majesty's service, without paying them what is just for such intolerable work. And if now and again they give them something for that reason, it is a hoe or an axe or a

cheap blanket or some other thing of such slight value to pay for their work, which involves carrying a cargo on their shoulders from the fort to the Province of Apalachee, which is eighty leagues distant, and the same to return. . . . And in addition to this, in order to employ them further, they detained them in St. Augustine for as long as they wish . . . with very short rations, such as giving them only two pounds of corn a day and giving them for pay, at the most, one real for each day of work, which sum is usually given them in the form of old rubbish of little or no value or utility to them. Add to this the further vexation or injury of being snatched by force from their homes and villages, not only for tasks at the fort but also for work for private citizens, and this in the rigor of winter (when they come naked) or in the middle of summer, which is when they are most occupied in the labor of their crops on which solely depends not only their sustenance and that of their wives and children but also the victuals necessary for the relief of the garrison. . . . Each year from Apalachee alone more than three hundred are brought to the fort at the time of the planting of the corn, carrying their food and the merchandise of the soldiers on their shoulders for more than eighty leagues with the result that some on arrival die and those who survive do not return to their homes because the governor and the other officials detain them in the fort so they may serve them and this without paying them a wage. . . . This is the reason according to the commonly held opinion that they are being annihilated at such a rate. (Moral 1676)

Complaints against such abuse of the Indians in Apalachee were made by the friars as early as the 1640s. In the early 1650s the treasurer confirmed the validity of the friars' charges. During the Rebolledo visitation of 1657 the Indians themselves spoke up against this exploitation. The chief of Cupaica, for example, while pledging that his vassals were ready to do their part in the king's service and to assist the friars, said that his tribesmen were willing to go for the planting at St. Augustine but that they objected to being required to carry cargo while going to fulfill that duty. "For which reason," he observed, "even though thirty or forty Indians from each jurisdiction might wish to go of their own will, half of them forsake it, fearing the loads there have always been, since these provinces gave their obedience to His Majesty" (Rebolledo 1657a:87). Some of the friars appear to have been among the worst offenders in this exploitation. The same chief of Cupaica, Baltasar, went on to remark that even though the friar who served them in 1657 was "very attentive in excusing them from the continuous freight-carrying, the predecessors have troubled them greatly in this particular, fetching them fifty at a time for cargo, both to the city of St. Augustine and for loading frigates at the port for this province. And [they have acted] in the same fashion in sending them to the provinces of the pagans of Apalachocoli and Chacatos to barter for deerskins and other things, on which trips some have died by the wayside without confession, because of the excessive work involved in it" (Rebolledo 1657a:87).

Some of these friars apparently tried to monopolize the trade with the Indians as well, forbidding the Indians to barter with the soldiers or the merchants from St. Augustine. When ships arrived at St. Marks the friars purchased all the trade goods that the ships brought, then sold them to the Indians at twice the price the Indians were accustomed to pay when they bought directly from the shipboard merchants. As an added injury, the friars required the Indians to carry the trade goods up from the port and to carry the proceeds from the trade back to the port without being paid for their work; if the shipboard merchants had handled the trade, they would have paid the Indians for such work.

Although three of the six provisions in the regulatory code issued by Governor Rebolledo dealt with these abuses, they do not seem to have had much effect except in diminishing abuses by the friars. These regulations provided that

> no Indian be obliged to go burdened to the fort of St. Augustine, as has been the custom until now, unless there first precedes an order for it from the governor . . . except for the bedding and provisions of any soldier who is dispatched by his excellency, and the case in which some Indian voluntarily desires to carry a load, which he may do, on his being paid for his just work, and in no other way . . . likewise, that no person may prevent or impede the said Indians from being able to trade freely with any Spaniards whatsoever, and let them be paid for what they carry to the sea; and let no person leave to trade with the neighboring pagans without first having permission from the said señor governor or from his lieutenant who resides in those provinces. (Rebolledo 1657a:89)

These regulations still imposed some burden on the Indians and left considerable discretion to the governor's lieutenant in Apalachee. Shortly after the visitation, friars in Apalachee noted that the natives were annoyed at having to feed the soldiers without being paid and also at the lieutenant's order that each mission plant from 50 to 100 pounds of maize for the soldiers' sustenance and in some places two jugs of wheat as well (Moral 1657). The regulations issued in the wake of the 1694 visitation imposed even greater burdens on the Indians and explicitly stated the natives' obligations under the labor repartimiento. Once the needs of the fort at St. Augustine had been met from the pool of laborers made available under the repartimiento, all the Spaniards living in Florida as well as the members of the garrisons who had family to support were to be given Indians from the remaining pool of available laborers to work their fields, on condition that the Indians be paid punctually for their work. On the matter of cargo bearing, the new regulations stipulated "that no person whatsoever, of any whatsoever state, quality or condition he may be, is to have the Indian carry for him, unless he pays him for his work; and to the soldiers who come and go on the service of His Majesty, there is to be given only one so that he may carry his bed and supplies; let them [the soldiers] give them what they may have without oppressing them or annoying them for it; and to those who may come on their own private business, to deal and contract that which they freely wish to give them" (Florencia 1695:87).

Among all these forms of compulsory labor, that of cargo bearing was the one to which both the natives and the friars objected most frequently and strenuously. In addition to the rigors involved, it appears to have been an especially demeaning type of labor for the natives, although it was well established before the arrival of the Spaniards. Boniface noted that, among the Timucua, those engaged in such labor apparently formed a despised class, portrayed by the French at Fort Caroline in the 1560s as *berdaches,* "transvestites," who adopted the dress and social role of women in the Indian tribes (Boniface 1971:180–181). This class was found among other tribes as well, and it is likely that the Apalachee were aware of its association with cargo bearing even if they did not have such a class (Hudson 1976:269)

The introduction of Spanish settlers in Apalachee in the 1670s led to many evils beyond those already discussed.[5] Stock from the Spanish ranches destroyed the crops of some of the native villages or required the maintenance of a constant guard to fend off the animals. Although the visitor in 1695 ordered a number of the ranches moved to points more distant from those villages, his orders were ignored with impunity by some relatives and friends of the authorities. It became customary for many settlers to compel Indian men and women to work for them, often without pay. Juana Caterina de Florencia, the wife of deputy-governor Jacinto Roque Pérez, was one of the worst offenders in this regard, requiring the village of San Luis to furnish six women for the grinding of meal every day without payment, another Indian to bring in a daily pitcher of milk from the country, and other services. She even slapped the face of one hapless chief who failed to bring her the expected fish one Friday. One

5. There is a possibility (but no evidence to date) that the Spanish settlement in Apalachee began before the 1670s. Governor Rebolledo's plans for the expansion of the garrison and for the building of a fort there in the 1650s included the establishment of a civilian Spanish community as a bulwark against what was perceived as a growing threat from an expansive and revolutionary Cromwellian England.

of the worst cases reported involved the entrepreneur Marcos Delgado, who carried off three women by force from the village of Candelaria to work on his ranch. To the village leaders' request for their release, he replied that he had the previous visitor's permission to keep them there. The Taman leader's petition to the visitor that he order the Spanish settlers to refrain from carrying off women by force to serve against their will suggests that it was not an uncommon occurrence. This same leader complained that another of the women of his village, Chuguta Francisca, had been dismissed by the adjutant Diego Ximénez without being paid, after having served him for a time and worked as well in the preparing of the meals at his ranch (Florencia 1695; Hinachuba 1699:26–27; Hinachuba and Andrés 1699:24–26).

Within the village economy itself, additional labor demands were made on the ordinary Indians who did the work. They were expected to sow separate fields of corn and wheat for the support of the priest and the children who lived at the convent and to finance the purchase of ornaments and vestments for the church. They worked still other fields for the support of the widowed, the poor, the incapacitated, and the soldiers while they were on expeditions. They also had to plant and care for fields for the chief and the other leading men as well as the parish interpreter and some of the leading ball players during the time that the game was permitted. The villagers also assumed the obligation of supplying their priest with meat, fish, and firewood. In 1677 Domingo de Leturiondo, as visitor, added still another burden to many of the villages by calling for the establishment of a school to be supported by the planting of yet another field by the community labor pool (Florencia 1695; Leturiondo 1678; Matheos 1687b:50–53; Solana 1687a:17–39).

The records reveal little about the status of the chiefs at the various levels as collectors or payers of tribute and as administrators of the communal food supply. The evidence that some of the principal chiefs were able to amass considerable quantities of foodstuffs seems to suggest that they levied tribute from the chiefs of the satellite villages under their jurisdiction as well as from the people of their own village. For one or more of Deputy-Governor Antonio Matheos's expeditions into the Apalachicola country in search of the English traders, some of the Apalachee chiefs provided the provisions for a sizable force of Spaniards and natives. Their compensation was to be a share in the expected booty. On other occasions chiefs in Apalachee sold quantities of grain on credit to officials at St. Augustine (Florencia 1695; Guerrero 1687: 104–105; Matheos 1687b:52).

The best source on the economic position of the principal chiefs and on the possible tributary relations between them and the most prestigious provincial chiefs are the accounts of one of the many conflicts between Matheos and the native leaders at San Luis, Matheo Chuba and Vi Ventura. At some point during Matheos's administration, when the community granary at San Luis was empty, the lieutenant attempted to persuade the native leaders to support his proposal to borrow grain from another village on the understanding that the loan would be repaid from the following year's harvest from the community field at San Luis. The two native leaders were asked apparently to act personally as cosigners, in effect, for the repayment of the loan. When Matheos broached the idea, the native leaders appear to have assented. But on learning that Matheos had struck a deal with the chief of Cupaica to borrow 150 arrobas of corn (almost two tons), Matheo Chuba and Vi Ventura reversed themselves. Alarmed, perhaps, at the size of the loan, they expressed misgivings about the wisdom of such a step, as they put it, "because they did not know whether they would gather the wherewithal to pay for it from the said community field" (Chuba 1687:31; Matheos 1687b:52).

If we presume that the corn proffered by Cupaica's chief was from his personal stock rather than from Cupaica's communal supply, it would indicate, first, that he was in control of a considerable quantity, especially since he expressed a disposition to lend even more if it were needed. The incident might also possibly be construed as an indication that San Luis's chief did not collect any tribute from the other principal chiefs in virtue of his position as head chief, at least during mission times. If Cupaica's chief owed any annual tribute payment to San Luis, that in itself would seem to have been at least a partial guarantee of the loan's repayment. On the positive side, there is no evidence that the chiefs of either San Luis or Ivitachuco received tribute because of their position of preeminence among the chiefs.

That the chiefs had considerable though not exclusive control over the distribution of the contents of the community storehouse is reflected in a 1695 regulation issued by the visitor Florencia. It provided that the community grain supply be held under a double lock. The chief was the custodian of one of the keys. The other was to be in the hands of a native elder chosen by the lieutenant. The regulation spelled out clearly the uses to which these provisions could legitimately be put: for poor widows and orphans, for feeding the Spanish soldiers while they were on His Majesty's service, for the purchase of ornaments for the church and tools for the service of the council houses, for feeding those who tilled the community field, and for seed for planting.

The account of another conflict between Matheos and Matheo Chuba and Vi Ventura suggests that in the mind of Matheos there was some commingling of the communally owned provisions and the personal possessions of those leaders that would justify their being requisitioned for the commonweal in emergencies. During the same or some other shortage of corn in the communal storehouse, Matheos ordered Vi Ventura, as inija, to find some to restock that granary. When he reported that there was none to be had, Matheos ordered the confiscation of the small supply Ventura had in his own granary and dispatched soldiers to collect it. On seeing the small amount Ventura had for his family, the soldiers, more compassionate than their commander, left it untouched, informing Matheos that they had found none. Matheos badgered Matheo Chuba similarly, insisting that he sell a cloak of some value that he owned in order to buy corn to restock the communal granary (Bentura 1687: 37–38; Chuba 1687:31; Florencia 1695; Matheos 1687b:52 ff.). It is not possible to ascertain whether there was any foundation in law or custom for Matheos's demands on the goods of the leaders or whether, more likely, it was just another example of the arbitrary behavior that led to his removal from office.

The one available detailed accounting of the requisitioning of labor in Apalachee suggests that the burden was distributed rather equitably. The larger villages of San Luis, Escambé, Ocuia, and Ayubale each supplied three carpenters, Ivitachuco and the midsized villages of Patale and Tomole each provided two, and the smallest settlements, Bacuqua, Capoli, and Oconi, provided only one each. Aspalaga was not represented, and neither were the villages of non-Apalachee (Matheos 1687a:77). More such paysheets must be found before any firm conclusions can be drawn on this topic. It is likely, however, that such demands for labor were heavier at San Luis than elsewhere in the waning years of the mission era because so many of the Spanish ranchers were based at San Luis and because it was the seat of government and of the garrison, Accordingly, it is probable that the inhabitants of San Luis bore the brunt of providing the labor to cut lumber for the fort in 1688 or 1689, which was then allowed to rot while the carpenters were diverted to build a short-lived fort on the Chattahoochee. Inasmuch as Governor Torres y Ayala launched his expedition for the exploration of Pensacola Bay from San Luis, the village probably supplied many of the natives who accompanied that expedition. When the same governor resurrected the project to build a fort at San Luis, the Indians were called upon anew to cut lumber and to build the blockhouse. Because they were near at hand, San Luis's inhabitants probably had to furnish a larger than average contingent. Upon completing the blockhouse, they were pressured into using the lumber left over to build several houses for the deputy-governor's brother-in-law and other Spanish settlers. These continual demands for labor, uncompensated as well as compensated, and the requisition of some of the natives' houses and fields were responsible for the withdrawal of the natives from that village in the late 1690s to a site in the woods a league distant from their former homes (Boyd, Smith, and Griffin 1951:21–30; Torres y Ayala 1693a:229–237).

Throughout the Spanish New World the repartimiento labor draft gradually gave way to a free labor system that was transitional to the emergence of the debt-peonage system of labor procurement. By the time of the destruction of the missions, that process had begun among the Apalachee. In time and with the steady decline of the population of Timucua and Guale, the Apalachee who wanted to escape the more onerous burdens imposed by the repartimiento labor pool, to secure better wages, and to perform work such as ranching that was more to their liking began to contract voluntarily to labor on a ranch or farm or in the service of an individual. Such employment, for a more or less lengthy period of time, often was at some distance from their home villages. During the 1694 visitation one of the most frequently voiced complaints in almost all of the Apalachee villages was the plea of abandoned wives that measures be taken to compel or secure the return of long-absent husbands who were working in Timucua, Guale, or St. Augustine. Twenty-nine Indians were identified by name as having left families behind to work outside of the province (Florencia 1695). The single men so absent, who may have been similarly numerous, were not mentioned, on the whole. Another device used to escape the labor draft was to move within the province to a village outside of the jurisdiction of one's home village, especially to a satellite village, which was not on the royal road. Such moves were prohibited in the 1694 visitation. Others simply moved into the woods away from the settlements, and some fled to British territory (Florencia 1695; Hinachuba 1699:26–27; Hinachuba and Andrés 1699:24–26; Leturiondo [1700]:198). The consequences—a reduction of the productive population within the province—produced a reduction in the size of the labor pool available for the repartimiento and, thus, a heavier burden for those remaining who were called on more frequently. Although the visitor Florencia forbade married men to leave their families to work outside the province, it is not clear how effectively the regulation was enforced.

A number of additional factors that had some impact on the economy of the Apalachee region merit investigation: (1) payment to the soldiers of the garrison in Apalachee and to the friars from the *situado*, the irregularly furnished subsidy from royal funds in Mexico, which paid most of the salaries and other expenses involved in maintaining the Spanish presence in Florida; (2) payments in goods from the special fund for providing gifts for the Indian leaders; (3) trade of the Spanish authorities, the friars, and the Indians with the non-Christian Indians in the territories bordering on Apalachee; (4) trade to and from Apalachee with Havana and St. Augustine; (5) the productive impact and the extent of the activity of the Spanish settlers and the soldiers in Apalachee; and (6) the degree to which tithes were collected by the friars from their Indian charges and how the funds were used. Unfortunately, little work has been done on the economy of the Apalachee region, and few documents dealing with these topics have been made easily available. What follows is the fragmentary information that is available currently.

Tools, glass beads, small bells, flour, occasionally firearms, and, above all, cloth seem to have constituted the bulk of the goods brought into Apalachee by the Spaniards as trade goods or as gifts to the Indians. On the whole the Spanish authorities sought to restrict the distribution of firearms to the Indians of their territories, but by the mid-1670s a considerable number of firearms seem to have reached Apalachee by way of the trade with Cuba. In the 1677 expedition against the Chisca, the villages of San Luis and Cupaica each provided 15 harquebusiers for a force of about 190 Indian warriors (Fernández de Florencia 1678). About a decade later Governor Marquez Cabrera commented that the Indians were acquiring firearms from the ships docking at St. Augustine, observing that he would not try to take away the guns already acquired but that he would see to it that this trade was ended (Marquez Cabrera 1686). About 1700, Alonso de Leturiondo remarked, concerning the Apalachee, "Their arms are the bow and arrow, which they handle with great skill, and, today, they use firearms as do the Spaniards, and, in Apalachee, they maintain their arms as well as do the best trained officers" (Leturiondo [1700]:199).

A remark in 1680 by the governor that cloth was what passed for currency in Apalachee seems to have been well founded (Hita Salazar 1680b). The leaders of the expedition against the Chisca were rewarded with gifts of cloth. The clothing among the booty found in the English traders' warehouse near Caveta during Antonio Matheos's second 1685 foray into the Apalachicola country was distributed to the native leaders present. A number of the unpaid debts and disputes resolved by Joaquín de Florencia in 1694 involved the trading of cloth or garments. An early eighteenth-century memorandum accounting for 500 yards of *jergueta* (a coarse woolen cloth) sent to San Luis's deputy-governor gives the value of various items in terms of yards of cloth (Boyd, Smith, and Griffin 1951:46–48; Florencia 1695; Guerrero 1687:104–105; Hita Salazar 1678b; Vega 1687:107–108).

Deerskins also seem to have served as currency. The penalty to be paid by chiefs for the violation of one of the regulations issued by the visitor Florencia in 1695 was a fine of 12 deerskins (Florencia 1695). The trade in deerskins was probably never large in Spanish Florida because Spain never provided the kind of market that existed among the English and French.

There is evidence that some Spanish currency was in circulation in Apalachee. Some of the financial disputes brought before Florencia in 1694–1695 seem to have been resolved by payment in pesos. Marcos Delgado, who provided some of the victuals for Governor Torres y Ayala's overland expedition to Pensacola Bay, was paid 170.5 pesos in pieces of eight. Those who supplied the horses and pack saddles were paid in a similar fashion, as were the natives who made the trek to Pensacola Bay as warriors, scouts, or workers to open the trail and tend to the horses. For this enterprise the governor brought more than 3,000 pesos with him from Mexico. Of course not all of it was spent on the expedition, but the surplus was to remain in Florida and be discounted from the subsidy. The Indian carpenters who worked on the building of a galliot on the River Tacabona during the 1680s and those who supplied corn and made or supplied the hardware were paid apparently in pesos (Delgado 1693: 254; Florencia 1695; Matheos 1687a:77; Torres y Ayala 1693a, 1693c:229, 257, 259).

Rum, a trade item generally much in demand in the eighteenth century, is rarely mentioned before the destruction of the missions. Bushnell suggests that upon the opening of the Suwannee River just after the mid-seventeenth century for trade with Menéndez Marquez's La Chua ranch, some of the ships from Havana brought rum that was distributed in Apalachee (Bushnell 1978a: 424). But such cases, if they occurred, must have been rare; complaints against this item do not appear in any of the visitation records or letters by the friars. Speaking about Florida's mission Indians in general, Bishop Calderón stated positively, "Their only drink is water, and they do not touch wine or rum." He also mentioned cacina as one of their beverages (Díaz Vara Calderón 1675:12).

Apalachee's trade with St. Augustine followed three separate channels (fig. 6.1). The first and oldest was the overland route via the Royal Road, which was based on existing Indian trade paths. The second and most important for heavy and bulky goods was the sea route around the tip of the peninsula, a voyage of about 700 miles, which took two weeks when conditions were favorable. The third was part maritime, part fluvial, and part terrestrial. Native canoes ferried supplies from the Wakulla River, St. Marks, or the Wacissa along the Gulf coast to the mouth of the San Martín River (Suwannee), ascending this stream to some point in the vicinity of its confluence with the Santa Fé; then the cargo continued on to St. Augustine via the royal road on pack animals or on human backs. There are no statistics available to show which route was most commonly used. Although Boniface characterized the maritime route as St. Augustine's major supply channel from Apalachee, he also states that the Suwannee route was preferred because of the difficulties and dangers of the sea route (Boniface 1971:167–169, 172–177).

St. Augustine's first commercial contact with Apalachee probably followed the prehistoric Indian trail. Boniface noted that in Florida these native paths were probably of greater importance than in other parts of North America because Florida's underlying limestone had left the region with a dearth of fluvial

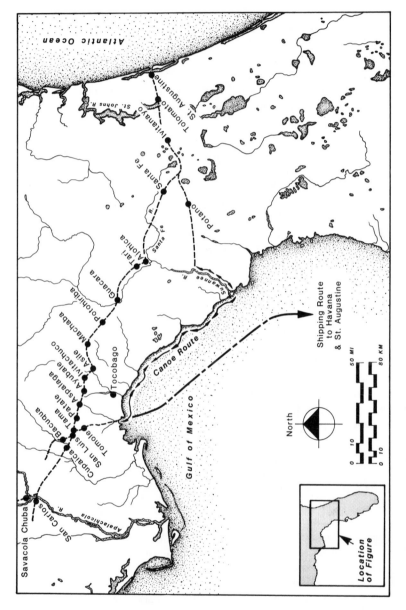

Fig. 6.1. Missions and trails of North Florida.

channels for canoe transportation. The Spaniards improved these trails sufficiently to allow the rapid passage of military patrols, dispatch riders, pack
animals, and eventually even oxcarts (Boniface 1971:174–176). Bushnell observed that in the 1680s, Enrique Primo de Rivera obtained a contract for
hauling provisions between St. Augustine and western Timucua and Apalachee. With the professed objective of relieving the natives of the onerous task
of transporting the clothing, the vestments, and the royal stipend sent for the
friars, he offered to carry these things to their destination for the sum spent by
the Crown each year for the corn given to the Indians who did that work. He
said that, if necessary, he would accept payment in clothing, at cost, from the
royal stock on hand in St. Augustine, estimating that corn was worth four reales per arroba. He was also responsible for making the road passable and
succeeded in doing so for the stretch extending eastward from San Luis as far
as the vicinity of present-day Gainesville. Because Rivera failed to make the
part between San Francisco de Potano and St. Augustine equally passable,
Governor Quiroga y Losada appears to have suspended the contract, and as
far as the available records indicate no further work was done to improve the
road or to reinstitute this service (Bushnell 1981:105; Quiroga y Losada
1688a:221–223). The western portion of the road remained passable. When
the Spaniards and the remaining Apalachee abandoned the province in the
summer of 1704, the church ornaments that were salvaged and other baggage
from San Luis and from Ivitachuco were carried by oxcart as far as San
Francisco de Potano. There the baggage from San Luis, which was to continue on to St. Augustine, was transferred to mules and packhorses (Bushnell
1979:12–13; Solana 1704b).

There is no clear statement of the route followed by the royal road in its
passage through Apalachee, either graphically or in the form of an itinerary.
The earliest useful maps showing the native trails date from the eighteenth
century. Presumably they preserved the Spanish trails in part at least. Late in
the mission period Ocuia was mentioned as not being on the royal road. The
following reconstruction of the road is based on the route that appears most
frequently in the mission lists and our knowledge of sites identified with most
of those missions. Some attention has been paid as well to the topography
surrounding those sites and to the location of the eighteenth-century trails. On
these bases we can presume the trail to have run from Cupaica south-southeast
to San Luis and then to Tama, Patale, Capoli, Aspalaga, Oconi, Ayubale, and
Ivitachuco, the eastern terminus within the province. Based on the itineraries
and on eighteenth-century trail maps, however, there seems to have been a
northerly trace that was part of the trail into west Florida and that ran eastward from Cupaica to Bacuqua and then Patale. Eighteenth-century maps
show this route as the main trail and the one through San Luis as a spur. Bacu-

qua was possibly a crossroads for separate trails that passed to the north and the south of Lake Jackson. The northern trail led to a crossing on the Flint River and thence to the Apalachicola's country. The southern trail linked Bacuqua to Cupaica. From there it led to the crossing of the upper Apalachicola at the site of the Christian Sabacola's village that was later occupied by Christian Chacato. From there the trail headed toward the 1674 site of several Chacato villages in the vicinity of Marianna and thence westward to the territory occupied jointly by Chisca, Chacato, and Pansacola. Eighteenth-century maps show another major trail that proceeds southward from Apalachee near the Gulf coast and parallels that coast. Mission era sources make no mention of such a trail, but it may be the route that Naváez followed in his trek toward Apalachee.

Soon after the establishment of the first missions in Apalachee, Governor Horruytiner began sending pilots overland to the Apalachee coast to take soundings from native canoes in a search for a suitable landing spot and a channel that would make it accessible to oceangoing vessels. His successor informed the king that on April 8, 1639, the first ship sailed from St. Augustine and came in sight of the Apalachee coast in under 13 days (Horruytiner 1637; Vega Castro y Pardo 1639b). How many ships followed it during the 65 years until the destruction of the missions is unknown. In the early 1650s, while Pedro Benedit Horruytiner served as interim governor, four or five shiploads of foodstuffs were brought from Apalachee to St. Augustine to meet needs arising from delays in the arrival of the situado. There are indications that from the beginning the greater accessibility of the Havana market made it more attractive to those who were exporting Apalachee's surplus produce. In the 1650s Governor Rebolledo found it necessary or profitable to forbid the export of produce to Cuba until St. Augustine's needs had been met (Rebolledo 1657c, 1657d). Rebolledo's critics portrayed his restrictions on trade as monopolistic in intent (Council of the Indies 1657a, 1657b:131–132). Boniface noted that the ships using the sea route to St. Augustine had to contend "with the variable currents, reefs, and shoals along the Gulf coast of Florida, not to mention the ever-present dangers from storms and pirates." He observed also that St. Augustine suffered a chronic shortage of ships, frequently having to rely on the launch that was used to lighter goods across the harbor bar for the longer voyage to St. Marks and Havana. It may only be coincidence, but on two out of three occasions when pirate ships stopped at St. Marks, they encountered Spanish vessels there (Boniface 1971:173; Leturiondo 1678:584; Olds 1962).[6]

6. Records show that the enemy ships arrived in the mid-1650s, in June 1677, and in March 1682. The last two intruders captured trading ships there.

The few records available highlight the difficulties of shipping in this area. In December 1646, Captain Juan Francisco de Florencia successfully brought the frigate *San Martín* from Apalachee to St. Augustine with supplies for the garrison. A generation later the frigate of Ignacio de Losa, requisitioned by the governor while it was in Apalachee so that it might bring a load of badly needed corn to St. Augustine, was forced by a storm to beach on the Calusa coast. At that time lack of rain had eliminated St. Augustine's corn harvest and the royal frigate was late. When that frigate arrived a month later, it was dispatched to Apalachee to take on a load of corn (Guerra y Vega 1668a, 1668b; Leturiondo [1670]). The available records do not indicate whether its voyage was more successful than that of de Losa's ship. The only guide to the nature of Apalachee's trade with St. Augustine is a document reproduced by Mark F. Boyd indicating that in 1703 Apalachee sent 1,238 measures of corn and 150 of beans to St. Augustine by way of two sloops.[7] The same document indicates that other individuals brought two hogs, 32 chickens, eight deerskins, and eight arrobas of tallow, without indicating the mode of conveyance or the route followed (Boyd, Smith, and Griffin 1951:46–47).

Boniface mentioned the Suwannee River as the preferred water route for sending produce from Apalachee to St. Augustine, but he did not indicate the volume of this trade. From the late 1670s at least, the Tocobaga handled the shipment of goods on the Suwannee River portion of this maritime-fluvial-terrestial route (Boniface 1971:174, 199, 218). The Leturiondo visitation record reveals that the Tocobaga who settled in Apalachee at Wacissa played a role in this trade. When Leturiondo persuaded some Yustaga to move eastward to found the new village of Santa Rosa de Ivitanayo on the royal road between San Francisco de Potano and the river crossing at Salamototo, he contracted with those Tocobaga to transport the migrants' corn and other goods by that fluvial route as far as a place called Pulihica. The chief of Santa Fé pledged to move those goods the remaining distance by horseback. The few available records indicate that for coastal navigation westward from St. Marks the Spanish authorities relied on the Chine. When the Chine's presence in Apalachee was first mentioned, they were living in association with Pacara and Amacano at the mission of Asunción del Puerto, said to be on the path to the sea, four leagues from Tomoli (Díaz Vara Calderón 1675:8–9; Hita Salazar 1675b; Leturiondo 1678:596, 598–599). The name of the mission and its stated distance from Tomoli suggest that it was on or near the coast, possibly near St. Marks or in the vicinity of Wakulla Springs. Later references to the

7. Boyd interprets measure to mean *fanega*, which he defines as a bushel or slightly more. Boniface, citing Boyd as his source, inflates the 1,238 measures of corn into 1,800 bushels, the 150 measures of beans to 230 bushels, and the 8 arrobas of tallow into 2,000 pounds.

Chine mission give different names to their village and definitely place them inland from the coast closer to San Luis; they are still located south of that mission on the road to the sea, indicating that they may have played a role in the maritime activity originating on Apalachee's coast or at least served as the province's fishermen.

Not enough information is available on the Apalachee economy to permit confident judgments about the purchasing power and the standard of living of either the average Apalachee native of the working class or the members of the leadership element. Similarly there is little data on the cost of necessities or of the iron tools, firearms, powder, cloth, beads, and bells introduced by the Europeans. The most we can have currently is a fragmentary glimpse of the natives' earning power and the prices of a number of common items at a specific time.

The daily wage of those compelled to labor under the repartimiento regime was one real per day plus a ration of food. As the wage was often paid in goods chosen at the discretion of the employer, many workers probably did not receive the full equivalent of the reales due to them. Frequently the goods were items of little utility or poor quality, which the worker would find difficult to barter or sell if he wished to dispose of them (Leturiondo [1700]:187–189; Moral 1676). On the occasions when workers were compensated fairly in cash or in its just equivalent in goods that were in demand, most of what the worker earned probably could be used to purchase desired European commodities or livestock, inasmuch as workers received a minimal food ration.

The length of the usual repartimiento labor stint in Florida is not known. Such projects as the building of the various forts at St. Augustine and the planting, tilling, and harvesting of crops for soldiers at the fort with families to support were the most common uses of the repartimiento labor. In Mexico, each adult male had to be available for about 45 days per year, usually a week at a time at various intervals. At any one time, only a small proportion of the men from a village were supposed to be called upon, and ideally heads of families were to have time free to cultivate their own fields (Meyer and Sherman 1979:170). For labor at St. Augustine some of these regulations were impractical and were probably ignored. Fray Moral's criticisms of the abuses of the system and the 1682 synod's third article suggest that the workers were often kept in St. Augustine beyond the legal time period at the whim of the authorities (Moral 1676; Leon n.d.).

For the building of the first fort at St. Marks around 1680, however, these rules appear to have been followed. The governor reported that the work force was being rotated every eight days (Hita Salazar 1680b). Those engaged as carpenters in the mid-1680s for the building of the galliot on the Rio Tacabona worked a minimum of 10 days and a maximum of 31 days. Twenty-three days was the most common stint. Of the 21 carpenters, 10 put in that number of days on the project. Because this work took place during the planting season, it and the cutting of the lumber created hardships for the natives. These hardships were one of the items in the litany of complaints lodged against Antonio Matheos.

Whoever converted 200 pounds of iron into nails and a set of chains on the galliot project received 11 pesos for the work. The iron cost 14 pesos, exceeding the cost of the labor for transforming it into the finished products. The two women who prepared food and the two young men who ground corn appear to have been paid less than the others. The four of them conjointly received 57 reales, about 14 each if the division were made equally. Although the number of days they worked is not specified, presumably they were there for the same three-and-a-half to four weeks as most of the workers. The rations that were purchased consisted only of corn, beans, and butter. Twenty pesos were spent on corn and three on the butter and beans. In terms of wages paid and foodstuffs purchased, this one project put 110 pesos or 882 reales into the local economy (Matheos 1687a:77).

Presumably those working voluntarily on a contract basis away from their communities received a somewhat higher compensation than the one real per day earned by the carpenters. During the 1694 visitation Ocolasi Lorenzo, who had worked for an unspecified time planting for a Spaniard, complained that his employer still owed him nine pesos for his work. A native from Cupaica placed a claim of 15 pesos for a pack saddle he had made for the royal works. Another native mentioned 6 pesos as the fee owed him for breaking in a young mare (Florencia 1695).

The following is a selection of the price or equivalent value of a number of items in Apalachee during the last two decades of the mission era.

4 bundles of tobacco for 2 pesos
8 bundles of tobacco for a shovel
a mare for 30 pesos
a bronze image of Our Lady for 8 reales or 1 peso
a painted wooden tray for a hatchet
a fowling piece for 2 harquebuses
a lined coat or cloak for a blanket, a pound of powder and 16 strings
    of thick beads (Florencia 1695)

1 real, or 1 day of compulsory labor, bought 5 pounds of salt beef
3 pesos or 3 1/2 weeks work for a calf big enough to eat

8 pesos for a steer (1693)

2 reales for a cheese

4 reales for a cowhide (Delgado 1693:254)

25 pesos for a stallion and about half that price for a draft ox (Bushnell 1981:28)

16 to 20 pesos for a hog versus 4 pesos prior to the early 1670s
(Leturiondo [1700]: 177–178)

20 yards of jergueta for 80 measures of corn

15 yards of jergueta for 15 measures of wheat

2 deerskin for 1 yard of jergueta

4 chickens for 1 yard of jergueta

36 measures of corn for 9 yards of jergueta

25 pounds of tallow for 1 yard of jergueta

2 hogs for 8 yards of jergueta (Boyd, Smith, and Griffin 1951:
46–47).

The last of those figures, one hog for 4 yards of jergueta, establishes the price
of jergueta as one peso per yard based on the old price of 4 pesos per hog.
That price is corroborated by Alonso de Leturiondo who gave the going price
of jergueta in Florida as one silver peso, commenting that it cost the merchant
only 2 reales per yard in Mexico and another real to place it in Florida. A
conga mestiza, or middling fine woolen blanket, sold for 4 pesos in Florida,
an ordinary blanket for 2 pesos, and a fine quality blanket for 8 pesos. He
gave the price of maize during times of shortage at 3 pesos per arroba or about
one real per pound. In the mid-1650s, Governor Rebolledo allegedly bought
maize and beans in Apalachee for 2 reales per arroba but sold them to the
Crown for the soldiers in St. Augustine for 8 reales (San Antonio 1657b). He
listed the price per yard of various cloths: Rouen linen at 12.5 silver reales;
ordinary *Bretaña* (a fine linen) at 8 to 10 reales; coarse Tlascala flannel (*bayeta*)
at 20 reales; Castilian flannel at 4 or 5 pesos; Granadan taffeta at 14 to 20
reales; and Tlascalan *palmilla* (a blue woolen cloth) at 3 pesos. A pound of
rice sold for 2 reales, an ounce of vanilla for 6 to 8 reales, a 4–5-pint flask of
aguardiente for 5 pesos, and a pair of shoes for 12 or 14 reales. Whether these
prices were typical is not clear; Leturiondo referred to them as tremendously
inflated as a result of shortages, often artificially created (Leturiondo [1700]:
188–189). Some indication of the change in prices and of the cost of various
manufactured articles is provided by a list from the early 1650s that gives the

sums paid for various items and persons that were sold when Governor Ruíz de Salazar's wheat farm was dismantled:

22 large plow-oxen sold for 40 pesos apiece
8 stallions and mares at 100 pesos each
45 head of swine at 4 pesos each
a large wooden serving table for 4 pesos
a used whetstone at 8 pesos
6 wooden benches for 6 pesos
a lamp for 1 peso
a machete *urbarrena* and a short thick lance at 4 pesos
3 wooden beds for 6 pesos
13 pieces (?) of used iron for 117 pesos
4 used spades for 8 pesos
7 used axes for 21 pesos
3 chisels for 2 pesos
2 hammers for 5 pesos
4 barrels for 4 pesos
3 cazuelas with feet for 9 pesos (cazuelas de manos)
2 saws and 1 handsaw for 5 pesos
2 used tablecloths for 5 pesos
a pewter plate for 2 pesos
2 machetes for 4 pesos
2 chocolate-stones for 5 pesos [a cylindrical stone for grinding the chocolate]
8 used iron spurs or goads for 24 pesos
2 iron chains for 8 pesos
an Angolan Black named Ambrozio, 30 years of age, for 500 pesos
a mulatto named Francisco Galindo, who at present is the superintendent of the said hacienda, for 600 pesos

These examples demonstrate that a member of the chieftain class who engaged in the raising of horses, cattle, and hogs could accumulate a significant amount of wealth from such an enterprise. Because they were free from the tax imposed on Spanish ranchers, we do not know the size of their herds.

One source of potential wealth that was not available generally to the Apalachee was the enslavement of their fellow Indians, which the Creek used effectively in their trade with the English. Long before the Spanish missionization of Apalachee, enslavement of the natives had been outlawed by the Crown. In frontier and primitive areas it was tolerated, however, and on several occasions was authorized by Florida's governors, in part to discourage the practice of scalping and the wanton slaughter of women and children who were taken prisoner. There is no evidence that any such prisoners were brought back as slaves from the 1677 expedition against the Chisca, but in the 1695 raid into Apalachicola country in retaliation for the Apalachicola's attack on San Carlos de los Chacatos, about 50 natives were captured in one of the villages that was taken by surprise. Those who had captured them were permitted to keep them as slaves (Torres y Ayala 1695:224–227). The few statistics available on exports from Apalachee also do not reflect any massive slaughter of deer or of fur-bearing animals for their skins such as occurred among the natives who traded with the English settlers. Even in postmission times, when the authorities dealing with the Creek had established a store at St. Marks in the hopes of inducing the natives to commit themselves to a Spanish allegiance, the governor complained that not only were they unable to match the English prices but that the skins did not have the same marketability either in Cuba or in Spain as they had in the North (Montiano 1746).

Among the Indians of the Southeast in general, the major portion of the hard work of the farm and household seems to have fallen to the women. While the men prepared the soil for planting, they seem to have spent much of the rest of their time in the hunt, at war, or in the discussion of village affairs in the council house or square ground. Of Florida's Indians, Bishop Calderón remarked in 1675, "They are fleshy, and rarely is there a small one, but they are weak and phlegmatic as regards work" (Díaz Vara Calderón 1675:12; Hawkins 1982a:21, 55–57, 478, 1982b:71; Hudson 1976:264–265, 312–313). Among the eighteenth-century Creek this attitude seems to have intensified, if anything, as a result of the gifts with which the competing European nations plied them and of the emphasis on hunting and warfare to secure skins and pelts and scalps to trade to the English settlers for the European goods on which they had become dependent. Hawkins found them strongly resistant to the government's plans in the late 1790s for settling them down as farmers and stockmen.

By contrast the Apalachee, like the Cherokee, seem to have adjusted rather easily to working on a steady basis at farming, ranching, and carpentering, much as would European farmers and workers. The French at Mobile were particularly impressed by the industriousness and the dependability of the Apalachee who migrated there in 1704. The Carolinians also commented favorably on the willingness to work and the discipline of those who accompanied Colonel Moore to the English territory earlier that same year ([Bienville] [1726]:536; Hawkins 1982a:67; Higginbotham 1977:192; Johnson et al. 1708; Raphael 1725(2):482). The fleeting glimpses we have of the province's economic life in the 1680s and 1690s, and to some extent even earlier, project a similar picture (Florencia 1695; Leturiondo [1700]; Solana 1687a:17–39). Naturally the mission regime and Spanish demands had much to do with this. But a question arises: Was there already some development under way before the mission period as a result of the Apalachee's heavy dependence on agriculture and sedentary existence that predisposed them to accept these changes without much resistance?

Chapter 7

The Population of Apalachee

THERE IS considerable diversity of opinion on the size of Florida's aboriginal populations during the two centuries after their first contacts with Europeans and Africans and the pathogens that the intruders introduced. Until the 1970s the conservative approach of authorities on the Indians of the Southeast suggested a small population for Florida and for Apalachee in particular during the protohistoric and the early historic or mission periods.[1] Henry Dobyns noted that Daniel G. Brinton set the tone in the mid-nineteenth century by maintaining that the aboriginal population for all of Florida never was much higher than 10,000 persons and by dismissing as hyperbole the chroniclers' accounts that de Soto's forces faced that many warriors in one encounter (Dobyns 1983:50). Brinton's point of view seems to have put a straitjacket especially on those writing from ethnographical and anthropological perspectives. Until the 1970s it seems to have kept most of them from even considering the possible validity of data that did not conform to this premise. For the early part of this century Dobyns observed that this bias included historians as well, remarking that "Early twentieth-century anthropologists and historians showed a pronounced (and unjustified) tendency to regard Colonial population reports as uniformly exaggerated" (Dobyns 1983:51).

Accordingly, two authorities on the Southeast, James Mooney and John R. Swanton, suggested a relatively small population for the region, and their estimates for Apalachee were no exception. In his *Indians of the Southeastern United States*, map 3 (seemingly covering the period 1600–1650), Swanton credits the Apalachee territory with a population of 5,000. He rejected as

1. The term *protohistoric* will be used in the sense assigned to it by Henry Dobyns in his 1983 book, *Their Number Become Thinned*. He used it to signify the 1512–1562 period of intermittent contact between Florida's natives and the Europeans prior to the beginning of sustained contact.

grossly exaggerated the friars' estimates of 16,000, 30,000, 34,000, and so on (see table 7.1). He conceded that in the late sixteenth century it might have been 1,000 higher than his estimate (Swanton 1922:118, 1946:4, 91). This low figure is still echoed by some. Kathleen Deagan (1976) suggests a figure of 5,000 to 6,000 during the mission period. Such low population estimates for Apalachee leave little scope for the devastating impact of various diseases, introduced by the Europeans and Africans, on Florida's natives who had no immunities to them. The work of Woodrow Borah and Sherburne Cook on the demographic destruction suffered by various Indian populations of Latin America indicates that the same diseases must have made serious inroads in Florida as well, even though the devastation may not have been as severe.

Influenced by Borah and Cook's pioneering work, modern scholars such as Charles Hudson and J. Leitch Wright have begun to postulate a larger population for the Southeast in general. Milanich and Fairbanks place the population at the time of the Narváez and the de Soto expeditions at a minimum of 25,000, but they keep faith with Swanton by noting that "By the height of the mission period, about 1675, this number had declined to about 5,000" (Milanich and Fairbanks 1980:230). Dobyns suggests still larger populations for Florida as a whole, and, by extension, for Apalachee. Using diverse techniques he hypothesized two possible aboriginal population figures for the early sixteenth century. Using what he characterized as standard demographic and ecological techniques, he arrived at 697,000 persons as a likely total among the Timucua, Calusa, and Apalachee. On the basis of detailed ethnohistorical regional analysis, he hypothesized the possible existence of a total population as high as 919,600 for those three groups before disaster struck in the form of a series of pandemics and epidemics resulting from Old World pathogens to which the American natives were susceptible. He identifies 722,000 of that total as Timucua and 97,600 as Calusa, leaving 100,000 as the hypothetic population of Apalachee in 1517. Working with the hypothetical Timucua figures, he theorized a 95 percent decline in that people's population within the first century of their exposure to the new diseases, positing a total of only 36,750 Timucua in 1618 (Dobyns 1983:204–208, 293–294). Although Dobyns did not apply this measurement to the Apalachee, it is curious that the same procedure would reduce the hypothetical 100,000 Apalachee to the 5,000 posited by Swanton and by Deagan.

The assessment of the validity of Dobyns's theses is beyond the scope of this work and my present capabilities. I believe, however, that his population estimates are too high, particularly because no archaeological evidence shows the concentration of populations in large villages that such expansive demographic estimates would seem to demand. His ideas on Florida demography do at least make it clear that protohistoric Florida possessed a much larger

Table 7.1. Population estimates for Apalachee

Year	Estimated population	Source	Assessment
ca. 1517	100,000	Dobyns	Probably too high
1570	20,000	López de Velasco	Too low
1590s	6,000	Swanton	Much too low
ca. 1600	At least 25,000	Milanich and Fairbanks	Realistic
1608	Over 30,000[a]	Fray Martín Prieto	Realistic
1612	Innumerable	Governor	
ca. 1617	30,000	Fray Luis Gerónimo	
1633	16,000	Governor	
1638	16,000[b]	Friar	
1673	8,000–9,000	Friar	
1675	8,220	J. Fernández de Florencia	A little too low[c]
1675	ca. 10,520	Bishop Calderón	Realistic[d]
1676	5,000	Friar and Swanton	Too low
1689	ca. 9,600	Ebelino de Compostela	
1703–1704	ca. 8,000	Spanish authorities	
1704	2,000	Swanton	Too low
1704	5,700	Deagan	
1704	7,000–8,000	French sources	
1704	10,200+	Wright	Too high
1705	None left in Apalachee		

a. Based on his estimate of the size of the crowd assembled to greet him.
b. A parish census, it possibly included only mission villages.
c. Florencia apparently was of this opinion, but as a village-by-village, round-figure estimate by Apalachee's lieutenant it is probably among the most reliable.
d. Based on an estimate of Apalachee's share of the total number of confirmations that were recorded individually.

population than traditional authorities have accorded it. I am skeptical also of Dobyns's assessment of the impact of the various epidemics that he theorizes spread quickly from Mexico or the Caribbean Islands to Florida and of the evidence on which he has based some of these epidemics. He is on particularly weak ground when he uses such evidence as a seemingly offhand remark by Juan Fernández de Florencia when he was explaining to the governor why he had used round-figure estimates rather than a censuslike technique for his 1675 tabulation of the population by village: "I have not taken a census and they die daily, for which reason, I have said a little more or less" (Fernández de Florencia 1675a). While admitting that Fernández meant this statement to be understood somewhat figuratively, Dobyns went on to argue, "Still it is indicative of an epidemic in progress, even if Fernández merely supposed that

Native Americans died frequently" (Dobyns 1983:281). Nonetheless, works of Dobyns and others do establish that the population estimates by the friars and by the Spanish officials for Apalachee can no longer be rejected out of hand.

Based on the population established for Apalachee in 1675 by the Florencia list and by the number of confirmations reported by Bishop Calderón for that same year, it seems reasonable to accept the figure of 25,000 Apalachee for the early seventeenth century, when peaceful contact began on a more or less regular basis between the Apalachee and the Spaniards. Milanich and Fairbanks suggest that figure as the province's early protohistoric population. Any lower figure, particularly Swanton's postulate of a mere 5,000, would leave no room for the devastation of the population that is known to have occurred from periodic epidemics, the stresses imposed by the Spaniards' labor demands, and the social trauma resulting from the disruption of the Indians' traditional pattern of living.

One of the models developed from the studies of population decline in Mexico posited a minimum of about a 90 percent decline before the population level stabilized in the mid-seventeenth century. Inasmuch as the contact in Apalachee was not as prolonged or intense or exploitative and Apalachee's population was not as densely congregated, the decline of its population would probably not have been that steep.

The Apalachee's direct contacts with the Spaniards of the Narváez and de Soto expeditions may not have been disastrous epidemiologically simply because they were almost entirely of a hostile nature. Such close contact, when it occurred, usually led to quick deaths in battle before any germs could spread. The fighting and, even more, the loss of much of their food supply doubtless took a toll. Sooner or later the Apalachee's trade encounters with neighboring tribes that had closer contact with the Spaniards must have introduced some of the new diseases, if they had not been got directly from the men with Narváez, de Soto, or Lucas Vásquez de Ayllón. The de Soto chroniclers record that some settlements in the territory of Cofatichique had been depopulated before de Soto's arrival. For this protohistoric period Dobyns provided no hard evidence of epidemics that had broken out among the natives of Florida but offered only speculation that Calusan visitors to Cuba could have brought back smallpox or other viruses to which the natives had had no exposure (Dobyns 1983:250, 254–259) or that disease carriers traveled overland from Mexico along native trade routes. Cabeza de Vaca records that Narváez and his men became ill shortly after they left Apalachee for Aute. The timing of this unspecified illness, which surfaced only long after their arrival in Florida, suggests that it was picked up locally as they trudged through the swamps and ponds of the coastal lowlands (Núñez Cabeza de Vaca 1964:

34–36). In the reports from the 1559 attempt by Tristán de Luna to colonize the Gulf coast, Dobyns sees evidence of the disappearance of many of the flourishing Indian chiefdoms described by the de Soto chroniclers. He concluded, "The general collapse of the good society that Native Americans had known for centuries in the brief period of twenty years indicates that demographic catastrophe struck the peoples of the Southeast between 1542 and 1559" (Dobyns 1983:267–268).

Whatever was the impact of such cataclysms on the population in Apalachee, some of the first estimates of about 30,000, made by the early seventeenth-century friars, were probably accurate. Based on findings for Latin America's Indians and others, there had to be at least 25,000 Apalachee to allow the survival of about 7,500 three-quarters of a century later, particularly since, once the mission era had begun, the province must have had some disastrous epidemics because of close contact with Europeans and blacks as well as some spillover from documented epidemics that ravaged neighboring Timucua.[2] Epidemics from Timucua must have become a serious problem after the introduction of the labor repartimiento in 1647, as it required large numbers of Apalachee to travel overland through Timucua for periods of work in and around St. Augustine. The hardships of the trip itself, intensified by the heavy cargoes they were assigned to carry, took a heavy toll on the natives.

The earliest recorded eyewitness estimate of the Apalachee population places it at more than 30,000. This number is supposed to have assembled at Ivitachuco in 1608 to welcome the first friars on their peace-making mission (Oré 1936:116). In 1612 the governor described Apalachee as a land "where there are innumerable people." Another friar's estimate in 1617 also put the population at about 30,000 (Fernández de Olivera 1612b; Gerónimo 1617). In 1633 the governor estimated the population at more than 15,000 or 16,000 (Horruytiner 1633), probably a realistic figure for that time, because it was seconded by a friar writing in 1676 about the rapid decline of the population. He mentioned that a church census for 1638 listed the population at more than 16,000, whereas the Lenten census of 1676 showed only 5,000 left in the province (Moral 1676). Two years after the governor's estimate, a friar posited a probably unrealistic level of 34,000, claiming that 5,000 had already been Christianized (Friar 1635). The author of the 1676 census seems to have understated the population to emphasize his point, as he was writing to Spain to stress the need for the appointment of a Protector for the Indians in Florida (Moral 1676).[3] Earlier in the 1670s a Franciscan official, asking for more

2. The available records contain few references to epidemics that had occurred in Apalachee, but beyond a doubt some of those recorded for Timucua spread to Apalachee.
3. The Protector was a special official within the bureaucracy whose duty was to look out for and defend the interests of the natives. The Crown refused to sanction the appointment of such an

friars for Florida, mentioned that eleven settlements had already been formed in Apalachee containing 8,000 to 9,000 Indians (Franciscan Commissary General 1673).

Swanton and those who follow his population estimates accept the 5,000 figure as valid but reject the one for 1638 cited by the same friar. They give no explanation for accepting one and rejecting the other. The acceptance of the figure of 5,000 in the context in which it occurs seems to require some justification. From the preceding year of 1675 there are two seemingly more reliable estimates of Apalachee's population that establish a figure well above 5,000. In the same phrase in which Swanton remarks that "The most reasonable is an estimate of 5,000 made in 1676, though it is possible that a hundred years earlier there were a thousand more," he goes on to observe, "and Mooney suggests 7,000 in 1650, including a few other tribes, while Governor Salazar's mission by mission estimate made in 1675 gives a total of 6,130" (Swanton 1946:91).[4] How Swanton derived that total from Governor Hita Salazar's list remains a mystery (see Swanton 312: table 2): for some reason he understated by more than 2,000 the total population given on the list. On that list, drawn up for the governor by Juan Fernández de Florencia, the populations given for the 11 missions inhabited by the Apalachee add up to 7,580. The three villages of non-Apalachee that were mission centers contained another 640 natives (Fernández de Florencia 1675a), for a total of 8,220. The total number of natives in the province at this time was probably another three hundred or so higher still, inasmuch as the Tocobaga were already settled at Wacissa, near Ivitachuco. They were not mentioned by Florencia because their village was not a mission center then or later. By 1677 some Tocobaga— 20 or so—had been buried at Ivitachuco because they had become Christians on their deathbeds (Leturiondo 1678:561–563). The lieutenant's listing of the population, which was done in round figures, mission by mission, by a man who was on the scene, merits more credence than the friar's global estimate written in Madrid and cited in a polemical context in which he was trying to emphasize the plight of the natives.

The validity of Florencia's figures as evidence of a population considerably larger than 5,000 is supported by the other population indicator from 1675. In that year Bishop Calderón administered confirmation to 13,152 natives in the four provinces of Guale, Timucua, Apalachee, and Apalachicola (Díaz Vara Calderón 1675:12). Inasmuch as mission activity had begun in Apalachicola only during the preceding year, almost all of those confirmed

---

official for Florida (except on an ad hoc basis when a native accused of serious crime needed a "public defender"), maintaining that existing officials were capable of serving as "Protector".

4. This is the Florencia list referred to earlier in this chapter.

would have been from the three older provinces, and about four-fifths of that total were from Apalachee. Governor Salazar's listing of the population of the three provinces, village by village, gives a total of only 10,260. All or part of several of the coastal villages, whose population contributed to that total, were non-Christian and would not have been part of the bishop's 13,152 who were confirmed. So possibly as many as about 10,520 were confirmed in Apalachee in 1675 (Díaz Vara Calderón 1675:12; Fernández de Florencia 1675a). Bushnell mentioned that the authors of the governor's census thought that the figures that they arrived at were low (Bushnell 1978b:4–5): perhaps they did not count those working in St. Augustine and on the ranches or the placeless persons of mixed blood, who might not be counted as members of the Indian community even though they lived among the Indians.

Unfortunately for purposes of comparison, the other listing of the villages' population, from 1689, gives the number of families per mission rather than the number of individuals, a total of 1,920 families (Ebelino de Compostela 1689). The three principal mission provinces of Guale, Timucua, and Apalachee had a total of 2,696 families. The census was made by the friars at the request of their bishop so that he might inform the king of the population of the various parts of his diocese of Santiago de Cuba. The bishop translated the total by families to individuals by assuming an average of five persons per family.[5] For Apalachee that would signify a population of about 9,600 individuals, exclusive of the Tocobaga because nonmission villages were not included in this census.

The two mission villages to the west of Apalachee (San Nicolás de Los Chacatos and San Carlos de Sabacola) contained another 100 families. The figures registered by the bishop both for Apalachee and for the other provinces raise some serious questions, which no one, to my knowledge, has yet addressed or even remarked upon. The figure of 9,600 is 1,380 above the 8,220 given for 1675 by the lieutenant's list, for a time period for which the conventional wisdom maintains that there was a steady decline in the population. Of course, as noted, the 1675 census probably understated the population. The figure of 10,520 confirmed in Apalachee, extrapolated from Bishop Calderón's statistics, would allow for a decline of about 1,000 in the province's population over that 15-year period.

Another disturbing feature of this 1689 census is its reversal of another trend that is usually taken for granted—the more rapid decline of the population in Guale and Timucua than in Apalachee. In 1675 Apalachee contained slightly more than 80 percent of the total population of those three provinces.

5. Kathleen Deagan (1978) used the figure of 4.5 persons per family to compute the numbers of individuals.

In this census, Apalachee's portion fell to 72 percent of the total. Even more incomprehensible, if one accepts these 1689 figures and the bishop's assumption of five persons per family, is the indication that the populations of both Guale and Timucua were rising in absolute terms. This development is particularly contraindicated for Guale; both historical and archaeological records seem to show it losing population during this interval as a result of English attacks and disease. Governor Salazar listed 12 settlements in Guale in contrast to the six mentioned on the bishop's 1689 list. As a result of the pressures from the Carolinians and from the natives allied with them, many of the Christianized natives from Guale moved into eastern Timucua during this period while others migrated inland or to English territory shortly before 1689, during the governorship of Marques Cabrera (Deagan 1978:105–107). This subject, accordingly, needs considerably more study. The location of some of the parish censuses that seem to have been made periodically, if not annually, during Lent might be an invaluable aid for resolving these problems.

If one accepts as reasonable the bishop's figure of 9,600 people in Apalachee's missions in 1689, and if one allows for similar attrition over another 15-year period, the estimates of a population of about 8,000 in 1703–1704 before the missions' destruction are probably close to the actual numbers. In mid-July 1704, while pondering the decision to abandon the province in the wake of the destruction of most of the missions in Apalachee, the Council of War held at St. Augustine posited a population of 8,000 in the 14 mission villages just before they were destroyed (Council of War 1704:56–59). This figure no doubt included the losses suffered during the year and a half of strife that served as a prelude to the climactic conflicts of January–July 1704: at least 200 warriors (possibly up to 400) lost in October 1702 at the rout that occurred on the Flint;[6] an unknown number of casualties from the Apalachicola's 1703 raid in which Ocuia was destroyed and probably a major portion of the approximately 500 prisoners taken in that attack; and the 170 recorded as having died in an epidemic that swept San Luis in that year (Albuquerque 1703; Romo de Urisa 1702; Zúñiga y Zerda 1704a:48–50). Although no mention is made that the epidemic spread to other villages, it seems unlikely that it would be confined to that one village in view of the proximity of so many of the other settlements and of San Luis's role as the headquarters settlement.

Here, as in their earlier estimates, authorities differ on the size of Apalachee's population at the start of 1704. Swanton maintained his conservative approach: "The figures given by Moore (1,300 free Indians plus 100 slaves) and Bienville (400 Indians) indicate that there were about 2,000 at the time

---

6. An 800-man Spanish-led Apalachee force on its way to a reprisal attack on the Apalachicola encountered an English-led Apalachicola force that was moving down for a raid on the missions. The Apalachee fled in panic after stumbling into a trap set by their foes.

when they were destroyed (1704)" (Swanton 1946:91). Once again Swanton seems to have maintained a selective approach in his use of population statistics. Although he mentioned that Bienville, writing from Mobile, stated that the English had killed or made prisoner 6,000 or 7,000, Swanton added, "The English estimate is not far wrong" (1946:90). Inasmuch as Bienville wrote this letter on September 6, 1704, presumably after having talked with the Apalachee who had just arrived in Mobile, Swanton's out-of-hand rejection of Bienville's estimate seems to require some explanation, particularly because the same estimate was made by the Spanish officials when the surviving Apalachee in French and Spanish territory are included. It is not clear if Swanton was aware of the more expansive claims made by Moore in his second letter.[7] The Library of Congress copies of both of Moore's letters were cited by Verner Crane, whose work Swanton had consulted. Deagan (1976), in a brief item in a population table, is more expansive here than Swanton. Her estimate is based on Boyd's calculations from the figures cited by Colonel Moore in his two letters. In a rough approximation of Boyd's figures, Deagan presents the population in 1702 as 5,700, observing in a footnote that this is "A rough estimate based on Moore's enumeration of captured and killed Indians (5,500) with an additional 200 who escaped." Her figure of 5,700 fails to take into account the considerable number of Apalachee who remained in the province until the second wave of attacks in June and July, long after Moore had returned to South Carolina with his captives. J. Leitch Wright presents the most expansive estimate: "It is not possible to be precise about the fates of all the Apalachees. Most of them, probably 10,000 or more, ended up in Carolina as slaves or tributaries." His 10,000 do not include the Apalachee who fled to Mobile and to Timucua in July 1704. He estimates that about 200 remained in Apalachee amid the charred missions (Wright 1981:114–115).

Another approach to calculating a rough estimate of Apalachee's total population is to use 1,500, the number of native warriors in the province in the wake of the 1702 disaster on the Flint. Inasmuch as the leader of the expedition who gave that figure mentions that only 300 returned with him, his estimate probably did not include the additional 200 whom Bushnell records as having straggled back later "without so much as their breechclouts" (Bushnell 1979:7; Romo de Urisa 1702). Using 1,700 as the number of relatively ablebodied males as the base for a rough projection, one could reasonably calculate a minimum population of more than 6,000 at the beginning of 1703. On the assumption that the men led more dangerous lives, there must have been at least 2,000 women to match those 1,700 men, and the other 300 or so who

---

7. Swanton cited only the B. R. Carroll version of Moore's letter to Governor Johnson taken from a Boston newspaper.

were probably working out of the province. Choosing the arbitrary but seemingly reasonable estimate of 1,200 of those women as married and fertile, and two children per couple, would point to a population of 6,400. Disabled warriors and the elderly would add to that total.

If one uncritically accepts the figures given by Moore, they also suggest a population approximating the 8,000 level. In his second letter Moore claimed that he brought away 300 men and 1,000 women and children to be settled as free allies in the Carolina territory, that he killed or enslaved 325 men, and that he enslaved 4,000 women and children, for a total of 5,625 people (Moore 1704b:888–891).[8] When Moore departed, probably sometime in February 1704, there was still a native population of some significance left in the province. Ivitachuco and Escambé appear to have escaped Moore's attack more or less unscathed. San Luis suffered some casualties and some desertions as well, but its population was probably still relatively intact. Patale was still in existence and, along with Aspalaga, bore the brunt of the second attack in June and July 1704. Consequently, significant portions of their inhabitants are not included in Moore's figures. Much of the population of the village whose inhabitants had fled survived into 1705. Even a few of the Ocuians survived to take part in the final encounters of June and July (Council of War 1704:56–59; Guzmán 1704:61–64; Solana 1704a:50–55; Zúñiga y Zerda 1704b:55–56, 1705). Using the 1689 census of families and making allowances for considerable attrition of the population in the interval by decreasing the number of Ivitachuco's families from 200 to 125, Oconi's from 80 to 40, Escambé's from 400 to 250, San Luis from 300 to 200, Patale's from 120 to 60, and Aspalaga's from 50 to 25, this still leaves 700 families, which would project a total population approaching 3,000 at a minimum.[9] Added to Moore's 5,625, this remnant provides a figure relatively close to the 8,000 posited by the Council of War.

Admittedly, there is a considerable element of speculation in this approach to establishing the size of the population in 1704. Particularly troubling is the questionable reliability of Moore's accounting and the round figure of 8,000 advanced by the Council of War. However, these multiple approaches and sources always arrive at a figure in the vicinity of 8,000, which suggests that it is possibly a reliable estimate of the size of the population. In any event, it seems indubitable that the estimate of 2,000 or so that some have advanced as the number of natives in the province on the eve of the destruction of the missions is much too low (Bienville 1704:27; Swanton 1946:91).

8. As noted in detail in chapter 12, there are serious reasons for doubting the validity of Moore's claim of having taken 4,000 women and children as slaves.
9. San Luis is mentioned as having 200 families at the time of the evacuation of the province (Boyd 1951:70).

The available records do not provide even a hint of the degree of mestization that occurred between the Apalachee and the Spanish soldiery. As a garrison site, San Luis would likely be the one most affected. Some attention has been given to mestization in St. Augustine, but the findings do not permit any useful inferences for San Luis. The visitors' repeated proscription of concubinage suggests that it was common. In view of the social predominance of the Spaniard, the result must have been a significant number of mestizo progeny in places where Spaniards were present. The emigrés to Mobile made an obscure reference to this phenomenon as one of their reasons for wishing to stay among the French, remarking that at San Luis they had not been masters of their wives and noting that since they had been living among the French it had not been a problem. This could have been simply a reference to the Spanish settlers' insistence that the Apalachee women do various chores for them, but that is not a likely prospect.

One aspect of population changes in Apalachee during the mission period that merits attention is the differing trends from village to village. Some villages declined abruptly in population, while others rose sharply or showed moderate declines or increases that left the relative ranking of the missions by size considerably different in 1689 from what it had been in 1675 (see table 7.2). There is no ready explanation for this phenomenon.

The 1675 list shows San Luis with 1,400 people as the most populous mission in Apalachee, followed by Ivitachuco with 1,200.[10] Ocuia and Cupaica jointly held third place with 900, Ayubale and Aspalaga shared fourth with 800, and Tomole with 700 was in fifth place. The remaining missions in descending order were Patale with 500, Oconi with 200, Bacuqua with 120, and Capole with 60. The settlements inhabited by non-Apalachee all ranked with the smaller villages showing populations of 300 or fewer.

The 1689 tabulation gives the number of families per mission rather than the number of individuals. To facilitate comparison, the bishop's estimate of five persons per household will be used to expand the count by families into one by individuals. Even a quick glance at the result reveals a perplexing mélange of changes, both absolute and relative, during the 14 years that separated the two head counts. San Luis, although gaining slightly in population in absolute terms, slipped into second place with 300 families or 1,500 individuals, losing out to Cupaica, which, with 400 families, had more than doubled its size since 1675. At 250 families (1,250 people), Ayubale showed strong growth as well, moving into third place. Ivitachuco's moderate decline to 200 families (1,000 people) caused it to slip into a tie for fourth place with

---

10. One version of the 1655 list mentions Ivitachuco as having a population of 2,500. Populations are not given for any of the other missions in 1655.

Table 7.2. Population by mission in 1675 and 1689

| | | 1689 | |
Mission	1675	Families	Persons
San Luis	1400	300	1500
Ivitachuco	1200	200	1000
Cupaica	900	400	2000
Ayubale	800	250	1250
Ocuia	900	200	1000
Tomoli	700	130	650
Patale	500	120	600
Oconi	200	80	400
Tama	300	80	400
Bacuqua	120	50	250
Aspalaga	800	50	250
Capole	60	30	150
Place of the Chine	300	30	150
Nativity of Our Lady	40		
San Nicolás de Tolentino	100 Chactos 30[a]		
San Carlos	300 Chactos 100[a]		
San Nicolás de los Chacatos		70	350
San Carlos de Çabacola		30	150

a. Figures given in 1675 by Bishop Díaz Vara Calderon.

Ocuia. Although Ocuia showed a moderate increase of 100 individuals to reach 1,000, it fell a notch in relative terms from its tie with Cupaica for third place in 1675. Aspalaga suffered a massive loss: its 800 people of 1675 shrank to 250, tumbling it from a tie for fourth place to a tie for eighth with Bacuqua. Although Tomole declined by 50 to 650 people, it remained in fifth place, and with a moderate increase of 100 to the 600 level Patale stayed in sixth. At populations of 400 and 250, respectively, both Oconi and Bacuqua doubled their size during this interval. Capoli remained the smallest village inhabited by Apalachee, although it grew spectacularly from 60 to 150. However, such growth is not reflected in a complaint by Capoli's chief in 1694 asking that four errant husbands working in St. Augustine be required to return to their wives. He stated that these men were missed by the village as well as by their wives because the village had no more than 20 men, some of whom were elderly (Florencia 1695:66–67). Among the non-Apalachee, Tama grew by 100 to 400, while the Chine mission declined by 50 percent from 300 to 150 persons (Ebelino de Compostela 1689; Fernández de Florencia 1675a).

The reasons for these changes, and above all the reasons for the lack of a pattern, remain a mystery. Although one would expect uniformity in a region as compact as Apalachee, the sharp decline manifested by a few missions is possibly attributable to the differential impact of epidemics, which hit some settlements more severely than others. There is some evidence that inter-village contacts may not have been as frequent as one might think in view of their proximity to one another. In looking closely at events at Patale and San Luis in the last week or so before Patale's destruction in July 1704, one is struck by the fact that, even though Patale was captured by an English-led Creek force on the night of June 23 and its convent was burned at that time, San Luis became aware of it only five days later (Solana 1704a:50–55). While Cupaica's people lived on a site west of the Ochlockonee River, they may have enjoyed an isolation that protected them from the ravages of some epidemics.

More disturbing are the absolute increases in the population of villages such as Cupaica that went counter to the general trend toward decline. In the case of Bacuqua, it is known that the authorities were encouraging its growth because of its small size and its position as a frontier village. It is possible that similar encouragement was given to Cupaica, which also occupied an exposed position, particularly in its trans-Ochlockonee location, in regard to the Apalachicola with whom relations were deteriorating during the 1680s. The very remoteness of such sites may have attracted migrants from other villages or from neighboring peoples. That there was some population movement from one village to another is reflected in a 1694 regulation requiring the permission of the governor's deputy for such moves in the future, on the grounds that some of those moving did so to escape the consequences of crimes or mis-demeanors they had committed in their home villages. The same regulations prohibited moves to villages such as Ocuia that were not on the royal road (Florencia 1695).

The relative remoteness of such sites may have freed their inhabitants from some of the more importunate and unauthorized demands for labor from Spanish settlers, soldiers, and the governor's deputy. While situated west of the Ochlockonee, Cupaica would have offered such attractions. The posting of a sentinel at the river would have allowed ample time to send a warning to scatter into the woods to escape such a labor draft while the official concerned was searching for a means to cross the river. Such locations facilitated migra-tion out of the province when disenchantment with Spanish rule became se-vere enough. A considerable but unspecified number did just that, migrating to Apalachicola country during the administration of the unpopular Antonio Matheos, just as many Yamasee left Guale for English territory during the same period. It is likely that the Apalachee wife of the so-called Emperor Brims of the Creek as well as the Apalachee wife of one of his sons were part of that emigration. Matheos's successor was able to induce most of the mi-grants to return to their home villages.

Although the relative stability of Ocuia's population might be attributed to the protection from imported pathogens offered by its remoteness, such an argument loses much of its force in the face of Patale's similar stability. It appears to have occupied something of a crossroads position on several trails within the province and on one heading north out of the province. The drastic decline in the population of the Chine mission may indeed be a function of its location "on the road to the sea from San Luis," as it was described on one mission list. That would make it a prime target for shipborne maladies introduced at St. Marks. Tomole's slight decline in population may have happened for a similar reason, as it was at least occasionally a way station for travelers from St. Marks to San Luis (Barreda 1693:265; Fernández de Florencia 1675a). As some of the 1675 inhabitants of the Chine mission were Yamasee, the decline may also be attributed in part to their departure to Candelaria to join the Tama, with whom they seem to have had some affinity. The changes in the Chine mission's name suggest that it moved to a new site on such occasions, and a move might have led the Yamasee to affiliate with another village. Ivitachuco's decline might also be attributable in part to its exposure to disease as the eastern gateway to Apalachee for all the Spaniards coming overland from St. Augustine as well as for natives returning from their labor stint in St. Augustine.

Some of Aspalaga's abrupt decline may be associated with dissatisfaction with a second move of the village site that may have occurred after 1675. As noted earlier, the mission appears to have been moved at some time between 1657 and 1675 from a position west of Ocuia to one east of it. There is some indication that, late in the mission period, Aspalaga may have slipped farther south. On the two 1675 lists, Aspalaga is bracketed between Ocuia and Oconi, and during the 1677 visitation Leturiondo stopped there between his visits to those places. In the 1694 visitation the Upalucha ranch was the visitor's stopping place between Ocuia and Oconi, and he passed to Aspalaga from Capoli, then from Aspalaga to Tomole. In the 1698 visitation Ayala went to Aspalaga from Tomole. It is possible that the Aspalagans were shunted farther south to make way for that ranch. The existence of discontent among the Aspalaga is indicated by the fact that the son of the chief of "Old Aspalaga" was among those who joined the Creek attackers of his fellow tribesman in 1704 (Florencia 1695; Solana 1704a:50–55). Several of the late eighteenth-century maps show the site of Aspalaga at the confluence of the St. Marks River and one of its tributaries. But, curiously, they show a second village site farther north bearing the name Yapalaga or Ypalaga (Tesar 1980,1:331, 334). This might indicate that in one or another of the mission's moves some of its inhabitants remained on the old village site or returned to it later, having become dissatisfied with the new one.

Even though there is no documentary support, the most plausible source for the impressive growth of villages such as Cupaica, Ayubale, and Bacuqua is the immigration of non-Apalachee into these villages, in a process similar to that which is known to have taken place in eastern Timucua. Several archaeologists have suggested such immigration as an explanation for this growth. There apparently is archaeological evidence for this intrusion in some of the Apalachee villages such as Patale. If there was a Yamasee tribe known as the Ilcombe, as Swanton maintained in 1922, that fact might indicate that both Cupaica's growth and the reference to it as Ilcombe late in the mission period were the result of a heavy influx of Yamasee. However, little evidence supports that thesis, and Swanton does not mention the "Yamasee Ilcombe" in his 1946 work. The references in the Carolina records to the Ilcombe, who were in South Carolina from 1706 to 1711, indicate clearly that, whatever may have been their tribal affiliation, they had recently come from "enemy territory," that is, either Spanish or French territory.

In summary, all of the unexplained anomalies associated with this 1689 population listing suggest that it needs more study. In his cover letter the bishop revealed that his list was based on registers that he had received from the pastors of the diocese so that he might fulfill a royal order for an accounting of the parishes and of the number of parishioners, Spanish and Indians, in the diocese (Ebelino de Compostela 1689).

One of the demographic questions whose resolution apparently must await archaeological research is the manner of distribution of the population between the principal village and the satellite villages of each missionary center and, concomitantly, the distribution of people between those villages and the surrounding countryside under their jurisdiction. For example, the 1,400 people indicated as inhabitants of San Luis in 1675 were distributed in four or five separate villages, San Luis and its three or four satellites, and in isolated homesteads or small clumps of homesteads scattered through the countryside. Currently, there is no documentary or archaeological evidence available that reveals how those people were apportioned among the villages or how many belonging to one of those villages lived at the village center and how many lived scattered through the countryside as seemingly portrayed in two remarks by the Fidalgo of Elvas: [from Ivitachuco] "Thenceforward the country was well inhabited, producing much corn, the way leading by many habitations like villages. . . . The Campmaster, whose duty it is to divide and lodge the men, quartered them about the town, at the distance of half a league to a league apart" (Elvas 1904 (1):47). For the head village of Anhayca Apalachee to which the latter remark refers, the opportunity to discover the size and the distribution of its sections likely has been lost under Tallahassee's parking lots, stores, houses, and public buildings. But the current work on the central site of Anhayca's political successor, San Luis, and on the Patale site offers an opportunity for possibly determining how much of the population lived at or close to the mission center. Possession of such information would be a start toward answering some other questions.

There is surprisingly little documentary evidence about the epidemiological mechanisms by which Apalachee's and Florida's populations were reduced so drastically. Only three of the references to epidemics seem definitely to refer to Apalachee. In 1657, Governor Rebolledo indicated that Apalachee had been affected by the epidemics that ravaged Timucua and Guale during the years immediately preceding, noting, however, that the effect had been less drastic in Apalachee. He remarked that there were few Indians left in Guale and Timucua because so many had died in recent years "with the sickness of the plague and of small pox" and that even in Apalachee the population had diminished (Rebolledo 1657a:111). This is a reference to the smallpox epidemics that ravaged Florida for at least ten months in 1655 (Rebolledo 1655). It is not clear whether the governor meant to include the unidentified epidemic of 1649–1650 as well. In 1703, it is recorded that 170 people perished in an epidemic at San Luis. Although the third reference is not so unequivocal, it is reasonably certain that Apalachee is being referred to in Governor Torres y Ayala's 1693 report to the viceroy from Pensacola Bay that "the state of these provinces of Florida is exceedingly bad and . . . they are suffering from the same epidemic as in New Spain" (Torres y Ayala 1693b:223). When he wrote, the only parts of Florida that the governor had seen were Apalachee and the territory between it and Pensacola Bay. It seems reasonable to assume, however, that most of the epidemics that swept Timucua had an impact on Apalachee, particularly in the seventeenth century.

At least two separate epidemics struck Florida between 1613 and the beginning of 1617, carrying off half the natives who had been converted as well as a considerable number of soldiers. The evidence appears in two sources. The first is a note (in English) in the Lowery transcripts: "Owing to the unhealthfulness of the country many of the soldiers sicken and die." [11] Lowery's extract (in Spanish) from a January 1617 note by the Florida friars in chapter is more informative.

> We find that from four years ago down to the present, there have died on account of the great plagues and contagious diseases that the Indians have suffered, half of them, in the which Your Majesty has had a very great part in the growth that was given to heaven. For with the help of the twenty-two Religious which Your Majesty sent . . . to these regions

11. Lowery's note is based on a 1615 letter by Governor Juan Treviño Guillamas. Lowery transcribed only a sentence or two in Spanish from that letter.

five years ago, a very rich harvest of souls for heaven has been made in the midst of this great number of deaths. There remain alive up to eight thousand Christians, at least, probably more than [eight than] less. (Treviño Guillamas 1615; Florida Friars in Chapter 1617)

Although Dobyns mentions the statement by the friars, noting that they observed that "half of the Native Americans there had perished of *repeated* episodes of epidemics and contagious diseases [italics mine]," he seems to argue that there was but one protracted epidemic, which he identifies on rather weak evidence as bubonic plague. Smallpox, he argued, spreads to all susceptible individuals very quickly, whereas the plague, because of its dependence on a flea vector, typically does not spread rapidly to all susceptible individuals in a linear fashion (Dobyns 1983:278–279). That smallpox did not spread in this fashion in Florida is indicated by Rebolledo's reference to the 1655 outbreak. Writing in October of that year, he observed that over the previous ten months there had been "a *series* of smallpox plagues which have affected the country" (Rebolledo 1655). In Dobyns's line of argument, bubonic plague accounts better for the length of this calamitous episode than smallpox would. However, simply taking at face value the friars' reference to "great plague*s* and contagious disease*s* [italics mine]," the protracted nature of this demographic disaster could be explained by the numbers of plagues and diseases. The use of the words *plagues* and *contagious diseases* and of plurals for both seems to indicate that at least two distinct maladies were involved and that multiple episodes of each or more than one plague and more than one disease were involved. The information in the available documents does not permit identification of the "plagues and contagious diseases." In view of the protracted nature of these epidemics and in view of the fact that they seem to have involved western Timucua, it seems to be all but certain that Apalachee was affected by one or more of them.

The documents record the outbreak of a second epidemic in 1649 and 1650 that carried off a number of Spaniards, including governors, treasury officials, company commanders, and friars. Dobyns identified this pestilence as yellow fever, basing his conclusion largely on the heavy toll it took among the European population and on the belief that this plague was then raging in various parts of the Caribbean basin, including Cuba. Bushnell suggested that typhus might have been involved as well in this epidemic. Swanton states that the documents do not reveal whether the illness also spread to the natives (Bushnell 1978a:419; Dobyns 1983:279–280; Swanton 1922:338). Dobyns's assumption that it did seems reasonable, particularly in view of the remark by one of the friars that during 1649 and 1650 many of his colleagues had died of the plague (Ponce de León 1651). Chatelain recorded that the 1655 smallpox outbreak carried off all the Crown's black slaves (Chatelain 1941:56). Of the same epidemic, Rebolledo wrote that its impact on the natives had been so great that they could not be counted on for labor to bring needed lumber from the nearest forests for the repair of the fort at St. Augustine:

> The necessary wood must be cut and brought from the forests by Indians. This necessitates too much work for them as the distance which it must be carried on their shoulders is long. I now consider this manner of bringing it impossible because of the high mortality rate which has been the result of a series of plagues of smallpox which have afflicted the country for the last ten months. Many died as a result of this and of the trials and hunger which these unfortunate people have suffered, and the province is quite destitute. (Rebolledo 1655)

In 1659 the incoming governor reported that a recent epidemic of measles had killed 10,000 of the natives. A second document, referring to events that occurred in the late 1650s, mentions that the western Timucuan missions of San Francisco de Potano, Santa Fé, San Martín, and San Juan de Guacara had been depopulated by the combined effects of a pestilence and the fighting and flight to the woods associated with the 1656 rebellion in Timucua (Aranguíz y Cotes 1659; Leturiondo [1670]).[12] Although it is not entirely clear if the pestilence referred to is the smallpox or the measles outbreak, or both, the fact that the governor moved to reestablish these communities only at the end of 1659 suggests that the measles epidemic was the major factor. The proximity of the mentioned towns to Apalachee and the fact that some of the rebel Timucua sought refuge and support in Apalachee seem to assure the spread of the illness or illnesses to Apalachee.

Still another plague was recorded as having caused so great a mortality in 1672 as to hinder the progress of work on the fort at St. Augustine. In this context the acting governor wrote in 1674 that the natives were "weak and unfit for this type of work . . . and there are few of them because of the contagion that occurred two years ago" (Boniface 1971:108). This illness remains unidentified, though Dobyns suggests influenza as a possibility on the basis of reports that New Mexico had suffered an outbreak of some pestilence in 1671 that killed both natives and cattle (Dobyns 1983:286).

Dobyns posited still another epidemic in Apalachee and Timucua in 1675

---

12. The document is a report drawn up in Spain commenting on the service record of Captain Juan Fernández de Florencia. It states that on November 19, 1659, Florencia was ordered to go to the provinces of Yustaga and Timuqua to repopulate and resurrect the settlements that had become depopulated because some of the natives had died from the plague and others had fled to the woods.

on the basis of Juan Fernández de Florencia's remark concerning the exactitude of his count of the mission populations. Florencia explained that they were not a census or head count but a round-figure estimate, as head counts were pointless inasmuch as "they die daily." Admittedly his remark could indicate an epidemic in progress, but, as noted earlier, it is rather tenuous evidence for such an assumption. Even more tenuous is Dobyns's inference of the possibility of another epidemic in Apalachee in 1686. His evidence is the occurrence of a typhus epidemic in Guatemala during that year and Marcos Delgado's report that, during the expedition he headed that year, half its members came down with fevers. Dobyns suggested that the typhus epidemic could have been widespread throughout Spanish North America (Boyd 1948:188; Dobyns 1983:282–283).

For the 1613–1617 epidemic Dobyns indicates a 50 percent mortality rate, for that of 1649 a rate of about 33 percent. He says the rate for the other epidemics is unknown (Dobyns 1983:283, table 27). If the governor's estimate of 10,000 victims for the 1659 epidemic is accurate, it indicates high mortality. Dobyns suggests that the impact of the 1659 epidemic might have been heightened by the appearance of influenza as well as measles.

For the sixteenth century Dobyns suggests strongly the possibility that Florida's natives were affected by the first great smallpox pandemic that spread from the Caribbean islands and Central Mexico between 1519 and 1524 and that they suffered a 50 percent mortality from it. He suggests almost as strongly that the pestilence that the de Soto chroniclers said had depopulated a number of Cofitachique towns one or two years before de Soto's arrival had probably spread to Florida's natives as well. He also suggests that a considerable number of additional epidemics may have occurred during the century, but he offers no hard evidence in support of his assertions (Dobyns 1983: 254–260, 262–264). Nonetheless, the spread of the first smallpox epidemic from Cuba to Florida is a distinct possibility. In the first half of the eighteenth century, natives from the Keys and from the Tequesta region seem to have made frequent trips in their dugouts to Cuba without incident, showing that such trips were feasible. Archaeological evidence for sixteenth-century contacts between the natives of South Florida and those of Cuba increases the likelihood that such contagion did occur, with the same disastrous results. In the first half of the sixteenth century, the native populations of many of the Caribbean islands were all but extinguished, principally through such epidemics.

Of course, once the French and then the Spaniards established themselves on the Atlantic coasts of Georgia and Florida, the possibility of contagion increased enormously. As a layman in the field of epidemiology, I wonder whether, in light of Apalachee's and the Southeast's rather scattered settlement pattern, epidemics would always have spread as widely or whether they would have had the same intensity as they did in crowded, urbanized Central Mexico. Considerable protection would have been provided by the extensive unpopulated buffer zones that seem to have separated the territories of many of the people of the Southeast. The juxtaposition of Apalachee's eastern frontier and Yustaga's western villages was definitely an exceptional situation, but the variety and multiplicity of epidemics suggested by Dobyns, and the frequency with which French and English as well as Spanish ships landed along the coasts from Florida to South Carolina, indicate that at least one epidemic did have a calamitous impact on Apalachee during the sixteenth century.

To date, no archaeological evidence shows the numerous groups of sizable populations that would have been called for to support Dobyns's postulate of repeated halving of the population in the 100 years between 1517 and 1618 (Dobyns 1983:283–288). He suggests that during that time a hypothetical 722,000 Timucua were reduced to a mere 36,750, largely by disease (Dobyns 1983:287–288, 293). Working backward from the 16,000 for Apalachee given by two sources in the 1630s and using Dobyns's "Schematic Reconstruction of Approximate Depopulation Trend of Florida Native Americans, 1519–1617," one would come up with a population of 261,000 Apalachee at the start of that period (Dobyns 1983:287). Such a total is far greater than that which Dobyns himself seems to suggest, but even the 100,000 he indicates as Apalachee's population at the beginning of the protohistoric period would require a very large number of sizable villages. To date, archaeologists have not encountered the remains of even one village in Apalachee that contains more than a few houses on one site. On the other hand, the archaeological and the historical study of the sixteenth- and seventeenth-century settlement patterns of Florida's natives are still in what might be termed "the Age of Discovery." Although Apalachee is one of the areas along with Potano that has received the most attention, there has been no extensive work as yet on the native housing portion of any Apalachee village for that period. In the supposedly populous province of Utina, only two mission sites have been located. There is currently no ready formula for resolving this discrepancy between the conclusions suggested by the documents and demographic theory and the evidence drawn from the archaeological site exploration, which points in the opposite direction.

In his work on the Creek frontier, David Corkran suggests one settlement pattern that would allow for a large population in Apalachee and be compatible with the archaeologists' failure to uncover any extensive concentrations of artifacts. It shows the dwellings scattered four to a block in ten block-sized rectangles around the square ground and the adjacent chunkey yard (Corkran 1967:8). A village of 1,000 inhabitants formed in that fashion would have its dwellings spread over a vast area, particularly if all the blocks were not immediately contiguous. Surface-collecting surveys conducted over the area included in such a "village" might well produce so few artifacts as to lead one to believe that no sizable villages existed.

Archaeologists hope that the forthcoming excavations of the presumed village areas at the center of the San Luis and the Patale sites will provide information helpful for at least a start toward the resolution of this problem. A 1985 year-long survey of approximately 60 square miles around one of the Patale sites by Stephen Bryne revealed a "notable" "intensity of settlement in this small area. . . . Some 117 sites were identified." They ranged from farmsteads to hamlets to villages to towns (Marrinan and Bryne 1987:6). Both the documents and the hypotheses advanced by Dobyns concerning the population-carrying capacity of Florida's fauna and flora for a people who were significantly dependent on horticulture in addition to hunting and gathering suggest a population that numbered in the tens of thousands.

That there was initially a large population is reflected in the Spanish officials' perplexity over the high rate of mortality that had already occurred by the start of the mission era in Apalachee. After observing that Florida lacked the usual mechanisms of harmful exploitation that were major causes for such mortality, namely, the *encomienda,* the *obraje,* or workshop, and the mines, the governor in 1630 remarked that Florida's Indians are "the best treated in America because they do not pay tribute. A few work in the soldier's sowings, but are paid for their labor. The Crown spends much money in gifts to the caciques each year, so that the Indians are the least worked and the best treated in the Indies, yet they die here as elsewhere" (Boniface 1971:81–82).

One of the more impressive indicators, perhaps, of the relative density of Apalachee's population, even during the mission period, and of the intensive exploitation of its agricultural potential is Captain Daniel E. Burch's observation in 1823 while he was establishing the route for the Pensacola–St. Augustine highway: "That part of Florida between the Ocholockony and Suwannee rivers appears to have once sustained a dense population, as the forest is entirely of second growth wherever the lands were susceptible to cultivation. There are also appearances of the lands having been cultivated in several places east of the Suwannee" (Burch 1823:93).

Chapter 8

Apalachee and Its Neighbors

AMONG the natives of south and central Florida with whom the first Spanish expeditions were in contact, the Apalachee had a reputation for bellicosity and military prowess. In their reactions to both the Narváez and the de Soto expeditions they lived up to their fame. Despite the prolonged presence of both expeditions in their territory, the Apalachee never came to terms with the intruders. In contrast to some of the other tribes the Apalachee continued to harass the Spaniards until the intruders departed (Fernández de Oviedo y Valdéz 1904:80; Hernández de Biedma 1904:5; Núñez Cabeza de Vaca 1964: 12–13, 24, 30). Garcilaso recorded that when the survivors of the de Soto expedition recounted their experiences with the Apalachee, "They commented upon the fierceness and unconquerable passion disclosed by the Indians of Apalache" (Vega 1951:627). This warlike reputation must have preserved them reasonably well from disastrous incursions by neighboring peoples because those neighbors spoke with respect of the Apalachee's fighting skill, and there were no fortifications around the Apalachee villages at this time, in contrast to the earlier period of the mound builders.

Nonetheless, hostilities between the Apalachee and their neighbors seem to have been perennial. At the time of the Narváez expedition, the Apalachee were at war with the neighboring Timucua (Núñez Cabeza de Vaca 1964:22, 29). When the Spaniards renewed contact with them early in the seventeenth century, the Apalachee were again, or still, at war with those neighbors (Oré 1936:114–117). In the 1630s, at the time of the establishment of the first permanent mission there, the Apalachee were at war with various neighbors to the north and west of their territory despite the considerable distance that seems to have separated the diverse tribal settlements on this side (Vega Castro y Pardo 1639b).[1]

1. The de Soto accounts depict the nearest settlement to the north as a minimum of three days' journey in contrast to the Timucuan settlements of Yustaga Province, which were quite close.

One cause of this endemic warfare was the existence of a warrior caste among the Apalachee and some of their neighbors. As it was with the Apalachicola, the first step toward entry into that caste was probably to be accorded a war name. That distinction could be achieved simply by being present at an encounter in which an enemy scalp was taken (Hawkins 1982a:70). Among the Apalachee, one who had achieved warrior status was known as tascaia. Entry into that class and advancement within its ranks depended on one's killing specified numbers of the enemy. The taking of one scalp sufficed for one to become a tascaia. Some of the ranks were noroco, hita tascaia, and nicoguadca. Three scalps earned one the rank of noroco. To achieve the status of nicoguadca, the warrior had to have killed seven tascaias and three hitas tascaias.

The practice of scalping appears to have been closely associated with this system of military rank. Exhibiting a scalp, telling the details of the encounter in which it was taken, and ceremonial dancing with the scalp were traditional proofs furnished by the warrior in support of his claims for advancement (García 1695:174 ff.; Paiva 1676). Scalping was one of the aboriginal customs that most perturbed the Spaniards, and they urged the adoption of some other criterion for advancement within warrior ranks (García 1695:174 ff.; Zúñiga y Zerda 1701:35–36). Nevertheless, it was so strongly rooted in the mores of the Apalachee and some other Florida Indians that it survived throughout the mission era.

The Spaniards succeeded, at least initially, in abating the continual intertribal warfare, playing the role of peacemakers between the Apalachee and some of their neighbors. The principal purpose of the first Franciscan foray into Apalachee territory in 1608 was ending hostilities between the Apalachee and the western Timucua, hostilities that the friars viewed as an obstacle to success with the Timucua. Peace was established at a mass assemblage of the Apalachee population and their leaders at Ivitachuco that same year (Oré 1936:114–117). A generation later, shortly after the launching of the formal mission effort in Apalachee, the Spaniards again served as peacemakers, ending the existing hostilities between the Apalachee and the neighboring bands of Chacato, Yamasee (Amacano), and Apalachicola (Vega Castro y Pardo 1639b).

After that success, the major remaining threat to peace in the region was a group identified by the Spaniards as Chisca. The Spaniards characterized them as a warlike people originally from New Mexico who gloried in their bellicosity and who wandered freely through the various provinces of the Southeast.[2] Although the authorities then were hopeful of persuading them to

2. De Soto a century earlier had encountered elements of this nation in north-central Mississippi. His chroniclers designated them as Quisquis. The accounts of the Juan Pardo expeditions of the 1560s place them in the Appalachian Mountains of Tennessee between the Nollachucky

settle down as allies of Spain (Vega Castro y Pardo 1639b), their efforts failed. Less than a decade later some Chisca incited the pagan Apalachee to revolt in an abortive effort to throw off Spanish control and to halt the growing Christianization of the tribe (Royal Officials 1647a). For the rest of the mission period the Chisca were to remain a thorn in the side of the Spaniards and of the Christianized natives of these western regions, whether they were Apalachee, Chacato, or Chine (Fernández de Florencia 1675b, 1678).

With this one exception, the arrival of the Spaniards initiated four decades of generally peaceful relations between the Apalachee and their non-Christian neighbors immediately to the west and northwest. Trading expeditions from Apalachee, organized either by the friars, the soldiers, the Spanish authorities, or the Indian leaders, appear to have gone to the villages of the Apalachicola with some regularity (Leturiondo 1672; Rebolledo 1657a:87, 89). In 1672, Captain Domingo de Leturiondo reported that the Indians of the province of Apalachicola were submissive to the governor's lieutenant in Apalachee; he said that soldiers went regularly to Apalachicola villages and that it was possible to trade among them with complete security. In the late 1640s Governor Bento Ruíz de Salazar himself journeyed to the Apalachicola country (Leturiondo 1672; Rebolledo 1657d). In the early 1660s the governor's deputy in Apalachee, Pedro de Ortes, accompanied by a body of infantry, set out to explore the province of the Chata (apparently, the Choctaw), which was believed to be beyond that of the Apalachicola. He dispatched a courier to contact the Chata when he reached Casista, then the last place in the province of Apalachicola, and four caciques came to Casista to pledge obedience, but they told him not to advance into their land because they were short of food. Accepting their evasion, Ortes left that exploration for another time, giving the visitors some beads and the corn that he had so that they might plant it (Ramirez 1687:108–110).

As a consequence of the growing English presence in South Carolina, at the time that Leturiondo wrote so confidently, developments were occurring that would soon interrupt that peaceful intercourse. Apalachee and the territory beyond it suddenly assumed greater importance, at least in the eyes of the Spanish officials in Florida, as a barrier to the spread of British influence

---

River and the Wautaugun and Holston rivers and identify them as a source of gold or copper for the natives to the south and east (DePratter, Hudson, and Smith 1983:132–134). Testimony taken by Governor Canzo in 1600 from two Indian women native to that interior region, which they left as girls at the time of the second Pardo expedition, also identified the Chisca Mountains as a source of gold and silver ornaments used by their people. In addition they described the Chisca as very white, ruddy, and blue-eyed with red or reddish blond hair and as natives who went about clothed and resembled Flemings. Alonso de Leturiondo, talking about the Chisca, referred to them as Caribs.

into the interior and, above all, against their pushing to the Gulf of Mexico from their coastal base in South Carolina.[3] In 1674, for the first time, the friars moved to establish a permanent presence among the Chacato and the Apalachicola to the west-northwest of the province of Apalachee. They established three missions, one on the Apalachicola River, just below the confluence of the Flint and the Chattahoochee rivers, to serve some of the Sabacola who had expressed an interest in becoming Christians, and the other two farther west-northwest in the vicinity of Marianna in the Chacato villages of San Nicolás de Tolentino and San Carlos de Yatcatani.[4]

The site of San Nicolás was a large cavern described as capable of housing more than 200 people; it contained a large spring and was well lit from three natural apertures in the walls of the cave (Barreda 1693:267–268; Díaz Vara Calderón 1675; Hita Salazar 1678b; Torres y Ayala 1693a:231, 255). Both San Nicolás and San Carlos were exposed sites and consequently were short lived. A revolt arose there in 1675 because those who wished to remain pagan resented the friars' pressure on them to become Christians and especially because the friar at San Nicolás rebuked two warriors, one for adultery and the other for polygamy, and moved to strip the latter of three of his wives. The revolt involved an attempt on the friar's life inspired by elements from both villages.

As in the 1647 Apalachee revolt, the Chisca were deeply involved. One of the ringleaders, Juan de Diosale, was referred to as a great tascaya, the son of a Chisca, greatly feared because he was part Chisca and had a following among the Chisca, some of whom were always to be found at his house. In enlisting support, the plotters threatened the recalcitrant that they would have the Chisca come and kill them all.[5] Upon the arrival of a relief force from Apalachee under the governor's deputy, the conspirators fled to a prearranged refuge at Tavasa. To prepare such a retreat for themselves, in case it should be needed, they had sent gifts both to Tavasa and to Achito. Although several of them later returned to be tried, and, although the majority of the villagers remained loyal, the governor, writing in August 1675, considered the missions there terminated. He probably regarded them as indefensible because of their distance from San Luis. Sometime before the fall of 1677, the inhabitants of both Chacato missions near Marianna abandoned their settlements. In

3. Conversely, the English settlers saw the Spanish presence, especially in Apalachee, as an obstacle to their thrust to the Gulf and into the lower Mississippi valley.
4. There is passing reference to a third settlement, San Antonio. It appears to have been a small village, and it was not a mission center but only a *visita.*
5. At this time, Chisca, Chacato, and Pansacola (or some of them at least) were living in amity. The Chisca settlement much farther west, which was the target of an Apalachee expedition two years later, was shared with Chacato and Pansacola.

that year an Apalachee expedition that stopped at both sites spoke of them as abandoned and deserted. They carefully reconnoitered the village of San Carlos, however, looking for Chisca, observing that they used it regularly as a stopping place on their raiding expeditions (Fernández de Florencia 1675b, 1678; Hita Salazar 1675b).

For a considerable period of time before 1676, the Apalachee had suffered nighttime raids for slaves by bands of Indians they were unable to identify further than that they were Chisca or Chichimeco.[6] Stimulated perhaps by the growing English demand for Indian slaves, the raiders became bolder; in 1676 successive raids against Ivitachuco, against the Chine at Chacariz, and against Cupaica established Chisca as the culprits.

Once the crops had been harvested, Indian leaders at San Luis proposed a retaliatory expedition against a palisaded village of the Chisca far to the west. San Luis and Cupaica responded with 160 of the 190-man expeditionary force. Another 18 came from the settlements of Chine and Chacato, which were located on lands that were under the jurisdiction of San Luis. The leaders of the nine other Apalachee villages turned a deaf ear to San Luis's appeal for support, for reasons that were left unexplained in the report on the expedition. Three of those nine villages provided a total of only six warriors, who volunteered without any encouragement from their chiefs.

During the night of the eighteenth day out from Apalachee, guided by the Chacato scouts and trail guides, the expedition reached the Chisca settlement. Because the village housed Chacato and Pansacola as well, the Chacato could choose not to participate in the attack on their fellow tribesmen. Five of eight Chacato took that option. Despite the fact that the inhabitants were still awake at three in the morning, apparently dancing around huge fires maintained both within and outside of the palisade, the attackers retained the element of surprise until almost the last moment, when a Chacato sentinel spotted them and gave the alarm. Having found the village too large to be surrounded (the village was described as being over 300 paces in length per side around the circuit of the palisade), they took the village by storm with a mass attack along one side of the palisade, killing and wounding a considerable number of the inhabitants. Many of the enemy were burned alive in the structures in which they had taken refuge. Ultimately the survivors fled across the stream below the bluff on which the village was located.

Five Apalachee were killed and 40 wounded. Because of the magnitude of their casualties, the Apalachee made no effort to continue the attack, even

6. This is one of the occasions when the Spaniards (and, in this case, the Apalachee as well) use these tribal names to indicate diverse peoples. Swanton and Anglo-Americans in general consider Chisca, Chichimeco, and Yuchi to be simply different names for the same people.

though the Chisca continued to shoot arrows across the narrow stream into the remains of their village. On the third day after the encounter the Apalachee torched what was left of the village and started home. A troop of Chisca who came out onto the trail to challenge them were dispersed by the inija Bentura from San Luis and the captain Don Bernardo from Cupaica, whose shots struck down two Chisca warriors.

Although sanctioned by the lieutenant, this expedition was initiated and organized entirely by the Indian leaders from San Luis and Cupaica. The lieutenant provided ammunition, powder, and musketballs, but no Spaniards accompanied the expedition, not even a friar to serve as chaplain. Upon its return, the lieutenant took down a report on the exploit in the Apalachee tongue precisely as it was given to him by the expedition's leaders. In forwarding that report to Spain, the governor suggested that its leaders be rewarded by the Crown with gifts of clothing, and that request was granted (Fernández de Florencia 1678; Hita Salazar 1678b; Junta 1680).

From that report, from two journals that record a 1693 overland trek from San Luis to Pensacola Bay, and from other sources, it appears that the Apalachee were not accustomed to venturing much beyond the Apalachicola River into the territory directly west of them. Both expeditions relied on Chacato as guides and scouts. When buffalo were encountered, it was the Chacato who killed them (Barreda 1693:272; Fernández de Florencia 1678; Torres y Ayala 1693a:230, 237). In the winter of 1698–1699, when one of the Spanish settlers at San Luis set out to hunt buffalo, he was accompanied by a band of 40 Chacato (Hinachuba 1699:26–27). These incidents could indicate that the Apalachee were not familiar with buffalo hunting.

During this period there do not seem to have been buffalo in northwest Florida any farther east than the area just west of the Chipola River. In his 1686 expedition, Marcos Delgado began to encounter buffalo west of the Chipola River, and it was somewhat farther west that the 1693 expedition first encountered them. A decade or so after the depopulation of the region resulting from the destruction of the Apalachee and the Timucuan missions, Diego de Peña, on his way through those areas to visit the Apalachicola on the Chattahoochee, reported killing buffalo on repeated occasions from east of the Santa Fé River to the chicasas of the western Apalachee missions and the Lake Jackson prairie. He described those regions as abounding in cattle, particularly buffalo (Boyd 1949:14–18).

The Apalachee also showed unfamiliarity with the sympathetic magic employed by the Chisca. On their trip homeward they encountered four shells placed in a clearing along the trail together with some pots of boiled herbs. They had to consult the Chacato on the meaning of that assemblage; the Chacato informed them that it was a charm designed to prevent their finding their way back to their own land so that they would die of hunger on the trail (Fernández de Florencia 1678).

The Indians' report on this expedition clearly illustrates the difficulties experienced when sizable bands of warriors struck out at enemies who lived some distance away. The Apalachee appear to have been able to carry regular rations for no more than four of five days of travel beyond their base of operations. It took them three days to reach Santa Cruz de Sabacola on their trek from Apalachee; they spent two days there to reprovision themselves. Four days after resuming their march west-northwest, they had exhausted their food supplies except for a little tolocano. They consumed a handful of it at midmorning, and that was their only sustenance for the next two days, after which they ate nothing for a day or so until they killed a cow buffalo. Having consumed it before they reached their destination, the Chacato, less committed to the expedition's goal than the rest, began to complain among themselves of the hunger and toil. They murmured that the Apalachee were boys who did not know how to fight, who would flee on coming face to face with the Chisca and imperil the lives of all. They made plans to abandon the enterprise by slipping away in the morning soon after they returned to the trail. Having overheard their plans and complaints, the Apalachee leaders admonished them to endure the difficulties with Christian resignation, warning them that they would carry them on by force, if necessary, until they had guided them to the Chisca settlement. On their return trip a relief column from Apalachee met them with food the day after their stopover at one of the abandoned Chacato villages (Fernández de Florencia 1678).

This Apalachee initiative against the Chisca was a prelude to two decades of conflict that began in 1685 and culminated in the destruction of the missions and the depopulation of the province. After that campaign, the Christian Sabacola, whose chief, Baltasar, had joined the expedition with a small contingent of his warriors, seem to have found it advisable to return to their village site along the middle Chattahoochee with their fellow Apalachicola. This move led to the dispatch of three friars in 1679 to establish a mission there, which also bore the name Santa Cruz de Sabacola.[7] The friars' leader was the veteran Fray Juan Ocón, who had been the pastor of the earlier village of Santa Cruz de Sabacola in 1675 when the wounded friar from the Chacato mission sought refuge there. Only a few days after their arrival at Sabacola the friars were ordered out by the cacique of Caveta, who was the head chief among the Apalachicola. They complied, and Governor Salazar instructed his deputy in Apalachee to accept the friars' expulsion with good grace and to continue to treat the Apalachicola as friends (Bolton 1925a:119; Hita Salazar

7. John Tate Lanning's reference to this effort as occurring in 1680 is obviously in error.

1680a, n.d.; Royal Officials 1680). His more militant and irascible successor, Juan Marques Cabrera, sent two friars back to Sabacola accompanied by 11 soldiers. They were received in a hostile fashion and withdrew after only a few months of futile waiting for the Indians' attitude to change. Governor Cabrera's threats of reprisals led to a compromise under which the Christianized Sabacola returned downriver to found a new settlement named Santa Cruz de Sabacola, which was a little distance above the confluence of the Flint and the Chattahoochee, about one-half league inland from the west bank of the Flint. By this time their old village site on the west bank of the Apalachicola just below the junction of those two rivers had been appropriated by a group of Chacato, who had formed another mission village called San Carlos de los Chacatos (Bolton 1925b:46–47; Boyd 1949:19; Marques Cabrera 1682).

This temporary papering over of the rift between the Spanish authorities and the majority of the Apalachicola was threatened in 1685 when Dr. Henry Woodward and a number of other English traders from South Carolina appeared among the Apalachicola. The governor's violence-prone deputy in Apalachee, Antonio Matheos, led a force of Spanish soldiers and Apalachee warriors into the Apalachicola's territory. Having set out in September 1685, they passed through the chicasa of Sabacola El Grande and the 11 inhabited towns of Jalipasle, Ocone, Apalachicola, Achito, Ocute, Osuchi, Ocmulgee, Casista, Colone, Caveta, and Tasquique. Angered by the Apalachicola's lack of cooperation in handing over the traders, Matheos wished to burn a number of the villages but was dissuaded by the Apalachee leaders and one of the Spanish soldiers who were with him. He contented himself with consuming or destroying their supplies of food and chickens and with sacking their houses (Bolton 1925a:121; Ximénez 1687:30).

On being informed of the traders' emergence from hiding to circulate freely again in those Apalachicola towns nominally subject to the Spanish Crown, Matheos hastened back in December 1685 with a force of up to 600 Indians and between 30 and 40 Spanish soldiers for a second try at capturing the elusive traders.[8] This time he carried orders from the governor to destroy any of the Apalachicola towns that overtly flaunted the Spanish demands for the surrender of the Englishmen and the severance of all dealings with them. With the exception of Chief Pentecolo's village of Apalachicola, the natives adopted the strategy of abandoning their villages upon the approach of Matheos. Despite his use of torture to obtain information concerning the where-

---

8. The testimony from a number of the soldiers present in the second expedition varied in some details. The estimates concerning the size of the Indian force ranged between "over 100" to 600. They differed also on the number of deerskins and other pelts expropriated, the quantity and color of the wool socks found in the Englishmen's storehouse, and even on the identity of one of the villages that was destroyed.

abouts of the seven English traders, Matheos's only success on this expedition was commercial. In the woods near Caveta he found a storehouse belonging to the English traders, and he appropriated its considerable quantity of deerskins and other pelts and its small amount of trade goods. While he sojourned at Caveta during several weeks of winter rains, trading parties arrived from Tiquipache and Atossi (in the Upper Creek country) to barter an additional quantity of animal skins, *guaypiles,* and other goods.

Through the influence of Chief Pentecolo, the headmen of seven of the Apalachicola settlements (Ocmulgee, Osuchi, Ocute, Achito, Ocone, Jalopasle, and an unnamed small village) were persuaded to meet with Matheos at Caveta in order to pledge to have no further dealings with the English and to be pardoned for past violations of this order. The four northern towns of Colone, Casista, Caveta, and Tasquique refused to appear or to make any such pledges.[9] Before his return to Apalachee, Matheos torched these four towns and destroyed their stores of food, causing concern among the Apalachee that this tactic sooner or later would bring retribution in kind on their own villages (Bolton 1925a:122; Guerrero 1687:104–105; Jorge 1687:110–111; Lanning 1935:178–180; Luxán 1687:111–13; Ramírez 1687:108–110; Vera 1687: 107–108). The majority of the eight towns that reaffirmed their loyalty to Spain appear to have been united linguistically as speakers of some variant of Hitchiti, closely related to the language of the Apalachee themselves, while three of the recalcitrant northern towns spoke Muskogee and the fourth, Tasquique, probably spoke Yamasee (Boyd 1949:25; 1952:113–114, 117; Swanton 1922:215).

Although even the destroyed towns soon asked for pardon and mercy, they continued to deal with the English traders, prompting Matheos to launch a third futile expedition in 1686. Under the next governor, who initially tried conciliation and apology for the excesses of his predecessor, all the villages renewed their pledges of allegiance to Spain but also continued to protect the English traders. The Spaniards dispatched two more futile expeditions before building a fort in the midst of the Apalachicola settlements to house a garrison of soldiers and Apalachee Indians to monitor the Apalachicola's compliance with Spain's demands and to be in a position to move quickly against any English traders who might appear.

In response many of the Apalachicola abandoned their settlements on the Chattahoochee to move eastward to the Ocmulgee, closer to the English.[10]

9. One witness identified the burned villages as "Cabeta, Casista, Viuchi and Colomo," another as "Osuchi, Casista, Taisquique and Caveta."

10. In the foreword to his 1953 publication of a number of documents on the Apalachee in *The Americas,* Boyd indicates that considerable numbers of the Apalachicola remained on the Chattahoochee (pp. 459–460).

There, by and large, they threw off even the pretense of submission to the Spanish authorities and began the series of raids and attacks in which the missions beyond St. Augustine and most of their inhabitants would disappear in just over a decade. At the end of 1691 the governor reported that planting and harvesting had been short because of the continual raids by non-Christian Indians. In 1691 the fort built at such cost in 1689 was abandoned and destroyed, as the Spanish and Apalachee garrison was ordered withdrawn. Four years later, to retaliate for an attack on the Christian Chacato, Governor Torres y Ayala dispatched a force of seven Spaniards and 400 Apalachee against the new Apalachicola settlements on the Ocmulgee. Finding most of the villages abandoned and destroyed in anticipation of their arrival, they only captured about 50 Indians (Bolton 1925a:123–125; Lanning 1935:182–184; Quiroga y Losada 1688b:219–221, 1690a, 1691b; Torres y Ayala 1695).

Around the turn of the century, peace treaties were worked out by the Apalachee to permit the restoration of trade with the Apalachicola and other neighboring non-Christian tribes. However, this objective was frustrated by the Spanish authorities' severe restrictions on that trade, forbidding the purchase of anything introduced by the English and the export by the Apalachee of horses, silver, or any other item that the Apalachicola might find marketable in their dealings with the English (Ayala Escobar 1701:33–34; Zúñiga y Zerda 1702:36–38). Angered by these restrictions, the Apalachicola tortured and murdered three members of an Apalachee mission who had gone to their land with peaceful intentions. This atrocity, together with an Apalachicola attack on the Timucua's mission village of Santa Fé in the spring of 1702, provoked the Apalachee to strike back by sending a force of 800 warriors led by a Spanish officer and accompanied by a few Spanish soldiers into Apalachicola country. En route they fell into an ambush set by a smaller but well-armed force of Apalachicola led by an Englishman, which had been on its way to raid some of the missions. In a disastrous rout the Apalachee suffered heavy losses. Most of the 300 who escaped left their arms behind, returning demoralized to await the catastrophe in which the Apalachee mission system would disappear less than two years later (Albuquerque 1703; Bolton 1925a:126–127; Romo de Urisa 1702). The Colonel Boll map put the toll of killed and captured at 600 (Chatelain 1941:map 8).

An undetermined number of the Apalachee were taken prisoner. A Christian Chacato woman living in Achito, who reached San Luis several days after the battle, reported that she passed through a place in which the returning Apalachicola force had camped for the night and, from the many withes that they left behind, she realized that they had many captives with them (Solana 1702). Many, if not all, of those captive Apalachee were sent on to South Carolina, apparently for sale as slaves. On January 23, 1703, the Carolina

Commons House of Assembly debated whether the Apalachee who were taken by the Cavetans and the English traders were to be considered "plunder to be divided within the Act for raising the sum of two thousand pounds for carrying on an expedition against St. Augustine" (Salley 1934:72–73). The Commons House of Assembly's *Journal* reported that this motion was voted down but provided no additional information about the fate of those captives.

As a prelude to the final assaults of 1704, a hostile force attacked the village of Ocuia in 1703. The governor's note reporting that event has not yet been found. We know of that note from a passing reference in the governor's March 1704 letter to the Crown reporting Colonel James Moore's attack on the province. The governor stated that in the incursions made since the lifting of the 1702 siege of St. Augustine, "San Joseph de Ocuia in Apalachee, Pilitiriva, and San Francisco have all been destroyed and many Indians killed, and in all they have carried off more than 500 prisoners" (Zúñiga y Zerda 1704a: 48–50).[11] In reporting the disastrous 1702 encounter on the Flint, the lieutenant had mentioned Ocuia as one of the frontier villages (along with Bacuqua and Escambé) that was in danger. He suggested its removal to the road so that it would be more accessible to relief forces (Solana 1702).

In contrast to these hostile relations, a number of bands from neighboring tribes were settled peacefully within Apalachee territory, particularly during the mission era. If the Oconee, the group most often mentioned in this respect, settled in Apalachee, they seem to have come prior to the mission era. San Francisco de Oconi appears on the first mission lists. Its inhabitants claimed that their settlement was the first place in the province into which Christianity entered. The name Oconi attached to the mission appears to be the only reason for considering its inhabitants to be other than Apalachee. It may legitimately be asked if that conclusion is justified.

The Spaniards never indicated Oconi's inhabitants as other than Apalachee. This failure contrasts sharply with the pains they took to identify the tribal affiliation of the other non-Apalachee groups who established settlements there, namely, the Yamasee, the Tama, the Chine, the Capara, the Chacato, and the Tocobaga. Such villages were usually referred to as San Carlos *of the* Chacatos or as San Pedro *of the* Chines. San Francisco was always referred to as San Francisco of Oconi and never as San Francisco *of the* Oconees. The fact that two mission villages, generally recognized as Apalachee, had satellite villages bearing the names of other neighboring tribes— the village of Pansacola, a satellite of Aspalaga, and Sabacola, a satellite of Ocuia—also argues against Oconi being other than Apalachee. It might also be noted that in the inquiry into the origins of the Apalachee ball game in the

11. Boyd (1951:188) identified Pilitiriva as San Pedro de Potohiriba. San Francisco was Potano.

1670s, one of the authorities consulted by the two Apalachee researchers was the inija of the village of Oconi. Inasmuch as the Oconee were Hitchiti speakers like the Apalachee, the use of language cannot resolve this problem, although it might be noted that the same interpreter was always used to interview the inhabitants of San Francisco de Oconi as was used in the known Apalachee villages. In addition, in contrast to the villages clearly identified with non-Apalachees, San Francisco de Oconi supplied workers for various purposes alongside the villages that were indisputably Apalachee.

In summary, at no time is any differentiation made between the people at San Francisco de Oconi and the other Apalachee, which is something that cannot be said in relation to the villages of the Chine, Chacato, Tama, and other non-Apalachee villages (Díaz Vara Calderón 1675:8–9; Florencia 1695; Hita Salazar 1675b; Leturiondo 1678; Rebolledo 1657a:91, 97–99). In the absence of other evidence and in the face of the Spanish practice of calling attention to the non-Apalachee inhabitants of other alien settlements, it cannot be assumed that Oconi is not an Apalachee village.

Presumably, when these non-Apalachee groups settled within Apalachee, the immigrants and the leaders of the Apalachee town on whose lands they settled reached some agreement about the newcomers' rights and obligations. The villages seem to have been jealous of intrusions even with respect to the hunting lands under their jurisdiction (Florencia 1695; Leturiondo 1678).[12] As noted earlier, the Chine and Chacato, on occasion at least, were settled on lands belonging to San Luis. The Tama village was also located within the same jurisdiction. On another occasion a band of refugee Chacato was temporarily lodged in the village of Cupaica. The one agreement that we have knowledge of governing such intrusive settlements was worked out between the Chacato and the leaders of San Luis. It established the terms for the Chacato's reoccupation of a village site within the jurisdiction of San Luis that they or other Chacato had possessed earlier. The Chacato were granted a free gift of the lands associated with the village site for the purpose of cultivation and an unrestricted right to hunt deer, hens, and other birds and animals with the following exceptions and restrictions. They were to hunt bears only in company with the inhabitants of San Luis, and only at a time they set, and were to have their share of the meat only from the animals they themselves killed, that share to consist of breast, stomach, and back. From the better cuts San Luis would allot the Chacato a portion sufficient for the Chacato to fulfill their obligations to their priest. Any bearskin was to go to the cacique of San Luis, as was the skin of any panthers they killed, but the Apalachee did not

---

12. During the 1677–1678 visitation, Ychutafun's chief complained that people from Oconi were
    hunting on their land.

want any of the panther meat. The hunting of a particular white bird was prohibited but, should they kill one, they were to present it at the council house and make the customary atonement. The harvesting of grapes and nuts was to be done in conjunction with the Apalachee at times they set. The Chacato could keep what they themselves gathered, and might harvest other fruits whenever it suited them (Florencia 1695).

There is some indication that the Tocobaga settlement at Wacissa was established without the prior acquiescence of the Apalachee. In 1678 the visitor Leturiondo instructed the latter not to disturb the settlement, as it rendered great service to the Crown by manning canoes for trade with St. Augustine by way of the Suwannee.

Chapter 9

San Luis: Village, Fort, and Mission

THIS CHAPTER contains a detailed view of the physical layout of the Apalachee village San Luis de Talimali. As the Spaniards' administrative headquarters, the home of one of the most important chiefs of the province, and the largest of the missions, San Luis merits special attention. It is a measure of its importance that it is the one village whose existence and location were never lost sight of. It probably was typical of the rest of the larger Apalachee villages, except for the features resulting from the presence of the lieutenant and the Spanish soldiers and ranchers.

The Christian name of San Luis first appears in the records in 1654 and 1655: It received passing mention in 1654 in a letter written in Timucuan, and it appeared in 1655 as San Luis de Apalachee on the Díez de la Calle list. As noted, the San Luis de Jinayca of 1657 probably represented the same corporate entity as de Soto's Anhayca and Fray Prieto's Inihayca. The village's last appearance under that historic name was in 1657. When next mentioned in the available records, 18 years later, it was identified as San Luis de Talimali, the name it retained from that time. To date, no explanation has been advanced for this name change.

The name San Luis may indicate that it was one of the earliest of the missions founded in Apalachee. It may have been a tribute to the governor Luis Horruytiner, under whom the formal mission era began. Cupaica, founded in 1639, is known to have been named San Damián for the incumbent governor, Damián de Vega Castro y Pardo, who was godfather at the baptism of the village's chief, Baltasar (Vega Castro y Pardo 1639a). Because of the importance of Jinayca as the seat of the "lord of the province" and because of its chief having journeyed to St. Augustine in 1608 to render the province's obedience to the Crown, it would have been likely, along with Ivitachuco, to have been among the first chosen to become mission sites.

Jinayca's predecessor, identified only by the name of Apalachen, was de-

194

scribed by Cabeza de Vaca, who was there with Narváez in 1528, as a town that "consisted of forty small houses made low and set up in sheltered places because of the frequent storms. The material was thatch. They were surrounded by very dense woods, large groves, many bodies of fresh water in which so many and so large trees were fallen that they form obstructions rendering travel difficult and dangerous" (Núñez Cabeza de Vaca 1966:35). The site seems to be distinct from the one described by the de Soto chroniclers. Garcilaso described the village where de Soto wintered as a "village which consisted of two hundred and fifty large and good houses . . . [with] the habitations of the Cacique, which were located on one side of the town and as royal dwellings had advantages over all the others. In addition to the principal town there were many more scattered throughout the vicinity at a half league, one, and one and a half, two, and at times three leagues apart. Some comprised fifty or sixty dwellings and others a hundred more or less, not to mention another great number which were sprinkled about and not arranged as a town" (Vega 1951:184). The Gentleman of Elvas described the village of Anhayca Apalache thus: "The Campmaster, whose duty it is to divide and lodge the men, quartered them about the town, at the distance of half a league to a league apart. There were other towns . . . On Saturday, the twenty-ninth of November, in a high wind, an Indian passed through the sentries undiscovered and set fire to the town, two portions of which, in consequence, were instantly consumed" (Elvas 1904:47, 49). This settlement would appear to be a much larger one situated in more open country than the one portrayed by Cabeza de Vaca. And it accords more with the settlement pattern as sketchily portrayed for the mission era.

There San Luis was described as surrounded by four satellite villages belonging to its jurisdiction. In 1675 San Luis and its satellites contained about 1,400 people (Fernández de Florencia 1675a; Leturiondo 1678; Rebolledo 1657a). That same year Bishop Calderón recorded that "In the mission of San Luis . . . resides a military officer in a country house defended by pieces of ordnance and a garrison of infantry" (Díaz Vara Calderón 1675:9). The bishop's "country-house" was probably the blockhouse or strong house, which the chief of San Luis promised Governor Rebolledo that he would build to house the enlarged garrison. San Luis is known from various sources to have possessed a council house. It no doubt conformed to the general description provided by Calderón of a structure built of wood "and covered with straw, round, and with a very large opening in the top." "Most of them," he added, "can accommodate from 2,000 to 3,000 persons. They are furnished all around the interior with niches called barbacôas which serve as beds and as seats for the caciques and chiefs and as lodgings for soldiers and transients" (Díaz Vara Calderón 1675:13).

Beyond that reference there is little information available on the housing of the soldiers at San Luis, and little is known about their presence there in the early years of the mission period. It does not appear that soldiers accompanied the first two friars in 1633, although one would have expected them to in view of the repeated remarks in the 1612 era concerning the need for the soldiers because of the natives' hostility toward the friars and the chiefs' inability to control unruly tribesmen.

The soldiers

Soldiers were not placed in San Luis until 1638, early in the term of the successor to Governor Luis de Horruytiner, the governor who brought the friars to Apalachee in 1633. The garrison remained there as well under the following governor, Benito Ruíz de Salazar, and under his interim successor, Nicolás Ponce de León. Shortly after the accession of Pedro Benedit Horruytiner as interim governor late in 1651, the soldiers were withdrawn at the request of the friars (Fernández de Olivera 1612a, 1612b; Martínez 1612; Rebolledo 1657a:109–110, 1657e).[1]

At the time of the Apalachee uprising early in 1647, when Pedro Horruytiner was serving as acting governor, the soldiers of the Apalachee garrison were not in Apalachee proper but were at Ruíz de Salazar's wheat farm near Asile, on the edge of Apalachee, tending to their wheat plantings. It is not clear whether that move was a temporary one or whether Ruíz de Salazar made his ranch the headquarters for the soldiers. Some of the comments concerning that enterprise indicate that the soldiers were there for much of the time that the farm was in operation, but remarks by the friars picture the soldiers as traveling around Apalachee as commercial agents for Ruíz de Salazar. And, inasmuch as Governor Rebolledo considered Asile to be part of Apalachee, he would not have considered their presence on the wheat farm as an absence from Apalachee. Having been outside of the province when the revolt began, the soldiers escaped unharmed, in contrast to the lieutenant and his family, who were attending festivities at Bacuqua, where the revolt started.

There is no indication where or how the lieutenant and his small force were domiciled at San Luis before 1657. Comments made during the Rebolledo visitation indicate that it was the custom of the soldiers to visit and spend time in some of the villages. On those occasions, presumably, they were lodged in the village council house as any other guest would be. The visitation record established that while they were on such trips they were fed by the Indians of the village concerned, but probably, from the time of the lieutenant's

---

1. Governor Rebolledo's remarks indicate that the lieutenant was also withdrawn from Apalachee at this time.

arrival in San Luis in 1645 or 1646, both the lieutenant and the soldiers had a residence and defensive structure. From that time the lieutenant appears to have established his headquarters at the site to which the chief of San Luis moved his village in 1656, because a later document states that the lieutenants had always resided there. Presumably this location was chosen for its elevation, the expanse of level land on the hilltop, and the presence of springs along the northeastern base of the hill, and because it was not very distant from the head village of San Luis prior to the 1656 move (Rebolledo 1657a: passim; Royal Officials 1647a, 1647b). That the need for a blockhouse was mentioned in 1612 when the establishment of the permanent Apalachee mission enterprise was first considered makes it equally likely that some such structure was built even earlier, soon after the arrival of the first soldiers.

Various secondary sources, such as Chatelain and Lanning, speak of a fort having been built at San Luis between 1640 and 1650; Chatelain adds that it was manned by 12 soldiers but cites only two secondary sources as the authority for his statement, an article by Boyd and Lanning's *Spanish Missions of Georgia*. Boyd offers no evidence for his statement, and Lanning presents only a muddled reference to the building of a fort at San Luis, which seems to pertain to the 1650s rather than to the 1640s (Chatelain 1941:133n.9; Lanning 1935:206, 274n.15). In speaking of the conflict between Governor Rebolledo and the friars in the mid-1650s over the governor's alleged mistreatment of the Indians, Lanning states that "Although Governor Rebolledo contended that he always paid the Indians for the work he required, the friars showed that for ninety-six days of labor on the wood work of the *presidio* at San Luis de Apalache they received pay for only twenty-five. . . . It irked the friars that the governor elected to leave a dozen soldiers in the *presidio* at San Luis" (1935:206). Lanning does not cite his documentary source for this information but offers only this confusing explanatory comment in a footnote: "Built in the time of Governor Benito Ruíz Salazar between 1645 and 1650" (1935:274n. 15).

Lanning's statement raises the question of why, if the fort was built in Governor Salazar Vallecilla's time, there were 96 days of labor on its woodwork done at Governor Rebolledo's behest. Lanning's source was a mid-1657 letter to the governor by six of the friars. It establishes that the 96 days of labor involved the preparation of lumber for the fort at St. Augustine (Moral et al. 1657).

The primary sources I have read seem to rule out the existence of any fort at San Luis immediately before 1657 and to negate the presence of Chatelain's 12 soldiers during the 1640s. Governor Rebolledo's intensive lobbying of the native leaders in 1657 to win their approval of the expansion of the garrison to 12 men and to gain their acquiescence to the building of a blockhouse there implies that the existing force was considerably less and that there was no blockhouse or fort there before that year. It is possible that deputy governor Claudio Florencia's house was sufficiently well constructed and armed to merit being referred to as a fort; no evidence has been advanced to indicate that that was the case, but logic and common sense seem to point in that direction.

Soon after assuming the governorship, Rebolledo began to reverse his predecessor's policy of giving the friars, the only Spaniards in Apalachee, free rein over the natives. His first move was the dispatch of a lieutenant with two soldiers to administer justice to the natives, settle their disputes with one another, and protect them from what Rebolledo regarded as the excesses of the friars. Some time after this lieutenant's arrival, an English ship reaching St. Marks was able to obtain provisions from the natives in exchange for knives, hatchets, and other goods. On learning of the ship's presence, the governor dispatched a 30-man force under Captain Gregorio Bravo as a temporary expedient to bolster the position of his lieutenant, who had rallied the native forces to discourage any intention the intruders might have had of establishing themselves on the Apalachee coast or of moving inland.

This incident, along with the developments in England, the 1656 revolt in Timucua, and the fear that the unrest might spread to Apalachee, served Governor Rebolledo as a pretext for a stronger Spanish presence in Apalachee than what the friars desired. He expressed particular alarm over the Puritan domination of England by Oliver Cromwell and his military and conservative-radical gentry in 1653; these elements were the chief Spaniard-haters in England and were also the most aggressive in colonizing and piracy. In 1655 an expedition dispatched by Cromwell the preceding year captured Jamaica after suffering a disastrous rout in its attempt to seize control of Santo Domingo. To forestall a similar move against richly endowed Apalachee, Rebolledo felt that the Spanish presence there had to be expanded greatly.

That expansion would begin with the stationing of a 12-man force in Apalachee under the lieutenant and with the construction of a blockhouse. Ultimately, Rebolledo envisioned the construction of a true fort in addition to the simple blockhouse. He intended a considerable increase in the size of the garrison once he had overcome the friars' objections and the natives' reluctance. The capstone was to be the creation of a Spanish settlement in Apalachee that would solidify Spain's hold on the food and labor resources of this province, which was so vital for the survival of St. Augustine itself. Without such strengthening of the Spanish presence, he argued, the English enemy could occupy a port such as St. Marks, fortify it, and become strongly entrenched, before the officials at St. Augustine would be able to do anything about it. With such a base, he continued, the English could threaten the treasure fleets and other shipping in the Gulf between New Spain and Havana. He believed that strengthening the Spanish presence in Apalachee would make the province a springboard from which to begin the conversion of the neighboring provinces of the Apalachicola and the Chacato, who had both expressed an interest in receiving friars (Parry and Sherlock 1968:58–61; Rebolledo 1657a:94, 96, 98, 101, 108–114, 1657e).

The opposition of the friars and others and their influence with the Crown helped to bring about the deposition and arrest of Rebolledo before he could put much of his plan into operation. During his 1657 visitation of Apalachee, Rebolledo had lobbied its native leaders vigorously to agree to the expansion of the garrison and to the building of a blockhouse. Various chiefs expressed support for the building of such a blockhouse, and the chief of San Luis pledged to build a capacious and strong house for the soldiers. The available documents do not indicate when he fulfilled that promise. The next mention of such a structure was in a letter of Bishop Calderón's, in which he speaks of a strong fortified country house at San Luis (Díaz Vara Calderón 1675:8; Rebolledo 1657a: 94, 96, 98, 101). During the intervening period this structure ceased to be a bone of contention between the friars and the governors and no further lobbying was done for the building, so it appears that the chief fulfilled his promise without undue delay.

But the chief balked at raising the garrison to 12 men, alleging a lack of food to meet the needs of additional soldiers because of the difficulties (unspecified) of the preceding winter and the disruptions occasioned by his having just moved his village. He suggested that six soldiers and a corporal would be enough for the present (Rebolledo 1657a: 115–118).[2] This was a significant setback for the governor. During the visitation, the chief of San Luis was the only Apalachee leader who genuinely approved of the garrison's expansion and took the initiative in asking for more soldiers. Encouraged by the friars, all the Apalachee leaders opposed the governor's plans at a subsequent meeting convoked by the chief of Ivitachuco and held at San Luis (Moral et al. 1657). Although Rebolledo, at the height of the controversy, told the Franciscan provincial that he would return to the regime of two soldiers and the lieutenant until he heard from the Crown on this issue, the governor seems to have forgotten his pledge, keeping a 12–man garrison in the province (Matter 1972:183, 185–186; Rebolledo 1657a: 107–114, 121–123). The friars at this time and for some time thereafter not only opposed the ex-

---

2. This suggestion appears in two of four letters to the governor by soldiers in Apalachee that are appended to the visitation record along with many other items relating to the controversy over the building of the blockhouse and the expansion of the garrison. Pearson (1968: 116–117) attributed this conversation to the chief of Bacuqua, although admitting that the chief was not mentioned in the soldiers' letters.

pansion of the garrison but clamored for its complete removal from the province (Franciscan Friars 1664; Moral et al. 1657; Rebolledo 1657a:passim).

On the basis of the fragmentary research available on the garrison at San Luis, its size seems to have fluctuated sharply after 1657. Using several notes written in 1659 by Governor Aranguíz y Cotes, Matter reported that in that year the governor spoke of putting up to 30 men in Apalachee (Matter 1972:187). Whether he did so is not indicated, but Griffen commented on one of the documents he listed in his calendar for the Stetson Collection that by 1662 the number had risen to 40 (Aranguíz y Cotes 1662a).[3] This sudden expansion undoubtedly was associated with the expedition during that time, led by Pedro de Ortes, to explore the Choctaw country (Ramírez 1687:108–110). By mid-1668 the garrison had shrunk once more to 12 men (Arguellas 1668; Guerra y Vega 1668c). In October 1671, Governor Cendoya reported that Apalachee had a force of 25 men, but just over a year later it was reported as 19 men, a level that it appears to have maintained until at least 1675 (Matter 1972:192–194). At some point before the end of Governor Hita Salazar's term in 1680 the garrison again shrank to 12 men (Hita Salazar n.d.), but by the early part of that year it had risen again to 24 (Hita Salazar 1680c).

Bushnell reported that, in response to the growing threat from the Carolinians, there were 45 men in the garrison by 1682 (Bushnell 1978b:2). A more immediate reason for the additional men was the rising tension between the Spanish authorities and the Apalachicola. The tension grew out of the Cavetan chieftain's ejection of the friars who had attempted to establish a mission at Sabacola on the Chattahoochee in 1679 and Governor Marques Cabrera's decision to attempt to reestablish the mission by sending back two friars with 11 soldiers. Although both the friars and the soldiers withdrew after only a few months, because the majority of the Apalachicola remained hostile to the mission effort, the garrison was probably maintained at this higher level. Apalachee and the Apalachicola country suddenly assumed greater importance for the Spaniards as the Carolinians began their attack on Guale and their push inland toward the Apalachicola country and as the French drove to establish a presence on the Gulf.

The fort at St. Marks

The major cause for the expansion of the garrison in Apalachee in 1682 was probably the destruction that year of the short-lived first fort at San Marcos de Apalachee. It had been built several years earlier to protect the coastal approach to the province. As in the mid-1650s, the appearance of an English

---

3. Matter also gives this number, presumably having obtained it from the document itself.

ship in that port in June 1677 had pointed up the need to improve the province's defenses. On this occasion the intruders carried off a frigate belonging to Diego de Florencia with its cargo of deerskins and trade goods. Before dawn on March 20, 1682, another pirate ship anchored off the fort and, on seeing a supply ship behind the fort, resolved to attack. There were only the commandant and a five-man garrison in the fort, and it was taken easily and quickly when someone inside opened its gate to the attackers. Doris Olds speculated that this was not the usual garrison. Ten or twelve Spaniards and a few Indians would seem a more likely number in normal times.

By coincidence, Andrés Pérez, the lieutenant from San Luis, had arrived after nightfall, accompanied by several soldiers and an unspecified number of native warriors.[4] Having been denied entry to the fort, the lieutenant and his companions spent the night in the nearby settlement. On learning of the attack on the fort, they beat a judicious retreat inland, leaving those in the fort to fend for themselves.[5]

In addition to the six defenders, three friars and the captain of the supply ship were taken prisoner in the fort. Two of the friars had come down to meet the third, who had come in on the supply ship. Some of the prisoners, including one of the friars, were soon released to go to San Luis to demand ransom for the freedom of the others. After waiting in vain for about two weeks for the ransom, the pirates departed; they took only the commandant and a young soldier, having released their other prisoners. After about two months at sea, the commandant and the soldier were put ashore in Cuba to make room for three women whom the pirates had captured during a raid on several coastal estates.

Before leaving, the pirates stripped the San Marcos fort of everything that was useful and portable and destroyed what they left, including the fort itself (Boyd 1936:4–5; Leturiondo 1678:584; Olds 1962:10–20; Wenhold 1956: 301–314). The details on the building of that fort and on what was done to replace it are shrouded in mystery and confusion. The need for a fort there was suggested as early as 1657.[6] Governor Aranguíz y Cotes, in 1659, ap-

---

4. In an article on the fort, Boyd describes the garrison at the time of the pirates' attack as having no fewer than 45 Spaniards and 400 natives. His source for those figures is not clear, but they seem unrealistically high for an area so remote and infrequently visited. It is possible that he interpreted the presence of the lieutenant as indicating that the entire garrison from San Luis was present.

5. Wenhold suggested that the fort commandant's refusal to admit the lieutenant hints at strained relations between the two (1956:309n.9).

6. In their opposition to Governor Rebolledo's plan to build a blockhouse at San Luis, some of the friars suggested that the blockhouse be placed at the port to put distance between the soldiers and the natives. Rebolledo may have contemplated building a fort at the coast in addition to the blockhouse he wanted at San Luis.

pears to have been the first governor to press the project, considering it so urgent that he offered to have a fort built there at his own expense. The suspicious Crown authorities demurred, asking for information on the need, the suitability of the site, and, above all, the cost (Olds 1962:6–7). Although succeeding governors also supported the project, the Crown did not give its approval until June 20, 1676, and then did so without providing any funds for the project. Governor Hita Salazar appears to have made an effort to begin work in the preceding year, but he reported that he had failed because of the lack of financial resources. He estimated that about 10,000 pesos would be needed and sent a list of the items—bells, knives, beads, and red and blue cloth—that would be useful for hiring native labor (Cendoya 1672; Guerra y Vega 1673; Hita Salazar 1675c, 1676). Spurred on by the appearance of pirates on the Apalachee coast in 1677, Governor Salazar appears to have begun work on a temporary structure with local resources that same year without waiting for the Crown to provide funds (Wenhold 1956:305–306).[7] According to Olds, Governor Salazar started to build the fort in 1678 and probably finished it by April 7, 1679 (Olds 1962:14). There is no evidence in the Griffen calendar to pinpoint when the fort was built. The calendar does indicate that the makeshift fort was in existence by March 1680 and that Governor Salazar was still vainly waiting for authorization, funds, and supplies for building the more elaborate and substantial redoubt that he had proposed (Hita Salazar 1680d). The fort that the pirates destroyed was this temporary structure made of logs and painted with lime to make it appear more substantial to someone viewing it from afar.

Boyd went on to say that, soon after its destruction in 1682, the fort at St. Marks was rebuilt under the direction of the engineer Juan de Siscara. Boyd even reproduced a tracing of a map from the Buckingham Smith Collection, which he admitted bears no date but which, he stated, was ascribed to April 28, 1685. Boyd speculated that "It more likely is the plan referred to in the letter of Marques Cabrera to Charles II, dated St. Augustine, Oct. 7, 1682," then described the new fort and mentioned Captain Francisco de Fuentes as its first commander. He concluded his remarks with the observation that "We lack information regarding the fate of this fort during Colonel Moore's victorious raid into Apalachee in the winter of 1704" (Boyd 1936:4–5).

The reason for that lack of information is that the fort seems never to have been built—at least in this period. Two documents reproduced by Boyd in his later work on the destruction of the missions seem to establish that fact clearly. The first is a royal cedula dated November 4, 1693, in which the mon-

---

7. Wenhold implies that it was this structure that was captured and destroyed by the pirates in 1682.

arch wrote, "We are informed that the Governor Pablo de Hita Salazar in his time constructed a wooden fort in the port of San Marcos, as you may know; and if it is not built as is supposed, you are to build it" (Royal Cedula 1693:20). In response Governor Torres y Ayala, in April 1696, informed the king that the only structure at St. Marks was a wooden watchtower, observing, "Neither did I find the fort built by the Governor Don Pablo de Hita Salazar, as it was burned and cut down by the enemy in the government of Don Juan Marques de Cabrera" (Torres y Ayala 1696:21–22). Had another fort already been built to replace it, the governor would certainly have mentioned it. Neither did Governor Torres y Ayala carry out the orders to build such a fort at San Marcos. Various sources indicate that in 1702 and 1704 two soldiers from the San Luis garrison were regularly posted as sentinels at the watchtower at San Marcos. If there were a fort and garrison at San Marcos, it would not have made sense to rotate soldiers from San Luis for such duty.

The absence of a fort at San Marcos is stated even more unequivocally in 1688 in the governor's covering letter that he sent with the Apalachee chieftains' letter to Charles II that they had written in their own language. After reporting the chiefs' willingness to build a wooden blockhouse at San Luis, the governor added that they were ready also to build a "stone watch-tower in the port of San Marcos, because it is not suitable for a fort and has no other defense" (Quiroga y Losada 1688c).

Although the rift with the Apalachicola was papered over temporarily by the establishment of the Christian Sabacola village just above the confluence of the Flint and Chattahoochee and by the Apalachicola's return to a nominal allegiance to the Spanish Crown, the breach reopened in 1685 after the appearance of English traders among the Apalachicola. Over the next four years, Spanish-Apalachee expeditions made five forays into Apalachicola territory in a futile hunt for the traders whose presence was reported to the lieutenant by the native spies he and the friars had posted there. Although these large armed search parties consisted largely of Apalachee warriors, they generally included 30 to 40 Spanish soldiers (Bolton 1925a:119; Lanning 1935: 176–181; Solana 1687a:17–39). The dispatch of that large a force of soldiers on such prolonged expeditions would seem to have demanded some further expansion of the garrison beyond the 45-man level to avoid leaving the province almost entirely undefended during the interim. The governor is known to have dispatched at least nine more soldiers to Apalachee when he ordered the second foray into Apalachicola country (Crane 1956:35; Luxán 1687: 111–113).

That San Luis must have had a relatively large pool of soldiers during this period is indicated by the additional demands that were placed on it. In 1686, at the height of this military activity by the San Luis garrison, Marcos Del-

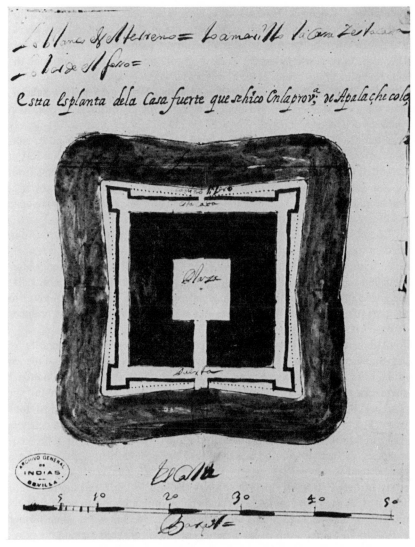

Fig. 9.1. The fort among the Apalachicola.

gado's expedition to search for the La Salle colony also departed from San Luis, drawing a few of its men from there. It eventually returned to San Luis from the Upper Creek country, after hearing from the Choctaw that they would not be able to supply them with any food. In 1689 the building of a fort in the heart of Apalachicola country placed another drain on the force at San

Luis (see fig. 9.1). When that fort was completed, 20 Spanish soldiers and 20 Indian warriors remained behind to staff it (Corkran 1967:51–52; Lanning 1935:182–183; Marques Cabrera 1687a; Quiroga y Losada 1690a). According to Lanning (1935:183), when the fort was abandoned after two years, its 20 soldiers were withdrawn to St. Augustine to be ready for a feared French attack. Alonso de Leturiondo made no mention of such fears, attributing the withdrawal rather to Governor Quiroga y Losada's recognition of "the difficulties that he had in sending the provisions by a very swift river of the said province of Apalachocoli [and] that no matter how much he cultivated the Indians [there], they did not respond but rather drew apart totally from communication with the Spaniards." Leturiondo also noted an additional motive: "Also, seeing how much at risk those few soldiers were in a place where many of the enemy could come against them . . . he saw himself obliged to withdraw the soldiers once again after they had suffered many misfortunes and much hunger in the said garrison" (Leturiondo [1700]:175). Still another factor may have been the Crown's disapproval of his having made this expenditure without its permission. The 1693 overland expedition by Governor Torres y Ayala to explore Pensacola and Mobile bays probably placed even more demands on the military resources of San Luis.

By 1702 the size of the garrison had diminished again, to 31, two of whom were always posted as sentinels at the watchtower at St. Marks (Tepaske 1964:108). By the beginning of 1704, however, the number of soldiers at San Luis had risen again to about 47, and on the eve of the cataclysm of late June and early July that number had been increased by 23, recruited from a relief ship from Pensacola. At the time of this final encounter, the San Luis garrison proper numbered 43, two having been killed in the earlier clash with Moore's forces at Ayubale and two, who were taken prisoner, having been burned at the stake. In those final engagements, 12 of San Luis's 43-man garrison were killed along with 10 of the Pensacolan recruits. Eight of the San Luis soldiers were burned at the stake in Patale, and two died in battle there. Two from San Luis and five Pensacola recruits were killed on their way up from St. Marks, having taken the royal road rather than the river as they had been instructed (Boyd 1951:15; Council of War 1704:56–59; Royal Officials 1704a:59–61; Solana 1704a:50– 55; Zúñiga y Zerda 1704a:48–50).

Upon the abandonment of San Luis the village and the blockhouse were destroyed by fire, but part of the stockade around the village failed to burn (Landeche 1705:82–85). For the remainder of the First Spanish Period there was no further activity at San Luis. In 1705, Admiral Landeche and his force spent two days at the ruins of San Luis (Landeche 1705:82–85). On his trip to the Apalachicola country in 1716, Diego Peña camped there for the night (Boyd 1949:18), and he probably did so on his other trips to the same region. Around the mid-1720s, a Spanish reconnoitering crew spent some time on the site of San Luis looking for a place to rebuild a fort in the Apalachee heartland as the nucleus for a renewed settlement of the province. They left some stakes driven into the ground to mark the site where the fort was to be built (Montiano 1745), but there is no evidence that any construction followed this activity.

A description of the San Luis area

None of the extant documents provide much of a physical description of the village of San Luis or of its immediate environs during the mission era. The investigation into the conduct of Antonio Matheos as lieutenant in Apalachee in the 1680s provides several fleeting glimpses of parts of the village or its surroundings. After being upbraided by the lieutenant, one of the Indian leaders was described as having gone "to his lodge and plaza crying, and that the Spaniards who lived around the said plaza, had consoled him." The image is that of an open square surrounded by Matheo Chuba's house, the houses of a number of Spaniards, and possibly the houses of other Indians (Ximénez 1687:35). This plaza would seem to be distinct from and at some distance from the plaza fronting the main council house of the village, which is where Matheo Chuba's incident with the lieutenant occurred. The fact that the plaza or square is spoken of as that leader's plaza might mean that each leader had his own plaza, also possibly surrounded by the residences of Spaniards living in San Luis.

Another of the witnesses in this inquiry, Vi Ventura, principal inija of San Luis, mentioned two incidents that give us a faint glimpse of the village and of its nightly routine:

> And that on another occasion on getting up at ten o'clock at night, this witness found, in relation to the Indian sentinels that it is the custom to maintain in the council house and plaza of this place, that people were missing, whom I sought out and called, reproaching them and telling them the evil that they did and that they should not let it happen again . . . and that that same night the said lieutenant had punished the said Indians with blows for having found them negligent, and that some days later, when the said lieutenant was walking alone far from the house of His Majesty, the Indian night patrol, seeing him one night at midnight told him [Bip Bentura] in the Council house that they had come upon the said lieutenant, and that, having challenged him 'who goes there', he had not replied, and that then they had approached and recognized the said lieutenant. (Bentura 1687:37–38)

This passage indicates a rather extensive open area around the village unless the lieutenant was a very foolhardy individual. The event occurred a few years before the building of the fort and blockhouse. Consequently, the "house of His Majesty" is probably the fortified country house mentioned in Bishop Calderón's letter of 1675.

Another description that implies the existence of an extensive stretch of open ploughed fields between San Luis and Tomole appears in a passage from the 1693 journal of Friar Rodrigo de Barreda:

> After getting into port (San Marcos de Apalache), we landed and took lodgings in some wretched huts where we remained until boats were brought from the province to transport us to a village within the same jurisdiction called Tomoly. This hamlet . . . is about six leagues from Apalachee through beautiful open pine groves. In the afternoon of the holy day of Our Lord [Corpus Christi] mentioned, the journey was made to the village of San Luis de Talmaly through a district furrowed with ploughed fields two leagues from Tomoly. (Barreda 1693:265)

The playing field for the ball game must have been a major feature of the village landscape. The ball game manuscript indicates that it was close to the main council house and an integral part of the village, and we can assume that it was on high ground. The manuscript recorded that in the three years from 1670 through 1672 the ball posts at San Luis, Patale, and Bacuqua were all struck by lightning and burned.

If any analogy can be drawn between the layout of the mission-era Apalachee villages and those of the Creek towns of the late eighteenth century, it should be noted that Corkran, relying on Bartram, shows the chunkey-yard occupying the very center of the village adjacent to the public buildings with the dwellings of the Indians ranged around it in little squares that comprised four family plots per square. These little squares were miniature reproductions of the public square and maintained its symmetry. Each family plot contained one to four buildings. Plots that had four buildings also formed a miniature square in one corner of the family plot. If four buildings were present, they were the winter lodging and cooking room, the granary and food storage area, a combination summer house (upper story) and storage area (ground floor), and a warehouse, the last found only where the proprietor was a wealthy man engaged in trade (Corkran 1967:8). Such may have been the arrangement around Matheo Chuba's plaza.

At the San Luis site a low-raised area is still clearly visible as a circular ridge surrounding a broad flat plazalike area, which the archaeologists exploring the site have named the "Great Circle." An augur survey revealed a concentration of daub and pottery within the series of low ridges that form the Great Circle and an absence of the same in the flat area. The survey's results suggest that the raised area represents part of the village surrounding the main plaza. Shapiro noted that "A gridded town is suggested by alignments of pottery and burned clay, especially on the northeast side of the plaza." That section of the village area had a high concentration of Spanish pottery. Almost no Spanish pottery was found in the suspected village area on the southwest side of the plaza, but that area had a large amount of Indian pottery (Shapiro 1985a:13–14; personal communication, May 1986). Shapiro concluded that "This distribution suggests ethnic (Apalachee vs. Hispanic) and/or economic differentiation within the village." A concentration of pottery, burned clay, and wrought iron nail fragments at the northwest end of the plaza has been suggested as the site of the church and convent. On the opposite—southeast—end of the probable plaza is what is believed to be the site of the council house. This flat platform, perhaps of artificial construction, appears to be surrounded by borrow pits. The first block excavations there revealed the existence of a substantial structure that was probably a round council house 36 meters in diameter that looked very much like the Creek rotunda pictured by Bartram. The 1986 excavations confirmed the conclusions drawn from the 1985 fieldwork on the council-house site. The burned-cob pits under the benches or beds followed the southwest wall to what is presumed to be an entrance facing the setting sun. Cob pits were found along the north wall, though not continuously. A Spaniard described the smaller Gualean variety he had slept on in 1595 as a continuous bed extending all around the wall, raised more than a yard above the ground. In summarizing his conclusions from the data obtained and analyzed to date, Shapiro noted that "Importantly it appears likely that the town as a whole conforms to a gridded plan oriented approximately 45 degrees west of north. Although San Luis had many more Apalachee than Spanish inhabitants, the gridded town indicates a degree of planning and administration that conforms more closely with Hispanic than with Apalachee settlement structure" (Garcia 1902:195; Shapiro 1985a:12–14, 18–19, personal communication, May 1986).

The location of the fort was already known from nineteenth-century accounts and from earlier excavations. It occupied the northern end of the site. Immediately to the southwest of the fort site, pottery was found to be abundant in an area that lacked both burned clay and nails. Inasmuch as its advantageous topographic setting on a high, flat part of the hill seems to rule out its having been a refuse dump, it is believed that the area may have been a marketplace or have had some other nonresidential function (Shapiro 1985a: 11–12).

The extant descriptions of the Apalachee's villages mention only two structures for the ordinary Indians' plots, the dwelling and the *garita,* or food storage area. Bishop Calderón described the native dwelling as round in form, "of straw, without a window and with a door a *vara* high and half a *vara* wide." He indicated that the garita stood to one side of the dwelling supported by 12 beams (Díaz Vara Calderón 1675:12–13). It appears to have been elevated. Again, if any parallel can be drawn, it should be noted that the village of Chisca, Chacato, and Pansacola attacked by the Apalachee in 1677 was described as having "corn cribs and high platforms" where many of the women and children had taken refuge, only to be burned alive there as the structures caught fire (Fernández de Florencia 1678). Archaeological research has revealed that the dwellings were between 5.5 and 7.5 meters in diameter (John Scarry, personal communication 1985). A fire pit in the center of the house provided sufficient warmth to enable the Indians to sleep without blankets. The bishop described their beds as frames made of reed bars and covered with bearskins (Díaz Vara Calderón 1675:12).

In mission times, at least, in addition to the traditional public buildings—the principal council house, the church, and the convent—there also was a public granary to hold the foodstuffs for feeding the poor, the orphaned, and the visiting soldiers as well as for equipping and maintaining the church. There is evidence that such public granaries existed in premission times as well (Laudonnière 1975:15). At San Luis with its large garrison this granary would likely have been a structure of considerable importance. It is mentioned in the mid-1680s documents dealing with the disputes between Antonio Matheos and the native leaders at San Luis and also in the regulations issued by Joaquín de Florencia at the termination of his visitation of the province. Article five of those regulations stipulated that

> They are to observe and maintain, relative to the community field of each village, that once its produce is collected, it is to be placed in the community storehouse, of which the principal cacique is to have one key and the other, the elder whom the lieutenant of this province names; and its distribution is to be in assistance of the poor orphans and widows, who do not plant a field for themselves and in order to feed the soldiers who go on the service of His Majesty; and in order to buy some ornaments for the church as well as to purchase hoes and hatchets for the service of the council houses and the work of the said field. (Florencia 1695)

In Garcilaso's account of the de Soto expedition, there is reference to what appears to have been a capacious multistoried building in the principal village of a separate district about one league distant from Anhayca Apalache. He records that some of the natives there took refuge in "the highest part of a house which was very different from all the others and appeared to be a temple." It was near the main plaza and large enough to enable them to ride in and out on their mounts (Vega 1951:254–255).

Building the blockhouse and stockade at San Luis

The first specific mention of plans for the building of a blockhouse in Apalachee dates from 1656–1657, when Governor Rebolledo lobbied the village
chiefs to support the idea in order to counter some friars' opposition to it (Rebolledo 1657a:passim). The chief at San Luis responded with a promise to
build a "strong and capacious house" for the troops stationed there (Rebolledo 1657a:116–119). The fulfillment of that promise, presumably, was
the fortified country house mentioned by Bishop Calderón. It also probably
served as the residence of the governor's lieutenant and is the "government
house" referred to in the mid-1680s (Bentura 1687:37–38).

In the year 1688 the newly arrived governor, Diego de Quiroga y Losada,
approached the Apalachee chiefs with the idea of building a proper fort at San
Luis and a stone watchtower at St. Marks. In a dispatch to the king, forwarding letters in the native tongues of Apalachee and Timucua written by the
chiefs of those provinces, the governor reported that, as a demonstration of
their zeal to excel in serving the king, "all the caciques of Apalache have
offered to me that, on my supplying them with tools, they will build a wooden
blockhouse at their expense, for the infantry that serves there on garrison
duty, along with another stone watch tower in the port of San Marcos, because
it is not suitable for a fort and has no other defense" (de Quiroga y Losada
1688c). In their letter the chiefs repeated that pledge but made it clear that the
suggestion for the two projects had come from the governor. They added the
qualification that the governor had pledged help with not only tools but also
assistance with "everything necessary" (Chiefs of the Apalachee 1688).
Shortly thereafter the Indians cut and prepared a quantity of lumber for the
project, but during the rest of the term of Governor Quiroga the Spanish authorities did nothing to forward it. Quiroga's successor found that lumber already weakened by decay (Torres y Ayala 1696:21–22). Initially, at least, the
failure to move forward on the work was probably occasioned by the diversion
of many of the region's abler carpenters for the building of the Spanish fort in
the Apalachicola country in 1689.

Shortly after the accession of the next governor in 1693, the Crown informed him of the native leaders' pledge to his predecessor and ordered him
to carry out the projects. To assure the prompt execution of those orders, the
Crown, a few weeks later, instructed the other royal officials at St. Augustine
to monitor the governor's execution of those orders and to keep Madrid informed of his action or inaction in the matter (Royal Cedula 1693:20; Royal
Officials 1696:20– 21). Although those orders were issued in November and
December 1693, it was not until October 1695 that construction of the blockhouse began.

The available documentation describing the building of the fort or portraying the structure while it still stood is surprisingly scant. Boyd reproduced a 1696 letter by the governor in which he informed the king that the project had been completed except for a third part of the roof. The only details provided on the nature of the structure were that timber was utilized in its construction, that it then contained two guns, and that it was sufficiently capacious to shelter both the garrison and the inhabitants of the village on nights when the alarm was sounded, a frequent occurrence at that time. To date, the governor's letter of July 3, 1697, reporting the completion of the blockhouse has not been located. From the royal cedula, in which its receipt was recorded, it is known that the governor, after repeating the comment on the fort's capaciousness, again mentioned that it possessed two pieces of artillery, adding that they were placed on two *travesos* that projected from the house.[8] He also informed the Crown that the construction had cost the king 304 pesos and 2 reales (Menéndez Marquez and Florencia 1697:22–23; Royal Cedula 1698:23–24; Torres y Ayala 1696:21–22). A report by the treasury officials indicated that almost two-thirds of that sum went for the purchase of nails and for the fabrication of large and small spikes and some necessary tools. They described it as a wooden blockhouse and added the detail that the 2,000 nails purchased were for the shingles for the roof (Menéndez Marquez and Florencia 1697:22–23).

During Governor Torres's residencia, one of the soldiers who had seen the blockhouse described it as an offensive and defensive fort provided with four bastions with two pieces mounted on top and a wall gun in the guardroom. He testified that its center was made of walls of mud, which he described as "the best material there is for that country," and that it was sheathed all around with boards about three fingers thick, or about two inches (Fuentes 1700:85). The only other somewhat contemporaneous description of the fort, that by Admiral Antonio de Landeche, who visited the site one year after the fort had been destroyed, conflicts with the foregoing in some details. He described the blockhouse as having been sheathed with palm posts rather than with two-inch-thick boards, and he portrayed the posts as having been "*masiado con adobes de baro*," which Boyd translated as "backed with clay bricks."[9] Landeche's drawing of the blockhouse shows no bastions at its corners and gives

---

8. The word *travesos*, which Boyd left untranslated, appears to refer to a bastionlike structure that would permit the defenders to enfilade anyone approaching the blockhouse. In one of the other contemporary descriptions of the fort, the travesos are described as *baluartes*, "bastions" or "bulwarks." Traverse, the English equivalent, has been defined as "a barrier (as a bank of earth) across part of a defensive area, to give protection from enfilade fire" (Arana and Manucy 1977:62).

9. I have not encountered the word *masiado* elsewhere. The closest likely equivalent is *macizado* which could be translated as "supported by," "solidified by," or "firmed by."

no indication that the roof was shingled. He gave the number of artillery pieces mounted on the blockhouse roof as eight instead of the two mentioned in the testimony given in 1700 (Landeche 1705:82–85 and plates I and II).

Upon completion of the blockhouse, work on the fort appears to have stopped. There is no mention of anything other than the wooden blockhouse in the correspondence reporting its completion, so it appears that this may have been all that was envisioned initially. Five more years passed before the start of the construction of the outworks around the blockhouse to convert it into a proper fort. Those outworks consisted of a stockade of upright logs, fronted by a moat and backed by a banquette terreplein. The work on these improvements began in October 1702, after the demoralizing rout suffered by a Spanish-led Apalachee expedition in an encounter with an Apalachicola force on the banks of the Flint (Romo de Urisa 1702; Solana 1702).

Shortly thereafter the governor issued orders for the building of a stockade to enclose the church and convent and an additional stockade to connect the convent with that enclosing the blockhouse (Zúñiga y Zerda n.d.:44–45). The only indication that some of this work was completed is the report by Landeche, who observed that "the blockhouse was demolished in such a manner that there remained only some portions of the stockade which . . . the flames . . . did not reach" (Landeche 1705:82–85). This comment and a drawing by Landeche of the fort and its setting indicate that the stockade around the blockhouse had been completed before the attacks in 1704.

At the time that he ordered the building of the stockade around the church and convent, the governor also directed that all the corn held by individuals be collected so that it might be stored in the blockhouse (Zúñiga y Zerda n.d.: 44–45). At the time of the destruction of the blockhouse, whatever corn had been stored, if any still existed, was probably not considerable. Depending on the time that it struck, the epidemic suffered by the inhabitants of San Luis in 1703 may have interfered with the planting for that year. Because of the destruction and demoralization created by Colonel Moore's attack during the winter, no corn was planted at San Luis in 1704.

The church furnishings

An inventory of the church plate and vestments that the Spanish soldiers brought out with them when they abandoned San Luis indicates that many such articles from a number of the missions were being kept at the blockhouse for security, in addition to the corn. In discussing this inventory, Bushnell implied that all of the inventoried silver and vestments belonged to San Luis. She speculated that, if all the 14 missions possessed amounts similar to that inventoried by Manuel Solana, the retreating commander, "the portable church property in Apalachee must have been worth over 37,000 pesos before the wars—a sum that represented 296,000 days of labor to a common Indian" (Bushnell 1979:12; Solana 1704b:151).

It is unlikely that the church at San Luis was as richly endowed as Bushnell's remark implies. First of all, the memorandum drawn up by Solana says that the silver came from the "churches" of the Province of Apalachee. The most telling indication, however, that the silver came from a number of missions is the presence of seven monstrances. A single mission church in such a poor and remote area was unlikely to have seven exemplars of this costly and relatively little-used article for religious services.[10] Another feature of this inventory that indicates multiple sources is the repetition of the pattern of sevens or of numbers close to seven, for example, seven monstrances, seven chalices with their patens, plus another three with theirs,[11] eight lunettes to administer the Viaticum, seven silver storage vessels, seven crosses of peace, six large silver crosses, and six nine-rayed halos for the Infant Jesus (Solana 1704b:151).

Fortunately, there also exists something of a guide to the holdings of the average mission with which these figures can be compared. In 1681, on the orders of the governor, an inventory was made listing most of the holdings of the 34 Indian missions in existence. It showed that the average mission possessed one silver monstrance,[12] two silver chalices, one silver lunet for the Viaticum, and one silver procession cross. In 1681, fewer than half the missions had even one silver deposit vessel, and only slightly more than half owned one silver cross of peace. Accordingly, it is improbable that San Luis alone would have seven of each. In 1681 the average mission had either one silver halo or one silver crown. In 1704 sixteen halos or crowns were taken away from San Luis by the departing soldiers. The 1704 inventory mentions 17 silver chrism vials. In 1681 the average mission possessed one and a half

10. The monstrance is used principally during the service known as Benediction of the Blessed Sacrament and for the Exposition of the Eucharist in Processions on Corpus Christi or in services such as the Forty-Hours Adoration.

11. This document is not very legible in places. In translating it, Boyd read the first "their" as "six." Inasmuch as the two words in Spanish, *sus* and *seis*, are not that dissimilar, either his reading or mine could be justified. It makes more sense to have as many patens as chalices because they go together in matched sets to hold the host and the wine during Mass. I found the second "theirs" completely illegible but thought it logical. Boyd rendered the word as *two*, adding after it the word *paten*.

12. Apalachee appears to have been unusual in this respect as only one of the seven monstrances that were saved was made of silver, the rest of cheaper gilded metal. Strangely, no gilded monstrance was noted on the 1681 inventory, even though its composers saw fit to enumerate lamps and censers of brass, items that would seem to be of less monetary and artistic value than a gilded monstrance.

vials (Robles et al. 1681:148–150). Even allowing for some increase in the number of items held by each mission through acquisitions made during the intervening quarter of a century, the conclusion is inescapable that the sacred vessels and other silver items removed in 1704 were drawn from a number of mission stations and not from San Luis alone.

Assuming that the furnishings were distributed more or less evenly over the various missions, those two inventories of 1681 and 1704 make it possible to establish the standard equipment of the average mission church in Apalachee at the end of the seventeenth century. As the headquarters mission with a small Spanish community, some of whom must have had some financial resources, San Luis probably was somewhat more richly endowed than the average mission. Even the brutal Antonio Matheos, despite his taunting of the native leaders for their intense involvement in church affairs, was religious enough to pledge 100 deerskins from the booty he captured near Caveta to, as one witness put it, "give them as an alms to Our Lady of the Conception, which is in the convent of San Francisco of the village of San Luis de Apalachee," adding, "And, in fact, he gave what they were worth to the steward of the brotherhood of Our Lady" (Guerrero 1687:104–105). Based on those inventories, the following listing is the standard equipment of the average mission church in Florida at the end of the seventeenth century (Robles et al. 1681:148–150; Solana 1704:151):

One monstrance, probably of silver, except for the Apalachee missions,
      where less expensive gilded monstrances seem to have predominated
Two silver chalices
Two missals—one for Requiem Mass
Nine or ten sets of chasuable, stole, and maniple of diverse colors
Seven or eight antependiums of diverse colors
Six albs of white linen
Seven handbells
Two or three large bells
Eight brass candlesticks
One or two copes
Five or six altar cloths
Seven amices
Seven or eight palls
Eleven corporals of starched linen
Five burses
Eleven or twelve chalice veils
Two surplices
Three or four rochets

Five cinctures

One long decorated stole

One coverlet for the altar

One silver lunette for the Viaticum

Ceramic or glass cruets and a 50 percent chance of having a set of silver cruets and a silver plate to hold them

One or two silver chrism vials (17 of these were among the objects removed from Apalachee in 1704)

One altar lamp, either of silver or brass (As only 12 are listed for the 34 missions, some locally made ceramic ones may have been used in the other missions. Three silver lamps were removed in 1704. If any brass lamps existed, they were left behind.)

One silver procession cross, or more probably, one made of less expensive metal (Only five silver procession crosses were mentioned on the 1681 list, but eight were removed from Apalachee in 1704, indicating that there were far more of them in Apalachee than elsewhere.)

One thurible, one incense boat, and one spoon for the incense, either of silver or brass. (Some brass censers and boats apparently were left behind in 1704, as only five silver thuribles were removed in 1704.)

Two religious banners. One of those at San Luis is known to have had an image of the Blessed Virgin on one side and an image of the crucifix on the other.

Two engravings depicting a religious scene

Five or six statues (The convent at San Luis had a statue of Our Lady of the Conception.)

Thirteen pictures or paintings depicting Christ or the saints or some religious scene

Four cornialtares [13]

A wooden missal stand and, possibly, a fancy coverlet for it

One cedar chest for storing vestments

Possibly a large chest of drawers for storing vestments

One silver crown or halo (The 16 removed from Apalachee in 1704 indicate that Apalachee's missions had far more than the usual number of these.)

Possibly a procession lantern

---

13. To date I have not discovered the nature of this item. In 1681 there were 149 of them in the 34 missions. Father Antonio G. Leon suggested that cornialtares might be the three alter-cards, containing prayers and the Last Gospel, used formerly at Mass. One was placed at each corner and the largest one in front of the tabernacle.

Possibly a canopy, and one silver deposit vessel
Possibly one silk humeral veil
One or more linen hand cloths
Possibly one ritual
One veil or curtain
Possibly a press for making hosts
And possibly a mirror, though few places had this item

Even a cursory glance at this list shows that, for a relatively poor frontier area, Florida's mission churches were well endowed with needed furnishings. Contrary to the inference made by Bushnell, not all of these were purchased by the sweat of the natives. The Crown supplied many of the basic items, such as chalices and vestments, Bishop Calderón donated some, and some were hand-me-downs from Spain and the richer New World provinces.

Both inventories omit a few items that would be part of the normal equipment of a functioning church. The most striking omission is altar stones, an item that the devout would not want to see profaned. Inasmuch as they contained the relic of some saint, one would expect that they would have been salvaged or buried, as were the large bells. Because they were usually made of marble, however, their weight may have prevented their being salvaged.[14] In view of its survivability, this item will probably be found on sites today, whether it was left in place or buried. Another unexpected omission on both lists is ciboria, the vessels used to hold the consecrated wafers for distribution to the faithful during Communion. The 1681 inventory contains one item, "five gilded sagrarios," that might be ciboria. In view of the small number mentioned, however, and because they were included in the same sentence with items of furniture, namely, holy-water basins and mirrors, these sagrarios were probably gilded tabernacles. Only five holy-water basins are listed on that inventory, but no baptismal fonts were mentioned (Robles et al. 1681: 148–150). As neither brass nor silver candlesticks were mentioned among the items removed from Apalachee in 1704, some made of brass were probably left behind. The 1681 inventory tallied 265 brass candlesticks for the 34 missions. Some of those indubitably were in Apalachee missions. The failure to mention ciboria suggests that those used in Florida were made of some cheap metal with a light gilding on the inside of the cup. It is not clear whether the gilded tabernacles were made of metal or wood, but the fact that they were deemed worthy of mention suggests that they were made of metal.

14. The usual altar stone in more recent times was a square to rectangular slab of marble about one inch thick varying in size from that of a large slice of bread to that of a medium-sized cutting board. It contained a cavity in the center into which the relics of a saint were cemented.

The number of items that are mentioned in the 1681 inventory but not on the 1704 list raises some interesting questions, particularly about the fate of the durable items that could not be destroyed entirely by fire, such as brass thuribles, lamps, and candlesticks. At the conclusion of his inventory, Solana stated that there were many more church vestments and furnishings that they could have salvaged had they sufficient horses and people to carry them. He revealed that these articles were "burned and destroyed, except for many bells which remained there buried" (Solana 1704b:151).[15] Five weeks earlier, while still in Apalachee, Solana reported that he had ordered the felucca that he had sent to Pensacola bearing the Spanish women and children from San Luis to return to transport the images and ornaments so that they might not have to be burned (Solana 1704a:50–55). But a letter by Pensacola's commandant indicates that the felucca did not sail from St. Marks until July 23, 1704 (Guzman 1704). That would seem to have precluded a return before Solana's withdrawal and explains Solana's burning of many of the church furnishings. Although the bells are the only things mentioned as having been buried, it would not have been that difficult to bury some of the brass items or even the cedar chests full of the richer vestments and the more elaborate missals. As resistant as cedar is to rot, such chests could have preserved their contents for a considerable period of time if steps had been taken to keep moisture out.

For the period between the destruction of the fort and village of San Luis in 1704 and the development of the property in the nineteenth century—sometime after the United States acquired title to the Floridas—a number of individuals have left references to features of the site or even brief descriptions of the surviving remains and the surrounding terrain. The earliest description of the ruins, as noted, dates from 1705. Enough of the remains of the fort were still visible then to enable one of Admiral Landeche's subordinates to make a sketch of its appearance and location.[16] The admiral noted that parts of the stockade had not been consumed by the flames because of the lack of resin in the wood. Unfortunately, he had little else to say about the status of the remains or the layout of the complex. His comments that his party spent an uncomfortable two days there during the summer rains because they had only shelter enough to protect the arms and the powder gives the impression that few, if any, structures had been left standing. That nature had already regained

15. At least some of those bells were recovered when the Spaniards returned to San Marcos de Apalachee in 1718.
16. In the preparation of that sketch some of the detail probably was provided by the members of the party who had been in Apalachee before the destruction of the missions. Their presence is indicated by the admiral's remark that those sent out to reconnoiter the villages adjacent to San Luis were guided by persons familiar with the region. Nonetheless, serious questions have been raised as to the reliability of the sketch as a true representation of the orientation of the mission and the relative positions of its structures.

control of the village sites is indicated by the admiral's remark concerning the inspection of the nearby villages, "of which were found no more trace than the statement of the guide that in those spots they were situated" (Landeche 1705:82–85). If this statement is understood literally, it would raise serious questions about the claims of early nineteenth-century observers that the outlines of the fort and the crumbled walls of the village structures could still be detected. Indeed, the most specific of these descriptions is the latest one, dating from the early 1830s, by General E. Parker Scammon, a U. S. army officer:

> About three miles from the town of Tallahassee, is the ruin of an old Spanish fort, which in by-gone days bore the name of San Luis. Its site is a ridge of land somewhat higher than the surrounding country, bounded on three sides by a narrow stream of running water, and on a fourth descending by a gentle slope, until lost in the thick mazes of a swampy hammock at its base. The crumbled walls embrace an area of near twenty acres of ground, on which may yet be traced the narrow streets of a small village. Three or four hundred yards to the north of the principal work, and connected with it by a covered passage, is a large square redoubt, with small bastions. The ancient parapet has long since crumbled to a mere mound of earth, and borne trees of more than a century's growth, whose decayed trunks now half fill the ditch at its foot. From the remains of an old postern, a path leads down a steep bank, to a small spring of clear water, which was arranged to supply the garrison, when not confined within the walls of the fort. (Scammon 1840:44)

One does not know what credibility should be given to this description of the site, as the remainder of this two-paged article is an almost completely fantasized account of the last days of the fort and the Spanish withdrawal, which does not make even an accidental approximation to the truth on any point beyond the fact that the Spaniards abandoned the post. In a flowery style, Scammon wrote of the fort's having been put under attack and strict siege by the natives, then of a treaty with the natives that permitted the Spanish garrison to withdraw toward the Apalachee coast. He concluded with a description of the massacre of the garrison by the natives, who were incensed by an explosion that killed many of them while they were celebrating their victory within the confines of the surrendered fort (Scammon 1840:44). Not one of those statements is true.

Scammon probably recorded what he had been told by Tallahasseans of that era concerning the demise of the fort. The two other specific references to the site, those by John Lee Williams and Captain Daniel G. Burch, which antedate General Scammon's account, are marred by equally garbled tales concerning the abandonment and destruction of the fort. Both accounts were garnered from an ancient Indian, who claimed to have been a participant in the war in which the missions were destroyed. Inasmuch as Burch was in Tallahassee about 1823, the Indian would have had to be at least 119 years old just to have been alive at the time of the destruction of the missions. A point that lends a certain credibility to General Scammon's 1833 description of the site is his account of his return to the site in 1865. He remarked that the features he had noted earlier were no longer visible, as both the site and the land around it had long been a cotton field. The preliminary archaeological work carried out in 1984–1985 also suggests the possibility that the village had narrow streets laid out in a grid pattern like that which Scammon had described (Shapiro 1985a:13, 18). In 1892, reminiscing about the two visits, Scammon wrote:

> The plan of the work was a square of about one hundred and fifty feet, with a small bastion at one of the angles. The walls had been formed of adobes . . . that now appeared to be only mounds of hard earth, perhaps ten feet wide across the top, and two or three feet higher than the *terre-plein*. . . . On two sides the outer faces of the work were flush with the steep slope of the bluff. On the other two the ditch was yet some two or three feet deep. . . . Though but a few yards distant from a post road, the old fort was completely hidden from it by the foliage of shrubs and trees. (Boyd 1953:466)

After reproducing this passage, Boyd observed that Scammon "also described a depression in the earth which appeared as a prolongation of the ditch to the northwest, traceable as far as the Ochlockonee River." He continued, "Although he [Scammon] interpreted this as a covered way to the fort and hence related to the fortification, it more likely was the eroded course of the former Spanish trail to Escambé." Such a depression is still visible on the south-facing slope on the west side of the San Luis property. Boyd noted further that Scammon "told of slight linear depressions, regularly spaced and parallel, about thirty feet wide, visible through the open wood, crossed at right angles by others similar, identified as the streets of a town occupying a large area." Boyd theorized that the "clay wall observed by Scammon was doubtless the banquette backing of the posts of the palisade" and commented further:

> Of the various early observers of the San Luis site, Scammon furnished the only particulars relating to the detached village area to the south-

ward of the stockaded blockhouse. His mention of crumbled walls (evidently of another banquette) about the village area, which was connected with the blockhouse by a covered passage, would indicate that orders conforming to Governor Zúñiga's memorandum were prepared and executed, and that as executed, the supplemental fortifications were more extensive than originally contemplated.(1953:466–467)[17]

The richness in the details provided by Scammon's account, the seeming conformity of some of those details with the instructions issued by the Spanish governor, and the fact that some of the features he describes can still be recognized suggest that some part of his description of what he saw in the early 1830s is reasonably accurate or at least worthy of being considered in the archaeological investigation of the site.

John Lee Williams and Captain Daniel E. Burch are the authors of the other two early nineteenth-century descriptions of the San Luis site by men who are known to have visited it. At various times Williams described the site as

situated on a commanding eminence at the north point of a high narrow neck of highlands surrounded by a deep ravine and swamp . . .

On a commanding hill about half way from Oclockney to Tallahassee. The south line of it measured 71 paces, the north 55, the east and west ends about 46. It had bastions near the angles, and in the spring about 50 feet down the ravine, east of the works, we discovered the breach of a six-pound field piece, and near it another piece of the same dimensions, from which the muzzle was broken.

Fort St. Lewis was situate [sic] two miles west of Tallahassee. Its form was an irregular parallelogram; the eastern and longest side was 52 paces. Within the moat, two brick edifices had been erected; one sixty by forty, the other thirty by twenty feet. There were bastions at each corner. The outward defenses are extensive. A covered way led to a spring, in a deep ravine, under the northeast wing of the fort. Here we discovered two broken cannon, one of them having only the muzzle broken off; this has been removed to Tallahassee, and again wakens the echoes of the distant hill on days of rejoicing. Many articles of old iron have been discovered about this old ruin. Before it, trees and grape

17. The orders referred to are those ordering the building of a stockade around the church and convent and another connecting that complex with the stockade around the fort. The crumbled walls around the village, of course, might simply be the collapsed walls of the houses and not a banquette.

vines grow, in the order in which they were planted: the rows are distinctly traced, although overrun with a more recent forest. (Boyd 1939:265–266, 1951:2–3; Griffin 1951:140; Williams 1827:33)

The following are Burch's impressions from his visit to the site a few days after Williams's visit there:

Fort St. Louis, at least its ruins, situated about 6 miles east of Ockolockony, and N. by W. 25 miles from St. Marks. This place has more the appearance of having been a fortified town than a mere fortification. . . . Fort St. Louis was built on an elevated spot of ground around a hollow, from the bottom of which issue 2 springs that furnish an abundant supply of water, but which after running but a few yards, again sink into the ground. One of these on being opened by Captain Burch, displayed the wooden box or trunk in which it had been enclosed; they were overshadowed by a beautiful live oak tree. (Boyd 1951:3)

Griffin reproduced another anonymous description of the site that was written in 1825:

At Fort St. Louis, about 2 miles west of Tallahassee, have been found remnants of iron cannon, spikes, hinges, locks, etc., which are evidently of Spanish manufacture, and which have not been much injured by the rust.

Within the principal fort, for the outworks seem to have been numerous and extensive, are the ruins of two brick edifices, one was about 60 feet by 40, the other was about 30 by 20. These are in total ruins, and nothing but a mound appears where the walls stood, composed wholly of broken bricks, which have been composed of a coarse sandy clay and burned in the modern fashion. Yet on the very walls of these buildings are oaks 18 inches in diameter. On the same hill, and in fact within the outworks of this fort, are to be seen grape arbors in parallel lines, which still maintain their pristine regularity. (Griffin 1951:141)

Even a hasty perusal of these early nineteenth-century accounts and the comparison of them with Admiral Landeche's description of the site reveals that they both agree and disagree on a number of important details. Among the differences, the most significant involve the size and shape of the palisade surrounding the blockhouse. Both the drawing and the dimensions provided by Landeche indicate a regular rectangle, 238.63 feet long on the north and

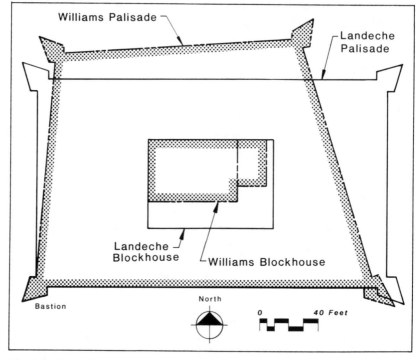

Fig. 9.2. Fort palisades and blockhouse drawn in accord with the dimensions given
        by Landeche (1705) and Williams (1827).

south sides and 131.6 feet long on its west and east sides. When those dimensions are used to draw the rectangle to scale, the result is a rectangle that is
much more oblong than the one provided on Landeche's map (see fig. 9.2). In
the drawing on the map the proportion of the two axes is roughly 3 to 2; in the
dimensions given by Landeche it is 9 to 5, indicating a structure that is almost
twice as long as it is wide. Williams described the palisade as forming an
irregular parallelogram with a south side that was 52 feet longer than the north
side. In one statement Williams portrays the east and west sides as of equal
length, which would be possible only with a trapezoidal figure. In a second
statement, the one in which he described the fort as an irregular parallelogram, he stated that the eastern side was about 20 feet longer than the western
one. Using either of Williams's sets of dimensions, the resultant figure is considerably less oblong than the one indicated by Landeche's dimensions and, of
course, is not a rectangle. Scammon does not appear to have measured the

palisaded area, which he described as a square of about 150 feet. The differences between these descriptions of the size and shape of the fort are such that they can be resolved only by archaeological exploration of the site.

The other major difference between Landeche's and Williams's descriptions centers on the blockhouse. Landeche described and portrayed it as a single building 85 feet by 57.5 feet faced with palm posts backed by clay bricks with a double layer of planks on its roof. Williams and the anonymous observer (who might well have been Williams) saw the remains of two structures, one 60 by 40 feet and the other 30 by 20 feet (Griffin 1951:141; Williams 1827:33). Both described the structures as made of brick, but the anonymous observer added the detail "burned in the modern fashion." [18] Although the overall length and width given by Williams approximates that of the structure described by Landeche, Williams's blockhouse would have a definite jog in its profile, where the smaller building abutted the larger one (following John W. Griffin's suggestion that the appearance of their having been two buildings resulted from the use of bearing walls within the blockhouse to support the roof; Griffin 1951:143– 144). The resolution of this difference also will have to await the thorough archaeological exploration of the site.

One other divergence of some significance involves the palisades other than those around the blockhouse. Landeche's map shows no other defense features except for what appears to be a stockade around the church. The descriptions left by Burch and by Scammon suggest that there were rather extensive fortifications in the village area as well. Burch remarked that "This place has more the appearance of a fortified town than a mere fortification." Scammon referred to the village as the "principal work" and indicated that it was connected to the fort by a "covered passage" (Boyd 1951:3; Scammon 1840:49). Although that expression is susceptible to various interpretations,[19] it suggests that the governor's orders for the building of a stockade to connect the church complex with the fort may have been carried out. It is worthwhile to note Scammon's observation that the palisade on two sides of the fort was on the edge of a steep decline and that he saw a moat only on two sides of the fort (Boyd 1953:486). One might infer from it that the steep fall-off of the terrain

18. Scammon, on the other hand, agrees with Landeche in describing the bricks as adobes, while the soldier Fuentes portrayed the interior walls as made of mud or clay, which could be an imprecise way of saying adobes.

19. Some have suggested an open or covered trench that would provide shelter from the attackers' fire or one whose approaches could be swept by fire from the fort. The most obvious is a stockade. The diagram for the 1718 fort at St. Marks uses that name, *covered passage*, to designate the open parade area immediately behind the stockade around the fort.

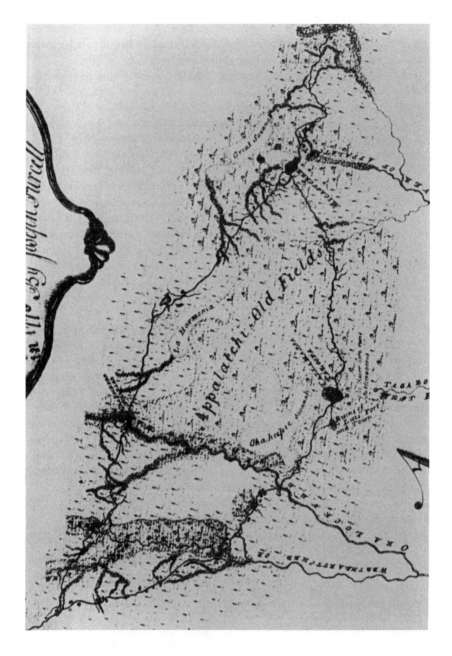

Fig. 9.3. The Stuart-Purcell map of 1778.

either rendered the moat unnecessary on those two sides or led to such erosion from the clay of the banquette as to fill the moat in the century and a quarter that had elapsed since the destruction of the fort. The absence of a moat on the west side would also offer a possible explanation for failure during the 1948 site exploration to find the west moat with the test trench that was dug.[20]

Perhaps the most surprising comments of the early nineteenth-century observers are the statements that "trees and grape vines grow, in the order in which they were planted: the rows are distinctly traced, although overrun with a recent forest," and that "in fact within the outworks of this fort, are to be seen grape arbors in parallel lines, which still maintain their pristine regularity" (Griffin 1951:140–141). Presumably the statements had some foundation in fact or in the perception of the observers, but they are difficult to accept in view of the relatively short life span of fruit trees and in view of the propensity of unpruned grapevines to form tangled masses of foliage. One would expect that over 120 years many other trees would have grown up to break the pattern and to shade out the less vigorous fruit trees.

The eighteenth-century visitors to the San Luis site, after Landeche, provide almost no data concerning its appearance. Diego Peña, who stopped there overnight in 1716, recorded only that he had killed two buffalo there. Lieutenant Pittman visited the site in 1767 and observed about the former fort only that "One can trace out the ditch and theire remains many broken pieces of Ordnance, and an entire bell was taken from thence some little time since by the Indians" (Boyd 1934:117, 1949:18). The location of the village and fort is indicated on the Stuart-Purcell map of 1778 (fig. 9.3), which shows the main trail passing about one mile to the north of the San Luis site. However, a lesser trail branches off the main one about two miles northwest of San Luis, passing by or through the northern edge of the site to connect it with the Seminole town of Tallahassee Taloofa, which appears to have occupied the site of

20. Another possible explanation is that the test trench dug in 1948 did not extend far enough west to cross the west moat. If I have correctly interpreted Griffin's comments in *Here They Once Stood*, that may be the case. If Griffin was correct in assuming that his Square 0 was in the east moat, the 180-foot east-west line he marked off from Square 0 plus the 35 feet of trench that was dug westward from the west end of that 180-foot line added up to only 215 feet. At the south wall of the palisade, if one accepts Williams's figures, the east and west palisades were 230.75 feet apart. According to Landeche's figures, the distance between them was 238.63 feet. This distance seems to leave that 1948 trench shy of the west moat, particularly when one takes into consideration the fact that the distance from the middle of one moat to the middle of the other would be a few feet more than the distance from palisade wall to palisade wall, which Williams's figures presumably represent. There is also the uncertainty as to whether the paces in which Williams calculated the distance represented a standard measure or the space that he covered in one step. The results given by the latter could fluctuate considerably, depending on the length of a person's legs and the vigor of his stride.

present downtown Tallahassee, astride the Monroe Street ridge from the capitol complex northward. About two-thirds of that Seminole settlement appears to have been north of the southern branch of the Pensacola–St. Augustine road.

Perusal of the few published sources dealing with the Tallahassee region during the Second Spanish period proved to be unrewarding. I have not had the opportunity to consult the voluminous archival sources for that period in the P. K. Yonge Library. However, the observations of Bruce Chappell on the scope of those records suggest that they might be a fruitful source of additional information on the San Luis site and the sites of some of the other missions as well as on human activity in the area during that period.

Chapter 10

Alienation and Demoralization, 1682–1702

THE SUDDEN collapse of Spain's Apalachee mission system in 1704 before a relatively small force of Englishmen and their native allies resulted from a series of developments from the early 1680s to 1702 that had left the natives of Apalachee alienated and demoralized. Among those factors five were especially prominent.

One factor was the irrational conduct of Antonio Matheos, the governor's deputy in Apalachee at the start of this period. Another was the steadily increasing demand on the Apalachee's time, labor, and resources for military and exploratory missions to the west, northwest, and north and for special fort and shipbuilding projects. These demands increased an already heavy and growing burden associated with the labor repartimiento. The third factor was the growing economic competition from and oppression by the Spanish settlers in the province and the governor's restrictions on trade with the Apalachicola. The fourth was the frequently unfulfilled promises to remedy the abuses of which the natives complained. And, last, on the eve of the final attacks came a disastrous rout of a sizable Spanish and Apalachee force that had been dispatched to avenge an Apalachicola attack on the Timucua village of Santa Fé and the Apalachicola's murder of three Apalachee traders.

Although the Apalachee probably had reasons enough for discontent before the 1680s, their experiences under Antonio Matheos and the governor's deafness to their complaints gave a special edge to that discontent. On at least one occasion Matheos pushed the inhabitants of San Luis to the verge of revolt. His perennial brutality and tyranny impelled a considerable number of the Apalachee to seek refuge among the Apalachicola rather than endure the insults and the cudgelings that he administered so freely, with little provocation and without respect for the status of his victims. In one of the most unsettling of these incidents Matheos clapped into irons two of San Luis's principal leaders, Matheo Chuba and the inija, Bi Bentura, when they asked for permission to go to St. Augustine to complain to the governor about his deputy's conduct. Only those leaders' calming of the agitated Indians who came to ask what they should do and the intercession of some of the Spaniards prevented a possibly serious incident. On separate occasions Matheos directed obscene and insulting words at Matheo Chuba that the latter affirmed left him speechless. After calling a general assembly of the caciques and other leaders, Matheos addressed them as rogues, liars, and cuckolds on learning that those chiefs had written to the governor asking for his removal.[1] In fits of anger he often struck caciques and Indians alike about the head with a club that he was accustomed to carry with him (Solana 1687a:22–23, 28–29, 31–36, 38–39).[2] The arbitrariness of his conduct is reflected in the testimony on several of these incidents:

> And that on one occasion the said lieutenant, Antonio Matheos, said that everyone had to come out for the preparation of the fields and for the work of sowing, and that he had learned that the people had not gone out for it, and that the said governor *ynixa* was to blame, and that, if in the future the Indians missed the said work, he would hang him. . . . And that some days later, when the said lieutenant was walking alone far from the house of His Majesty, the Indians' night patrol, seeing him one night at mid-night, told him in the council house that they had come upon the said lieutenant and that having challenged him, who goes there, he had not replied, and that then they had approached and recognized the said lieutenant, and that, after having heard the major *chacal* of the King, he said to the aforementioned lieutenant, your person is the talk of the Indians who met you alone at night. For which the said lieutenant ordered the summoning of the said witness and said to him that they had dared talk about him, which no one was to do, and chastising him with a walnut club, he injured and cracked his head. . . . And that on another occasion the said lieutenant had told him to look for corn for some persons to plant and that the said witness had responded that he did not have any or know whence to look for it. To which he repeated, then go look for it because I order it. And the said *ynixa* again repeating that he did not have any to spare, he told him to give what he

---

1. Interestingly, similar charges were made against Guale's lieutenant less than a decade later during the 1695 visitation, and that lieutenant's arbitrary actions led similarly to flight by Guale and Yamasee.
2. The testimony against Matheos's intolerable conduct was given by both Spaniards and Indians.

had in his house. And the said witness replying that if he gave the little that he had, I could not plant for my family. At that the said lieutenant ordered three soldiers to take the corn that he had in his storehouse. And the said soldiers, seeing that it was little, . . . left it, telling him, we will tell the lieutenant that you did not have any. (Bentura 1687:37–38)

The sheer volume of the complaints against Matheos forced Governor Juan Marques Cabrera, who had appointed him, to send an inspector to investigate them. That he had intended it to be a mere formality to protect himself rather than a serious investigation is indicated in remarks by the man appointed to conduct a second investigation into Matheos's conduct:

In the city of San Augustín of Florida on the 23rd day of the month of April of the year 1687, the notary, Alonso Solana . . . certifies . . . that on the 18th day of the month of September of the past year of 1686, the captain and sergeant-major, Juan Marques Cabrera, delivered to me . . . an *auto* provided by His Excellency . . . for the inquiry . . . and for the presentation of witnesses, among whom was one Matheo Chuba, an Indian leader of the said province of Apalache, who, on being questioned . . . declared that all the natives of the said province were very unhappy with the said lieutenant because he treated them badly . . . which testimony, on being seen by the governor moved him to call in the sergeant-major Domingo de Leturiondo, and in great anger and annoyance he ordered him to reject the said testimony and that the Indians were to be asked to express their opinion only on whether the said lieutenant prevented them from hearing Mass and attending Christian doctrine and whether he had removed some fiscals from the villages, and, that they were not to be asked anything else, with the said declaration by the said Matheo Chuba remaining in the hands of the sergeant-major. (Solana 1687b:28–29)

Shortly after this episode the governor, who was engaged in a controversy with the friars as well, panicked and fled to Cuba. These actions led to the reopening of the investigation under his interim successor and to the removal of Matheos from his post.

Two threatening problems that probably contributed to keeping the governor and his deputy on edge and led to incessant demands for the Indians' labor were the growing influence of the English from South Carolina on the Apalachicola Indians of the Middle Chattahoochee River, who were nominally vassals of the Spanish monarch, and the reports of French activity along the Gulf coast and in the lower reaches of the Mississippi valley. To check on the

French, Matheos ordered the building of a galliot on the Tacabona River. Although the Indians who did the carpentry were paid one real a day for their labor, the timing of the project and the haste with which it was launched imposed a severe burden on them. One of the soldiers stated under oath that "it was a considerable hardship for the natives and the other persons who worked on building the galliot; for the said carpenters, he knows, went down to work with their own tools and without food supplies for some days and that between twenty and thirty of the said natives went down to carry the lumber from the forest . . . being absent from the sowing of their fields" (Matheos 1687a:77; Romo de Urisa 1687:22–23). Matheos's report on the expenses associated with this project gives no indication that those who cut and carried the lumber were paid. Work on the galliot was suspended before the vessel was completed, and it was never resumed. The Indians eventually removed the nails it contained.

To search for the French, Governor Cabrera dispatched Marcos Delgado in August 1686 on an overland trek that was launched from the village of Escambé in Apalachee. The Apalachee contributed 40 warriors under Chief Alonso Pastrana, the head chief of Patale (Boyd 1937:5–6; Marques Cabrera 1686b, 1687a). It is possible that the Apalachee were asked to supply some porters as well.[3]

In a futile attempt to capture the English traders who began to appear in the Apalachicola towns along the Chattahoochee in 1685, Matheos made three forays into that territory, two of them launched in the last four months of that year. On the first he was accompanied by 250 Indians from Apalachee and on the second by 600. On the second expedition, and probably on the first as well, the Apalachee chiefs supplied the foodstuffs for this force at their own expense. Frustrated by his lack of success in capturing the English traders and angered by the steadfast refusal of the leaders of four of the principal Apalachicola towns to meet with him or sever their contacts with the English traders, Matheos burned those four towns and destroyed their stores of food. He had wanted to do so on the first expedition but had been dissuaded by the Apalachee leaders and Spanish soldiers with him, who argued that such drastic action would bring retaliation in kind against Apalachee, particularly because one of the towns was Caveta, the village of the head chief of the Apalachicola (Bolton 1925a:119–124; Guerrero 1687:104–105; Jorge 1687:110–111; Luxan 1687:111–113; Ramírez 1687:108–110; Solana 1687b; Vera 1687:107–108). Before the end of the decade two more expeditions into the Apalachicola country were made, for a total of five (Bolton 1925a:123–124).

---

3. Sabacola, apparently procured from the village located near the juncture of the Flint and the Chattahoochee, were the only ones mentioned as serving as porters.

During the same period when the Apalachee were placed under these demands, they were also bearing an increasing burden under the labor repartimiento. The building of the stone fort at St. Augustine was under way, and pestilence had sharply reduced the native populations of both Timucua and Guale. During the 1680s the flight of the remaining natives in Guale and the attacks of the English and their Indian allies forced Spain to abandon the traditional Guale territory. By 1690 the northernmost Guale mission was on Amelia Island (Wright 1981:111–112), so Apalachee bore the brunt of St. Augustine's demand for labor for the fort and for the farms of its soldiers and settlers. The expansion of the garrison at San Luis and the growth of Spanish ranching in the province meant additional demands for labor there as well.

Nonetheless, the Apalachee chieftains were so relieved to be free of Antonio Matheos and so contented by the new governor's conciliatory gestures toward them and the Apalachicola that they allowed themselves to be persuaded in 1688 to build a substantial wooden blockhouse at San Luis and a stone watchtower at St. Marks on the coast at their own expense, except for the tools, which the governor was to supply (Chiefs of Apalachee 1688; Quiroga y Losada 1688c). But the mismanagement of even the blockhouse project led to friction and discontent. A substantial quantity of wood was cut and made into planking for the structure. But before work could begin, the governor resolved to deal with the problem of the Apalachicola's continued contacts with the English traders by placing Spanish soldiers and Apalachee warriors along the middle Chattahoochee in their midst. There, after two months of labor in 1689, a hundred Apalachee carpenters completed a blockhouse protected by a moated stockade. It was staffed with 20 Spanish soldiers and 20 Apalachee warriors.

After an initial pretense of acquiescence to the demands that they sever their contacts with the English, many of the Apalachicola in those villages moved eastward to settle with the Uchee on Ocmulgee Creek to be closer to the English settlements and to escape Spanish supervision.[4] As a result of this

---

4. In a 1953 article introducing some new documents from the era of the destruction of the missions, Boyd noted that it has been the common belief that this move eastward by the Apalachicola represented a general exodus of the natives from the Chattahoochee River valley. He suggests that the emigration was limited to the four towns burned by Antonio Matheos in 1685. Although some of the Apalachicola remained on the Chattahoochee in the early 1690s, the migration to the Ocmulgee River seems to have involved a greater number of towns than the four suggested by Boyd. A 1708 document drawn up by South Carolina's Council reported the existence of 11 towns on the Uchisi River. The continued presence of some of the Apalachicola on the Chattahoochee is suggested by incidents that took place in 1701 and 1702. A Spanish and Apalachee force that set out in October 1702 to retaliate for affronts by the Apalachicola headed for the Chattahoochee River, not to the Ocmulgee region as had the 1695 retaliatory expedition. The Apalachicola force that it encountered had been dispatched

move they began to be known as Creek among the English and eventually as Yuchi or Uchisi among the Spaniards, from the name of the Chisca settlement that they found already established there; it became a member of the Creek Confederacy. Before long the governor withdrew his forces from the Chattahoochee, ordering the destruction of the fort, even the filling in of the ditch. With their antipathy toward the Spaniards and the Apalachee thus reinforced, the Apalachicola joined the Yamasee in an active war against the missions of Apalachee and Timucua that would culminate in the almost complete destruction of the missions slightly more than a decade later (Bolton 1925a:124; Quiroga y Losada 1690a; Torres y Ayala 1696:21–22).

The arrival of the next governor in 1693 brought renewed labor demands. He proceeded to Apalachee from Mexico to organize a large overland expedition to Pensacola Bay and points beyond it, for which the Indians were called upon to provide warriors, porters, and trailblazers (Torres y Ayala 1693a: 230–232). The following year, in retaliation for the frequent raids made by the Apalachicola, and particularly as a reprisal for a recent attack on the Chacato village of San Carlos on the Apalachicola River in which 42 Christian Chacato had been carried off, a force of 400 Apalachee and seven Spanish soldiers moved against the Apalachicola. They found all but one of the villages abandoned and torched (Torres y Ayala 1695). The new governor resurrected the plans for the building of a blockhouse at San Luis. The lumber cut earlier had decayed so new wood had to be cut, but by mid-1697 the blockhouse had been completed (Boyd, Smith, and Griffin 1951:20–24).

By the 1690s, probably earlier, the growth of Spanish ranching activity, especially in the western reaches of Apalachee province, created a number of economic problems for the natives. In some villages their crops suffered severely from the free-roaming stock from the ranches. At times the Spanish settlers demanded work from the natives without paying them for it, and occasionally they even carried off native women to work on their ranches against their will (Florencia 1695; Hinachuba 1699:26–27; Zúñiga y Zerda 1700a: 30–32). Before the expansion of the Spanish settlements, a number of enterprising Indians had conducted a flourishing trade in ham, bacon, lard, nuts, and other produce of the province. The Spanish settlers not only began to compete with the natives, but they also forced many of them to sell their produce at low prices, gradually excluding all but the most powerful from the trade with St. Augustine (Leturiondo [1700]; Royal Cedula 1702; Zúñiga y

---

from the Chattahoochee River town of Achito. The fact that Achito had just hosted a general meeting of the chiefs of the Creek Confederacy suggests the continued presence of a considerable number of Creek towns in that region (Solana 1702; Romo de Uriza 1702; Boyd 1953: 468–472).

Zerda 1700:30–32). Both Governor Torres and his successor dispatched a special visitador to investigate the reports of abuse of the natives. The man chosen for both missions was related to a number of the offending ranchers and monopolists as well as to the lieutenant, so the native leaders were reluctant to voice their complaints to him. Although Governor Joseph de Zúñiga in November 1700 ordered his lieutenant to see that all abuses ended, the continued complaints of the native leaders and their friends within the Spanish community indicate that little was done. The orders for the redress of these grievances were ignored by royal officials with family ties to the offending parties (Ayala y Escobar 1698; Hinachuba 1699:26–27; Ponce de León 1702:27–29). On his second mission the inspector not only did not try to remedy matters but also sharply restricted the potential for renewed trade between the Apalachee and the Apalachicola and other non-Christian tribes with whom they had just celebrated peace treaties in part for this purpose (Ayala y Escobar and Solana 1701:33–34; Hinachuba 1699:26–27).

An atrocity committed by one of the well-connected Spaniards in Apalachee, Francisco de Florencia, contributed directly both to provoking the Apalachicola attack on Apalachee and to demoralizing its inhabitants. While on a buffalo hunt with 40 Chacato, Florencia encountered a band of Indians coming to Apalachee from Taisquique to trade buffalo skins, deerskin shirts, and other goods. Learning where the Indians intended to spend the night, Florencia and his party fell upon them at midnight, killing 16 of the 24 and carrying off the goods that they had intended to trade. On returning to Apalachee, Florencia brought the stolen deerskin shirts to Ayubale to be painted. In reporting this atrocity early in 1699, the chief of Ivitachuco prophesied, "It is certain that the deed is such that all of us will have to pay for these activities" (Hinachuba 1699:26–27). It was probably no accident that when the major assault on Apalachee was launched in 1704, Ayubale was the attackers' first target, even though it was not the most exposed or accessible of the mission villages.

The episode that seemed to contribute most to the demoralization of the province was a disastrous rout suffered by its forces in 1702. In retaliation for an Apalachicola attack on the Timucuan mission village of Santa Fé and the earlier murder of three Apalachee traders, a band of 800 Apalachee led by a Spanish officer and accompanied by a few Spanish soldiers set out to attack Apalachicola towns along the Chattahoochee. En route they fell into an ambush set by a band from Apalachicola province that was on its way to attack Apalachee and were defeated disastrously. Only 300 of the Apalachee returned directly from the fray, and they had had to leave most of their arms on the field of battle. After that disaster the expedition's leader reported that, counting both the boys and the old men, he could now muster only about

1,500 fighting men; he had few arms to equip them, and their morale was low because they expected additional attacks by the Apalachicola (Romo de Urisa 1702; Zúñiga y Zerda 1702).

On the same day as the ambush, the governor's deputy in Apalachee expressed serious concern about the defensibility of the province because its villages were so spread out and the houses in each village were scattered widely over a circumference of three or four leagues. In a "circle-the-wagons" proposal, he advised moving the small frontier village of Bacuqua to a point closer to San Luis and similarly suggested relocating Escambé to a site between Tama and Tomoli, one league from San Luis. He also mentioned plans for building a stockade around San Luis. Additional concern about Bacuqua and Escambé grew out of the report of a Christian Chacato woman who had escaped from Achito. She reported that the Apalachicola leaders intended to make those villages their first targets in a projected attack on the province (Albuquerque 1703; Solana 1702).

Boyd says that the lieutenant's recommendation to move those two villages seems to have been carried out. He based his conclusion on the 1705 depiction of the fort and village of San Luis and the surrounding terrain by a member of Admiral Landeche's party. It seems to place Bacuqua to the southeast of San Luis rather than north of it, as it is known to have been at an earlier time (Boyd, Smith, and Griffin 1951:plate I). Boyd also based his judgment on the remark by Manuel Solana in July 1704 that Escambé was then within cannon shot of San Luis (Boyd 1953:460–461). If this depiction is accurate, then it appears that Bacuqua had been moved, as suggested by the lieutenant. Questions have been raised, however, that throw serious doubt on the assumption that the drawing was meant to be an accurate depiction of the locations of the identified features. The orientation of the San Luis site in relation to Apalachee Bay and to the points of the compass seems to have been distorted by 180 degrees. Not much can be based on the remark about the location of Escambé beyond the fact that the village had been moved eastward from a location west of the Ochlockonee that it had occupied in 1693.

Although the inhabitants of Ayubale, the first village attacked by the Apalachicola in 1704, resisted heroically until they ran out of ammunition, alienation and demoralization took a toll on the inhabitants of most of the rest of the Apalachee villages, facilitating the work of the attackers. News of the Apalachee's discontent traveled as far as Charleston. When Colonel Moore broached his plan to attack Apalachee, the South Carolina authorities were encouraged by reports of serious disaffection toward the Spaniards among the Apalachee. The authorities ordered Moore to induce as many Apalachee as possible to relocate voluntarily to British territory by offering them their freedom rather than simply killing or enslaving them, as Moore seems to have contemplated initially. In response to that offer, the entire population of at least two villages went over to the English-led invaders without a fight. The chief of Ivitachuco bought temporary safety for his people by delivering the church plate and a quantity of foodstuffs to the attackers. Tortures inflicted by the Indians allied with the English on prisoners induced more Apalachee to desert to the invaders, further lowering the morale of the remaining Spaniards and Indians. On the eve of the final major encounter during the second campaign in June 1704, the Indians refused to face the enemy unless the Spaniards agreed to fight with them on foot. In the heat of the battle, a rumor among the Apalachee warriors that the enemy was encircling them caused most of the Indians to abandon the field. So mistrustful did the surviving Spaniards become of their erstwhile allies that most of the Indians who straggled back to the blockhouse at San Luis seeking refuge were turned away unless they had come in the company of a Spanish soldier (Boyd 1951:15–19; Solana 1704a:50–55).

The best illustration, perhaps, of the alienation and demoralization among the Apalachee at the time is the frank exchange of views between some of the native leaders and Manuel Solana, recorded by the latter after this second attack and defeat. Seeing that many of the surviving natives were fleeing to the woods to escape a rumored third invasion, Solana addressed them, warning them that in fleeing to the woods they were going forth to perish. He suggested that if they wished to leave their lands and property, they would do better to go to the vicinity of St. Augustine, driving their cattle before them. He assured them that the governor would welcome them, if he wrote proposing this move, and would provide them with lands there. He recorded their frank response:

> To all of which they replied to me that they were weary of waiting for aid from the Spaniards: that they did not wish merely to die; that for a long time we had misled them with words, [saying] that reinforcements were to come, but they were never seen to arrive; that they know with certainty that what the pagans say, will happen as they say, because all that they have said up to now has been done . . . and that if we do not believe what the pagans say, that we who remain in the blockhouse, they well know, remain to die; that if they go, it will not be to the Spaniards, and if they remain until the return of the enemy, it will be in order [to go] against us, and they will burn us within the blockhouse, while they escape with their lives. (Solana 1704a:50–55)

Without any apparent rancor, the Spanish authorities, in ordering the abandonment of the province, acknowledged the justice of that statement:

> It has also been found that the Indians have been justified in saying they have been expecting one confusion after another, as a consequence of

the promises made to them that help would be sent them shortly. Up to this time none has arrived, for none of the promises made them could have been fulfilled. In the repeated invasions made in this region during three years, there have been more than three thousand killed, and a great number of captives have been carried off. (Council of War 1704:56–59)

Spain was not in a position to send aid, even if it had wanted to. It was wracked by the War of the Spanish Succession, both a civil war and an international war involving Europe's major powers, over whether a French Bourbon or an Austrian Hapsburg would control Spain and the resources of its empire.

Chapter 11

Indian and Spanish Interaction and Acculturation

WHEN FLORIDA'S mission system was destroyed at the start of the eighteenth century, this corner of Spain's far-flung empire was well on its way toward the formation of its own culture based on the fusion of Spanish and aboriginal elements. Had the Creek and Carolinian attacks not ended the process so abruptly, Florida's native contribution probably would have had a distinctly Apalachee flavor because of the preponderance of the Apalachee among Florida's surviving mission population in 1700. I will look in some detail at this inchoate new culture and at the nature of the contacts between the two cultures that produced the mix.

The principal Spanish agents for the modification of the native culture were the friar and the soldier, though the Spanish settlers probably had some influence as well. The mechanism of the natives' influence on Spanish culture in the region is more difficult to define. In part, certainly, it resulted from the isolation and poverty of Florida, the small size of the Spanish population, and its reliance on the natives for domestic service, construction work, and agricultural labor. To some degree, especially in the more remote areas such as Apalachee, native influence probably flowed from the fraternization between the Spanish soldiery and the native leadership element. In other parts of the Spanish and Portuguese New World, the intermarriage or cohabitation of the Iberian male and the Indian female was a major source of the cultural cross-fertilization that has given much of Latin America its distinctive character. For Florida as a whole, and particularly for Apalachee, the role of such alliances in this process is unknown, inasmuch as data concerning the incidence of mestization is virtually nonexistent.

The initial contacts between the two ethnic groups in the first half of the sixteenth century gave no inkling of such an outcome. The Apalachee remained steadfastly hostile to the brutal soldiery of both the Narváez and the de

237

Soto expeditions, showing a single-minded determination to expel the intruders. From his contacts with the Apalachee not long after de Soto's departure, however, Fontaneda saw something in their attitude or character that induced him to make a remarkably accurate prediction. Among all of the Indians of the Southeast of whom he had become aware, the Apalachee seemed to him to offer the best prospect as candidates for Christianization and incorporation into the Spanish world, if properly approached (d'Escalante Fontaneda 1976:38).

One can only speculate about what moved some of the Apalachee in the first years of the seventeenth century to ask that missionaries be sent to live among them. The desire for European goods probably was an important factor and another likely was their loss of faith in the adequacy of their view of the cosmos in the wake of the decimation of the population by the diseases introduced by the European and the African. There are indications that the chiefs saw Spanish support as an opportunity to enhance their control which had probably been weakened by the demographic disasters of the preceding century. To the degree that the chiefs functioned as priests, their power would have been undermined because of the erosion of faith in the old ways produced by those disasters.

The formal process of acculturation began in 1608 with the visit of the first friars to Ivitachuco on a mission of peace, but acculturation probably remained localized and minimal in its impact until some years after 1633, when the first permanent missions among the Apalachee were established. Thus, any significant blending of the two cultures had progressed for only a little more than half a century before disaster struck in 1704. During those years, the most important Spanish influence resulted from the natives' contact with the Franciscan friars.

The term used to denote the principal mission station in each district, doctrina, is indicative of the cultural exchange function exercised by the friars. In a narrow sense the word means the place where the catechism and other basic Catholic beliefs were taught to the Indians. In a broader sense, however, the root of the word indicates that the friars of the doctrina were primarily *teachers* seeking to indoctrinate the natives in the rudiments of Spanish civilization, of which the Catholic faith was a basic ingredient. Their teaching encompassed much more than religion, extending to the natives' agricultural practices and resources, language, mores, mode of dress, conduct of war, and other matters.

Not unexpectedly, Spanish influence on the natives appears to have been most intense in the realm of religious belief and practice. Taken out of context, an embittered friar's complaint in the late 1680s that the Apalachee had no appreciation of the faith or sense of the law of God and never would might lead one to believe that the friars had little impact (Friar at Bacuqua 1687). The testimony of the French, however, who had contact with the Apalachee emigrés from San Luis and Escambé at Mobile, indicates that in the practice of their new faith the Apalachee were almost thoroughly acculturated and scarcely distinguishable from Europeans who had been Christians for centuries ([Bienville] [1726]:536; McWilliams 1953:133–135).

It is probable that the emigrés from those two villages along with those from Ivitachuco and possibly Oconi, were the most acculturated of the Apalachee because of their contact with the Spanish soldiers and the friars, and in San Luis and some of the other westernmost missions there was additional contact with the Spanish ranchers during the last quarter of the seventeenth century. Ivitachuco probably owed its high degree of acculturation in part to its early Christianization, from 1608 to 1612, to the use of much of its male population in a rotating labor force on the Spanish ranches of Timucua and in St. Augustine, and to its close contact with western Timucua, which had already been Christianized before the formal launching of the Apalachee missions in 1633. A confident grasp of the essence of the new faith was reflected in the Ivitachuca chief's assessment in 1657 that their current pastor's fomenting opposition to the soldiers contradicted the message and example of charity to all given them by their previous pastor, Fray Pedro Muñoz (Rebolledo 1657a:100–101).

In material matters, the Spanish intrusion had its greatest impact in agriculture, not as much in changing the natives' methods of farming or their basic crops as in enriching them. Because of the Spanish influence, the natives added many new cultigens to their diet and learned new activities, such as the raising of chickens, dairy farming, and animal husbandry in general. No exhaustive work has been done yet to identify the exotic cultigens brought to Apalachee by the Spaniards, but there is archaeological or documentary evidence for the introduction of wheat, barley, chickpeas, European greens, various aromatic herbs, peas, sugarcane, garlic, peaches, pears, medlars, figs, pomegranates, quince, and European grapes (Boniface 1971:123; Castilla 1740; Leturiondo [1700]:200–201). Bolton's remark that most cultivated plants then known to Europeans were introduced to the Spanish missions can probably be applied to Apalachee (Bolton 1917:57).

The natives seem to have been introduced to the production of chickens and hogs early in the mission period. Indeed, once peace had been established between them, the Apalachee probably began to secure hogs and chickens by trade with the Timucua. It is not clear whether Apalachee was already in the market at mid-century, but the fall of the price of hogs to the four-peso level by 1651, when the stock of Governor Ruíz de Salazar's farm was sold off, suggests that it may have been.

Cattle seem to have been slower to arrive. That they were introduced before the arrival of the Spanish settlers at San Luis in the 1670s is indicated by export statistics for the middle of that decade, which reveal that Apalachee exported 150 hides and 3,800 pounds of tallow to Havana in 1675. By 1681 the number of hides exported had risen to 700, and in the same year more than 5,000 pounds of tallow were sent to Havana from Apalachee (Boniface 1971:200). One of the friars in Apalachee is mentioned as owning stock at some time before 1657 (Rebolledo 1657a:97–98). Governor Ruíz de Salazar's farm on the border of Apalachee in the last half of the 1640s had a considerable number of hogs, cattle, and plow oxen. In view of the farm's proximity to Ivitachuco, it is possible that some of the hogs were sold in Apalachee. Raising chickens and hogs appears to have become widespread among the natives, but the degree to which the ownership of cattle spread among the natives beyond the leadership class, at least on any significant scale, remains unknown. In July 1704, Manuel Solana, in a speech to persuade the remaining natives to withdraw with him to St. Augustine, did mention that they might bring their cattle (Solana 1704a:50–55).

The only reference to the production of salted beef and to the manufacture of cheese involves a Spanish rancher from Bacuqua, but some of the natives likely became familiar with these processes as they worked on the Spanish ranches (Delgado 1693:254). The natives were already familiar with smoking and drying meat over a fire, but with the introduction of hogs they also became acquainted with the use of salt in combination with smoking in the production of ham and bacon. They learned to manufacture lard and butter, and they probably learned the technique of producing jerky if they did not already know it.

Although there is no mention of goats or sheep in Apalachee, these animals were so much a part of Spanish agriculture that it seems likely that they were introduced. Some had been brought to St. Augustine as early as 1567. On the basis of a 1686 report that the Indians had become proficient in making cordovan leather, Boniface concluded that goats had been introduced in at least one of the missions (Boniface 1971:200).

Horses were probably the last domesticated animal to be introduced into Apalachee in any quantity, and apparently they were never numerous. While organizing his overland expedition to Pensacola Bay in 1693, Governor Torres remarked on the scarcity of horses in Apalachee, but most of the approximately 70 horses that accompanied the expedition came from Apalachee (Torres y Ayala 1693a:229, 231). Horses were numerous enough in the province in the 1690s to have become an item of trade with the Apalachicola (Ayala Escobar and Solana 1701:33–34; Bushnell 1979:6; Zúñiga y Zerda 1702:36–38). The ownership of horses by Apalachee's leadership class is indicated clearly in the 1694 visitation. One of the civil complaints at Escambé involved the village chief's sale of three horses to one of the Christian Chacato Indians temporarily housed in his village as refugees. Shortly after the turn of the century the governor reported confidently that the 25 horses he had asked the chiefs to furnish for sale to the Crown for a cavalry company would arrive shortly. The visitation record also reveals the existence of communal herds of cattle as well as ownership by individual natives (Florencia 1695).

The degree to which the introduction of iron led to the replacement of the natives' wooden or stone farm tools is not clear. The metal hoe (more like the modern mattock) replaced the Indians' wooden tool for digging (Boniface 1971:123), and metal axes and knives seem to have come into common use. The degree to which oxen and the plow were used for turning the soil also remains unclear. On his 1693 trip from Tomole to San Luis, Friar Rodrigo de Barreda mentioned passing through a district furrowed with ploughed fields two leagues from Tomole (Barreda 1693:265). These may have belonged to Spaniards rather than to natives, but the use of the term *digging Indians* to designate the natives sent to St. Augustine to plant for the soldiers there seems to indicate that, on the whole, they continued to follow their traditional practices of tilling the soil even when working for the Spaniards. In addition, the involvement of most of the village work force in the planting of the fields for the maintenance of the priest, for the adornment of the church, and for meeting community welfare needs points to the persistence of the traditional methods, even for relatively large operations in which the use of oxen and the plow would most likely have replaced them (Bentura 1687:37–38; Roque Pérez 1687:32–33).

Little information has surfaced concerning the friars' influence in introducing the Apalachee to new crafts and skills. A certain amount of ironworking was done in the province. Anvils are known to have been used in some of the villages, and nails, spikes, and tools for construction projects were made on site; but it is not clear whether the blacksmiths were Indian or Spanish. The two blacksmiths who made the hardware for the fort at San Luis were not identified; neither was the maker of the hardware for a galley-building project on the Tacabona, despite the identification of all the Indian carpenters on the project by name and by village of origin (Boyd, Smith, and Griffin 1951:23; Matheos 1687a:77). Inasmuch as nails and spikes were used in building churches and convents, some natives must have learned simple blacksmithing when church building was at its peak. Speaking in a general sense about such activity in more distant mission areas, Governor Quiroga (1687–1693) observed that the merest beginnings of forges or blacksmiths' shops had been established by the natives many years earlier to eliminate the need for going to St. Augustine to repair small iron tools, but that the natives' poverty prevented them from expanding the shops into more ambitious operations (Quiroga y Losada 1688a:221–223).

Apalachee is not mentioned specifically as the site of a forge, but in view of its distance from St. Augustine and our knowledge that nails, spikes, and tools were made there, it appears likely that it had a forge or two. That the natives were already familiar with the hammering out of objects made of copper would have facilitated their acquisition of these additional metal-working skills. They were sufficiently interested in nails, either to use on their structures or to rework into something else, to travel to the coast to salvage the nails used in the unfinished ship on the Tacabona.

We know that the Spanish presence led to some enhancement of the Apalachee's skill in tanning leather. Before their contact with the Europeans, the Indians of the Southeast, in general, possessed considerable skill in the dressing of skins. De Soto's companions spoke with admiration of the well-tanned multicolored skins used by the natives to make moccasins, leggings, and breechclouts. In order to produce soft and pliable leather, they scraped and soaked the skins in water and then treated them with the cooked brains of a deer or some other animal. This treatment produced a fine white leather, but it had the drawback of being unsuitable for exposure to moisture, which caused it to harden and shrink on drying. To be used in moist circumstances, such skins required further treating by smoke and dung. This treatment produced a durable but smelly leather which provoked one European observer to remark that the odor was so unpleasant as to discourage even a rat from gnawing at such skins unless it were blessed with a good stomach (Swanton 1946: 442–447).

Swanton's account of the natives' skin-dressing skills does not indicate whether the use of tannin from tree bark was familiar to the Indians before their contact with Europeans. He mentioned their use of water in which red oak bark had been boiled but did not reveal whether the practice had prehistoric origins. The natives were not familiar with the use of oil for softening leather (Swanton 1946:335, 443). We can presume that the Apalachee possessed similar skills to those characteristic of other natives of the Southeast before the arrival of the Europeans; Narváez, for example, encountered painted deerskins from Apalachee in South Florida (Núñez Cabeza de Vaca 1964:12–13).

Governor Quiroga identified Apalachee as one of the places where some of the natives had acquired the art of producing fine leather and leather of the cordovan-type for making shoes. The raw material was in such short supply in the area, however, that none of the natives practiced the trade on a regular basis. Instead they processed leather only as they needed it for themselves or when there was some demand for it. Quiroga observed that this locally produced leather was used by some of the soldiers to make shoes (Quiroga y Losada 1688a:221–223). There is some question as to how widespread this skill was in Apalachee. A request in 1703 by the governor to his deputy at San Luis for 40 tanned hides brought the response that such hides for making shoes were not to be found in the province because enemy incursions had removed those who possessed that skill (Solana 1703:41). Apalachee chieftains Don Patricio of Ivitachuco and Don Andrés of San Luis several years earlier gave a different reason for the departure of at least one tanner. They complained to the king that the deputy-governor and the Spanish settlers at San Luis had compelled the mico of La Tama, whom they characterized as new in the faith and skilled in tanning, to prepare skins for them without paying him for his work, and that, as a consequence of this injustice, the said chief had deserted to the English (Hinachuba and Andrés 1699:24–26). In commenting on the hides exported from St. Marks and other parts of Florida in the 1674–1694 period, Boniface speculated that they were almost certainly unprocessed, noting that most were referred to as *cueros al pelo* (probably raw hides with the hair on) (Boniface 1971:203, 219). These comments about the tanners indicate that, particularly for the dressing of the skins of wild animals, the Apalachee continued to employ the traditional methods with which they were familiar.

The friars sought to introduce the Apalachee to the technique of weaving cotton cloth so that they might protect themselves from the winter cold more adequately and dress more decently. The Spanish authorities repeatedly requested the importation of either Tlascalans or Indians from Campeche to impart this skill to the Apalachee, remarking that cotton was already being grown in the province. But no Indians were dispatched from Mexico for that purpose, despite the Crown's approval of the suggestion on at least one occasion. What little cotton was grown was produced as a curiosity for amusement or for spinning into thread.

The Indians of the Southeast possessed a rudimentary form of weaving but had not developed the shuttle (Council of the Indies 1702; Hita Salazar 1678a; Leturiondo 1673; Royal Cedula 1676; Siguenza y Góngora 1693:162–167). In his description of the Indians encountered at Pensacola Bay, Father Sigüenza y Góngora mentioned seeing balls of yarn made from buffalo hair and a well-woven sash made of the same material (Sigüenza y Góngora 1693:162–167). The Apalachee doubtless possessed similar skills, but that was the limit of their weaving skills. By the end of the mission period, yarn was one of the products occasionally exported by Apalachee. In January 1703, the governor asked the lieutenant to send him about 600 skeins of coarse yarn along with a number of other items. The lieutenant replied that the yarn was being made and that as much as could be readied would be sent with the labor detail that would be dispatched for St. Augustine's spring planting (Solana 1703:41–42). Bishop Calderón characterized the mission Indians in general as "clever and quick to learn any art they see done, and great carpenters as is evidenced in the construction of their wooden churches which are large and painstakingly wrought" (Diáz Vara Calderón 1675:12). The Apalachee had a reputation as good carpenters. Their placement of the huge major support posts for the San Luis council house reflects both skill and precision. The profiling of two of the postmolds of these deeply rooted posts reveals a difference of only two centimeters in the distance above mean sea level of the base of these tree trunks (Gary Shapiro, personal communication, May 22, 1986). Much of their skill in working with wood probably antedates the mission period, but it was no doubt enhanced by the acquisition of new iron and steel tools such as the saw, the adze, augurs, and chisels. These new tools do not seem to have altered the natives' methods of constructing their own buildings. The Apalachee's basic architectural styles appear to have remained unchanged through the mission period, but in the building of the churches and convents they followed European models to some degree. These buildings were rectangular rather than round, like the natives' houses and lodges, and were multiroomed in contrast to aboriginal building styles. Iron nails and spikes were used to fasten together the framework, and hardware such as locks and sliding bolts were attached to the doors of these structures as were metal hinges (Morrell and Jones 1970; Smith 1951a, 1956:56–60, 62–66).

Beyond these changes, even these European-inspired structures generally followed the native building style, relying on wattle and daub for the lower part of the side walls and interior partitions and thatch for the remainder of the wall and for the roof. Occasionally, however, planking was used for one or more of the walls. Some of the lumber left over from the building of the fort at San Luis was used by the Indians to build a number of houses for the Spaniards in the village (Hinachuba and Andrés 1699:24–26; Morrell and Jones 1970:33, 36). In some cases, a stucco finish was applied to the exterior portion of the wattle and daub wall and then painted white with a coating of lime (Morrell and Jones 1970:35). Without making it clear whether he is talking about a specific group, Alonso de Leturiondo reported that it was the Indians' custom to decorate the walls of their lodges and churches with great naturalness with multicolored murals depicting their battles and their stories (Leturiondo [1700]). Lime-whitened walls would have provided an ideal background for such artwork. That the Apalachee were accustomed to painting on deerskins suggests that their aesthetic impulse also found this outlet. Timucua appears to have been the source of many of the pigments used in the murals, however. Leturiondo noted that the natives extracted "very fine and light powders of all colors which they use to make pigments" from a place called Aramazaca on the hacienda of Dona Luisa de Los Angeles y Argüellez (Leturionda [1700]:201). For the floors of the church and the convent the native practice of using hardened packed clay was followed.

Not enough archaeological work has been done on the natives' dwellings and council houses of the mission era to examine the extent of European influence on building techniques. Except for the work begun at San Luis early in 1985, no council house of the period has been excavated to establish whether any European novelties were used in these native structures (B. Calvin Jones, personal communication, April 19, 1984). The excavation of San Luis's council house has revealed no nails or spikes. The relative scarcity and cost of metal in Florida probably prevented any widespread use of these items in native building projects. The San Luis council house has the configuration of the classic Creek rotunda (Shapiro 1985b; personal communication May 1986).

The Spaniards had little impact on the making and use of pottery by the natives. In contrast to the English from Carolina, as Boniface noted, the Spaniards did not supply metal cooking and food utensils to the natives as trade items—not surprising inasmuch as the use of earthenware vessels was still a part of the Spanish culinary tradition (Boniface 1971:188–189). Indeed earthernware vessels were still being used for shipping and storage, for example, the famous Spanish *tinaja,* or olive jar, was used for shipping wine and oil. Accordingly, this area is one where the Spaniards borrowed from the natives, adopting their cooking utensils as well as the foods that were prepared in them. This adaptation is reflected in a letter by the commandant at St. Marks in the mid-1740s mentioning the arrival there of two formerly Christian Sabacola women. He noted that they were of invaluable assistance to the garrison in making native pottery and in gathering food such as oysters and potatoes (Montiano 1756). As reflected in this instance the Spaniards' adoption of the natives' cooking and eating utensils was also to some degree a consequence of the poverty of Spanish Florida and the Crown's failure to keep it adequately supplied.

Although missionization did not lead to the displacement of native pottery, Spanish influence did bring about some changes in it. A distinctive pottery style linked to the Apalachee missions (but found beyond the borders of Apalachee as well) reached its full development during the mission era. It is known as Leon-Jefferson Ware for the two counties whose boundaries today enclose most of the Apalachee's territory. Initially thought to have belonged exclusively to the mission period, Leon-Jefferson Ware is now believed to antedate the mission era in some of its important characteristics. The annular ring type of base used in various pottery types of Leon-Jefferson Ware—such as Miller Plain, Jefferson Plain, and Mission Red Filmed—and the vessel forms on which it was used (plate and bowl) are direct copies of the European-inspired majolica-ware from Mexico found in association with it. The pitcher form and the Miller Plain pitcher handles were also copied from Spanish models.

Hale G. Smith observed that it is difficult to say whether these types of vessels were wheel-made (Smith 1951c:26; 1956:63–64, 112, 123–127, 1968:316–319). There apparently is no direct evidence for the introduction of the potter's wheel among the Indians of the region (James Miller and Gary Shapiro, personal communication, April 9, 1984). Other types of clay vessels produced here during the mission period show clearly the natives' continued use of the traditional coil method of manufacture (Smith 1951b:165–166).

There is evidence that some of the pottery made during the mission period was harder than that made earlier, indicating the introduction of improved firing techniques. In some cases, there was a decline in the aesthetic quality of mission-era pottery, but, as noted, it was to be expected because this feature was intimately linked with aboriginal tribal lore and religion (Smith 1951a: 129, 1956:26). This decline was not, however, universal. Some attribute it to the disruption of clan ties and traditional village organization that resulted from the Spanish intrusion and from the rapid population decline and to the fact that women (who were the pottery makers) were forced to look beyond the usual sources for their mates (Gary Shapiro, personal communication, October 1984).

In contrast to the neighboring Creek, who, under English influence, largely replaced the traditional bow and arrow with firearms, the Apalachee's traditional weapons were not displaced by those of the Spaniards. For most of the warrior class the primary weapons remained the bow and arrow and hatchet. Spanish officials sharply restricted the natives' access to firearms, but there has been a tendency to overplay the effectiveness of their control. The unsupervised trade between Havana and Apalachee provided the Apalachee with significant quantities of arms. Probably all of the native leadership had access to firearms, but the majority of the warriors continued to rely on the bow and arrow. The makeup of the 1677 anti-Chisca expedition probably indicates the degree of the spread of firearms among the Apalachee: 30 of the 190 warriors carried firearms (Fernández de Florencia 1678).

At least two of the leaders had become sufficiently familiar with their guns to have become good marksmen. When the Apalachee started toward home, a Chisca force appeared on the trail. With one shot each, Don Bernardo from Cupaica and Bi Bentura of San Luis killed two of the enemy and put the rest to flight. By 1700 the Apalachee had become familiar enough with the use of firearms to prompt Alonso de Leturiondo to remark that, although their principal weapon was still the bow and arrow, which they handled with great skill, "today they use firearms as do the Spaniards, and, in Apalachee, they maintain their arms as well as do the best trained officers" (Leturiondo [1700]: 199). In the final encounter in 1704 between the Spanish and Apalachee force and the English-led Creek invaders, 93 of the Apalachee warriors carried firearms and only 60 were archers (Solana 1704a:50–55).

Leturiondo went on to remark that the Apalachee "also use some hatchets that they bear attached to the leather belt worn about the waist [*en la petrina*] with which they remove the scalp of those whom they kill" (Leturiondo [1700]:199). It is likely that, because of the Spanish influence, that hatchet was often iron rather than stone or that, when an iron hatchet was lacking, an iron or steel knife was used for scalping. There is evidence that a favorite instrument for scalping was a scalpel made from a sharpened reed.

The impact of the Spanish authorities' condemnation of the practice of scalping is difficult to evaluate. In the expedition against the Chisca, the Apalachee leaders were able to restrain their warriors from scalping their victims, but as late as the end of the seventeenth century scalping was still being practiced by the Timucua, who had been exposed to European influence for a considerably longer period than had the Apalachee (García 1695:172 ff.; Zúñiga y Zerda 1701:35). As Leturiondo noted, scalping was still in use among the Apalachee as well in 1700. In response to an incident of Timucuan scalping, the governor issued a general order forbidding the practice in the territories under his jurisdiction and specifically mentioning Apalachee as one of the provinces to which this order was directed. As the public display of scalps was closely linked to entry into and advancement within the warrior class, the governor ordered that some other criteria be established for the recognition of warriors' achievements (Zúñiga y Zerda 1701:35–36).

Equally difficult to assess is the validity of Willey's suggestion that the Apalachee were easily defeated by the Creek led by Moore because "the old war patterns were probably extinguished or suppressed" (Willey 1949:489). From the establishment of the missions among them until the English arrived in South Carolina, the Apalachee had an unwonted period of peace. Undoubtedly, that they were no longer constantly honing their skills as warriors had some impact on their confidence and expertise. But from the 1670s on, they had been blooded repeatedly, and, until the attacks that led to the obliteration of their villages, they do not seem to have been wary of taking the field to seek redress for grievances. In 1700, Alonso de Leturiondo could still write that "The Indians of those provinces, and principally the Apalache, have been and are the most valiant of all those lands. . . . They are so bloodthirsty that, if some Indian from their village is killed by one from another, they do not rest until they revenge the killing either on the one who did it or on someone else from his village" (Leturiondo [1700]:199–200). The introduction of Christianity and European civilization doubtless had some effect in diluting the Apalachee's warrior spirit displayed so boldly against de Soto and Narváez in the sixteenth century. Moore's easy victory in 1704, however, was more the result of the Apalachee's inferior firepower and their demoralization from the recent defeat on the Flint and the report of the tortures inflicted on those taken prisoner at Ayubale. In addition, they were greatly outnumbered because they could not bring together in one place their still substantial number of warriors.

It is not possible to ascertain the degree to which Christian teaching and the Spanish emphasis on legalism curbed the practice of family, clan, or village retribution for the death of a fellow tribesman. In the formal visitations of the provinces, one of the questions often addressed to the chiefs was whether they had any unpunished crimes such as murder or concubinage to report. Invariably the answer was no. The chiefs' complaints usually involved civil matters or abuse of power rather than crimes of violence or offenses against societal sexual mores. There was one exception, a case, associated with the 1695 visitation of Timucua, involving a scalping that may have been a murder. If it was murder, it was not for revenge. If it was not murder, it indicates that the custom of seeking private justice, even for relatively trivial affronts, was still alive but had been modified to express itself through the Spanish legal system.

This interesting case was touched on briefly by Bushnell in her article on Don Patricio de Hinachuba. A Timucua named Santiago from Potohiriba brought to his village a scalp he claimed to have taken from one of four Creek warriors he had encountered in the woods. He was soon accused of having removed it instead from the head of a putative Chacato woman.

Accepting the argument advanced by Santiago's public defender, Bushnell suggested that the missing Chacato woman was invented by Don Patricio and the Apalachee who committed perjury for him and that the murder charges were trumped up by Don Patricio to strike back at Santiago. Shortly before this incident, Santiago had stripped some poachers from Don Patricio's village of two bearskins and grease from animals taken on lands belonging to San Pedro. Don Patricio sought to retaliate by leading a number of his warriors into San Pedro to seize from Santiago property equivalent to the lost bearskins and lard. Santiago had rallied enough support from his fellow villagers to thwart Don Patricio's designs.

The record of the trial inquiry left me in doubt about whether the story concerning Don Patricio was the invention of a pettifogging public defender or whether, indeed, the Chacato woman was real and had been murdered by Santiago so that he might add another scalp to his bow. When Santiago first appeared with the scalp and his story of its origin, the governor's deputy at Santa Fé appears to have been sufficiently suspicious to launch the investigation that provided Don Patricio his opportunity for revenge, if that is what it was (García 1695;172 ff.; Zúñiga y Zerda 1700a).

A disturbing feature of the case is Don Patricio's investigation into it that paralleled and meshed with the inquiry conducted by the lieutenant for western Timucua. Don Patricio sent an Ivitachucan to Potohiriba to investigate the case, and this man followed Santiago himself as a witness in the lieutenant's inquiry. Machaba similarly sent an agent to Potohiriba to look into the matter. He found what was believed to be the remains of the Chacato woman at the arroyo called Ygiura Yvita, one league west of Potohiriba on the trail to Machaba. The testimonies against Santiago by the Machaban leader and Don Patricio's agent were among the most damning. The record of the inquiry attached to the Florencia visitation does not indicate the outcome of the trial, but testimony given in 1700 by a number of witnesses during Governor Torres's residencia shows that Santiago was found guilty and was serving a sentence of forced labor at St. Augustine for the crime.

One hopes that this judicial inquiry was typical of investigations into other crimes or conspiracies, that other prosecutors and public defenders did their work as zealously as they had here, and that other records will come to light to provide valuable insights similar to those provided in this case. This instance shows that Florida's natives had become sufficiently acculturated to move comfortably within the Spanish legal system.

The persistence of the custom of private revenge for murder is illustrated by an incident in 1705 in which three Timucua killed three of four Apalachee they encountered on the La Chua cattle range. Diego Peña reported from Potano that two of the Timucua had fled and that the third had sought asylum in the convent to escape the Apalachee who had come seeking revenge (Peña 1706).

On a broader scale the revenge syndrome can be seen as a psychological weapon in intertribal relations. When the Apalachacola attacked an Apalachee village or, in 1702, when they assaulted the Timucua village of Santa Fé, the Apalachee felt, as fellow Christians, a need to strike back in order to prevent similar attacks on their own villages which they felt would follow unless the Apalachicola were punished (Zúñiga y Zerda 1702:36–38).[1]

It is not clear to what degree the native practices associated with the preparation for war—the war dance, the black-drink ceremony, the abstinence from food and sex—persisted under the mission regime. Alonso de Leturiondo mentioned one part of the Apalachee's preparations for battle: "To give battle they dress themselves elaborately after their usage, painted all over with red ochre and with their heads full of multi-colored feathers" (Leturiondo [1700]:200). No such preparations are mentioned specifically elsewhere. The account of the anti-Chisca expedition states simply that, when approaching

1. The Apalachicola had recently killed three Apalachee traders in their midst, a definite consideration in the Apalachee's decision to strike back.

the enemies' palisaded village, "[we] pulled off the trail to a high place to prepare ourselves, to inspect our arms, to pull ourselves together, and all we leaders joined together in consultation concerning what we should do" (Fernández de Florencia 1678). In the record of preparations for the expedition, there is no mention of any of these elements. The one practice recorded as having survived was the pep talk or harangue by the Indian leaders to their troops. On the first day of their march out from San Luis, they stopped for a time upon reaching the Ochlockonee to assess their strength and to be addressed by their leaders, who reminded them that they were men capable of defending their villages, women, and children and assured them that, because they were Christians, God and his most holy mother would favor them in the upcoming battle. After 18 days on the trail, they found the palisaded village of the Chisca, Chacato, and Pansacola during the night, and their leaders addressed a second exhortatory message to them just before the attack at about three in the morning. The influence of the Spanish crusading approach to war and of the mission is reflected in the banner that led them into battle: it was emblazoned on one side with the crucifix and on the other with a portrait of Our Lady of the Rosary, to whom there was apparently a special devotion at San Luis (Fernández de Florencia 1678).[2]

The Spanish influence on the native warrior is reflected in the title of the leader of the native militia in most of the villages: captain in the Spanish infantry, a title of which they apparently were intensely proud. In some cases it was the chief who bore that title, but at San Luis and Ivitachuco it appears to have been held by a leading man other than the chief (Fernández de Florencia 1678; Rebolledo 1657a). No friar is shown to have accompanied that 1677 expedition as chaplain. In the other military events on which we have detailed accounts, the friars are recorded as playing significant roles. Fray Angel de Miranda directed the defense of Ayubale, and Fray Juan de Parga addressed a lengthy sermon in Apalachee to the troops just before their unsuccessful counterattack against the forces of Colonel Moore. In 1704, the friars accompanied the forces into battle (Cruz 1705:74–75; Zúñiga y Zerda 1704a:48–50).

By the time of the destruction of the missions, the Apalachee's speech had been influenced considerably by Spanish. The French who met the emigrés in Mobile described them as speaking a mixture of their native tongue and Spanish. Some of the literate leadership, such as the royal interpreter, Diego Salvador, and the chiefs of Ivitachuco, were probably fluent in Spanish. Con-

2. As they were about to attack, the native leaders reported seeing a great light about as high as a man and with a blue spot in the middle. Some sources view this episode as a reflection of the natives' belief in the miraculous. However, it is recounted matter-of-factly with no such explicit implication. And indeed it worked against them, as it enabled one of the Chacato sentinels to spot them and sound the alarm.

versely, some of the Spanish soldiers, such as the lieutenant in Apalachee in the 1670s, Juan Fernández de Florencia, were fluent in the native tongue. Many of the friars, on the other hand, do not seem to have become proficient in the language, making necessary the use of interpreters for hearing confessions, teaching catechism, and performing other clerical duties. This failure was a frequent complaint of the governors (Ferro Machado 1688; Higginbotham 1977:194; Quiroga y Losada 1690b).

Acculturation led many among the leaders in Florida to abandon the use of their native surnames. More of the leaders in Apalachee seem to have clung to their native names than did those in Timucua. Thus, long after Christianization, one encounters Patricio and Bernardo Hinachuba, Matheo Chuba, Pedro Osunac, and Nicolás and Feliciano Tafunsaca to balance Alonso Pastrana, Juan Mendoza, and Diego Salvador. Among the ordinary Apalachee, preservation of the native surnames appears to have been the rule, again in contrast to other Christianized groups. The first census after the destruction of the missions, in 1711, showed all but one name in the Apalachee village near St. Augustine to have a native component (Córcoles y Martínez 1711). There was no effort made to force the natives to learn Spanish, a fact reported critically by a visitador in 1688 who lamented that the friars were teaching religion classes to the natives in their own tongue rather than in Spanish (Ferro Machado 1688).

Medicine appears to have been one field in which the Apalachee resisted acculturation rather persistently. They continued to have recourse to the shaman and sowed a field for him despite the condemnation of these practices by the Spanish authorities. As late as the 1694–1695 visitation, it was found necessary to issue a regulation stipulating that the caciques were "not to consent to, tolerate, or conceal curing after the pagan manner; and they are not to sow or dig the field for such curanderos as is the practice" (Florencia 1695: 87–88). This continued recourse to the shamans is not surprising in view of the epidemics of European-introduced diseases that swept through the mission villages and in view of the fact that the Europeans probably had little to offer them that was any more effective.

Alonso de Leturiondo mentioned two medicinal herbs as the most important in Florida, royal and white *itamo* and one called *chitubexatica* by the natives. Everyone carried the latter while traveling, he affirmed, because of its efficacy in promoting the healing of various types of wounds no matter how deep or numerous they might be (Leturiondo [1700]:200). A century earlier itamo was mentioned apparently under the name "Royal *Guitamo*" as indigenous to Tama and Ocute in the Georgia piedmont (Mendez de Canzo 1600).

In the other parts of the Spanish New World, mestization was a principal source of acculturation of the natives and of their loss of their identity as Indians. There is little concrete information concerning the incidence of this phenomenon in Apalachee. One suspects that some so-called natives, like the royal interpreter Diego Salvador, who bore exclusively Spanish names, held Spanish military commissions, and were literate and bilingual, may have been the product of an alliance or marriage of a Spanish soldier and an Apalachee woman from one of the tribes' leading families.[3] The Spaniards' evident admiration for the Apalachee would seem to have fostered such alliances. Such a background gave a son the opportunity to become fluent in at least two languages or even more if his father were posted to St. Augustine or to the Gualean or Timucuan garrisons, to learn to read and write, and to become rather thoroughly Hispanicized after the fashion of the Inca Garcilaso de la Vega. The only positive references to such mixing of the two groups are of the most oblique character. One of the friars' arguments for removing the soldiers from Apalachee was the suggestion that the presence of unmarried soldiers made the natives concerned for their wives and daughters, while the presence of soldiers with families increased the natives' labor burdens. One of Lieutenant Matheos's criticisms of the Apalachee men was that, when their wives were caught in adultery, they were not men enough to take vengeance on the offender; rather, once the offender had been officially chastised for his misdeeds, the husband often went home arm in arm with the one by whom he had been cuckolded as though nothing had happened (Matheos 1687b:50 ff.). The most direct reference to this phenomenon is the enigmatic remark by the Apalachee emigrés in Mobile that among the French they were masters of their wives in a fashion that they had not been among the Spaniards (Bienville 1706:25).

Sexual mores seems to be one area in which Christianization considerably modified what was regarded as acceptable behavior. There are few references to the customs and taboos of the Apalachee on this subject, but their ethical standards are likely to have been similar to those of their neighbors, about some of whom we have more concrete information. The free-wheeling conduct associated with the dance on the night before the raising of the ball post permitted the men to touch and fondle any women who were there, suggesting that in pre-Christian times the Apalachee probably shared the relaxed sexual mores and weak marriage bonds attributed to the neighboring Apalachicola, to whom they were related culturally (Hawkins 1982a:62). Among the Creek there were no taboos against premarital sex; adultery was forbidden, but

---

3. It should be noted, however, that the Spaniards were usually careful, particularly in official documents, to designate one's ethnic status correctly. A mestizo would not normally be referred to as an Indian. In fact, generally, even a thoroughly acculturated Indian ceased to be referred to as "Indian." He became a "Ladino"; it signified one who was ethnically Indian but culturally European.

the marriage bond was fragile and divorce easy to obtain. Unsatisfactory marriages were dissolved easily at the time of the Green Corn ceremony (Hudson 1976:200, 232). The existence of polygamy among the neighboring Chacato was illustrated dramatically by the 1675 revolt in the Chacato missions. It was provoked by an overzealous friar's imprudence in stripping a newly converted Chacato of three of his four wives (Hita Salazar 1675a). It is likely that similar customs prevailed among the Apalachee before they were thoroughly Christianized.

Some lapses from the new ethical standards are hinted at occasionally in the visitation records in statements that deny the existence of any such problems at the time of the visitation and indicate that, when they do arise, the village leaders deal with them promptly. This close control and the assessment by the French that the Apalachee were proper Catholics indicate a rather complete acculturation in this respect. It seems to be indicated as well by the frequent complaints recorded in the 1694 visitation by wives whose husbands were away working in other provinces (in one case for ten years) who requested that the absent husbands be required to return to their villages to resume their conjugal obligations. In response the visitor decreed that in the future, married Apalachee men were not to work outside of the province and established a heavy fine for caciques and lieutenants who tolerated this practice (Florencia 1695).

The Spanish impact on many of the complex and central features of Apalachee culture and society remains unknown because the matter received no attention or earned only the most fleeting reference in the available documentation. A prime example is the clan system and the role it played in questions of peace and war, in the choice of marriage partners, and in the determination of the divisions within the towns. The system did not receive even passing mention except for the possible reference to it in the ball game manuscript noted by Bushnell. There, in the presentation of the challenge to a game, the home team was said to have painted themselves black to represent the dark and strong animals such as the panther, wolf, and bear from which they believed their ancestors had sprung. Father Paiva noted that *cuy,* or "panther," and *nita,* or "bear," were common surnames at San Luis, and Bushnell speculated that the panther and bear clans may have been the most common clans at San Luis (Bushnell 1978b:13; Paiva 1676). Father Paiva then observed that the opposing team would paint itself with different colors representing other animals such as the deer and the fox (Paiva 1676). If the ball game played as central a role in the life of the Apalachee as it did later among the Creek, and if it was as intimately connected to the division of the realm of the Apalachee into white and red units as it was among the Creek, then the banning of the ball game would certainly have had an impact. But in the absence of documentary evidence one can do no more than indicate that there was some influence and speculate as to its nature.

A little more is known of the impact of the Spanish presence on political organization. Whatever the nature of the areawide authority among the Apalachee before they accepted Spanish overlordship, the creation of the post of deputy governor resident at San Luis definitely brought a change. The deputy governor assumed the role of top political official in the province, and the Indian leaders referred to him as their "war captain." He and the governor who appointed him became the final authorities and arbiters in such situations as determining matters of peace and war, settling questions of disputed chieftainships, moving villages and creating new ones, admitting non-Apalachee groups into the territory, and determining the relations of the Apalachee with their neighbors. In theory the governor's deputy was prohibited from interfering with the day-to-day administration of the village, but in practice, in the short run at least, there was probably little to prevent such interference. The complaints elicited by the administration of Antonio Matheos in the 1680s are the best illustration of this interference, although his actions ultimately led to his removal when the governor who appointed and supported him fled to Cuba.

In contrast to Timucua and Guale, for which Spanish intervention in the choice of chiefs has been documented (Milanich and Fairbanks 1980:225), there is no evidence of Spanish interference in Apalachee, except possibly in the wake of the 1647 uprising. Disputes over a chieftainship did open the door to Spanish intervention and influence, but in the cases that were recorded the Spanish authorities seem to have been conscientious in consulting the native leaders to assure that the rightful claimant, in accord with the natives' customs, was installed (Florencia 1695; Leturiondo 1678:546–547).

Charges of substantial interference by the governor's deputy are few, except in the notorious case of Antonio Matheos, whose conduct ultimately led to his removal. His case does illustrate the helplessness of the native leaders and society, short of flight or revolt, against abuses of power by the governor's lieutenant as long as he had the governor's support. This helplessness is further demonstrated by the unsuccessful efforts of the chief of Ivitachuco to secure redress for the natives at San Luis from the losses and the abuse inflicted on them by the Spanish settlers there. The Crown's good intentions were no match for the inertia of the bureaucracy and the entrenched vested interests of the Spanish settlers, who had numerous ties of blood and marriage to the local bureaucracy (Ayala y Escobar and Solana 1701:33–34; Bushnell 1979:3–5; Hinachuba 1699:26–27; Hinachuba and Andrés 1699:24–26; Leturiondo [1700]; Ponce de León 1702:27–29; Royal Cedula 1700:29–30; Zúñiga y Zerda 1700a:30–32). The situation in Florida illustrates the validity of the maxim that in dealing with their overseas empire the kings of Spain possessed wide vision but short arms (Spain 1873(3):2055).

The nature of the relations between the friars and natives and the friars' influence over them deserves special attention because of its pervasiveness. Unfortunately, despite the major role the friars played in extending Spanish control over the region and in effecting acculturation, the documentation for their conduct and its influence is surprisingly scanty. Much of what we have is suspect or questionable, at least in its impartiality, as most of it comes from two controversial governors who were at odds with the friars. One of those governors was removed and placed under arrest by the Crown; the other ultimately deserted his post. Under both there was serious discontent among the natives and much flight from Spanish-controlled territory.

The account of Rebolledo's visitation of the province has the first extensive record of relations between the friars and the Indians. With the exception of two friars who received high praise, the Indian leaders were uniformly critical of the friars they mentioned. In contrast the leaders praised the soldiers uniformly. And, surprisingly, they all endorsed the governor's plan to expand the garrison and build a blockhouse at San Luis. One wonders if the actions portrayed were typical of the conduct of most of the friars, and one suspects that the criticism was orchestrated. Only such a supposition seems to account for the contrast between the angelic behavior attributed to the soldiers and the brutal conduct ascribed to the friars. Keeping these reservations in mind, however, the criticisms of many of the friars probably can be accepted at face value, as portraying their general approach to the evangelization and the acculturation of their Indian charges.

First and foremost, the friars did regard the natives as their "charges" once a mission had been established, that is, they could be given minority status with relation to the friar, similar to that between parent and child. As *gente sin razon* (people incapable of rational behavior) Indians were considered legally as minors and wards of Crown and church (Meyer and Sherman 1979:212). The natives' acceptance of baptism was thought by the friars to allow them further rights over the natives: to establish norms of conduct; to discipline the Indian for departures from those norms; and to prohibit long-established native customs that were an integral part of his culture, such as the ball game, dances, and the native curing rituals, whenever the friar considered them incompatible with the natives' acceptance of Christianity. This minority status was even used as a pretext for some bullying in the pursuit of these goals and to prevent renunciation of their acceptance of Christianity, once that commitment had been made.

The Indians' criticisms also reveal that some friars exploited the natives (at times bordering on the inhumane) to help meet the financial needs of the mission or to bring in supplies they felt they needed or that they simply desired. The Indians' charges of exploitation are most suspect of being spurious, inspired as they were by Rebolledo. He was accused of serious financial abuse of the soldiers and seems to have followed the tyrants' practice of trying to hide his own crimes by accusing his opponents of similar ones. In outlawing customs such as the ball game and even some innocent dances, some of the friars resorted to ridiculing the natives' customs in the presence of Spaniards. A few of the incidents simply reflect bad temper by the friars concerned.

The chief at Bacuqua complained that on one occasion the friar from Patale rudely interrupted a celebration to which Bacuqua's leaders had invited their counterparts from San Luis before they went on to Patale for a fiesta. The friar, he alleged, smashed all the pots of food that they had been preparing and sent the celebrants scurrying, without having warned them that they were doing something evil. At San Luis the chief complained that earlier, when the village's leaders ignored their friars' orders forbidding them to give food to the soldiers, the two friars stationed there upbraided the leaders in a manner that offended them deeply. For violating that order one of the friars had whipped Captain Antonio García, a leading man who was a cousin of the chief, and also had laid hands on the chief himself, attempting to throttle him. The chief concluded with an accusation against the incumbent, alleging that this short-tempered friar had smashed their pots for storing cacina along with the jugs they used for making it, when, on one occasion, they did not prepare his beverage as quickly as he wished.

At Aspalaga the chief complained of an equally short-tempered and violence-prone priest, whose outburst was triggered when the village ignored his prohibition of even their lawful dances. The chief charged that the prohibition had been delivered in an uncivil and insulting manner. When the friar came to the principal lodge and found the villagers flaunting his order, he seized a cudgel and used it to shower blows on the ribs of a leading man, the chief's brother-in-law, desisting only when his weapon shattered. When the irate friar kicked the chief, who was seated beside the drummer for the dance, the rest of the Indians prudently took to their heels. The chief also accused the same friar of having ordered the whipping of an Indian to the point that he was bathed in blood, merely because the native, pleading illness, had asked the priest's steward to excuse him from delivering a package for the priest to a village in Timucua—this despite the fact that the steward had secured another to perform the chore.

At Ocuia the chief arraigned a former pastor, Fray Miguel Sánchez, for avarice, noting that he had shipped the convent's corn supply to Havana, supposedly to buy furnishings for the convent. Instead the villagers saw it transformed into trade goods, such as beads, glasses, and knives. He accused the same friar of tying Chief Gaspar, of Ocuia's satellite village of Sabacola, to the door of the church and whipping him abusively for having missed Mass because of illness. Ocuia's chief had noted that, even if the Sabacolan leader had not been ill, the proper routine was to bring such a lapse to the attention of the principal chief and the other satellite village chiefs so that they might see to it that he fulfilled his religious obligations. Despite this experience the chief mentioned with regret that Ocuia had not had a resident friar for some time.

At Ivitachuco the chief paid tribute to a former pastor, Fray Pedro Muñoz, one of the cofounders of the Apalachee mission in 1633. He described him as a priest who had taught them with great love, instructed them that they should love their neighbors as themselves, and set an example by feeding arriving soldiers from his own table whenever the Indians were short of food. The Ivitachucan chief's principal complaint was that the current pastor taught the opposite doctrine, forbidding the villagers to give the soldiers any sustenance and discouraging them from doing any work on the roads that would make the soldiers' passage easier (Rebolledo 1657a:passim).

To redress the abuses revealed by the various chiefs, the governor, on completing his visitation of the first village, Cupaica, issued a six-point regulatory code: Indians could not be obliged to carry cargo to St. Augustine without an order to that effect from the governor, except in the case of bedding and provisions of soldiers dispatched by the governor; no one was to forbid the Indians from voluntarily feeding such soldiers; no one was to prevent or impede the natives from trading freely with any Spaniard; Indians were to be paid for carrying any goods to St. Marks; no trading expeditions were to be sent to the neighboring non-Christian provinces without the permission either of the governor or of his deputy in Apalachee; no one was to forbid or restrict the natives' licit customary dances or to ban the playing of the ball game at its customary time, as long as these diversions did not interfere with their farm work or other necessary occupations; when caciques and other leaders were guilty of transgressions, their punishment was to be left to the governor; and in the buying and selling of the produce of the land, existing prices were to be maintained (Rebolledo 1657a:89–90).

That these regulations were issued at the beginning of the visitation suggests that the governor, on his journey westward to Cupaica, had already talked with the chiefs of most of the villages—adequate reason for regarding the chiefs' complaints against the friars with skepticism. The complaints against Rebolledo sent to the Council of the Indies indicate that many of Florida's Spaniards were terrified by this governor. In many cases the chiefs' complaints are probably not representative of the everyday conduct of a typical friar but rather an elicited response to a governor who had just executed a number of Timucuan chieftains for the 1656 rebellion. The governor suspected that some of the Apalachee chiefs might have been in sympathy with the rebels and let it be known that he was ready to forgive and forget; he also indicated that he would be pleased by any horror stories concerning the behavior of the friars that the chiefs might offer (Council of the Indies 1657a, 1657b:130–135; Rebolledo 1657a:89–90).

For the next quarter of a century there do not appear to have been any similar complaints voiced against the friars. The only mention of mistreatment of the Indians occurs in a 1664 note by various friars complaining of the soldiers' continued presence in Apalachee and alleging that their principal function has been to conduct trading expeditions to the non-Christian tribes for the benefit of the governors. This trade, the friars maintained, placed a heavy burden on the natives who were required to serve as porters and caused considerable discontent on their part (Franciscan Friars 1664). During the 1677–1678 visitation of Domingo de Leturiondo, the natives voiced no complaints against either the friars or the soldiers.[4] There were three principal issues to which Leturiondo directed his attention: the renewal of the orders for the extinction of the Apalachee's ball game; the restriction of the natives' freedom to move their domicile from village to village, requiring them to obtain the lieutenant's permission for such moves, unless they wished to move to Bacuqua; and the setting up of schools in a number of the villages for the education of the children (Leturiondo 1678).

During the governorship of Juan Marques Cabrera, from 1680 to 1687, the volume of complaints of clerical mistreatment of the natives rose once more. The main burden of this governor's complaints involved the friars' punishment of chiefs and leaders, as well as ordinary Indians, by whipping and the friars' imposition of unpaid labor on the natives beyond what was required to meet the needs of the community. Whipping was the penalty for transgressions as trivial as missing Mass on Sunday (Marques Cabrera 1683, 1687b; Royal Cedula 1681). On one occasion, the governor charged, an Apalachee Indian at Oconi died of a whipping ordered by Fray Blas Robles (Marques Cabrera 1686a). The governor also complained that some of the friars in this era were still bent on curbing the natives' penchant for dancing (Marques Cabrera 1683).

Marques Cabrera's regular successor, Governor Diego de Quiroga y Losada, continued to criticize the friars' treatment of the Indians. He charged the Father Provincial, Pedro de Luna, with having sent some Indians from Ivitachuco to St. Augustine as cargo bearers without giving them any food or money for the journey. He complained of the indiscriminate use of whipping as a punishment, alleging that the brutality of Fray Domingos Santos, pastor at the village of Tama in Apalachee, had virtually depopulated that mission.

4. Perhaps, more correctly, the complaints that they made were not recorded. In the 1694–1695 Florencia visitation there is mention that in 1677 during the visitation the depredations of Marcos Delgado's cattle had elicited complaints from the natives whose crops were destroyed by those cattle. These complaints do not appear in the record from 1677.

He also mentioned that three friars (one of whom served in Apalachee) had been withdrawn from their missions for firing shots at their terrified parishioners (Quiroga y Losada 1691a).

In the 1694–1695 visitation, however, the natives themselves voiced no such complaints against the friars. In the one incident involving punishment that was recorded there, the chief of Patale complained that an Indian named Niquichasli Adrián had prevented him from punishing some women. On admitting that he had done so, Niquichasli justified his action by pointing out that the matters for which the chief had wanted to punish the women were trivial ones. He revealed that it was actually the priest who had intervened to block the chief, doing so at Niquichasli's behest.

The major complaints presented by the natives in this visitation involved requests by wives for the return of absent husbands who had been away from their families for varying periods of time working in Timucua, St. Augustine, and Guale; requests by the natives for the satisfaction of unpaid debts owed them by fellow Indians, Spaniards, and the Crown for sales and trades of goods or services rendered; and requests for action by the visitador to force the Spanish ranchers, whose cattle was destroying their crops, to move the herds far enough away to prevent damage.

The visitation revealed that, in addition to the temporary forced labor contingent drawn off under the repartimiento, a growing proportion of the labor force was being contracted to work outside the province on a long-term basis, in what amounted, for the individual involved, if not his family, to entry into a money economy. The number of the complaints over unpaid debts indicated a significant amount of commercial activity, particularly by the native leaders in the sale of horses, tobacco, and pack saddles and the bartering of firearms, clothing, and other commodities. The visitation also disclosed that some of the chiefs were employing natives from villages other than their own as foremen for their ranching operations. The immediate settlement of some of the unpaid debts by cash payments indicates that some hard currency was in circulation in this frontier region; so does the prohibition of the export of silver in the trade with the Apalachicola issued a few years later by Governor Zúñiga. The most striking illustration of this monetary acculturation of the Apalachee is the arrest of two of their number in St. Augustine in this period for manufacturing and passing counterfeit tin coins.

An understanding of and continued respect for the matriarchal system is reflected in a decision by the visitador. The chief of Oconi requested that one of his vassals, who was married to an Ivitachucan woman, be permitted to move back to Oconi so that he might be installed as their sacristan, because no one in Oconi was suitable for the post. The visitador granted the request but only on condition that the wife freely consented to the move, specifying that such a move was not to be forced on her. The same outlook is reflected in the resolution of the cases of the absent husbands. All of them were required to abandon their jobs outside of the province and to return to their wives. There was no suggestion that the wives should move to the husband's place of employment, and for the future no married Apalachee males were to be allowed to accept employment outside of the province under the pain of heavy fines on the chiefs or on the governor's deputy who consented to violations of this rule (Ayala y Escobar and Solana 1701:33–34; Florencia 1695; Zúñiga y Zerda 1700a).

Although there were no complaints against the friars about the problems cited in 1657, the visitador did deal with similar issues in the regulations he issued on completing his circuit of the villages. No one except a soldier on official business was to employ a native as a cargo bearer without paying him for his work. Control over the food in the community storehouse was given jointly to the village chief and an elder chosen by the governor's deputy, each of whom would hold a key to separate locks on that structure. Permission of the governor's deputy was required for anyone going to trade with the Apalachicola. The governor's deputy was forbidden to interfere with the chiefs' and elders' administration of their villages. If he found them overstepping their bounds or if they were alleged to have committed some crime, the lieutenant was not to punish them but rather to bind them over to the governor along with the evidence against them. No one was to prohibit the licit dances or even to specify the hour or times at which they might be held, except during the Lenten season when they were not to be held. Whenever the prohibited obscene dances were indulged in, the lieutenant was to discipline those responsible. The regulations authorized the assignment of "planting Indians" to the Spanish settlers in the province and to the soldiers of the garrison so that they might produce the food needed to sustain their families, but they stipulated that the natives were to be paid punctually for their work (Florencia 1695:87–88).

An overall assessment of the tenor and the results of the Franciscans' tutelage of the Apalachee is difficult to make. When put to the test by the Anglo-Creek attacks in 1704, a considerable number of the Apalachee were sufficiently disenchanted with the friars or the Spaniards, or both, to join the enemy in their assault on the mission villages or at least to agree, under a certain amount of duress, to relocate to English-held territory. On the other hand, the inhabitants of the villages that were assaulted resisted bravely. When their ammunition ran out and they had to surrender, those singled out by the Carolina-led Indians for torture and burning at the stake endured their suffering stoically, solaced by their faith. When the Spaniards decided that the province would be abandoned as no longer defensible, a number of Apalachee—

roughly equivalent to the number that moved voluntarily to Carolina—were sufficiently influenced by the faith the friars had brought to choose freely to remain in Spanish-controlled territory or to migrate to French-controlled Mobile where they could continue to practice that faith. The best perspective, perhaps, for assessing these criticisms of the friars is that reflected in a 1697 letter to the king by Governor Torres y Ayala. He reported having heard that "there were a very few friars, who, forgetful of their rules and vows," exploited their native parishioners, selling bacon, lard, tobacco, and so forth, produced at the doctrina, for their own benefit. But he then assured the king that very few of the religious engaged in such activity and stated that "We consider all the rest to be most exemplary and good *doctrineros.*" In conclusion, the governor remarked that most of the friars distributed among their parishioners the greater part of the salary given them by the king (Torres y Ayala and Royal Officials 1697).

There is little evidence on relations between the Spanish soldiers and the natives and the impact of those Spaniards on them. That certain soldiers were admired and esteemed by the natives probably is indicated by the natives' adoption of Spanish surnames as well as saints' names, for example, Juan Mexía (at least two took his name), Andrés García, Lorenço Moreno, and Alonso Pastrana. It is also shown by the pride with which those natives who held captains' commissions used the title. It is known that some of the soldiers at St. Augustine and Santa Elena married Indians. One suspects that the same occurred in Apalachee, especially when the garrison expanded. An interesting aside to this subject is provided by the soldiers' view of the Indians evinced in their testimony during the investigations into the conduct of Antonio Matheos. In one phase of the investigation, the soldiers who were witnesses were asked what they thought of the veracity and the reliability of the Indian leaders who had testified. The soldiers were divided in their opinions. Some declared that they would not dare to affirm anything concerning the caciques, "as they are very fickle people," or because "now they say one thing, and then they deny it." Others maintained that they were honorable men of good character and reputation and God-fearing men of truth, whose word was equally as trustworthy as that of the Spanish soldiers (Guerrero 1687:104–105; Luxán 1687:111–113; Ramírez 1687:108–110; Ximénez 1687:103).

Apalachee dress appears to be a custom that was influenced significantly by the Spanish presence, at least toward the end of the mission period. As late as the mid-1670s, Spanish authorities were commenting on the brevity of the everyday Apalachee attire, noting that the men often wore only a deerskin breechclout and, if anything more, an unlined coat of serge or a blanket and that the women used only a knee-length skirt woven of Spanish moss or a shoulder-to-ankles tunic made of the same material. Bishop Calderón boasted that in 1675 in the three provinces, he had persuaded 4,081 women he encountered naked from the waist up to don the longer version of those garments (Díaz Vara Calderón 1675:12). Just five years later cloth may have begun to reach the province in some quantity. Toward the end of 1680, reporting the progress on the fort at St. Marks, Governor Hita Salazar suggested that goods such as cloth provided the best means of paying the rotating work crews that put in eight days at a time, observing that "Clothing is what passes for money here" (Hita Salazar 1680b). Clothing figured in a number of the unpaid debt claims presented to the visitador Florencia (Florencia 1695). A document from the period of the destruction of the missions records that a 500-yard bolt of cloth was used to purchase a variety of items from corn and beans to tallow and chickens, bearing out Governor Hita Salazar's remark in 1680 about clothing serving as currency in Apalachee (Boyd, Smith, and Griffin 1951: 46–48). A French observer described the Apalachee who migrated to Mobile in 1704 as dressing in the European fashion, the women in cloaks and skirts of silk stuff and the men in cloth overcoats (McWilliams 1953:134–135). This, of course, was their Sunday church dress, but the remark of this observer and others that there was nothing uncivilized about the Apalachee except their hybrid language of Spanish and Apalachee implies that for workdays as well they dressed in the European fashion.

One other area of possible European influence during the mission period is the Apalachee's introduction to alcohol. Although there is no mention of it, there seems to be no question that it was introduced in some limited fashion, at least within the Spanish community, and in quantities sufficient for the natives to have become acquainted with it, those at home and those sent to St. Augustine. The prevalence of blackberries and grapes and other fruit such as peaches would have provided an opportunity for local production of alcohol. But if it was being consumed by the natives to the point of becoming a problem, it did not elicit any comment or complaints from the friars or from the Spanish authorities. Bishop Calderón observed positively that the mission Indians did not touch wine or rum (Díaz Vara Calderón 1675:12). In her article on the Menéndez-Marquez cattle barony in the Potano region, Bushnell suggested that rum was introduced there via the ships from Havana that plied the Suwannee. Inasmuch as the same ships often docked at St. Marks as well, it is possible that they brought rum to the Apalachee region. It is not likely, however, because the presence of the friars and of the governor's deputy at San Luis would permit much closer surveillance than was possible in the areas of riverine commerce along the Suwannee. In the brief listing of the property lost by Diego de Florencia in 1677, when pirates seized his merchantman at St. Marks, alcoholic beverages were not mentioned (Leturiondo 1678:584).

In the period after the destruction of the missions, when Spanish forces returned to St. Marks, the authorities began to furnish and to sell rum to the Creek in order to compete with the English for their trade and allegiance. But those authorities remarked on the unpleasantness of having to deal with drunken Indians, and it suggests a frame of mind that probably would have led them to restrict the natives' access to alcoholic beverages in the regimented society of the mission era (Montiano 1738c; León 1747). The only reference linking the Apalachee to alcohol involves only two late survivors at St. Augustine in the dismal postmission era. The governor remarked that all 46 of the Indians at Nombre de Dios were badly addicted to alcohol and were leading wretched lives of dissolution and disorder, observing that the continued attachment to Christianity of the Timucua and the two Apalachee among them made them the best of a bad lot (Montiano 1738a). Considering the existence to which these refugees had been reduced by the constant raids of the English and their Indian allies, such a result is not surprising.

Burial practices are an obvious area in which mission experience would influence native customs. Except for the Lake Jackson mound era, little is known about premission Apalachee burial practices. Cemeteries have been discovered at the sites of several Apalachee missions. Individual graves were placed in tight rows with the bodies extended and hands clasped or folded across the breast in the Christian fashion. The relatively few grave goods encountered were items of personal adornment and associated primarily with children: multicolored European glass beads, rolled sheet brass beads, and grooved dumbbell-shaped shell pendants. Children usually were buried in a section of the cemetery apart from the adults (Jones 1970).

Chapter 12

Destruction of the Missions and Dispersion
of Their People

IN THE short span of the seven months between January and August of 1704, the Apalachee region was stripped of a native population of at least 4,000. Most of the contemporary references speak of a population of 7,000. The attacks responsible for this tragedy have been described as marking "the greatest slave raid ever to occur in the South, or probably in the United States, with the possible exception of de Soto's *entrada*" (Wright 1981:141). Hundreds were killed, thousands were claimed to have been enslaved, and more than 2,000 were forced into exile in order to preserve their freedom or their lives.[1] About 14 prosperous mission villages and their two dozen or so satellite settlements were reduced to ashes along with a number of Spanish ranches.

Within a decade of the removal of this human population, buffalo, which earlier had not been found east of the Chipola River, roamed freely over the province's savannas and uncultivated cornfields. In half that time, English-inspired native slave raiders reached to the Florida Keys to spread terror among the peninsula's remaining aboriginal population.

In this exodus, Apalachee's inhabitants scattered to the north, east, and west. The greater part moved north, principally to South Carolina, but some migrated to the Upper and Lower Creek country of Georgia and Alabama. According to some authorities many of those taken to Carolina as slaves were soon exported to the West Indies or to New England (Crane 1956:113–114). Three to four hundred of those who survived the 1704 attacks moved eastward, initially to the Potano region, but continued assaults on them there forced the remnant to seek refuge near St. Augustine. During Moore's attack,

1. Including earlier encounters back to at least 1702, one Spanish official put the death toll at 3,000, but that figure seems too high.

the people of another village escaped briefly by wandering about in the forests of Timucua, but in 1705 they were tracked down and almost exterminated by Indians allied with the English. A somewhat larger group from western Apalachee, drawn mainly from San Luis and Escambé and from the Christian Chacato, moved westward to Pensacola and Mobile (Boyd 1953:461–462; Bushnell 1979:12–16; Florencia et al. 1707:85–89; Higginbotham 1977: 189–191; Moore 1704b). That group appears to have fared best in that a few of their descendants are known to have survived and to have maintained their tribal identity for more than a century, although eventually they dispersed to Louisiana, Texas, and Mexico, where some of their descendants may yet survive. For the majority of those forced to leave Apalachee in 1704, the path to extinction as a people was a short one.

Problems of the documents

Composition of a satisfactory account of the destruction of the settlements and of their inhabitants' fate is hampered by the serious inadequacies of the available records. Except in depicting the tortures and deaths inflicted by the English-led native warriors on some captives, Spanish accounts are generally vague and laconic. The English records are equally so and contradictory in addition. Considering the numbers alleged to have been involved in this migration, there is relatively little trace of the 1704 influx of Apalachee natives in the records of the Carolina colony.

The most important English sources, Colonel James Moore's two accounts of his exploits, create the most serious problems. Moore's accounts, in his letters to the Carolina governor and to the colony's lords proprietors, not only differ from the Spanish reports but also conflict with each other. For example, in the extant versions of his two letters Moore described the number whom he enslaved in Apalachee variously as 100 and as more than 4,000 and the number whom he led off as free immigrants as 300 and as 1300. The differences between Moore's accounts and the Spanish reports and between Moore's two accounts involve the number of villages that surrendered unconditionally, the number of villages that agreed to relocate to Carolina in exchange for keeping their freedom, the number of villages whose inhabitants were annihilated, the number of free Apalachee who migrated to Carolina, and the number of natives who were carried from the province as slaves.

Differing versions exist of both of Moore's letters to complicate the problem additionally. The discrepancies range from insignificant differences in spelling, capitalization, punctuation, wording, and paragraph division to significant ones involving the numbers of villages and individuals who suffered one fate or another and other substantive matters. There are significant discrepancies between two of the three versions of Moore's letter to the governor that are available. The two available versions of Moore's letter to the lords proprietors also contain significant discrepancies, but those latter differences are not as important for the purposes of this chapter as are those in the discordant versions of Moore's letter to the governor. The most readily available copy of one version of Moore's letter to the governor, that presented by Mark F. Boyd in *Here They Once Stood,* is marred additionally by serious errors introduced presumably by Boyd's copyist. The discrepancies in the copies of these two letters and the uncritical use that has been made of the letters in some earlier works constitute a valuable lesson in historiography.

Boyd's published transcripts are the most accessible source for both of Moore's letters. The other published source, B. R. Carroll's *Historical Collections of South Carolina,* contains Moore's letter to the governor. The other sources are manuscript collections at the Library of Congress and at South Carolina's Department of Archives and History, which contain copies or extracts of both letters (see appendix 12 for transcripts of all of these versions and of Boyd's copies of the Library's version, marked to show the points at which they differ significantly).

None of the available exemplars is an original or known to be directly linked to the original version or versions of these letters. Carroll's copy of Moore's letter to the governor is possibly the oldest. It was derived from a copy of the letter published in May of 1704 by a Boston newspaper. The South Carolina Archives' copies, made in 1895 by W. Noel Sainsbury, an employee of the Public Records Office, are copies of copies made originally in South Carolina in 1737–1738 by Governor William Bull as part of a lengthy series of documents providing information requested by London to refute the claims to Georgia that Spanish authorities were pressing at that time.[2] The pedigree of the Library of Congress' copies is more obscure. A Library official wrote that the collection containing its copies was purchased from an unidentified source in 1915 and that the copyist's identity was not known. The Library official revealed that its copies were in a six-volume collection of "transcripts of Great Britain, Board of Trade Spanish Records (Miscellaneous Manuscript Collections—1788)" and suggested that the original materials were British

2. Both of these copies are labeled as extracts. The Archives officials did not know the fate of the letter Governor Bull had used to make the copies he sent to England. The copies of Moore's letters in the Archives appear to have been little used. To my initial request whether they had copies of Moore's letters, the Archives responded that they were unable to locate any copies and that their search for data about the letters revealed that prior to Verner Crane's use of the Library of Congress copies, scholars had relied on the Carroll version. Subsequently, I learned from William Snell's dissertation that the Archives had a copy of at least one of Moore's letters, and I obtained it.

Board of Trade Records held by the Public Record Office (Hutson 1984). Only one of the Library's letters is identified as an extract, although both cover the same ground as do the Archives' copies.[3] Although Boyd cited the Library of Congress' collection as the source of his copies, his transcription of Moore's letter to the governor follows the Carroll version at a few points.

Whether the Archives' and the Library's version of either of these two letters had a common ancestor is an open question. Although the Archives' copies, on the whole, have the same wording and word order as do the Library's copies, the marked differences in spelling, capitalization, and punctuation, coupled with several significant discrepancies in wording, raise questions that leave the issue in doubt. The wider differences between those two versions and the Carroll version raise more questions that cannot be resolved satisfactorily. At the very least, the nature of the discrepancies suggests that an editor or copyist took considerable liberty with the original text, if it was the same text from which the Archives' and Library's versions may have descended.

The significant differences among the versions and Boyd's copies

Comparison of Boyd's transcription of Moore's letter to Governor Johnson with the Library of Congress' version reveals several significant errors in Boyd's copy. In the most striking departure from his source, Boyd reduced the five towns that surrendered unconditionally to two towns. The Library's and the South Carolina Archives' versions' rendition of Moore's point of departure as "the Ockmulgees" was changed to "the Ockmulgee" by Boyd, influenced possibly by Carroll's "the Ockomulgee." After describing his defeat of the Spanish garrison's challenge to his invasion, Moore noted that "We have a particular Account of 168 Indian Men Killed and taken in this Fight and Flight. The Apalatchee Indians say they lost 200 wch we have reason to believe to be the least." Boyd omitted the words "to be," potentially altering the meaning. In Moore's statement, "The number of free Apalatchee Indians wch are now under my protection," Boyd changed "now" to "not." And, finally, Boyd changed the Library's version's "Pansicola" to "Pensacola."[4]

3. In response to a request for information, the Public Record Office replied that they found no reference to Colonel Moore's two letters in the standard guides for their material and that they would need more specific references in order to locate them. A search of the "Historical News" section of the *American Historical Review* for the 1915 period revealed the following note: "The Library has completed for the present its invaluable series of transcripts from British archives numbering about 175,000 folios and is proceeding with similar copying in Paris and Seville" (*American Historical Review* 21:668).

4. The other versions have Pensacola as well.

Comparison of the Carroll version with the Library's and Archives' veisions reveals significant differences between the Carroll version and the other two. The above-mentioned "free Apalatchee Indians, wch are now under my Protection, bound with me to Carolina, are 300:" of the Library's and Archives' versions appear in the Carroll version as "are 1300, and 100 slaves." The ransom paid by Ivitachuco's chief to escape attack by Moore was described in the Carroll version as "his church's plate, and ten horses laden with provisions" in contrast to the Library's version's "his Church Plate & led Horses loaden with Provisions."[5] In Carroll, Ivitachuco's chief was called "cassique of the Ibitachka" in contrast to the Library's and Archives' "King of the Attachookas." Similarly the Library's version's "Aiavalla" became "Ayaville" in the Carroll version.[6] The Carroll version gave the number of Apalachee killed in Moore's assault on Ayubale as 25 rather than the 24 mentioned in the other versions. Comparison of the copies of these versions in appendix 12 will reveal other discrepancies in the wording that are of lesser importance.

In his transcription of Moore's letter to the lords proprietors, Boyd made only one significant change in the Library's version that was his source. To the passage "and put them out of a Capacity of returning back again alone In this Expedition I brought away 300 Men, and 1000 Women and Children have killed," Boyd added a period after "alone" and a comma after "Children." Inconsistently, Boyd placed the period in brackets to show that it was not in his source, but failed to do that with the comma, even though that minor change altered the meaning to say that the 1,000 women and children were brought away rather than killed. It is conceivable that the editor or printer, rather than Boyd, made that change. In his schematic comparison of the statistics contained in Moore's two letters, Boyd listed the 1,000 women and children as having been killed rather than as having been brought out as free persons along with the 300 men.

Significant discrepancies appear as well when one compares the Library's version of Moore's letter to the lords proprietors to that of the Archives. In the passage quoted in the preceding paragraph "returning back again alone" is "returning back again alive," in the Archives' version; the word "free" appears before "300 Men:" and there is a comma after "killed."[7] Equally significant discrepancies between the two versions occur in the passage that appears in the Library's version as "who cannot now (as I have Seated Our Indians) come at me that way, must they must March thro' 300 Indian Men Our Friends." In the Archives' version "come at me" is "come at us;" the first "must" of "must they must" is "but;" and "300 Indian Men" is "900

5. The Archives version spelled "led" as "lead" and Boyd changed "loaden" to "leaden."
6. The Archives version rendered the name as Aiaivalla.
7. In the Archives version "killed" was rendered as "kill'd."

Indian Men." Comparison of these versions in appendix 12 will reveal additional differences in the wording that are of lesser significance.

Analysis of the differences between the Library's and Archives' versions of Moore's letter to the governor and the Carroll version produces neither a ready explanation for the divergences nor even an indication of which is more reliable overall. In some cases the Carroll variant seems the more logical or acceptable, and in other places the Library's and Archives' versions seem correct. The Carroll version's date for Moore's arrival before Ayubale (December 14) is obviously a copyist's error. If one assumes that Moore penned the originals for both the Carroll and the Library-Archives version, then the only logical explanation for the variant forms Moore gave to the name of Ayubale (Aiavalla, Ayaville) and Ivitachuco (Attachookas, Ibitachka) is that he had not fixed firmly in his mind the manner of rendering these unfamiliar names. His use of the title "King" for the chief of Ivitachuco in one version and the title "cassique" in the other also has a plausible explanation. The Carolinians customarily gave the title "King" to the chiefs of important villages. "Cacique" is the title Moore would have heard used by the Indians, particularly the Apalachee who accompanied him on his return to Carolina. This variance suggests that the diverse versions of this letter were made by Moore at different times and possibly that the copy sent to the Boston newspaper was made by someone other than Moore. The Carroll version's reference to the ransom paid by Ivitachuco's chief as "ten horses laden with provisions" makes much more sense than that of the Library, "led Horses loaden with Provisions." But the agreement here between the Library's and the Archives' version (except in spelling) gives the Library's version credence as well. There is no logical explanation for the discrepancy between the Library's version and the Carroll version concerning the number of towns whose people were annihilated. Both versions seem to be incorrect on the basis of Moore's statement in his letter to the lords proprietors that the only natives that he enslaved or put to death were those taken in battle or in Ayubale.

Although the Library's and the Archives' versions of Moore's letter to the governor agree on the figure of 300 free Apalachee who voluntarily accompanied Moore to Carolina, the 300 seems to be in error. The figure of 1300 in the Carroll version is corroborated by the Archives' version of Moore's letter to the lords proprietors and by another contemporary source, Colonel Robert Quary. Writing from Virginia on May 30, 1704, Colonel Quary made the following comment on Moore's exploits:

> This late expedition in South Carolina under Col. James Moore against the Apalacy Indians, was a brave action; and will be attended by this good consequence, to secure that Province from any attempt of the Spanyard or Indian against them by land, this nation of Indians being

the chief that the Spaniard depended on for that design. Col. Moore marched with a great body of our friendly Indians and about 50 Englishmen; they killed a great number of the Enemy, brought a great number of them prisoners, besides 1300 that come voluntary with them to live under the protection of ye English Government.[8] (Quary 1704:145)

Also, as late as 1715, the free Apalachee in South Carolina still numbered more than 600. Copyist's error seems the most plausible explanation for the figure of 300 that appears in the Library's and the Archives' versions and for their omission of any mention of the natives enslaved.

Carroll's figure of 100 slaves seems too low, however. Quary alluded to those enslaved simply as "a great number." When mentioned in conjunction with the 1,300 free Apalachee, 100 would not seem to fit that description and it is contradicted by Moore's other statements about the number he enslaved. Those statements range from a low of about several hundred[9] through the unspecified numbers from the four towns allegedly that surrendered "without conditions" to the extravagant claim of more than 4,000 men, women, and children.

The data contained in Moore's two letters presents still other problems. The most serious problems arise from attempts to match the details furnished by Moore about the number of villages that surrendered unconditionally, or were destroyed, or which agreed to relocate with facts established by other sources and with his claims about the number of natives, free and enslaved, who accompanied him on his return to Carolina. He listed 300 men and 1,000 women and children as free migrants; 4,000 women and children as slaves; and 325 men either killed or enslaved, a total of 5,625. Although that total of slave migrants is high, it could be accounted for from the province's general population pool. But the missions recorded reliably as not having fallen to Moore or joined him en masse contained so much of the total population that no combination of the remaining missions could provide the more than 4,000 people Moore claimed to have enslaved. Three of the four most populous settlements (Cupaica, San Luis, and Ivitachuco) were still relatively intact when Moore returned to Carolina. Two others, Patale and Aspalaga, retained enough of their inhabitants to invite an assault by a second group of Creek in June 1704, several months after Moore's departure. Both Moore's account and

---

8. Quary's source, of course, may have been the Boston newspaper account rather than a communication from Charles Town.

9. The several hundred include the 168 to 200 prisoners taken by Moore at Ayubale and a part of the 200 he claimed to have killed or captured during his encounter with the forces from San Luis.

a Spanish source document the survival into 1705 of the inhabitants of an additional mission who fled into the woods, accompanied by their pastor Fray Domingo Criado (Bienville 1704:27; Council of War 1704:56–59; Higginbotham 1977:191; Moore 1704a, 1704b; the Royal Officials 1704b:61–62; Solana 1704a:50–55; Zuñiga y Zerda 1704a, 1704b:48–50, 55–56).

Studying an augmented version of Boyd's schematic illustration of the data contained in Moore's two letters can help in better appreciating the problems posed by these conflicting sources and in resolving those problems to the extent that that is possible. Table 12.1 will include the pertinent information from the Spanish and the French sources as well, and with it we can compose a reasonably satisfactory account of the fate of the missions and of their inhabitants, using the points of agreement between the sources and the points that are not open to question.

All of the sources agree that the first target of Moore's attack, Ayubale, was taken by assault. There is no reason to question his claims of 200 taken prisoner there, 20 to 25 killed in the assault, and an additional 200 taken by the Creek in the outlying portions of that mission. There is no evidence concerning the fate of the remainder of Ayubale's large population. In 1689, it was reported as having 250 families (Ebelino de Compostela 1689). In reporting its capture in February 1704, Governor Zúñiga described it as "one of the largest places in Apalachee" (Zúñiga y Zerda 1704a:48–50). In order even to begin to account for the more than 4,000 whom Moore claimed to have enslaved, the remainder of Ayubale's population would have to be included somehow.

The major part of the native force of 400 that accompanied the Spanish troops to recapture Ayubale probably was drawn from San Luis, Patale, and Escambé, although only the first two are mentioned in connection with this engagement. In addition to the 168 to 200 Indians Moore mentioned as having been killed by his forces in this second battle, Spanish sources allege that more than 40 of the men taken prisoner were burned at the stake by Moore's Indian allies in the wake of the battle (Cruz 1705:74–76; Fuentes de Galanca 1705:77–78; Solana 1705:79–82).

Although Ivitachuco's ransom is not mentioned in the Spanish sources, there is no reason to question Moore's assertion that Ivitachuco's chief agreed to hand over that mission's church plate and some provisions. It seems to be stretching a point, however, to describe this action as a surrender, as Moore does, inasmuch as Ivitachuco's forces remained in control of the village and its people. More likely, in view of his losses in taking Ayubale and in turning back the relief force from San Luis, Moore did not want another encounter with a large and well-defended settlement such as Ivitachuco, particularly since few of his Indian allies showed any disposition to participate in the as-

Table 12.1. Comparison of Moore's letters and Spanish and French reports

Moore's letter to governor	Moore's letter to proprietors	Spanish and French reports
Ayubale taken by assault	Same	Same
Ivitachuco makes peace	Ivitachuco surrenders upon condition	Ivitachuco survives
5 places surrender unconditionally	4 places surrender unconditionally	5 places destroyed and the people of 2 leave voluntarily
All the people of 3 places are in my company	All the people of 4 places agree to relocate	Mention that 50 or so Apalachee joined the enemy
Part of the people of 4 places agree to relocate; San Luis one of the 4 places	Same	Vague reference to only 4 places being left and that those who emigrated were established in 4 places
Destroyed all the people of 2 towns (and 4 towns in the Carroll version)	Killed or enslaved only those taken at Ayubale or in battle	People of Ayubale, Tomole, Capoli, Tama, and Ocatoses carried off
Burned 1 town, whose people fled		People of 1 place fled to the woods with Fray Criado

Only Ivitachuco and part of San Luis are left; 28 to 30 whites left	Only 300 Indians and 24 whites are left	Enemy came no closer than 2 leagues to San Luis
300 free Apalachee bound with me to Carolina (Carroll version has 1,300 free and 100 slaves)	300 free men and 1,000 free women and children locate to Carolina. Boyd read this as 300 free men relocated and 1,000 women and children killed	More than 600 Christian Indians carried off
	325 men killed or enslaved and 4,000 women and children enslaved	
At Ayubale the English captured 52 men and 116 women and children and killed 24 men (Carroll has 25)	English took 200 alive and killed 20 at Ayubale	Some of Patale, Aspalaga, and Escambé's people and the Chacato mentioned as surviving
During the attack on Ayubale, Creeks killed or captured the same number in the plantations		
Killed 168 to 200 Apalachee in the encounter with San Luis's forces sent to the relief of Ayubale	Killed or captured 200 in this encounter	Ocuia was destroyed before Moore's arrival

sault on the walled compound at Ayubale. He gave his casualties as the reason for not having attacked San Luis.

Moore's claims concerning the places whose chiefs and entire populations accepted his offer of freedom of person and property in exchange for their relocating to Carolina find partial substantiation both in the Spanish reports and in other English sources, but his claims and the Spanish sources present other, serious problems. The most obvious discrepancies are in Moore's giving the number of places accepting these terms as three in one letter and four in the other, while the Spanish governor asserted that of the five places destroyed, the population of two left voluntarily. The figure of four villages seems more reliable because subsequent English and most Spanish sources say the emigrés to Carolina were established there in four settlements (Florencia and Pueyo 1704: Wallace 1934(1):202; Zúñiga y Zerda 1704a:48–50).[10] The discrepancy between the Spanish governor's two villages and Moore's four could be accounted for if two of the places claimed by Moore were satellite villages rather than mission centers. However, the validity of such an assumption is not easy to sustain in view of the excellence of Moore's intelligence concerning Apalachee; the Spanish governor would not likely consider satellites as separate entities.

Existing records do not permit more than conjecture concerning the identity of Moore's four villages. The mention in the *Journal of the Commissioners of the Indian Trade* of the presence of the Tomolla King in connection with a dispute over the enslavement of one of his subjects seems to point to San Martín de Tomole as one of them (McDowell 1955:4–5). Some uncertainty remains, however, in view of a statement in October 1705 by Governor Zúñiga in which he lists Ayubale, Tomole, Capoli, Tama, and Ocatoses as places from which people were carried off by the invaders. By elimination, Bacuqua, San Pedro de los Chines, and the Tocobaga settlement at Wacissa seem most likely the other candidates for this category, inasmuch as they are not mentioned either as surviving Moore's attack or as having had their inhabitants carried off.[11] Bacuqua, a small, vulnerable frontier town, would have abundant reasons to accept such terms, as would the equally small place of the Chine. Even though the governor spoke of Ocuia as having been destroyed along with several Timucuan villages before Moore's attack, the number of people cited as having been carried off in that 1703 attack suggests that some of its population survived. If so, it could also be a possibility for inclusion as one of the four villages. That Bacuqua was another may be indicated by the

10. One of the Spanish sources says three.
11. An undetermined number of Tocobaga are known to have gone to Mobile at some time before 1718, and there were a few Tocobaga near the coast when the Spaniards returned to San Marcos de Apalachee in 1718.

fact that Diego Peña encountered its chief, Adrián, as a person of influence among the Lower Creek in 1717 soon after the Yamasee uprising of 1715 in which the free emigré Apalachee in South Carolina also participated (Boyd 1952:116–118, 121, 123, 126: Crane 1956: 170, 180–181).

Both of Moore's letters state that part of the people of four towns agreed to relocate in exchange for their freedom,[12] and San Luis is specifically mentioned as one of them (Moore 1704a, 1704b). Patale was referred to as a small village at the time of its destruction in June 1704, which may mean that it was another; it had been a medium-sized village of 120 families in 1689 (Fuentes 1705:80; Ebelino de Compostela 1689). The mention of the presence of the Ilcombe King and the recording of a dispute concerning the enslavement of an Ellcombe man in South Carolina might indicate that Ilcombe or Cupaica was another source of these towns (McDowell 1955:4, 60). If one were to include in this category the Apalachee who became rebels, joining in the attack on their fellow tribesmen, Aspalaga might be yet another; the son of the chief of Aspalaga the Old is mentioned as having been killed in an encounter with a loyal Ivitachucan force, along with a rebel warrior from Tomole (Solana 1704a:50–55). It is more likely, however, that the rebels were from a number of villages, drawn from those with particular grievances against the Spaniards and from the social misfits produced by all societies. Manuel Solana reported that the punishment of the Spanish soldiers captured in July 1704 (burning at the stake) was done at the urging of the rebellious Apalachee (Solana 1704a: 50–55).

Moore's claims concerning the villages that allegedly surrendered to him unconditionally, together with his assertions about the number of Indians he allegedly enslaved, present the most serious problems. In his letter to Governor Johnson, Moore mentioned that only two towns surrendered unconditionally; but in his letter to the proprietors, he stated unequivocally that four towns surrendered to him unconditionally, and he provided such rich details that he makes the latter account convincing. In his second letter, he mentions resting at Ayubale for four days after the two battles there because some of his men were neither fit to march nor to be carried. During this pause he reached his agreement with Ivitachuco. On the fifth day he marched to two more forts,[13] both of which were delivered to him without conditions, along with their inhabitants, who became prisoners at discretion. After spending the night at one of those places, he marched on the next day to two more forts, both of which were delivered to him with their people without conditions, and

12. The Carroll version says three towns.
13. Moore used this term to describe the walled compound within which the village's church and
    convent were located.

he spent two nights in one of these two settlements. Yet in another passage, Moore stated that he enslaved only those taken at Ayubale and those captured in battle. And his statement that, in endeavoring to bring away free as many Indians as he could he had drastically reduced the plunder his men had hoped for, leads to the same conclusion.

However, Moore's version of two villages surrendering in this manner is more consonant with Governor Zúñiga's report that when Moore withdrew, he left five places destroyed, the population of two of which had left with him voluntarily. Subtracting Ayubale as well from those five settlements leaves only two as possibilities for unconditional surrender (Moore 1704a, 1704b; Zúñiga y Zerda 1704a:48–50). A little more than one and a half years later the governor repeated the assertion that Moore's Indians had carried off the people of five villages, on that occasion identifying the villages as Ayubale, Tomole, Capoli, Tama, and Ocatosis (Zuñiga y Zerda 1705). In his earlier letter the governor also affirmed that Moore had turned back when he was two leagues from San Luis (Zúñiga y Zerda 1704a:48– 50). This fact would seem to eliminate Tama as a candidate for unconditional surrender, if it still occupied the same site as it had in 1675: In that year Fernández de Florencia placed it as slightly over one-half league from San Luis, while Bishop Calderón, rounding his figures, gave it as one league (Ebelino de Compostela 1689; Fernández de Florencia 1675a). If evidence cited earlier is valid, indicating Tomole as one of the villages whose people left voluntarily, then only Capoli and Ocatosis could be the villages surrendering unconditionally. Reducing the villages from which slaves could be drawn to these two plus Ayubale poses insuperable difficulties in accepting Moore's claim that he carried more than 4,000 natives back to Carolina as slaves.

Even with four villages that surrendered unconditionally, it is hard to begin to approach the figure of over 4,000, inasmuch as after Moore's departure three of the four largest settlements (San Luis, Ivitachuco, and Cupaica) were still in existence with a substantial portion of their populations. Capoli was a very small village, having only 30 families in 1689 and only 20 men in 1694 (Ebelino de Compostela 1689; Florencia 1695). The identity of Ocatosis is unknown. Matching geography with Moore's description of his march to the four settlements that he claimed surrendered unconditionally indicates Tomole, San Pedro de los Chines, and the Tocobaga village as the most likely possibilities. The place of the Chine was no larger than Capoli, and the population of the Tocobaga was about 300 people (Ebelino de Compostela 1689; Florencia 1695). Geographically both Tama and San Carlos de los Chacatos would be possibilities for this category, but their proximity to San Luis seems to rule them out. The Chacato village is also ruled out because 250 of its inhabitants survived both Moore's attack and the June–July campaign to migrate to Mobile (Bienville 1704:27, 1706:25, [1726]:535).

Moore's claim that the population of one village fled at his approach is confirmed by Spanish sources (Florencia et al. 1707:85–89). His statement that he destroyed all the people of two towns is not confirmed in any other source (except possibly in the governor's claim that 3,000 natives had been killed) and seems to be contradicted by his own letter to the proprietors in which he said that he did not enslave or put to death "one man, woman or child but what were taken in the fight or in the Fort I took by storm" (Moore 1704a). No town other than Ayubale is mentioned by Moore or by the Spaniards as having put up a fight at his approach.

Moore's claim that when he left Apalachee only Ivitachuco and part of San Luis survived and that only 300 Indians and 24 to 30 whites were left is patently false. Spanish and French sources indicate that substantial portions of the populations of Escambé and of the Chacato still existed along with some part of the population of Patale and Aspalaga. Ivitachuco by itself still had more than 300 inhabitants when the Spanish abandoned the province in July 1704. About 800 residents of the San Luis area migrated to Mobile at this time. Others from Escambé stopped at Pensacola; still others remained in the vicinity of their destroyed villages at the time of the Spanish withdrawal (Bienville 1704:27, 1706:25; [Bienville] [1726]:536; Council of War 1704: 56–59; the Royal Officials 1704a:59–61; Solana 1704a:50– 55; Zúñiga y Zerda 1704b:55–56, 1704c).

Moore's claim that he enslaved 4,000 people is suspect on other grounds. First, there is a tremendous disproportion between the number of men and the number of women and children he mentioned. Even taking into account the number of men killed in battle and the probability that men would be more prone and able to flee to preserve their lives and freedom, Moore's figures seem out of proportion.[14] The governor's council, in its listing of the Indian slave population in South Carolina in 1708, gave the proportion of 500 men to 600 women and 300 children—less than two to one, a far cry from Moore's thirteen to one. A more serious problem is the total of only 1,400 Indian slaves in South Carolina in 1708 given by that report, an increase of just over 1,000 in excess of what the colony possessed in 1703. When this number is viewed in light of speculation by Snell and others that most of the Apalachee slaves must have been kept in Carolina, it leaves at least 3,000 of Moore's claimed 4,000 to be accounted for (Snell 1972:60n9, 96, table I).

Unfortunately for the resolution of this problem, Snell's statement seems to be pure speculation. The assembly, around the time of the Apalachee expe-

14. The fact that the men who were captured were likely to be put to death by their captors was a definite incentive to flight once the battle was lost. Women and children could expect nothing worse than slavery unless illness or injury prevented their keeping pace with their captors. A woman and a child were killed by their Creek captors on this pretext as the second attack force withdrew from the province in July 1704.

dition, imposed an export tax of 20 shillings on Indians exported from the colony, but until the Tuscarora War there is only one recorded instance when that duty was paid: for one slave exported to Antigua on May 17, 1703, by Governor Nathaniel Johnson (Snell 1972:60 and appendixes).[15] This scarcity of recorded exports seems to be Snell's reason for assuming that most of the Apalachee slaves were retained in South Carolina. Although he records Moore's figure of 4,000 slaves, he makes no attempt to account for the 3,000 who are not reflected in the increase of 1,000 or so in the Indian slave population during that five-year period when more such slaves were brought into Carolina from other parts of Florida and from the Chickasaw raids on the Choctaw.

Closer examination of the 1708 report presents a serious challenge to Moore's claim of over 4,000 slaves. The figure of 1,400 Indian slaves appears in a report drawn up by the governor and his council in response to a request from the queen through the lords proprietors for periodic reports on the colony's affairs. In the prologue to the report they state that the information they are furnishing is based on a careful inquiry into the present state and circumstances of the province. Their report begins, "The number of ye inhabitants of this province of all sorts are computed to be nine thousand five hundred & eighty souls." They break that number down into numbers of free white men, women, and children; white indentured men and women; Negro slave men, women, and children, and Indian slave men, women, and children. The free Indians were not included in the total because the councilors intended to discuss each of those allied groups individually later in the report.

In this opening comment, the councilors went on to discuss the changes that had occurred in the makeup of the population during the preceding five years:

> The freemen of this province by reason of the late sickness brought here from other parts though now very healthy & small supply from other parts are within these five years last part deceased about one hundred free women about forty white serv[ts] for the aforesaid Reasons & having completed their servitude are deceased fifty white servants women for the same reason thirty white children are increased five hundred negro men slaves by importation three hundred negro women slaves two hundred Indian men slaves by reason our late Conquest over the French and Spaniards and the success of our forces against the Appalaskye and other Indian engagem[ts] are within the five years increased to the number

---

15. Governor Johnson paid the duty for two such slaves that he exported on that occasion, but the payment for only one was recorded. Snell also notes that there are few legal records indicating the retention of many Apalachee slaves in the colony.

of four hundred and the Indian women slaves to four hundred and fifty negro children to six hundred and Indian children to two hundred. (Johnson et al. 1708(5):203–204)

This statement indicates clearly that, as a result of the raids into Apalachee and attacks on other Indian groups during that period, the Indian slave population increased by no more than 1,250, a total that included others in addition to the Apalachee. Admittedly, nothing is said of slave exports here, but it seems that if they were as massive as would be required to meet the numbers claimed by Moore, they would have elicited some comment in such a detailed report.

Data from Spanish sources allow us to say with some certainty that when Moore left Apalachee he had with him the surviving population of Ayubale, Tomole, Capoli, Tama, and Ocatosis. Similarly, from Moore's letters and the Spanish sources, it can be said that the people from Ayubale and probably those from two more villages left as slaves and that those of two other villages left as voluntary emigrants, besides those from San Luis who deserted. The five villages of San Luis, Ivitachuco, Patale, Aspalaga, and Escambé were still existing in some fashion. One village's people had fled to Timucua. It is unlikely that those enslaved by Moore numbered many more than 1,000. The Colonel Bull map of 1738 put the number of Spaniards and Indians killed or captured by Moore at 800 (Chatelain 1941:map 8).

The second attack of 1704

The exclusively Spanish sources for the second attack on Apalachee, in June 1704, are more informative than all the sources for the first assault in January. They indicate that Patale and Aspalaga were captured by the invading forces. Escambé also was occupied and destroyed, but before the attack most of its populace had taken refuge at San Luis on orders of the lieutenant. At this time some outlying part of San Luis also came under attack. Some of the enemy swept around to the south of San Luis, capturing seven Spaniards who had come up from St. Marks on the Royal Road. Concerning casualties among the loyal Apalachee, Manuel Solana reported that the Indians told the cacique of San Luis "that the missing number seven, and that from the village of Escambé five [are missing]. The number of those who went forth from other villages is not known, nor whether any are missing" (Council of War 1704: 56–59; Royal Officials 1704a:59–61; Solana 1704a:50–55; Zúñiga y Zerda 1704b:55–56). When this second enemy force withdrew, only the villages of San Luis and Ivitachuco were left, along with much of the population of Escambé and at least part of the Chacato population. Except for the cacique and people of Ivitachuco, who remained loyal to the Spanish monarch, the majority of the remaining natives were thoroughly demoralized and disillusioned with the Spaniards over the disasters that had beset the province under their leadership and over their unfulfilled promises of relief. In view of the reports that their enemies would soon return with a larger force to complete the annihilation of the inhabitants, some of the remaining natives began to flee to the woods. In reply to a warning from the governor's deputy that in doing so they would only perish in the wilds and to his invitation that they seek refuge at St. Augustine, the natives replied that they were weary of waiting for Spanish aid and reinforcements that never arrived. They remarked frankly that if they left the province, they would not go to another Spanish-controlled area; if they decided to remain, it would be in order to join with the enemy in their attack on the Spaniards in the blockhouse (Solana 1704a:50–55).

Shortly after this frank exchange of views, the native leaders of San Luis led a caravan of about 800 natives—most of the remaining population of San Luis, part of the population of Escambé, the remaining Christian Chacato of Apalachee, and a few non-Christians from a refugee Yamasee village—on an overland trek westward to Pensacola, driving their remaining cattle before them (Higginbotham 1977:191). With them was a Frenchman from Mobile who had brought an invitation from Bienville to settle near that recently established French outpost. These emigrés reached Pensacola around July 28, 1704. Eight Spanish families from the San Luis region had already arrived there by sea (Guzmán 1704:62–64; Ruíz de Cuenca 1705:70–72).

The governor's deputy, on July 8, suggested the abandonment of the province, giving as his reasons the disastrous rout of the Spanish-Indian force that had gone out to challenge the invaders at Patale, the declaration by San Luis's leaders that they would no longer fight alongside the Spaniards, and the rumors concerning the proximate arrival of a third invasion force. At a Council of War in St. Augustine on July 13, the Spanish officials and officers adopted his suggestion, ordering the immediate abandonment of the province and the withdrawal of its population either to St. Augustine or to San Francisco de Potano, where they might join with the remaining population of western Timucua to form a strong outpost (Council of War 1704:56–59; Solana 1704a: 50–55).

At the end of the month San Luis and its blockhouse were destroyed, and the surviving soldiers headed toward St. Augustine with the church treasure that had escaped capture and such possessions as could be carried in the available oxcarts. A small band of drovers, who headed for Pensacola with cattle they had bought at San Luis, were overtaken and killed by a band from the third attack force that had reached San Luis on August 2, just two days after the departure of the remnant of the garrison (Zúñiga y Zerda 1704d:65–67).

The retreating soldiers were then only 16 leagues away, at San Pedro de Poto-hiriba, but the attack force made no attempt at pursuit. At San Pedro the Span-ish force caught up with the inhabitants of Ivitachuco, who had set out earlier under their chieftain, Don Patricio de Hinachuba. The portion of Escambé's population that had remained in the province to welcome the invaders was captured or killed (Zúñiga y Zerda 1704d:65–67, 1704e:67–68). This assault apparently completed the depopulation of the province.

Summary

From this analysis of the data provided by the documents and of the contra-dictions by which the documents are marred, some conclusions can be drawn concerning the fate of the various settlements during the two attacks of Janu-ary and June 1704, but the necessarily conjectural nature of many of those conclusions should be kept in mind.

The attack began with the capture of Ayubale by assault. It is likely that most of its large population beyond the 400 or so killed and captured in the assault were also taken prisoner. Consequently, it probably provided the largest contingent of the slaves taken by Moore. Ivitachuco escaped attack and probably served as a refuge for a few who escaped from the more easterly settlements before their surrender. The number of refugees cannot have been large, however, because only about 400 natives were in Ivitachuco at the time of its abandonment, which is not a large number for a town that had once rivaled San Luis in size but had seen a decline in its relative position. It is not recorded whether its inhabitants burned their village at the time of their depar-ture. Unless it had been moved to the vicinity of San Luis, Bacuqua seems likely to have been one of the villages whose chief and populace agreed to relocate to Carolina, although it was never mentioned by name in the records of the attacks. Ocuia reportedly was destroyed before Moore's arrival, but some of its inhabitants apparently survived to participate in the final encounter with the invaders on July 4, 1704 (Higginbotham 1977:191). Accordingly, Ocuians were probably among the natives who joined the final eastward and westward exodus, although it is not clear in which band they departed. The inhabitants of one village fled at Moore's approach, and Moore burned the village. Their reprieve was only temporary, however, because they were sur-prised at their Timucuan refuge sometime in 1705, and most were killed (Flo-rencia et al. 1707:85–89; Moore 1704b). Capoli, Tomole, and Tama are men-tioned by the governor as settlements whose inhabitants were carried off by the invading Indians (Zúñiga y Zerda 1705). Neither Capoli nor its people are mentioned again, but, because it is the next village to the west of Ayubale on the royal road, it was probably one of the settlements that Moore said surrendered unconditionally. The next town to the west along that road, Tomole, probably was another. Tama's proximity to San Luis seems to rule it out also as one of the villages surrendering unconditionally, and it is likely to have relocated voluntarily. This surmise appears to be borne out by the reappearance near St. Augustine in the wake of the Yamasee uprising of a village named Nuestra Señora de Candelaria de la Tamaja, headed by a Yamasee-speaking chief named Antonio de Ayala and containing some Christian Yamasee (Ayala y Escobar 1717). It is supported as well by Diego Peña's mention in 1717 of the presence of a Christian Taman from Apalachee named Augustus who was headman of some hamlets in the Lower Creek country (Boyd 1952:116). San Pedro and the Chine are not mentioned in the records, but the settlement's proximity to Tama makes it a strong possibility for unconditional surrender or voluntary relocation. Proximity to San Luis would have protected San Carlos de los Chacatos from attack, if it had been reestablished. Its inhabitants migrated westward with the people from San Luis and Escambé (Higginbotham 1977:191). The Tocobaga settlement is not mentioned in the records from this era, but its population appears to have been destroyed or dispersed. When Spanish forces returned to San Marcos in 1718, they found a very small number of Tocobaga on the Wacissa River (Primo de Rivera 1718a, 1718b).[16] As people associated with water, they or the Chine may have belonged to the village referred to as Ocatoses. In 1719, two Tocobaga were recorded as having returned from Mobile dissatisfied with their treatment by the French (González de Barcia Carballido y Zúñiga 1951:374–375).

Some of San Luis's population defected to the enemy while Moore was in the province. Mistreatment at the hands of the Spanish settlers and the latters' usurpation of some of their property in the village were undoubtedly the reasons. Inasmuch as the expeditions for the relief of Ayubale and Patale were mounted there, its warriors apparently bore the brunt of the casualties, especially in the first of these encounters. Three of its inhabitants, two of them leaders, were singled out for torture by their captors, enduring their ordeal with exemplary faith and courage until they died (Cruz 1705:74–76; Fuentes de Galanca 1705:77–79; Moore 1704b; Solana 1704a:50– 55, 1705:79–82).

The village of San Luis and its fort were destroyed by the Spaniards themselves when they withdrew. The bulk of the mission's surviving native population migrated westward. A few seem to have accompanied the garrison eastward, as indicated by the eventual emergence of an Apalachee hamlet near St. Augustine bearing the name San Luis, with a man named Osunac as its chief. Although such surnames were not confined to any one village, Osunacs or Usunacas are recorded as part of the leadership element at San Luis and at

16. There appear to have been fewer than 25.

nearby Cupaica (Ayala y Escobar 1698; Córcoles y Martínez 1711; Florencia 1695). Apparently Cupaica was not threatened by the invaders until June 1704. Inasmuch as most of its inhabitants had obeyed the lieutenant's order that they seek refuge in San Luis, only a few were captured or killed when the invaders destroyed Escambé in late June 1704. Some of Escambé's remaining population joined San Luis's in the trek to Pensacola. Others, who remained behind when the garrison left, were killed or captured early in August by a third attack force. Patale and Aspalaga also fell to the invaders during the second attack. Those who survived the assaults on these two settlements were probably either murdered or enslaved, except for two from Patale who eventually escaped to alert San Luis about the presence of this second attack force and its planned assault on Escambé.

Chapter 13

Exile and Extinction of the Apalachee

A GENERAL EXODUS of the surviving Apalachee population resulted from the 1704 attacks on the province. The majority moved northward with the invaders. The remainder of the surviving population moved eastward to Timucua and the vicinity of St. Augustine or westward to Pensacola and Mobile.

The eastward migration

The Apalachee who migrated eastward appear to have been among the least fortunate of the groups forced to leave their homeland in 1704. Before the end of 1705, most of the inhabitants of the unidentified village whose people had fled during Moore's attack had been massacred in their sylvan refuge in Timucua. For most of the Ivitachuca who left in July, life would be almost equally short and brutal. Their leader, Don Patricio Hinachuba, initially declined the governor's invitation to settle them in the vicinity of St. Augustine. Instead he chose to settle his people and a few Timucua below San Francisco de Potano at a place called Abosaya. Don Patricio had advised the governor to concentrate western Timucua's population at San Francisco, which, as the residence of the governor's deputy, had a small Spanish garrison (Bushnell 1979:13; Council of War 1704:57–58; Horue 1705:73; Junta of War 1705; Zúñiga y Zerda 1705). This concentration of forces, he hoped, would deter attacks by the marauding native allies of the English, while the abandoned Spanish ranches in the area could furnish meat until crops could be planted and harvested. The fortified main house of one ranch, La Chua, provided additional security, as some soldiers were posted there to secure meat and horses for St. Augustine's garrison.

Don Patricio's hopes were dashed within weeks as new bands of raiders struck San Pedro and San Matheo, the two missions north of San Francisco, and came within view of La Chua's blockhouse, not long after he had completed the stockade around his new settlement of Ivitachuco at Abosaya. Although a French privateer's attack on a plantation near Charles Town moved South Carolina's governor to propose a truce, the respite was brief. Before the end of that winter of 1704–1705, small bands of Creek again began to appear in the vicinity of La Chua.

Late in May 1705, Don Patricio informed the governor that he had news from the governor's deputy at San Francisco that enemy forces were coming to destroy both San Francisco de Potano and the new village of Ivitachuco at Abosaya. Don Patricio appealed for provisions, munitions, six muskets, and a dozen Spanish soldiers to help him and his men resist. In response the governor dispatched Francisco de Florencia with a small Spanish force (Bushnell 1979:14–15; Hinachuba 1705:473–474; Horue 1705:72–72; Ruíz de Cuenca 1705:70–72; Zúñiga y Zerda 1704f:68–69, 1705).

Soon after Florencia's arrival, Don Patricio journeyed to St. Augustine to lobby for more supplies, leaving Florencia in charge of defending the village. The expected enemy attack, by a force numbering 200, occurred while Ivitachuco's chief was in St. Augustine. On learning of the village's plight, the governor immediately dispatched a relief force of 100 to accompany Don Patricio on his return. Before it had marched very far, that force was twice diverted from its initial goal to deal with additional marauding bands of Creek operating closer to St. Augustine. The Spanish force was defeated and dispersed in the second of those encounters. Before the second encounter Don Patricio and his small band of warriors had set out alone for La Chua. On arriving there, they received word from Florencia that they should not attempt to enter Ivitachuco unless they were accompanied by a large force. While vainly awaiting the arrival of the defeated relief force, Don Patricio's band found themselves besieged for a time in La Chua's blockhouse. When Don Patricio was able to reenter his village, he found food in short supply and many of his people ill. At some point during the winter of 1705–1706, Don Patricio and his people abandoned the village for the imagined security of the environs of St. Augustine (Boyd 1953:461–462; Bushnell 1979:14–16; Florencia 1705a: 474, 1705b:474–475; Florencia et al. 1707:87–88; Florencia and Pueyo 1706a:475–476; [Hinachuba] 1705:473–474; Zúñiga y Zerda 1705:16).

Not all of the problems at Ivitachuco-Abosaya were caused by the enemy. In mid-January 1706, before their departure for St. Augustine, Diego Peña reported from Potano that on New Year's Day, three Timucua, who had gone to La Chua, killed three of four Apalachee whom they encountered there hunting cattle. Although wounded by a hatchet blow, the fourth escaped to tell his compatriots.

On arriving at St. Augustine, the refugee Ivitachucans did not set up a village of their own but sought shelter in a number of existing small native villages that had been established a little to the south of the city. There, early in the spring of 1706, Don Patricio and many of his people were killed in a new wave of attacks. Others were taken prisoner, and a few escaped. These attacks were described by the royal officials in terms that implied a Creek design to annihilate the few surviving members of the Apalachee nation who had remained loyal to Spain (Bushnell 1979:16; Florencia and Pueyo 1706a: 475–476).

During this same interval the two remaining western settlements of San Francisco de Potano and Santa Fé were similarly assaulted. Although they were able to hold out and eventually received relief, they asked for and were granted permission to withdraw to the vicinity of St. Augustine (Florencia and Pueyo 1706b:477–479). This move reduced the Spanish presence in East Florida to a narrow area close to St. Augustine.

By the time of the census of January 1711, the 400 or so Apalachee who had left their homeland in mid-1704 with Don Patricio or with the San Luis garrison appear to have been reduced to 48 individuals, 31 men, 11 women, and 6 children (3 boys and 3 girls). The boys belonged to the Chinacossa family. Although the 48 people are listed by name, their villages of origin cannot be identified with certainty. Perusal of earlier listings of individuals reveals that the same surnames are found in several villages. The name of the village, "San Luis de Thalimali alias Abosayan," indicates that its population was drawn from San Luis as well as from Ivitachuco (Córcoles y Martínez 1711).

This census's listing of the surviving natives by name reveals the Apalachee's pertinacity in preserving their native surnames, in contrast to the Ibaja and Timucua, most of whom are listed by Spanish names. Only one Apalachee woman had abandoned her native surname. The others, including the children, bore Christian first names and a native surname (Córcoles y Martínez 1711).

The Apalachee represented only about 10 percent of the native population clustered within a pistol shot of the fort. The total included 400 Indians, of whom 105 were non-Christians. The other hamlets were Santa Caterina de Guale, composed of Ibaja speakers, Santo Tomás de Santa Fé alias Esperansa, composed of Timucua speakers, Tolomato, San Juan del Puerto, Nombre de Dios, and Salamototo (Córcoles y Martínez 1711).

The crushing of the Yamasee uprising in South Carolina, in which the free Apalachee there had participated, brought a new influx of Indians to the vicinity of St. Augustine. The census taken by the governor in 1717 shows that the number of native hamlets had increased to ten and that several of those listed in 1711 had either disappeared or undergone a change of name. Yamasee predominated among the newcomers. In the space of six years the Apalachee population had almost doubled, but it is not clear how many were newcomers.

The Apalachee village known as San Luis de Talimali in 1711 was known, by 1717, as Our Lady of the Rosary of Abosaia (or Jabosaia). Its cacique in 1717 was Don Pedro de Osunaca, who in 1711 had been listed as "the old cacique." The incumbent in 1711 had been one Hina Juan de Hita. Its population had shrunk by one-third, to 31, but, inasmuch as the 1711 imbalance between men and women had been rectified, this decline probably resulted, in part at least, from the departure of some of the mateless warriors. In 1717, Abosaya had one other leading man, twelve Christian women, and three boys and four girls listed as "Doctrina children." Also joined to it were two non-Christian women of the Chasta nation.

Apalachee were to be found in a number of other villages. The Timucua village of Our Lady of Sorrows had 20 Apalachee warriors. The non-Christian Yamasee settlement of Pocosapa was listed as the residence of "thirty-four warriors . . . of the Apalachino and Timucuan tongues and three Christian women of the Yamasee and Apalachino tongues." The Timucua village of Nombre de Dios had three Apalachee men and four women of that tribe, and the women were described as having been among 16 who came from Salamototo (Ayala y Escobar 1717; Oliveira y Pullana 1716). These other Apalachee raise the prospect that in 1711 there were more Apalachee in the St. Augustine region than the 48 residents of San Luis, particularly in view of the royal officials' remark that when the Ivitachucans abandoned the Potano region of St. Augustine, they did not establish a place of their own but scattered among other tribal hamlets (Bushnell 1979:16; Florencia and Pueyo 1706a: 474–476).

The great disproportion between the numbers of Apalachee men and women reflected in these two censuses, together with the lack of children, obviously portended the rapid disappearance of the Apalachee at St. Augustine as a separate people, particularly in view of the matriarchal structure of most of these southeastern tribes. It meant that the children of the Apalachee men who were forced to go outside the tribe for wives would be identified with their mothers' people.

One of the other new villages mentioned in this census bore the name Nuestra Señora de Candelaria de la Tamaja. It was peopled by Yamasee, a mixture of some Christian and a considerable majority of non-Christians. The name of the settlement, the tribal affiliation of its inhabitants, the Christian faith of a number of them, and the Spanish name of its principal chief, Antonio de Ayala, all suggest that the Christians among them were former residents of the Apalachee village of that name who had fled from South Carolina after the collapse of the widespread Indian revolt initiated by the Yamasee. The chief and 28 others were Christians. Inasmuch as one of them was identified as a new Christian, the other 27 presumably were Christians of long standing (Ayala y Escobar 1717).

In addition to the natives who came to St. Augustine to settle, the disruption of Indian ties with the English produced by the Yamasee revolt brought such other groups as the Lower Creek to St. Augustine as visitors. During 1717 in particular, the city repeatedly hosted parties of Creek that came to pledge or reaffirm their allegiance to the Spanish monarch and to be regaled and feasted at the governor's table. One of the most frequent visitors was Adrián, chief of the former Apalachee village of Bacuqua, who came with a large party of Lower Creek in April. He returned with some of them in July and made the journey again in September, carrying a message to the governor for Diego Peña, who had been sent by the governor on a mission to win the "Emperor" Brims's firm commitment to the Spanish cause.

On the third visit, Chief Adrián was accompanied by 46 other Apalachee from the Lower Creek country. Adrián was an intimate of the pro-Spanish elements among the leaders of the Lower Creek, particularly of Chiscalachisle,[1] chief of the town of that name built in 1716 just above the confluence of the Flint and the Chattahoochee, and of Chipacasi,[2] usinulo and heir to Brims.[3] Except for two Bacuquan vassals of Chief Adrián, nothing is said of the town of origin of these Apalachee. At this time a number of Apalachee were living dispersed through the Lower Creek country (Boyd 1952:126; González de Barcia Carballido y Zúñiga 1951:358; Tepaske 1964:202). Presumably, most, if not all, of them had fled from South Carolina because of their participation with the Creek in the so-called Yamasee War. Emperor Brims's wife was a Christian Apalachee, as was the wife of Chipacasi. As Chipacasi's mother, Brims's wife was probably part of the Apalachee exodus to the Creek country in the 1680s during Antonio Matheos's tyrannical rule as the governor's deputy in Apalachee. That background is probably reflected in her pro-English stance (Corkran 1967:52, 62–63).

1. There are myriad renditions of this name, among them Tascaliche, Chalquilicha, Talichasliche, Chislacasliche, Chasliquasliche, and, in many of the English sources, Cherokeeleechee or Cherokee-killer. There is some confusion concerning his identity and that of the people of his town, which was built on the site of the short-lived Christian town of Sabacola of the 1680s. Crane (1956:255) identified his people as Creek from Palachocola Town; Corkran said they were Apalachee. The most reliable designation is probably that of the Spanish governor who identified him as chief of the province of the Uchices (Ayala y Escobar 1717:37).

2. This name also appears in many variants such as Tsipacaya, Sincapafi, and, in English sources, as Seepeycoffee. Tepaske refers to him as Brims's nephew, but overwhelming evidence points to him as Brims's son. His being named successor to Brims was a departure from the matriarchal line of succession.

3. Brims, alias Yslachamuque, was the principal chief of Coweta and eventually was acknowledged as head chief of all the Creek. Governor Ayala identified him as "Usinjulo and mico—heir of the great chieftainship of the province of Cabetta, whom all those nations and vassalls had in the same esteem and veneration as the Spaniards hold the prince our Lord" (Ayala y Escobar 1717:36–37).

When next mentioned, in 1723, the St. Augustine Apalachee's hamlet was referred to as the village of Moze. A more informative reference stems from the governor's visitation of the native towns in December 1726. San Luis was then the name given to the Apalachee's settlement. It was described as possessing a church and convent of straw and a population of 87, of whom 78 were old Christians and the others recent converts. There is no indication of how many of them were Apalachee; 36 were men, 27 women, and 24 children (Benavides 1726). It seems certain, because of the increase in the number of women and the presence of recent converts, that some of them were not Apalachee. A later source confirms this conclusion, mentioning that a surviving remnant of the Yamasee from the village of Tama had sought refuge with the Apalachee at this time.

The Carolinian-inspired genocidal campaign against the Yamasee was at its height in the early 1720s. It received new impetus after 1724, when several Yamasee killed Ouletta, the pro-English son of Brims.[4] In a particularly catastrophic attack on November 1, 1725, the Uchise killed many of the Yamasee and carried off others. Plague completed the carnage, leaving Moze with only three inhabitants (Benavides 1727a; Bishop of Cuba 1728; Bullones 1728; Corkran 1967:71; Council of the Indies 1727). Early in 1729, the bishop of Cuba informed the king that the native population had declined to such a point that the numbers in the four surviving hamlets would not suffice to create one doctrina worthy of the name or the money (Bishop of Cuba 1729). Either the bishop was overly pessimistic or St. Augustine received a new influx of Indians, for a decade later the number of hamlets had doubled to eight, containing 340 natives. The only Apalachee mentioned among the survivors were two males living at Nombre de Dios (Horcasitas y Güemes 1739; Montiano 1738a). At the time of the transfer of St. Augustine to the British, five of the approximately 80 Christian Indians who departed with the Spaniards were Apalachee (Deagan 1976; Gold 1969:81–82). By 1766 only 53 of the Florida natives were still alive (Gold 1969:81–82). What became of them in Cuba is unknown.

The northward migration

In the destruction and dispersion of the population of Apalachee in 1704, by far the greatest number migrated northward, voluntarily or involuntarily. Determining the numbers involved in that migration and the village of origin of the migrants is difficult. Establishing the fate of the majority of these emigrants is equally troublesome.

4. Until that time, Brims had opposed the break with the Yamasee demanded by the English.

The least is known about those who remained among the Creek from the beginning. During the attacks at least 50 Apalachee rebels actively joined the enemy against the Spaniards and their fellow tribesmen. Fourteen of those rebels died in subsequent skirmishes, and four were captured. One of the dead rebels was from Tomole, and another was the son of the cacique of Aspalaga the Old (Solana 1704a:50–55). There were likely additional defections during the last encounter with the Creek, on July 4, 1704, when the Apalachee warriors abandoned the field en masse shortly after the enemy had been engaged. Presumably all of these rebels migrated to Upper or Lower Creek towns and were adopted as members of the various tribes there. In 1717 Diego Peña reported that the Apalachee as well as the Yamasee were living dispersed among the Creek, rather than concentrated in one or more areas (Boyd 1952:123). The 1708 Carolina census stated that several families of Apalachee were living in some of the eleven towns along the Ochasee River.[5]

By 1717 their number would have been considerably augmented by the exodus of the Apalachee from South Carolina at the end of the Yamasee War (Crane 1956:254–255). During his 1716 trip to the Apalachicola country, Diego Peña reported the presence of some Christian Apalachee somewhere below the village of Sabacola on the west side of the lands between the Flint and the Chattahoochee and five days north of Chislacasliche's new village just above the confluence of the Flint and the Chattahoochee. They owned some prairies there. One day's journey farther north, he spent the night with other Apalachee who lived on a small farm belonging to the cacique of the town of Apalachicola. The farm was some distance south of that chief's town. Without giving any further information concerning their location, Peña stated that there were many Apalachee in the province at the time (Boyd 1949:20–22, 25). During his 1717 trip, Peña sojourned at a hamlet headed by a Christian Taman from Apalachee named Augustus. It lay four days north of the village of Chislacasliche. His next stopping point was a cattle ranch owned by some Apalachee, which was one day's journey from the Taman's village. It was probably the Apalachee-owned prairie two leagues below Sabacola where he had stopped during the preceding year (Boyd 1952:114, 117–118).

The fact that one of the upper branches of the Oconee River is known as the Apalachee River suggests that at some time a band of Apalachee lived in that area, particularly as it was once known as the South Oconee River. However, none of the archaeological sites in the area has revealed any artifacts indicative of their presence. In the course of his research on the Joe Bell site at the junction of the Apalachee and the Oconee, Mark Williams gave some attention to the origin of the name "Apalachee" for that river and was unable to

5. Ochasee River is Ochesee Creek, the former name of the Ocmulgee River.

find any record of its having been used for that stream any earlier than the 1780s. He dated the last native occupation of the Joe Bell site as 1630 to 1675 (Williams, personal communication 1984).

The return to Apalachee

Some of the Apalachee in the Creek country eventually settled near Pensacola, and from there some soon moved to the vicinity of the new Fort San Marcos de Apalachee established by José Primo de Rivera in 1718 (González de Barcia Carballido y Zúñiga 1951:366, 368, 372–373, 378). The Spanish authorities made repeated efforts to induce the Apalachee of the Creek country and some of the Creek themselves to resettle Apalachee, particularly the area of the abandoned missions (Ayala y Escobar 1718; Boyd 1952:199; Primo de Rivera 1718a). Chief Adrián promised that he would round up all the Apalachee that he could and bring them down to found a new settlement near the fort at St. Marks (Primo de Rivera 1718a); there is no direct evidence that he did so, although it remains a possibility. In 1719, while the head chief Juan Marcos was recruiting settlers for Apalachee among the Pensacola Apalachee, he mentioned that an Apalachee settlement had been established near St. Marks, but there is no indication where those Apalachee came from. As Juan Marcos had just come from St. Augustine it is possible that he had recruited them from St. Augustine's Apalachee community or from the considerable number of Apalachee from the Creek country mentioned as being in St. Augustine as visitors in September and October 1718.

Among the natives, the Yamasee showed the greatest interest in relocating to Apalachee in order to escape the incessant attacks from the Uchise bands partial to the English. In mid-1718, Rivera spoke of the intent, once their crops were in, of a group of Yamasee who had settled at the site of the Chacato village of San Carlos on the Apalachicola to move to the forest of Sarturcha in the vicinity of the fort (González de Barcia Carballido y Zúñiga 1951:378; Primo de Rivera 1718a). In the 1723 list of the missions, the only natives mentioned as present in Apalachee are the Amapexas, 12 children and 79 adults.[6] In the 1726 list, however, the Apalachee reappear along with the Yamasee residents of the village of San Juan, which was served by the fort's church of San Marcos. Its population of 46 included 16 men, 17 women, and 13 children, all but one of whom were Christians. In 1728 it still had between 30 and 40 people. There was a larger village named San Antonio, with its own straw church and convent, containing 146 Yamasee, of whom 48 were recent converts and the remaining 98 non-Christian. It had 66 men, 51 women, and

6. Presumably a band of Yamasee.

29 children (Benavides 1726). By 1728 this village had lost all its women and children and contained only 80 warriors. Now referred to by the name of Tamasle, it had been forced to surrender to the Uchise when its defenders exhausted their ammunition. The 80 warriors had been able to escape and seek refuge at the fort two leagues away (Bishop of Cuba 1728; Montiano 1745).

By 1739 the natives living near the fort at San Marcos were reduced to one village named Tamasle, containing an unspecified number of Catholics and non-Christians (Horcasitas y Guemes 1739; Montiano 1738d). One source in 1736 put its permanent population at 20 to 30 Indians (Auxiliary Bishop of Florida 1736). After 1739 the only mention of Tamasle is a brief reference in a 1747 letter by the governor; he mentions only Yamasee as inhabitants of the village (Montiano 1747). Swanton identifies Tamasle with the Tama-Yamasee, although he leaves open the possibility that its people were Sawokli, his name for the Sabacola (Swanton 1922:12, 1946:180, 189). A year or two earlier the commandant at the fort mentioned the recent arrival of two formerly Christian women, one of whom had two children and the other the widow of the leader of Sabacola. He found them of invaluable assistance in making native pottery and in gathering such food as oysters and potatoes (Montiano 1756). It is possible that they were among the five Indians from the towns of Sabacola and Tamasca recorded as having been granted permission to leave for Cuba with the Spanish garrison when it withdrew in 1764 after delivering the fort to the British (Gold 1969:158–159).

In the half century after the Spanish return to Apalachee, Spain proved unable to attract or preserve any significant number of natives in the area. One reason was the failure of its authorities to keep their promises to put a settlement of Spaniards in Apalachee, to build a new fort there, and to equip it with a well-stocked store. This point was driven home sharply by the Creek leader Chocate, citing as an example that at one point a Spanish party had gone to San Luis, marked out an area on which to rebuild the fort, and left many stakes driven as an expression of Spain's intentions to build it and to send families to settle in that area. But, he concluded, none of this came to pass, not even the establishment of the store that they had asked for (Montiano 1745).

That activity at San Luis appears to have taken place in the latter half of the 1720s. In 1727 the governor advised the king that, on the basis of a reconnaissance of the Santoucha forest and of the old villages of Ivitachuco, San Luis, and of the Chacato and Chine, he considered the site of San Luis to be the most desirable because of its better breezes, more fertile lands, abundance of lumber, and valuable water (Benavides 1727b). A decade later another governor chose the site of La Tama, paying similar tribute to its fertility, sweet water, and other attributes (Montiano 1738c). That nothing came of these plans and projects resulted from Spain's overextension and from the Spanish view of Florida as a peripheral province without the intrinsic value to justify such expense when it was weighed against the needs of other areas making similar demands on Spain's resources. A store eventually was established at San Marcos, but it was unable to compete effectively with its British counterparts (Montiano 1745).

This talk about reestablishing a Spanish presence in the former mission region of Apalachee appears to have misled Boyd into assuming that the talk led to action. In a 1939 article, Boyd observed that "The impression has been general, that following this [Moore's] assault, the missions were extinguished. There is no positive reason to believe this, and from the Spanish side there are encountered fragmentary data which lead to the suspicion that the effect of Moore's raid may not have been as permanently devastating as he boasted." From that cautious speculation Boyd passed to the positive assertion that

> It would appear that in the course of time the frailes gathered together considerable numbers of their scattered charges, and reorganized the *doctrinas* or mission villages, perhaps on different sites. This view is confirmed by a letter from Governor Don Antonio de Benavides to the King, written from San Marcos de Apalache on the 8th of February, 1732, in which are listed eight settlements of Timuquan Indians bearing the XVIIth century names, and thirteen villages of Apalachee Indians which perpetuate the names of the villages of the previous century. This letter discusses plans for colonization in Apalachee, with the establishment of a *villa* or *ciudad* at La Tama and the construction of fortifications at La Tama and San Marcos. (Boyd 1939:278–279)

Only the last sentence of Boyd's statement is supported by the document he cites. The sentence in which the 13 Apalachee villages are named begins, "The thirteen places of Apalachee Indians of which the province alluded to *was composed* [*se componia*] are the following" (Benavides 1732). The governor's and other documents definitely indicate that after 1704 the only native or mission villages established in Apalachee territory under Spanish auspices were the two villages in the vicinity of the fort at San Marcos. The contemplated settlement and fort on the former site of the Mission of La Tama were to be inhabited by up to 500 Canary Islanders rather than by Indians, but that project never passed beyond the proposal stage. From 1736, for example, just four years after the document cited by Boyd, there is a positive statement by the auxiliary bishop of Florida that, just as the non-Christian Indians from the interior who come down to St. Augustine occasionally to pledge obedience were a fraud, coming only for a handout and then returning to their ties with the English, the same occurred in Apalachee. He said that there were only 20 to 30 Indians there, at the fort at San Marcos, and that the rest were with the English (Auxiliary Bishop of Florida 1736). There are two separate mission lists for 1738, one giving an account of the native villages and the other a report on the friars serving in Florida. Only two friars are mentioned as serving in Apalachee. One was chaplain in Fort San Marcos; the other was stationed in the settlement of Tamasle, which was not far from the fort (Montiano 1738a, 1738d).

When the Spanish authorities renewed friendly contact with the Creek in this post-1715 period, the Creek still held an undetermined number of Christian Indians as slaves. Although their tribal derivation is not mentioned, most were probably from Apalachee. On at least two occasions when Brims was pressed for the release of these captives, he evaded the question. The Spaniards were more successful with the Upper Creek, securing the release during 1718 of 15 Christian natives held as slaves by the Talapuces (González de Barcia Carballido y Zúñiga 1951:361, 369–370). The freed natives appear to have gone to Pensacola. Although the enslaved Apalachee as well as the free Apalachee who remained among the Creek disappeared as a distinct people during this period, their genes probably persist among some of today's Seminole in Florida and among the Seminole and the Creek forced to migrate to Oklahoma.

The emigrants to South Carolina

Most of the emigrants from Apalachee who headed northward in 1704 journeyed to South Carolina. These migrants included 1,300 free Indians and an undetermined number of others destined to be slaves, although, as J. Leitch Wright and others have observed, the distinction between the freemen and those to be enslaved was not always clear (Wright 1981:114). The number enslaved was probably far smaller than the more than 4,000 claimed by Moore. An additional number of natives from Apalachee lost their freedom in the second and third attacks on the province in June, July, and August 1704. A few were enslaved in 1705 during the attack on the Ivitachucan settlement near St. Augustine and in the Creek 1706 attack on Pensacola. Although the Creek attack forces were almost entirely Indian, some of their captives were probably sold to the Carolinians when the Creek brought in the scalps of the Christian natives and Spaniards whom they had killed for the bounty paid by the English authorities. Selling fellow Indians into slavery had become one of the Creek's principal means of supporting their developing taste for European wares. They could obtain as much for one slave as for a year's accumulation of deerhides (Crane 1956:109–114). It is my opinion that the total number of Apalachee enslaved in this period was under 1,000. As noted in chapter 8, an unspecified number of Apalachee were in South Carolina by January 1703, more than a year before the massive influx of Apalachee. They probably were captured in the battle on the Flint in September 1702 and arrived toward the end of that year. On January 23, 1703, the Commons House of Assembly voted down a motion that they should be considered as "plunder to be divided within the Act for raising the sum of two thousand pounds for carrying on the expedition against St. Augustine" (Salley 1934:72–73). There is no further information concerning the fate of this first group of captive Apalachee brought to Carolina.

Unfortunately, not a great deal more is known about the fortune of the surviving Apalachee population that arrived in South Carolina in 1704, neither of the free immigrants nor of those who came as slaves. As might be expected, we have almost no information on the fate of the slaves.

The colonial assembly was responsible for preserving the freedom of some of the native immigrants from Apalachee. The Commons advised Governor Nathaniel Johnson to instruct Moore to strive to win over the Apalachee by peaceful means, having been informed that they would be open to such overtures. Accordingly the assembly suggested that some of the Apalachee should be brought back as free Indians. Although Snell describes Moore as reluctant to keep his promise, the majority of the 1,300 to whom such terms were extended were settled along the Savannah River to serve as part of a native buffer force against any attack on the colony from the south (Covington 1972:376; Salley 1934:121; Snell 1972:58). Whatever Moore's reaction was, the person accused in the colonial assembly with seeking to thwart this policy was John Musgrove, who was charged during the 1706 session with obstructing the governor's orders under which the free Apalachee were authorized to settle along the Savannah River. Musgrove's maneuvers moved Apalachee chiefs to complain about him. He also was charged with using the governor's name, while he was among the Apalachee, to pretend that "he had Sometime Orders from him to go to warr" (Salley 1939:22).

Evidence on the number of Apalachee settlements in South Carolina is scanty and conflicting. Shortly after the arrival of the immigrant Apalachee, the Commons House of Assembly discussed its policy toward them and resolved

That the Governor be advised that the appalacha Indians brought in by Col. Moore, be taken into the protection of this Government; and for the present that they continue at the *places* now settled. But further advise that with all convenient speed, both the Caciques of our friendly Indians, among whom they are settled, and the Caciques of the Appalachas be sent for, that inquiry be made whether the Yamasee Indians, now brought from the Spaniards are more inclined to continue where they now live or to come down and settle here with their nation, and they willing to entertain them. (*Journal of the Commons House of Assembly* 1704:232; italics mine)

The indication, then, is that there was more than one settlement of Apalachee at that time. A Spanish document of November 1707 states clearly that, from those carried off, three villages of just Apalachee had been formed (Royal Officials 1707). But in a description of the various Indian tribes subject to South Carolina in 1708, a source in the colony reporting to the lords proprietors speaks of the Apalachee as living on the Savannah River in a "considerable town" containing about 250 men "who behaved themselves very submissive to the government." There is a clear implication that they were concentrated in one town in contrast to the 150 male Savanna, who are mentioned as living on the river just below the Apalachee and scattered in three separate towns (Salley 1947 (5):208, 247). Covington identifies the location of that one village as near New Windsor, South Carolina, at a site just south of present-day Augusta, Georgia (Covington 1972:376). The only other free Apalachee mentioned in the 1708 source were several families living in 11 towns along the Ocmulgee River. J. Leitch Wright was of the opinion that some of the free Apalachee were scattered around the South Carolina countryside as well (personal communication, February 1984).

Initially, at least, the English seem to have been mistrustful of the Apalachee immigrants. In the same resolution of April 1704 in which the Commons brought the Apalachee under their protection, they also took the precaution of ordering the following:

And also, further advise that the Indian traders be commanded and the said Appalachees advised to a free trade for Gunns and amunition shall not be granted to them, till we are better assured of their sincerity to us and that we may not lye open to such barabous [*sic*] cruelty as hath been committed by some of them. Wee also advise that the Appalachee Indians be not employed as Burtherners by the Traders no further than the Savana Towne. (*Journal of the Commons House of Assembly* 1704:232)

Shortly after their arrival some of the Apalachee apparently gave them cause for concern. At the Commons session of April 27, 1704, members agreed to consider a request from Colonel Moore for satisfaction for the loss of three of his slaves, who had been killed by the Apalachee, apparently in Charleston. After debating the matter the next day, the Commons resolved

That Col. Moore be paid out of the Publick Treasury the sum of 150 12S . 6 . for the loss of 3 slaves killed and goods taken away by some of

the Appalatchee Indians brought down into this settlement as burthen-
ers, the Appalachee Indians being but lately reduced and come into us,
and therefore, not able to make him satisfaction. (*Journal of the Commons House of Assembly* 1704:236)

As early as September 3, 1704, Governor Zúñiga reported that some of the
Apalachee carried off by the enemy were already escaping (Zúñiga y Zerda
1704d:65–67). In June 1707, the same assembly approved Thomas Nairne's
motion that a gratuity of five pounds be paid to Shamdedee, a St. Helena Indian, because the latter's brother had been killed by an Apalachee slave. The
assembly's profession of hope that this gratuity would serve as "an encouragement to other Neighbor Indians to be Diligent in pursuing and apprehending
run away slaves" suggests that runaways were a common problem (Salley
1940:63).

However, it appears that they soon won the confidence of their hosts to a
greater degree. During their relatively brief sojourn in the Carolina territory,
the Apalachee engaged extensively in hunting; they were employed by traders
as pack bearers, were pressed into service as field hands at harvest time, and
fought alongside the English as warriors in the Tuscarora War (Barnwell
1908:30; Covington 1967:14, 1972:376). They also were incorporated into
the permanent defense system under English officers to take them to the coast
if danger threatened there (Crane 1956:87–88). A heavy traffic in skins developed between the new Apalachee villages and Charles Town, and the route
became known as the Apalachee trail (Covington 1972:376–377). Concerning the Apalachee's role as pack bearers, the members of the Governor's Council commented in 1708, "These people are seated very advantageous for
carrying our trade. Indians seated upwards of 700 miles off are supplied with
goods by our white men that transport them from this river upon Indians'
backs" (Salley 1947, 5:208).[7]

Despite the council's contentment with the Apalachee, they were not always treated justly by the Carolinians. In some cases, the wives and children
of free Apalachee warriors were sold into slavery while those warriors were
off fighting the Tuscarora at the side of the English settlers. On other occasions, free Apalachee were forced to work on the farms of traders at harvest-
time (Covington 1967:14; McDowell 1955:4). As early as the Commons session of 1706–1707, charges were lodged in that assembly that John Musgrove
had arbitrarily enslaved or received as slaves a considerable number of free

7. In this document the name Apalachee is spelled Appalatchyes. It appears to have been the
   most common rendering of the name in English at this time and probably reflects the way the
   natives' pronounciation sounded to English ears.

Indians, some clearly identified as Apalachee and others possibly Apalachee. The following is part of the charge filed against Musgrove:

> 2nd. It is alledged and charged . . . that he arbitrarily and of his own accord took and Receiv'd Sixteen Illcombee and Wacoca ffree people and made them his Slaves upon pretence that he would thereupon Sett the rest free when they were none of them at that time slaves and that he the said John Musgrove in a like arbitrary and forcible manner tooke six of the I:Awellies [*sic*] a ffree aplacia people and made and sold them for Slaves.
>
> 3dly It is alledged and Charged upon the said John Musgrove that he arbitrarily and of his own accord tooke tooke [*sic*] a ffree Indian woman belonging to the Coolenne Towne and brought her as a Slave to the Savannah Town and that he tooke a ffree Toomelean and made her a slave.
>
> 5thly [*sic*] It is alledged and Charged upon the said John Musgrove, That he the said John Musgrove arbitrarily and of his own accord tooke at one time Eight Worstera free people and made them Slaves.
>
> 6thly It is Alledged and Charged upon the said John Musgrove, that he the said John Musgrove arbitrarily and of his own Accord threatened the lives of the Tuckesaw Indian King and another unless they would give him ffour Slaves . . .
>
> 7thly It is Alledged and Charg'd upon the said John Musgrove that he arbitrarily and of his own Accord tooke away ffrom the Illcombeans or Wacoca Indians two Slaves one horse and Some say Six and others say Sixteen ffree Indians and made them Slaves upon the pretence that the said Illcombean or Wacoca Indians had killed Severall of his Cattle.[8]
>
> Lastly It is alledged and Charged upon the Said John Musgrove that notwithstanding the ffree people of the Appelachies were by the Governrs Order to Sett down Some where on the Savanah River, he has hindred and given the greatest discouragement he could ffor their so doeing. of which Abuse their Casseiques did Complain or were Comeing to Complaine to the Governr. (Salley 1939:21–22)

Of the groups mentioned in this source only the I:Awellies are identified clearly as Apalachee. They may have been from Ayubale, which is the Apala-

---

8. A blank space was left before "Indians" with the evident intention of filling it in with the name of the tribe when learned. This is a footnote by Salley, who also noted that there was a blank space on the page between the 3rd and 5th allegations which was evidently left to be filled in later.

chee village name that most clearly approximates I:Awellies, and this spelling is not far removed from the forms Aiavalla and Ayaville used in Colonel Moore's two letters. The Toomelean woman could well have been from Tomole, and the Illcombeans could well have come from the Apalachee village of that name. The name Wacoca could be a corruption of Bacuqua. The derivations of the Illcombeans and the Wacocans are open to other interpretations. First, this source seems to be using the names Illcombeans and Wacocans interchangeably. Second, Swanton (1922) identifies Ilcombe as one of the ten Yamasee towns spoken of in early South Carolina documents. In his 1946 work, however, he gives a different listing of these ten Yamasee towns in which there is no mention of Ilcombe.[9] The sources he cites in his 1922 work are from the "Proceedings of the Board Dealing with Indian Trade" and hence probably posterior to the above sources as that board was formed in 1710. Swanton (1922) mentions the Wakokai as one of the Muskogee or Creek peoples. The references to the Illcombeans both in the Commons journal and in the later Board of Indian Trade records seem to imply that they arrived later than 1704, that they came to Carolina from an "enemy" territory, where they had been under attack, and that they had been given the option of relocating as free men. Although the references are too sketchy to support a definitive judgment on their origin, it is my feeling that they were from the Apalachee village of Ilcombe originally and came to South Carolina from either the Apalachee colony at Pensacola or from one of the Apalachee settlements above Mobile. In an earlier meeting during that session, the Commons had resolved that

> Upon debate concerning the Illcumbee Indians it is the opinion of this House that the Illcumbee Indians be declared free people . . . and that your Honrs be pleased to send for the Indians now in Town and signifie it to them . . . and that a present of fforty or ffifty pounds may be made to them by your Honr for their conducting them out the Enenies Countrey into this Government. And we further desire your honr to remove the said Illcombees ffrom the place they now Sett down in to Some other place as your Honrs shall think fitt. (Salley 1939:13)

Shortly after charges were filed against Musgrove, similar charges of unjust enslavement of the natives were alleged against three other English settlers:

> It is alleged and charged. They the said John Pight, Anthony Probert, and James Lucas . . . artibrarilly . . . bought of an Indian named Tomichee ten Indians which were free and made slaves of them

9. In 1946 it disappears completely from his index in contrast to the 1922 work where it is mentioned as both a Yamasee and an Apalachee town.

2nd it is alleged and charged that the same three men bought or otherwise procured these several Indian free people knowing them to be free and made them slaves Viz

       7 Waucoogau free people bought of Toomichau [10]
       2 Illcombee free people of D°
       2 free people of the Tookesa king
       1 Toomela free boy bought of D°
       1 free Ilcombe woman and her sister
       2 Tomillee free woman by name Collose and Aukilla
       1 Tomillee boy. In all 20 free people. (Salley 1939:27)

On this list, the name Waucoogau—presumably a variant of Wacoca—is even more reminiscent of a corruption of Bacuqua, or Vacugua as it occasionally was rendered in the Spanish texts. The name Tomillee could also be a corruption of Tomole; the names of the two Tomillee women are not among the Apalachee names that have survived. The indictment of these three men closed with the charge that they had persisted in holding these natives as slaves despite the government's orders that they be freed and, prophetically, as the Commons put it, "to the great danger and hazard of this Colony by provoking the Indians in such a manner."

Despite the strictures of this assembly in 1707, the abuses continued. When the commissioners for the regulation of the Indian trade began their initial sessions on September 21, 1710, to consider the complaints by the Indians, most of the first cases that they heard involved Apalachee. The first case involved an Apalachee named Ventusa and his wife, who claimed that they had been enslaved unjustly by Phillip Gilliard. The board held that they should be free until such time as Gilliard could prove the contrary. There is no record in the board's journal that he tried to. Two other male Apalachee were granted their freedom under similar circumstances. In the fourth case, involving an Ellcombe Indian named Wansella, the native was to be free until John Pight could produce an order from the government authorizing his enslavement. The Apalachee also presented a complaint that Captain Musgrove had gone to their town in the spring demanding Indians to work on his land and beating them when they did not comply. It is not clear whether any action was taken against Musgrove on this occasion; it is doubtful that the commission did. Despite his contumacious abuse of the natives, Musgrove was soon to become a member of the commission. Other Apalachee complaints involved

---

10. One wonders if there is any connection between this collaborator with the worst elements among the English settlers and the Tomochichi, leader of the Yamacraws in Oglethorpe's time, in view of the similarity of their names and affection for the English.

the abduction and beating of Indian women and of those who intervened to try to halt the beatings (McDowell 1955:3–5).

Although the commission seems to have made an effort to rectify some of the abuses, its members do not seem to have done enough, inasmuch as the Apalachee were one of the many Indian groups who joined the Yamasee in the 1715 uprising (Crane 1956:170). There is no record that any effort was made to convert the free Apalachee during their stay in Carolina, although Captain Thomas Nairne did apply to the English Society for the Propagation of the Gospel for missionaries for them and other natives (Crane 1956:145–146).

The sources provide only sketchy information on the Apalachee's role in the Yamasee War, particularly in its early weeks. Crane implies that they were involved almost from the beginning. In June 1715, they were a major contingent of a Creek-led force that swept to within a dozen miles of Charles Town, destroying many plantations, one ship, and the Pon Pon bridge over the Edisto River (Crane 1956:170, 173, 180–181). This last great push of the natives into Carolina was led by Chigelly, the head warrior of Caveta and Brims's brother (Corkran 1967:59).

The Apalachee who survived the Yamasee War joined the Caveta, Palachicola, Savana, Yuchi, and Oconee in moving not only from the Savannah River region but in withdrawing from the Ocmulgee River area to return to the banks of the Chattahoochee that the Apalachicola among them had occupied before 1690. As noted, the Apalachee involved in this exodus spread rather widely, some settling among the Creek, others near Pensacola; still others moved on to Mobile to join the Apalachee who had been established there since 1704 (Crane 1956:254–255). Some undoubtedly accompanied the Yamasee who flocked to the vicinity of St. Augustine, and some of them may have returned to their native Apalachee with the Yamasee. It is not clear how many were involved in this exodus. At the time of the uprising, the 1,300 free Apalachee who had relocated to Carolina in 1704 had been reduced to 638: 275 men, 243 women, 65 boys, and 55 girls. Some of these were probably killed or captured during the uprising. Those who were captured were shipped outside the colony as slaves (Covington 1972:378). There is no indication whether any of the Apalachee enslaved in 1704 were able to take advantage of the uprising to secure their freedom. That they did or that considerable numbers of these slaves had been escaping earlier may be reflected in a 1722 act designed to discourage the importation of Indian or Negro slaves from Spanish territory. It imposed a duty of £150 current money on such slaves (Snell 1972:102).

Almost nothing is known with certainty about the fate of the Apalachee who migrated to Carolina as slaves in 1704. However many slaves Moore brought with him, it is almost certain that additional levies of enslaved Apalachee were dispatched to the Carolina market from the captives taken in the attack of June–July 1704 that completed the destruction of the province, from those of the 1705 attack on the fugitives who had fled to Timucua from Moore's attack, and from those of the almost contemporaneous attack on the Ivitachuca living near St. Augustine. Despite the massive influx of Indian slaves from various parts of Florida during these years, the Indian slave population of Carolina increased by only a little more than 1,000 between 1703 and 1708 (Lauber 1913; Snell 1972:96, table I).[11]

Despite this relatively small increase, some authorities believe that many or most of the enslaved Apalachee were kept in Carolina and not sold out of the colony. Snell takes this position, saying that "most of the Apalachees must have been kept in Carolina," although he admits that there were few legal records that indicated their retention. J. Leitch Wright was also of the opinion that a considerable number of the Apalachee slaves were retained in South Carolina, suggesting that diligent research in the probate records and in the British records would turn up some evidence of this (Snell 1972:60; J. Leitch Wright, Jr., personal communication, February 1984). Philip Morgan, who has worked with the probate records and the British records, noted that when Indians are mentioned, their tribal affiliation is not specified (personal communication, February 9, 1987).

Covington and Converse D. Clowse, on the other hand, hold that only a few of the Indian slaves were kept in South Carolina. They argue that, compared to blacks, they had little value as workers, not being able or willing to meet the pace demanded of them in field work, and that the chief utility derived from enslaving them was the quick profit to be obtained from exporting them and ridding the countryside of real and potential enemies.[12] They offer no evidence to support their position, however, and observe that the records contain little information about the export of slaves (Clowse 1971:65, 108; Covington 1967:14). Despite a law imposing a duty on Indian slaves exported from the colony before the influx of enslaved Apalachee, the records before 1712 show that that duty was paid only on two Indian slaves who were exported in 1703. Snell also records that from 1704 to 1708 there were only four bills of sale and three wills that mention the disposition of Indian slaves, commenting that, with an increase of 1,050 in the Indian slave population during this time, many must have changed hands without any legal paperwork (Snell 1972:60–61). A minimum of 19 Indian slaves were involved in those seven documents. Although Snell cites Moore's claim of over 4,000 slaves, he does

11. Snell gives the total Indian slave population as 350 in 1703 and as 1,400 in 1708. On page 60 of the text he puts the increase at 1,000, but in a footnote on pages 60–61 he speaks of an increase of 1,400 during this period.
12. The relative ease with which the Indians could escape from slavery and return to their people would be an additional motive for shipping them to the West Indies or elsewhere.

so without comment. With an increase of only 1,050 in the Indian slave population from 1703 to 1708 and his belief that most of the slaves were kept in the
colony, some explanation seems to be needed.

Whatever the number of exported slaves, most are usually said to have
gone to the West Indies and particularly to Barbados, although New England
and New York also are mentioned as destinations (Covington 1967:15–16).
Crane believed that most were exported and that New England was a significant market. There are reasons to doubt that South Carolina exported Indian
slaves to the West Indies in this period. In the 1708 report to the lords proprietors, South Carolina's officials comment on the colony's population and
economic activity, but in the section dealing with the exports to Barbados,
Jamaica, and other areas in the West Indies, they make no mention of Indian
slaves being shipped there. By contrast, "Boston, Road Island, Pennsilvania,
New York and Virginia" are noted as places to which the Carolinians were
exporting Indian slaves (Salley 1947 (5):203, 205). Moreover, although Barbados especially is often mentioned as providing a market for such exports,
Jerome Handler, an authority on slavery in Barbados, lists only Arawak and
other Amerindians from the Caribbean Islands and Guiana as Amerindian
slaves used there. In addition, he indicates that the use of Indian slaves
in Barbados had all but disappeared by the early eighteenth century when
the Apalachee became available (Handler 1969:38–64: Handler and Lange
1978). None of the other secondary sources that I consulted mentions the
presence of Indian slaves in the West Indies for this time period (Gardiner
1971; Handler 1970, 1971). Wright, on the other hand, who believes that
most of the enslaved Apalachee were retained in South Carolina, states that
"Documents such as custom records, export licenses, and West Indian plantation records" exist that "indicate that aborigines were shipped to the islands
and other mainland colonies" (Wright 1981:148, personal communication,
1985). In view of the diversity of opinion on this issue, it would be a fruitful
topic for further research.

The records concerning the destiny and the life of the enslaved Apalachee
who remained in South Carolina are also scarce and uninformative. There are
a few references to Apalachee children being purchased by ministers who baptized them after teaching them to read and write. The need for christening
them was questioned by some on the supposition that most of the Apalachee
had already been baptized by the friars before they were enslaved by the English (Wright 1981:193). The possibility of church records serving as a source
of information on the Indians held as slaves was eliminated by a 1704 church
act, which provided that the parish registers should not list births, christen-
ings, marriages, and burials of Indians and blacks. The law merely confirmed
existing colonial practice (Snell 1972:62).

There seems to be no information on the number of Apalachee among the

more than 1,000 Indian ₔslaves that were added to the population of South
Carolina between 1703 and 1708. In addition to the influx of enslaved Apalachee, the English-inspired slaving raids in the post-1704 period scoured what
was left of Timucua and reached deep into central and southern Florida, as
well as scourging the Choctaw country (Crane 1956:81–86). These developments and the attitudes that spawned them are aptly illustrated in the correspondence of Thomas Nairne. In 1705 he boasted, "We have these two . . .
past years been intirely kniving all the Indian Towns in Florida which were
subject to the Spaniards" (Crane 1956:81). Three years later he would attest:

> Yo' Lordship may perceive by the map that the garrison of St. Augustine
> is by this warr reduced to the bare walls their cattle and Indian towns all
> consumed Either by us In our invasion of that place or by our Indian
> subjects since who in quest of Booty are now obliged to goe down as
> farr on the point of Florida as the firm land will permit they have drove
> the Floridians to the Islands of the Cape, have brought in and sold many
> hundreds of them and dayly now continue that trade so that in some few
> years thay'le reduce these Barbarians to a farr less number, there is not
> one Indian town betwixt Charles Town and Mowila Bay except what are
> prickt, in the mapp, only am uncertain of the number of the Floridians.
>   Our friends the Talopoosees and Chicases Imploy themselves in
> making slaves of such Indians about the lower parts of the Mississippi as
> are now subject to the French the good prices the English traders give
> them for slaves Encourage them to this trade Extremely and some men
> think it both serves to lessen their numbers before the French can arm
> them and it is a mor Effectuall way of civilising and Instructing then all
> the efforts used by the French missionaries. (Nairne 1708(5):196–197)

In 1710 Nairne added that "there remains not now, so much as one village
with ten Houses in it, in all Florida, that is subject to the Spaniards" (Crane
1956:81). In reality he was modest. By 1711 the terror inspired by the raids of
the Yamasee and the Uchise had reached the Keys, whose inhabitants began
asking for refuge in Cuba (Valdés 1711). Although an Indian slave sold for
only half the price of a black, an adult Indian still brought in £18 to £20 or in
Barbados supposedly (if any of them actually were sent there) 75 gallons of
rum, as much as or more than a good deer hunter could earn in a year from
skins (Covington 1967:15; Crane 1956:113).
    There is also a dearth of information about the work to which the enslaved
natives were assigned and their rate of mortality. It is probably safe to assume
that their mortality rate was at least as high as that of the free Apalachee in
Carolina, whose number had been halved in ten years.

It is likely that Apalachee were among the 309 exported Indian slaves on whom duty was paid in 1715 and 1716 (Snell 1972:appendix II). Here as elsewhere Snell does not indicate the location to which they were exported or whether the records provide such information.

The westward migration

The best documented of the Apalachee emigrés of 1704 are those who journeyed westward to Pensacola and Mobile. In the wake of the final defeats suffered by the Spaniards and the Apalachee in late June and early July, the native leaders of San Luis led a caravan of about 800 natives, comprising most of the remaining population of San Luis, part of the population of Escambé, the remaining Christian Chacato from Apalachee, and a few non-Christian Yamasee, on an overland trek westward to Pensacola, driving their remaining cattle before them (Higginbotham 1977:192–93; Zúñiga y Zerda 1704d: 65–67, 1704e:67–68). These emigrés reached Pensacola around July 28, 1704. The eight Spanish families from the San Luis area had already arrived by sea. The Spanish commander was somewhat concerned by this additional large influx of mouths to be fed. He welcomed the newcomers, however, and on learning of their intention to move on to Mobile he pleaded with them to stay even though he had little to offer in the way of food or arms, only promises. Shortly after their arrival, he announced that the half-pound daily ration of bread would be reduced beginning on August 1 in order to stretch the flour supply past the end of the year. This move probably dissolved whatever doubts may have existed for those who had determined to continue on to Mobile. Before the end of August, a number of Apalachee leaders from San Luis de Talimali and a number of headmen from the Chacato, accompanied by a friar from Pensacola, had arrived in Mobile (Bienville 1704:27; Guzmán 1704: 62–64; Higginbotham 1977:189, 191–192; Ruíz de Cuenca 1705:70–72). Although he had earlier invited the Apalachee to emigrate to French territory, the French commander was particularly surprised to see the contingent from the head village of San Luis, who had been associated closely with the Spaniards for so long (Higginbotham 1977:189–190).

Most of the refugees from San Luis and most of the Chacato made the move to the Mobile area at this time. Only those from Escambé and a few of the Talimali remained at Pensacola (Higginbotham 1977:191–192), and most of them would follow their compatriots to French territory by 1706. Writing 20 years after the event, Bienville placed the number of Apalachee immigrants at 500 men and the Chacato at half that number ([Bienville] [1726]:535–536). In his report to Pontchartrain, written soon after they had begun to arrive, he placed the number of Apalachee immigrants at 400 and the Chacato at about half that number. Bienville noted on different occasions that the Chacato came from St. Joseph's Bay or from near Pensacola rather than from Apalachee (Bienville 1704:27).

Bienville assigned lands to the Apalachee at some distance up the Mobile River from his fort, one league below the confluence of the Alabama and the Tombigee at the present Mount Vernon landing. Only about 200 of the immigrants moved to this site. The other half of the group remained across the bay from present-day Mobile on Baptizing Creek. The Chacato were assigned lands at the mouth of the river at a site then called Oigonets, which would be taken over by the French in 1711 when they moved the town of Mobile to its present site (Higginbotham 1977:192–193).

The immigrants reached Mobile at a time when yellow fever was raging, and the malady spread to the Apalachee settlements. They began to bring their sick children to the fort for baptism; the first baptism recorded for the newly created parish at Mobile was that of a young Apalachee child on September 6, 1704 (Hamilton 1976:109; Higginbotham 1977:193).[13] The new curé, Father Alexandre Huvé, himself down with yellow fever, along with the other two priests then in Mobile, was not enthusiastic about this sudden increase in the number of his parishioners whose devout Catholicism made them clamor for service. To a friend he wrote, "You cannot believe the trouble the Apalachee are causing us. They are constantly asking for sacraments, and we cannot understand them anymore than we can make ourselves understood" (Higginbotham 1977:193).

From the remarks made about them by French observers, this group of Apalachee appear to have been acculturated at the time of their arrival in Mobile. They are described as speaking a mixture of Apalachee and Spanish (Higginbotham 1977:194). Bienville described them as good Catholics, fairly civilized, laborious and skillful, little given to hunting (Bienville [1726]: 536).[14] Various French authorities remarked on the Apalachee's insistence on being furnished with a priest, noting that they threatened to return to Spanish territory if this demand were not met (Council of Commerce of Louisiana 1721:303; Raphael 1725:482). Penicault described them as dressing in the European fashion, in a civilized style. He also considered them devout and remarked that there was nothing savage about them, except their mixed language of Alibaman and Spanish (Hamilton 1976:109; McWilliams 1953: 134–135). They eventually overcame that barrier among the French to being

---

13. Higginbotham identifies the child as a girl and Hamilton as a boy. The former seems more reliable because his source was the Mobile parish register, while Hamilton seems to be relying on John Gilmary Shea's work.

14. Penicault, however, characterized the eight Apalachee who accompanied the Sieur de Waligney on a 1710 hunting expedition as good hunters.

considered completely civilized by adding a knowledge of French (and Mobilian as well) to their achievements (Covington 1964:222). One of the most lavish French tributes to the character of these Apalachee emigrés is that made by the Capuchin Superior in the Louisiana Territory. After noting that the company maintained a missionary among them, he remarked that

> It is important for the welfare of the colony that there always be one because these people, very zealous for religion, would abandon the post, if they were left without a priest, and as they are of all the Indians the only ones on whose fidelity we can count with certainty, they are of great assistance to us principally in the place in which they are established fifteen leagues from Mobile up the river whence they can easily inform Mobile of the movements of the other Indian nations to take us by surprise. Besides they are hard working and industrious people who are employed advantageously in case of need. (Raphael 1725:482–484)

He went on to advise that they be shown more consideration by the French authorities, not only because they merited it but also because generous treatment would facilitate the conversion to Christianity of the Apalachee's non-Christian neighbors on the Mobile River. In conclusion he noted, "The contrary is the practice, for while considerable presents are given to the pagan nations, we are content to pay this one a very modest salary for its work. This makes the others say that if they should become Christians they would become slaves of the French like the Apalachees" (Raphael 1725:482–484).

However ungenerous the French remuneration may have been, the Apalachee's treatment at the hands of the French seems to have been sufficiently satisfactory for them to resist the blandishments of the Spanish authorities, who offered inducements for them to return to Spanish territory. In mid-1706, Bienville reported that he had attracted the remainder of the Apalachee and Chacato from the vicinity of Pensacola, remarking that the commander at Pensacola had offered considerable presents to the chiefs of those two nations to secure their return and that those leaders had refused them, saying that the French assisted their allies better than did the Spaniards and furnished them arms. They reminded the commander that among the Spaniards they had not been masters of their wives, whereas among the French they could be at rest on the matter (Bienville 1706:25).

In terms of the number who survived, these Apalachee immigrants did not fare well. In contrast to the Chacato, they were apparently devastated by the yellow fever they encountered upon their arrival. In his *Memoirs*, Bienville reported that of the 500 men who arrived in 1704 and thereafter, only 100 remained in 1725 because of the ravages of disease. Although they escaped the 1704 epidemic, the Chacato population shrank even more drastically. By 1725 the original 250 people had been reduced to 40 ([Bienville] [1726]:526–527, 535–536; Higginbotham 1977:193–194).

Little is known about the sites occupied by the Mobile Apalachee or their activity or fate after their arrival. At the time of the decision in 1710 to relocate Mobile to its present site, one of the smaller Talimali villages upriver, located just below the settlement of the Little Tomeh, was moved downstream to the south side of the mouth of the St. Martins River (today's Chickasabogue or Chickasaw Creek).[15] That move was to enable its inhabitants to assist in the construction of the new fort because they were considered the most skilled and diligent of France's native allies in the region (Hamilton 1976:158; Higginbotham 1977:457).

Some time before 1733, however, the inhabitants of this site, known in later times as the St. Louis tract, were required to move, or chose to, to the east side of Mobile Bay. That tract, probably named for the Apalachee parish dedicated to that saint, was granted to an M. Diron in 1733 (Hamilton 1976:158). As late as 1725, the Apalachee village just below the junction of the Alabama and the Tombigbee was still in existence ([Bienville] [1726]:536; Raphael 1725:482–484).

Apalachee appear to have been associated at one time or another with a number of sites east of the town. Unfortunately, the references to these are fragmentary. The Apalachee who abandoned the St. Louis tract (probably about 1718 according to Hamilton), when John Law's company was forcing the growth of the colony at an extravagant pace, ultimately settled on the eastern mouth of the Tensaw River, which still bears their name. Hamilton (1976:111, 124, 158, 270–271, 513–514) mentions a number of other sites across the river from Mobile associated with the Apalachee.

At the time of the relocation of Mobile in 1710, the Chacato, whose village was located within the new town site chosen for Mobile, were moved farther down the bay to Dog River, where they were assigned a new site one-quarter of a league up the river (Higginbotham 1977:459). There is little mention of them in the records. They also were viewed as good Catholics and were valued by the French as warriors. They are mentioned as speaking a dialect distinct from Apalachee but, like that of the Apalachee, it was heavily larded with Spanish ([Bienville] [1726]:535; Higginbotham 1977:310, 313).

If the second relocation since 1704 forced on the Apalachee of St. Louis parish near Mobile occurred in 1718, as Hamilton suggests,[16] it apparently

15. Hamilton locates this site between Three-Mile Creek and Chickasabogue (which was called St. Louis River under the French) and states that it covered about 22,500 arpens.

16. Barcia, in his chronicle for the year 1718, speaks of the Apalachee as still living near Fort St. Louis, one league from Mobile, the site to which they had transferred when Mobile was moved downriver.

induced some of them to return to Pensacola that year. There is some indication, however, that their departure gave rise to ill feeling toward them among their compatriots who remained in French territory. Not long after they arrived, the Apalachee at the new village of Nuestra Señora de la Soledad y San Luis near Pensacola heard a rumor that the Apalachee living at Fort St. Louis, a league from Mobile, intended to destroy the new settlement. When told of the rumor by Indians, who also said that Bienville had intervened to forestall such an attack, the Spanish commander at Pensacola was skeptical, believing that if Soledad were to be attacked by the Mobile Apalachee or by any other Indians subject to the French, it would be at the instigation of Bienville. The Spanish commander was sufficiently concerned over the rumors to order the inhabitants of La Soledad to fortify their settlement to enable it to withstand a first assault long enough to allow time for aid to be sent from the Spanish garrison at Santa María de Galve, should such an emergency arise (González de Barcia Carballido y Zúñiga 1951:372).

No such attack occurred in 1718. But in the following year an amphibious French force of 600 men, supported on land by an Indian force of more than 700, took Pensacola itself. No attack was made on the Apalachee village, and the surrender terms provided in article 10 of the agreement that "The Apalachee Indians of the village of Nuestra Señora de la Soledad were not to be molested, [but] rather, treated as vassals of the King, and allowed to go where they would with their wives and children" (González de Barcia Carballido y Zúñiga 1951:379–380). The Apalachee apparently remained there during the brief French occupation of Pensacola. Early in August 1719, a Spanish expedition from Cuba regained control. A nephew of Bienville, who reached Pensacola on August 11 at the head of an Indian relief force, finding the town and fort in Spanish hands already, agreed to depart peaceably. On the night before his departure, he and his Indian force went to the Apalachee settlement to sleep (González de Barcia Carballido y Zúñiga 1951:384–386; Noyan 1719:252).[17]

That the Apalachee village just above Mobile was moved across the bay around 1718 may also be indicated by the sudden disappearance of Apalachee entries from the Mobile parish register of baptisms at this time. From 1718 through 1720 there were no entries, and beginning in 1721 far fewer Apalachee baptisms were recorded there than had been before 1718 (Hamilton 1976:109–112). Swanton attributed this reduction to the return of many of the Mobile Apalachee to Pensacola (Swanton 1922:126–127). More likely explanations for at least part of this decrease seem to be that the Mobile Apalachee moved to a site from which it was difficult to reach Mobile and that, during some part of this 1718–1721 period, they were deprived of the ser-

17. This event suggests that relations between the French Indians and the Pensacola Apalachee were friendly again, if indeed they had been disturbed in 1718.

vices of a priest of their own. The priest who had served them since 1704, Father Huvé, was in France for a visit at some time during this period. Father Le Maire, who filled in for him, does not seem to have learned Apalachee, which may also have had some impact on the records. After Father Huvé's return from France, he appears to have been ailing, and, therefore, he went back to his homeland in 1721.[18]

During this period the Apalachee went as a group to Antoine Le Moyne de Chateaugué, threatening to return to Pensacola if their requests for a priest to serve them were not met. The threat moved the council to respond at once; on February 8, 1721, it appointed a Discalced Carmelite, Father Charles of St. Alexis, as their priest. Father Charles assumed the title "Curé des Apalaches," one his predecessor had never used. Hamilton suggests that Father Charles and his successors probably kept a separate register for their Indian flock, but if there was such a register, it has disappeared. The last entry of an Apalachee baptism in the Mobile parish register was for an Apalachee girl in 1751. The existence of their village is mentioned as late as 1762 in the recording of the death of a Joseph Cook while crossing from the Apalachee to Mobile (Hamilton 1976:110–112; O'Neill 1966:117, 125).

The acculturation of these Apalachee is particularly reflected in the practice of their religion. Penicault observed that they conducted divine services like the Catholics of France, reverently hearing Mass and singing the psalms in Latin. Their principal festival was the feast of St. Louis celebrated on August 25. They solemnized the occasion with special religious ceremonies followed by festivities to which they invited both the neighboring Indians and the French. They regaled their guests with plenty of meat and other foodstuffs, and after an evening service of Vespers and Benediction of the Blessed Sacrament, they held a dance at which all—men, women, and children—wore masks. In commenting on their dress, Penicault noted that their only departure from the European custom was that women were bareheaded. He described the women's hair as long and black, woven into one or two plaits hanging down their backs after the fashion of Spanish girls. If their hair was very long, however, it was folded up to the middle of their backs and tied with a ribbon. Their village contained a church with a baptismal font (McWilliams 1953:133–135).

Swanton mentioned the upriver Apalachee settlement near the Mobilian Indians as having been broken up by the Alibama and concluded that this made them take refuge near the newly built second Fort Louis (Swanton 1922:127). There is some question about the reliability of his information, which he derived from Hamilton, who, in turn, used the not-always-reliable John Gilmary Shea. The only attack by the Alibama in this period, mentioned

18. Hamilton says he left in 1727, but Huvé was no longer serving them early in 1721.

in the more carefully researched work of Higginbotham, is an attack in May 1709 against the Mobilian village at the fork of the Mobile and Tensaw Rivers, two years before the Apalachee village moved to the vicinity of the new site for Mobile. This move, according to Higginbotham, was for the purpose of using the Apalachee as workers on the fort. In coming downriver to attack the Mobilian village, the Alibama did have to pass the Apalachee settlement, but there is no mention of the Apalachee being involved even in the French-led pursuit of the raiders by the Mobilians and Little-Tomeh. In addition, a map reproduced by Higginbotham shows the upriver Apalachee village as continuing to exist until 1763.[19] Higginbotham spoke of the migrants as coming from "one of the smaller villages of the Talimali . . . then located upstream from the present town site just below the Little Tomeh" (Higginbotham 1977:383–385, 457).

In 1763, at the transfer of the French territory east of the Mississippi River to the British, the Apalachee in the Mobile area migrated westward, departing in September 1763 to settle on the Red River near Nachitoches (Hamilton 197:568). Little is known about this colony. Covington recorded that by 1804 there were only 14 families there. Sometime during their stay in Louisiana they invited the Tensa band from Alabama to settle near them. In 1803, the Tensa's chief and Valentine Laysard, who was reputed to be the agent of the Apalachee's chief, Etienne, sold most of the tribal land to two merchants who in turn sold it to an Isaac Baldwin. When the United States assumed control of the Louisiana Territory, Baldwin was attempting to evict the Apalachee. Although the Indian agent who heard the case awarded most of the disputed land to the Apalachee, Baldwin continued to harass them, moving his slaves onto their land, burning their wooden huts, and destroying their other improvements. This activity induced some of the colony to migrate to Texas in 1827. The last written evidence of their existence is in a note in 1834 which the Apalachee leaders sent to the U.S. secretary of state requesting an agent and money due them from the United States (Covington 1964:222–224).

At the time of the 1704 migration of the refugee San Luis Apalachee and the Chacato to Mobile, the Apalachee from Escambé, a few of the Chacato, and possibly a few from San Luis remained at Pensacola. By 1706, most, if not all, of these refugees had also moved on to French territory along with the Pensacola and Tawasa (McWilliams 1953:102). It is not clear if any natives of Apalachee were among the few Indians in the vicinity of the town when Pensacola came under attack in 1707. If so, they were probably killed or enslaved in the attacks of 1707, 1708, or 1711 (Corkran 1976:56; Crane 1956:86, 88–90; Higginbotham 1977:308).

There is no further mention of the Apalachee in connection with Pensa-

19. According to Corkran (1967:57) there were no further attacks while the French remained on the Gulf coast.

cola until 1717. That influx was doubtless a result of the emigration of the free Apalachee from South Carolina after the Yamasee War. Initially they had scattered through the Lower and Upper Creek country, forming a major element along with the Yamasee in the pro-Spanish faction among the Creek (Boyd 1949:19–23, 1952; Crane 1956:254–255). The triumph of the pro-English faction, which had an influential champion in the Apalachee wife of Emperor Brims, the Chieftainess Qua, probably brought about the return of many of these emigré Apalachee to Spanish territory (Swanton 1922:124–125). To some degree the move was probably encouraged as well by the Creek, who thought the Apalachee's past ties with the Spaniards and their status as Christians would facilitate the success of the Creek overtures to the Spaniards and the French. It also lessened the danger that the Apalachee would spy on the Creek for the Spaniards concerning the Creek's continued dealings with the English.

The outcome of the Yamasee War set the stage for intensified international rivalries in this area of the old Southwest for the remainder of the colonial era, with the focus of the struggles in the newly repopulated land of Apalachicola on the Chattahoochee, where the trails from Charleston, Apalachee, and Mobile all met. In the wake of the uprising, English prestige was momentarily eclipsed, while that of the French and Spanish grew. In the midst of the war Creek and Yamasee turned to St. Augustine and Pensacola for trade goods and ammunition (Crane 1956:254–255). Even after peace was restored between the Creek and the English, the Apalachee could play a role in the development of Brims's policy of maintaining peace with all his European neighbors and not tying himself too closely to any of them, in order to preserve a balance of power in the region that served the Indians' interests.

Accordingly, while Governor Ayala was entertaining Chief Adrián of Bacuqua and a number of Lower Creek chieftains in St. Augustine, Don Gregorio de Salinas was hosting a large group of Tallapoosa and Apalachee at Pensacola. In order to strengthen the renewed ties, and also, probably, to relieve the pressure on his chronically short food supplies, Salinas dispatched a number of the Apalachee and some of the Upper Creek headmen to Mexico in 1717, to impress them with the grandeur of the viceregal capital and to give more solemnity to their renewal of their profession of allegiance to the king of Spain. While they were in Mexico, the viceroy named one of the Apalachee caciques, Juan Marcos, as governor of all the Apalachee, in the hope that it would enable him to promote the resettlement of the province. Texjana, the warrior captain of the Talisi village of the Tallapoosa, was given the title of "Campmaster General" among the Creek (Crane 1956:255; González de Barcia Carballido y Zúñiga 1951:359–361).

Upon their return from Mexico, Juan Marcos and Texjana hastened to the

Creek country to meet with Emperor Brims and to try to persuade some of the Upper Creek to settle in the vicinity of Pensacola, as Diego Peña at the same time sought to persuade Chief Adrián and the Apalachee among the Lower Creek as well as some of the Lower Creek themselves to repopulate Apalachee. Juan Marcos also sought the release to him of the Christian Indians still held as slaves by the Upper and Lower Creek. The Upper Creek showed no interest in moving to Pensacola, but the Tallapoosa did release 16 Christian Indians whom they held as slaves to return to Pensacola with him. Chief Adrián, supported by Chislacaliche and by other leaders among the Lower Creek, urgently requested the governor of Florida to build a fort in Apalachee at San Marcos, pledging that, given this security, they would settle in the province. In response, Governor Ayala, early in February 1718, dispatched Don José Primo de Rivera with 70 soldiers and skilled workmen to build the desired fort at San Marcos (Ayala y Escobar 1718; González de Barcia Carballido y Zúñiga 1951:360–370).

Upon his return to Pensacola via Mobile, Juan Marcos led the 70 Apalachee in Pensacola five leagues from the Spanish settlement to found a native village on the River Chicsas;[20] he called the new settlement Nuestra Señora de la Soledad y San Luis. He attracted still others, presumably from the Creek country, to swell the population of the new village to more than 100. Still others arrived from the Apalachee villages near Mobile; he probably had influenced them on his way through Mobile to Pensacola. Early in April 1718, on returning from a trip to St. Augustine, Juan Marcos led many of the inhabitants of La Soledad back to Apalachee to a new Apalachee village that had been created in the vicinity of Fort San Marcos (González de Barcia Carballido y Zúñiga 1951:372–378).

Strangely, in his reports to the governor written on April 28 and August 3, 1718, José Primo de Rivera did not mention Chief Juan Marcos or this new village to which Marcos brought the Apalachee he recruited from La Soledad. Neither are any Apalachee mentioned as being at St. Marks in the 1723 census. However, Rivera does mention the arrival of Chief Adrián in May with the chief of Caveta. Rivera was much impressed by Adrián, who promised to round up all the Apalachee he could find to come to establish a settlement adjacent to the new fort. Rivera also reported that a group of Yamasee, who were then settled at the chicasa of the Chacato, wished to settle in the forest of Sartouche about one and a half leagues from St. Marks.[21] They had had some

20. This probably should be River of Chiscas.
21. It is not clear whether this chicasa is the one near San Luis or the one just below the junction of the Flint and Chattahoochee. In view of the reference to discord with Chislacaliche, the latter seems more likely to be the one referred to because Chislacaliche's village was above the confluence of those rivers.

discord with Chislacaliche and were also being harassed by the Uchise whom he led (Benavides 1723; Primo de Rivera 1718a).

Despite the fact that on his departure Chief Juan Marcos had assured the Apalachee remaining at La Soledad that he would return shortly, the Apalachee attempted to elect a new chief. Unable to agree on a candidate, they appealed to the commander at Pensacola in order to avoid a disturbance. After restoring calm, he entrusted the Franciscan superior with the responsibility of persuading them to abandon their disputes. Sometime after the Spanish recapture of Pensacola, Chief Juan Marcos brought word that Chipacafi was willing to bring his supporters and friends to assist the Spaniards there in their struggle with the French and their Indians, should that help be needed. Urged by the commandant to return as quickly as possible with all the Creek and Apalachee he could recruit, Juan Marcos left for Caveta accompanied by a Spanish soldier-interpreter. Before they could return, Pensacola fell to the French once again. Soon after the Spanish surrender, Juan Marcos and the soldier arrived with 60 Indians. On seeing the destruction, the soldier surmised what the outcome had been. After ordering the Indians to return home, the soldier went on to Pensacola to give himself up (González de Barcia Carballido y Zúñiga 1951:387, 391–393). There is no mention of the fate of the remaining Apalachee at La Soledad during this second French attack, which was preceded by harassing raids by the French Indians from Mobile. There is no further mention of Juan Marcos or of the Pensacola Apalachee until the time of the transfer of Pensacola to the English (Covington 1972:382; González de Barcia Carballido y Zúñiga 1951:389–394).

At that time, the Crown designated Veracruz, New Spain, as the destination of Pensacola's inhabitants. On September 3, 1763, the entire Spanish population there boarded eight ships. They were joined by 40 families of Christian Indians, who totaled 108 individuals referred to as Yamasee Apalachino. For many years they had been living near Pensacola in the villages of Escambé and Punta Rosa. It is likely that some of them had migrated to the Pensacola region from the native villages in the vicinity of Fort St. Marks in Apalachee to escape the continual Uchise raids on that area. On learning of the Spanish withdrawal in 1763, they asked to be evacuated along with the Spaniards because they feared annihilation by some of the neighboring non-Christian tribes, particularly the Tallapoosas, who sought their extinction.

The move to their new home in Mexico proved to be scarcely less traumatic. Less than half the emigrés survived the sea and land journey to their ultimate destination. Immediately after they landed at Veracruz, the Pensacola merchant to whom the governor had entrusted the Indians' possessions for shipment absconded with them to sell them in several Caribbean ports. Although a major portion of the natives' valuables or their monetary equivalent were recovered, the process caused a prolonged and costly sojourn in Veracruz. The cost of the pursuit and recovery of the Indians' property was an additional drain on their resources. Of the 40 families that left Pensacola, only a portion of 22 survived—17 men, 16 women, 3 boys, and 11 girls. The property with which the merchant absconded was valued at 2,844 pesos and included household goods, glass, mats, seeds, plain and cordovan sheepskins, and even the clothing belonging to the daughter of one of the chiefs. By the time they reached their new village of San Carlos de Chachalacas in Tempoala, 1,314.5 pesos out of the 2,844 had already been spent. The immigrants were stranded more than six months in Veracruz before the Spanish officials moved to organize a search for the embezzler and the missing property. The viceroy commissioned a Lieutenant Pedro de Amoscotigue y Bermudo for those tasks and also appointed him "Protector of the Christian Indians of Pensacola," instructing him to protect, guide, and assist them in setting up their new community in New Spain. In all they were forced to tarry at Veracruz for 15 months before heading for the district of Tempoala, where the Spanish authorities had had local builders construct a village for them around a typical Spanish square.

Well intentioned though it may have been, the manner in which the building project was handled provided an additional source of grief and financial loss for the natives. In building the village, and especially its church, the Spanish officer appointed as their protector employed expensive Spanish laborers and materials for the construction of the church without consulting the natives who were to bear its cost. On learning of what had been done, the natives protested that they could have built the church themselves with little expense using materials available in the nearby forests. This project, instead, subtracted another 1,129 pesos from the natives' resources. The new village and its lands occupied 172 acres on the Rio de Chachalacas, which surrounded it on three sides.

From the time of their arrival until February 1766, each Yamasee tribesman received one and a half reales per day for subsistence. The Crown also supplied various agricultural implements and tools needed by the settlers to become self-sufficient. As among the Creek, most of the farm and household work was done by the women. The local authorities remarked on the lack of appeal of physical labor to the men except that involved in hunting. They also accused the newcomers of neglecting the cultivation and protection of the communal plots to concentrate on their individual plots. Out of respect for the role of hunting among them, both as a source of food and as a means of earning the traditional marksmanship honors that brought prestige to the hunters with the most game, the viceroy granted them special permission to hunt as requested by their appointed protector, ignoring the protests of the local ranchers.

There is no indication of the proportion of Apalachee blood that flowed through the veins of the emigrés. Even though Gold lists the 47 survivors by name, none had a recognizable Apalachee name, and almost all had exclusively Spanish names. Only the fact that one of their Florida villages was named Escambé suggests that a considerable proportion of them may have been of Apalachee origin. There are indications that miscegenation was making considerable inroads among the group. When the remaining funds and the designated lands of San Carlos were divided among the surviving emigrés, several Spaniards were among those receiving allotments. Gold records that the viceroy authorized the settlement of a dozen Creoles from Pensacola in the community. Most were soldiers who had already been married to Yamasee women or who had declared their intention to do so.

Gold's last reference to this community of Florida emigrés was for the year 1774. In that year a local hacendado brought suit charging that the Crown had illegally deprived him of the lands on which the village of San Carlos was located. He asked that the immigrants be removed or that he be compensated for his loss. Gold concluded his study of the emigrés' fate with the observation that "Although the Apalachinos suffered a number of socio-economic calamities in New Spain, the unfortunate events were really circumstantial and coincidental rather than the result of Spanish policy. The royal officials of New Spain actually revealed obvious concern in the attempts to settle the Indians comfortably in San Carlos" (Gold 1969:101–102, 1970).

During most if not all of the period 1704–1763 the Apalachee's village sites in their homeland remained deserted, used only as campsites by the Spanish expeditions passing through the region. Despite projects for the resettlement of some of the Apalachee mission sites in the mid-1720s and in the 1730s, no new settlements appeared. The only known settlements for this period under Spanish auspices are the two native villages that sprang up in the vicinity of Fort St. Marks and those of two small groups of Tocobaga (Primo de Rivera 1718a). The Creek ancestors of the Seminoles appear to have used the province solely as a hunting ground and as a corridor for reaching the apparently richer hunting grounds and pastures of the Alachua prairie. Occasionally some visited Fort St. Marks to trade, receive presents, or simply take scalps (Montiano 1745). The beginnings of the Seminole settlements at Lake Miccosukee and Tallahassee Talofa probably antedate the departure of the Spaniards in 1763, but I have seen no evidence in the few Spanish records that I have viewed from the period. That possibility is suggested, however, by Lieutenant Pittman's mention that two Indian towns were on fine soil in Apalachee at the time of his visit only four years later in 1767 (Boyd 1934:118).

In view of the character they demonstrated from the time of their contact with the Narváez and de Soto expeditions to the early years of their exile after 1704, the Apalachee deserved a better fate than dispersion and death as a distinct people. Despite the harsh reception they gave to the first Europeans who intruded on their territory, they appear to have been a hospitable people. When the Spaniards spoke of them it was almost invariably in tones of admiration for their qualities. Let us hope that the resurgence of interest in these people that has occurred over the last two decades, particularly in archaeological research, will enable them to live on as more than a name attached to a mountain chain, a bay, and several rivers.

Appendix 1

Chronology for San Luis and Apalachee

1528   A Spanish expedition led by Pánfilo de Narváez established the first recorded European contact with the hostile Apalachee. Its chronicler believed they had visited its main village, Apalachen, a small village of 40 houses.

1536   Álvar Núñez Cabeza de Vaca, one of the four survivors of the Narváez expedition, reached Mexico and provided the first written description of the land of the Apalachee.

1539   The expedition led by Hernando de Soto reached Apalachee in early October, crossed the province from east to west, and settled for the winter at Anhayca Apalachee, seat of the lord of the province, which represented the same corporate entity as the mission-era village of San Luis. De Soto built additional houses in the village for his men and erected a fortificaton to protect it. On November 29, an Indian slipped through the sentries to set fire to the village, two portions of which were instantly consumed because of a high wind.

1540   In early March, de Soto left Anhayca, heading northward, without most of the Indians from South and Central Florida whom he had impressed as porters. They had died from exposure to Apalachee's comparatively harsh winter.

1607   Some of the Apalachee asked the Spaniards to send missionaries.

1608   The first Franciscans were welcomed at Ivitachuco by the entire population of the province. They were able to establish peace between the warring Timucua and Apalachee. The chief of Inihayca, whose village would become the future mission of San Luis, was chosen by the assembled chiefs to visit the governor at St. Augustine as their representative.

319

1612   Spanish authorities rejected the Apalachee's request for a permanent mission. Not all the Apalachee favored the presence of the friars; the hostility had forced the friars to withdraw twice between 1608 and 1612. Some Apalachee leaders asked the friars to designate a a place to set up a cross. By this time, the natives had built churches after their own fashion in some of the villages to be ready when the friars would be available.

1625   Apalachee had begun to send food supplies to St. Augustine.

1633   In October the first two friars arrived to establish a permanent mission presence among the Apalachee. As one of the important villages the mission of San Luis de Jínayca was likely established soon after their arrival, possibly named for the incumbent governor, Luis Horruytiner.

1638   The first soldiers were sent to Apalachee. A Lenten census of the province put the population at 16,000.

1639   The chief of the village of Cupaica was converted and a mission established in his village. The mission was named San Damian de Cupaica in honor of the governor, who served as the chief's godfather. It is the only Apalachee mission with a definite foundation date. As a result of the efforts of the governor, the neighboring Amacano, Chacato, and Apalachicola made peace with the Apalachee. After two years of taking soundings on the Apalachee coast for a suitable place for a port and a channel giving access to it, maritime contact between Apalachee and St. Augustine was established. The first ship made the run in 13 days, opening the prospect that Apalachee could relieve St. Augustine's constant need for food.

1640s   Early in this decade the mission effort in Apalachee expanded dramatically.

1643   A brisk trade between Havana and Apalachee had begun.

ca. 1645   The post of deputy governor of the province of Apalachee was created and Claudio Luis de Florencia named as the first incumbent. Some sort of fortlike residence was probably built for him and his family.

1647   By the start of the year the soldiers appear to have been withdrawn to the governor's farm near Asile. At the time eight villages contained missions. On February 19 a Chisca-inspired uprising by the non-Christian Apalachee began at Bacuqua, and it was joined by some recent Christian converts. The deputy governor, his wife and children, and three of the friars were killed by the rebels and seven churches and convents destroyed. In March a Spanish-Timucuan relief force met the rebels on Timucua soil. The rebels withdrew after a day-long battle, but the Spanish returned to St. Augustine convinced that additional forces would have to be recruited in Cuba to regain control of the province. The acting governor went to Yustaga with a few soldiers to try to prevent the spread of the revolt there. Learning that the rebels had become dispirited and that the older converts among the Apalachee leadership had regained control, he slipped into Apalachee and, within a month, negotiated its submission to Spanish rule once more. Twelve of the rebel ringleaders were executed and 26 others sentenced to forced labor at St. Augustine. The introduction of the labor repartimiento was part of the amnesty agreement.

ca. 1648   This period marks the first recorded visit of a governor to the province. He also visited the neighboring province of the Apalachicola, beginning regular commercial intercourse between the provinces that flourished until the early 1680s.

ca. 1651   The soldiers were withdrawn from the province at the request of the friars.

1651   The mission of San Luis was mentioned by name for the first time.

ca. 1652   The friars and some of the Indian leaders harvested wheat from the abandoned farm near Asile established by Governor Salazar y Vallecilla and began to plant their own wheat in Apalachee.

ca. 1655   The appearance of an English ship at St. Marks spurred concern for the province's security that led to the return of the soldiers and expansion of the garrison.

1655   The mission of San Luis was mentioned as one of nine missions existing in the province.

1656   The chief of San Luis de Jinayca moved his village to be near the Spaniards. There appears to have been some unrest in the province, a spillover from the uprising in Timucua at the time, but the Apalachee did not participate in that revolt, as is often stated in secondary sources. It is likely that there was some ill feeling toward the chief of San Luis because he had close ties with the Spaniards and because he led the opposition to Apalachee support of the Timucuan revolt.

1657   Governor Diego de Rebolledo came to the province in January on a formal visitation of its ten principal mission villages, which were identified by name along with approximately 25 satellite villages. San Luis was identified alternately as San Luis de Jinayca and San Luis de Nijajipa, and two of its satellite villages were identified. The garrison at San Luis was doubled to 12, and a blockhouse or fortified country house was probably built at this time to house the deputy governor and the soldiers. The governor forbade any export of foodstuffs from Apalachee until St. Augustine's needs were met.

ca. 1662   The Chacato asked for missionaries again, probably as a result of their contact with the expedition to the Upper Creek country led by Pedro de Ortes. (They had also asked for friars in the late 1640s and mid-1650s.)

1662   The size of the garrison was temporarily expanded to 40 as San Luis became the base for an exploratory expedition to the country of the Upper Creek.

1668   The size of the garrison at San Luis was reported as 12 men.

1671   Governor Cendoya reported the size of the garrison as 25 in October.

ca. 1672   The ball post on the playing field at San Luis was struck by lightning and burned, as had happened at Patale two years earlier and at Bacuqua in the same general period.

1672   By late in the year the size of the garrison was down to 19, and it stayed there until at least 1675. At some time before 1680 it declined again to 12.

1674   A number of non-Apalachee were revealed to be living in the vicinity of San Luis, and missions were established among them. They were identified as the Tama, Yamassee, Amacano, Pacara or Capara, and the Chine.

1674–   San Luis became the base for the establishment of missions to the
1675   west for a group of Sabacola living on the Apalachicola River and Chacato living in the vicinity of present-day Marianna.

ca. 1675   Governor Hita Salazar apparently inaugurated the settlement of Spanish families in the vicinity of San Luis by making a number of land grants. The creation of a Spanish community in that area was first contemplated by Governor Rebolledo in the mid-1650s.

1675   San Luis was revealed to have a population of 1,400 natives within its jurisdiction, making it the most populous district in the province. The name "San Luis de Talimali" was recorded for the first time, and the old name "Jinayca" disappeared from the records. Bishop Calderón made a pastoral visit to San Luis and the other Apalachee missions and mentioned the existence of a fortified country house there.

1677   At a formal assembly at Tomoli the leaders of the province reluctantly endorsed a resolution outlawing the Apalachee's traditional ball game. This move was instigated by San Luis's pastor, Fray Juan de Paiva, and abetted by one of the village's principal leaders,

Juan de Mendoza, who was coauthor of a research paper on the game and its origins. In September the leaders at San Luis, supported by the chief of Cupaica, organized a successful expedition against a Chisca stronghold in West Florida which had served as a base for nocturnal slave-raiding attacks on Apalachee settlements. After the beginning of the English settlement, Carolina served as a market for these slaves. The presence of the Tocobaga living at Wacissa, near Ivitachuco, was mentioned for the first time. English and French pirates appeared in the port of San Marcos in Apalachee.

ca. 1678   A temporary wooden fort was built at St. Marks, designed to hamper anyone trying to enter the harbor again as pirates had in 1677.

1681   Relations between San Luis and the Apalachicola began to deteriorate when friars at Sabacola on the Chattahoochee, whom the Spanish governor attempted to impose on the Apalachicola by force of arms, had to withdraw.

1682   Reflecting that friction, the garrison at San Luis was expanded to 45 men. French corsairs sacked and destroyed the new fort at St. Marks in Apalachee.

1683   A map believed to have been drawn in 1683 shows a village of Chacato located just to the west of San Luis, as well as locations of the other missions.

1685   A period of strained relations had begun between the native leaders of San Luis and its deputy governor because of his arbitrary and brutal conduct, disparagement of Indian customs, and interference in administration of the village. A number of dissatisfied Apalachee migrated to Creek country. Leaders at San Luis petitioned the governor for removal of the deputy governor. Relations with the Apalachicola, which seemed to have improved in the early part of the year, deteriorated seriously in the second half as English traders from Carolina came to the Apalachicola towns. Their presence prompted five armed expeditions from San Luis in a vain attempt to capture them. On the second expedition in 1685–1686 four Apalachicola towns were sacked and burned by a force of Spaniards and Apalachee.

1686   An exploratory expedition was launched from Apalachee to search for the French in the lower Mississippi valley.

1687   Early in the year the deputy governor was removed from office when the governor who had appointed him deserted and fled to Cuba. In March, Governor Marques Cabrera appointed the soon-to-be-deposed lieutenant of the province of Apalachee to lead an expedition of 25 Spaniards and 100 Apalachee to explore the Bay of Espirito Santo (Pensacola).

1688   Plans were made to establish an elaborate blockhouse for the expanded garrison at San Luis. Apalachee's chiefs pledged to do the work without charge if the Crown would supply tools and food for the workers. Lumber was prepared for the project. Four chiefs from Mobile came to San Luis to pledge obedience to the Spanish monarch and to request land to settle in the area.

1689   The building of a fort on the Chattahoochee by Apalachee carpenters led to the temporary abandonment of plans to build a fort at San Luis and a watchtower at St. Marks. A census by families showed that Escambé's population of 400 families had surpassed San Luis's 300 families, making it the most populous district in the province.

1691   Spanish and Apalachee forces destroyed their recently built fort on the Chattahoochee and withdrew to Apalachee territory at San Luis.

1693   San Luis served as the departure point for the overland expedition, led by Governor Laureano de Torres y Ayala, to explore Pensacola and Mobile bays. Apalachee provided horses, salt beef, and cheese for the expedition. In November the Crown ordered Governor Torres y Ayala to resurrect the plan to build a fort at San Luis and a stone watchtower at St. Marks.

1694   The Chacato village just below the confluence of the Flint and the Chattahoochee was attacked by a band of Apalachicola, and more than 40 of its inhabitants were carried off as slaves.

1695   In January the Chacato refugees from that village, then living at the trans-Ochlockonee site of Escambé, received permission to reoccupy their former village site near San Luis, where they had lived in the early 1680s. Spanish soldiers led an Apalachee expedition against the Apalachicola living along the Ocmulgee in retaliation for their attack on the Chacato village. They found only the ashes of the Creek villages and captured no more than 50 Apalachicola.

1696   By April the blockhouse portion of the fort at San Luis had been completed except for part of its roof; work had been suspended to permit the Indians to plant their crops. Frequent nocturnal harassment by enemy natives forced the soldiers and the inhabitants of the village to seek shelter within the blockhouse. Marcos Delgado moved his ranch to a former site of Patale.

1697   By July work on the blockhouse had been completed. Only the outworks remained to be finished.

1698   Late in the year the natives of San Luis became seriously alienated from the Spaniards because Spanish settlers had expropriated some of the natives' houses and lands and were making constant demands on them for uncompensated labor (forcing native carpenters to build several houses for Spanish settlers with the lumber left over from the building of the fort).

1699   By February the inhabitants of San Luis had moved their village to a site that was one league from the existing village, in an expression of their discontent with the settlers. Early in the year Francisco de Florencia and a band of Chacato, while on a buffalo hunt, murdered and robbed most of a band of Tasquique who were on their way to San Luis to trade. This attack set up the Apalachee for retaliation, especially the village of Ayubale to which stolen deerskins had been taken by the Chacato to be painted. Diego Ximénez moved his ranch to an abandoned site of the village of Escambé, three leagues from San Luis.

1701   Suspicious of peace treaties between the Apalachee and their Apalachicola neighbors that permitted a resumption of trade, the Spanish authorities put restrictions on that trade, interdicting the sale of horses or the export of silver from Apalachee. In the wake of the unprovoked killing and scalping of some Mayaca by an expedition of Timucua and Iguaja, the governor issued orders to the Christian Indians of Florida, including the Apalachee, that they were no longer to take scalps or dance with them in the council house and instructed his subordinates to work out with the natives some other criteria for the acquisition of warrior status and for advancement within warrior ranks.

1702   Angered by Spanish restrictions on trade in horses, the Apalachicola broke the peace treaties, murdering three of four Apalachee envoys in their midst and devastating the Timucua village of Santa Fé. In the second half of the year a Spanish-led Apalachee force on its way to retaliate for those acts of hostility was ambushed and routed, losing most of its arms and many able-bodied warriors. In October the governor's deputy announced plans for building a stockade around the fort at San Luis and considered the relocation of Bacuqua and Escambé to more defensible sites closer to San Luis.

1703   The mission of San Joseph de Ocuia was attacked and destroyed by a raiding band of Apalachicola who also struck into Timucua.

1704   In January, Colonel James Moore, at the head of a force of Carolinians and their Creek allies, attacked and captured Ayubale, defeated a Spanish and Apalachee relief force from San Luis, and accepted the surrender of a number of the other villages, some unconditionally and others on terms. Without attacking San Luis or the villages closest to it, Colonel Moore withdrew, accompanied by 1,300 voluntary emigrants and an undetermined number of Apalachee carried off as slaves. In late June and early July a second Creek attack force assaulted most of the remaining settlements in Apalachee, taking Patale, Aspalaga, and Escambé and even an outlying part of San Luis. Most of Escambé's population escaped by seeking refuge at San Luis. A Spanish-Apalachee relief force was routed at Patale on July 4. The Creek left without assaulting the fort or Ivitachuco. In mid-July most of the surviving natives of San Luis and Escambé, along with the Chacato, moved westward toward Pensacola and Mobile, following the Spanish civilians, who had already left for Pensacola by sea. By the end of July the remaining soldiers at San Luis and a few natives left for St. Augustine after destroying the fort and the village of San Luis, catching up by August 2 with the withdrawing Ivitachuca at San Pedro de Potohiriba. On August 2 a third Creek attack force reached San Luis, killing or capturing the portion of Escambé's population that had remained behind to welcome them and pursuing and killing the cattle drovers from Pensacola, who were herding cattle they had purchased in Apalachee toward that settlement.

1705   In August, after landing at St. Marks, Admiral Landeche visited the site of San Luis and sent parties from there to explore other former mission sites. They found no signs of cattle or human habitation in the parts of the province they visited.

1716   Diego de Peña was the first Spaniard recorded as having returned to the province since 1705. On his overland trek to Apalachicola country, he camped at the site of Patale and San Luis and at the trans-Ochlockonee site of Escambé.

1718   Spanish soldiers returned to Apalachee but built their fort and settlement at St. Marks rather than inland. Unsuccessful efforts were made to persuade the surviving Apalachee and the lower Creek to occupy the former Apalachee mission sites. Some Apalachee from an undetermined location, along with some from Pensacola, established a settlement near Fort St. Marks in Apalachee. A few Tocobaga were reported to be living at Wacissa and at the mouth of the Aucilla on an island. Some Yamasee living on the site of the old Chacato village on the Apalachicola moved to the vicinity of Fort St. Marks to establish a village there.

ca. 1725   Spaniards reconnoitered at the San Luis site preparing to re-establish a settlement there; they drove stakes to mark an area for rebuilding the fort, but their plans were never carried out.

1728   There occurred in this year the last mention of the presence of Apalachee in one of the villages near Fort St. Marks. The Yamasee village of Tamasle lost all its women and children to attacking Uchise, but 80 of its warriors were able to seek refuge in the fort when their ammunition was exhausted.

1738   San Luis, Tama, and other former village sites were again reconnoitered as possible locations for the repopulation of the province, and the Tama site was selected, but once again the planned settlement of the province stalled.

1764   The Spanish garrison withdrew from St. Marks. Five Indians from the towns of Sabacola and Tamasle were given permission to leave with the Spanish forces.

Appendix 2

Translation of the Ball Game Manuscript

AMONG the sources providing information on the Apalachee, the ball game manuscript is indisputably the most valuable extant document for the light that it throws on their culture and customs. It is particularly significant for the San Luis site because the friar who penned it was pastor of the San Luis doctrina at the time he led the campaign for the abolition of the ball game. One of his two closest collaborators in the preparation of the manuscript and in the conduct of the campaign was the parish interpreter for San Luis, the Apalachee leader Juan Mendoza. The other, Diego Salvador, seems to have spent much of his time at San Luis as the royal interpreter. Consequently, San Luis and its people figure significantly in a number of the scenes and events described by Father Paiva and the two interpreters.

For the most part, this manuscript does not present any major problems for the transcriber or the translator. The script is legible in most places; only occasionally does the poor legibility of a word or two pose serious problems. More serious problems arise because of Father Paiva's convoluted and elliptical style and the passion with which he composed this piece. His emotions, at times, caused him to break his chain of thought in midsentence to interject an expression of dismay or to recount an anecdote. He had a tendency to use pronouns for which there were no clearly identified antecedents. These problems are aptly summarized in Amy Bushnell's observations in an article on the ball game: "Certainly it is a translator's nightmare, full of flashbacks and derailings, copyists' errors, garbled syntax, and unanchored pronouns, not to speak of smatterings of Apalache, Timucuan and Latin. . . . The polemic Deutero Paiva was rapidly written to the point of incoherence" (1978b:14–15). As noted in chapter 3, in my opinion the evident rapidity of its composition and the passion that inspired it adequately account for those problems, eliminating the need to posit a Proto and a Deutero version by Fray Paiva. The layering in the document can be explained by Paiva's having incorporated much of the work of the two native interpreters with his own, interlarding sizable pieces of it with his own observations, reminiscences, and hortatory arguments for the extinction of the game. Fortunately, relatively few passages are so difficult that they completely defy a translator's efforts to decipher Paiva's message. One peculiarity, which I have reproduced, is his use of single (at times, paired) parentheses, all of which face to the left.

Although this document has been translated on several occasions, none of those translations has been published. I have had access to photocopies of the typescript of two of the existing translations, those by Julian Granberry (n.d.) and Evelyn Peterson (1976). Their works are commendable, but both are too freely translated. Consequently, I felt that there was still a need for a careful translation that would be as literal as feasible while still conveying the thought of the original as clearly and as readably as was possible. As expected, my rendition differs significantly from both in a number of passages.

In view of the prominence of San Luis and its people in this manuscript, the current exploration of that site under the direction of the Bureau of Archaeological Research also seemed to create a need to make this important document more readily available. Within those parameters, I have sought to follow the guidelines Fray Marcelo de San Joseph set for himself almost 300 years ago when he translated from Apalachee into Castilian the one document for which we have the natives' original text. Early in 1688 the friar wrote to the king that he had translated the chiefs' letter to the monarch "just as it is and sounds," noting, "And even though I could have touched up its unpolished manner of chatting with our King and lord, nevertheless, I decided not to change the style, even though I could have polished it without betraying its substance." Whenever I have added words to the original text for purposes of clarity, I have placed them in brackets.

In December 1984 I initially translated this document, in a somewhat less literal form, from my rough transcription of the Ball Game Manuscript that appears in the record of the Domingo de Leturiondo Visitation of the Provinces of Apalachee and Timucua in 1677–1678. That transcription was rough because it was the first seventeenth-century Spanish document with which I had the pleasure of wrestling, and it remained rough because my plans for translating this text were put aside before I had the opportunity to smooth out those rough spots. Most of the words and passages that were not deciphered in the 1976 transcription were clarified during a brief reexamination of the manuscript in March 1985 and through a hasty perusal of portions of the Jeannette Thurber Connor transcription of the same document. Both my 1976 transcription and the 1985 reexamination were done from the Stetson Collection photostat of that document in the P. K. Yonge Library of Florida History of the University of Florida.

In closing I must note that the manuscript's title might be misleading if it causes the reader to infer that the ball game was confined to the Apalachee and the Yustaga. There are indications that the same game was played among the other groups of Timucua as far east as Potano. During his visitation, Leturiondo sought to proscribe the game in those provinces as well. In pleading for the right to continue to play the game, the Timucua argued only that their game had been freed of its pagan and superstitious accoutrements and of the violence that marred Apalachee's games, not that it was a different game.

Origin and Beginning of the Game of Ball that the
Apalachee and Yustagan Indians Have Been Playing
since Pagan Times until the Year of 1676. The Reverend
Father Friar Juan de Paiva, pastor of the doctrina of San
Luis de Talimali, brought it to light. May it be for the
honor and glory of God. Amen.

In the pagan times of this Apalachee nation there were two chiefs, whose experiences I am going to recount, who in their [time of] blindness lived close to one another as neighbors. One was named Ochuna nicoguadca, whom they say is Lightning Bolt. And the other Ytonaslaq, a person of banked fires. And in his understanding both [are] the names of demons, which they have held as such, especially for Ytonanslalaq.

The latter had an orphaned granddaughter named nico taijulo, woman of the sun. The leading men, who are those who are in charge of the place, the aldermen, as we would say, sent her out for water every day. She became pregnant in this employment and gave birth to a son and hid him among some bushes, where the panther, the bear, and the jay found him. And they brought him to itonanslac, his great-grandfather. And they told him how his grand-daughter, Nicotaijulo, had given birth to that child. He then ordered that they should not say anything to anybody or reveal that his granddaughter had given birth. He was given the name Chita. They do not know what it means, nor have I been able to discover it. He was reared to the age of twelve with this name, and [then] it was changed and he was given another, which was Oclafi, Baron of water. This is their way of speaking. He was reared with that name until the twentieth year. And [then] it was taken from him and he was given another, which was eslafiayupi. Neither did they know what this one meant.

331

They say they are ignorant of it.) The which young man excelled everyone in courage and in his skill with the bow and arrow and in the game of *quicio* [chunkey], which all these nations play, which is [played] with two long poles about three yardsticks in length and a flat and round stone.

Ochuna Nicoguadca harbored suspicions that that young man was the son of Taijulo because his shamans had told him, or, prognosticated, as we would say, that the son to which Nico taijulo gave birth was destined to kill him. And in order [to learn] if perchance this was so, he tried to see if he might kill him. And he set the following three traps for him, so that he might perish in one.

Take note that the Ytonanslaq had commanded his great-grandson that, concerning everything that they ordered him to do or that happened, that it was important for him that he should let him know about it before he obeyed it. And, accordingly, [when] he was ordered first that he should go to a certain place where there was a large and very deep sinkhole, that he should obtain flints there for arrowheads, and that they should not be from any other place, the young man went at once and told his great-grandfather of what they were ordering him [to do]. And he said to him, son, this spring is very deep. You cannot obtain the flints from it without risking your life. He gave him some beads [made] of shell and told him to give those beads to a little bird that would be there diving and ask for the flints from it. And so he went, gave it the beads and asked it for them [the flints]. And it gave them [to him], and he brought them to Ochuna Nicoguadca. He ordered him secondly to go to a certain thicket where he would find a canebrake of bamboo, and that he should cut canes there, and bring them for arrows. The young man went and told his great-grandfather what they had commanded of him. The old man said to him, Son, there are many poisonous snakes in that canebrake, you would be running great danger. What you can do is form hoops from the grapevines and carry them along. And when the snake comes, throw the hoop where it is crawling. Then it will chase the hoop and you [can] rush up and cut the canes. With which he did just that. He went, cut his canes, and he brought them. Thirdly and lastly, he ordered him to go to a certain place where he would find a nest of eagles in a tree, that he should go and kill the parents and bring back the fledglings. The youth went and informed the old man and he gave him the advice that follows. And it was that he should bring some gourds with him that he might put on his hands and on his head, and, that he should bring a lariat with him, and, that when he should see the eagle about to bite him, he should let go with the aforesaid lariat. And that is what he did. He went and killed the eagles and brought the young ones and presented them to Ochuna Nicoguadca. On seeing that he could not kill him, he arranged then that they should play the ball game. This is how it had its beginning. And it is in this fashion. = =

They send a courier, challenging the place with whom they are going to play, citing the day, and with how many players, let's say forty or fifty more or less, in accord with the people to be had. It has to be [played] at midday or at two in the afternoon, and, in the summer. And in winter they do not play. It is to eleven strikes with the ball that they fire at the pole. And it must be with the foot. And as I understand it, one holds the ball with the hand, lets it fall, and, lifting it up with the foot and giving it a kick upwards, one fires the said ball, which will be the size of a musket-ball, [or] a little larger. If it remains on the pole it is worth two. They all crowd together like a clump of pine-cones, naked as when their mother bore them, except for a deerskin breechclout that covers their private parts, and, [with] their hair braided. And a leading man throws the ball in the midst of all of them, who are erect and with their hands raised. It falls into the hand of someone. And they fall upon one another at full tilt. And the last to arrive climb up over their bodies, using them as stairs. And, to enter, others [step on] their faces, heads, or bellies, as they encounter them, taking no notice [of them] and aiming kicks without any concern whether it is to the face or to the body, while in other places still others pull at arms or legs with no concern as to whether they may be dislocated or not, while still others have their mouths filled with dirt. When this pileup begins to become untangled, they are accustomed to find four or five stretched out like tuna; over there are others gasping for breath, because, inasmuch as some are wont to swallow the ball, they are made to vomit it up by squeezing their windpipe or by kicks to the stomach. Over there lie others with an arm or a leg broken. In this exercise, the fashion in which I have described it is but a sketch of what took place, because their faces are like a living fire from this exertion and from the midday sun. What damage must not be done to these bodies [from this]! And they resuscitate them by dint of a bucket of water. What kind of a remedy is this, when they have their pores open in this fashion? How can these wretches stay alive thus? Accordingly, they are destroying themselves and this nation is being extinguished. And all this is only a sketch!

When the courier left, it was obligatory that he go in the following fashion, that he be in the guise *dosuai*, which is the raccoon,[1] with his tail, and stained with black, [with] something like horns(?)[2] on his head, and his face painted with red and his body stained with black and with raylike streaks of red, so that they looked like the devil himself. As for me, I say that each time

1. The Spanish word used here, *tejon*, means badger in modern Spanish. North Florida is not part of the badger's range, so raccoon, suggested by the references to black, seems a more appropriate translation. *Dosuai* is probably the Apalachee name for the animal.
2. The Spanish word seems to be *guerrios. Cuernos,* or horns, is the closest equivalent to it that makes sense in modern Spanish. The Jeannette Thurber Connor transcription (n.d.) of this document has *Quernos.*

that I saw them, they represented the image of the devil. And, when the challenge was not accepted, there was a ceremony whereby the trappings were removed, and he came slinking back without entering the plaza, except with all the instruments put away and hung from the shoulder on a little stick. But, if it were accepted, he would enter in the aforesaid guise, and with rattles or little bells or cowbells making a great harmony with the instruments, calling out so that they might come out to receive him. And, having accepted the challenge, Ytonanslac called to all his vassals, who were the panthers, wolves, and bears, all the dark and strong animals. And thus they use Cuy Juan as a surname. Cuy is the panther. Nita Agustin is the bear and equally *seteris pauper*, etc.[3] And it was their understanding, as the players proceeded and descended from the plaza and the ball pole, that these were their very ancestors from whom they were descended. And accordingly, these all entered painted with black, representing those animals. And the rivals painted in other colors, different from these, representing other animals such as the deer and the fox. They all came and entered into the plaza naked as their mothers bore them except for a little breechclout with which they covered their private parts.

And it is where the greatest assembly of people is to be found, as I shall speak about farther on. And from time to time they let out howls, like wolves. And, with these sights [before you], consider now, for the love of God, I ask each one of you, "How does such a game appear to you?" and "Whom) would such a game not appall?") Could this fail to hold something from their pagan times concealed in it!

His players having come together, Ytonanslac gave them the rules so that they would not lose. And they are those which follow. And they are kept inviolate, so I understand. And should they cease to do so, they consider it inevitable that they would lose. And as proof I shall tell you what happened to me in a certain place to which I used to go to say Mass on Sundays because of the absence of its priest. I came to the place having only recently arrived [in Florida]. And those of this place had lost two important games and they were about to play another one that Sunday. And there was a soldier there, who today is an Inactive Captain, and he told me that the Indians were very demoralized because they considered it a certainty that they would lose. And, on being asked the reason, he told me, "Because they have not been assembling at night 'to sleep the ball,' and because they were not opening the church for them as [they did] formerly." On taking note of all this, I pretended not to understand.)

3. This name appears to be in Latin. *Pauper* definitely means poor, or meagre, and by extension little. The closest equivalent to *seteris* that I could find was *saetiger*, which means bristly or boar. *Saet-* is sometimes written as *set-*. Inasmuch as the boar was introduced into the Southeast by the Spaniards, the use of this name would have been a phenomenon of the historic period.

The first rule [is] that the players are not to sleep the night before they have to play. I have been given to understand that, if they are to play on a Sunday, during the night of the Saturday before they have to play, if the players do not keep the vigil and carry out the practices I shall speak about farther on, because, if one should feel something in his hand and go to sleep, it would be easy for someone else to take it away from him.) And, thus, if he slept, it would be a sign that he would lose. And they did it thus. And they would remain in vigil all night long, all bunched together and seated) on some low benches, speaking very softly. And from time to time they let go with some wolf howls. And these were made occasionally from midnight on. And at once the dogs of the place, which are not few, would accompany them, howling. And I will let each one imagine what this seemed like in the silence of the night. As for me, I say that it gave me the horrors and a start. And it made me wonder how that could be good, that it was impossible that it should fail to conceal or to contain some abuses and superstitions. And, when I questioned some of the priests about it, they told me that they [the howls] gave them the sign for when they should be playing all piled together. But, despite this, I did not desist in believing the contrary, because what did the sign have to do with not sleeping and with the giving of those howls from time to time. = =

The second [rule is] that they should order four or five elderly men to go to sleep. And, that, early in the morning, they should tell what they dreamed about to the leading man or to whomever the ball-game courier reported to. And it is said that, if one dreams that the enemy entered from a certain direction and killed them and took what they had, it is a bad dream. Consequently, they are not to put the benches for the players on that side, because they would lose. And, if the other one said that he dreamed that a very gallant chief entered from such a direction with many gifts that he distributed among them, it was a good dream. The benches for the [players][4] should be placed on that side.

The third [rule is] that they must make a new fire and that they are not to approach it; nor are they to use it for anything other than what it is destined for, because to use it so, they believe without a doubt, would make them lose, even if it were [merely] for smoking tobacco.[5] And they must carry it [the new fire] to the ball game in some bundles of lighted palm-thatch.[6] They are accustomed to place this in front of themselves.

4. This word or something more seems to have been omitted by the seventeenth-century copyist in going from one page to another. In the Spanish text the last line of this page ends in a dangling fashion: "por aquella parte se ponian los asientos a los." The next page begins with the third rule.

5. For purposes of literalness, it should be noted that the Spanish expression here is *chupar*, "to suck," rather than *fumar*, "to smoke."

6. The Spanish here, "en unos mechones de guano encendido," could be rendered also "in some bundles of lighted Spanish moss."

The fourth [rule is] that, on entering into the plaza, they should not enter with all the people who have consented of their own accord to play. If it was arranged for fifty persons, let them enter with four or five less. And when they ask them if you have all the people assembled, let them say they do not, that they lack so many. And if they then command them to include [some] from the young men and from the other people who are there, it would appear to be considered as a good sign that they will win. And thus he did it. And thus they have continued doing it. And this and all the rest [is] the worst of it in our view, as will be seen. This occurs in all the places of Apalachee, being common and equal in all the province. And because they were considered simple people *suiaj* they passed for such, when it was us in effect who were the simpletons.[7]

They entered the plaza and, on being asked if their people were assembled and at full strength, those on Ytonanslac's side said "no," that they were short so many people. The rivals told them that they should choose from those young men who were in the vicinity. They called to eslafiayupi, the son of Nicotaijulo, he who killed the eagle and tricked the snakes, etc., and who gave the appearance of being ill, leaning up against a post, wrapped with a cloak of feathers. And upon his entering the game, the battle was begun. And when those of Ytonanslac had reached seven, eslafiayupi let out a thunderous roar and they were all terrified. And eslafiayupi was recognized for Nicoguadca, who is the Lightning-flash, son of Nicotaijulo and of the sun, who is nico. And since then it has remained for an omen that the first who arrived at seven would win because Nicoguadca helped him. And the rivals lose heart at once. And they were accustomed to tell this story every night, sometimes in the council house and sometimes under the ball post.

After having lost at the ball [game], Ochuna Nicoguadca challenged Nicoguadca to play at *el quisio* which is the game which, at the beginning, I said all these nations play, which is with a stone and two poles, for, as I say, he challenged Nicoguadca, and having won from him all that he had, they say that he tried to ensnare him and he pretended to the aforesaid Ochuna Nicoguadca that he was thirsty and wanted to go to drink.[8] And they say nico-

---

7. I was not able to decipher the not very legible word that I have written as *suiaj*, which follows *por simplasos*, "simple people."

8. From this point to the end of the paragraph the story line seems to become confused. As a result various sections of it have been rendered differently by the three people who have dealt with it. In the Granberry (n.d.) version Eslafiayupi challenges Ochuna Nicoguadca to the game of chunkey and wins it as well. It is Eslafiayupi who pretends to be thirsty, and it is he who finally is killed by Ochuna Nicoguadca. In the Peterson (1976) version of this passage and in the Bushnell article on the ball game, Ochuna Nicoguadca challenges Eslafiayupi to a game of chunkey and wins it and pretends to be thirsty. But it is Eslafiayupi who emerges

guadca hit the ground with the stick's sharp end [and] made water spring forth and said to him, "Drink." At this point he pretended to need to relieve himself.[9] And Nicoguadca fashioned a little thicket for him and said, "Over here." And finally he said he was going to light a tobacco and entered into a house and opened a hole [in the wall] and fled to Apalachocolo. And Nicoguadca then went in search of him with his warriors. And they say that he formed much fog, cold mists, [and] frost, etc.[10] But despite it all he vanquished him and killed him and his warriors. And his vassals fashioned the ball pole for him that is shown here on this page, the nature of which, with God's help, I shall go on explaining,

[It was at this point that the graphic of the goal post was inserted in the text. See figure 3-2.]

concerning the [ ][11] with which he killed the eagle. At the foot of this pole they are to place or bury a scalp from a dead person in memory of Ytonanslac, its founder, great grandfather of Nicoguadca. The little sticks with which they adorn[12] it have to be of sassafras and of no other wood. They have to raise it

---

victorious at the end in tracking down and killing Ochuna Nicoguadca. My rendition of these murky passages differs in places from both of these earlier versions. There seems to be no doubt that Ochuna Nicoguadca challenged Eslafiayupi to the game of chunkey and won it. Consequently, Granberry's version seems to be in error on this point. However, I agree with the Granberry version that Eslafiayupi pretended to be thirsty. Although both Peterson's and Bushnell's versions make more sense logically on this point, in terms of what one would expect the story to be, their rendition seems to be ruled out grammatically by the phrase "fingio al tal Ochuna Nicoguadca." There Ochuna Nicoguadca is clearly the indirect object of the verb *fingio*, "pretended," not its subject. Jeannette Thurber Connor has, I believe, pointed the path out of this maze. In a penciled note on the typescript of her transcription of this document (p. 12), she observed, "The friar forgets to explain that after Eslafiayupi killed Nicoguadca he took his place and his name. From now on he calls Eslafiayupi Nicoguadca." If one applies that last sentence to the remainder of this paragraph beginning with "And they say Nicoguadca hit the ground" to interpret this Nicoguadca as the former Eslafiayupi, one has a satisfactory story.
9. The Spanish here reads "Aqui fingio tener necessidad corporal de usar desualbadañar." I could not locate the word *albadañar*, but the meaning is clear.
10. The Spanish here is "nieblas frios gelos."
11. The copyist may have omitted something here. "Explaining," the last word preceding the illustration, is followed by a comma. The illustration fills the lower two-thirds of the page. The next page begins with the incomplete phrase "concerning the with which he killed the eagle," which is followed by a period.
12. The Spanish verb here, *estofan*, has in modern Spanish the literal meaning "to quilt," "to put embossed painting on a gilt ground," or "to size carvings before gilding." On the drawing of the goalpost, the word *atari* is written in minuscule letters under each of the sassafras pegs that adorn each side. And there is a tassellike appendage on each peg.

with wild grapevines, and not with anything else, even though they might have ropes, as happened to me when I gave them ropes. They answered me, "No," that the former were stronger and that they were [used] in memory of those which he [Eslafiayupi] carried with him, when he went for the arrow shafts, from which he made the hoops with which he tricked the snakes. Consequently, they made and established this ball post of the devil to the honor of Nicoguadca, to put it better, with all its frauds, as is seen. And this is not the end of it, as will be seen. And this has been the acclaimed and celebrated, etc. [ball game].

Let us begin now, bringing to light all its virtues. First of all, let me say of them, that to list all of them, would be an infinity, because they are as many as [the great number] of deceitful teachers they have and have had. And I call to your attention that everything that you see written here is [written] by two interpreters, who are considered among the most loyal among them, as has been learned by experience. And it has been [read] in the presence of some leading Indians and chiefs. And all in unison confess and state that this is indeed truly what was done in all of Apalachee, no less in one place than in another, because a pole like the one you see, this is set up in all the places, with the baubles with which they decorate it and which they hang from it. In all they sleep the ball. They dance in all. And in all they enter in the fashion in which I have painted it, giving the howls that I have spoken about in the very same way. And they were accustomed to play in all the places after a similar ceremony. I will tell about this farther on.

Abuses and omens and superstitions for the raising of the ball pole. And this was their greatest fiesta. Firstly, when they have put it together, but without the little sticks with which they adorn it, as we would put it, [when it is] in embryo, its crown must be toward where the sun rises, and the hole for it was made on that side, because if they placed it on another as they were doing it they considered it an omen that they would lose. And the eagle had to be looking toward the setting sun.

Secondly, that it had to be raised with wild grapevines, as I have said.

By the third [rule], that before it is raised, the warriors have to be dancing around the pole to the sound[13] of a drum and occasionally giving howls like dogs and at other times barking, and at others doing as would wolves.

The fourth, that after these warriors have danced, six women must enter with another six warriors and they must remain dancing until the pole is put in place.

---

13. Peterson (1976) rendered this passage, "The warriors have to be dancing to the sun with a tambourine around the ball post." The Spanish is clearly "al *son* de um tamboril," or "to the sound of a drum." The Connor transcription also has *son*.

And fifth, that the men must pull the wild grapevines from one side and the women from the other. And no one must remain in her house.[14]

The sixth, that a young woman, she must not be married, must be there with a crooked-headed bat, which is in effect a bamboo a yard and a half in length, split and doubled over, as is seen in the margin,[15] which is [that] with which the women play their ball. And the latter [young woman] must be performing ceremonies under the pole while they pull on it, etc., and while they are raising it. They say that it was in memory of Nico tai Julo, the mother of Nicoguadca.

[Seventh.] And, that as the pole is on the point of being set upright and put in place, the usinulo, which signifies beloved son, thus they speak of the son of the chief, who alive or dead, such a one has to be the son of the principal chief of the place, because these places have three or four little places, each one [of which] has its chief. San Luis, for example, is the principal place. It has joined to it, San Francisco, San Bernardo, and San Agustín. Consequently, the usinulo of the place of San Luis must be the one who must perform the ceremony I shall speak about. When they are lifting it, as I have said, he must make the *gua* to the pole, which is what we would call the "reverence."[16] And it is in the following fashion. Placing his hands together straight, he says three times, gua, gua, gua, which is the salutation that they make to the chiefs. And, immediately, he must pour out *cacina*. Take note now that this usinulo is the person whom they love and reverence and respect most. Surely now, this making of the gua, offering of cacina to that pole, etc., What mystery does it hold? It was their idol.) Does it appear to some that it [was] not? And if some understand this [to be] licit? Not me! Thanks be to God. And, accordingly, I would lose my life before I would consent to that.)=

The eighth. That the night before the day that they had to raise the pole, there was permission[17] so that anyone whatsoever could touch and fondle, etc. anywhatsoever woman that was present, whether married or single, when she came to the dance that night. The which was not to defend herself, because if she did not consent, they considered it certain that all the games that were played on that pole that they were raising, they would be destined to lose. For which reason the leading men went about solicitous, begging them not to de-

14. In Spanish *ninguna,* "no one," is clearly feminine.
15. The indicated illustration does not appear in the margin of this page of this copy, but in 1976 I saw a second copy of the manuscript in the P. K. Yonge Library that had a drawing that somewhat resembled a lacrosse stick.
16. This word might also be rendered as "the salutation" or as "the God bless you" or "blessings." The Spanish term here is *Salve,* which is the Roman greeting "Hail" or "Hello," familiar to us as the opening words of the hymn "Salve Regina."
17. The Spanish here is *salvo conduto,* or "safe conduct."

fend themselves, that they might have pity on them and on their husbands and brothers, etc., because they would lose what they had.[18] Of this they assured me, that they had done this themselves. With all [this], I ask [you], Whose counsel is this? Oh powerful God!

The ninth. That at the foot of this ball pole, they had to place a skull or a scalp of a dead person, as I have already said, in memory of its founder, [in memory] of Ytonanslac, the father of the ball players. [Such were the] abuses, omens, and superstitions that they had when they played this bedeviled game!

First of all the ball must be of deerskin taken from the area of the animal's hooves, because it was said that the deer has all of his strength in his feet and his hands. And when the ball is [made] from the hooves, it infused their vigor in the one who caught it. And they filled this ball with clay, and set it out to dry. Afterward, as a result, one could not tell the difference between it and a shot.

The second. That the Usinulo, man or woman, and I have already explained who the usinulo is, that he is the son of the chief and in their language is called beloved son). And this person at once begins to fast. And it is in the following manner. He must not eat anything more than a little bit of onsla, which is the same as weak *atol*.[19] And he must not eat anything else. And there is a designated number of spoonfuls that he is to drink from that onsla. No one was to approach to drink who was forbidden, because they would lose). Neither must the fire with which it was cooked be used for anything else other than to cook this onsla and to imbibe[20] tobacco. And [for] the aforesaid faster, the tobacco which he inhales[21] must not be of our [type], but of theirs, which they call *acchuma fina*, mixed with another, which they call *atabac*. And, although they always use this, when they do not have tobacco, or to mix with what they have, nevertheless, they are not to imbibe their acchuma fina without this other one. And this fire on which this onsla is cooked must be new).

The third. That in some places they are accustomed to place hair from people whom they have killed in the ball. And they say that it was to bewitch.

The fourth. That the chief of the place that was playing had to fast the night before the game, in this manner). At the setting of the sun or later they gathered in the *bujio*,[22] which is to say, the houses of their government. They place benches for the players. And they are low, some logs hollowed out un-

18. A reference to the natives' custom of wagering on the outcome of the game.
19. *Atol* is probably Nahuatl. It was used in Mexico and Cuba to designate a gruel made by pounding maize into flour and boiling it in water or milk.
20. The Spanish word here is *bever*, "to drink."
21. Here once more the Spanish is *chupar*, the primary meaning of which is "to suck."
22. Modern dictionaries spell it *bohio* and define it as an Indian hut or a humble hut for the

derneath, without legs.[23] And they are to put them in front of the place with which they are playing. They give me to understand that, if the place lies to the north, they place the benches toward the south so that they will come to have their faces toward the north. And the dancers have to go out by the south side, letting out squeals[24] [or yells], and indicating the direction with their arm extended. And the drummer and he of the marua[25] and the women, all must be facing toward the place with whom they are to play, because, they say, if they were to turn their backs, it was a sign that they had to lose. Accordingly, they placed the fasting chief behind these benches of the players. And they placed fires between the chief and the players, [which] had to be new. And the latter was not to be used except by the chief for inhaling tobacco. And that had to be from theirs, *hachuma fina*, and not from ours, and *q de forsi ore*[26] it had to be mixed with the atabac herb or leaf, that I spoke of above. The aforesaid fasting chief must remain seated all night long on that bench, giving advice to his players, etc., reminding them also that they were men and not women, that once they catch the ball, they should not let go of it, even though they killed them. And they said *Maquiliqui*.[27] And I heard them say this not once, but many times. And not in San Luis.[28] Thus it will be, as in fact it was. And from time to time, little by little, they must keep giving him cacina, even though he may not want it). What he did when he was very full was to throw it up. And he was constantly inhaling tobacco, of which I have spoken.

And at times other times.[29] If this chief were a strong man, and even when he was not, he entered the game, having endured this exercise.

Negroes in the West Indies, but in seventeenth-century documents from Florida it is used most commonly to indicate a council house.

23. In Spanish *sin pies*, literally, "without feet."

24. The Spanish here is *Jipidos*, which I have not found in the modern dictionaries but which I recollect having encountered in a Spanish-American novel as indicating something like a rebel yell. Its onomatopoeic quality suggests that as well. As the verb *gipar*, it was used in this sense in the inquiry into the 1675 Chacato revolt. Diocsali, one of the ringleaders, is described as yelling like a Chisca giving a war whoop. Granberry (n.d.) and Peterson (1976) translated it as "sigh."

25. I did not find this word in the dictionary. Granberry (n.d.) and Peterson (1976) render it as "rattles," which makes sense in the context.

26. This page contains some not very legible passages, one of which is this. It could be a corruption of afortiori.

27. Presumably this and *chacalica* below are Apalachee words.

28. Peterson (1976) added the word "only" here, rendering it, "And not only in San Luis." Although this seems to make more sense, the word "only" does not seem to be there. Granberry (n.d.) rendered it as I have.

29. My rendition of this not very legible passage is somewhat conjectural. I transcribed it as *Y*

The fifth. On receiving news of these fasts, the rival place at once performs the *chacalica*, which in our speech is the "countermeasure".[30] And, as I have said, on receiving news of these fasts, or of other things that they did, for, for these purposes they had their spies, either from the men or from the women. At once the rival village sought to kill a turkey or a squirrel or a raccoon.[31] And it must not be from one of those animals that the rest say, will not do. And they immediately set it to cooking in such a way that the bones fall loose and what results in something like a mush. This [mess], of three or four days in the making, they poured into containers and carried it to the spot where they were staining their bodies and painting themselves. And with this fetid stew they liquefy the clay for staining, or whatever else they used for painting themselves. And it was so foul-smelling that they tell me that they could not stand it. And, that on entering into the plaza, they say that as soon as the rival side smelled them, they lost heart [or swooned].[32] And, consequently, the fast, which they had made as a countermeasure, etc. now no longer had any force. =

The sixth. When the courier came and told the people for the last time that they were to play, he counted that [the team] of the rival village, and [prepared] an equal number of sticks of the size of the finger of the hand. And, tying them all together like an *asesito*[33] he threw them into a pot. And they ordered the making of cacina. It must not be of those from the sea coast, which is the one that is commonly drunk, but, rather, that of the forest from here up. And once the cacina is made, it is poured into that pot with those little sticks in the name of the rival players so that they may become weak and not have strength. And if, perchance, this pot were uncovered, while they were playing, they considered it certain they would lose. =

The seventh. The night they kept a vigil for the ball, the leading men asked whether there was anyone or some who felt anxiety or fear. And, if there were, they sent a man satisfactory to them to the rival village with whom they were to play. He carried a scalp of a dead person to bury under the ball pole where they must play, or, if he could, that he might throw it into the players' fire. If he could achieve this last) [feat], they considered it to be certain that

---

abese otras mas. Peterson (1976) rendered it "Most of the time" and Granberry (n.d.) as "In the majority of cases."

30. The Spanish here is *contra de contra.*

31. Again, the Spanish here is *tejon,* which in modern dictionaries is the badger.

32. The Spanish verb here is *desmaiaban,* which can signify either.

33. I was unable to find such a word in Spanish. The Connor transcription also has the same spelling. Possibly it was meant to be *hacecico* or "small sheaf." Peterson translated this passage as "all gathered together in a bundle," and Granberry rendered it freely as "binds up the sticks and throws them into a pot."

they would not lose. And they were so blind that, even though they lost, they were not disabused).

Let us turn now to the entertaining story of how the beloved and dear Nicoguadca ended his days). They say that when he wished to die, or, to put it better, the time to deceive them, he called all his leading men. And, once they were assembled, he said to them, "Now I am about to die. He who might wish to be Nicoguadaca now and remain in my place must kill seven warriors and three *hitas tascaias*.[34] And, having achieved this, he will be Nicoguadca). As my children have told me, those from San Luis, that not long ago there died an Indian named Talpagana Luis, who had a staff or club[35] the size of a *benoble*.[36] And, on the tip of the said pole some scalps, and some painted. And I asked who [or possibly, what] that was. And they told me that he [or it] was *Itatascaia* and now they have confessed to me that he was Nicoguadca.[37]

While I was priest of this *doctrina*, the year of seventy-one, I left [to become] guardian of the convent of St. Augustine. And, during this time, while the Reverend Fray Francisco Maillo was its priest, this Indian died, and they still tell me that he said that he would have to come back and burn the ball post. As though by the just judgments of God Our Lord, a lightning bolt fell that year and burned that of San Luis. And another year, another fell and burned that of Bacuqua, it having happened two years before that another had fallen in Patale and burned another pole? [*sic*]. He [Nicoguadca] went on with his discourse and told them, "What I charge you today is that as soon as I die you should throw my body into some large pots with squashes, melons and watermelons and fill them with water. And put them on the fire until they boil very thoroughly so that I may leave with that steam, having been converted into mist [or smoke].[38] This is for when you have your fields sown. I will remember you and give you water. And, accordingly, when you hear it thunder, it is a sign that I am coming. And thus, they say, did he go, and that he did it. And up to the present, they, and particularly the old ones, continue to believe that when it thundered Nicoguadca was on his way to give them water. And who doubts but that many of their children and relatives, being so easily influ-

34. The second of these words means warrior, apparently an Apalachee word. The *Hita tascaia* seems to be one of the upper ranks within the warrior caste.
35. The Spanish here is *baston*, which could also mean a cane. It is known from other sources that some of the Apalachee leaders regularly carried some kind of a staff or swagger stick, at least while they were in the council house.
36. I have not found this word in my modern Spanish dictionaries, but I have encountered it in other seventeenth-century documents from Florida in contexts in which it definitely has the meaning of cudgel or club.
37. Here both words seem to be used in the sense of a title of rank, and in the case of Nicoguadca it also seems to indicate him as the lightning-bolt deity.
38. The Spanish here is *humo*.

enced, have not believed this, especially when we looked the other way, and they were not taken to task nor reprehended [for it], and persisted in this blindness, deceived by the devil. Blind! Dumb![39] I do not say deaf, because if they were ignorant concerning all this, how could they be reprehended for it and how could they hear the opposite of these abuses? So, for the love of God, I ask that we view this with charity. Let us see, as will be seen farther on, whether such a game can be permitted). What I feel is that after they have learned [the truth] and they have wanted to speak against he who does not abandon them [the abuses]. I do not know on what they can base this. Let us give many thanks to God that it has been taken away from them. I for my part do not know whether it will cease? [*sic*] For this reason I am asked, "What motive did I have for trying, with such effort, to bring about the abolition of this bedeviled game?" One might say, "With the help of Our Lord." When his Excellency Señor Don Gavriel Días Vara Calderón came on his visit, having seen the youths in this place of San Luis, by chance, playing that game, not as it was played with other places, he sent for his secretary, so that he might see that pileup, and what sort of game [it was], and the kicking, and the climbing over one another as if it were upon a stone staircase. The aforesaid Don Pedro came and told him how bestial it was and his Lordship kept observing it with all his attention and afterwards commanded that all the poles be knocked down, that that was a barbarous and bestial game, and contrary to all common sense, and damaging to the human qualities of these wretches. With entreaties and petitions, I begged him to suspend the execution of his order for the present, [convinced] (?)[40] that for the present he had not uncovered any evil [in it], neither had we in the meantime to make (?) legs, as they say, so that we might be able to abolish it. Because I had then seen the cedula of Her Majesty, May God hear her, in which she ordered that the natives of these regions should not be deprived of any of their dances or other games as long as they were not contrary to the law of God Our Lord or to their education.

I spoke as a Catholic. Consequently, His Grace gave me every consideration. Consequently, for the reasons mentioned and others, it appeared to me that I had good reason [for my stand], even though I had some minor misgivings. After another year, which was that of seventy-six, the province was on the point of being lost, all as a result of this game. My conscience began to bother me with the weight of scruples concerning them [His reasons for defending the game] and to make me responsible for everything that could happen. For the lord bishop had ordered the cutting down of the poles, and, at my

39. In the sense of mute.
40. The Spanish here is *lleno*, which ordinarily means "full."

request, suspended his order because I assured him that there was no risk. It was the will of God himself that I found myself as priest in a place of which I can say, "There are Indians of common sense and satisfaction." I called on those whom I considered to be most trustworthy and questioned them about the beginning and origins of this game. With this, infinite thanks be to God, I went about drawing out what they themselves have seen, with the two interpreters, which is all this [the contents of this manuscript] and much more, which I shall not go into, lest I be fatiguing. And from other interpreters, who were in the habit of coming here to San Luis, so it was said, and they confessed to me that it was true that this was done and much more. And, the beginning of this game and of its origins, Diego Salvador said, "Was told to him by the chief of Samoche,"[41] who is still living today, and by an *inija* from Ocone. And afterward the one in Yvitachuco verified all of it. And Mendoza has told me that his father told him all this story and that he had seen a pole raised in San Diego, a place of Tomole, and that there he had seen the pouring out of cacina and the making of the gua to the pole, the usinulo, and the rest. They say that this is *ymulisla*, or as we would say it, these [are] their customs in Apalachee).

At once I found myself supported by the governor, Don Pablo de Ita Salazar, and by our Reverend Father Provincial, Fray Francisco Perete, who accepted it, as they should have, assured consequently that what my children told me was true. And as you will see, in an assembly of the chiefs, which the Captain Juan Fernández de Florencia[42] held, in order to thank them on the part of the governor for the good work that the chiefs had performed, who had knocked down the poles and put the holy cross in their place. Diego Salvador said to all of them in my presence [that it was true], and all of them also said that it was true, being, the Captain Juan Fernández and the Captain Juan Sánchez de Uriza and many others. And despite all this, [its abolition] has not failed to arouse its controversies. Not on the part of the Indians. I will say one [thing] that is the most fundamental, and it is, that they say that it was true that they had them [all those pagan practices], but that they no longer had recourse to them. To which I respond, "But who was responsible for their abandoning them? Who was it that made them understand this? Who was it that chided them so that the pole in honor of Nicoguadca presently no longer is seen, so that they may no longer be seen to sleep the ball or keep the vigil for it, and so that they are not seen to enter [the plaza] painted in the manner that I have spoken of. And this, until the present day, up to the last game that they played.

41. A satellite village belonging to the jurisdiction of Tomole.
42. Florencia was the governor's deputy in Apalachee at the time of Paiva's campaign against the game.

Accordingly, this being the case, just as they abandoned it, when they saw that they were applauding him, so also from his method [43] they are bound to abandon it, when we are watching them and following them closely [as with] (?) their doctors, who cure with a thousand cunning tricks, with both the priests and the lieutenant chiding them and even subjecting them to forced labor for a time to make them mend their ways. And despite the fact that there is no remedy to make them abandon it. For there are those who are not ignorant that, inasmuch as the Indian is the child of fear), how (?) are they from their own self-love (?) [44] to abandon this game, hobbled [by] such great self-interest, when it is recognized that the Indian is so interested, and when they are confessing it with loud voices, that it is true, Blessed be God! The game has been abolished with all love and calm. The Indians themselves with loud voices [recognize] how good this is for their souls as well as for their bodies. Let us give God a thousand thanks for so great a benefit.

Let us see what resulted from playing this infernal ball game. The first, the many disagreements and the scant peace that have resulted from this devilish game. Nobody denied this truth to me. To it they simply reply that it is a matter of good policy that some places should be at odds with others. Policy of the devil, a Luciferian [philosophy] of government! For it is opposed to the doctrine and teaching of Christ [who said] "Beloved disciples, my peace I leave unto you, my peace I give unto you." In the end, peace was the most valuable gift he left entrusted to us. And that which the angel announced to the shepherds, "Glory be to God on the highest and peace to men of good will." For what policy can be good, that does not seek for peace, but rather discord. So erroneous a doctrine, that involves such blindness, is enough to make one shed tears of blood. They tell me that it is one of the reasons that they wrote to the governor, asking that he not abolish the game. I do not know that it is true. I only know that it was told to me by a trustworthy person.

Third. It is a barbarous game, that only people lacking the knowledge of God could play—for many reasons, that I shall go on giving you, and, for the many lamed, broken legs, persons without the use of one or both hands, blinded in one eye, broken ribs, and other broken bones, such as we are presently observing in the province. And not just a few, but many! And, in some cases, people who have been killed in the said game. I can give testimony about two that I am aware of in the place of San Luis.

43. The words appear to be *de su metodo*. The rendition of this sentence and of the several following is conjectural in places because of the combination of tortuous syntax and words that are difficult to decipher.

44. My rendition here is conjectural. The Spanish could be *de su amor proprio, de su nome proprio,* or something else. The word *proprio* is the only word in this phrase that is clear. And the problem is compounded by the elliptical and convoluted style of the rest of the sentence. It is possible that some copyist omitted something here.

Fourth. That, because of the harm when they played thus, there was a risk that not just one, but that many misfortunes could result, as I saw in the year seventy-six. In five successive games not one concluded without becoming a live war, from which it was resolved that the best path was to abandon it. And there is no doubt that worse calamities would have followed, if soldiers had not been present at the games. And they say this is good policy? They must have forgotten the words John the Evangelist [records that Christ] spoke to his disciples, when he said to them simply, that they should love one another, and they, reflecting on this, said to him, "But, Lord, do you teach us nothing more than that we should love one another?" And he said to them, "And, if you should do this, it will suffice." Could [any other course] be good policy?

Fifth. That while an Indian was a ball player, they dug his field for him and they built a house and a storage-crib for him. And he had license to practice any sort of roguery. And, no matter what it was, the chiefs and leading men overlooked it all and covered it up, with no heed to the law of God, and without reporting it to the friar or to the lieutenant, fearful that, if they punished him, he would move to another village. The truth will come out. Let us all acknowledge it.

Sixth. And, while this harmful game was being played, it was the rule that there would be theft because they left their houses, which are such that they do not have padlocks or other hardware. Nor does the single entrance which the house and the storehouse possess, have any door in it. The most they do is to put a few boughs across it and all go to see this infernal game. And also, at times, because those who wager are such great rogues they walk off both with that which is theirs and with what belongs to another, and, in winning, they lose. And when it comes to setting matters to right, a great deal [of work] is necessary. And, at times, this cannot be achieved, because they do not know who the culprits are.

Seventh. That they lose many of their crops. And villages [perish] because they do not prepare their fields at the proper time. Because they are so totally absorbed in this infernal game, that they become so addicted to it that it becomes the center of every vice and evil, so that at times it was necessary for the lieutenant of this province to send *chacales*[45] or soldiers to some places to order them to prepare the fields so that they might not perish. And despite this, the place that had many games would experience hunger that year, because it lost.

Eighth. That once it was announced that there was a ball game, they all foolishly ran to see it. They went whichever way they chose. The husband took off by one path, the wife by another. And if they had a daughter or sons,

45. These were native officials, similar to the *fiscal* of Spanish municipal governments, who seem to have served as overseers for communal labor projects.

each one chose his own path, except that they all went to see the ball [game]. The husband did nothing to prevent his wife or his children from going with whomever they pleased and to wherever they pleased. They all ran off heedlessly. [On one occasion] when the village of San Luis was playing with Ybitachuco in the plaza of Ocuia, which was something over four leagues more or less from this, it happened to me that I found myself alone [at San Luis] with the sacristan and a young boy, without any other people in the place. And I would not give the sacristan permission to go there, nor the boy, as this would have left me there alone.

Ninth. That, at times, and [indeed], most of the time, some poor Indians went with their children without intending to gamble. [There] they would be given something, so that they might lay a bet, without paying any heed to the consequences that might emerge as a result from this infernal game or [how] they would grow, nor to how great an offense it was to God Our Lord, and to how contrary it was to his holy law. Nor did they take heed that it [the winnings] was the harvest of the devil and *sente suio a nois*.[46] They also tried to get them to play and went about seeking out the players, rewarding them and flattering them, which amounts to the same thing as welcoming evil men and idlers, because, on average, the great ball player was a lazy lout. I have known more than one of that ilk in all of the places that I have administered. Nor, did I arrive yesterday, as they say, for it was fourteen years since I came to the land. And, of those fourteen years, I have spent only seven at San Luis. The rest of the time I have been in other places, teaching, or to put it better, administering, because, I, what doctrine could I teach? And accordingly, the thanks [are owed] to God [alone]. I am not ignorant of any of this. And I have seen it all. I know most [of the places] of the province. But, let us keep to the subject at hand. And, it is a ridiculous and frivolous thing which they [the opponents of the game's abolition] say, that the land would rise up and that the Indians would not dig or work. This alludes to the [experience] in Japan, when St. Francis Xavier converted the kings and grandees, their Bonzes predicted to them that they would lose their kingdoms and that they would sacrifice the obedience of their vassals, who would turn to another King. And for the common people whom he converted they foretold famine and wars. And it appears to me that this alludes to That, just because they have been forbidden so fiendish and sacrilegious a game, one with so many abuses and evils, they predicted that the land would revolt. "What have we come to?" I ask, "to adjust ourselves to their laws and abuses in preaching the evangelical law to them, in correcting their vices, in teaching them virtue? Who would believe this! For

---

46. This was not very legible. Peterson (1976) transcribed this conjecturally as *senso suio* and also made no attempt to translate it.

the love of God! For the [love] of his most holy mother! By the wounds of our Señor Father St. Francis![47] Tell [me] of one single virtue possessed by the ball game that these [people] play. Tell me about it. For if you can point out just one to me, I shall be quiet. They will not find any to tell me. Consequently, I shall not keep quiet."

God's church would have been in a fine fix, if, out of fear, it had ceased to preach the holy gospel and to correct and to chastise evil and to teach virtue. There is no other course to follow. Hence I am not worried that they will attack these walls. And for the last time I say and make it clear that this game was invented by the devil and that one could establish that by its effects, even if there were no other evidence. Accordingly, the abuses and distressing discords [show it] to be the focus of lust, the ruin of the constitutions of these poor souls, and, what makes my heart weep the most, this people is and is known to be so docile, as they are on the present occasion, and as they have been on many others. I have seen it and experienced it, above all now. For, having (?) *********[48] formed an assembly of the chiefs and leading men and other people of influence from this place of San Luis, which is far from being the least in Apalachee, but [is] rather the greatest, and among the most important and loyal, and, having proposed to them that they abolish the ball game, laying out the reasons, and with Diego Salvador, who is the King's interpreter, reading this notebook to them [written] in his hand[49] and having heard them, my children told me that everything which the interpreter had set forth was true, that not all the forms of the chacalica chacalica[50] [sic] which is the countermeasure, that not all of these were resorted to in any one place, but rather, that one would be used here, and another over there, and [still] another over yonder, that this was in accord with [what] they had [from] their masters.[51] And yet, that presently it was being done according as they knew and consequently had heard. And before[52] making up my mind, I assembled them on

47. This is a reference to the stigmata or crucifixion wounds of Christ which St. Francis is believed to have exhibited during his life.

48. The last two words of the text are very badly blurred. For the initial word I was able to decipher only the first letter and the last two, a****do, which is probably *aciendo*. Nothing of the second word could be deciphered.

49. Taken literally this would seem to say that the interpreter had been either the author or the amanuensis for the entire manuscript. Paiva obviously is the author of the polemic portion. Diego Salvador and Mendoza seem to have been responsible for most of its native lore. As royal interpreter, Salvador may have made the copy for the lieutenant, Florencia, which Leturiondo commandeered for his visitation record.

50. Given in Spanish as the *contra de la contra*.

51. The term the Spaniards commonly used to designate the shaman or pre-Christian native intellectual leader who was the guardian and repository of the people's cultural traditions.

52. In my transcript the preposition here is *antes*, which means "before." In their translations

two occasions, as I have said, and they ratified what they had already said, replying to me that I was their spiritual father, that I came to teach them the road to their salvation, to instruct and to enlighten them as to [how] to save their souls through the means that he was teaching them, and not in order to condemn them. And, accordingly, that they must not do anything other than what I might wish, inasmuch as it was above all for the welfare of their souls and bodies. And they gave me this reply in the presence of the two interpreters. And they said that they understood how beneficial it was for them to abandon the ball game, and, accordingly, that they would abandon it at once.

Let it be seen now that everything that I said was correct. And [as witness to this], the two interpreters signed it, both the one for the church and the one for the King, so that for all time, it would be evident. For they were the ones who had testified that this is a copy that is in concordance with its original, which remains in my possession. Done in San Luis de Talimali on the twenty-third of September, the year of sixteen hundred and seventy-six. Diego Salvador holata Juan Mendoza=

Diego Salvador holata juan mendoza

I, the Captain Mrn^a Lorenzo de la bora, Notary clerk de Ver^{da} and I give true testimony as to how the interpreters Diego Salvador and Juan de Mendoza examined this notebook, which they said was the same one that contained the abuses and superstitions of the Apalachee ball game, which was being played up to the day that this notebook was brought to light. And, so that this may be evident, I give the present affirmation in the place of San Luis de Talimali on the twenty-sixth day of the month of December of the year sixteen hundred and seventy-seven.[53]

Mrn Loxenzo de la bora (Rubric)
[Martín Lorenzo de Labora]
Notary Clerk of Record

[The following documents, which throw some additional light on the genesis of this manuscript, appear in the Leturiondo visitation record in the pages immediately preceding the ball game manuscript.]

---

both Granberry and Peterson at this point have "after." In Spanish this would be *despues,* which bears no resemblance at all to *antes.*

53. The reason for the discrepancy of over a year between the date on this document and the date on the preceding one signed by the two interpreters is that the latter certification of the authenticity of this copy of the ball game manuscript was made for its inclusion in the Domingo de Leturiondo visitation record. That visitation occurred near the end of 1677 and the beginning of 1678.

[Folio 566.]

In the place of San Luis de Talimali of the Province of Apalachee on the twenty-sixth day of the month of December of the year one thousand six hundred and seventy-seven the Señor Sergeant-major Domingo de Leturiondo . . . stated that, in view of the ball game's having been extinguished in these provinces, as is made clear more at length in the *autos* of the visitation of the Village of Tomole in the general assembly of all the chiefs and leading men of the province that was held [there], and that it is appropriate for its better *apxoue*^{on} that the Captain Juan Fernández de Florencia hand over a notebook that is in his possession, (in which was set forth all the abuses that were practiced in the said game, for which reason it has been ordered to be abandoned forever), so that the interpreters who set it down and who brought it to light may Authenticate it and so that thus [authorized], it may be placed in these autos, so that it may be evident how legitimate were the causes for extinguishing it. And let the said lieutenant be notified so that he may hand it over. And by this auto I provide such an order. And I sign and certify it.

Domingo de Leturiondo
before me Lorenzo de Labora

[Folio 566 back.]

. . . At once, without a delay, in conformity with what was ordered by his excellency the said Sergeant-major Domingo de Leturiondo, the said captain Juan Fernández de Florencia, Lieutenant of these Provinces, handed over the notebook contained in the *auto*, brought written on sixteen pages. Of this I give witness.

Martín Lorenzo de la boxa
Notary of the visitation

AUTO

In the said place on the said day, month and year the Sergeant-major Domingo de Leturiondo . . . / [folio 567] stated that the sergeant-major Diego Salvador and Juan de Mendoza, who brought to light the notebook of the abuses which the ball game contained, saw it and recognized it to be the same one that the captain Juan Fernández de Florencia had handed over, and having recognized that it was the same one, let them put their report in these autos, and let them sign it with their n^e [probably *nombre*, or "name"], so that it may be evident in all of this, and his excellency provided [and] ordered this and signed. I give witness of this.

Domingo de Leturiondo
Before me Mxn Lorenzo dela bora, notary

In the said place of San Luis de Talimali on the said twenty-sixth day of the month of December of one thousand six hundred and seventy-seven, in fulfillment of the *auto* of his excellency, what was contained in it was read and made known to Diego Salvador and Juan de Mendoza. And they stated that it was precisely what they had brought to light and they signed it with their n^{es} [names]. Of this I give witness.

Diego Salvador holata Juan Mendoza
before me Mxn Lorenzo de Labora, notary

[Folio 568.]
And to Reverend Father mai° franc^{co} de Florencia

I place in your hands the ball game which the Apalachino Indians have been playing so barbarously until God Our Lord was pleased that they should come forth from the blindness in which the demon held them. Concerning which, from this point on, I say adios with infinite thanks, for I became the principal instrument to make it be overturned and to come crashing down, and so that such a tribute to the devil might be ended, I did not cease to give thanks to his divine Majesty. Having recognized the favors that he has done me, for by my intervention its destruction was begun when it seemed to be impossible that such a game could be destroyed or taken away. It caused horror and struck fear [into us], holding out the prospect of disastrous uprisings similar to that faced by St. Francis Xavier while he was converting the Japanese, when their Bonsos promised them misfortunes and calamities. It is to God that credit must be rendered that it was taken from them with the fullness of love with all gentleness, without having any discord or contradiction . . . From San Luis, on the 28th of May of 1677. . . . your brother

Juan H^z de Florencia [Hernández]

[The ball game manuscript begins immediately following this letter on folio 569 down to folio 584 covering precisely the sixteen pages mentioned in one of the preceding documents. However it is really double that number as these pages are numbered only on the front side.]

In chapter 3 it was noted that the account of the final contest between the two Nicoguadcas has been translated in different fashions. For those who might wish to judge for themselves how best to handle the passage, the following is my transcription of the Spanish text.

Abiendo perdido Ochuna Nicoguadca a la pelota, desafio a Nicoguadca a jugar a el quisio que es el juego que al principio dijo jugaban todas estas naciones que es con una piedra y dos varas, pues como digo desafio a nicoguadca y abiendole ganado todo q^{to} tenia disen que trato de meterlo a trampa y fingio al tal Ochuna nicoguadca que tenia sede e queria yr a bever y disen dio (?) nicoguadca con la vara de punta en el suelo hiso brotar agua y dijole, Veve. Aqui fingio tener necessidad corporal de usar de su albadañar. Y Nicoguadca la formo un montesillo y dijole hasta aqui. Y por postre dijo yba a ensender un tabaco y entro en una casa y abrio un agujero y se fue a Apalachocolo y entonces Nicoguadca fue en su busca con sus tascaias y el disen le formo muchas nieblas frios gelos M*****^{a}mas con todo, lo bencio y lo mato a el y a sus tascaias y sus basallos le formaron el palo de pelota que se be aqui en esta plana. . . .

Appendix 3

Villages in Apalachee during the Mission Era (with variant names and spellings)

Villages	Satellites
San Lorenzo de Ivitachuco, Ybitachuco, Ibitachuco, Bitachuco, Vitachuco, Hibitachuco, Ybitachua	San Juan, San Nicolás, San Pablo, Ajapasca
San Luis de Xinayca or San Luis de Nixaxipa[a] or (from 1675 on) San Luis de Talimali, Talmaly	Abaslaco, San Augustín, San Francisco, San Bernardo
San Cosme y San Damian de Cupaica,[a] San Damian de Cupaica, San Cosme y San Damian de Yecambí (Icabí, Yscambí, Escabí), Ilcombe, Cupahica, Acpayca, Escambé	Nicupana, San Lucas, San Pedro, Faltassa, San Cosme
San Martín de Tomole, Thomole, Tomoli, Tomoly	Ciban, Samoche, San Diego
San Joseph de Ocuia, Ocuya, Ocuux	Sabacola, Chali, Ajapaxca
San Juan de Aspalaga,[a] Azpalaga, Espalaga	Pansacola, Nipe (or Jipe), Sabe, Culcuti
San Pedro y San Pablo de Patale, San Pedro de Patale, San Pedro y San Pablo de Kpal, Patali, Petali	Ajamano, Talpahique or Talpatqui(?)
San Francisco de Ocone, Oconi	San Miguel
San Antonio de Bacuqua,[a] Santa María de Bacucua, Vacuqua	Guaca

Santa María de Ayubale, Concepción de Ayu-   Cutachuba
bale, Nuestra Señora de la (Puríssima) Con-
cepción de Ayubale, Ayubali, Ajubale,
Aiubale
Santa Cruz de Ytuchafin (or Hichutafun), Santa
Cruz y San Pedro de Alcantara de Ychutafun,
Santa Cruz de Capoli, Capoli, Capole
La Purificación de Tama, Candelaria, Nuestra
Señora de la Candelaria, Nuestra Señora de
Candelaria de Tama, Thama, Tamaja
San Carlos de los Chacatos[a]
Assumption of Our Lady[b] (Amacano, Chine,
and Pacara or Capara)
Nativity of Our Lady[b]
San Pedro de los Chines
San Antonio de los Chines[c]
Medellín (appears only on a 1683 map)
Ocatoses (or Ocatacos)[d]
Settlement of the Tocopacas at Vacisa
San Marcos de Apalache[e] (the port)
Tamasle (a postdestruction settlement near St.
Marks; Yamasee)
San Juan (postdestruction settlement near St.
Marks; Yamasee and Apalachee). It was
served by the church at St. Marks.
Apalachee appears as Apalache, Abalache, Ha-
balache, Aba Lah chi, and Palache.[e]

---

a. These villages are known to have been moved at least once during the mission era. At least two
separate moves are recorded for Escambé.

b. These villages were mentioned only once (on the 1675 lists). They may have disappeared or
they may be identical with one of the other villages listed, such as that of the Chine or
Medellín.

c. It is not clear whether the change of name here, from San Pedro de los Chines, signifies a
second Chine village or a change of location for San Pedro de los Chines.

d. Ocatoses may represent a geographical place-name that stands for one of the above-mentioned
villages rather than a separate village. It could be identical with Assumption of Our Lady or
Nativity of Our Lady rather than a separate village.

e. The use of *b* rather than *p* appears in the document written in Apalachee and among Spaniards
who spoke Apalachee.

Appendix 4

Mission Villages to the West of Apalachee Province

San Nicolás de Tolentino: Chacato mission about 25 miles west-northwest of
the Apalachicola River located in a large cave with a spring issuing
from one of its walls. Mission there survived only from 1674 to 1675.

San Carlos: Chacato mission about ten miles farther west. It was equally
ephemeral and contemporaneous with San Nicholás.

San Antonio: Chacato satellite village in the same area.

La Encarnación a la Santa Cruz de Sabacola (also known as Santa Cruz and
Santa Cruz de Sabacola): on the west bank of the Apalachicola just
below the confluence of the Flint and the Chattahoochee, from 1674 to
1677 and possibly a little beyond that date.

Sabacola: at the Lower Creek village of that name on the middle Chattahoochee a few leagues below the falls. Friars were allowed to remain there
only three days in 1679; then they returned for several months in 1681
backed by soldiers.

San Carlos de los Chacatos: located about 1681 on the Apalachicola River
apparently on the site of the 1674 Sabacolan mission. Survivors abandoned this site in 1694 after it was attacked by the Creek. The site was
occupied briefly about 1716–1718 by a band of Yamasee, who then
moved down near St. Marks.

Santa Cruz de Sabacola: established about 1682, among the Christian Sabacola, who migrated from their village on the Middle Chattahoochee to
a site a little to the west of the Flint River and just above the junction of
that river with the Chattahoochee. Referred to as San Carlos de
Çabacola in 1689 and as Savacola Chuba in 1690, the last time that it
is mentioned. In 1715 the site was reoccupied for a few years by the
refugees from the Creek town of Palachicola on the Savannah River
under Chislacaliche (Cherokeeleechee in English texts).

Appendix 5

Apalachee Mission Villages, Their Population, and Distances between Villages

Cupaica: 900 people, 1675; 400 families, 1689

90 leagues to St. Augustine (1655)

1 league to San Luis and 2 leagues to Bacuqua (1675, Hita Salazar and Calderón lists)

Due north of and close to San Luis (1683 map)

3 leagues from San Luis and west of Ochlockonee (1693)

3 leagues from San Luis and 2 to Bacuqua (1697)

3 leagues from San Luis to a former site of Cupaica (1699)[a]

Within cannon shot of San Luis (1704)

Bacuqua: 120 people, 1675; 50 families, 1689

Moved half a league by permission (1657)

2 leagues from Patale (1675), both lists

Three cattle ranches were close enough for their cattle to harm the village's crops in 1694, one of them between Bacuqua and Patale.

9 leagues from Ocuia (1697) and 2 from Cupaica

San Luis: 1,400 people, 1675; 300 families, 1689; 200 families, 1704

88 leagues from St. Augustine (1655)

Moved (1656)

1 league to Cupaica and half a league

357

plus to Candelaria (1675, Hita Salazar
list)

1 league to Cupaica and 1 league to Purificación de Tama (Candelaria) (1675,
Calderón list)

Half a league east of Chacato village
(1683 map, 1695 list)

3 leagues from Cupaica (1697 list)

Natives reported to have withdrawn to
site 1 league from San Luis
(1699–1702)

3 leagues from Patale (1716)

San Martín de Tomole:
700 people, 1675; 130
families, 1689

87 leagues to St. Augustine (1655)

2 leagues to Tama and 2+ to Capoli
(1675, Hita Salazar list)

1 league to Tama and 2 to Capoli (1675,
Calderón list)

Considerably east and slightly southeast
of San Luis and due south of Tama
(1683 map)

Governor Torres stopped there on way to
San Luis from St. Marks (1693).

1.5 leagues from Aspalaga and also from
Tama (1697 list)

Diego Peña passed Tomole and Tama on
a 3-league trek from Patale to San
Luis (1716).

Patale: 500 people, 1675;
120 families (1689)

84 leagues to St. Augustine (1655)

4 leagues from Ocuia and 2 from Bacuqua (1675, Hita Salazar and Calderón
lists)

A considerable distance due west of
Ocuia with a slight bias toward the
northwest—most northerly of all
(1683 map)

4 leagues from San Luis in 1696 to former site of Patale to which M. Delgado moved his cattle ranch in that
year[b]

1.5 leagues from Capoli and from Aspalaga (1697 list)

Described as a "small" village (1704)

3 leagues to San Luis (1716)

Aspalaga: 800 people, 1675;
50 families, 1689

86 leagues to St. Augustine (1655)

1 league to Oconi and 1.5 to Ocuia
(1675, Hita Salazar list)

1 league to Oconi and 2 to Ocuia (1675,
Calderón list)

Appears to have been west of Ocuia on
1655 and 1657 lists and between
Ocuia and Oconi, east of Ocuia, by
1675

Between Oconi and Ocuia west-northwest of Oconi (1683 map)

1.5 leagues from Patale and from Tomole (1697 list)

Ocuia: 900 people, 1675;
200 families, 1689

84 leagues to St. Augustine (1655)

1.5 leagues to Aspalaga and 4 to Patale
(1675, Hita Salazar list)

2 leagues to Aspalaga and 4 to Patale
(1675, Calderór. list)

4+ leagues to San Luis (1676)

9 leagues from Bacuqua and 3 from
Oconi (1697 list)

Oconi: 200 people, 1675; 80
families, 1689

77 leagues to St. Augustine (1655)

1 league to Aspalaga and half a league to
Ayubale (1675, Hita Salazar list)

2 leagues to Aspalaga and 1 to Ayubale
(1675, Calderón list)

3 leagues to Ocuia and 2 to Ivitachuco
(1697 list)

Ayubale: 800 people,
1675; 250 families, 1689

77 leagues to St. Augustine (1655)

1.5 leagues to Ivitachuco and half a
league to Oconi (1675, Hita Salazar
list)

Ivitachuco: 2,500 people, 1655, and 1,200, 1675; 200 families, 1689

1 league to Ivitachuco and 1 to Oconi (1675 Calderón list)
1 league to Ivitachuco and 3 to Capoli (1697 list)
1 league to Ivitachuco (1716)

75 leagues from St. Augustine (1655), the same as Asile
1.5 leagues to Ayubale (1675, Hita Salazar list)
1 league to Ayubale and 2 to Asile (1675, Calderón list)
1 league to Ayubale and 2 to Oconi (1697 list)
1 league to Ayubale (1716)

Capoli: 60 people, 1675; 30 families, 1689; 20 men, 1694

2 leagues from Tomole on both lists (1675)
3 leagues to Ayubale and 1.5 to Patale (1697 list)
On the road between Ayubale and Patale (1716 list)

Tama or **Candelaria:** 300 people, 1675; 80 families, 1689

Half a league to San Luis and 2 leagues to Tomole (1675, Hita Salazar list)
1 league to San Luis and 1 league to Tomole (1675, Calderón list)
Half a league to Chine village and 1.5 leagues to Tomole (1697 list)
On the road between Patale and San Luis (1716)

Assumpción del Puerto: 300 people, 1675, including Capara, Amacano, and Chine; 30 families of Chine, 1689, not necessarily in the same location

4 leagues from Tomole (1675, Calderón list)
Mentioned only as being on the path to the sea from San Luis (1675, Hita Salazar list)
Place of the Chine was half a league from Tama (1697 list)

Nativity of Our Lady: 40 people, 1675

2 leagues from San Luis toward the Apalachicola country (1675, Hita Salazar list)

San Carlos de los Chacatos: provided about 250 migrants to Mobile in 1704

Half a league from San Luis
Established sometime between 1675 and 1677
Abandoned sometime after 1683
Reoccupied (?) sometime after 1695

Escambé: (trans-Ochlockonee site)

Described by Governor Torres as 3 leagues from San Luis across the Yellow River and 12 leagues southwest of the Chacato village on the Apalachicola (1693)
On the same trek Friar Barreda placed it a little more than 2 leagues from San Luis, northwest of San Luis on a trail that took them 1.5 leagues to the river crossing and then about 1 league east of the Palos (Taluga) River and 9 leagues east of the Apalachicola opposite the Chacato village there.
Late in 1694 its chief asked for permission to move the village back to the site it had occupied prior to moving across the Ochlokonee, but as of 1697 they had not moved back.
3 leagues from San Luis (1697 list)
Diego Peña described it as 1 league across the Ochlokonee from his campsite on the Lake Jackson prairie (1716).

a. Diego Jiménez had moved his cattle ranch to that abandoned site by 1699. It was was 5 leagues from the former site of his ranch, which was close enough to Bacuqua in 1694 for his cattle to cause problems for that village's crops.

b. This site was about 1.5 leagues from the site of his former ranch which was possibly the Bacuqua site abandoned in 1657.

Appendix 6

Apalachicola Villages with Which the Apalachee Had Contact

1675 Calderón list

Santa Cruz de Sabacola el Menor or La Encarnación a la Santa Cruz de Sabacola on the Apalachicola River just below the junction of the Flint and the Chattahoochee; formed by chief and people of Sabacola El Grande in 1674.

Chicahûti, Sabacôla, Ocôni, Apalachocôli, Ilapi, Tacûsa, Usachi, Ocmûlgui, Ahachîto, Cazîthto, Colômme, Cabita, Cuchiguâli: These 13 towns are described as being on the Chattahoochee 30 leagues to the north of the Christian Sabacola village of Santa Cruz.

In the Province of Toâssa: Toâssa, Imocolâsa, Atayâche, Pacâni, Oslibâti, Afaschi, Escatâna, Atâssi, Tubâssi, Tiquipachi, Achichepa, Hilâpi, Ilantâlui, Ichopôsi (Díaz Vara Calderón 1675:9–10)

1685 Antonio Matheos's lists

Sabacola El Grande, Jalipasle, Oconi, Apalachicola, Achito, Ocute, Osuchi, Ocmulgee, Casista, Colone, Caveta, Tasquique

Those villages that attended a conference with Matheos arranged through Chief Pentecolo of Apalachicola: Ocmulgee, Osuchi, Ocute, Achito, Apalachicola, Oconi, Jalipasle, and an unnamed small village (possibly Sabacola).

These nonattending towns were burned by Matheos: Caveta, Casista, Tasquique, Colone. (Guerrero 1687; Lanning 1935:267)

1695 Letter of Governor Torres y Ayala[a]

The governor mentions that the 50 warriors who attacked the Chacato village on the Apalachicola some time before this were from Sabacola, Apalachicola, and Tiquipache. In retaliation a Spanish-led Apalachee expedition marched to the Apalachicola country to plunder and burn. Among the towns mentioned as having suffered this fate were Cavetta, Cassista, Ocmulgee, Taisquique, Uchichi, and the places of those of Oconi. (Torres y Ayala 1695)

1702

Achito, departure point for Creek force that routed the Apalachee on the Flint in that year

1716 Diego Peña expedition

Diego Pêna mentioned that the province of Apalachicolo had ten villages, which he encountered in the following order proceeding upriver:
1. Chislacasliche's place on the site of ruins of the Sabacolan village just above the confluence of the Flint and Chattahoochee;
Five days' journey upriver he camped on prairies between the Flint and Chattahoochee belonging to some Christian Apalachee, 2 leagues distant from
2. Savacola, where he spent the night, then proceeded to a small farm occupied by Apalachee that belonged to the chief of Apalachicolo, which was 2 leagues to the north;
3. Apalachicolo, 6 leagues from Caveta;
4. Achito;
5. Ocmulgee;
6. Uchi, where they speak a different language than the others, for which there are only 2 or 3 interpreters;
7. Tasquique, where they speak Yamasee;
8. Casista, where they speak Muskogee;
9. Cavetta, where they speak Muskogee; all the others speak the same language (Hitchiti) except the Sabacola, who have a distinct language but also speak Apalachee;
10. Chavajal. (Boyd 1949:21–25)

364

Appendixes

Diego Peña's 1717–1718 expeditions

Diego Pêna mentions in passing: Chislacasliche's place; Apalachicolo; Uchis; Euchitto (Achito); Oconi; Caveta; Casista; Chavagali.

He mentions the following as planning to move to Apalachee close to St. Marks: Tasquique (of the Yamasee tongue); Euchitto (of the Uchisi tongue [Hitchiti]); Uchi (a different language—only two interpreters for it); Apalachicolo (of the Uchisi tongue); Oconi (of the Uchisi tongue); Sabacola (part Christian). (Boyd 1952)

1738 list of gifts

Gifts were distributed at St. Marks to the leaders of the 14 towns that make up the Province of the Uchise and Cabeta: Tamaxle the Old; Chaschdve (a new pueblo); Chalaquiliche; Jufala; Sabacola; Ocone; Ayfichito; Apalachicole; Ocmulgee; Osuchi; Chioja; Casista; Cabeta; Tamasle the New. (Toro 1738)

1745 list of the 14 towns of the Province of the Uchises

In the order of their location along the banks of the river where they were situated:

Zalacasliches, Yufala, Savacola, another Savacola, Ocone, Apalachicola, Ajachito, Chaquitpe, Chiaja, Ocmulgee, Osuche, Yuches, Casista, and Caveta. Witnesses say only three of these villages were hostile to the Spaniards: Ocone, Chiaja, and Ocmulgee. (Montiano 1745)

a. Serrano y Sanz (1912:224–227) presents a similar letter bearing this date which mentions only Cavetta, Oconi, Cassista, and Tiquipache and does not identify the attackers of San Carlos.

Appendix 7

Some Apalachee Names

At San Luis

Usunaca Andrés or Don Andrés, principal chief
Holata Juan Mendoza, a leader
Vi (or Bip) Ventura, inija
Usunaca Monica, married to Chuguta Juan
Pedro Ventura
Alap Adrián
Antonio Acuipa Feliciano

At Abaslaco

Usunaca Juan, chief
Usunaca Matheo, heir

At Cupaica

Bernardo Ynachuba (Hinachuba), chief in 1677
Juan Mexía*
Inacusa Sa Bernardo
Pansaca Pedro
Chocolaga Juan
Vi Adrián
Chocoluga Santiago
Holata Santiago
Chuguta Mariana, a Chacato
Guaca Joseph, a Chacato[1]

At Faltassa

Tafunsaca Martín, chief
Tafunsaca Feliciano, heir
Nicolás Tafunsaca, brother
Tafunsaca Bauptista, parish interpreter
Osunaca Pedro Garcés, usurping chief, 1669–1677

At Bacuqua

Juan Mexía,* chief (Cui Juan Mexía——uncertain whether he is the same
    person)
Ocolasli Jucege
Itam Martín

At Patale

Alonso Pastrana,* principal chief in 1680s
Ynaja Benito
Osunac Favian
Pansacola Miguel (two had this name)
Pansaca Baptista
Asta Alonso

At Tomole

Paslali Alonso
Pansaca Juan Mendosa
Pansacola Julian
Ocolasli Baltasar
Chislic Antonio

At Capoli

Hinacchuba Adrián, chief, 1695
Don Patricio Non Juluchba, chief, 1687
Chuguta Marcelo
Chinocosa Jucege
Chaepa Evangelista
Abaiaga Nxnd

Abaiaga Martín
Abaiaga Vicente

At Ayubale

Savacola Adrián, *jinija*, 1695
Usunaca Jucege, his son
Chuguta Antonio
Ynac Ygnacio
Pansacola Juan
Choaito Pedro
Ocolasli Martín

At Aspalaga

Ynac Andrés
Ocolasli Juan, married to Afac Grabula
Hijnac Andrés, married to Ychu Francisca
Afac Nicolás
Hipahala Esteban, son of Afac

At Ocuia

Pansac Baptista
Pansac Manuel
Faquit Alonso
Nicquichasli Adrián
Usunaca Sebastian, chief of Ichasli

At Oconi

Cui Francisco
Savocola Caurenti
Paiasqui Antonio
Pansaca Luis

At Ivitachuco

Don Luis Ybitachucu, principal chief, 1657
Don B^{ra} (Bentura) ybita chuco ho lah ta,[2] chief, 1688

Don Patricio Hinachuba, chief, 1695, alias Nan hulu chuba, Don Patricio
Nicquichasli Antonio, ensign
Lorenço Moreno,* captain, 1657
Pedro Muñoz,* chief of San Pablo, 1657
Marecule (or Maviule) Gabriel
Castogola (or Castocola) Sevastian
Ycho Sevastian
Paslali (or Paslaxali) Lorenzo
Ocolasli Antonio
Baua Alonso
Guasa Pedro
Esfan Juan
Hinija Luis, elder
Hinija Luis, elder
Inija Sevastian[3]

At Tama

Chuguta Francisca (female)

Village of origin not specified

Hubabpt (or Ubapt) Gaspar, royal interpreter, 1694–1695
Cui Juan Mexía
Pansacola Mexía
Chuguta Alonso

At the Apalachee village near St. Augustine in 1711, San Luis de Talimali, alias Abossaya

Hina Juan de Hita, the chief
Viunac Pedro, the old chief[4]
Savacola Bernardo

Adult males	Adult females
Usunac: Don Juan	Hinachuba María
Hinachuba Francisco	Usunac Maxina
Pansacola Evangelista	Usunac María Solana
Icho Marcos	Usunac Cicilia
Ispalala Martín	Chinocosa Maxina
Ispalala Juan	Chinocossa Francisca

Icho Joseph
Afac Francisco
Afac Ambrosio
Jolata Francisco
Panzacola Francisco
Alap Antonio
Ocolasli Juan Monzón
Cuy Bernardo
Opalossa Juan
Alap Gaspar
Lagnachi Melchor
Ocolasli Bautista
Pallali Juan Arguello
Ocollali Santiago
Ocolagli Simón
Chinocossa Dionisio
Alap Julian
Usunac Alonsso
Panzaca Antonio
Castocola Juan
Isfane Mario
Cuy Juan

Afac María Cruz
Alap Manuela
Alap María
Panzacola María Cruz
María Candelaria

Boys

Chinacossa Juan
Chinacossa Francisco
Chinacossa Silvestre

Girls

Afac Michaela
Castacola Ana
Isfane Juana

From the foregoing lists it is clear that the same surnames occur in different villages. The surname Chuguta was found at Tama and among the Chacato as well as in the Apalachee villages. Husbands and wives appear to have kept their own surnames. In the two instances in which we have the names of father and son, their surnames are different, suggesting that children may have taken their surnames from their mothers. This conclusion also seems to be borne out by the cases where we have lines of succession of uncle to nephew, as in the Tafunsaca line at Abaslaco, where uncle and nephew have the same surname.

Two families in particular stand out here as occupying leadership roles, the Hinachuba and the Usunaca. Hinachuba is probably a modification of Ybitachuco, the surname used by that town's ruling family in 1657 and 1688. And Non Juluchba is probably another variation of the same surname. We encounter Hinachubas as chiefs at Ivitachuco, at Capole, and at Cupaica. In Cupaica the Hinachuba form of the name emerges as early as 1677. Osonacas or Usunacas appear as chiefs at San Luis, at Abaslaco, a satellite of San Luis, at Ichasli, as the usurping chief for an eight-year period at Faltassa, a satellite of Cupaica, and as heir to the inija of Ayubale.

It also should be noted that in the lists of the ordinary Indians, both male and female, the Usunacs and Hinachubas appear at the top of the list. And the one male Usunac whose name appears in the ranks is given the title of "don."

1. Guaca was also the name of the satellite village of Bacuqua mentioned in the 1657 visitation record.
2. In the Spanish version it appears as Don Bentuxa, cacique de Ybitachua.
3. Inija here appears to be a surname rather than a title of office.
4. By 1717 he was the chief again. On this occasion his name was spelled Don Pedro Osunaca.

Appendix 8

Explanatory Notes for Figure 2.1

THE geographic features in figure 2.1 were traced from a map of the province prepared by Charles Poe, who also was responsible for determining the location of San Luis. B. Calvin Jones provided the information that helped to determine the location of Ivitachuco as well as those of a number of other villages. I established the locations of the remaining missions by using Ivitachuco and San Luis as anchor points and by applying information on the known mission sites and the distances given on the two 1675 mission lists and in other documentary sources. A site marked by a triangle has been definitely identified as representing a mission site through site reconnaissance or digging, or both, largely as a result of the efforts of B. Calvin Jones. A mission site marked by a circle is one whose location is based on documentary sources only. The final version of the map in the figure was prepared by Charles Poe from my rough sketch.

Ivitachuco: Location is based on both documentary sources and archaeological evidence that there was a village on that site. One documentary source indicates that Ivitachuco was located elsewhere at some time prior to the 1640s.

Ayubale: The site indicated was identified tentatively as that of Ocone by Hale G. Smith in 1951. Calvin Jones has made the identification definite.

Oconi: A site identified with Oconi has been found. However, its placement on the map is based on the 1675 data on its distance from Ayubale and Aspalaga and on the study of a topographic map for the likeliest hilltop site with access to water that fitted both stated distances from reference points.

Aspalaga: Placement of the site is based on Morrell and Jones (1970) who

371

explored it. An alternative site, marked by a circle, is included because of the possibility that Aspalaga in the 1650s occupied a site farther west than the one definitely identified. Documentary sources suggest that this alternative is probably the case.

Ocuia: The placement of Ocuia is based on the 1973 article by B. Calvin
Jones reporting the excavation on the site he discovered in 1968. The
site is just south of Burnt Mill Creek, a spring-fed stream that insured
the inhabitants a year-round water supply. Its elevation is about 120
feet above mean sea level and about one kilometer north of the Cody
Scarp, the divide between the Tallahassee Hills, where all the Apalachee missions were located, and the coastal lowlands (Jones 1973).
There is documentary evidence suggesting that Ocuia occupied a different site at some time.

Patale: Two known sites are identified with Patale. The westernmost is the
Buck Lake Road site. Since I was not aware of the exact location of the
second Patale site, I located it on this map by information derived
from conversations with Calvin Jones and Gary Shapiro. The Buck
Lake Road site appears to be the earlier of the two and to have been
used as the point of reference for stating the distance to Ocuia on the
1675 lists.

Bacuqua: Locating a possible site for Bacuqua poses the most serious problem
of all the sites on the map. On the basis of existing data on its location
in the 1670s, all that can be said with any certainty is that it lay somewhere along an arc swinging from the vicinity of the Tallahassee Memorial Hospital along Betton Road and north along Thomasville Road
through the area just west of that road up to Lake Hall, from there
through Killearn Estates to the area north of Long Pond and south of
Tom John Pond. In terms of topography and access to water, there are
many likely sites in that area. I chose the vicinity of Lake Hall because
some artifacts have been found in that general area and documentary
references indicate that the village was on the frontier, that it was the
northernmost of the missions, and that it was on or close to a trail
coming into the province from the Lower Flint River region. Its suitability as a location for Spanish cattle ranches indicates that it was surrounded by lands with abundant meadowland and adequate access to
water as would likely be found around the earlier Lake Jackson settlement. Before 1657 Bacuqua is known to have been located on another
site whose soil and firewood had become exhausted. Data from the
1690s, when Cupaica was located west of the Ochlockonee, also raise
some problems inasmuch as Bacuqua is posited as still 2 leagues from
Cupaica, as it was earlier. This information seems to require the re-

moval of Cupaica to a site west of Lake Jackson or to the land bridge between Lake Jackson and Lake Carr, or vice versa.

Cupaica: A site for this mission has been identified. We know that Cupaica changed its location at least two times and possibly more. The location of the trans-Ochlockonee site for Cupaica is based solely on documentary data and study of the topographical maps. Archaeologists have found no indications of its trans-Ochlockonee location or even of where the trail to the west crossed that river. During the 1694–1695 visitation, Cupaica's chief asked permission to move his village again. In 1697 its distance was given as 3 leagues from San Luis and 2 from Bacuqua. The trans-Ochlockonee site was about 3 leagues from San Luis as well. By 1699 a cattle ranch had been established on some abandoned site of Cupaica that was 3 leagues from San Luis. By 1704 Cupaica had been moved to a site described as being within cannon shot of San Luis, but as late as 1702 its location was described as on an exposed frontier.

Tama: The location of Tama on this map is conjectural. The documents and the topography permit its being located on a number of points on an arc running from the heights of Florida A & M University through Capitol Hill or Myers Park and out along North Monroe Street to the vicinity of Lake Ella. I have ruled out the A & M site by placing the Chine village there. B. Calvin Jones believes that Myers Park is perhaps the most likely site as it has produced many Apalachee artifacts, although no signs of a Spanish presence. I also found that site attractive in a number of respects, for example, the 1730s references to its fine waters suggest proximity to the Cascades. I placed it along North Monroe Street in order to accommodate the prevailing conjectures about the most probable site of Tomole, the data concerning Tama's location in relation to Tomole and Patale, and my belief that Capoli was located along the Old St. Augustine Road.

Tomole: Because Tama is the most important reference point for the location of Tomole, a number of possible sites might be chosen for it, ranging from the vicinity of Lake Munson and McBride Slough, to Six-Mile Pond and Campbell Pond, to the area southeast of it where the Truck Route swings north. The scarcity of acceptable agricultural soils and the restricted number of water sources are, however, limiting factors. I have chosen the fairgrounds site on the basis of B. Calvin Jones's belief that it is the most promising because it has yielded many Apalachee artifacts. As yet, no signs of a Spanish presence have been found there.

Capoli: B. Calvin Jones has found a definite site for this village, with signs of both a Spanish and an aboriginal presence. The placement of the village on this map, based on the documentary evidence, is conjectural.

Assumpción del Puerto: The location of the village on the map is conjectural, as no site has been identified yet. The location of the site depends on the location chosen for Tomole. Its stated distance from Tomole on Bishop Calderón's list would permit its being located at a number of points along an arc based on that distance. It is likely that it was on or close to the trail to St. Marks. If the present road to St. Marks runs relatively close to the original trail, that would put the village in the vicinity of Crawfordville. However, B. Calvin Jones believes that the poor potability of the water in that area would have discouraged settlement there. He suggests a site farther east, closer to Wakulla Springs.

San Carlos de los Chacatos: The location shown here is based on the distance as stated in the records, on its depiction in relation to San Luis on the 1683 Spanish map, and on topographical considerations. Archaeologists have found a probable site for this village. The same factors govern the choice of the Florida A & M University location as the site for the Chine village.

Nativity of Our Lady: Because of the paucity of data, this mission village has not been included on the map. Its stated distance from San Luis seems to place it on the banks of the Ochlockonee in an area where the soil appears to be most unpromising for agriculture. That may have been a factor in its having been mentioned only on the 1675 Hita Salazar list.

Tocobaga: Missions were never established at the Tocobaga villages. As the villages are mentioned on a number of lists, however, it seemed useful to indicate their location. The Wacissa site's location is conjectural and based solely on documentary sources. The two sites closer to the coast are as depicted on maps of the St. Marks region.

Chine: The location of this village is conjectural and based solely on documentary sources and study of the topography.

San Luis: The location of San Luis is, of course, definite; it is the one Apalachee mission site whose location was never lost. There is evidence, however, that before 1656 the native village and the mission were located at a different site and that just before the start of the eighteenth century the natives had withdrawn from the San Luis site to some location about one league away. There are a number of suitable sites for both the earlier and the later village within a one-league radius of San Luis. The recent discovery of part of de Soto's winter camp not far from the state capitol complex suggests that Anhayca Apalache occupied the hill on which the capitol is located.

St. Marks: In the period before 1704, the port of St. Marks does not seem to have been the site of a mission. In 1693, Friar Barreda described the lodgings there as "wretched huts." Shortly after the return of the Spaniards to St. Marks in 1718, a mission was established.

Appendix 9

Spanish Weights and Measures and Their U.S. Equivalents

Unit of measure	Where used	U.S. equivalent
Arroba	Spain	25.36 pounds
	Spain	3.32 gallons (oil)
	Spain	4.26 gallons (wine)
Carga	Mexico (=2 fanegas)	5.15 bushels
	Spain (Castile)	6.3 bushels
Dedo	Spain	⅟₄₈th of a vara or Spanish yard
Fanega	Spain	1.58 bushels
	Mexico	2.57 bushels
	Mexico	8.81 acres
Legua (league)	Mexico	2.60 miles[a]
Pipa or pipe		126.6 gallons
Quintal	Mexico	101.44 pounds
Vara (yard)	Cuba	33.39 inches
	Mexico	32.99 inches
	Spain (Alava)[b]	32.90 inches

Sources: for dedo, see Mariano Velázquez de la Cadena, Edward Gray, and Juan L. Iribas, *New Revised Velázquez Spanish and English Dictionary,* revised by Ida Navarro Hinojosa (New York, 1960), p. 227. All other information is from Juan Villasana Haggard, *Handbook for Translators of Spanish Historical Documents.*

a. Roland Chardon (1980:294–302) indicated that in the sixteenth century, Spaniards used two different measurements for a league: the common one was 3.45 miles and the legal one was 2.63 miles.

b. In Spain the length of the vara differed slightly from province to province. Alava's was shared by some others and seemed to be a median value.

Appendix 10

Standard Spelling for Native and Spanish Names

Amacano
Apalachee
Apalachicola
Asile
Aspalaga
Aucilla
Ayubale
Bacuqua
Canzo
Capoli
Casista
Caveta
Chacato
Chattahoochee
Chisca
Cupaica
Escambé
Faltassa
Gonzalo
Ivitachuco
Lake Miccosukee

Mikasuki
Ochlockonee
Oconi
Ocuia
Pacara
Patale
Sabacola
Salazar
San Juan
San Lorenzo
Tacabona
Talimali
Tama
Tocobaga
Timucua
Tomole
Vallecilla
Wacissa
Yamasee
Ychuntafun
Yustaga

Appendix 11

A Catalog of Native Leaders

1657

Diego Salvador, royal interpreter for both Apalachee and Timucua for at least the 1656–1677 period, filling that function for both Rebolledo's and Leturiondo's visitations as well as for the inquiry into the 1675 Chacato revolt; literate; one of the authors of the research piece on the ball game; in 1677, held the rank of sergeant-major; village of origin and native surname not known.

At Cupaica

Baltasar, principal chief (not clear if he was the same chief Baltasar baptized in 1639)
Bentura, chief of Nicupana
Martín, chief of Faltassa
Bentura, chief of San Cosme
Lucas, chief of San Lucas

At Bacuqua

Alonso, principal chief
Martín, chief of Guaca

At Patale

Baltasar, principal chief
Francisco, chief of Ajamano
Alonso, chief of Talpahique

At San Luis

Francisco Luis, principal chief
Antonio García, captain and the chief's cousin; literate
Antonio de Ynija, a leading man
Pedro García, a leading man
Gerónimo, chief of Abaslaco
Francisco, chief of San Francisco

At Aspalaga

Alonso, principal chief
Manuel, chief of Pansacola
Christobal (Xpobal), chief of Sabe
Santiago, heir of chieftanship at Jipe

At Thomole

Antonio, hinija, governor in the absence of its principal chief
Bernardo, chief of Ciban
Diego, chief of San Diego
Bernardo, chief of Samoche

At Ocuia

Benito Ruíz, principal chief
Gaspar, chief of Sabacola
Santiago, chief of Ajapaxca
Jerónimo, chief of Chali

At Oconi

Francisco Martín, principal chief
Alonso Martín, chief of San Miguel

At Ayubale

Martín, principal chief
Alonso, his brother and a leading man
Adrián, a leading man of Cutachuba

At Ybitachuco

Don Luis, principal chief; nephew of the chief of Asile; literate, signing his name as Don Luis Ybitachucu; name and signature first appear on a 1651 deed.
Andrés, chief of San Juan, an uncle of Don Luis

Pedro Muñoz, chief of San Pablo
Thomás, chief of San Nicolás
Lorenço Moreno, captain; literate
Francisco and Santiago, leading men

At Asile

Gaspar, principal chief, uncle of Don Luis
Manuel de Asile, chief in 1651
Lázaro, leading man, father of the chief of Sabe

1677

Juan Mendoza, coauthor of the ball game research piece; held rank of captain at San Luis; listed first among the leaders of 1677 expedition against the Chisca.

Matheo Chuba, field master; one of the leaders of the 1677 anti-Chisca expedition; a leader at San Luis, in the mid-1680s twice referred to as "governor" of San Luis; taunted by Antonio Matheos for close ties with the friars; a number of Spaniards had houses on his plaza; in the 1680s seemed to be doing much of the work of the inija along with Bip Bentura, the man designated as holding that position; literate; still alive in 1695.

Bip Bentura, a leader of the 1677 anti-Chisca expedition; not literate; principal inija at San Luis in the mid-1680s, active in running the village at that time, also referred to as "governor" and as "order-giver"; 50 years old in 1687, still alive in 1695; also referred to as San Luis's head chacal.

Bernardo Ynachuba (Hinachuba), principal chief of Cupaica and the fourth leader of the 1677 anti-Chisca expedition; held rank of captain.

Tafunsaca Martín, principal chief of Faltassa, a satellite of Cupaica; died in 1669, designating an absent nephew, Tafunsaca Feliciano, as his successor.

Tafunsaca Feliciano, on arriving to claim the chieftainship of Faltassa, found that a determined usurper had been installed and did not then press his claim; died some time thereafter.

Nicolás Tafunsaca, brother of Feliciano; inija of Nicupana in 1677 and successfully pressed his claim to the chieftainship of Faltassa against the usurper in that year.

Tafunsaca Bauptista, parish interpreter at Cupaica in 1669; a witness to the last will of the dying chief of Faltassa along with Bernardo Ynachuba, Cupaica's head chief.

Osunaca Pedro Garcés, usurping chief of Faltassa for eight years (1669–1677); admitted his usurpation in the last year.

Francisco Luis, principal chief of San Luis in 1686; not clear if he was the Francisco Luis who was head chief in 1657; if he was, in 1686 he was fit enough to contemplate a trip to St. Augustine to complain about Antonio Matheos.

Alonso Pastrana, head chief of Patale in the mid-1680s; literate; led the native forces on one of Antonio Matheos's forays into the Apalachicola country in search of the English traders there; 49 years of age in 1686; still chief in 1688.

Quuy Olata Baltasar, identified by Chief Alonso Pastrana in 1687 as a chief at Bacuqua whom Antonio Matheos had struck with a cane because the chief had allegedly defrauded an Indian woman there.

Don Patricio Non Juluchba, chief of Capoli in 1687; not literate; 42 years old in 1687.

Osunaca Juan, chief of Abaslaco, a satellite of San Luis; not literate; was to join Francisco Luis and Matheo Chuba on trip to St. Augustine in 1686 to complain to the governor about Antonio Matheos's conduct and ask for his removal; 50 years old in 1687.

1688

Don Bentura, Chief of Ybitachuco; on B. Smith's facsimile of the Apalachee chiefs' letter to the king in their own tongue, signed his name as Dn Bra Ybitachuco holahta.

Don Patricio, chief of Santa Cruz; also signed the letter to the king even though he appears to be the chief of Capoli who, while testifying against Antonio Matheos, said that he could not write.

Don Ignacio, chief of Talpatqui, also a signer of the letter to the king.

Don Matheo Chuba and Don Alonso Pastrana, also letter signers.

Holata Juan Mendoza, the fifth signer; Holata here may represent his family surname rather than signify that he was a chief; still alive in 1695.

1694–1695

Don Bicente, chief of Escabí
Juan Mexía, chief of Bacuqua
Juan Mexía, chief of Ocuia
Usunaca Sebastian, chief of Ichasli
Cui Juan Mexía, supported Usunaca Matheo's claim describing himself as

chief and as older than Usunaca Matheo; this Cui Juan Mexía may be one of the two Juan Mexías mentioned above.

Pansacola Mexía and Chucuta Alonso, named by Usunaca Matheo as able to testify to the legitimacy of his claim.

Hinachuba Adrián, chief of Capoli, also spelled Hinaccuba (the name of Ivitachuco's Don Patricio was given the form "Ygnhac Chuba" on the 1698 visitation list); at the time of the Florencia visitation he had not been installed even though he was the legitimate heir; after confirming his claim, Florencia had him installed.

Don Andrés, principal chief of San Luis, coauthor of 1699 letter to the king; full name is Usunaca Andrés.

Don Patricio Hinachuba, chief of Ivitachuco; the other coauthor of the 1699 letter to the king; literate; bilingual; killed in battle early in 1705.

Usunaca Juan, still chief of Abaslaco in 1694, but his heir, Usunaca Matheo made an unsuccessful bid to oust him, claiming the incumbent was a usurper; Florencia upheld Usunaca Juan's claim.

Alonso, chief of Tomole

1698

At Ibitachuco

Don Patrizio Ygnhac Chuba, principal chief and field master
Niquichasli Antonio, a headman
Aque Ju°, a headman

At Ayubale

Ushina (?) Coaleixo, chief
Michasle Ebanjelista, a headman
Hina Adrián, a headman

At Oconi

Hina Alonso, a chief
Osonaca Ju°, a headman
Hina Alonso, a headman

At Ocuya

Osunaca Lorenzo, principal chief
Ymixa Mexís, a headman
Cui Bernardo, a headman

At Bacuqua

Usunaca Mexía, principal chief
Hina Felipe, a headman

At Escabí

Hina Bicente, chief
Esfana Labentura, a headman
Bis (?) Bautista, a headman

At San Luis

Osunaca Andrés, chief
Michasle Franc co, a headman
Mila Ysfani Alonso, a headman

At Thomoli

Osonaca Alonso, chief
Ysfania Alonso, a headman
Cui Patriburio, a headman

At Espalaga

Osonaca Benito, principal chief
Ysfani Bentura, a headman
Bi Ju°, a headman

At Capoli

Hinachuba Adrián, chief
Sabacola Feliziano, a headman
Cui Esteban, a headman

1704

Antonio Acuipa Feliciano, inija of San Luis, one of the Indians burned at the stake by Colonel Moore's Indians; he bore up heroically under the torture, preaching to his tormentors.
Luis Domingo, another Indian from San Luis singled out for torture.

1711

Hina Juan de Hita, chief of San Luis de Talimali; alias Abossaya, name of the village of refugee Apalachee at St. Augustine.

Viunac Pedro, referred to as "the old chief"; by 1717 apparently the chief again with his name as Pedro Osunaca.

Savacola Bernardo, leader in San Luis de Talimali; alias Abossaya.

1717

Adrián, chief of the former village of Bacuqua, then living among the Creek; a frequent visitor to St. Augustine and St. Marks during the next two years; served as interpreter for Diego Peña in his 1717 contacts with the Creek, translating from Apalachee into Uchisi; Barcia reports him as having visited St. Augustine as early as 1711.

Marcos, one of the party of Apalachee and Creek leaders sent to Mexico City to visit the viceroy; there named head chief and governor of the Apalachee; directed the foundation of the Apalachee settlement of San Luis de Soledad near Pensacola in 1718; led some Apalachee from that village to take part in the foundation of a new Apalachee settlement near St. Marks; when Pensacola came under French attack in 1719, raised a small force in the Creek country to assist in its defense but upon his arrival found that it had fallen.

Note: The script for some of these names is not very legible, and the rendition of those with question marks is tentative. Also some of the letters *m* should be rendered *n* instead. In one of the Usunacas, the *n* looked very much like an *m*. Usunaca and Osonaca are variants of the same name. The Ygnhac in Don Patricio's name appears to be a variant of Hina. It is not clear whether all of the other Hinas are related to the Hinachubas, or whether the numerous Usunacas also are related. However, the predominance of those two names among those in positions of power, together with the identification of those two names with the two principal villages of San Luis and Ivitachuco, suggests that they may represent two leading families in this era.

Appendix 12

Variant Versions of Colonel James Moore's Letters about His Assault on Apalachee

APPENDIX 12 contains copies of the versions of Colonel Moore's letters to the governor of South Carolina and to the lords proprietors that are held by the Library of Congress and the South Carolina Archives, along with the versions published in Boyd, Smith, and Griffin, *Here They Once Stood* and in Carroll's *Historical Collections of South Carolina*.

To highlight the divergences, the Library of Congress version will be compared to that in the South Carolina Archives and points of difference that are of historical significance will be marked with a degree symbol (°). Words or phrases found only in one of the versions will also be so marked. Differences in spelling and capitalization will not be noted except for the variant spellings of Ivitachuco. Divergences in punctuation will be marked only when they alter the meaning significantly.

Boyd's version of the two letters will be compared with the Library of Congress version that Boyd cited as his source. Historically significant points at which Boyd's version diverges from its alleged source will be marked with an asterisk (*) unless the language follows the Carroll version. Boyd's borrowings from the Carroll version will be marked with a dagger (†). Carroll's version of the letter to the governor will be compared to its counterpart in the Library of Congress and the significant divergences indicated thus.°

Library of Congress Version

Extract of Col° Moore's Letter to the Lords Proprietors 16 April 1704

I will not trouble Your Lordships with a Relation of the many Hazards and Difficulties I underwent in my Expedition against Apalatchie but beg leave to let you know what I have done there.

By my own Interest and at my own Charge I raised 50 Whites, all the Government thought fit to spare out of the Settlement at that time; with them and 1000 Indians, wch by my own Interest I raised to follow me, I went to Apalatchie. The first place I came to was the strongest Fort in Apalatchee, wch after Nine Hours Storm I took, and in it 200 Persons alive, and killed 20 Men in the Engagement.° I had killed 3 Whites and 4 Indians: of the last there were but 15 ever came within Shott of the Fort. The next Morning the Captain of the Fort of St Lewis and Governor of the Province of Apalatchee, with all the Forces of Whites and Indians he Could raise in the Province came and gave me Battle in the Field; after half an hours Fight we routed them, and in the Fight and Flight killed Six Spaniards, one of which was a Fryar; took the Captain and Governor and Adjutant General and Seven Men Spaniards Prisoners, and killed and took 200 Indian Men. In this Fight my Captain was killed and 11 of my Indians. I lay in the Field of Battle four days, some of my wounded Men, not being in a Condition to March, or to be carried any way° in this time.° The next strongest Fort was surrendered to me upon Conditions. On the 5th day I marched to two more Forts, both wch were delivered up to me, without Conditions, & the Men Women and Children of the whole Town, wch were in it, Prisoners at Discretion. In one of these° Forts I lodged one Night; the next day I marched to two more Forts, both wch with the People that were in them were delivered to me without Conditions, as were the two other Forts. In one of these I lay two Nights, here I offered freedom of Persons and Goods, to as many Kings, as with all the People under their Government° would go along with me, and live under and subject themselves to Our Government. On these Terms four Kings and all their People, came away with me; and part of the People of four more Kings; wch I have planted among Our Indians, and put them out of a Capacity of returning back again alone° In this Expedition I brought away 300 Men,° and 1000 Women and Children° have killed,° and taken as Slaves 325 Men, and have taken Slaves 4000 Women and Children;° tho' I did not make Slave, or put to Death one Man, Woman or Child but what were° taken in the Fight, or in the Fort I took by Storm. All wch I have done with the loss of 4 Whites and 15 Indians, and without One Penny Charge to the Publick. Before this Expedition we were more afraid of the Spaniards of Apalatchee and their Indians in Conjunction with the French of Missisippi, and their Indians doing us Harm by Land, than of any Forces of the Enemy by

Sea. This has wholly disabled them from attempting any thing against Us by Land, the whole Strength of Apalatchee not exceeding 300 Indians and 24 Whites, who cannot now (as I have Seated Our Indians) come at me° that way, must° they must March thro' 300° Indian Men Our Friends, wch were before this Conquest of Apalatchee (for fear of the Spaniards and their Indians)° every day moving to the Northward of Us.

That Colony of the French wch is Situated on the River Missisippi, are not the French we have reason to fear; they have seated another° Colony on a River called Coosa Six days Journey nearer us than Missisippi, and not above 50 Miles° from us than Apalatchee. These French and their Indians (if suffered to live where they are now) will be no less a dangerous Enemy to us in Peace, than in War, it being much easier for them to Cut off Our° Settlements from this Place, than it is for the Canada Indians to Cut off the Inland Towns in New England.

Col° Moores Letter to Sir Nathaniel Johnson 16. April 1704

May it please Your Honour,

To accept of this short Narration of what I, with the Army under my Command, have been doing since my departure from the Ockmulgees, wch was on the 19th of Decr On the 14th of January at Sun rising we came to a Town, a strong and almost regular Fort, called Aiavalla.° At Our first Approach the Indians in it fired, and shot Arrows at Us briskly, from wch we hid and Sheltered Ourselves under the Side of a great Mud Walled House, til we could take a View of the Fort, & consider of the best way of assaulting it, wch we concluded to be by breaking open the Church Doors, which were a part of the Fort, with Axes.

I no sooner proposed this, but my Men readily undertook it, run up to it briskly (the Enemy at the same time shooting at them) were beaten off, without effecting it, and 14 White Men wounded. Two Hours after that, we thought fit to attempt burning the Church which we did, three or four Indians assisting Us in it we burnt it. The Indians in it obstinately defended themselves and killed us two Men Viz! Francis Plonden and Thomas Dale. After we were within their Fort a Fryar, the only wch in it, came forth and beged Mercy: In this We took 26 Men Alive and 58 Women and Children,° the Indians took about as many more of each sort. The Fryar told us we killed in the two Storms 24 Men.

The next morning the Captain of St Lewis's Fort with 23 Whites and 400 Indians came to fight us, wch we did, beat him, and took° eight of his Men Prisoners. And as the Indians (wch say they did it) tell us, killed 5 or 6 Whites; We have a particular Account of 168 Indian Men killed and taken in this Fight and Flight. The Apalatchee Indians say they lost 200, wch we have reason to believe to be the least. In this Fight Captain John Berringer, fighting bravely in the Head of Our° Men, was killed at my Foot. Captain Fox died of a Wound given him in Our first Storming of the Fort.

Two days after I sent to the King of the Attachookas (who with 130 Men was in his strong and well made Fort) to come to me to make his Peace with me, he did it, and compounded for it with his° Church Plate & led Horses loaden with Provisions. After this I marched thro' Five Towns, wch have all strong Forts and Defences against small Armies, they all submitted and surrendered their Forts to me without Conditions. I have now in my Company all the whole People of three Towns, and the greatest part of four more; We have totally destroyed all the People of two Towns, so that we have left in Apalatchee but that one Town wch compounded with me. Part of St Lewis's and the People of one Town wch run away altogether, their Town, Church, and Fort, we have burnt. The People of S^t. Lewis's wch remain, come unto me every Night. I expect, and have Advice, that the Town, wch compounded with me, are coming after me. The waiting for these People make my Marches slow; for I am willing to bring away° free, as many of the Indians as I can; this being the Address of the Commons to° order it so. This will make my Mens parts of Plunder (wch otherwise might have been 100 p man) but small, but I hope with your honours' Assistance, to find a way to gratify them for their bold and stout Actions, and their great Loss of Blood. I never saw, or heard of a stouter or braver Thing done than the Storming the Fort, it hath regained the Reputation we seemed to have lost under the Conduct of Captain Mackie, the Indians having now a mighty Value for the Whites.

Apalatchee is now reduced to that feeble and low Condition, that it neither can supply S^t. Augustine with Provisions, or disturb, damage or frighten Our Indians living between us and Apalatchee, and° the French. In short we have made Carolina as safe, as the Conquest of Apalatchee can make it.

If I had not had so many Men wounded in Our first Attempt, I had assaulted St Lewis's Fort in wch is now but 28 or 30 Men, and 20 of these came thence from Pansicola to buy Provisions the first Night after I took the first Fort.

On Sunday the 23^d of this Month I came out of Apalatchee Settlement, and am now about 30 Miles in my way home, but do not expect to reach it til about the middle of March; notwithstanding my Horses will not be able to carry me° Cherokee Nations°.

I have had a dirty, tedious and uneasy Journey, and tho' I have no reason to fear any Harm from the Enemy, thro' the Difference between the Whites and the Indians, between Indian and Indian, bad way and false Alarms, do still labour under hourly Uneasinesses. The number of free Apalatchee Indians, wch are now under my Protection, bound with me to Carolina, are 300; the Indians under my Command killed and took Prisoners in the Plantations, whilst we stormed the Fort, as many Indians as we and they took and killed in the Fort.

I am etc
Ja. Moore

South Carolina Archive Version

Extract of Colonel Moore's Letter to the Lords Proprietors 16th April 1704

I will not trouble Your Lordships with a relation of the many Hazards and difficultys I underwent in my Expedition against Apallachee, but beg leave to let you know what I have done there.

By my Own Interest and at my own Charge, I rais'd fifty Whites all the Government thought fit to Spare out of the Settlement at that time, with them and one Thousand Indians, which by my own Interest I raised to follow me, I went to Apalachee. The first place I came to, was the Strongest Fort in Apalachee, which after nine hours Storm I took, and in it Two hundred Persons alive, and kill'd 20 Men, in this Engagement° I had kill'd three Whites and four Indians of the last there was but fifteen ever come within Shott of the Fort. The next Morning the Captⁿ of the Fort of S^t. Lewis and the Governor of the Province of Apalachee, with all the Forces of whites and Indians he could raise in the Province came and gave me Battle in the Field; after half an hours' fight, we routed them, and in the Fight and Flight kill'd Six Spaniards, one of which was a Fryer, took the Captain and Governor and the Adjutant General, and Seven Men Spaniards Prisoners, and kill'd and took Two Hundred Indian Men, In this Fight my Captain was kill'd and Eleven of my Indians. I lay in the Field of Battle four days, some of my Wounded Men not being in a Condition to march, or be carried any way;° in this time the next strongest Fort was Surrender'd to me on Conditions, on the fifth day I march'd to two more Forts, both which were delivered up to me without Conditions, And the Men, Women and Children of the whole Town, which were in it Prisoners at Discretion. In one of the Forts I lodg'd one night the next day I march't to two more Forts, both which with the People that were in them, were delivered to me without Conditions, as were the two other Forts. In one of these I lay two Nights; here I offered freedom of Persons and Goods to as many Kings, as with all the People under their Government would go along with me, and live under, and Subject themselves to our Governments°, on these Terms four Kings with all their People came away with me. And part of the People of four more Kings, which I have planted among our Indians, and put them out of a

Capacity of returning back again alive°, In this Expedition I have brought away free 300 Men° and 1000 Women and Children,° have kill'd ° and taken as Slaves 325 Men, and have taken Slaves 4000 Women and Children,° tho' I did not make Slaves or put to Death One Man, Woman or Child, but what were kill'd° and° taken in the Fight, or in the Fort I took by Storm All which I have done with the loss of 4 Whites and 15 Indians, and without One penny Charge to the Public. Before this Expedition we were more afraid of the Spaniards of Apalachee and their Indians in Conjunction with the French of Mississcipi, and their Indians doing us harm by Land, than of any Forces of the Enemy by Sea, this hath wholly disabled them to Attempt any thing against us by Land, the whole Strength of Apalachee not exceeding three hundred Indians and 24 Whites, who cannot now (as I have seated Our Indians) come at us° that way, but° they must march thro 900° Indian Men our Friends, which before this Conquest of Apalachee were (for fear of the Spaniards and their Indians° every day removing to the Northward of us.

That Colony of the French which is Seated on the River Mississcipi, are not the French we have reason to fear, they have Seated a° Colony on a River called Coosa six days Journey nearer us than Mississipi, and not above 50 Miles further° from us than Apalachee. These French and their Indians (if Suffered to live where they are now) will be no less a dangerous Enemy to us in Peace than in Warr, It being much easier for them to Cut off our Out° Settlements from this place, than it is for the Canada Indians to Cut off the Inland Towns of New England.

Extract of Colonel Moore's Letter to Sr Nathaniel Johnson 16th April 1704

May it Please Your Honour

To accept of this Short Narration of what I with the Army under my Command have been doing since my Departure from the Ockmulgees, which was on the 19th of December. On the 14th of January at sun rising we came to a Town, a Strong and almost regular Fort, called Aiaivalla,° at our first Approach the Indians in it fired and Shott Arrows at us Briskley, from which we hid and Sheltered Ourselves under the side of a great Mud Wall'd House till we could take a View of the Fort and Consider of the best way of assaulting it, which we concluded to be by breaking open the Church Doors, which were a part of the Fort with Axes.

I no Sooner proposed this, but my Men readily undertook it run up to it briskly, (the Enemy at the same time shooting at them) were beaten off without effecting it and 14 White men wounded. Two hours after that, we thought fit to attempt burning the Church which we did, 3 or 4 Indians Assisting us in it, We burnt it; The Indians in it obstinately defended themselves and kill'd us two Men Viz! Francis Plowden and Thomas Dale, after we were within their Fort A Fryer the only which in it, came forth and beg'd Mercy: In this we took 26 Men alive and 58 Women and° The Indians took about as many more of each Sort. The Fryer told us we had kill'd in the two Storms 24 Men.

The next Morning the Captain of S' Lewis's Fort with 23 Whites and 400 Indians came to fight us, which we did, beat him and took him° and ° Eight of his Men Prisoners, and as the Indians (which say they did it) tell us, kill'd 5 or 6 Whites. We have a particular Account of 168 Indian Men killed and taken in the Fight and flight. The Apalachee Indians say they lost 200, which we have reason to believe to be the least in this Fight, Captain John Berringer fighting bravely in the head of our [own?][1] Men was kill'd at my Foot, Captain Fox died of a Wound given him at our first Storming of the Fort.

Two days after I sent to the King of the Attachookas, (who with 130 Men was in his strong and well made Fort) to come to me to make his Peace with me, he did it and Compounded for it, with the Church Plate, and lead Horses Loaden with Provisions. After this I marched thro five Towns, which have all Strong Forts and defences against small Armys, They all Submitted and Surrend'd their Forts to me without Conditions. I have now in my Company all the whole People of Three Towns and the greatest part of four more. we have totally destroyed all the People of two Towns so that we have left in Apalachee, but that one Town which Compounded with me, Part of S' Lewis's and the People of one Town which run away altogether. their Town, Church and Fort we have burnt. the People of S' Lewis's which remain come in to me every Night. I expect and have advice that the Town which Compounded with me are coming after me. The Waiting for these People make my marches Slow, for I am willing to bring away with° me° free as many of the Indians as I can this being the address of the Commons to° Your° Honour° to order it so. This will make my Men's Parts of Plunder (which might otherwise have been 100£ p Man,[2] but small, but I hope with your Honour's Assistance to find a way to Gratify them for their Bold and Stout Actions and their great loss of Blood. I never see or heard of a stouter or braver thing done than the Storming the Fort, it hath regained the Reputation we seemed to have lost under the Conduct of Capt. Mackey, the Indians having now a mighty value for the Whites.

1. The photostat of this document is a poor one and one can make out that there is a three-letter word here only with great difficulty. Hence my rendition here is tentative. The word "own" does not appear in the library's version at this point. As the punctuation photostated very poorly in places my rendition of the punctuation is tentative in places.
2. The close-parentheses appears here in the library's version. I was not able to detect any sign of the close-parentheses here or elsewhere in this photostat.

Apalachee is now reduced to that Feeble and low Condition, that it can neither Supply St Augustine with Provisions or disturb damage or frighten our Indians living between us and Apalachee or° the French, in Short we have made Carolina as safe as the Conquest of Apalachee can make it.

If I had not so many Men wounded in our first attempt, I had assaulted St Lewis's Fort, in which is now but 28 or 30 Men and 20 of these came thence from Pançicola to buy Provisions the first night after I took the first Fort.

On Sunday the 23rd of this Month I came out of Apalachee Settlement, and am now about 30 Miles in my way home; but do not expect to reach it 'till about the Middle of March, notwithstanding my Horses will not be able to carry me to° the° Cherokee Mountains°.

I have had a Dirty, tedious uneasie Journey. And tho' I have no reason to fear any harm from the Enemy, thro the Differences between the Whites and Indians, between Indian and Indian, bad way and false alarms, do still labour under hourly uneasynesses. The Number of free Apalachee Indians, which are now under my Protection bound with me to Carolina are 300. The Indians under my Command kill'd and took Prisoners in the Plantations whilst we Stormed the Fort, as Many Indians as we and they took and kill'd in the Fort.

I am

Your Hon^s

Most Faithful Oblig'd humble Servant

Ja. Moore

The Boyd Version

Col° Moore's Letter to Sir Nathaniel Johnson 16 April, 1704

May it please Your Honour,

To accept of this short Narrative of what I, with the Army under my Command, have been doing since my departure from the Ockmulgee*, which was on the 19th of December. On the 14th of January at the Sun rising we came to a Town, a strong and almost regular Fort, called Aiavalla [Ayubale]:* at our first Approach the Indians in it fired, and shot Arrows at Us briskly, from which we hid and Sheltered Ourselves under the Side of a great Mud Walled House, til we could take a View of the Fort, and consider of the best way of assaulting it, which we concluded to be by breaking open the Church Doors, which were a part of the Fort, with Axes.

I no sooner proposed this, but my Men readily undertook it, run up to it briskly (the Enemy at the same time shooting at them) were beaten off, without effecting it, and 14 white men wounded. Two hours after that we thought fit to attempt burning the church, which we did, three or four Indians assisting us in it we burnt it. The Indians in it obstinately defended themselves and killed us two men, viz., Francis Plowden† and Thomas Dale. After we were within their Fort a Fryar, the only [white]† within it, came forth and begged mercy: In this we took 26 men alive and 58 women and children, the Indians took about as many more of each sort. The Fryar told us we killed in the two storms 24 men.

The next morning the Captain of St. Lewis's Fort with 23 Whites and 400 Indians came to fight us, which we did, beat him, and took eight of his men prisoners. And as the Indians (which say they did it) tell us, killed 5 or 6 whites. We have a particular account of 168 Indian men killed and taken in this fight and flight. The Apalatchee Indians say they lost 200, which we have reason to believe* the least. In this fight Captain John Berringer, fighting bravely in the head of our men, was killed at my foot. Captain Fox died of a wound given him in our first storming of the fort.

Two days after I sent to the King of the Attachookas [Ivitachuco]* (who with 130 men was in his strong and well-made Fort) to come to me to make his peace with me, he did it, and compounded for it with his church plate and led horses leaden* with provisions. After this I marched thro' two* towns, which have all strong Forts and defenses against small armies [sic], they all submitted and surrendered their Forts to me without conditions. I have now in my company all the whole people of three towns, and the greatest part of four more; we have totally destroyed all the people of two towns, so that we have left in Apalatchee but that one town which compounded with me, part of St. Lewis's and the people of one town which run away altogether, their town, church, and fort, we have burnt. The people of St. Lewis's which remain, come unto me every night. I expect, and have advice, that the town which compounded with me, are coming after me. The waiting for these people make my marches slow; for I am willing to bring away free, as many Indians as I can, this being the address of the commons to order it so. This will make my mens part of plunder (which otherwise might have been £100 per man) but small, but I hope with your Honour's assistance, to find a way to gratify them for their bold and stout actions, and their great loss of blood. I never saw, or heard, of a stouter or braver thing done than the storming of the fort; it hath regained the reputation we seemed to have lost under the conduct of Captain Mackie, the Indians having now a mighty value for the whites.

Apalatchee is now reduced to that feeble and low condition, that it neither can supply St. Augustine with provisions, or disturb, damage or frighten our Indians living between us and Apalatchee, and the French. In short, we have made Carolina as safe as the conquest of Apalatchee can make it.

If I had not had so many men wounded in our first attempt, I had assaulted St. Lewis's fort, in which is now but 28 or 30 men, and 20 of these came thence from Pensacola† to buy provisions the first night after I took the first Fort.

On Sunday the 23rd of this month I came out of Apalatchee settlement, and am now about 30 miles in my way home, but do not expect to reach it til about the middle of March, notwithstanding my horses will not be able to carry me [to the]* Cherokee Nations.

I have had a dirty, tedious and uneasy journey, and tho I have no reason to fear any harm from the enemy, thro the difference between the Whites and the Indians, between Indian and Indian, bad way and false alarms, do still labour under hourly uneasinesses. The number of free Apalatchee Indians, which are not* under my protection, bound with me to Carolina, are 300; the Indians under my command killed and took prisoners in the plantations, whilst we stormed the Fort, as many Indians as we and they took and killed in the Fort.

I am &

Ja. Moore

Extract of Colonel Moore's letter to the Lords Proprietors, 16 April, 1704

I will not trouble Your Lordships with a relation of the many hazards and difficulties I underwent in my expedition against Apalatchee, but beg leave to let you know what I have done there.

By my own interest and at my own charge I raised 50 whites, all the Government thought fit to spare out of the settlement at that time; with them and 1000 Indians, which by my own interest I raised to follow me, I went to Apalatchee: The first place I came to was the strongest Fort in Apalatchee, which after nine hours I took, and in it 200 persons alive, and killed 20 men in the engagement. I had killed 3 whites and 4 Indians; of the last there were but 15 ever came within shot of the Fort. The next morning the Captain of the Fort of St. Lewis and Governor of the Province of Apalatchee, with all the force of Whites and Indians he could raise in the Province came and gave me battle in the field; after half an hour's fight we routed them and in the fight and flight killed six Spaniards, one of which was a Fryar; took the Captain and Governor and Adjutant General and Seven men Spaniards prisoners, and killed and took 200 Indian men. In this fight my Captain was killed and 11 of my Indians. I lay in the field of battle four days, some of my wounded men not being in a condition to march, or to be carried any way in this time. The next strongest Fort was surrendered to me upon conditions. On the 5th day I marched to two more Forts, both which were deliverd up to me, without conditions, and the men, women and children of the whole town, which were in it, prisoners at discretion. In one of these Forts I lodged one night; the next day I marched to two more Forts, both [of] which with the people that were in them were delivered to me without conditions, as were the two other Forts. In one of these I lay two nights, here I offered freedom of persons and goods, to as many Kings, as with all the people under their government would go along with me, and live under and subject themselves to our Government. On these terms four Kings and all their people, came away with me, and part of the people of four more Kings; which I have planted among our Indians, and put them out of a capacity of returning back again alone [.] In this expedition I brought away 300 men, and 1000 women and children,* have killed, and taken as slaves 325 men, and have taken slaves 4000 women and children; tho I did not make slave, or put to death one man, woman or child but what were taken in the fight, or in the Fort I took by storm. All which I have done with the loss of 4 whites and 15 Indians, and without one penny charge to the publick. Before this expedition we were more afraid of the Spaniards of Apalatchee and their Indians in conjunction* the French of Mississippi, and their Indians doing us harm by land, than of any forces of the enemy by sea. This has wholly disabled them from attempting anything against us by land, the whole strength of Apalatchee not exceeding 300 Indians and 24 Whites, who cannot now (as I have seated our Indians) come at me that way, must they must [sic]* March thro' 300 Indian men our friends, which were before this conquest of Apalatchee (for fear of the Spaniards and their Indians) every day moving to the Northway of us.

That colony of the French which is situated on the River Mississippi, are not the French we have reason to fear; they have seated another colony on a river called Coosa six days journey nearer us than Mississippi, and not above 50 miles from us than Apalatchee. These French and their Indians (if suffered to live where they are now) will be no less a dangerous enemy to us in peace than in war, it being much easier for them to cut off our settlements from this place, than it is for the Canada Indians to cut off the inland towns in New England.

The Carroll version

Account

To the Governour of Carolina:

May it please your honour to accept of this short narrative of what I, with the army under my command, have been doing since my departure from the Ockomulgee°, on the 19th of December.

On the 14th of December° we came to a town, and strong and almost regular fort, about Sun rising called Ayaville.° At our first approach the Indians in it fired and shot arrows at us briskly; from which we° sheltered ourselves under the side of a great Mud-walled house, till we could take a view of the fort; and consider of the best way of assaulting it: which we concluded to be, by breaking the church door, which made a part of the fort, with axes. I no sooner proposed this, but my men readily undertook it: ran up to it briskly, (the enemy at the same time shooting at them,) were beaten off without effecting it, and fourteen white men wounded. Two hours after that, we thought fit to attempt the burning of the church, which we did, three or four Indians assisting us.° The Indians° obstinately defending themselves, killed us two men, viz. Francis Plowden° and Thomas Dale. After we were in their fort, a fryar, the only white° in it, came forth and begged mercy. In this we took about° twenty-six men alive, and fifty-eight women and children. The Indians took about as many more of each sort. The fryar told us we killed, in the two storms of the fort, twenty-five° men.

The next morning the captain of St. Lewis Fort, with twenty-three men and four hundred Indians, came to fight us, which we did; beat him; took him° and eight of his men prisoners; and, as the Indians, which say° it, told us, killed five or six whites. We have a particular account from° our° Indians° of one hundred and sixty-eight Indian men killed and taken in the fight;° but° the Apalatchia Indians say they lost two hundred, which we have reason to believe to be the least. ° Capt. John Bellinger° , fighting bravely at the head of our men, was killed at my foot. Capt. Fox dyed of a wound given him at the first storming of the fort. Two days after, I sent to the cassique° of the Ibitachka°, who, with one hundred and thirty men, was in his strong and well made fort, to come° and make his peace with me, the° which° he did,° and compounded for it with his church's plate, and ten° horses laden with provisions. After this, I marched through five towns, which had all strong forts, and defences against small arms.° They all submitted and surrendered their forts to me without condition. I have now in my company all the whole people of three towns, and the greatest part of four more. We have totally destroyed all the people of four° towns: so that we have left the° Apalatchia° but that one town which compounded with° one° part of St. Lewis;° and the people of one town, which run away altogether: their town, church and fort, we burnt. The people of St. Lewis came° to me every night. I expect and have advice that the town which compounded with me are coming after me. The waiting for these people make my marches slow; for I am willing to bring away with° me,° free, as many of the Indians as I can, this being the address of the commons to° your° honour° to order it so. This will make my men's part of plunder (which otherwise might have been 100£ to a man) but small. But I hope with your honour's assistance to find a way to gratifie them for° their° loss of blood. I never see° or hear° of a stouter or braver thing done, than the storming of the fort. It hath regained the reputation we seemed to have lost under the conduct of Robert Macken°, the Indians now having a mighty value for the whites. Apalatchia is now reduced to so° feeble and low a condition, that it can neither support St. Augustine with provisions, nor distrust°, endamage or frighten us°:° our Indians living between° the Apalatchia and the French. In short, we have made Carolina as safe as the conquest of Apalachia can make it.

If I had not° so many men wounded in our first attempt, I had assaulted St. Lewis fort, in which is about 28 or 30 men, and 20 of these came thither from Pensacola° to buy provisions the first night after I took the first fort.

On Sabbath°, the 23rd instant°, I came out of Apalatchia settle,° and am now about 30 miles on my way home; but do not expect to reach it before° the middle of March, notwithstanding my horses will not be able to carry me to° the° Cheeraque°'s Mountain°. I have had a tedious° duty°, and uneasy journey; and though I have no reason to fear any harm from the enemy, through the difference between the whites°, and between Indians and Indians, bad way and false alarms, I do° labour under hourly uneasiness. The number of free Apalatchia Indians that are now under my protection, and bound with me to Carolina, are 1300°, and° 100° slaves°. The Indians under my command killed and took prisoners in the plantations, whilst we stormed the fort, as many Indians as we and they took and killed in the fort.

°Dated° in the woods° 50° miles° north° and east° of Apalatchia.°

THE END

Glossary

Acchuma fino—Indian tobacco.

Alabama—An Upper Creek tribe, whose language is one of two to which Apalachee is believed to be most closely related. "As shown by their language and indicated by some of their traditions," Swanton noted, "[the Alabama] were connected more nearly with the Choctaw and Chickasaw than with the Creek. Stiggins declares that the Choctaw, Chickasaw, Hitchiti, and Koasati languages were mutually intelligible, and this was true at least of Choctaw, Chickasaw, and Koasati" (Swanton 1922:191).

Amacano—Non-Apalachee natives with whom the Apalachee were at war in the 1630s. By 1674 the Amacano had settled in Apalachee and were part of a mission in association with the Capara and the Chine. Swanton believed they may have been Yamasee.

Amapexas—The only natives mentioned as present in Apalachee in 1723. Presumably they were Yamasee. A group called Macapexos were living in a village near St. Augustine in 1726 (rendered as Amacapiras by Swanton [1946:195] and Macapiras by Geiger [1940:133]) in association with the Chiluca of San Buenaventura.

Apalachicola—The name applied by seventeenth-century Spaniards to the natives living along the Chattahoochee River, known later to English and Americans as Creek or, rather, Lower Creek. The Spaniards also used the name to identify a specific village along that river that once seemed to occupy a leadership position among the Hitchiti-speaking villages there. Based on the Lamhatty testimony, Swanton (1946:92) also applied the name to four towns (Ephippick, Aulédy, Socsósky, and Sunepáh) on or near the Apalachicola River when they were attacked by Indians allied with the English. The inhabitants carried off were

399

settled on the Savannah River at a place later known as Palachocolas.
After the Yamasee War they established Chislacasliche on the former
site of Sabacola Chuba just above the confluence of the Flint and the
Chattahoochee rivers. The Diego Peña journals reveal that contemporaneously there was still a separate village of Apalachicola a little over
six days' journey north of Chislacasliche's town. Chislacasliche was
identified in 1717 as chief of the province of the Uchises (Ayala y Escobar 1717:37).

Atabac—A tobacco substitute prescribed for certain ceremonies associated
with the ball game.

Atequi—A native name for the interpreter used by Spanish officials dealing
with the Indians and by the friars for communication with their flocks.
In some circumstances the *atequis* seem routinely to have handled
clerical functions such as catechetical instructions. The position often
attracted natives from the leadership class who were literate as well as
bilingual. The term's linguistic origin is unknown. It was used by the
Spaniards before they began the evangelization of Apalachee, usually
in the form *athequi*. In the form *yatiqui* it was found later among the
Creek as well.

Barbacoa—A native term, probably Arawak, used by Spaniards to designate
variously the principal fire in the council house, the niches in the
council house wall used for seating and sleeping, the bed frame of reed
bars in the natives' houses, and, possibly, the platform for smoking
meat and fish.

Batea—The name given to the kneading trough in most parts of America.

Buhio or *bohio* or *bujio*—The name, probably Arawak, used by the Spaniards
to designate both the council house and the hut of the Apalachee. The
council house was known as the *buhio principal*.

Cacina—The native tea used by the Apalachee and other Indians of the
Southeast, made of the toasted and powdered leaves of the yaupon
holly. It was similar to South America's yerba mate.

Calusa or Calos or Carlos—The most important South Florida natives, living
around Charlotte Harbor and the mouth of the Caloosahatchie River.

Capara—See Pacara.

Casista—The Spanish name for an important Lower Creek town, known in
English sources as Kasihta. Swanton (1946:143) identified it as one of
the two great tribes constituting the larger part of the pure Muskogee
element among the Lower Creek.

Caveta or Cabeta—Spanish name for Coweta, the other great pure Muskogee
town of the Lower Creek and the uppermost of these towns on the
Chattahoochee both geographically and politically for much of the

second half of the seventeenth century. It led the opposition to a Spanish alliance.

Chacal—An Indian official, at times identical with the inija, but not always, who served as a sort of overseer directing community work. His duties seem to have been akin to those of the Spanish municipal official known as the *fiscal,* and the Spaniards often used the words *chacal* and *fiscal* interchangeably. For Guale and neighboring Timucua a Carmelite based in Mexico (García 1902) used the word, spelled *jacal,* to signify a large round community building in the Asao towns that was made of whole pines without branches and poorly stripped of their bark with their tops bunched together like the ribs of a parasol. In this sense the term is probably of Mexican origin and meant Indian hut or wigwam. Kessell (1979:105) used the term to describe the temporary structure built by the Pecos to serve as the first church at the mission at Cicuye.

Chacato—The name applied by the Spaniards to an eastern offshoot of the Choctaw, apparently long separated from them, who in the seventeenth century lived in the Florida Panhandle in the vicinity of Marianna and at times in association with the Pansacola. Some moved to Apalachee shortly after being missionized. Swanton believed the Choctawhatchee River was probably named for them. In modern works they are usually referred to as Chatot.

Chasta—Two women of the nation were listed as living at the Apalachee village of Abosaia (near St. Augustine) in 1717. Swanton does not mention a Chasta nation. Possibly they were Chasee, a division of the Lower Yamasee.

Chicasa—The native name applied to the site of an abandoned village and to its surrounding lands. It probably is an Apalachee term.

Chichimeco (occasionally spelled Chichumeco)—The name applied by the Spaniards in Florida to certain bands of warlike, savage, and somewhat nomadic Indians. English sources and Swanton identify them with the Yuchi, but the Spaniards seem to have regarded them as a group distinct from the Yuchi, although related to them. In one document a Spanish official spoke of a group of Chichimeco identifying themselves by that name and spoke of using a Yuchi as an interpreter to communicate with them. There are repeated references to these people as "eaters of human flesh." Consequently, the Florida Spaniards' Chichimeco appear to be the Westo of the Savannah River area, of whom Maurice Mathews remarked in 1671, in describing the natives of coastal South Carolina, that they instilled such fear in the others that they were "Affraid of ye very footstep of a Westo which they say eat people and are great warriors." The same inference of cannibalism may have been intended when A. Leturiondo ([1700]: 177) referred to the Chisca as Caribs. In Mexico both the Spaniards and the sedentary civilized natives used the name Chichimec as a generic designation for most of the uncivilized natives of the central highlands north of the Aztec and Tarascan territory. The Aztec themselves, before their absorption of the high civilization of central Mexico, had been regarded as Chichimec. Among the Mexican natives the name meant "people of dog lineage." In 1662, Governor Aranguiz reported that a band of Chichimeco, who said they were from Jacan (Virginia), swept through the province of Guale wreaking havoc, then passed to the provinces of La Tama and Catufa. When the Spaniards took four of them prisoner, they brought in some Chisca from Apalachicola as interpreters.

Chine—A group of non-Apalachee natives who settled in Apalachee in the seventeenth century. Most modern authorities identify them with the Chacato, but the Spaniards do not seem to have used the names interchangeably. When the Spaniards needed pilots for sailing along Florida's Gulf coast toward Pensacola, they used the Chine. They probably were a band of Chacato, however, and may have taken or been given the name Chine from the Chief Chine recorded by Fray Barreda and Governor Torres y Ayala as having served with his son as pilot on the ketch that formed the maritime arm of the governor's expedition to Pensacola Bay. In the governor's journal they are mentioned in association with the Chacato as people with a knowledge of the territory between Pensacola and Mobile. Claraquachine is one of the names for the Ochlockonee (Milán Tapia 1693:283), and Penicault reported a group of Apalachee who reached Mobile late in 1705 (probably Cupaicans from Pensacola), stating that they were from a village near the River of Tolacatchina (McWilliams 1953).

Chisca or Ysica—A widely dispersed, warlike, nomadic people who were, at times, a thorn in the side of the Spaniards and the Christian Apalachee and Chacato. They appear to be the same people identified by eighteenth-century Spaniards as Yuchi and by the English as Uchee and Euchee. However, Diego Peña (Boyd 1952) spoke of the Uchisi and Uche tongues as separate languages. Chisca were involved in the 1647 revolt in Apalachee and the 1674–1675 troubles in the Chacato missions. A Chisca settlement in West Florida attacked by the Apalachee in 1677 was shared by Chacato and by Pansacola. Juan Pardo encountered Chisca in the Tennessee mountains in the 1560s, and de Soto's Quisquis are believed to have been Chisca. See also Chichimeco.

Chuba—An Apalachee term that apparently means "big," "great," or "powerful." It also was spelled *cuba, chua,* and probably *chuco* and appears to be the same word as the Creek *thlucco.* It formed part of the name of one of the influential families in Apalachee.

Cuy—The Apalachee word for panther. It appeared commonly as a surname, as in Cuy Bernardo.

Doctrina—The name used by the Spaniards to designate a principal mission center in Florida.

Ducat—11 reales.

Encomienda—An assignment of tributes and services from an Indian community to favored individuals or reserved to the Crown itself. The system was designed practically to assure an adequate supply of foodstuffs and Indian labor for the Spanish community and theoretically to provide a framework for the Christianization and acculturation of the natives.

Garita—The Spaniards' name for the Apalachee's food storage structure. In modern Spanish it means "sentry box," "porter's lodge," or "privy."

Gua—A native gesture of reverence made with the hands placed together straight. The word *gua* was pronounced while making the gesture. It was also used as a salutation to the chief, seemingly like the Roman *Salve.* It also appears as a woman's name: The Apalachee wife of Emperor Brims of the Creek (chief of Caveta or Coweta) was named Gua.

Guale—The Spaniards' name for the people who occupied the Georgia coast from St. Andrews Sound to the Savannah River. The name was also applied to a village in the vicinity of St. Catherines Island known to the French as Ouade. The Guale were one of the first native groups of Spanish Florida to be missionized. The dominant element among them, Swanton believed (1946:135), was Muskogee, but he felt there probably were Hitchiti-speaking natives among them as well. The Guale were known to the Timucua as Ibaja, Iguaja, and Yupaha, and the Spaniards at times used those names for them. In the Leturiondo *Memorial* ([1700]) the name is accented (Gualé).

Guano—In Spanish Florida, the word for Spanish moss and for palm thatch, rather than its usual meaning of bird dung.

Guaypil or *guayapil*—A loose dress for Indian women mentioned as an article of trade between the Apalachee and the Apalachicola late in the mission period.

Hina—An Apalachee word that possibly means "power." It was joined with "chuba" to form the surname Hinachuba, used by what appears to have been Apalachee's leading family.

Hitchiti—The name applied to a particular village and to a broad group of peoples who at one time were probably the most important tribe in southern Georgia and their language the prevailing speech from the Chattahoochee River to the Atlantic Ocean. Most of the Apalachicola or Lower Creek were Hitchiti speakers. De Soto's Ocute are probably the ancestors of the later Creek village of Hitchiti. The name Hitchiti does not appear in the Spanish records.

Holata—A native term meaning "chief," which appears in some Apalachee documents. It may have some connotation of head chief, because in the Apalachee chiefs' letter of 1688 to Charles II, written in their own tongue, only the chief of Ivitachuco styled himself *holahta*. Although it also appears with Juan Mendoza's name, he put it before his name, which may indicate that it was his native surname; it does appear elsewhere as a family name. The other chiefs who signed the letter called themselves *caciques*. The connotation of head chief is also suggested in the body of the letter, where the appellation *holahta chuba* is used to designate the king. There it would have the sense of "big," "powerful," or "head" chief. In the Apalachee text it also appears in combination with the word for governor. The two texts in Apalachee run thus: *Pin holahta chuba pin Rey* and *holahta Governadori*. The word *pin* apparently means "our." Some Timucuan chiefs also used the title *holata* to designate their position.

Hurimelas or *Junumelas*—*Hurimelas* is the name used by Bishop Calderón to describe the fire hunt, which served to clear the fields of grass and weeds in preparation for spring planting. He mentions that it occurred in January. *Junumelas* may be the Apalachee term for the practice. The term appears in the 1657 visitation record. When Governor Rebolledo visited Aspalaga on January 20 to hold an inspection, he found that the village's leaders and most of its people were away for something referred to as "the Junumelas."

Ibaja or Iguaja—See Guale.

Inija (also spelled *hinija, inixa, henija, enixa*)—The title used by the Apalachee to designate the second-in-command in the native political hierarchy. The inija appears to have been responsible for such tasks as directing community labor and seeing to the posting of sentries and night patrols. There is some evidence that they were also the guardians of native traditions such as the origins of the ball game. The Apalachicola had a similar official. Inija also occurred as a surname.

Ita tascaia—One of the ranks within the warrior class.

Koasati—One of the two tribes to whose language Apalachee is believed to have been most closely related. The tribe first appears in history in the de Soto narratives under the name Coste or Acosta, living on an island in the Tennessee River, probably Pine Island.

Maestre de campo or field master—A military rank corresponding to a present-day colonel.

Mikasuki—A prominent Seminole tribe composed of Indians speaking Hitchiti. Although their name does not appear in the documents I consulted from the first Spanish period, they may have begun to settle around Lake Miccosukee before the Spanish withdrawal in 1763.

Muskogee—The dominant people in the Creek Confederacy by the second half of the seventeenth century and a general name that includes most of the tribes whom the Spaniards encountered in the mid-to-lower Southeast. In Florida and Georgia all the people whom the Spaniards met were Muskhogean except the Timucua and the natives of South Florida below Tampa Bay. The name Muskogee does not appear in Spanish documents from the sixteenth and seventeenth centuries. Muskogee is the language of the non-Hitchiti-speaking Seminole.

Nicoguadca—The lightning bolt and the divine force associated with it, to which the goalpost in the ball game was dedicated. It also appears to have been the name for the highest rank within the warrior class, achieved by one who had killed seven *tascaias* and three *itas tascaias*. There is a suggestion in the ball game manuscript that when such a superwarrior was accorded that title, it indicated a belief that the supernatural force associated with lightning and rain had become identified in some fashion with him from then until the time of his death.

Nita—The Apalachee name for bear.

Noroco—A rank within the warrior class, achieved apparently by killing three people.

Ochete—A village in Apalachee mentioned by the Fidalgo de Elvas in the original Portuguese version of his narrative as 6 leagues (most modern translations mistakenly say 8) from Anhayca Apalachee on the way to the sea. The name Ochete was not mentioned in mission times. The only mission-era village in that vicinity was Assumpcion del Puerto, but it was mentioned for the first time in 1675 and its inhabitants were not Apalachee but Capara, Amacano, and Chine.

Oclafi—Lord of the water.

Oconnee—A tribe from Georgia's interior, some of whom formed a mission village on the Georgia coast. The name was also attached to one of the Apalachee missions, San Francisco de Ocone, and authorities such as Swanton have identified its people as Oconnee rather than Apalachee;

however, Spanish documents give no indication that they were other than Apalachee.

Onsla—A weak corn gruel, prescribed to be taken in a specified number of spoonfuls by the usinulo as part of ceremonies before the ball game to ensure victory.

Osachile—A village mentioned by Garcilaso as the westernmost one encountered by de Soto before he crossed into Apalachee. Garcilaso described it as separated from Apalachee by 12 leagues of wilderness and five days west of Ivitachuco, which Garcilaso placed deep in Timucua rather than in Apalachee. Swanton (1946:169) seems to identify the villagers with the later Osochi, whom he classified as Muskhogean stock (1922:11), but he does not explain how they changed from Timucua speakers into Hitchiti speakers. Under the spellings Ucachile and Uzachil the same village is mentioned by Ranjel and Elvas and also placed in Timucua.

Pacara—Mentioned only in 1675 by Bishop Calderón as one of three groups of non-Apalachee joined together in the mission of Assumpción del Puerto. That same year the lieutenant in Apalachee gave their name as Caparaz.

Pansacola—The name for the natives who lived on Pensacola Bay. Before the Spaniards established a presence there, the natives apparently had been almost exterminated by the neighboring Movilas with whom they had been at war. In 1693 Governor Torres y Ayala found only their abandoned village and two small bands of Chacato there.

Peso—8 reales.

Petrina—In Apalachee the name, probably of Spanish origin, for the sash across the breast in which the tomahawk was carried.

Rio de Lagna or Agna (Calderón) or Amarillo (Barreda and Governor Torres) or Lina (1683 map) or Lagino (anti-Chisca expedition)—Some of the names used to designate the Ochlockonee River. Rio Amarillo is the Spanish for Yellow River; the native name Lagna apparently meant the same.

Rio Tacabona or Tacavona—Appears to have been the St. Marks River, which also was called the River of Apalachee and Rio de el Toscache. The Wakulla was known as the Guacara, which was also the native name for the Suwannee. Rio San Martín was the name most commonly used by the Spaniards for the Suwannee.

Sabacola—The Lower Creek people known to the English as Sawokli, who were missionized by the Spaniards for a brief period in the 1670s and 1680s.

Sergeant-major—The equivalent of a present-day major.

Tafun—The word for town or village in Apalachee.

Tallapoosa—The general name used by the Spaniards in the first half of the eighteenth century for the natives we know as Upper Creek.

Tama or Tamali—One of the non-Apalachee people who settled in Apalachee by 1675 in the mission of Candelaria or Purificación, which they shared with a band of Yamasee to whom, some believe, they were closely related. Swanton (1946:189) suggests that they may indeed have been Yamasee. The Spaniards found them sufficiently different to refer to them by different names in 1675, and Swanton found them sufficiently different (1922:11) to classify the Tamali as Hitchiti-speakers, while placing the Guale and Yamasee after the Tuskegee as separate groups. The Tama are mentioned a number of times in the late sixteenth century and the first half of the seventeenth as living in central Georgia inland from the Guale coastal missions. In one document they were described as living on the edge or skirts of the mountains.

Tascaia—The general native name for warrior and apparently the entry rank within the warrior class achieved by killing one enemy.

Timucua—The general name used by the Spaniards for all the native peoples who occupied North Florida east of the territory of the Apalachee. The Timucua were composed of a number of autonomous provinces that were hostile to one another at times, as they were, for example, when the first Europeans arrived. Among the important divisions in mission times were the Saltwater Timucua (Saturiwa and Mocamo), Fresh Water, Potano, Utina, and Yustaga. The Saturiwa, whom the French encountered at the mouth of the St. Johns River, used the name Timucua, spelled Thimogna, to designate specifically the Utina living between the St. Johns and the Suwannee. In the early seventeenth century the Spaniards also used the name in this restrictive sense.

Tocobaga—"A generic term for the aboriginal peoples inhabiting the Florida Gulf coast from about Tarpon Springs to Sarasota at the time of European contact" (Bullen 1978:50). Some would extend their territory farther north and south, but that position is questioned seriously.

Tocopaca—The commonly used name for a group of Tocobaga Indians who established a village of about 300 at Vacissa, not far from Ivitachuco, around 1675. Plans for the fort at San Marcos de Apalachee in 1718 indicate that there were two small settlements of Tocopacas in the vicinity of Fort San Marcos, one on the shore of the bay a short distance to the west of the mouth of the St. Marks and the other a short distance upstream on the first waterway to the east of the mouth of the St.

Marks. There is no evidence that a mission was ever established among the Tocopacas. They handled coastal transport for the Spaniards from St. Marks to the Suwannee and up the Suwannee.

Tolocano—The Apalachee equivalent of K rations, apparently a mixture of parched corn, dried berries, and nut meats.

Uchee or Yuchi—The name most commonly used by the Spaniards during the first half of the eighteenth century to designate the people earlier referred to as Chiscas or Ysicas. The Uchee maintained the earlier Chiscas' inveterate hostility toward the Spaniards and the Spaniards' native allies.

Utina—The Timucua who occupied the territory between the St. Johns and the Suwannee north of the Santa Fé River. Utina probably extended well up into Georgia to the southern drainage of the Altamaha.

Yamasee—A Muskhogean people apparently scattered throughout the Southeast about as ubiquitously as the Chisca and, if the authorities are correct, like the Chisca, assuming a variety of names. There appears to have been a major concentration in southeastern Georgia just west of the Guale settlements. One or more bands of Yamasee had moved into Apalachee to settle by 1675. Others participated in the 1704–1705 attacks on the missions. Many moved to Spanish territory after the Yamasee War of 1715 in South Carolina.

Yuchi—See Uchee or Chisca.

Yustaga—Rendered variously as Ustaca, Yustega, Ustega, this group of Timucua were the Apalachee's closest neighbors. They occupied the territory between the Aucilla and the Suwannee, which was similar to the land of the Apalachee, with whom they seem to have shared some cultural traits, including the Apalachee ball game.

Bibliographic Essay

THE INFORMATION for this study has been drawn from a number of books, articles, unpublished papers, dissertations and theses, and collections of documents, published and unpublished, translated and untranslated. The one major published work to date on the Apalachee and on the missions among them is *Here They Once Stood: The Tragic End of the Apalachee Missions* by Mark F. Boyd, Hale G. Smith, and John W. Griffin (1951). In this book Boyd reproduced all or part of 45 documents that illustrate the last days of the mission era and the destruction of the missions in 1703 and 1704; Smith presented the findings from the excavation of the site of two mission buildings belonging to an Apalachee site in Jefferson County, Florida; and Griffin recorded the results of excavations he directed in 1948 of parts of the San Luis fort site. The only significant source for a broad view of the Apalachee and their culture is the unpublished preliminary draft of a brief article, "The Apalachee," written in 1976 by Kathleen A. Deagan for the *Handbook of North American Indians*. It has circulated among some scholars in mimeographed form. Since the late 1960s the discovery and archaeological exploration of a number of Apalachee mission and premission sites and the dissemination of some of the findings by state archaeologists L. Ross Morrell, B. Calvin Jones, Louis Tesar, and others has significantly expanded the corpus of information in a number of areas. Particular aspects of Apalachee life, culture, or history have received attention in several excellent articles by Amy Bushnell, a dissertation and article by Robert Allen Matter, a master's thesis by Brian G. Boniface, and an unpublished paper on the Apalachee farm by Elizabeth Purdum and Kenneth J. Plante. These works supplement the earlier articles and documents published by Mark F. Boyd, the documents published in Spanish by Manuel Serrano y Sanz, the translation of the Bishop Calderón letter by

Lucy M. Wenhold, and the material on the Apalachee in the works of John R. Swanton.

Additional information can be found in an unpublished series of translations and synopses of documents dealing with Apalachee that I prepared in 1976 for the Florida Division of Archives, History and Records Management. Three of the most important of these primary sources are the records of the official visitations of the province in 1657, 1677–1678, and 1694–1695. My translation of the 1657 visitation record and of several other documents that contain information on the Apalachee was published in *Florida Archaeology* in late 1986. Of equal value are the excerpts from the investigation into the complaints against Antonio Matheos, Governor Juan Marquez Cabrera's deputy governor in Apalachee, and from Matheos's suit against the interim governor who removed him, Pedro de Aranda y Avellaneda. These two sets of documents form part of the record of the residencia of Governor Marquez Cabrera.

Another major unpublished primary source is the manuscript describing the Apalachee and Yustaga ball game, composed by Fray Juan de Paiva in 1676. It appears in the 1677–1678 visitation records of Domingo de Leturiondo. Since 1976 was the three-hundredth anniversary of the composition of the ball game manuscript and was coincident with the bicentennial of the nation, the Bureau of Historic Sites and Properties thought it a fitting time to publish a translation of this valuable piece. After the bureau had entrusted the task to me, and after I had almost completed a rough transcription of the document, the bureau learned that Evelyn Peterson and Amy Bushnell had a prior interest in the document and decided to leave its translation and exploitation to them.

At some time prior to 1976, an unpublished translation of this manuscript had been made by Julian Granberry. During 1976, Evelyn Peterson produced a translation of the Paiva document, which has remained in manuscript. From her interest in the document, Amy Bushnell published a substantial article on the ball game in 1978. While I was revising this manuscript on the Apalachee for publication, I completed a translation of the ball game manuscript, believing that there was still a need for a literal and exact translation.

There follows a list of the major Spanish documents used in this study and translated or transcribed by me since 1976.

Governor Diego de Rebolledo to the King, 1657. AGI Escribanía de Cámara, leg. 155 B, no. 18. This is the record of Governor Rebolledo's visitation of the province and a considerable amount of correspondence between the governor and the friars dealing with the stationing of troops in Apalachee and the building of a blockhouse to shelter them. It also contains four letters to the governor by soldiers in Apalachee who were conducting an investigation there for him as well as lobbying the chiefs in support of the governor's plans for the expansion of the Spanish military presence.

Domingo de Leturiondo, Inspection of the Provinces of Apalachee and Timucua, 1677–1678. AGI Escribanía de Cámara, leg. 156 B, folios 519–616.

Fray Juan de Paiva, "Origin and Beginning of the Game of Pelota Which the Apalachee and the Yustacan Indians Have Been Playing from the Time They Were Unbelievers until the Year of 1676. It Was Brought to Light by the Reverend Father Fray Juan de Paiva, Pastor of the Doctrina of San Luis de Talimali." AGI, Escribanía de Cámara, leg. 156 C, folios 569–583.

Joaquín de Florencia, "General Inspection that the Captain Joaquín de Florencia Made of the Provinces of Apalache and Timucua . . . by Title and Nomination of Don Laureano de Torres y Aiala . . ." November 5, 1694. AGI, Escribanía de Cámara, leg. 157 A, cuaderno I, folios 44–205. Beginning with folio 172, this document consists of part of the record of two criminal cases. The first involved a Timucuan native who was alleged to have killed a Chacato woman who did not exist, if the "public defender" for the accused is to be believed. The second involved two Apalachee Indians residing in St. Augustine, who were accused of making and passing counterfeit coins made of tin to buy food. The first of these documents bears the following title: "Autos Made Officially from the *Ca.* Justice by the Adjutant, Andrés García, Lieutenant of the Province of Timuqua, against Santiago, Native to the Village of San Pedro. Year of 1695" (AGI, Escribanía de Cámara, leg. 157 A, cuaderno I, folios 172-189).

An assortment of pieces that have some relation to Antonio Matheos, excerpted for the Stetson Collection from the residencia of Governor Juan Marques Cabrera. They are from AGI Escribanía de Cámara, leg. 156 C, cuaderno E. In the Stetson Collection they are found in bundles 2770 and 2582.

Juan Fernández de Florencia, "Report Which the Principal Leaders Who Went to Make War on the Chiscas, Who Are Juan Mendoza, Matheo Chuba, Bernardo, the Cacique of Cupayca, and Bentura, the Inija of San Luis, Made in the Presence of Captain Juan Fernández de Florencia, and [Report] Concerning How the War against the Chiscas Originated." October 5, 1677. This report appears in a letter by Governor Pablo de Hita Salazar to the King, November 10, 1678, AGI SD 226, SC. Florencia took down their report in the Apalachee tongue and did not translate it into Spanish to forward it to the governor until

August 30, 1678. Although he forwarded the original to the governor, only his Spanish translation is included here. It appears in vol. 9 of the Lowery Collection.

Alonso de Leturiondo, Memorial to the King Our Lord in His Royal and Supreme Council of the Indies in Which a Report Is Given of the State in Which the Presidio of St. Augustín of Florida Happens to Be; of the Things that It Needs for Its Protection, Defense, and Preservation: For the Good Government and Punctual Service of His Majesty in Those Provinces. This work was published in Spain about 1700, and a copy appears in AGI Escribanía de Cámara, leg. 157 C, cuaderno I, Stetson Collection. My translation of this piece has been published in *Florida Archaeology* 2 (1986): 165–225.

In addition to the major sources that I translated, this study relies principally on the research notes, translations, and synopses that I prepared in 1976. It was supplemented by additional research and translation undertaken from 1983 to 1987. I have drawn much information and some ideas from the sources on this list, from others listed in the footnotes and bibliography, and from conversations with B. Calvin Jones.

Although the Spanish documents I used in archival sources in American collections bear the three-part numbering system used by the Archive of the Indies before 1929, I have converted the old numbers. In the several cases in which I could not find conversion equivalents or the data for extrapolating the new numbers on the conversion table prepared for the P. K. Yonge Library of Florida History (University of Florida, Gainesville) by Paul E. Hoffman, I kept the old numbers. The abbreviation SD following the AGI for Archivo General de Indias stands for Santo Domingo. The abbreviations following the serial number for each bundle are SC for Stetson Collection (P. K. Yonge Library of Florida History), WLC for Woodbury Lowery Collection (Library of Congress), JTCC for Jeannette Thurber Connor Collection (Library of Congress), and NCC for North Carolina Collection (University of North Carolina Library, Chapel Hill). For the Woodbury Lowery Collection I used transcriptions made from copies held by The Florida State University and the P. K. Yonge Library of Florida History. The former copy is contained on fewer microfilm reels than is the P. K. Yonge Library's copy. To lessen the problem of locating documents, I have used the volume number rather than the reel number whenever I had that information.

Because most of the documents used for this study were written at St. Augustine, the point of origin of the document will be noted only when it is other than St. Augustine. Published documents have been cited by the name and date of their author so that the reader will know when I used the document rather than the editor's or translator's interpretation of the document. The authors or scribes who wrote these documents varied their spellings of these letter writers' names. I have given them a uniform spelling.

Bibliography

Adair, James
    1930   *The History of the American Indians.* Edited by Samuel Cole Williams. New York: Promontory Press.

Albuquerque, Viceroy Duque de
    1703   [Letter to the King, Mexico, April 10, 1703.] AGI SD 865 SC.

Arana, Luis Rafael
    1964   The Alonso Solana Map of Florida, 1683. *Florida Historical Quarterly* 42:258–266.

Arana, Luis Rafael, and Albert Manucy
    1977   *The Building of the Castillo de San Marcos.* Eastern National Park and Monument Association for Castillo de San Marcos National Monument.

Aranda y Avellaneda, Pedro de
    1687   [Testimony of Witnesses He Presented in Antonio Matheos's Suit against Him.] AGI Escribanía de Cámara, leg. 156 C, pieza 25 (E. 20), folios 101–113. SC.

Aranguíz y Cotes, Governor Alonso de
    1659   [Letter to the King, November 1, 1659.] AGI SD 852 SC.
    1662a [Letter to the King, August 8, 1662.] AGI SD 852 SC.
    1662b [Letter to the King, September 8, 1662.] AGI SD 225.

Arguellas, Antonio de
    1668   [Letter to the King, July 6, 1668.] AGI SD 196 WLC vol. 8.

Auxiliary Bishop of Florida
    1736   [Letter to the King, August 31, 1736.] AGI SD 863 SC.

Ayala y Escobar, Juan de
    1698   [Autos of the Visitation of the Provinces of Timucua and Apalachee, January 24, 1698.] AGI Escribanía de Cámara, leg. 157a, *residencia* for Governor Laureano de Torres y Ayala. Microfilm roll 27-p, P. K. Yonge Library of Florida History.
    1717   [Letter to the King, April 21, 1717.] AGI SD 843 SC.
    1718   [Letter to the King, January 28, 1718.] AGI SD 843 SC.

Ayala y Escobar, Juan de, and Juan Solana
    1701   Auto of the Inspector Relating to the Apalachee, San Luis, February 22, 1701. In Boyd, Smith, and Griffin, 1951, 33–34, q.v.

Barnwell, John
    1908   The Tuscorara Expedition: Letters of Colonel John Barnwell. *The South Carolina Historical and Genealogical Magazine* 9:28–58.

Barreda, Fray Rodrigo de, OFM
   1693   Journal of Friar Rodrigo de la Barreda, August 3, 1693, Bay of Pensacola. In Leonard,
          1939, 265–282, q.v.
Bartram, William
   1955   *Travels of William Bartram.* Edited by Mark Van Doren. New York: Dover Publications.
Benavides, Governor Antonio de
   1722   [Letter to Andrés de Pez, November 10, 1722.] AGI SD 842 SC.
   1723   [Letter to the King, March 8, 1723.] AGI SD 865 SC.
   1726   [Testimony of the Investigation Made during the Visitation of the Indian Settlements
          near St. Augustine, December 1, 1726.] AGI SD 865 SC.
   1727a [Letter to the King, September 10, 1727.] AGI SD 844 SC.
   1727b [Letter to the King, September 10, 1727.] AGI SD 844 SC.
   1732   [Letter to the King, San Marcos de Apalache, February 8, 1732.] Buckingham Smith
          Collection, microfilm, P. K. Yonge Library of Florida History.
Bentura, Bip, principal *Inija* at San Luis
   1687   [Testimony by, in Solana, 1787a, q.v.] AGI Escribanía de Cámara, leg. 156, cuaderno
          E, folios 37–38, SC. [Elsewhere his name was given as Vi Ventura.]
Bienville, Jean Baptiste Le Moyne de
   1704   Letter to Phelypeaux de Maurepas Pontchartrain, September 6, 1704. In Rowland and
          Sanders, 1932, 3: 27, q.v.
   1706   Abstract of Letters, from Bienville to Pontchartrain, July 28, 1706. In Rowland and
          Sanders, 1929, 2: 25, q.v.
   [1726] Memoir [by Bienville] on Louisiana. In Rowland and Sanders, 1932, 3: 499–539, q.v.
Bishop of Cuba
   1728   [Letter to the King, Havana, September 1, 1728.] AGI SD 865 SC.
   1729   [Letter to the King, Havana, January 14, 1729.] AGI SD 865 SC.
Bolton, Herbert E.
   1917   The Mission as a Frontier Institution in the Spanish American Colonies. *American His-
          torical Review* 23:42–61.
   1921   *The Spanish Borderlands: A Chronicle of Old Florida and the Southwest.* New Haven:
          Yale University Press.
   1925a Spanish Resistance to the Carolina Traders in Western Georgia, 1680–1704. *Georgia
          Historical Quarterly* 9:115–130.
   1925b *Arredondo's Historical Proof of Spain's Title to Georgia.* Berkeley: University of Cali-
          fornia Press.
Boniface, Brian George
   1971   A Historical Geography of Spanish Florida, circa 1700. Master's thesis, University of
          Georgia.
Boyd, Mark F.
   1934   Apalachee during the British Occupation: A Description Contained in a Series of Four
          Reports by Lieut Pittman, R. E. *Florida Historical Quarterly* 12:114–122.
   1935   The First American Road in Florida: Pensacola–St. Augustine Highway, 1824. *Florida
          Historical Quarterly* 14:73–106, 138–192.
   1936   The Fortifications of San Marcos de Apalache. *Florida Historical Quarterly* 15:1–34.
   1937   Expedition of Marcos Delgado from Apalachee to the Upper Creek Country in 1686.
          Florida Historical Quarterly 16:2–32.
   1939   Mission Sites in Florida: An Attempt to Approximately Identify the Sites of Spanish
          Mission Settlements of the Seventeenth Century in Northern Florida. *Florida Histori-
          cal Quarterly* 17:255–280.

1948 Enumeration of Florida Spanish Missions in 1675. *Florida Historical Quarterly* 27:181–188.

1949 Diego Peña's Expedition to Apalachee and Apalachicolo in 1716. *Florida Historical Quarterly* 28:1–27.

1951 Fort San Luis: Documents Describing the Tragic End of the Mission Era. In Boyd, Smith, and Griffin, 1951, 1–104, q.v.

1952 Documents Describing the Second and Third Expeditions of Lieutenant Diego Peña to Apalachee and Apalachicolo in 1717 and 1718. *Florida Historical Quarterly* 31: 109–139.

1953 Further Considerations of the Apalachee Missions. *The Americas* 9:459–479.

Boyd, Mark F., Hale G. Smith, and John W. Griffin

1951 *Here They Once Stood: The Tragic End of the Apalachee Missions.* Gainesville: University of Florida Press.

Bullen, Ripley P.

1978 Tocobaga Indians and the Safety-Harbor Culture. In Milanich and Proctor, 50–58, q.v.

Bullones, Fray Joseph

1728 [Letter to the King, Havana, October 5, 1728.] AGI SD 865 SC.

Burch, Captain Daniel E.

1823 [Letter to General Thomas S. Jessup, December 1, 1823.] In Boyd, 1935, 93, q.v.

Bushnell, Amy

1978a The Menéndez-Marquez Cattle Barony at La Chua and the Determinants of Economic Expansion in 17th Century Florida. *Florida Historical Quarterly* 56:407–431.

1978b That Demonic Game: The Campaign to Stop Indian Pelota Playing in Spanish Florida, 1675–1684. *The Americas* 35:1–19.

1979 Patricio de Hinachuba: Defender of the Word of God, the Crown of the King, and the Little Children of Ivitachuco. *American Indian Culture and Research Journal* 3:1–21.

1981 *The King's Coffer: Proprietors of the Spanish Florida Treasury, 1565–1702.* Gainesville: University Presses of Florida.

Carroll, Bartholomew Rivers (editor)

1836 *Historical Collections of South Carolina Embracing Many Rare and Valuable Pamphlets and Other Documents Relating to the History of that State from Its First Discovery to Its Independence in the Year 1776.* 2 vols. New York: Harper and Brothers.

Castilla, Don Juan de, Scribe

1740 [Letter to Joseph de la Quintana, January 6, 1740.] AGI D 2565 SC.

Cendoya, Governor Manuel de

1672 [Letter to the King, December 15, 1672.] AGI SD 839 SC.

Chardon, Roland

1980 The Elusive Spanish League: A Problem of Measurement in Sixteenth-Century New Spain. *Hispanic American Historical Review* 60:294–302.

Chatelain, Verne

1941 *The Defenses of Spanish Florida, 1565 to 1763.* Washington: The Carnegie Institution, Publication 511.

Chiefs of Apalachee

1688 [Letter to the King, San Luis de Abalachi, 21st Day of the Moon that Is Called January.] Translated from the Apalachee by Fray Marcelo de San Joseph. AGI SD 839 SC.

Chuba, Matheo

1687 [Testimony by, San Luis de Talimali, May 29, 1687.] In Alonso Solana 1687a, q.v. AGI Escribanía de Cámara leg. 156, cuaderno E, folio 31, SC.

Clowse, Converse D.
   1971   *Economic Beginnings in Colonial South Carolina 1670–1720.* Columbia: University of South Carolina Press.
Córcoles y Martínez, Governor Francisco de
   1711   [Letter to the King, April 9, 1711, and "Memorial" of the Male Indians, Female Indians, Boys and Girls Which the Settlement and Place of San Luis de Talimali or Abosaya of the Apalachee Tongue Has Up Until Today, . . . 1711.] AGI SD 843 SC. [The memorial is a census of the village's population.]
Corkran, David H.
   1967   *The Creek Frontier, 1540–1783.* Norman: University of Oklahoma Press.
Council of Commerce of Louisiana
   1721   Minutes of the Council of Commerce of Louisiana. Biloxi, February 8, 1721. In Rowland and Sanders, 1932, 3: 303, q.v.
Council of the Indies
   1657a [Order for Governor Rebolledo's Removal and Imprisonment, Madrid, June 12, 1657.] WLC reel 3.
   1657b [Opinion Submitted to the King, Madrid, June 15, 1657.] AGI SD 6, SC. In Rebolledo 1657a, q.v.
   1657c [Opinion Submitted to the King, Madrid, July 7, 1657.] AGI SD 6, SC.
   1702   [Note, January 11, 1702.] AGI SD 853 SC.
   1727   [Report to the King, Madrid, March 30, 1727.] AGI SD 837 SC.
Council of War
   1704   Council of War, July 13, 1704. In Boyd, Smith, and Griffin, 1951, 56–59, q.v.
Covington, James W.
   1964   The Apalachee Move West. *Florida Anthropologist* 17:10–18.
   1967   Some Observations Concerning the Florida-Carolina Slave Trade. *Florida Anthropologist* 20 (1–2):10–18.
   1972   Apalachee Indians, 1704–1763. *Florida Historical Quarterly* 50:366–384.
Crane, Verner W.
   1956   *The Southern Frontier, 1670–1732.* Ann Arbor: University of Michigan Press.
Crawford, James M. (editor)
   1975   *Studies in Southeastern Indian Languages.* Athens: University of Georgia Press.
Cruz, Juan de la
   1705   Testimony of, June 9, 1705. In Boyd, Smith, and Griffin, 1951, 74–77, q.v.
Cumming, William P.
   1958   *The Southeast in Early Maps with an Annotated Check List of Printed and Manuscript Regional and Local Maps of Southeastern North America.* Princeton, NJ: Princeton University Press.
Deagan, Kathleen A.
   1976   The Apalachee. Department of Anthropology, Florida State University. [Draft of an article to appear in vol. 13 of the *Handbook of North American Indians,* edited by W. C. Sturtevant. Washington: Smithsonian Institution.]
   1978   Cultures in Transition: Fusion and Assimilation among the Eastern Timucua. In Milanich and Proctor, 89–119, q.v.
Delgado, Marcos
   1693   Bill of Sale, 1693, San Antonio de Bacugua. In Leonard, 1939, 254n.3, q.v.
DePratter, Chester B., Charles M. Hudson, and Marvin T. Smith
   1983   The Route of Juan Pardo's Explorations in the Interior Southeast, 1566–1568. *Florida Historical Quarterly* 61:125–158.

Díaz Vara Calderón, Bishop Gabriel

1675   *A 17th-Century Letter of Gabriel Díaz Vara Calderón, Bishop of Cuba, Describing the Indians and Indian Missions of Florida.* Edited and translated by Lucy L. Wenhold. Smithsonian Miscellaneous Collections, vol. 95, no. 16 (1936). [A photostat of the original also was viewed in the Stetson Collection, AGI SD 151.]

Díez de la Calle, Juan

1659   *Noticias sacras e reales de los dos imperios de las Yndias Occidentales desta Nueva España.* 2 vols. [Notes taken from it by Woodbury Lowery, WLC vol. 8. Serrano y Sanz, 1912, pp. 131–133, reproduced a slightly different version of this document, also taken from Díez de la Calle's work, it seems.]

Dobyns, Henry F.

1983   *Their Number Become Thinned: Native American Population Dynamics in Eastern North America.* Knoxville: University of Tennessee Press.

Ebelino de Compostela, Bishop Diego

1689   [Letter to the King, Havana, September 28, 1689.] AGI SD 151 SC.

Elvas, The Fidalgo of

1557   *Relaçam verdadeira dos trabalhos q̃ ho gouernador dõ Fernãdo de Souto e certos fidalgos portugueses passarom no descobrimẽto da prouincia da Frolida [sic].* Facsimile of the original Portuguese edition. Deland: Florida State Historical Society, 1932.

1904   *True Relation of the Vicissitudes that Attended the Governor Don Hernando de Soto and Some Nobles of Portugal in the Discovery of the Province of Florida,* vol. 1. Translated by Buckingham Smith and edited by Edward Gaylord Bourne. New York: A. S. Barnes.

d'Escalante Fontaneda, Hernando

1976   *Memoir of Dᵒ d'Escalante Fontaneda Respecting Florida.* Translated by Buckingham Smith. Annotated by David True. Miami: Greater Miami Bicentennial Project.

Fernald, Merritt Lyndon, and Alfred Charles Kinsey

1958   *Edible Wild Plants of Eastern North America.* Rev. ed. New York: Harper and Brothers.

Fernández de Florencia, Juan

1675a   [Letter to Governor Pablo de Hita Salazar, San Luis de Apalachee, July 15, 1675.] In Hita Salazar, 1675b, q.v. AGI SD 839 SC.

1675b   [Autos Concerning the Tumult of the Chacatos.] In Hita Salazar, 1675a, q.v. AGI Escribanía de Cámara, leg. 156, folios 119–142, SC.

1678   [Letter to Governor Pablo de Hita Salazar, San Luis de Talimali, August 30, 1678.] Report Which the Principal Leaders Who Went to Make War on the Chiscas, Who are Juan Mendoza, Matheo Chuba, Bernardo, the Cacique of Cupayca, and Bentura, the *Inija* of San Luis, Made in the Presence of Captain Juan Fernández de Florencia and Concerning How the War against the Chiscas Originated. In Hita Salazar, 1678, q.v. AGI SD 226 WLC, vol. 9. [This report by the Indian leaders was taken down by Florencia in the Apalachee language when the expedition returned to San Luis on October 5, 1677. A year passed before Florencia translated it into Spanish to forward it to the governor. An English version of the report is available in Swanton, 1922, q.v., and a Spanish version in Serrano y Sanz, 1912, q.v.]

Fernández de Olivera, Governor Juan

1612a   [Letter to the King, October 13, 1612.] AGI SD 229 SC.

1612b   [Letter to the King, October 13, 1612.] AGI SD 229 WLC, vol. 6.

Fernández de Oviedo y Valdéz, Gonzalo

1904   *A Narrative of de Soto's Expedition Based on the Diary of Rodrigo Ranjel, His Private*

Secretary, vol. 2. Edited and translated by Edward Gaylord Bourne. New York: A. S. Barnes.

Ferro Machado, Juan, visitador of Florida
1688 [Letter to the King, August 8, 1688.] AGI SD 229 SC.

Florencia, Fray Claudio de; Fray Simón de Salas; Fray Manuel de Urisas; Fray Antonio de los Angeles; Fray Domingo Vásquez; Fray Francisco de León; and Fray Andrés de Oramos
1707 Letter to the King, May 7, 1707. In Boyd, Smith, and Griffin, 1951, 85–89, q.v.

Florencia, Francisco de
1705a Letter to Andrés G. [Garcia], Ivitachuco [at Abosaya], August 23, 1705. In Boyd, 1953, 474, q.v.
1705b Letter to the Commander at San Francisco [de Potano], Ivitachuco [at Abosaya], August 27, 1705. In Boyd, 1953, 474–475, q.v.

Florencia, Francisco de, and Juan de Pueyo
1704 [Letter to the Viceroy (presumably), June 4, 1704.] In Testimony of *Autos* Made Concerning Various Measures Taken by the *Presidio* of Florida and the Rest. Viceroy of New Spain to the King, Mexico, June 6, 1706. AGI SD 851 SC or AGI 58–2–1/2, pp. 13238–13236. [This material cited here and subsequently with this backward-running page count is from the documents gathered for the residencia of Governor Joseph de Zúñiga y de la Cerda.]
1706a Letter to the King, April 30, 1706. In Boyd, 1953, 475–476, q.v.
1706b Letter to the King, August 13, 1706. In Boyd, 1953, 477–479, q.v.

Florencia, Joaquín de
1695 [General Inspection that the Captain Joaquín de Florencia Made of the Provinces of Apalachee and Timucua, Interim Treasurer of the Presidio of St. Augustine of Florida, Judge Commissary and Inspector-General of Them by Title and Nomination of Don Laureano de Torres y Aiala, Knight of the Order of Santiago, Governor and Captain General of the Said *Presidio,* and Provinces by His Majesty 1694–1695.] AGI Escribanía de Cámara, leg. 157 A, cuaderno I, folios 44–205, SC.

Florida Friars in Chapter
1617 [Letter to the King, January 17, 1617.] AGI SD 235 WLC, vol. 6.

Franciscan Commissary General
1673 [Letter to Francisco R. de Madrigal, Madrid, January 7, 1673.] AGI SD 848 NCC 3.

Franciscan Friars
1664 [Letter to the King, June 16, 1664.] AGI SD 848 WLC, vol. 8.

Friar (apparently)
1635 [Letter to the King, February 2, 1635.] AGI SD 225 WLC, vol. 7.

Friar at Bacuqua
1687 [Enclosure in Governor Diego de Quiroga y Losada to the King, May 20, 1691.] AGI SD 228 SC.

Fuentes, Francisco
1683 [Letter to Governor Juan Marquez Cabrera, in Governor J. Marquez Cabrera, 1683.] AGI SD 226 SC.

Fuentes, Manuel Jacomé
1700 [Testimony for the *Residencia* of Governor Laureano de Torres y Ayala, December 21, 1700.] AGI Escribanía de Cámara, leg. 157 A. Microfilm roll 27p, P. K. Yonge Library of Florida History.

Fuentes de Galanca, Francisco de
1705 Testimony of, June 9, 1705. In Boyd, Smith, and Griffin, 1951, 77–79, q.v.

Gannon, Michael V.
   1983   *The Cross in the Sand: The Early Catholic Church in Florida, 1513–1870.* Gaines-
          ville: University Presses of Florida.
García, Andrés
   1695   [Autos Made Officially by the Adjutant, Andrés García, Lieutenant of the Province of
          Timucua, against Santiago, Native to the Village of San Pedro. Year of 1695.] AGI
          Escribanía de Cámara, leg. 157 A, cuaderno I, folios 172 ff., SC. [This document is
          appended to the J. de Florencia visitation record of 1694–1695.]
García, Genaro
   1902   *Dos antiguas relaciones de la Florida.* Mexico: Tip. y Lit. de J. Aguilar Vera y Comp.
Gardiner, William J.
   1971   *A History of Jamaica from Its Discovery by Christopher Columbus to the Year 1872.*
          London: Frank Cass & Co. Ltd.
Gatschet, Albert S.
   1969   *A Migration Legend of the Creek Indians.* New York: Kraus Reprint Co. [Originally
          published, Philadelphia: D. G. Brinton, 1884.]
Geiger, Maynard
   1940   *Biographical Dictionary of the Franciscans in Spanish Florida and Cuba (1528–
          1841).* Franciscan Studies, vol. 21. Paterson, NJ: St. Anthony Guild Press.
Gerónimo, Fray Luis
   [1617] [Memorial.] AGI SD 235 WLC, reel 3.
Gold, Robert L.
   1969   *Borderland Empires in Transition: The Triple-Nation Transfer of Florida.* Carbondale:
          Southern Illinois University Press.
   1970   Conflict in San Carlos: Indian Immigrants in 18th-Century New Spain. *Ethnohistory*
          17:1–10.
Gómez de Engraba, Fray Juan
   1657a [Letter to Father Fray Francisco Martínez, March 13, 1657.] AGI SD 225 WLC vol. 7.
          In Rebolledo 1657a, q.v.
   1657b [Letter to Father Fray Francisco Martínez, April 4, 1657.] AGI SD 225 WLC vol. 7. In
          Rebolledo 1657a, q.v.
González de Barcia Carballido y Zúñiga, Andrés
   1951   *Barcia's Chronological History of the Continent of Florida.* Translated by Anthony
          Kerrigan. Gainesville: University of Florida Press.
[Granberry, Julian]
   n.d.   [Translation of the Ball Game Manuscript.] Photocopy of a typed manuscript with no
          date or attribution, in the possession of John Hann.
Green, Michael D.
   1979   *The Creeks: A Critical Bibliography.* Bloomington: Indiana University Press for the
          Newberry Library.
Griffin, John W.
   1951   Excavations at the Site of San Luis. In Boyd, Smith, and Griffin, 1951, 139–160, q.v.
Guerra y Vega, Governor Francisco de la
   1668a [Letter to the King, July 7, 1668.] AGI SD 233 WLC vol. 8.
   1668b [Letter to the King, August 8, 1668.] AGI SD 224 WLC vol. 8.
   1668c [Letter to the King, August 6, 1668.] AGI SD 224 WLC vol. 8.
   1673   [Letter to the King, January 25, 1673.] AGI SD 855 SC.
Guerrero, Lourenço
   1687   [Testimony of, 1687.] AGI Escribanía de Cámara, leg. 156, pieza 25 (E. 20), folios
          104–105.

Guzmán, Joseph de
  1704   Letter to the Viceroy, Santa María de Galve [Pensacola], August 22, 1704. In Boyd,
         Smith, and Griffin, 1951, 62–64, q.v.
Haas, Mary R.
  1978   The Position of Apalachee in the Muskogean Family. In *Language, Culture, and History: Essays by Mary R. Haas*. Stanford: Stanford University Press. [This article appeared originally in the *International Journal of American Linguistics* 15 (1949): 121–127.]
Hamilton, Peter J.
  1976   *Colonial Mobile*. Reprinted from the revised 1910 edition. Edited by Charles G. Summersell. University: University of Alabama Press.
Handler, Jerome S.
  1969   The Amerindian Slave Population of Barbados in the Seventeenth and Early Eighteenth Centuries. *Caribbean Studies* 8:38–64.
  1970   Aspects of Amerindian Ethnography in Seventeenth-Century Barbados. *Caribbean Studies* 9:50–72.
  1971   *A Guide to Source Materials for the Study of Barbados History, 1627–1834*. Carbondale: Southern Illinois University Press.
Handler, Jerome S., and Frederich W. Lange, with the assistance of Robert V. Riordan
  1978   *Plantation Slavery in Barbados: An Archaeological and Historical Investigation*. Cambridge: Harvard University Press.
Hann, John H.
  1986   Demographic Patterns and Changes in Mid-Seventeenth Century Timucua and Apalachee. *Florida Historical Quarterly* 64:371–392.
Hawkins, Benjamin.
  1982a *Letters of Benjamin Hawkins, 1796–1806*. Reprint. Spartanburg, SC: The Reprint Company. Originally published in 1916 as vol. 9 of the *Collections of the Georgia Historical Society*.
  1982b *A Sketch of the Creek Country, in the Years 1798 and 1799*. Reprint. Spartanburg, SC: The Reprint Company. Originally published in 1848 as vol. 3, part 1 of the *Collections of the Georgia Historical Society*.
Headlam, Cecil (editor)
  1916   *Calendar of State Papers, Colonial Series, America and West Indies, 1704–1705. Preserved in the Public Record Office*. London: His Majesties' Stationery Office.
Hernández de Biedma, Luis
  1904   *Relation of the Conquest of Florida Presented by Luys Hernández de Biedma in the Year 1544 to the King in Council*, vol. 2. Translated by Buckingham Smith and edited by Edward Gaylord Bourne. New York: A. S. Barnes.
Higginbotham, Jay
  1977   *Old Mobile, Fort Louis de la Louisiane, 1702–1711*. Mobile: Museum of the City of Mobile.
[Hinachuba, Don Patricio] (Cacique of Capoli)
  1687   [Testimony of, 1687.] AGI Escribanía de Cámara, leg. 156, cuaderno E, folios 38–39, SC.
Hinachuba, Don Patricio (Cacique of Ivitachuco)
  1699   Letter to Don Antonio Ponce de León, Ivitachuco, April 10, 1699. In Boyd, Smith, and Griffin, 1951, 26–27, q.v.
  1705   Letter to the Governor, Ivitachuco [at Abosaya], May 29, 1705. In Boyd, 1953, 473–474, q.v.

Hinachuba, Don Patricio, and Andrés [Usunaca]
  1699   Letter to the King, San Luis, February 12, 1699. In Boyd, Smith, and Griffin, 1951, 24–26, q.v.
Hita Salazar, Governor Pablo de
  1675a [Letter to the Queen, August 9, 1675.] AGI Escribanía de Cámara, leg. 156, folios 119–142, SC.
  1675b [Letter to the Queen, August 24, 1675.] AGI SD 839 SC.
  1675c [Letter to the Queen, August 24, 1675.] AGI Contratacion 3309, WLC reel 4.
  1676   [Letter to the Queen, April 26, 1676.] AGI SD 839 SC.
  1678a [Letter to the King, June 15, 1678.] AGI SD 855 SC.
  1678b [Letter to the King, November 10, 1678.] AGI SD 226 SC.
  [1679] [Letter to the King, undated.] AGI SD 226 WLC vol. 9. [The contents indicate that it was written in 1679.]
  1680a [Letter to the King, March 8, 1680.] AGI SD 226 WLC, vol. 9.
  1680b [Letter to the King, December 7, 1680.] AGI SD 226 SC.
  1680c [Letter to the King, May 14, 1680.] In Serrano y Sanz, 1912, 216–219, q.v.
  1680d [Letter to the King, March 6, 1680.] AGI SD 839 NCC 4.
  n.d.   [Letter to the King, undated.] AGI SD 226 WLC, vol. 9.
Horcasitas y Güemes, Governor Juan Francisco de
  1739   [Letter to the King, May 21, 1739.] AGI SD 866 SC.
Horruytiner, Governor Luis de
  1633   [Letter to the King, November 15, 1633.] AGI SD 233 SC.
  1637   [Letter to the King, June 24, 1637.] AGI SD 225 SC.
Horue, Don Miguel de, Royal Notary
  1705   Extract Made . . . from an Anonymous Letter for Submission to the Viceroy, New Vera Cruz, February 2, 1705. In Boyd, Smith, and Griffin, 1951, 72–73, q.v.
Hu, Shiu Ying
  1979   The Botany of Yaupon. In Hudson, editor, 1979, 10–39, q.v.
Hudson, Charles
  1976   *The Southeastern Indians.* Knoxville: University of Tennessee Press.
Hudson, Charles M. (editor)
  1979   *Black Drink: A Native American Tea.* Athens: University of Georgia Press.
Hudson, Charles; Marvin T. Smith; and Chester B. DePratter
  1984   The Hernando de Soto Expedition: From Apalachee to Chiaha. *Southeastern Archaeology* 3:65–77.
Hutson, James H.
  1984   [Letter to John H. Hann, July 10, 1984.]
Ibarra, Governor Pedro de
  1608   [Letter to the King, August 22, 1608.] AGI SD 224 WLC, vol. 6.
  1609   [Letter to the King, September 1, 1609.] AGI SD 128 SC.
Jaen, Diego de
  1695   Record of the Response by Diego de Jaen to the Charges Lodged against His Conduct as the Lieutenant of Guale by the Natives of that Province during the 1695 Visitation of Guale and Mocama Made by Don Juan de Pueyo. AGI Escribanía de Cámara, leg. 157 A, cuaderno I, folios 140–172, SC. Translated by John H. Hann, 1986. [A copy is on file at the Bureau of Archaeological Research, Tallahassee.]
Johnson, Governor Nathaniel; Thomas Broughton; Robert Gibbs; George Smith; and Richard Beresford
  1708   [Letter to the Lords Proprietors, Carolina, September 17, 1708.] In Salley, 1947, 5: 203–209, q.v.

Jones, B. Calvin
  1970   A 17th-Century Spanish Mission Cemetery Is Discovered near Tallahassee. *Archives and History News* 1 (4).
  1972   Colonel James Moore and the Destruction of the Apalachee Missions in 1704. Tallahassee: Florida Bureau of Historic Sites and Properties *Bulletin* 2:25–53.
  1973   A Semi-Subterranean Structure at Mission San Joseph de Ocuya, Jefferson County, Florida. Tallahassee: Florida Bureau of Historic Sites and Properties *Bulletin* 3:1–50.
Jorge, Julian
  1687   [Testimony of, 1687.] AGI Escribanía de Cámara, leg. 156, pieza (E. 20), folios 110–111.
Journals of the Commons House of Assembly of South Carolina.
  1704   [Photostat copies furnished by South Carolina Department of Archives and History.]
Junta
  1680   [Madrid, September 5, 1680.] AGI SD 226 WLC, vol. 9.
Junta of War
  1705   [Letter to the King, Madrid, August 29, 1705.] AGI SD 863 SC.
Kessell, John L.
  1979   *Kiva, Cross, and Crown: The Pecos Indians and New Mexico, 1540–1840.* Washington: U.S. Department of the Interior, National Park Service.
Labora, Lorenzo de
  1677   Certification by, December 26, 1677. In Leturiondo, 1678, q.v. AGI Escribanía de Cámara, leg. 156, SC.
Landeche, Admiral Antonio de
  1705   Letter to the Viceroy [the Duke of Albuquerque], Havana, August 11, 1705. In Boyd, Smith, and Griffin, 1951, 82–85, q.v.
Lanning, John Tate
  1935   *The Spanish Missions of Georgia.* Chapel Hill: University of North Carolina Press.
Larsen, Clark Spencer
  1987   Stress and Adaptation at Santa Catalina de Guale: Analysis of Human Remains. Paper presented at the 20th annual meeting of the Society for Historical Archaeology, Savannah.
Larson, Lewis H.
  1980   *Aboriginal Subsistence Technology on the Southeastern Coastal Plain during the Late Prehistoric Period.* Gainesville: University Presses of Florida.
Lauber, Almon W.
  1913   *Indian Slavery in Colonial Times within the Present Limits of the United States.* Studies in history, economics and public law, vol. 54. New York: Columbia University.
Laudonnière, René
  1975   *Three Voyages.* Translated by Charles E. Bennett. Gainesville: University Presses of Florida.
Leon, Antonio G. (translator)
  n.d.   Synod of the Diocese of Santiago de Cuba, Jamaica, Habana, and Florida, Bishop Juan Garcia de Palacios, 1682.
León, Juan Isidro de
  1747   [Letter to Governor Manuel de Montiano, Fort San Marcos, Apalachee, June 26, 1747.] AGI SD 2584 NCC.
Leonard, Irving (translator)
  1939   *Spanish Approach to Pensacola, 1689–1693.* Albuquerque: The Quivira Society.
Leturiondo, Alonso de
  [1700] *Memorial to the King Our Lord in His Royal and Supreme Council of the Indies in*

Which a Report Is Given of the State in Which the Presidio of St. Augustine of Florida Happens to Be; of the Things that It Needs for Its Protection, Defence, and Preservation: for the Good Government and Punctual Service of His Majesty in Those Provinces. [Published about 1700.] Copy in AGI Escribanía de Cámara, leg. 157 C, cuaderno I, folios 44–205 SC. Translated by John H. Hann, *Florida Archaeology* 2 (1986):165–225.

Leturiondo, Domingo de

[1670] [Partial Report of the Service Record of Captain Juan Francisco de Florencia.] AGI SD 233 WLC reel 4.

1672 [A paragraph extracted from a report by Captain Domingo de Leturiondo, Madrid, December 30, 1672.] AGI SD 848 WLC, vol. 8.

1673 [Letter to the King, Madrid, March 28, 1673.] AGI SD 226 SC.

1678 [Inspection of the Provinces of Apalachee and Timucua, 1677–1678.] AGI Escribanía de Cámara, leg. 156 B, folios 519–616, SC. Translated (in part) by John H. Hann, 1983. [Copy of translation on file at Bureau of Archaeological Research, Tallahassee.]

López, Fray Baltasar

1602 [Letter to the King, September 15, 1602.] AGI SD 235 SC.

Lorant, Stefan (editor)

1965 *The First Pictures of America Made by John White and Jacques Le Moyne and Engraved by Theodore de Bry with Contemporary Narratives of the French Settlements in Florida, 1562–1565 and the English Colonies in Virginia, 1585–1590.* Rev. ed. New York: Duell, Sloan and Pearse.

Luna, Fray Pedro de

1690a [Note, August 15, 1690.] An enclosure in Governor Diego de Quiroga y Losada, 1690b, q.v. AGI SD 228 SC.

1690b [Memorial of the Distribution and Assignment of the Religious, August 15, 1690.] An enclosure in Quiroga y Losada, 1690b, q.v.

Luxán, Pedro de

1687 [Testimony of, 1687.] AGI Escribanía de Cámara, leg. 156, pieza 25 (E. 20), folios 111–113, SC.

Lynch, John

1964 *Spain under the Hapsburgs.* 2 vols. New York: Oxford University Press.

McDowell, W. L. (editor)

1955 *Journal of the Commissioners of the Indian Trade, September 20, 1710–August 29, 1718.* Columbia: South Carolina Archives Department.

McSpadden, George E.

1956 *An Introduction to Spanish Usage.* New York and Toronto: Oxford University Press.

McWilliams, Richebourg Gaillard (translator and editor)

1953 *Fleur de Lys and Calumet, being the Penicaut Narrative of French Adventure in Louisiana.* Baton Rouge: Louisiana State University Press.

Manuel, Chief of Asile

[1654?] [Letter to the Governor of Florida.] In Ruíz de Salazar y Vallecilla, 1657, q.v.

Marques Cabrera, Governor Juan

1680 [Letter to the King, 1680. Report on the religious existing in the missions of Florida and on the villages in which there are *doctrinas*, December 6, 1680.] AGI SD 226 WLC, vol. 9.

1682 [Letter to the King, January 25, 1682.] AGI SD 226 WLC, vol. 9.

1683 [Letter to the King, June 28, 1683.] AGI SD 226 SC.

1686a [Letter to the King, March 20, 1686.] AGI SD 852 SC.

1686b [Letter to the King, October 6, 1686.] AGI SD 227 SC.

1687a [Letter to the King, January 3, 1687.] AGI 61–6–20/38 SC.

1687b [Letter to the King, February 28, 1687.] AGI SD 228 SC.

Marrinan, Rochelle A., and Stephen C. Byrne

1987 San Pedro y San Pablo de Patale: An Outlying Seventeenth Century Apalachee Mission. Paper presented at the 20th annual meeting of the Society for Historical Archaeology, Savannah.

Martínez, Fray Lorenzo

1612 [Letter to the King, September 14, 1612.] AGI SD 232 SC.

Mason, J. Alden

1957 *The Ancient Civilizations of Peru.* Baltimore: Penguin.

Matheos, Antonio

1686 Letter to Governor Juan Marquez Cabrera, San Luis, May 19, 1686. In Serrano y Sanz, 1912, 193–198, q.v. [Serrano y Sanz gives the date incorrectly as 1606.]

1687a [Memorial Concerning the Indian Carpenters Who Worked on the Galiot Which Was Built on the Tacavona at His Majesty's Expense and of the Foodstuffs that Were Also Expended on the Said Indians and the Other Carpenters, on the Manufacture of Sets of Nails and on the Said Project.] AGI Escribanía de Cámara, leg. 156 C, cuaderno E, folio 77, SC. Translated by John H. Hann, 1976.

1687b [Testimony from the Record of the Residencia.] AGI Escribanía de Cámara, leg. 156 C, pieza 25 (E. 20), folios 50–60, SC. [The Stetson photostat of this document begins after the document starts. For this reason it is not clear whether it was a written statement of his case presented by the deposed lieutenant of the province of Apalachee or whether it was testimony he gave for the *residencia*. In the photostating of this collection of documents, folios 40–49 were not reproduced.] Translated by John H. Hann, 1976. [A copy of the translated portion of this collection of documents is on file at the Bureau of Archaeological Research, Tallahassee.]

Matter, Robert Allen

1972 The Spanish Missions of Florida: The Friars versus the Governors in the "Golden Age," 1606–1690. Ph.D. dissertation, University of Washington.

Medina, Fray Juan de

1651 [Letter to the Governor of Florida in the Name of the Chiefs of Apalachee, December 29, 1651.] In Ruíz de Salazar y Vallecilla, 1657, q.v.

Medsger, Oliver Perry

1957 *Edible Wild Plants.* New York: The Macmillan Co.

Méndez de Canzo, Governor Gonzalo

1600 Report concerning La Tama and Its Lands and of the Settlement of the English, February 1600. AGI SD 224 in Serrano y Sanz 1912, q.v. Translated by John H. Hann, 1984. [A copy is on file at the Bureau of Archaeological Research, Tallahassee.]

1601 [Letter to the King, April 24, 1601.] AGI SD 235 SC.

Mendoza, Captain Juan de

1687 [Testimony of, 1687.] AGI Escribanía de Cámara, leg. 156, cuaderno E, folio 38, SC.

Menéndez Marquez, Francisco

1648 [Letter to the King, February 8, 1648.] JTCC reel 3.

Menéndez Marquez, Francisco, and Pedro Benedit Horruytiner

1647 [Letter to the King, July 27, 1647.] AGI SD 235 JTCC reel 4.

Menéndez Marqués, Thomas, and Joachin de Florencia

1697 Letter to the King, July 3, 1697. In Boyd, Smith, and Griffin, 1951, 22–23, q.v.

Meyer, Michael C., and William L. Sherman

1979 *The Course of Mexican History.* New York: Oxford University Press.

Milanich, Jerald T.
1978   The Western Timucuan: Patterns of Acculturation and Change. In Milanich and Proctor, 1978, 59–88, q.v.
Milanich, Jerald T., and Charles H. Fairbanks
1980   *Florida Archaeology*. New York: Academic Press.
Milanich, Jerald T., and Samuel Proctor (editors)
1978   *Tacachale: Essays on the Indians of Florida and Southeastern Georgia during the Historic Period*. Gainesville: University Presses of Florida.
Milán Tapia, Francisco
1693   Journal of Francisco Milán Tapia, August 1, 1693, Great Bay of Pensacola. In Leonard, 1939, 283–305, q.v.
Milling, Chapman J.
1940   *Red Carolinians*. Chapel Hill: University of North Carolina Press.
Montiano, Governor Manuel de
1738a   [Letter to the King, June 4, 1738.] AGI SD 865 SC.
1738b   [Relation of the Number of Missionaries . . . in This Province of Santa Elena . . . , June 23, 1738.] AGI SD 865 SC.
1738c   [Letter to Governor Juan Francisco Güemes y Horcasitas, August 8, 1738.] Montiano Papers, no. 75, p. 108v, M–119.
1738d   [Letter to Governor Juan Francisco Güemes y Horcasitas, October 26, 1738.] Montiano Papers, no. 89, pp. 119–119v, M–133.
1745   [Letter to the King, February 17, 1745.] AGI SD 862 SC.
1746   [Letter to the King, March 6, 1746.] AGI SD 862 SC.
1747   [Letter to the King, August 3, 1747.] AGI SD 2584 NCC reel 17–46.
1756   [Letter to the King, March 6, 1756, Witness of a Letter of the Commandant of Apalachee. . . .] AGI SD 862.
Moore, Colonel James
1704a   [Letter to the Lords Proprietors, 16 April 1704.] Great Britain, Board of Trade, Spanish Papers, Manuscripts, Library of Congress, vol. 5, pp. 888–891. [This is an extract, not the complete letter. A published version taken from this copy is in Boyd, Smith, and Griffin, 1951, 93–95, q.v.]
1704b   [Letter to Sir Nathaniel Johnson (Governor of Carolina), 16 April 1704.] Great Britain, Board of Trade, Spanish Papers, Manuscripts, Library of Congress, vol. 5, pp. 892–896. [A published version taken from this copy is in Boyd, Smith, and Griffin, 1951, 91–93, q.v. It contains some serious errors. A variant published version may be found in Carroll, 1836, q.v.]
1704c   [Letter to the Lords Proprietors, 16th April 1704.] Manuscripts, South Carolina Department of Archives and History. [This is an extract of the same portion of the letter contained in the Library of Congress extract, but it differs in some matters of substance as well as in spelling, punctuation, capitalization, and word order.]
Moral, Fray Alonso del
1676   [Memorial of Fray Alonso Moral Concerning (the Need) for Naming Someone to Be Protector of the Indians of Florida, November 5, 1676.] AGI SD 235 WLC reel 4.
Moral, Fray Alonso del; Fray Bernardo de Santa María; Fray Miguel Garcón; Fray Pedro Vázquez; Fray Francisco de San Joseph; and Fray Martín Lasso
1657   [Letter to the King, May 10, 1657.] AGI SD 235 JTCC reel 4; WLC, reel 3.
Moreno, Fray Juan
1673   [Petition to the Crown, Madrid, February 27, 1673.] AGI SD 848 SC.
Moreno Ponce de León, Fray Pedro

1648a [Letter to the King, July 9, 1648.] AGI SD 235 WLC reel 3.

1648b [Memorial to the King, July 21, 1648.] AGI SD 235 WLC reel 3.

1651 [Memorial to the King, September 7, 1651.] AGI SD 225 WLC reel 3.

Morrell, L. Ross, and B. Calvin Jones

1970 San Juan de Aspalaga (A Preliminary Architectural Study). Tallahassee: Florida Bureau of Historic Sites and Properties *Bulletin* 1:25–43.

Nairne, Thomas

1708 Letter to an Unidentified Lord, 10 July 1708. In Salley, 1947, 5:193–202, q.v.

Noyan, Mr. de

1719 Letter to Bienville, August 12, 1719. In Rowland and Sanders, 1932, 3:252, q.v.

Núñez Cabeza de Vaca, Álvar

1964 *The Journey of Álvar Núñez Cabeza de Vaca.* Translated by Fanny Bandelier. Chicago: Rio Grande Press.

1966 *The Journey of Álvar Núñez Cabeza de Vaca.* Translated by Buckingham Smith. Facsimile ed. Ann Arbor: University Microfilms. [Originally published in New York in 1871.]

Olds, Doris L.

1962 History and Archaeology of Fort Saint Marks in Apalachee. Master's thesis, Florida State University.

Oliveira y Pullana, Pedro de

1716 [Letter to Diego de Morales y Velasco, Havana, July 2, 1716.] AGI SD 843 SC.

O'Neill, Charles Edwards

1966 *Church and State in French Colonial Louisiana: Policy and Politics to 1732.* New Haven: Yale University Press.

Oré, Luis Gerónimo

1936 *The Martyrs of Florida (1513–1616).* Translated by Maynard Geiger. New York: Joseph F. Wagner.

Paiva, Fray Juan de

1676 [Origen y principio del juego de pelota que los Indios Apalachinos y Yustacanos an estado jugando desde su infidelidad asta el año de 1676. Sacó a luz Rev^{do} p^e fr Juan de Paiva, p^c (paroco or padre) de la dotrina de San Luis de Talimali. Copy made by Juan Hernández de Florencia, the lieutenant of Apalachee, authenticated by Diego Salvador and Juan de Mendoza, Royal and parish interpreters, respectively, and included by Domingo de Leturiondo as part of the record of his visitation of the provinces of Apalachee and Timucua, in 1677–1678.] AGI Escribanía de Cámara, leg. 156 C, folios 569–583, SC. [Fray Paiva's name is sometimes presented as Juan de Paina; it is spelled that way on one of the copies of this manuscript.]

Pareja, Fray Francisco de

1602 [Letter, September 14, 1602.] AGI SD 235 WLC reel 2.

Pareja, Fray Francisco de, and Fray Alonso de Peñaranda

1607 [Letter to the King, November 6, 1607.] AGI SD 224 SC.

Pareja, Fray Francisco; Fray Lorenço Martínez; Fray Pedro Ruíz; Fray Alonso Desquera; Fray Juan de La Cruz; Fray Francisco Moreno de Jesus; and Fray Bartolomé Romero

1617 [Letter to the King, January 17, 1617.] AGI SD 235 WLC reel 3.

Parry, J. H., and P. M. Sherlock

1968 *A Short History of the West Indies.* New York: Macmillan–St. Martin's Press.

Pastrana, Don Alonso (Chief of Patale)

1687 [Testimony of, 1687.] AGI Escribanía de Cámara, leg. 156, cuaderno E, folio 34, SC.

Payne, Claudine
  1981   A Preliminary Investigation of Fort Walton Settlement Patterns in the Tallahassee Red
         Hills. *Proceedings of the Thirty-seventh Southeastern Archaeological Conference*
         24:29–31.
Pearson, Fred Lamar, Jr.
  1968   Spanish-Indian Relations in Florida: A Study of Two *Visitas,* 1657–1678. Ph.D. dis-
         sertation, University of Alabama.
Peña, Diego
  1706   [Letter to Governor José de Zúñiga y Cerda, Potano, January 16, 1706.] AGI SD
         858 SC.
  1717   Letter to Governor Juan de Ayala Escobar, Sabacola, September 20, 1717. In Boyd,
         1952, 115, q.v.
Peñaranda, Fray Alonso de
  1608   [Letter to the King, January, 1608.] AGI SD 224 WLC vol. 6.
Pérez, Fray Francisco
  1646   [Memorial for His Majesty Presented by the Priest Fray Francisco Pérez of the Order of
         St. Francis Concerning the Shortage of Religious that Exists in the Province of Florida
         and a Summary of the Conference in Which the Council Proposes Its Increase, 1646.]
         AGI SD 235 WLC reel 3.
Peterson, Evelyn
  1976   [Translation of the Ball Game Manuscript.] Photocopy in the possession of John Hann.
Ponce de León, Don Antonio
  1702   Letter to the King, Havana, January 29, 1702. In Boyd, Smith, and Griffin, 1951,
         27–29, q.v.
Prado, José de, Treasurer
  1654   [Letter to the King, December 30, 1654.] AGI SD 229 SC.
Primo de Rivera, José
  1718a [Letter to Governor Juan de Ayala y Escobar, San Marcos de Apalachee, April 28, Au-
         gust 3, 1718.] AGI SD 843 SC.
  1718b [Letter to Governor Juan de Ayala y Escobar, San Marcos de Apalachee, August 3,
         1718.] AGI SD 843 NCC, reel 14-25.
Provincial and Definitors of the Province of Florida
  1617   [Letter to the King, January 24, 1617.] AGI SD 235 WLC reel 3.
Pueyo, Juan de
  1695   General Visitation of the Provinces of Guale and Mocama Made by the Capt. Don Juan
         de Pueryo by Title and Nomination of the Sr. Don Laureano de Torres y Ayala, Knight
         of the Order of Santiago, Governor and Capt. General of the City, Presidio, and Prov.ˢ
         of St. Aug.ⁿ of Florida for His Maj.ʸ. AGI Escribanía de Cámara, leg. 157 A, cuaderno
         1, folios 109–140, SC. Translated by John H. Hann, 1986. [A copy is on file at the
         Bureau of Archaeological Research, Tallahassee.]
Purdum, Elizabeth, and Kenneth J. Plante
  n.d.   The Apalachee Farm: An Ethnohistoric and Archaeological Reconstruction. Manu-
         script on file, Department of Anthropology, Florida State University.
Quary, Colonel Robert
  1704   Letter to the Council of Trade and Plantations, Virginia, May 30, 1704. In Headlam,
         1916, 145, q.v.
Quiroga y Losada, Governor Diego de
  1688a Letter to the King, April of 1688. In Serrano y Sanz, 1912, 221–223, q.v.

1688b   Letter to the King, April 1, 1688. In Serrano y Sanz, 1912, 219–221, q.v.
1688c   [Letter to the King, April 1, 1688.] AGI SD 839 SC.
1690a   [Letter to the King, June 8, 1690.] AGI SD 227 SC.
1690b   [Letter to the King, August 31, 1690.] AGI SD 228 SC.
1691a   [Letter to the King, May 8, 1691.] AGI SD 228 SC.
1691b   [Letter to the King, December 12, 1691.] AGI SD 228 SC.

Ramírez, Nicolás
1687   [Testimony of, 1687.] AGI Escribanía de Cámara, leg. 156, pieza 25 (E. 20), folios 108–110, SC.

Raphael, Fray
1725   Letter to the Abbe Roguet, New Orleans, May 15, 1725. In Rowland and Sanders, 1932, 2:482, q.v.

Rebolledo, Governor Diego de
1655   [Letter to the King, October 24, 1655.] AGI SD 852 SC.
1657a   Testimony from the Visitation That Was Made in the Provinces of Apalachee and Timucua and Ustaca Made by the Señor Don Diego de Rebolledo, Knight of the Order of Santiago and Governor and Captain General of These Provinces of Florida by His Majesty. AGI, Escribanía de Cámara, leg. 155 B, no. 18, SC. Translated by John H. Hann, *Florida Archaeology* 2 (1986): 81–145.
1657b   Letter to the King, September 18, 1657. In Serrano y Sanz, 1912, 202–205, q.v.
1657c   [Letter to the King, October 18, 1657.] AGI SD 233 SC.
1657d   [Residencia of Governor Benito Ruíz de Salazar Vallecilla, 1657.] AGI Escribanía de Cámara, leg. 155 B. Microfilm roll 27–F, P. K. Yonge Library of Florida History.
1657e   [Letter to the King, October 24, 1657.] AGI Escribanía de Cámara, leg. 155, no. 18. Microfilm roll 27–G, P. K. Yonge Library of Florida History.

Robles, Fray Blas de; Fray Martín Lasso; Fray Alonso del Moral; Fray Francisco Peyota; Fray Jacinto de Barreda; Fray Francisco Bejarano; and Fray Alonso de Arroio
1681   [Account of the Sacred Vestments and Treasures Which the Churches of the 34 *Doctrinas* of the Conversions of Florida Possess for Public Worship, June 16, 1681.] AGI SD 235 WLC vol. 9. Translated by John H. Hann in *Florida Archaeology* 2 (1986): 148–150.

Romo de Urisa, Francisco de
1687   Testimony of, San Luis, May 22, l687.] AGI Escribanía de Cámara, leg. 156, cuaderno E, folios 22–23, SC.
1702   [Letter to Governor Joseph de Zúñiga y la Cerda, San Luis, October 22, 1702.] AGI SD 858 SC. [Filed under 1707, pp. 13061–13059 (pp. 33–35 in the bundle).]

Roque Pérez, Jacinto
1687   [Testimony of, 1687.] AGI Escribanía de Cámara, leg. 156, cuaderno E, folios 32-33, SC.

Rowland, (Jerome) Dunbar, and A. G. Sanders
1929   *Mississippi Provincial Archives, 1701–1729, French Dominion*, vol. 2. Jackson: Mississippi Department of Archives and History.
1932   *Mississippi Provincial Archives, 1704–1743, French Dominion*, vol. 3. Jackson: Mississippi Department of Archives and History.

Royal Cedula [Spanish Crown]
1648   [Royal Cedula to Governor Diego de Villalva, 1648, Cuba.]
1651   [Royal Cedula to the royal officials of Florida, Madrid, December 5, 1651.] AGI SD 229.

1676   [Royal Cedula to the governor of Florida, Madrid, February 13, 1676.] AGI SD 834 SC.

1681   [Royal Cedula to Governor Juan Marques Cabrera, Madrid, September 27, 1681.] AGI SD 227 WLC vol. 9.

1693   Royal Cedula, Madrid, November 4, 1693. In Boyd, Smith, and Griffin, 1951, 20, q.v.

1698   Royal Cedula to Don Laureano de Torres y Ayala, Madrid, March, 1698. In Boyd, Smith, and Griffin, 1951, 23–24, q.v.

1700   Royal Cedula, Madrid, May 7, 1700. In Boyd, Smith, and Griffin, 1951, 29–30, q.v.

1702   [Royal Cedula to the governor of Florida, Barcelona, March 8, 1702.] AGI SD 836 SC.

Royal Officials

1647a [Letter to the King, March 18, 1647.] AGI SD 229 SC.

1647b [Letter to the King, May 22, 1647.] AGI SD 229 JTCC reel 3.

1680   [Letter to the King, January 29, 1680.] AGI SD 226 WLC vol. 9.

1696   Letter to the King, April 6, 1696. In Boyd, Smith, and Griffin, 1951, 20–21, q.v.

1704a Letter to the Viceroy, July 16, 1704. In Boyd, Smith, and Griffin, 1951, 59–61, q.v.

1704b Letter to the Viceroy, 18, 1704. In Boyd, Smith, and Griffin, 1951, 61–62, q.v.

1707   [Letter to the King, November 10, 1707.] AGI SD 847 NCC reel 11.

Ruíz de Cuenca, Bartholomé

1705   Declaration of, before the Governor of New Vera Cruz, January 20, 1705. In Boyd, Smith, and Griffin, 1951, 70–72, q.v.

Ruíz de Salazar y Vallecilla, Governor Benito de

1643   [Memorial, May 4, 1643.] WLC vol. 7.

1645   [Letter to the King, April 16, 1645.] WLC vol. 7.

1647   [Letter to the King, May 22, 1647.] JTCC reel 3.

1650   [Letter, July 14, 1650.] AGI SD 225 WLC, reel 2.

1657   [Residencia of.] AGI Escribanía de Cámara, leg. 155 B. Microfilm roll 27–F, P. K. Yonge Library of Florida History.

Salinas, Juan de

1619   [Letter, May 24, 1619.] AGI SD 225. [Abstract by W. Lowery.] WLC reel 3.

Salley, Alexander S. (editor)

1934   *Journal of the Commons House of Assembly of South Carolina for 1703.* Columbia: Historical Commission of South Carolina.

1939   *Journal of the Commons House of Assembly of South Carolina, November 20, 1706– February 8, 1706/7.* Columbia: Historical Commission of South Carolina.

1940   *Journal of the Commons House of Assembly of South Carolina, June 5, 1707–July 19, 1707.* Columbia: Historical Commission of South Carolina.

1947   *Records in the British Public Records Office Relating to South Carolina,* 5 vols. Columbia: Historical Commission of South Carolina, 1928–1947. [Volume 5 covers the period 1701–1710.]

San Antonio, Fray Francisco de; Fray Juan de Medina; Fray Esteban Martínes; Fray Jacintho Domíngues; Fray Alonso del Moral; and Fray Juan Caldera

1657a [Letter to Governor Diego de Rebolledo, August 4, 1657.] AGI Escribanía de Cámara, leg. 155 B, no. 18. In Rebolledo, 1657a, q.v.

1657b Letter to the King, September 10, 1657. AGI SD 235, WLC, reel 3.

San Joseph, Fray Marcelo de

1688   [Letter to Governor Diego de Quiroga y Losada, February 15, 1688.] In Quiroga y Losada, 1688c, q.v.

[Scammon, U. S. A., General E. Parker]

1840   A Leaf from Florida. *The Knickerbocker* 16:44–46.

Scarry, John
   1986   The Rise, Transformation, and Fall of Apalachee: Political Centralization and De-
          centralization in Chiefly Society. Paper presented at the 38th annual meeting of the
          Florida Anthropological Society, Gainesville.
Serrano y Sanz, Manuel
   1912   *Documentos históricos de la Florida y la Luisiana, siglos XVI al XVIII*. Madrid: Li-
          breria General de Victoriano Suárez.
Shapiro, Gary
   1985a Broad-scale Testing and Settlement Plan at a Seventeenth-Century Spanish Mission in
          North Florida. Report for the Florida Bureau of Archaeological Research, Tallahassee.
   1985b The Apalachee Council House at Seventeenth-Century San Luis. Paper presented at the
          Southeastern Archaeological Conference, Birmingham.
Sigüenza y Góngora, Don Carlos de
   1693   Journal of Sigüenza y Góngora, May 15, 1693, on Board the Frigate Nuestra Señora
          de Guadelupe, Anchored in the Harbor of San Juan de Ulua. In Leonard, 1939, 152–
          192, q.v.
Simpson, J. Clarence
   1956   *A Provisional Gazetteer of Florida Place-names of Indian Derivation Either Obsoles-
          cent or Retained, Together with Others of Recent Application*, edited by Mark F. Boyd.
          Tallahassee: Florida Geological Survey, Special Publication No. 1.
Smith, Hale G.
   1951a A Spanish Mission Site in Jefferson County, Florida. In Boyd, Smith, and Griffin,
          1951, 107–136, q.v.
   1951b Leon-Jefferson Ceramic Types. In Boyd, Smith, and Griffin, 1951, appendix, 163–
          174, q.v.
   1951c The Influence of European Cultural Contacts upon the Aboriginal Cultures. Ph.D dis-
          sertation, University of Michigan.
   1951d The Ethnological and Archaeological Significance of Zamia. *American Anthropologist*
          53:238–244.
   1956   *The European and the Indian: European-Indian Contacts in Georgia and Florida*.
          Florida Anthropological Society Publications 4.
   1968   Two Historical Archaeological Periods in Florida. *American Antiquity* 13:313–319.
Snell, William R.
   1972   Indian Slavery in Colonial South Carolina, 1671–1795. Ph.D. dissertation, University
          of Alabama.
Solana, Alonso, Notary
   1687a [*Autos* and Inquiry Made Concerning the Impossibility that Exists for Achieving the
          Exploration of the Coast of the Bay of Concepción, Which Is Called of the Holy Spirit,
          that Is Planned to Be Made from Apalachee.] AGI Escribanía de Cámara, leg. 156,
          cuaderno E, folios 17–39, SC.
   1687b [Testimony of, April 23, 1687.] AGI Escribanía de Cámara, leg. 156, cuaderno E,
          folios 28–29, SC.
Solana, Manuel
   1702   [Letter to Governor Joseph de Zúñiga y Cerda, San Luis, October 22, 1702.] AGI SD
          858 SC.
   1703   Letter to the Governor, San Luis, February 3, 1703. In Boyd, Smith, and Griffin, 1951,
          41–42, q.v.
   1704a Letter . . . to Governor Zúñiga, San Luis, July 8, 1704. In Boyd, Smith, and Griffin,
          1951, 50–55, q.v.

1704b [Memorial of the Silver Which the Churches of Apalachee Had, August 19, 1704.] AGI
       SD 858. [Photostat in Mark F. Boyd Collection, The Florida State University Library.]
       Translated by John H. Hann in *Florida Archaeology* 2 (1986): 151–152.
1705   Testimony of, June 9, 1705. In Boyd, Smith, and Griffin, 1951, 79–82, q.v.
Somoza, Fray Antonio de, and Don Francisco Fernández de Madrigal
1673   [Letter, San Francisco, May 2, 1673.] AGI SD 235 WLC vol. 9.
South Carolina Commons House of Assembly
1704   Journals. Photocopies furnished by the South Carolina Department of Archives and
       History.
Spain, Cortes
1873   *Diario de las sesiones de Cortes: Legislatura de 1821.* 3 vols. 2d ed. Madrid: Imprenta
       de J. A. Garcia, 1871–1873.
Spellman, Charles W.
1965   The Golden Age of the Florida Missions, 1632–1674. *Catholic Historical Review*
       51:354–372.
Sturtevant, William C.
1954   The Mikasuki Seminole: Medical Beliefs and Practices. Ph.D. dissertation, Yale
       University.
Swanton, John R.
1922   *Early History of the Creek Indians and Their Neighbors.* Bureau of American Eth-
       nology Bulletin 73. Reprint. New York: Johnson Reprint Corporation, 1970.
1946   *The Indians of the Southeastern United States.* Bureau of American Ethnology Bulletin
       173. Reprint. New York: Green Press Publishers, 1969.
Tepaske, John T.
1964   *The Governorship of Spanish Florida, 1700–1763.* Durham, NC: Duke University
       Press.
Tesar, Louis Daniel
1980   *The Leon County Bicentennial Survey Report: An Archaeological Survey of Selected
       Portions of Leon County Florida.* Miscellaneous Project Report Series no. 49, sections
       1 and 2. Tallahassee: Florida Division of Archives, History, and Records Management.
Toro, Alonso Marqués del
1738   [Letter, San Marcos de Apalachee, April 18, 1738.] AGI SD 2593 SC.
Torres y Ayala, Governor Laureano de
1693a Journal of Don Laureano de Torres y Ayala from the Expedition He Made Overland
       from San Luis de Apalachee to the Bay of Pensacola in the Year of 1693, Bay of Pen-
       sacola, August 5, 1693. In Leonard, 1939, 228–255, q.v.
1693b Letter to the Conde de Galve, Bay of Pensacola, August 5. In Leonard, 1939, 218–
       225, q.v.
1693c Letter to His Majesty, Bay of Pensacola, August 5. In Leonard, 1939, 256–262, q.v.
1695   [Letter to the King, March 11, 1695.] AGI SD 839 SC. [This document is also available
       in Serrano y Sanz, 1912, 224–227, q.v.]
1696   Letter to the King, April 15, 1696. In Boyd, Smith, and Griffin, 1951, 21–22, q.v.
Torres y Ayala, Governor Laureano de, and the Royal Officials Thomas Menéndez Marquez and
Joaquín de Florencia
1697   [Letter to the King, April 20, 1697.] AGI SD 230, JTCC, reel 4.
Treviño Guillamas, Governor Juan de
1615   [Letter to the King(?), 1615.] AGI SD 225, WLC vol. 6.
Valdés, Bishop Gerónimo
1711   [Letter to the King, Havana, December 9, 1711.] AGI SD 860 SC.

Valverde, Fray Miguel de, and Fray Rodrigo de la Barreda
  1674   [Certification by the Priests Fray Miguel de Valverde and Fray Rodrigo de la Barreda, San Nicolás (de los Chacatos), September 10, 1674.] AGI SD 234 SC.
Vega, Garcilaso de la
  1951   *The Florida of the Inca.* Translated and edited by John G. Varner and Jeannette J. Varner. Austin: University of Texas Press.
Vega Castro y Pardo, Governor Damián de
  1639a   [Letter to the King, August 12, 1639.] AGI SD 225.
  1639b   [Letter to the King, August 22, 1639.] AGI SD 225 SC.
  1643   [Letter to the King, July 9, 1643.] AGI SD 224.
Vera, Pedro de la
  1687   [Testimony of, 1687.] AGI Escribanía de Cámara, leg. 156, pieza 25, (E. 20), folios 107–108, SC.
Vi Ventura
  1686   [Testimony of, 1686.] AGI Escribanía de Cámara, leg. 156, cuaderno E, folio 67, SC.
Wallace, David Duncan
  1934   *The History of South Carolina.* 4 vols. New York: The American Historical Society, Inc.
Wenhold, Lucy L.
  1956   The First Fort of San Marcos de Apalachee. *Florida Historical Quarterly* 34:301–314.
White, Nancy Marie
  1986   Archaeological Survey in the Middle and Lower Apalachicola River Valley, Northwest Florida. Paper presented at the 38th annual meeting of the Florida Anthropological Society, Gainesville.
Widmer, Randolph
  1985   [General Observations of the Patale Skeletal Population.] Report to the Bureau of Archaeological Research, Tallahassee.
Willey, Gordon R.
  1949   *Archeology of the Florida Gulf Coast.* Smithsonian Miscellaneous Collections 113.
Williams, John Lee
  1827   *A View of West Florida Embracing Its Geography, Topography,* &c. Philadelphia: printed for H. S. Tanner and the author.
Williams, John Mark
  1984   The Joe Bell Site: Seventeenth-Century Lifeways on the Oconee River. Ph.D. dissertation, University of Georgia.
Wright, J. Leitch, Jr.
  1981   *The Only Land They Knew: The Tragic Story of the American Indian of the Old South.* New York: The Free Press.
Ximénez, Juan
  1687   [Testimony of, May 22, 1687.] AGI Escribanía de Cámara, leg. 156, cuaderno E, folio 30, SC.
Zúñiga y Zerda, Governor Don Joseph de
  1700a   Order, November 5, 1700. In Boyd, Smith, and Griffin, 1951, 30–32, q.v.
  1700b   [*Residencia* for Governor Laureano de Torres y Ayala, November 16, 1700.] AGI Escribanía de Cámara, leg. 157 A. Microfilm roll 27–P, P. K. Yonge Library of Florida History.
  1701   Order, March 14, 1701. In Boyd, Smith, and Griffin, 1951, 35–36, q.v.
  1702   Letter to the King, September 30, 1702. In Boyd, Smith, and Griffin, 1951, 36–39, q.v.

1704a Letter to the King, March 30, 1704. In Boyd, Smith, and Griffin, 1951, 48–50, q.v.

1704b *Auto,* July 12, 1704. In Boyd, Smith, and Griffin, 1951, 55–56, q.v.

1704c [Letter to the King, October 6, 1704.] AGI SD 858 SC. [Filed under 1707, pp. 12549–12546.]

1704d Letter to the King, September 3, 1704. In Boyd, Smith, and Griffin, 1951, 65–67, q.v.

1704e Letter to the Viceroy, September 10, 1704. In Boyd, Smith, and Griffin, 1951, 67–68, q.v.

1704f Letter to the King, September 15, 1704. In Boyd, Smith, and Griffin, 1951, 68–69, q.v.

1705   [Letter to the Viceroy, October 26, 1705.] AGI SD 857 SC.

n.d.   Memorandum [undated]. In Boyd, Smith, and Griffin, 1951, 44–45, q.v.

Index

Abalache (variant spelling), 124
Abaslaco, 32
Abortion, 95
Acchuma fina, 78, 340, 341, 399. *See also*
Tobacco
Acculturation, 237, 255, 260, 263; in agriculture, 239–41; in crafts, 241–45; in dress,
261–62, 306, 310; in labor system, 259;
linguistic, 250–51, 306; in medicine, 251;
through mestization, 251–52; in political
organization, 254; in pottery, 245–46; in
private justice ethos, 248–49; in religious
practices, 238–39, 306, 307, 310; in sex-
ual mores, 252–53; in warrior ethos,
249–50; in weapons, 246–48; in work
ethic, 158–59, 307
Ache, 129–30
Achito, 122, 184, 188, 189, 190, 231 n.4
Acorns, 131–32
Adrián, chief of Bacuqua, 288, 291, 312, 313
Adultery, 94
Agriculture, 126–27, 239–41
Alabama-Koasati language. *See* Koasati
Alabama language, 119, 120, 399. *See also*
Alibama (people)
Alibama (people), 310–11. *See also* Alabama
language
Alaiguita, 111
Alcohol, 127, 149, 262–63
Amacano, 16, 33, 399. *See also* Yamasee
Amapexas, 291, 399. *See also* Yamasee
Amelia Island, 231
Amoscotegui y Bermudo, Pedro de, 315
Andrés, chief of San Juan, 98
Anhayca Apalache, 24, 195, 319; link with
Inihayca and San Luis Inhayca, 27; seat of

government, 96, 97; site of, 26–27. *See
also* Iniahico; Iviahica; San Luis de Inhayca; San Luis de Jinayca
Animal husbandry: introduction of, 239–41,
290
Animals, European: introduction of, 133, 134
Antonio, alaiguita of Tupique, 111
Apalachee (people): in Apalachicola province, 172, 288, 290, 291, 294, 301,
312–13, 314; as carpenters, 46, 244; cattle
ranch on Chattahoochee, 290; as complex
chiefdom, 9, 97; demoralization of,
235–36; dispersion of, 264–65, 284–315
passim; enslaved in South Carolina,
295–305; exported from South Carolina,
302–3, 305; near Fort St. Marks
(post-1704), 313; games of, 71–73; in
Louisiana, 311; as migrants in Mobile, 306,
307; meaning of name, 124; names of individuals, 251, 365–69; peace with
Timucua, 11; as rebels, 290; near St. Augustine (post-1704), 285, 286, 287; settlements in South Carolina, 295–96; slave-
holding by, 43; Spaniards' admiration for,
6–7, 9; staying power of, 68; work ethic
of, 158; in Yamasee War, 301. *See also* Labor; Marriage practices
—revolts by: in 1638, 15; in 1647, 3, 14, 15,
16–20, 27, 140, 196, 320–21; in 1656, 22
Apalachee language, 9, 118–24, 186
Apalachee province: abandonment of, 4,
167–69, 264, 280–83, 284, 305; fame of,
5–6; immigration into, 173–74; importance of, 1–2; indefensibility of, 234; limits of, 2, 5, 27; most dense settlement, 1,
179–80; name for Indian hinterland of

437

Index

Apalachee (people) (*continued*)
Southeast, 5; origin of people of, 7; port
in, 15–16, 152; resettlement of, 291, 292,
293, 301, 316; return to, 291–94; unrest in
(1656), 22; valor and ferocity of people of,
5–7; withdrawal from, by natives and
Spaniards, 61, 326
Apalachee River (Georgia), 290–91
Apalachee Trail, 297
Apalachen, 5, 194–95
Apalachicola (province), 187, 200, 203, 205,
227, 231 n.4, 312, 323, 324, 325, 399–
400; alliance with English, 189, 230,
231–32, 233; interest in Christianization,
47, 184; language of, 119, 120, 122, 123,
189; move to the Ocmulgee, 189, 190, 231;
peace with Apalachee, 16, 182, 190, 233;
obedience to Spanish Crown sworn by, 32,
183, 189, 229, 231; request for friars by,
32; trade with Spaniards, 16, 32, 183; vil-
lages of, 362–64; visited by governor of
Florida, 16, 32, 183; war on, by Spaniards,
188–90, 230, 232, 233. *See also* Brims,
Emperor; Creek; Fort in Apalachicola province; Lower Creek; Matheos, Antonio;
Ruiz de Salazar Vallecilla, Benito de;
Trade: with Apalachicola province
Apalachicola (town), 119, 123, 188, 290
Apalachicola River, 33, 40, 47. *See also*
River of Santa Cruz
Armas, Fray Andrés de, 33
Aranguíz y Cotes, Alonso de, 201–2
Asile, 14, 55, 196; chief of, 17; under Apa-
lachee's jurisdiction, 31; location of, 30.
See also San Miguel de Asile
Aspalaga, 28, 31, 43, 173, 270, 275; capture
of, 279, 283; chief of, 256; moving of, 32,
39, 55–59; size of church of, 39. *See also*
San Juan de Aspalaga
Aspalaga the old, 57, 275, 290
Assumpción del Puerto, 36, 43, 45
Assumption of Our Lady, 35, 36, 37, 45
Aucilla River, 25
Ayala, Antonio de (Yamasee), 282, 287
Ayala y Escobar, Juan de: visitations of,
57–60
Ayubale, 28, 32, 58, 62, 233, 234, 275, 276,
279, 298; capture of, 271, 274, 281. *See
also* Concepción de Ayubale; I: Awellies;
Nuestra Señora de la Concepción de
Ayubale; Santa María de Ayubale

Bacuqua, 27, 31, 32, 43, 58, 60, 138, 139,
172, 196, 199 n.2, 275–76, 281; chief of,

256; moving of, 28, 54–55, 191, 234; as
site of Spanish ranch, 53. *See also* Delgado, Marcos; Our Lady of the Rosary
Ranch; San Antonio de Bacuqua; Santa
María de Bacuqua
Baldwin, Isaac, 311
Ball game: abolition of, 43, 73–74, 88–90,
91, 322–23, 344, 345, 346, 350, 351,
352; ball used in, 74, 80, 340; banned by
Bishop Calderón, 73, 86, 344; banned by
individual friars, 19, 73; body paint used
in, 75, 77, 342; cacina used in, 78, 80,
339, 341, 342; challenge ritual of, 77, 333,
334; as communal affair, 74, 80–81, 338,
346, 347–48; described, 74–76, 333; and
dream interpretation, 78, 335; fasting prescribed for, 78, 340, 341, 342; eagle's nest
in, 74, 75, 79; grapevines in, 79, 80, 88,
338, 339; and lightning, 79, 85, 336, 343;
magic used in, 74, 77, 78, 342, 349; new
fire for, 78, 335, 340, 341; origin myths of,
81–86, 332, 334, 336–37; paraphernalia
of, 74–75, 80, 333–34, 337, 338, 340,
342; playing field of, 80; pregame rituals
of, 74, 77–78, 87–88, 335, 340, 341;
privileges of players, 81, 347; religious
aspects of, 74, 85–86, 331, 334, 339,
343–44, 345, 348; social evils of, 74,
76–77, 80–81, 89, 346–48; as source of
intervillage disharmony, 76–77, 87, 346,
347; as substitute for war, 74; as summer
pursuit, 76, 333; tobacco used in, 78, 335,
340, 341; vigil for, 77–78, 334–35, 342;
violence of, 73, 76, 333, 346; wagering
on, 74, 347, 348; women's version mentioned, 73, 339. *See also* Ball game manuscript; Ball pole
Ball game manuscript: genesis of, 73–74,
87–89, 345, 350–52; links to San Luis,
73, 76, 77, 80, 85–86, 87, 88, 328, 329,
339, 343, 344, 345, 346, 348, 350–52;
problems of, 328–29
Ball pole: atari, 75–79; dances around,
79–80, 338–39; eagle on, 79, 338; nest
on, 74, 75, 79, 338; portrayed, 74, 75, 79,
337, 338, 339; raising of, 79–80, 338,
339–40; reverence to, 80, 339; sassafras
pegs on, 79, 337; shells on, 75, 79; and
worship of Nicoguadca, 79, 339, 343, 345
Baltasar, chief of Cupaica, 14
Baltasar, Sabacola chief, 47, 187
Baptizing Creek, 306
Barbacoa, 113, 195, 208, 400
Barreda, Fray Rodrigo de, 57, 207

Our Lady of the Rosary of Abosaia, 287
Our Lady of the Rosary ranch, 52, 53. *See also* Delgado, Marcos
Our Lady of Sorrows, 287
Oxen, 134, 137, 151, 157

Pacara, 36, 406. *See also* Capara; Yamasee
Paiva, Fray Juan de, 328, 329, 331; hostility to ball game, 87; campaign against game by, 73, 88–90; defense of game by, 73, 86–87. *See also* Ball game manuscript
Palachicola (people), 301. *See also* Apalachicola (town); Chislacaliche
Palisades, 25, 109, 181, 185, 212, 250
Palm berries, 131
Pansacola (people), 122, 184 n.5, 185, 250, 406
Pansacola (satellite village in Apalachee), 29, 47
Panther, 192–93, 334
Pastrana, Alonso, chief of Patale, 230
Patale, 28, 32, 54, 58, 62, 172, 173, 180, 205, 270; capture of, 275, 279, 283; chicasa of, 53, 60, 138, 139; possible move by, 55; size of church at, 39; two sites of, xii–xiii. *See also* San Pedro de Patale; San Pedro y San Pablo de Patale
Peace: introduced by Spain, 182, 183
Peace and War towns, 100, 101
Peaches, 133
Pensacola: Apalachee exiles in, 291, 294, 299, 312, 313; French attack on, 309, 314; migration from, 311; migration to, 291, 294, 301, 305, 307, 309
Pentecolo, chief of town of Apalachicola, 188
Peña, Diego, 57, 62–63, 120, 186, 225, 290
Pérez, Andrés, 201
Persimmons, 133
Peso, 406
Petrina, 406
Pine tar, 137
Pinoco, 129
Pirates, 201, 202, 262
Pittman, Lieutenant, 225
Plague, 175, 289
Plaza, 206, 207–8, 209
Plums, 133
Pocosapa, 287
Political independence, natives': loss of, 254
Political polarity, 96–97, 98
Political unity: early seventeenth century, 97–98
Polygamy, 12, 184
Ponce de León, Antonio, 59–60

Ponce de León, Nicolás de, 196
Population, xi, 11, 14, 23, 25, 26, 27, 30, 32, 37, 38, 39, 40, 96, 102, 195, 264; decline of, 161, 163, 164, 166, 180; distribution of, 174–75; estimates of, 160–61, 162–63, 164, 165, 167, 168, 169; of Guale, 166, 167; of Timucua, 166, 167; by village, 170–71, 172, 173. *See also* Swanton, John R.; Wright, J. Leitch
Port in Apalachee. *See under* Apalachee (province)
Potano, 11, 13, 91 n.9, 151; missionization of, 10; opposition to abolition of ball game, 91–92. *See also* Prieto, Fray Martín
Potohiriba, 248, 249. *See also* San Pedro de Potohiriba
Pottery, 245–46
Prado, José de, 21
Prices of labor and goods, 155–57
Prieto, Fray Martín, 97–98; evangelization of Potano by, 10; and peace mission to Apalachee, 10–11. *See also* Potano
Primo de Rivera, Enrique, 151
Primo de Rivera, José, 63, 291, 313
Principal chief, 101, 110, 111, 112
Principal village, 30, 31, 102
Productivity, 126, 132
Punta Rosa, 314
Purchasing power, natives', 154, 155, 156
La Purificación de Tama, 36–37. *See also* Candelaria; Nuestra Señora de la Candelaria de la Tama; Nuestra Señora de la Tama; Tama

Qua, chieftainness at Caveta, wife of Emperor Brims, 172, 288, 312
Quicio. *See* Chunkey
Quiroga y Losada, Diego de, 205, 210, 258–59

Ranches: damage to natives' crops from, 53, 143, 259; Indian, 53–54, 290; practices on, 138; Spanish, 232. *See also* Delgado, Marcos; Fernández de Florencia, Juan; Florencia, Francisco de; Jiménez, Diego de; Ruiz de Salazar Vallecilla, Benito de; Ximénez, Diego de
Ranches of San Joseph de Upalucha and of San Juan de Ochania, 52
Rebolledo, Diego de, 20, 30, 73, 152, 196, 321–22; in conflict with friars, 21–23, 197; deposition of, 23; friars accused by, 255–58; military presence in Apalachee increased by, 198–99

Talpagana, Luis, 85–86, 343

Tama (in Apalachee), 33, 35, 37, 51, 55, 62, 63, 192, 258, 274, 276, 279, 281, 282, 407; chief of, 243; fate of, in 1704, 61; language of, 121; plans for resettlement of site of, 292–93. *See also* Candelaria; Nuestra Señora de la Candelaria de la Tama; Nuestra Señora de la Tama; La Purificación de Tama

Tama (in Georgia), 251; request for friars by, 33; language of, 120–21

Tama (people): in Apalachicola Province (1717), 290

Tamasle (near St. Marks), 292, 294. *See also* San Antonio

Tanning. *See* Leather

Tascaia, 71, 182, 407

Tasquique, 188, 189. *See also* Taisquique

Tastanage. *See* "Great Warrior"

Tattooing, 93

Tavasa, 68 n.9, 184. *See also* Tawasa

Tawasa, 311. *See also* Tavasa

Tensa, 311

Tequesta: Indians of, 178

Texjana, warrior captain of Talisi, 312–13

Tesar, Louis, 26–27, 99

Thluco, 123

Thunder-god, 86

Timucua, 11, 13, 17, 21, 22, 28, 30, 31, 70, 73, 91, 92, 93, 95 n.11, 99, 161, 166, 167, 177, 179, 181, 182, 232, 239, 244, 248, 249, 407; decline in population of, 19, 23, 69; language of, 120, 121, 123, 124; people of, 285, 286; revolt by, 105; at war with Apalachee, 10

Timucua Alta, 13

Tiquepache, 49, 189

Tobacco, 133, 259. *See also* Acchuma fina

Tocobaga (in Apalachee): fate of, 61, 62; people of, 40, 41, 42, 52, 54, 61, 62, 165, 193, 282, 316, 323, 407; transport role of, 42; village of, 40, 41–42, 46, 193. *See also* Tocopaca

Tocopaca, 41, 407–8. *See also* Tocobaga

Tolocano, 131, 187, 408

Tolomato, 286

Tomole, 28, 32, 55, 57, 58, 62, 63, 274, 275, 276, 279, 281, 282, 290. *See also* San Martín de Tomole

Tools, iron, 241–42

Toomelean, 298, 299, 300

Toomichau, 299, 300

Torres y Ayala, Laureano de, 37, 49, 190, 203, 205, 324

Towns. *See* Peace and War towns; Villages

Trade, 16, 20, 32, 117, 147, 148, 155–56, 198; with Apalachicola province, 190, 233; with Cuba, 133, 134, 137, 152, 320; regulation of, 136–37, 142, 152, 227, 233, 257; with St. Augustine, 15, 19, 21, 42, 136–37, 144, 149, 151, 152, 153, 232, 233; in skins, 158. *See also* English traders

Trade goods, 134, 148

Trade routes, 149–51

Tuscarora War, 297

Tustunnuggee thlucco. *See* "Great Warriors;" Tastanage

Typhus, 176, 178

Uchisi, 232, 289, 291, 292, 304, 314; language of, 120, 123. *See also* Hitchiti

Uchisi River, 231 n.4

Unity, cultural and political, 97

Upper Creek, 294, 313

Usinulo, 78, 104, 123, 338, 340

Usunaca, Andrés, chief of San Luis, 98, 110, 243

Utina, 10, 11, 13, 91 n.9, 408

Vega, Garcilaso de la, 25, 96–97

Vega Castro y Pardo, Damián de, 14, 15, 16, 20, 25, 194

Velda phase, 9

Ventura, Vi, 145–46, 206. *See also* Bentura, Bi

Veracruz (Apalachee in), 314, 315

Villages: grouping of, 32; as major centers, 96–100; settlement pattern of, 25; territory of, 102–3. *See also* Principal village; Satellite villages; Settlement pattern

Visitations, 114, 115

Wacissa: site of Tocobagan settlement, 40, 41, 165

Wacissa River, 41, 42

Wacoca, 298, 299, 300

Wages, 154, 155, 230

War chief, 101–2, 112

Warfare: acculturation in, 249–50; decline in spirit and skills for, 247–48; endemic, 182; with neighbors, 181, 185–87, 188, 189, 190

War of Spanish Succession, 4, 60

Warrior ranks, 182. *See also* Nicoguadca; Nocoro; Scalping; Tascaia

War towns, 100, 101

Watermelons, 95

Weaving, 243–44

West Indies, 303

Wheat, 17, 19, 20, 127, 134, 142, 144, 196, 321

Whipping, 256, 258